P9-DID-142

BISON
BOOKS

Walter Johnson

Baseball's Big Train

Henry W. Thomas

Foreword by Shirley Povich

UNIVERSITY OF NEBRASKA PRESS
LINCOLN AND LONDON

♾ The paper in this book meets the minimum requirements of American National Standard for Information Sciences—Permanence of Paper for Printed Library Materials, ANSI Z39.48-1984.

First Bison Books printing: 1998
Most recent printing indicated by the last digit below:
10 9 8 7 6 5 4 3 2 1

Library of Congress Cataloging-in-Publication Data
Thomas, Henry W.
Walter Johnson: baseball's big train / Henry W. Thomas: foreword by Shirley Povitch.
p. cm.
Originally published: Washington, D.C.: Phenom Press, ©1995.
Includes bibliographical references (p.) and index.
ISBN 0-8032-9433-6 (pa: alk. paper)
1. Johnson, Walter Perry, 1887–1946. 2. Pitchers (Baseball)—
United States—Biography. I. Title.
[GV865.J6T46 1998]
796.357′22′092—dc21
[B] 97-35190
CIP

Reprinted from the original 1995 edition by Phenom Press, Washington, D.C.

FOR MOM

CONTENTS

Acknowledgments

Without the constant help and support of Carolyn Johnson Thomas over the years, this book would never have been more than wishful thinking on my part. Even when it was well under way, during those moments when I thought my reach might have exceeded my grasp, her unwavering faith kept me moving forward. Indispensable also were her intimate knowledge of the subject and the countless hours she devoted to various aspects of the project.

The aid and comfort of Karen and Bill Pearson and their family in the earliest stages of this endeavor helped get it off the ground, and their continuing interest and encouragement has been sustaining. The insights of Eddie Johnson and Barbara Johnson Pogue into the life of their father were an invaluable contribution, and their participation was a personal pleasure for me.

The dedicated work of editors Tom Simon, Neal McCabe, and Ed Johnson has improved this book substantially and in ways too numerous to mention. Offering important suggestions and weeding out pesky inaccuracies and blatant errors were Joe Wayman and my cousins Jim Johnson and Chuck Carey. In addition, Chuck's tireless work on the long-neglected prehistoric epoch of "Kid Johnson" in California led to some priceless discoveries. Frank J. Williams deserves special mention, not only for his definitive work on the statistics of Walter Johnson's major-league pitching career but for being so unselfish with the hard-earned fruits of his labor. Williams's game-by-game detailing of Johnson's career served as the roadmap for much of my research, never more than an arm's length away during any period of my work, and his analysis was often elucidating. William Ruiz's clever approaches to The Big Train's numbers were also revealing and useful.

Chuck Rideout of the Walter Johnson High School in Bethesda, Maryland, was not only of enormous aid to this particular project, but has made it part of his work to see that the spirit of Johnson's life, and not just the name, is his legacy to the students and community there. Phil Wood's involvement at every stage has been of great help. The boundless enthusiasm of Ed Charron always seemed to provide a boost at just the right time. Heartfelt thanks go to Shirley Povich, John Steadman, Bob Davids, and Tim Kurkjian for their special contributions. Paul Dickson and Saul Wisnia came through when I needed them.

The credit for making a silk purse of a book from a sow's ear of a dog-eared manuscript goes to Dan Rapoport, Merideth Menken, and Elizabeth Webber at Farragut Publishing Company, and Marc Meadows, Melton Castro and Robert Wiser of Meadows and Wiser Graphic Design. Jerry McCoy carefully and beautifully reproduced the photographs.

There are others, many others, whose contributions made this book much more than it would have been otherwise and without whose association it would have been less of a joy for me to put together. The good company and assistance of Russell Shew, Alan Alper, and Pete Frutkin helped ease the strain of many long days poring over microfilm at the Library of Congress, and when the limits of endurance had been reached they were usually available for a trek to Hagerstown and some real baseball. Last, but hardly least, is Bebe.

Introduction

He was, beyond doubt, the greatest pitcher that ever scuffed a rubber with his spikes. But he was much more than that. Walter Johnson had all the virtues commonly but not always truthfully attributed to athletic heroes: honesty, decency, dignity, thoughtfulness and a genuine modesty. A simple man, he was, in his way, a great man.

FRANK GRAHAM, BASEBALL MAGAZINE, FEBRUARY 1947

It was reading such statements that got me started on this book. I came to a curiously late appreciation of the story of Walter Johnson, considering that he is my grandfather. But he died in 1946 when I was eight months old, and my grandmother, Hazel Johnson, had passed away many years earlier. I saw quite a bit of his mother, my great-grandmother, Minnie Johnson, who lived to be 100 years old, and I knew his children (my mother, aunt, and uncles), but Walter and Hazel Johnson might as well have been 19th-century ancestors, little more than faces in old black-and-white pictures on the wall. It's not that I was unaware of his stature as one of the all-time baseball legends and Washington's greatest sports hero. I went to Griffith Stadium several times for ceremonies honoring Walter Johnson's memory, including an Old-Timers Day in 1959 when I stood on the first-base line representing the family. But I don't believe that my knowledge of him went much deeper than that of most kids my age growing up in the nation's capital during the '50s and '60s.

It was our sad fate to have the perennially last-place Washington Senators for a team at a time when baseball was more important to kids than it is today. Other sports were barely a blip on the screen then, although my buddies and I treated the fabulous Boston Celtics as our own because Nancy Auerbach was a classmate and we had been to her house and met Red. But one of the few things all long-suffering Senators fans, myself among them, could point to with pride was that the Greatest Pitcher of All Time had worn a "W" on his cap and sleeve his entire career.

Our family did have the scrapbooks, thirty oversized volumes containing thousands of articles, letters, telegrams, and other materials collected and meticulously assembled by Hazel Johnson, but for decades they sat undisturbed in a cabinet in the living room. Perhaps their sheer number was daunting, or maybe it was the forbidding black binding, but for some reason not once did I (or anybody else, for that matter) ever reach in, pull one out, and start reading—not even when baseball was just about the biggest thing in my life. Then, on a visit to the old home place one day years later, and again for a reason I can't explain (it might have been one of those Thanksgiving or Christmas dinners where everyone sits around afterward watching a football game), I did just that. Within minutes I was hooked.

Over the next few months I went through the scrapbooks one by one, and it wasn't long before I realized that the major treatments of Johnson's life and career to that point—a warmhearted but cursory 1948 book, *Walter Johnson, King of the Pitchers,* by sportswriter and children's author Roger Treat, and several long magazine profiles—had only scratched the surface of a truly remarkable man and the fantastic adventure that was his life. A biography worthy of the subject had to be done, I felt; the material between the covers of those scrapbooks demanded it. Years of research followed to fill in periods not covered by the scrapbooks and to search out whatever other sources of information I could find.

At times it seemed that these efforts would never bear fruit, but my dream of a comprehensive and entertaining biography of Walter Johnson never disappeared. It's been a real joy and privilege to spend so much time with him, and I hope I have done his story justice—it deserves no less.

Henry W. Thomas
Washington, D.C.

Foreword

When Henry W. Thomas chose the Walter Johnson story as the subject of his work, he had a rare, special, motivational interest—a blood relationship. The man so often acclaimed through the generations as the greatest ever to grace the major league pitching mounds was the writer's grandfather.

Thus was Thomas advantaged in his work. He not only dedicated himself to researching Johnson's career, he mined it, and profited from his access to the nooks of the family history and remembrances, dating from those times when Walter Johnson was a farm boy growing up on the plains of Kansas through those years when grandfather Johnson was putting more records in the books than any man who ever lived.

The upshot: Henry Thomas has written a biographical gem. It touches every base of the legend. The Johnson story was often told by baseball authors, by magazine writers and as excerpts in books. But never like this. Thomas has trumped them all.

I, too, have dabbled in the Walter Johnson story, in newspaper columns for the *Washington Post,* and in series, and as a contributor to books, and had the good luck to be there in his later World Series years. Captivated was I, not only by his unmatched pitching skills, but by the manner of the man, his modesty, humility, and humanity while surrounded by a game that in his era was the playing field of roughnecks.

For twenty years they were synonymous—The Washington Senators and Walter Johnson, but it was in high irony. The image of the Senators—who gave rise to the vaudeville joke "Washington, First in War, First in Peace, and Last in the American League"—was as the inept, hopeless teams of Johnson's early years, while Johnson in contrast was gaining his fame as the super pitcher of his time—one could make that all time—owner of the swiftest pitch ever known to the game, and inhibited always by his sensitivity that it could maim someone.

For years Walter Johnson was identified by baseball writers, in the slang of the time, as "The Big Swede." Despite no Swedes in his ancestry, Johnson accepted the appellation without protest. "I didn't want to offend anybody," Johnson once told me. "There are a lot of Swedes I know who are nice people." This book is about that kind of man.

Shirley Povich

CHAPTER ONE

Kid Johnson

When the Senators took the field it was behind the broad shoulders of Walter Johnson, and this time their hero did not fail them. In danger in every one of the four innings that he worked, he rose superbly to every emergency. In each succeeding crisis he became a little more the master, a little more the terrible blond Swede of baseball fable. Twice he struck out Long George Kelly when the game hung by a thread so fine that thousands in the tense, silent throng turned their heads away with every pitch.

To the victor belong the spoils. When future generations are told about this game they will not hear about Barnes, or Frisch, or Kelly, or even about Harris or McNeely. But the boy with his first glove and ball crowding up to his father's knee, will beg:

"Tell me about Walter Johnson."

BILL CORUM, NEW YORK TIMES, OCTOBER 11, 1924

Those assuming Walter Perry Johnson to be of Scandinavian origin could be excused the mistake. With his sandy brown hair, blue-gray eyes, fair complexion, finely chiseled facial features, and broad, strong frame over six feet tall—what else would they think? His Western Plains twang, though it lacked the lilting accent of the Nordic immigrant, would do nothing to change the impression. But Johnson's ancestry, as far back as it traces, is entirely of the British Isles: Johnson, Perry, Higbee, Bradley, Sheldon, Daugherty, Smith, McCullom, Cross, Lane, Skidmore; mostly English, some Irish, Scotch, and Welsh. Of course, the long history of immigration into and conquest of Great Britain from the Scandinavian peninsulas suggests that in the longer view the Swedish assumption might not be far off base after all. The predominance of fair features throughout the Johnson family, continuing to the present day, makes this seem all the more likely.

Of his nationality Johnson remarked, "Well, to tell the truth, we're just about as plain, old-fashioned American as could possibly be," and this is no exaggeration.[1] He was a 10th-generation American on the side of paternal grandmother Phoebe Higbee Johnson, their ancestor Edward Higby having arrived from England in 1645 to marry Jedidah Skidmore, who by that time had already been in the colonies for ten years. The Johnson line went back at least five generations to Samuel Johnson of New Jersey during the Revolutionary period. His mother's forebears, the Perrys, were also in that area at about the same time. The Johnson and Perry families, in fact, took remarkably similar journeys across the country: from New Jersey to Pennsylvania, then to Ohio, and finally on to the Great Plains, they traveled the well-established route of migration to the West. The great rivers, the Allegheny, Ohio, Missouri, and Mississippi served as the common "highways" taking people to a new life in the territories.

Johnson's maternal grandfather, John Lane Perry, survived four years with the Fourth Pennsylvania Cavalry in the Civil War, fighting at Bull Run, Antietam, and Gettysburg. At war's end he joined his parents in Ohio, and it was there he met Lucinda Bradley, whose own parents had died when she was an infant. They married in 1866 and moved the next year to Richmond, Indiana, where their first child, Minnie Olive, was born. In the spring of 1875, with five children in tow, John and Lucinda Perry moved westward to Dixon, Missouri.

Dixon was in the heart of an area terrorized by the infamous Confederate guerrilla bands of William Quantrill and "Bloody Bill" Anderson during the long and bitter Kansas-Missouri border war. Denied amnesty when peace was declared at Appomattox, the Missouri guerrillas returned home as outlaws. Some, like Cole Younger and the James brothers, stayed together to apply tactics learned during the war to the robbing of banks and trains. Minnie Johnson would tell the story of the time three tired and hungry strangers rode up to the Perry farm asking if they could stay the night in the barn. Her father agreed, but kept himself awake all night to make sure they didn't steal his horses. The next morning while Lucinda Perry made breakfast for everybody the men chatted with eight-year-old Minnie on the front porch. A bluejay landed on a fence some 20 yards away and one of them twirled his pistol and fired, dropping the bird with a single shot. After breakfast, the strangers thanked the Perrys for their hospitality and rode off. Later that afternoon a posse came by and the family learned that their guests had been none other than Frank and Jesse James.[2]

In March of 1884, John Perry moved his family, soon to fill out to ten children, across the border to Iola, Kansas. A short time later Minnie Perry met

Frank Johnson at a little country dance in nearby Humboldt, Kansas, and they were married on July 2, 1885. Frank's parents, Nathaniel and Phoebe Higbee Johnson, had only recently moved with their eight children to Kansas. Now the newlywed Frank and Minnie Johnson settled onto their own 160-acre farm in the Neosho Valley of Allen County, Kansas, about three miles north of the town of Humboldt. A year later their first child, Effie Belle, was born, and it was at the farm on November 6, 1887, that Walter Perry Johnson came into the world.

Walter Johnson would look back on his Kansas childhood as not only the happiest a boy could have but also as the best preparation for life.[3] Growing up on the Plains meant a certain isolation from the outside world, but there was much on the farm to keep a child occupied. The Johnson property, with its sturdy white clapboard house and several smaller buildings, sat on the east bank of the blue Neosho River, a place for swimming in the summer and fishing under the big willow trees all year. Young Walter chased hogs and chickens around the yard and tried to ride his father's colts, who didn't take kindly to his attempts at breaking them in.[4] Animals would be a major interest throughout Johnson's life, and by all accounts he had a natural way with them. "He was always catching wild animals and trying to tame them," his brother, Earl, recalled. "He was fearless as a youngster, and I remember once when my sister, Effie, and Walter and I saw a large gray wolf in a field. We got the dogs and chased the wolf into a den under a rock. Walter found another den a few feet away, crawled in and pulled out five young wolves. Had the dens been connected, the mother would have torn him to bits."[5] Hunting was also part of the pioneer life, though, and Walter learned to use a rifle as soon as he was big enough to aim it.[6] His prowess with another weapon was probably the first indication of an unusually sharp eye-hand coordination. "He was an amazing shot with a sling," Earl Johnson remembered, "and could hit squirrels up to 60 feet."[7]

The children accompanied Frank Johnson on his occasional trips into Humboldt and Iola to buy supplies, and getting away from the farm to see the sights of "the big towns" was a thrill. But on a small family farm there was no shortage of work to be done. The youngsters were assigned chores as soon as they were able to do them, and when they got older the boys helped with the harvests, putting in long hours in the fields with their father. In later years Johnson would credit his physical strength and endurance to the hard work and wholesome outdoor life of his youth.[8] The development of his personality and character, which would be such a prominent part of the Walter Johnson story, was no doubt largely due to the influence of his parents.

The expression "salt of the earth" could have been coined with Frank and Minnie Johnson in mind. Children of farmers, then farmers themselves, they were by all accounts an example of everything good and proud about a life working the land. Frank Johnson, though rugged and strong, was a quiet man with a philosophical, common-sense manner. He didn't believe in using a great deal of discipline on his children, preferring the application of praise and reason instead. As a result, the children wanted to please him.[9] "My father was a big man who didn't have much to say, but who was always sure of himself when he did say something," Walter Johnson recalled. "He always did his best to make things pleasant around home."[10] Minnie Johnson was practical, selfless, and friendly. She already knew a great deal about raising children from being the oldest in a family with ten of them. Neither parent drank, smoked, or cursed ("Goodness Gracious" was the worst anyone would ever hear from their oldest son), both remarkably free of vices of any kind, in fact, even though formal religion didn't play much of a role in their lives or in the moral instruction of the Johnson children. "It was wilderness country where we lived," Earl Johnson explained, "and churchgoing was difficult. But our father and mother taught us the Golden Rule, and we lived by it to the best of our ability. Walter, I believe, best of all."[11] "My good parents taught me a few simple truths in early life that I have tried to follow," was how Walter Johnson put it. Among the truths imparted by their parents were tolerance and a respect for others; just tend to your own business, Frank Johnson told them.[12]

At the peak of her son's fame many years later, Minnie Johnson was asked about his childhood. "Walter was always a model boy," she replied, "he's as good as they make them. He's always made friends. As a schoolboy he was the friend of everybody, and was never the kind who would pick a quarrel with anybody. In fact, he straightened out a lot of quarrels."[13] Formal learning began at the Crescent Valley School a mile and a half from the farm. In every kind of weather he walked along dirt roads to the one-room "little old-fashioned country school," as he later characterized it, where twenty or so farm children received their early education.[14]

It was here also that Johnson was introduced to sports, at first just tossing a rubber ball back and forth over the tiny building.[15] Later he joined the older boys playing "one o' cat" (a rudimentary version of baseball) in the school yard. The first evidence of an unusual talent was displayed one April morning during recess. A game was under way and it was Walter's turn to pitch, but the older boys, thinking him too young for the task, wanted to replace him. "I can do it," he protested, and to prove the point threw the ball with all of his might. Sailing far over the heads of the waiting players, it took one bounce before brushing the back of their teacher's head and bounding up against the school to break the biggest window in the building. "I was so frightened," Johnson remembered, "I honestly thought I would be sent to jail."[16]

The ability to throw hard was not something that Johnson ever had to develop. It was a gift, pure and simple. "From the first time I held a ball it settled in the palm of my right hand as though it belonged there," he told an interviewer, "and when I threw it, ball, hand and wrist, arm and shoulder and back seemed to all work together."[17]

At the turn of the century a severe drought devastated Allen County, forcing Frank Johnson to sell the farm on which the family had worked so hard for the past fifteen years. In April, 1901, they moved into Humboldt, renting a house in the southwest part of town. Bad luck followed a few days later when fire destroyed a small stable adjacent to the house, killing the cow they had brought with them.[18] Earning only a dollar a day working in Humboldt, Frank Johnson somehow managed to pay his bills and support the family, which had five children with the birth of Blanche Marie in August. "There was hard sledding in the Johnson home at times," recalled Walter Johnson, "but we were all the better for it."[19] He helped out by working as a hired hand for the new owners of the farm, earning $35 for the summer. At harvest time, he got 50 cents a day making hay. "I considered myself on the highway to prosperity," Johnson later joked.[20]

Thirteen-year-old Walter entered the eighth grade of the Humboldt city school that fall of 1901. He was a conscientious student, judging by his inclusion in the *Humboldt Union's* list of those with perfect attendance for the months of September and November. (This was apparently important to Frank and Minnie Johnson, as their other schoolchildren, Effie, Earl, and Leslie, also made the list.) The school had no ballfield, much less a baseball diamond, so the kids often played on the vacant lot behind a church.[21] Most of the time they just played in the streets of Humboldt, a situation against which the *Union* conducted a vigorous editorial campaign.[22]

Walter struck up a friendship with a neighbor and schoolmate, Dave Woods, who owned a homemade catcher's mitt, and afternoons and weekends they played catch in the street. Sometimes there were enough boys for a pickup game, in which Walter usually pitched for his crowd.[23] On one occasion the other team objected on the grounds that he had hit several players in these games. "We won't play if the wild Johnson kid is going to pitch," they insisted, but ran into a rare instance of documented contrariness on his part. "I got on my high horse," he recalled many years later. "'You [his teammates] told me I was going to pitch,' I said, 'and I'm going to pitch or there ain't goin' to be any game.' And with that, I laid right down flat on the pitcher's mound and refused to get up until they finally agreed that I could pitch."[24]

There is evidence of considerable interest in baseball in Humboldt at that time. "Baseball is the most popular game at school now," the *Union* declared. (It didn't say which sport had been displaced in their affections.) The town had a semiprofessional team, the "Greys," playing Sundays in a seven-team league. In 1901 they won their first 10 games before slumping to a 12–5 final record. The most exciting contest of the season occurred in October when a large crowd turned out to see the Greys challenge the "Original Boston Bloomers Ladies Champion Baseball Club of the World," which had their own train bringing along fences and a grandstand. The famous Bloomers were said to have been "defeating some of the best amateur clubs in the country," but were soundly trounced by the Humboldt boys, 19–4, in a game that took on even greater significance two days later when neighboring Iola lost to the Bloomers, 4–2. The defeat of the Boston Bloomers was no doubt the biggest event in Humboldt since Spanish-American War hero and vice-presidential candidate Teddy Roosevelt delivered a campaign speech at the train depot a year earlier. Whether young Walter Johnson paid the game much attention is unknown, but it is true that when he left Humboldt at the age of 14 he had yet to play in anything resembling a real game of baseball.[25]

In November, 1901, Minnie Johnson's brother, Cliff Perry, who had moved to California several years earlier, returned to Humboldt for a visit.[26] Cliff and older brother Frank Perry had found work in the oil fields of Southern California, and Cliff's accounts of the boom times there found a receptive audience in Frank Johnson. At that time many farmers were moving from the Plains, where they were at the mercy of the weather, to California and its huge irrigation projects.[27] When Cliff returned to the West Coast his brother-in-law went along to see for himself. Frank Johnson quickly found himself a job, and on April 23, 1902, Minnie Johnson and her five children boarded a train heading west.[28]

At the time, the only contact I had with baseball was playing Sundays on a semipro team called the Hoegee Flags. We were sponsored by a sporting-goods house, and on our backs we had flags of all nations. We played teams all over southern California, and I still remember the one that was the toughest. It was a team down by Santa Ana, for which Walter Johnson pitched. If people think Walter was fast later on, they should have seen him then. Whew! Most of the time you couldn't even see the ball![29]

FRED SNODGRASS

As the 19th century turned into the 20th, a second wave of migration poured into California, not after gold in the north this time but to southern parts in search of the "black gold"—oil. If less dramatic than the first, which had brought the colorful "Forty-Niners" a half-century before, this influx was to have a far greater and longer-lasting impact on the Golden State. Beneath the ground in certain sections of Southern California lay large deposits of oil, and the dawn of the automobile revolution in the 1890s brought increasing demand for it. In 1897, E.L. Doheny, who would achieve infamy as the instigator of the Teapot Dome scandal of the early 1920s, formed the Brea Canyon Oil Company to tap the huge reserves discovered there. Wooden oil derricks seemed to sprout everywhere overnight.

A strong, diligent, and sober man like Frank Johnson had no trouble making his way in the oil fields. Settling in the tiny village of Olinda twenty miles southeast of Los Angeles, he worked as a teamster and loader for the Santa Fe Oil Company, a partnership between Doheny and the Santa Fe Railroad. Johnson hauled supplies by horse and wagon six miles from Fullerton, with a population of 1,700 the nearest town of any size. The family lived on Olinda's main street in a house owned, like everything else on the oil leases, by the company.[30]

Compared to the isolated and sometimes precarious existence on the plains of Kansas, life in Olinda was bountiful. The houses had plumbing, electricity, and gas heat. Food of every variety was delivered by wagon from Fullerton, and the fenced backyards were big enough to keep cows, chickens, and other livestock. The nearby foothills of the coastal range mountains were full of rabbits, squirrels, quail, even deer and bear at the higher altitudes.[31] Warm sunshine came down through clear blue skies onto the velvet-green hills, and when the orange groves in Placentia were in blossom a sweet fragrance blanketed the area for miles around. The big social event in Olinda was the Saturday night dance at the company hall, where a small orchestra played until midnight and could be bribed into staying later.[32]

Minnie Johnson would look back on these years as the happiest of her long and eventful life. She was surrounded by family: her parents, John and Lucinda Perry, had moved there with their younger children; brothers Cliff and Frank were in nearby Fullerton; and there was her own still-growing brood, which filled out to six the next year with the birth of Chester Johnson.[33] Olinda was a wonderful place for children. One resident recalled growing up there at the turn of the century: "It was all kids and dogs . . . a happy place to play. A neighbor's dog was affectionately treated like a member of the family. At night the constant pumping of the wells would rock us all to sleep. Our parents told us that each creak of the pump whispered, 'five dollars,' 'five dollars,' 'five dollars,' until we finally dozed off." Children slid down gravel-pit hills on corrugated-metal sleds, and poked around the pumphouses for "trapdoor" spiders and their satin-like tunnels. There was cool, pure mountain water to drink straight from hillside springs. But for the boys of Olinda one pastime ranked in importance far above any other—baseball.[34]

While the Johnsons were making a new life for themselves in Olinda a great baseball boom happened to be taking place there. Drillers and other workers from the oil companies were organized into teams, and their Sunday games became a popular attraction for local residents. Wanting its name well-represented in these contests, the Santa Fe Oil Company made unofficial scouts of its managers, encouraging them to hire men with ballplaying skills. Jobs were created with the company "weed gang" that controlled fire hazards in the oil fields. Hoes and shovels in hand, the "ringers" would disappear out of sight into the countryside, when out came the real tools of their trade—bats, balls, and gloves. Aspiring ballplayers were soon coming to Olinda to apply for this easy work, and as the team improved it began to look farther afield for worthy opponents.[35] This was the great era of "town ball" in America. Every community with enough men to field a team challenged its neighbors, with the games often taking on a holiday atmosphere of bands, cookouts, special trains, and wholesale gambling on the outcome. For the people of these isolated localities, with little else in the way of entertainment, the contests were a passionate affair indeed.

Around the turn of the century the "Oil Wells" team of Olinda started taking on nines from nearby towns and semipro outfits from Los Angeles. Olinda didn't have a real ballpark, just a rough diamond laid out on a flat section of land, and as fan interest grew a more suitable place to play was needed. The problem was solved in 1903 when the town of Anaheim, two hours south of Olinda by horse and buggy, volunteered the use of its newly-constructed ballpark. The only locality in Orange County where serving alcohol was legal on Sundays, Anaheim and its saloonkeepers hoped to draw business from the crowds coming in for games. The arrangement proved a success and lasted for years, the Olinda Oil Wells becoming the "home" team at Anaheim's Athletic Park and bringing in the best ballclubs from a wide area of Southern California. Players dressed in the back of the bars while patrons in the front drank and placed bets on the outcome.[36]

One of the Oil Wells' biggest fans was Frank Johnson. And while it's not likely he contributed any business to the saloons, on any Sunday he could be found sitting along the foul lines rooting for his team. Alongside him always was his son, Walter.[37]

For two years after the move to Olinda, Walter Johnson's involvement in baseball was limited to being a spectator at these games in Anaheim. That and the typical boy's interest in the great stars of the major leagues. Years later when a new generation of youngsters was following *his* every move, Johnson recalled searching the papers for the latest exploits of Ed Delahanty, Wee Willie Keeler, Honus Wagner, Napoleon Lajoie, and a pair of pitchers with whom Johnson himself would forever be compared: Christy Mathewson and Cy Young.[38] He drove a team of horses for his father after school and during summers, apparently leaving little time for playing ball. "I never had a chance to play," was the only explanation offered for the fact that not until well into his 16th year did Johnson play baseball to any extent. He credited the delayed start for the remarkable resilience and durability of his arm: "By that time I had attained sufficient strength so that I could not hurt myself," Johnson explained.[39]

As the success of the Olinda team captured the imagination of the community, it also fostered a tremendous enthusiasm for the game among the youngsters. A dozen or so students from Olinda Elementary, Johnson's school for his first two years there, gathered each day on the "flat" to play baseball until the sun disappeared behind the hills.[40] Lacking the personnel for real games, they made do with the usual shorthanded versions, "numbers" and "one o' cat," although on occasion a bunch from a neighboring area would come over with a challenge. Initially Johnson's favorite position in these games wasn't pitcher. He preferred being the catcher instead, and his powerful arm made him a natural for it. That there was no mask or other protective equipment, which necessitated standing ten feet behind the batter, didn't discourage him from the job. But Frank Johnson, seeing the speed his son could put on the ball, suggested he try pitching. "But Papa," the boy countered, "they don't ever steal when I'm behind the bat."[41]

One day in the spring or early summer of 1904, a group of boys from the nearby orange groves came to the flat to take on the oil-field kids. Johnson started the game behind the plate as usual, but after three pitchers had been clobbered by the visitors he was sent to the mound in the fourth inning in a desperate attempt to stem the tide. "It was my first taste of real competition," Johnson recalled. "I soon found there was just as much pleasure in whipping the ball to the catcher as in shooting it to second base. And, as one after another retired on strikes, I found the pleasure even greater." He struck out 12 batters in all, and the boys on the flat had found themselves a new pitcher.[42]

Walter Johnson's throwing style—a short "windmill" windup in which he rotated his arm in a circle while standing straight up on the mound, then swept the arm behind his back as far as it would go before whipping it forward in a smooth sidearm-underarm arc—was unique unto him, his signature. Legendary sportswriter Grantland Rice called it "the finest motion in the game," for its simplicity and grace.[43] But despite its obvious effectiveness, it would be years before older players stopped trying to persuade him to change his delivery. It would never do in "fast company," they told him.[44]

Speed was there from the beginning, but Johnson wasn't satisfied with his control. He gathered up empty cans wherever he saw them and kept a supply in his wagon. On lunch breaks he would set up a row of cans on the side of the wagon and throw rocks at them from about ninety feet.[45] That was the full extent of Walter Johnson's "training" to develop his pitching skills, and all he ever needed, it seems.

He kept striking out the boys on the flat, and soon became the subject of some discussion in the stores and around the oil derricks, where baseball was always the hot topic. Joe Burke, a bookkeeper with the Santa Fe Railroad and player-manager of the Olinda Oil Wells, heard the stories and became the original "discoverer" of Walter Johnson. Several years later Burke wrote about it:

> Some of the boys got to talking in the office about the enthusiasm in the flat, and Jack Burnett [Olinda's big hitter, who would play in the major leagues] and I decided to go down and have some fun with the lads. Somebody told us that Frank Johnson's kid, Walt, was some heaver. Jack and I sauntered down and found Walt idly throwing to another kid alongside the store. I gave Jack a wink and asked Walt to throw us a few. He blushed, but was willing. I stepped to the imaginary home plate, posed a bit, and told Walt to let 'em come. They came. I made an attempt to bunt, missed, thought it an accident, tried another, missed it, got another and missed it. I gave way to the slugger. Jack squared away to put a crimp in the young blood, and the way he fanned the air has never been equalled in front of Walter Johnson from that day to this. Jack Burnett was the most surprised man in California, except myself and maybe Walt. [Johnson] took it all as a huge joke. He was never any else than good-natured, easygoing and smiling. We walked back up the hill, and Jack and I confided to each other that we were glad we had not invited the bunch down to watch us make monkeys of the kids.[46]

Not long after this impromptu "tryout," Johnson was given a more demanding audition pitching in a real game for Olinda. The date was July 24, 1904, and the Oil Wells were playing the Eureka team from Los Angeles. After six innings Olinda had piled up a commanding lead, so Burke decided to let some of the younger boys have some fun. "Go on in, Walt," he said. "Let's see what you can do." Johnson got up from where he had been watching the game and walked out to the mound. An even younger boy named Grover Collins, who was probably familiar with Johnson's pitching from the flat, was put in to catch, and the Oil Wells' regular infield was replaced by Olinda youngsters. What they did for uniforms is a mystery, but not the result.

"Walt turned things loose," Burke recalled, "and hanged if he didn't drub the Los Angeles bunch worse than we did."[47] The final score was 21–6. The number of hits and runs allowed by the 16-year-old wasn't reported, but the *Fullerton Tribune* did mention that "Johnson, the crack pitcher of the Olinda 'kid' team, fanned six men in the three innings which he worked." It was his first press notice. For the next six months, however, this one appearance remained the full extent of Johnson's semiprofessional career. Frank Johnson, concerned that his son was moving too fast and might hurt his arm, held him back from further work with the Oil Wells. "A wise old fellow," Joe Burke called the father.[48]

Johnson continued pitching for the boys on the flat, and in the fall of 1904 entered Fullerton Union High School. For some reason he had fallen behind in his schooling, leaving Kansas in the eighth grade and only now, two years later, moving up from middle school to the freshman class of the high school.[49] Perhaps his Kansas education had placed him at a disadvantage in the California school system, or working for his father had interfered with his studies. But he had stayed on track in the Humboldt City School, which was much larger than Fullerton's, and it doesn't seem likely that his parents would have allowed his education to be neglected even for work. With no reason to believe that Johnson, who by many accounts possessed an above-average intelligence, wasn't up to the demands of the schoolwork, this late ascension to the high school remains a puzzle.

"Walter Johnson and Grover Collins have been added to the list of professional players for the famous Olinda team," noted the *Fullerton Tribune* on February 2, 1905. With Frank Johnson apparently loosening the reins, the son asked the new manager of the baseball team, Tom Young, if he could play for them. The Oil Wells had just lost their crack battery to another club, which might have played a part in Johnson's asking, and it was almost certainly a factor in the young pitcher and catcher being added to the roster. By the time of the *Tribune's* announcement, Johnson had already started his first game for Olinda, an extra-inning complete game at that.

The Oil Wells took the train to Los Nietos, just outside of Whittier, to play the Rivera club (and their own 17-year-old destined for fame in the big leagues, catcher Fred Snodgrass) on January 29, 1905. Giving up nine hits and striking out eight, Johnson lost a 5–4 thriller in the bottom of the 11th inning on a home run by Rube Ellis, who would play for the St. Louis Cardinals. "Johnson was presented as a high school kid, but he is certainly a graduate in the science of delivering the ball," punned the *Whittier News.* Years later a witness recalled his impression of Walter Johnson's first start: "There was no uniform for him to wear, so they gathered some odds and ends. Always a husky youth, the shirt he wore was too short, so his shirttail was out after every pitch and his pants hit him well above the knees. They were too tight to buckle and his cap bobbed on his head. He took an awful ribbing, which he ignored, fanned every batter, and before he was through he had the entire crowd cheering for him."[50]

At the same time his semipro career was getting underway, Johnson also played several games for Fullerton Union High School. Coverage was sporadic and incomplete, but it's likely that he pitched in at least three games, and according to his own version of events he was the catcher in two others.[51] There was no one in the tiny school of some 60 students capable of holding Johnson's deliveries, so Grover Collins, although still in the grammar school, was drafted into service behind the plate for the Fullerton Union team.

The high school didn't win a game in which Johnson played, but the last one, on April 15, 1905, was a classic nonetheless—a 15-inning 0–0 tie with Santa Ana High School. Johnson struck out 27, his highest single-game total at any level, while yielding seven hits and three walks. Great as the performance was, he was outpitched by Santa Ana's ace, George Coleman, who allowed Fullerton a meager three hits and one walk while striking out 17. The game was called not for darkness but because of the sheer exhaustion of everyone involved. "Rooters were out in force for both sides and the grandstand was kept in a constant uproar applauding the brilliant work of the players," reported the *Santa Ana Evening Blade.* Santa Ana's captain, Garland Ross, recalled that "for the most part, we just went up to the plate, took our three swings, and walked back to the bench. I remember we all kept saying to the next batter, 'He ain't got a thing but a fast ball,' and that was true. But what a fast ball! It came up to the plate like a pea shot out of a cannon."[52] Santa Ana went on to win the Southern California high school championship, while Fullerton's season was over.

The Olinda Oil Wells were playing every Sunday, meanwhile, and Johnson was in the lineup consistently, alternating between right field, first base, and the mound. In his pitching debut at the home park in Anaheim on March 5 he again lost by the margin of 5–4, a victim of five errors by his teammates. Having given up only four hits and a walk, he was lauded for the performance by the *Anaheim Gazette,* which also tagged him with his first nickname, one that would stick with him for the next two years: "Far and away the most pleasant feature of the game was 'Kid' Johnson's pitching for the Olinda team. He remained cool-headed throughout the game . . . Johnson is a good find and he had a host of admirers upon his first appearance." On April 9 he struck out 11 Los Angeles Owls but lost again when they took advantage of his inexperience and that of a new third baseman, bunting six times in a row for four hits and three runs in the ninth inning to break up a 2–2 tie.

In his adolescence Johnson was the "awkwardest fellow on the team," Joe Burke remembered. "Many a time I have seen Walt pitch a superb game, and along toward the last a little bunt would come rolling down to him gently, like a zephyr from the western sea. Walt would start to get it, his feet were sure to tangle and Walt was sure to fall down on the ground. Tall and angular, his feet and hands were abnormally big, out of proportion to the rest of him. He afterwards grew up to his extremities. While he handled himself like a barnyard animal in fielding and baserunning, he was always a good batter, and he had that graceful swing of the shoulders and free action with his arm. He sure could pitch." Johnson's problems with coordination brought some teasing, but he handled that better than the bunts, according to Burke: "The Oil Wells bunch has no mercy on its friends, and boring into some fellow is a favorite pastime. Their joshing was rough-shod stuff, and Walt had a lot to take. He knew it and took his joshing like a man."[53]

On May 28 Johnson struck out a dozen of the Hoegees club from Los Angeles but was once again sabotaged by a leaky Olinda defense that allowed four unearned runs in the first two innings of a 4–2 loss. Although invincible for the rest of the game, he did hit three of the Hoegees who, "failing to find them with the bat, turned their anatomy toward the ball, getting it amidships," the *Gazette* noted. Two weeks later the Hoegees became Walter Johnson's first victims when he beat them, 9–4, on June 11 to finally pick up a win in his ninth pitching appearance (including three with the high school). The Olinda season ended July 30 with more than a thousand fans overflowing the Anaheim ballpark to see the Oil Wells play a Sioux Indian team from South Dakota. Like the Bloomer Girls, the Indians toured the country in their own train bringing everything with them, including 50 arc lamps to illuminate the field for the night game of a day-night doubleheader. Johnson won the day game handily, striking out ten Sioux, who then humiliated the locals under the lights in the evening contest, 17–5.

After the doubleheader the Olinda Oil Wells disbanded. Manager Tom Young was weary of exhorting the Anaheim crowds to "loosen their wallets" when the hat was passed to cover expenses. Interruptions in the games while Young and his players pleaded with the fans from the middle of the diamond had become an annoying but increasingly necessary feature of the contests. Independent of any company support now, and unwilling to try to charge admission to the games, the Oil Wells were dependent on the goodwill of their followers. But often after visiting teams had been reimbursed for transportation and meals, there was little or nothing left for the players.[54] Johnson, 17 years old and living at home, was unconcerned. "My share was often 50 or 75 cents, and frequently nothing," he recalled. "This, however, did not worry me as the keen enjoyment of the game was compensation enough."[55] But some of the older men who had been promised a regular salary departed for greener pastures. After the breakup Johnson joined the Rivera club, which had expressed an interest in him two weeks earlier when rumors of the demise of the Oil Wells first circulated. Also switching to Rivera was Guy Meats, who would be behind the plate for most of Johnson's semipro games over the next five years.[56]

Throughout Walter Johnson's career certain receivers took naturally to his pitching, unfazed by the unusual speed, while otherwise excellent catchers had a difficult time with it. His favorites were the former, of course, and Meats was the first of these. In an interview more than 50 years later Meats shared a surprising "secret" that was commonly expressed by Johnson's regular catchers over the years: "He was the easiest man I ever caught," Meats declared. "Despite his great speed, he threw a light ball, and his control was so perfect that you always got what you asked for. I could have caught him in a rocking chair." Of Johnson's unflappable disposition on the mound, Meats recalled: "If an umpire called a close one, Walter never took issue with him, because he believed that the umpires make mistakes the same as players do and the next one might be in his favor. He just tossed the next one over the plate in such a fashion that it left no doubt in anyone's mind. He never complained or noted an error behind him."[57]

As the summer of 1905 came to an end, instead of returning to the high school Johnson enrolled in the Orange County Business College, a bookkeeping and secretarial school in nearby Santa Ana. Almost 18 years old, an age at which most students are finishing high school, he might have felt himself too old to be going into the tenth grade. He studied bookkeeping at the business school, perhaps influenced by Joe Burke, who worked in that capacity for the Santa Fe Railroad. Johnson had taken a job at the grocery store in Olinda, and the owner, Maurice Ray, also encouraged him to continue his education.[58] He made four dollars a week doing general chores, and according to Guy Meats most of that went into the card games usually in progress in the back of the store. "He didn't drink or smoke," Meats recalled, "but how the son-of-a-gun liked to play poker! Any time there were four or more in a room, Walter would start a poker game, and he could draw to anything. He was such a soft touch for any amount. I could have retired on what he gave away."[59]

In October, Tom Young announced the reorganization of the Olinda Oil Wells now that "more favorable concessions" from Anaheim had been secured, possibly some kind of guarantee from the saloon owners.[60] The new deal had the effect of increasing the average kitty to about $25 per game, not a bad split for nine players considering that a roustabout in the oil fields started at $1.50 a day.[61] After a four-game stint with Rivera Johnson returned to the Oil Wells, this time as their front-line pitcher. On November 12 he crafted his first semipro shutout, a 1–0 1-hitter with 13 strikeouts. He also had two hits in three times at bat. "The best game of ball ever witnessed here," gushed the *Gazette,* "with Kid Johnson the star performer. The way he struck them out was wonderful. Johnson is no doubt one of the best amateurs in the state and has the stuff in him to send him up the line." Just how far "up the line" Johnson was to go neither the *Gazette* nor anyone else could have imagined, but this game was just the confidence-booster needed after an inconsistent first year and it started the youngster on a six-game winning streak.

On February 11, 1906, Johnson pitched one of his less sparkling victories of the winter, a 5–4 squeaker over Rivera in which he struck out 11 but was also touched for 10 hits. What made the affair memorable was the presence of two of the most important baseball men on the West Coast, Frank "Pop" Dillon, captain of the Los Angeles Angels of the Pacific Coast League, and Russ Hall, manager of the Seattle club of the PCL, the top professional circuit on the West Coast. Word of the Oil Wells' recent success, 9 wins in 11 games since starting up again, had gotten around and the men were there scouting for talent. Johnson wasn't told about them for fear it might affect his pitching, and when he was introduced to the pair after the game had no idea who they were. Joe Burke was particularly eager to see Johnson move up into faster company. "I felt sure that if he had half a chance he would develop into something really great," Burke recalled. "He was our kind of fellow. So when we heard that Dillon and Hall had their eagle eye on us, we gave the lad the best support there was in us. After the game I led a delegation of Oil Wells players to where Dillon had been sitting in the little grandstand directly back of the catcher.

'What did you think of the kid?', I asked him.

'Well,' said Dillon. 'He won't do yet. He telegraphs everything he throws.'"[62]

Johnson's style of swinging the ball back in full view before whipping it forward had convinced the major-league veteran Dillon that the youngster wasn't ready for the higher leagues, although Dillon's other criticisms about Johnson's trouble holding runners on base and general lack of experience were more pertinent. As if Dillon's rejection didn't hurt enough, Hall ignored Johnson completely while signing two others, outfielder Jack Burnett and third baseman Anson Mott, for Seattle. Three weeks later Hall was again on hand to see Johnson pitch, but it happened to be one of his worst outings of the season, a 5–3 loss to the same Rivera club.

Olinda's season ended in early April. Johnson finished with a record of 12 wins and 3 losses, all complete games, with 5 shutouts and an average of 10 strikeouts per game.[63] While many of his teammates were leaving for minor-league jobs or tryouts, it seemed the end of baseball for him for awhile. But just a week later Johnson's fortunes took a dramatic turn with the receipt of a telegram from Tacoma, Washington, with a job offer. Jack Burnett had been traded from Seattle to Tacoma of the Northwestern League, it seemed, and had told them about his hard-throwing Olinda teammate.[64]

Surprisingly, Johnson didn't jump at the chance to move up to the minor leagues. In an early example of the caution that would precede decisions throughout his life, and with little concern, apparently, that it might be his only chance, the matter was left entirely up to his parents. "Johnson has not decided yet whether he will enter the league this year or wait until next season," the *Fullerton Tribune* reported. Neither parent objected to their son trying his fortunes in Tacoma, though, and baseball fan Frank Johnson must have been thrilled. But some relatives and neighbors were horrified at the prospect, rushing to warn the Johnsons what might become of young Walter should he turn to baseball as a profession.[65]

CHAPTER 2

The Weiser Wonder

It was wild country in those days. Whenever I go to the movies and see a picture showing so-called "hard-boiled westerners", I just think of Idaho back in 1906 and wish some of those Hollywood directors had been with me up there.[1]

WALTER JOHNSON

Johnson took a train to Los Angeles for the connection north. He carried a leather satchel full of sandwiches his mother had made and a package with the new suit necessary, she had insisted, for meeting one's employer. It cost him twelve dollars, the savings of a lifetime. Arriving in Tacoma, Johnson ducked into the gent's room of a hotel near the station to change clothes. But along the way he had tucked the suit into the satchel, which was opened now to reveal a disaster. The beautiful garment had turned into a wrinkled rag. "If I'd slept in it a month, it couldn't have looked any worse," Johnson remembered. And if that wasn't bad enough, one of the sandwiches had broken free of its wrapping and saturated the suit with jelly. He reported to the baseball field in the clothes on his back.[2]

At that time there was another catastrophe on everyone's mind, of far greater consequence than a kid's mishap with a new suit. In fact, it was the worst natural disaster in the history of the United States—the San Francisco earthquake and fire of April 18–20, 1906, occurring just days before Johnson's arrival in Tacoma and not far away. As it would do for so many others in the area, the earthquake changed the course of his life. There was no hint of that at first as he signed up with Tacoma, joining a roster that listed only two other pitchers: 33-year-old veteran Ike Butler, who had blown his one chance in the major leagues with a 1–10 season at Baltimore in 1902, and Irv Higginbotham, who was ten years younger and would be moving up to the

St. Louis Cardinals later in the year. The Tacoma Tigers, recently shorn of their Pacific Coast League franchise, were newcomers this year to the Northwestern League, a circuit of four cities in the state of Washington: Tacoma, Spokane, Aberdeen, and Grays Harbor.

Johnson was with Tacoma by April 24 at the latest, when his presence there was first reported by the *Spokane Spokesman-Review*. The *Tacoma Ledger* carried a similarly brief mention the next day, adding only that he had played in the "California State League." Newspapers were taken up largely with the earthquake and its consequences, even the sports section, where there was much speculation about the fate of the Pacific Coast League. San Francisco had been the league's flagship franchise, its largest city, and the season was apparently over there. Fires still raged out of control as W. H. Lucas, president of the Northwestern League, told the *Portland Oregonian* that the Seattle and Portland PCL clubs would be welcome in the Northwestern League "should the Coast League find it impossible to continue."[3]

Tacoma's season opened on April 28 with a series against the Grays Harbor Warriors. Higginbotham and Butler won the first two games, the hitting star of which was Tigers first baseman Jack Burnett with two hits in each, including a home run in the first game and a double and triple in the second. A day off was scheduled for Monday, April 30, but the teams volunteered to play an unofficial exhibition game to benefit the Red Cross earthquake relief fund. Walter Johnson pitched and lost a 4–3 thriller, giving up 10 hits and a walk while striking out seven, a creditable first effort for the 18-year-old. Sixty-eight dollars was raised for the charity.[4]

The next day an article adjacent to the *Ledger's* account of the game reported the demise of the Pacific Coast League. Announcing the disbanding of his club, Los Angeles Angels owner Jim Morley declared that there was no chance the league would last another week. The Northwestern League was said to be reorganizing, adding the Seattle and Portland teams and picking up new players for the existing teams. "The circuit will begin to strengthen immediately from the defunct Pacific Coast League," the *Ledger* stated, "the pick of the players being taken." Tacoma owner George Shreeder added: "We will begin to strengthen right away from the other teams of the Pacific Coast League. The managers of the Northwestern teams will look over the field and pick the men they want."[5]

In anticipation of this flood of PCL talent, Tigers manager Mike Lynch released his young pitcher, Walter Johnson. And with his mind on the bigger things seeming to be in store for him, perhaps, Lynch didn't bother with any care for the boy's feelings. "He told me that so far as pitching was concerned, I would make a better outfielder," Johnson recalled.[6] As things worked out, the timing couldn't have been worse. Within days after he was let go, Northwestern League teams and their fans had second thoughts about adding the much stronger PCL clubs. Then the Pacific Coast League pulled itself together with financial assistance from the major leagues. In the end, both circuits continued on as before.[7] Lynch did replace Johnson with a pitcher from the PCL, a youngster named Finney who had failed at Seattle and would contribute little to the Tigers' pennant chase—certainly not enough to compensate for the damage to Lynch's reputation later when he became known as the man who had let Walter Johnson slip through his fingers.

The abrupt release from Tacoma was a crushing blow. Johnson had just begun to consider the possibility of a career in baseball,[8] but within the space of a few months now he had been summarily rejected by three of the most influential baseball men on the coast, all of them veterans of the major leagues. He also found himself a thousand miles from home with forty dollars, his week's pay at Tacoma, to his name, and nowhere to go.[9] The old job driving a team of mules in Olinda looked pretty good to him, but he wanted to stay in baseball if possible. So instead of going home, Johnson stayed in Tacoma, and once again a telegram from an old Olinda teammate came to the rescue. Oil Wells shortstop Clair Head had become a baseball itinerant, passing through the Southwest in the spring and the Northwest that summer trying to hook on with a team. Following a three-game tryout with Tacoma a few days after Johnson's release, Head had moved on again. His telegram was from the town of Weiser, Idaho, and he wanted Johnson to join him there.[10]

Weiser (pronounced "weezer") was a town of some 3,000 inhabitants on a bend in the Snake River in Southwestern Idaho, not far from the Oregon border. A hundred years earlier Peter Weiser, an original member of the Lewis and Clark expedition, returned to the area with a party of fur trappers to chart it for Clark's map of the Northwest.[11] The thriving mining and farming region was proudly called "The Fat Land of Weiser" by local boosters. In the heart of the Rocky Mountains, it was a wild and scenic place, surrounded on all sides by spectacular, rugged peaks and gorges. Weiser's population was equally picturesque, a melting pot of gold and copper miners, sheep and cattle ranchers, apple, potato, and sugar-beet farmers, cowboys, Shoshone Indians, Chinese railroad laborers, and a bit of everything else. "A big-hearted, hard-fisted town," Walter Johnson called it. The 15 saloons and several opium dens in operation there notwithstanding, "It kept itself in surprising order," he remembered. "There were few, if any, drunks to be seen on the streets."[12]

Early in April, 1906, six towns accessible to each other by railroad formed the Southern Idaho League, with games to be played on Sundays and holidays.

An old baseball field next to the racetrack in Weiser was spruced up and fenced in so a 25-cent admission could be charged. A manager was appointed by a committee of town leaders, ballplayers were recruited, and practices begun. Their only preseason game was lost to the Payette "Melon Chewers" (nicknames reflected the principal industries of the towns), and on April 28 Weiser's official season opened at home with a dismal 23–11 thrashing at the hands of their arch-rivals, the Caldwell "Countyseaters." In the next two weeks the Weiser boys defeated the Nampa "Sugar Beeters" and lost to the Boise "Senators" in close, low-scoring games. For the Boise game Weiser had a new man, Clair Head, playing third base. In its "All Around the Town" column on May 19 the *Weiser Signal* noted that "Walter Johnson of Los Angeles was among city arrivals yesterday."

"I was broke the day I landed at Weiser, Idaho. Not only that but I was hungry," Johnson remembered. "I stopped a stranger and asked for directions to baseball headquarters. 'Which team do you want?,' he asked. That sounded encouraging. This must be some town, I thought, to support more than one baseball team. But I soon discovered one was the high school team and the other represented the town." Johnson ran into Clair Head in front of the hotel, and by the next day had himself a job with the Bell Telephone Company of Washington County at a salary of ninety dollars a month. He did work there some in a clerical capacity, making himself useful around the office, but the job was really part of the business community's support for the team.[13] "I was assigned to what you might call the baseball department," Johnson explained. "My duties consisted of pitching for the town team every Sunday."[14]

He started earning his pay two days later, on Sunday, May 20, when the team journeyed south to the state capital of Boise. This time, with a new pitcher and catcher, Weiser trounced the Senators, 17–1, in front of a crowd of 1,000. Johnson ran into trouble in the first inning when two Boise hits and an error loaded the bases with one out. But a strikeout and groundout closed off the threat and the rest of the way was a breeze, Johnson allowing four hits and a walk while striking out seven. He scored three runs himself with three hits in five trips to the plate.

But the Boise newspaper, the *Idaho Daily Statesman,* mentioned Johnson's Weiser debut only in passing. It was fascinated instead by his catcher, a 250-pound, 53-year-old Weiserite playing ball again for the first time after a 15-year hiatus from the game. His name was E. Cornelius Uhl, but in Weiser everyone knew him as "Foxy Grandpa." Adding intrigue to the story, Uhl played under the name "Miller" and Johnson was listed as "H. Smith." Clair Head appeared in box scores for most of the season as "Roy Patterson." The phony names might have been used because these men had played ball elsewhere and teams in the Southern Idaho League were supposed to be made up of local talent.[15] But according to the *Statesman* Uhl was a Weiser resident, making the pretense unnecessary in his case, at least. He was also the star of the game, in the newspaper's opinion, and deserved much of the credit for Johnson's sterling performance also. Under the headline, "Old Timer Who Can Play Ball," his remarkable story was told:

It was all the fault of "Foxy Grandpa" Miller, who did the backstop act for the visitors. There was a time, so the old-timers in the baseball world assert, when Foxy Grandpa used to play ball regularly. But some 15 years or so ago, he felt his bones stiffening and he concluded to stop the strenuous life. He moved out to sunny Idaho, and established himself on a farm near Weiser. Just as a reminder of the old times, Foxy Grandpa went to town last Sunday and saw the game between Boise and Weiser. He was disgusted to think the Weiser team would be beat by such an aggregation as that from the capital. "Huh," he said, "I am old and fat and grey-headed, but I can play ball enough yet to beat that bunch." And Monday morning he began training, with the result that he was given a place behind the bat in yesterday's game. He coached up young Smith [Johnson] until the latter kept his head all the way through. Every time a Boise man got on a base—and there were very, very few—Foxy Grandpa would pull off some sort of an unexpected play and catch the runner napping.

Neither did Johnson's 12–0 one-hitter with a dozen strikeouts against Payette the following week catch the newspaper's attention in its continuing astonishment at the exploits of the ancient Weiser catcher, who went four-for-five at the plate. "'Foxy Grandpa' Miller was the star performer," the *Statesman* insisted, "the same as he was last week. He made a sensational long hit and, although he is not shaped for a sprinter, he reached third on it." But it was Johnson the large crowd had come to see, according to the *Weiser World*. "Everyone awaited the beginning of the game with intense interest," it reported, "to see Weiser's phenomenal pitcher, Johnson, twirl the ball over the home plate. The game began amid a roar from the spectators, which was occasioned by Payette's star batter striking at the first ball and Foxy Grandpa Miller holding it up to show him he had caught it several seconds before." At Emmett the next weekend Weiser inexplicably dropped back-to-back games Saturday (an exhibition) and Sunday to the last-place "Prune Pickers." Johnson's 2–0 defeat in Sunday's official contest, despite twelve strikeouts, would be his only loss of the season.

On June 10 the Weiser team and several hundred fans took the 50-mile train trip to Caldwell for the big game against their long-time rivals, who were undefeated in six games. From the start the Caldwell crowd voiced disdain for the third-place Weiser club and their 3–3 record. The blatant partisanship of the Caldwell band still amused Neil Uhl—Foxy Grandpa—years later: "Part of the band got in the stand, the other part got behind me," he remembered. "Whenever Walter started his delivery, the drums, trombones and other instruments would let out an awful howl. I stood it for some time and then when Walter let one of his fast ones loose, I made as if it was low to the right. It hummed by me and banged into a trombone and carried it clear across the road. I begged the gentleman's pardon and the small contingent of the band found its way back to the bandstand."[16]

Four innings into the game Weiser held a surprising 4–0 lead. As Johnson walked to the mound for the fifth, several Caldwell rooters came down from the stands and walked onto the field, verbally accosting the first baseman, Weiser Deputy Sheriff Lafe Lansdon. He gave it right back to them, but more fans came over and a shouting match ensued. Lansdon's brother Bob, the Weiser sheriff and manager of the baseball team ("both fine big western types," Johnson described the Lansdon brothers), walked over to order them away. Suddenly Lafe Lansdon was struck in the eye, and he retaliated. Set upon by two others, he knocked them to the ground, whereupon a general pandemonium broke loose. "A free-for-all if there ever was one," Johnson characterized the fight. He stayed on the mound while the action swirled all around him. "'You ain't much on roughin' it, is you?,' was the remark of a hard-looking customer who walked up alongside of me in the box," he remembered. "'To tell the truth, my friend,' I replied, 'I just joined the club, and I don't know which are our players and which are yours.'"[17]

The Caldwell sheriff and his deputies finally brought the melee under control, arresting the Lansdon brothers and another Weiser man in the process. Things turned ugly again when one of Caldwell's leading citizens began parading up and down in front of the Weiser section of the grandstand, shaking his fist. "There is not a respectable man or woman here from Weiser," he told them. "You are all toughs, hoodlums and prize fighters." In spite of the provocation, the visitors held their tempers and eventually got even. This man owned the hotel in Caldwell where more than 100 of the Weiser visitors had planned to have dinner. Instead, they went to the neighboring town of Nampa after the game, and gave their business to the hotel there.

The game itself ended in an easy 8–1 Weiser victory, after which the team was ordered by Caldwell's justice of the peace to a nearby barn for a "trial" where the guilty parties—all of them Weiser citizens, not surprisingly—were assessed a $10 fine.[18] It came out later that the fight had been arranged by gamblers with heavy bets on favored Caldwell, in an attempt to remove some Weiser players from the game.[19] Seeking to capitalize on Caldwell's shock over losing the game, and the strong feelings generated by it, several Weiser citizens offered to wager up to $1,000 each on their team in a rematch.[20] On Monday, Johnson was summoned to the office of Weiser's mayor. "Young fellow," he inquired, "do you think we can lick these fellows if we play another game?" Johnson replied that he thought they could, then listened as the mayor phoned his counterpart in Caldwell with the challenge, which was turned down.[21]

A week after the Caldwell episode Johnson held Emmett to three hits and struck out 13 in a bottom-of-the-ninth 1–0 win. That game ended the official season, Weiser posting a record of seven wins and three losses to finish second behind Caldwell's 9–1 mark. Play continued briefly with an unofficial "purse game" for $250 against Emmett on July 4. "'Too much Johnson' was the result," reported the *Signal.* "He didn't do a thing but pitch, say nothing and chew gum." In reality it was Emmett that didn't do a thing as Johnson no-hit them in a 5–0 win. The game was part of a spectacular day-and-night Fourth of July celebration for which a crowd of 5,000 people, "the biggest crowd ever gathered within her gates," poured into Weiser. Both teams marched in between the floats in a grand parade down the main street to a pavilion where U.S. Senate candidate William Borah (who would be the model for the Washington team's "Mr. Senator" logo in the 1950s) made a speech, after which the assemblage went over to the ballpark to see Johnson blank Emmett.[22]

Caldwell was issued another challenge, this time to a purse match on neutral grounds for $1,500, but got "cold feet," according to the *Signal,* which lamented that the first games of the season had been played "before the Weiser team was thoroughly organized." "'Kid' Johnson is regarded here as the greatest pitcher in Idaho," it added.[23] Johnson's Weiser record was seven wins against one loss, with four shutouts. He allowed 8 runs in as many games and struck out 79 in the 7 games where those totals were given. On July 10, with no more baseball scheduled in Southern Idaho, he went home to California.[24]

For the rest of the summer and early fall, Johnson pitched for Guy Meats's home town of Olive before Joe Burke reassembled the Oil Wells in November. They were the Anaheim Oil Wells now, representing that city in the newly-organized Southern California League that also included Pasadena, San Diego, San Bernardino, and four Los Angeles clubs. The only player not returning was Jack Burnett, who stayed in Tacoma after a fine season there.

As he turned 19 years old on November 6, 1906, Johnson's 6-foot, 1-inch frame was fast filling out with muscle, his gawky adolescence a thing of the past. "He was a magnificent athlete, weighing about 175 pounds, with long arms and powerful shoulders," Oil Wells teammate Bob Isbell recalled.[25] Johnson's development as a pitcher is reflected in his record for the 1906–07 winter season with Anaheim, in which he took one loss (by 1–0) in nine games. He threw three shutouts and allowed a total of 10 runs while striking out 101 batters in 74 innings But when the Oil Wells' season ended in March, 1907, there still didn't seem to be a place for him in professional baseball.

Rube Ellis, who had ruined Johnson's first Olinda start two years earlier with a home run for Rivera, tried to change that. An outfielder starting his second season with the Los Angeles Angels of the Pacific Coast League, Ellis had played for the Hoegees in the winter league and happened to face Johnson in one of his best performances, an 11-inning 0–0 tie on March 10 in which he struck out 17. When Ellis went to camp with the Angels a short time later, he mentioned Johnson to Pop Dillon, the Angels' manager now. Remembering his scouting trip to Anaheim a year earlier, perhaps, Dillon told Ellis to have Johnson come to Los Angeles and meet him at the Hoffman, a cigar store and billiard parlor that served as a hangout for Dillon and Angels owner Hen Berry, who had bought the franchise after the earthquake.[26]

"I was on time for the appointment and sat near the door where they would enter," Johnson recalled. "They came in a little while after I arrived and immediately started playing a game of billiards. They didn't ask for me and didn't seem to be much concerned whether I had come or not. I didn't feel as though I ought to go up and interrupt such important men. Pretty soon their billiard game was finished and they left without knowing I was present."[27]

Johnson's modesty and reserve, such widely-admired features after he became famous, were proving a handicap now. At the insistence of Joe Burke and others, while in Los Angeles Johnson paid a visit to the camp of the New York Giants, who were in spring training at Chutes Park (known later as Washington Park). "One morning I went to the ballpark alone," Johnson remembered. "Naturally, no one knew me as I took a seat in the old wooden grandstand and watched Christy Mathewson and all the famous stars go through their practice. I made several feeble starts in McGraw's direction, but at each move it seemed some Giant player would step up for a few words with his manager. I left the Los Angeles ballpark without as much as meeting John McGraw."[28]

So instead of going to New York or Los Angeles and the higher leagues, Johnson went back to the Snake River Valley of Southern Idaho for another season with Weiser, which had offered him a raise to $150 a month. They also wanted him to bring along Guy Meats and Billy Elwell, the Oil Wells' second baseman. In his recollections of this period Johnson would put the best face on the situation, noting that his return to Weiser was a "sure thing" and claiming that he "was pleased to play with them once more."[29] But unless his dreams of a career in baseball had been put aside—doubtful considering the nearly unbroken string of successes on the mound he had enjoyed in the past year—going back there must have seemed like another dead end. It turned out to be anything but.

At what point Cantillon came to a decision to give some credence to Johnson's admirer is not known, but it could well have been when he read: "This boy throws so fast you can't see 'em . . . and he knows where he is throwing the ball because if he didn't there would be dead bodies strewn all over Idaho."[30]

SHIRLEY POVICH

Whatever his thoughts about another season with Weiser from the standpoint of his baseball career, there's no question that Walter Johnson liked the town and its people. Of course, he returned as something of a celebrity after his earlier success there. "Weiser people began calling me 'Pardner' instead of 'Sonny'," he said.[31] As wild as the town could be, it never tried to entice him into the vices so widely available there, something he looked back upon with appreciation. "They never teased me to drink," he recalled, "though I could have had any saloon in town after some of the games I won for 'em. When they found out I had never tasted hard liquor, they said, 'Good boy, keep away from it always.'"[32]

The wild parts of Weiser that Johnson did enjoy were the mountains and rivers, and the great hunting and fishing there. Quail were everywhere, as in California, but there were also pheasant, a prized bird for sportsmen. Wise enough to stay away from the grizzly bears found at higher altitudes, he nevertheless got a big kick out of the tales spun by the iron-nerved hunters who did go after them. The cold mountain streams were alive with trout, beautiful to look at and delicious to eat, and on one expedition Johnson and three companions caught over 200 in a day.[33]

Interest in baseball was at a fever pitch as the season approached. "The people thought, talked, and dreamed of nothing but the game," Johnson remembered.[34] The ballfield had been greatly improved, the grandstand enlarged, and new navy-blue flannel uniforms ordered for the team. Never having picked up a nickname the previous year, they were now being called the "Kids" with none of them older than 25.[35] The league had expanded to eight teams with the addition of the Mountain Home "Dudes" and the Huntington, Oregon, "Railroaders." The excitement in Weiser intensified after lopsided victories in the first two games of the season, 13–1 over Payette on April 14 and 19–0 at Huntington a week later. In the two contests Johnson gave up five hits, walked none, struck out 27, and made four hits himself.

Suddenly telegrams began arriving from Tacoma, offering Johnson another chance with the Tigers. He ignored them, which made Mike Lynch even more determined until eventually he offered Johnson $350 a month, top of the scale for the minor leagues. This, too, was disregarded, as Johnson explained later: "I said from the start that I would never play again with Tacoma for people who, when I was with them, had never given me a fair chance to make good. I am sure I would not have gone back if my entire major league career had depended on my going."[36]

On April 28 the Caldwell "Champions" (in honor of their victorious 1906 campaign) came to Weiser for the first big game of the year. A crowd of 1,500 turned out to witness a stirring battle taken by Caldwell, 2–1. Johnson had 17 strikeouts, but Weiser left seven men on base to Caldwell's three. In spite of the strong feelings between the teams and their fans, the *Weiser Signal* noted, "The game was cleanly played, there being little rag-chewing and no gabfests or mid-diamond mass meetings."

The Kids returned to form the next week with a 10–2 pounding of Nampa in which Johnson struck out 14. The runs would be the last scored against him for almost two months. The first in a long string of shutouts came against Boise on May 19, a 6–0 one-hitter in which he struck out 19 batters, including 8 of the first 9.[37] "The Boise players went down before the mighty Johnson like grass before a reaper," said the *Daily Statesman.* Of his great strikeout record at Weiser, where he averaged almost 14 a game, Johnson said in 1914: "In those days I could pitch as swift a ball as I can now. Many batters don't care for speed, especially if the pitcher is a trifle wild. Many of the players were delighted when the umpire called them out on strikes. Others would take three weak swings, for fear the umpire might *not* call them strikes."[38]

With Weiser and Boise tied for second place behind unbeaten Caldwell, the competition heated up in earnest. "All the league teams are strengthening up, and the Southern Idaho League promises to furnish as fine ball playing as any league in the Pacific Northwest," the *Signal* reported, adding "but Johnson and the Kids are losing no sleep." Boise imported their own 19-year-old pitcher from California, Specs Harkness, who had blanked Olinda for the Hoegees in the 11-inning, 0–0 tie two months earlier. In three years he would be pitching for Cleveland in the American League, but in Boise on May 26 Harkness showed none of this ability, giving up eight runs in five innings of a 12–0 Weiser romp before a crowd of 1,800, the largest of the year in the capital. The following Sunday Johnson made Huntington a 5–0, two-hit victim. "They are a game bunch of losers and do not kick or complain at their fate, although the cellar yawns to receive them," the *Signal* complimented the Oregonians.

Monday morning, Johnson got a call from Nampa asking if he was available to pitch for them in a special game against Mountain Home that afternoon. For many years these towns had been engaged in a rivalry even more intense than that between Weiser and Caldwell, and Nampa, seeking immediate revenge for a close loss at Mountain Home on Sunday, had put up a $1,000 purse for a rematch. Johnson agreed, and with only five minutes to catch a freight train going to Nampa he tossed a few things into a bag, ran for the station, and jumped on the train as it was pulling out. When the conductor—a Nampa boy—discovered the pitcher's mission he told the engineer to stoke it up, and Johnson was delivered just in time to a frenzied scene. "In all the world series games I have pitched I never saw more enthusiasm than on that Monday afternoon," he recalled.[39]

A crowd of 1,100, including the Mountain Home band and 200 of their fans, had packed the Nampa ballpark. Stores closed for the day, and a holiday atmosphere had taken over. But it turned out to be no holiday for the Mountain Home Dudes as Johnson permitted them a lone base on balls—and no hits—in pitching Nampa to a 5–0 victory. With the $1,000 prize and another $3,600 from side bets in their pockets, Nampa partisans were in a mood to celebrate. "The Nampa fans were so delighted that a banquet was tendered our modest Walter at the Dewey Hotel, and the whole city was dressed in gala attire," the *Signal* reported. Johnson said later: "Believe me, the tar barrels burned in Nampa that night. Everybody was happy, from the babies in their cradles to the grey-haired grandmothers."[40]

His fourth shutout in a row (and second in two days) focused attention for the first time on Johnson's consecutive scoreless innings streak, although it was miscalculated by the *Signal* to be 48 instead of the actual 40. (This overstatement of eight innings would be perpetuated throughout by the *Signal* and repeated by many others.) The Weiser paper ran a prophetic profile of Walter Johnson at this crossroads in his career:

> [The streak] certainly means something to a young man of Johnson's disposition—quiet, unassuming, sober and industrious. He is a coming man of the baseball world. His services have been sought by the big[ger] leagues . . . and the bait would have dazzled the eyes of most youngsters, but not so with Walter. He is but 19 years of age, but he turned it down for the reason that he thought himself too young. Too

many youngsters are too willing to flutter around a manager's candle and fall at the first tryout, but Johnson knows himself and knows baseball. He plays as though there were no glory or excitement in it, but goes up against a game like it was a business proposition. He will break into the big leagues yet and when he does his good right arm will earn him thousands of dollars annually.[41]

On June 9, Johnson pitched his second no-hitter in a row (and the only perfect game of his career), striking out 18 in an 11–0 Weiser rout of the Emmett Prune Pickers. In 27 innings from Sunday to Sunday he had given up two hits and one walk while striking out 44. Picking up the *Signal's* error, the *Daily Statesman* boldly claimed that Johnson's 57 straight scoreless innings (actually 49) had broken the "world record" of 54, while failing to mention the basis for this assertion. (Doc White of the White Sox held the major-league record with 45).[42] Record or not, a 4–0 blanking of Nampa the next week extended the actual streak to 58 innings.

With Johnson's accomplishments piling one on top of another, notice of them eventually overcame both the remoteness of the region and a scant regard among baseball professionals for great records achieved in loosely-organized town leagues. The minor-league clubs of the Northwest were the first to be alerted of something special happening in their midst, and they responded, but by then Johnson had made up his mind not to go back to Tacoma nor, apparently, to anyplace else in the vicinity. In the first two weeks of June the *Signal* carried reports of "flattering offers," and Johnson's rejections of them, from Spokane of the Northwest League and Portland of the Pacific Coast League.[43]

In time tales of his prowess made their way farther afield, however. "Every now and then," Johnson recalled, "after watching me pitch a game some stranger would tell me that he liked my pitching, that he was from the east, and that he intended writing to the manager of this or that club about me. In two or three months, I think a hundred stray spectators paid me that sort of compliment, and a good many of them told me I ought to be in the Big League. I regarded that possibility, however, as quite too far away to give it any serious consideration."[44]

On June 17 a telegram arrived that required such consideration. "Walter Johnson, Weiser's phenomenal pitcher, today received a telegram from Joe Cantillon, manager of the Washington, D.C. club in the American League, asking him if he would accept a pitcher's position with the Washington team," the *Daily Statesman* reported. "The telegram stated Cantillon would pay Johnson's transportation to the national capital and gave Johnson assurance of a good salary. Johnson was asked for an immediate reply. He gave it and it was that he would stay with Weiser in the Idaho State League."

Johnson's caution now seemed to be bordering on the extreme, even if the *Daily Statesman* found much to admire in "this wise course, failure to observe which has spoiled many a young pitcher." Jack Burnett had no such reservations, and five days later the St. Louis Cardinals bought him from Tacoma for the largest price paid for a player in the Northwestern League to that point. Burnett had been a tremendous success at Tacoma, a fan favorite and the league's leading hitter and best first baseman.[45] Meanwhile, Walter Johnson carried on with Weiser, running his scoreless innings streak to 67 on June 23 with a 17–0 crushing of the Payette Melon Eaters.

On Friday evening, June 28, Johnson was strolling back to his boarding house from the ballfield, where members of the team gathered each night after dinner to practice for an hour or so before the sun went down. Suddenly a man stepped up to him, saying, "You had a lot of stuff on the ball this evening, but you were a little wild." Johnson was somewhat confused by the statement, because his control had been good as usual. (He had walked three batters in 11 complete games.) The man then introduced himself: Cliff Blankenship, a catcher with the Washington club of the American League. He wanted to know if Johnson would care to go to Washington to pitch for them. When Johnson answered that he didn't think so, Blankenship was incredulous. "Ain't you glad to get a chance in the East?" he asked, and was surprised again when Johnson said he had been there before. What team had he been with, Blankenship wanted to know. "No team," Johnson replied. "What I meant to say was I've been East before. I was born in Kansas." Expressing doubts about his ability to make good with Washington, Johnson added that he didn't want to go all the way there only to fail. Blankenship told the youngster to think it over some more and meet him again later that night.[46]

Johnson talked it over with Guy Meats. "Walter didn't want to go," the catcher recalled. "He just couldn't believe he was ready for the big leagues. He thought he might be pushing himself too fast." He would have to wire for his parents' advice, Johnson told Blankenship—hoping, according to Meats, that his parents would say no and end the matter there. But the next day the answer came back from Olinda: Frank and Minnie Johnson had no objection to their son going to Washington.[47] After mulling the proposition over some more, Johnson decided to take a chance, even though the idea still frightened him. "I was nothing but a green country boy," he said later, "and jumping to a city the size of Washington was a real sensation to me. I was about as nervous as it would be possible to be."[48]

Blankenship wanted to take his recruit with him immediately, but Johnson refused to leave until the end of Weiser's season in two weeks.[49] He also insisted on enough money in advance to get back home. A railroad man figured out it would take $250 to get East and back to California. Blankenship wired the team for that amount, but turned over only $100. "I never did find out who got the change," Johnson later joked. No contract was ever signed between them (contrary to a much-repeated but apocryphal tale of an agreement written out on a meat wrapper); surprisingly, there was no documentation of the arrangement at all. "They'll fix your salary up when you land in Washington," Blankenship assured Johnson.[50] The Washington catcher then left Weiser, preferring to be elsewhere when the townfolk discovered that their star was being taken away. Blankenship had pressed Johnson to make a decision the previous evening, in fact, in an attempt to depart without so much as spending the night.[51]

If the day he agreed to go to Washington was one of the most important in the life of Walter Johnson, the next day, Sunday, June 30, was without a doubt the biggest in the annals of Southern Idaho baseball. At the top of the league with a 9–1 record, Weiser stood a game ahead of reigning champion Caldwell, who had inflicted the Kids' only loss this year. The tight race combined with the years of rivalry and bad blood between the towns to turn the contest into an event of major proportions. A "Special Dispatch" in Sunday's *Daily Statesman* described the scene:

> Like the clans of the olden country came pouring in from every nook on their great fete days, so the people flocked to Caldwell today to see the greatest, fastest, and all-important game of baseball yet played in the Idaho State League or, for that matter, ever played anywhere in the state. The people, anxious to see the pitcher's battle they knew would take place on the Caldwell diamond today, flocked here in immense crowds from every nearby town. The Weiser special train was crowded to the guards and brought people from nearly every town on the railroad in Washington County. More than 2,000 persons crowded the ball grounds.

Betting, a prominent feature of any game in this league, reached unprecedented levels—$10,000 worth, in Johnson's estimation.[52] All week, Weiser partisans offered odds to all takers, even going to Caldwell to drum up more bets. So much money was riding on the game that Caldwell's gamblers held a council and decided to invest some more to improve their chances. Caldwell captain Eddie Hammond traveled to Butte, Montana, to sign up three Northwestern League stars, including Johnson's old Tacoma teammate Irv Higginbotham, who had pitched Aberdeen to the top of the league.[53] (He would finish the season at 29–12 with 295 strikeouts.) In addition, Caldwell arranged for Nampa to cancel its game with Payette and release Big Leaguer Hanson, the best catcher in the league, so he could sign with Caldwell to catch Higginbotham. Weiser's complaints about their opponent's "loading up" for the game fell on deaf ears, as it had become an increasingly common practice. Johnson had done it himself when he pitched for Nampa.

The game turned out to be the exciting pitcher's duel everyone anticipated. Higginbotham, who had shut out Spokane on June 21 and Butte on the 25th before losing to Butte, 2–0, on June 28—just two days earlier—was invincible. Fast, with a knee-buckling curve, he struck out eight of the first nine batters, 17 altogether, and allowed only two hits in 11 innings. Johnson walked two in the first inning but escaped harm with the help of a great catch by Weiser right fielder Tommy "Hungry" Higgins. He settled down to pitch a great game himself, giving up five hits and striking out 15 of the Champions. After 10 innings the game was still a scoreless tie.

In the top of the 11th Weiser had a man on third with two outs. As Hungry Higgins, a good hitter, set himself in the batter's box, Weiser's doctor suddenly rushed out from the stands. "$750 is yours if you score that man from third," he screamed to Higgins, waving the cash in his hand. Weiser players ran out from their bench and grabbed the doctor, who, it turned out, had bet $1,500 on the game. Rattled by the commotion, Higgins took a strike down the middle. On the next pitch the runner took off for the plate, but left too soon; having gone most of the way down the line, he turned around and headed back to third. But when Higginbotham's pitch got by the catcher momentarily, the runner reversed himself again, bolted for the plate, and was tagged out inches short of it after a spectacular slide.

Johnson, who had allowed Caldwell only three hits to that point, gave up back-to-back singles to start the bottom of the eleventh. The next batter hit an easy grounder to third, but in a desperate attempt to get the runner at home the third baseman drilled the ball squarely into his back instead. The run scored, Weiser lost the game, and Johnson's streak ended at 77 straight scoreless innings.[54]

The remainder of the Idaho State League season deteriorated into a travesty that made it impossible to determine the championship. There was much "loading up" and gambling all around, and more wrangling in the courts and the editorial pages than actual play on the ballfields. Johnson was true to his team, trying to stay until everything got straightened out. He shut out Mountain Home two days in a row, July 14 and 15, to win a three-game purse match for $2,500, then waited another week for a champion to be crowned and the season declared over. But when the league couldn't even figure out when that was, Johnson decided it was time to go.[55] After a final game against a team from Vale, Oregon, the day before (he didn't pitch, perhaps saving his arm for the big leagues), a large crowd of friends and admirers came to the Weiser depot on Monday evening, July 22, to see him off.[56] As Johnson said goodbye to Guy Meats and his other pals, there were tears in his eyes.[57] A group of Weiser fans had tried to convince him to stay, offering to set him up with a cigar store in the town square. Johnson thanked them sincerely but allowed as how the Washington offer might mean more to him in the future. "You know how you are at 19," he explained later. "You want to see things."[58]

CHAPTER 3

Phenom

Johnson turned to Cantillon and said, "Joe, I guess I was the worst busher that ever broke into the big leagues, wasn't I?" Cantillon replied, "No, you weren't, Walter. You had sense enough to keep your mouth shut, and that's more than most of them have."[1]

WASHINGTON POST, MARCH 25, 1917

"Washington . . . first in war, first in peace, and last in the American League!" It was one of those shopworn jokes of the kind, according to Washington sportswriting legend Shirley Povich, that killed vaudeville.[2] The humor was certainly lost on the long-suffering fans of the local baseball team. Things had gotten so bad that in March 1905, a committee of newspapermen was commissioned to come up with a new nickname for the team. The old one, "Senators," was thought to be a "hoodoo" (a curse) because in more than twenty seasons in the big leagues the team had yet to finish in the first division. The incongruous term "Nationals" was chosen, apparently in honor of the old Washington National League teams of the 1880s and '90s, although they, too, had been the doormats of the league.[3] Local sportswriters shortened it to "Nats," which sounded snappier and saved space in the headlines, but neither the fans nor visiting baseball writers took to the change completely, continuing to call them the "Senators" until 50 years later, when the owners finally gave in and made the name official once more. The plan seemed to work to a degree, nonetheless, as the team moved up to seventh place in 1905 and 1906.

Seeking to improve even further on this escape from the American League cellar, the Nationals hired Joe Cantillon to manage the team. All but forgotten today, during his 52-year career Cantillon was among baseball's most respected practitioners—and one of its truly colorful characters.[4] "Pongo Joe," as he was universally known, was playing professionally by the age of 17 and for the next 15 years bounced around various minor leagues and the "outlaw" California League as a good-field, no-hit second baseman and occasional manager. Cantillon built a reputation for the development of young talent, reportedly an influence early in the careers of both Amos Rusie, the "Hoosier Thunderbolt," and Rube Waddell, probably the game's fastest pitchers to that point.[5]

In 1895 Cantillon became an umpire in Ban Johnson's American Association, the position in which he would leave his most lasting mark on the game. It was the custom at that time for the catcher to move into the infield with no runners on base and fewer than two strikes on the batter. Pitches would go straight through to the backstop, and the umpire was responsible for retrieving the ball. But Cantillon refused to go along with that system, insisting that the catcher come back to get the ball each time, until eventually Johnson issued an edict requiring catchers to stay behind the plate. Games moved along at a quicker pace and the practice was gradually adopted by the other leagues.

When Ban Johnson and Charles Comiskey launched the American League in 1901, Cantillon helped acquire players for the new venture. As umpires in the fledgling circuit (he presided at the first game), Cantillon and Jack Sheridan played a crucial role in Johnson's campaign to stamp out rowdyism and enhance the respectability of the game. John McGraw, Baltimore player-manager and one of the new league's crown jewels among those "stolen" from the National League, was put out of a game for his typically bad behavior. Sheridan and Cantillon wired Johnson that McGraw's umpire-baiting and open contempt warranted a suspension, and Johnson—caught between his desire for decorum on the field and McGraw's importance to the prestige of the league—backed up his staff.[6] It was the start of a lifelong feud between the two baseball giants, McGraw jumping back to the National League to stay in 1902.

Normally it took the most drastic kind of provocation for Cantillon to toss a player out of a game; he preferred putting them in their place with devastating repartee and other methods. Clark Griffith told about the time Cantillon achieved this by relaxing the balk rule: A batter (McGraw, according to one version of the story), after complaining nonstop about Cantillon's decisions, singled. As the only umpire in the game, Cantillon moved behind the pitcher—Griffith—as the runner continued bombarding him with curses and epithets from first base. Suddenly Griffith was surprised to hear a voice whisper into his ear, "Go ahead, Griff, pick him off." Drawing the runner off base with a motion toward the plate, he quickly wheeled and rifled the ball to the first baseman instead. The baffled runner was quickly trapped and tagged and Cantillon waved him out, the indignant player screaming all the while "Balk! Balk! Everybody saw Griffith make a balk!" to no avail. After the next batter also singled, Griffith caught him off base in the same manner, but this time Cantillon called a balk and motioned the runner to go to second. Now it was Griffith's turn to protest, but Pongo Joe just grinned at him and admonished, "That stuff won't go now."[7]

As manager of the Nationals Cantillon cut a picturesque figure with his trademark red vest draped over his uniform and smoke billowing out from the big cigars he liked to smoke while entertaining anyone within earshot with endless stories from his long career in the game. Cantillon's patience would be sorely tested during his stay at Washington, but by all accounts his sarcastic wit remained up to the challenge. In a game with Detroit, Ty Cobb bunted twice in a row to the third baseman, who each time threw wildly past first. Further misplays allowed Cobb to score on both occasions, and after the second one Cantillon yelled out to his unfortunate infielder: "Listen, you, the next time Cobb pokes a bunt at you, grab the ball, run back to third base, and try and head him off there!" Following an ugly loss at St. Louis, as the team journeyed back from the ballpark Cantillon asked the driver how far they were from the river. Just a few blocks away, he was told. "Then head for the river and dump this wagonload of baseball garbage in it!" Joe snapped.[8]

In the first two months of Cantillon's initial season at the helm of the Nationals, the team was kept from the bottom of the American League only by the ineptitude first of the St. Louis Browns and then of the Boston Red Sox. But they dropped into last place in mid-June and spent the rest of the season solidifying their hold on it. Cantillon had inherited little more than an outfit of minor-leaguers masquerading as a major-league ballclub. The impoverished franchise had no budget for paid scouts, so early in June the desperate manager began sending players out in search of new material. Two weeks later hard-luck catcher Cliff Blankenship suffered his fourth injury of the season when a foul tip smashed a finger on his throwing hand, and Cantillon took advantage of the misfortune to send Blankenship on a scouting mission to the West. Several prospects in the more distant leagues had attracted Cantillon's attention, but the two primary targets were players Blankenship was instructed not to scout at all, just sign up and arrange their transportation to Washington.

The object of his first stop was Clyde Milan, an outfielder for Wichita in the Western Association who had played impressively when the Nationals lost an exhibition game there in the spring. Milan's two hits and terrific speed caught Cantillon's eye, but a .211 batting average in 1906, his first season in pro ball, had made him just another name to file away for future reference. This year he had raised his average 100 points to lead the league in hitting, and Nationals president Tom Noyes had received several letters from western friends touting him. Blankenship made a beeline to Wichita, purchased Milan's contract, and wired Cantillon that he had bought "a splendid player, guaranteed to make good in the American League."[9] In later years Milan would recall with a chuckle Blankenship's complaints about his next assignment: "I've got to go up in Idaho and inspect a pitcher named Johnson," he told Milan. "He's probably some big busher that isn't even worth the car fare to scout."[10]

Joe Cantillon first heard the name Walter Johnson not long after being appointed Washington manager in the fall of 1906. A former teammate of Cantillon's in the California League, Joe "Mickie" Shea, had seen Johnson pitch in California. Shea wrote to his old friend: "Johnson is a wonder and you had better get a string on him at once."[11] From their days together at Oakland in the early 1890s Cantillon knew Shea to be a no-nonsense type, but as the new manager of a team with limited resources he was in no position to send someone all the way to the West Coast to check out the tip.[12] Every big-league club kept a wastebasket full of letters from out-of-the-way places touting local "wonders" sure to make good in the majors.

In the spring of 1907 the Nationals' skipper heard from his old teammate again, this time from Idaho, where Shea was painting advertising signs for 20-Mule Team Borax, a national soap company. Johnson was now pitching for a team up there, it seemed, and Shea was ever more insistent in a series of letters and telegrams about the youngster's remarkable ability. Shea's persistence, and Cantillon's respect for his judgment, finally prevailed, and Pongo Joe dispatched the mid-June telegram to Johnson offering a job with the Nationals. Undoubtedly astonished when the offer was rejected, Cantillon instructed Blankenship that as soon as Milan was secured to go on to Idaho and bring Johnson back to Washington. "Shall I wire you how he looks?," the catcher asked. "No, bring him back," Cantillon told the catcher, "no matter how he looks."[13]

The Nationals were in New York on June 29 when Cantillon received word from Blankenship of the success of his mission. Perhaps because of the gaudy numbers coming in on Johnson's season in Idaho—75 straight shutout innings, 166 strikeouts in 11 games—his acquisition was heralded by Washington newspapers as a major event. That the team's new property was a teenager pitching in a town league, and no one with the Nationals had ever seen him throw in a game, didn't dampen their enthusiasm in the least. Multiple headlines topped the *Washington Post's* report the next morning:

"Secures a Phenom"
"Cantillon Signs Young Pitcher With Wonderful Record"
"Johnson His Name and He Hails From the Wooly West"

It was left to the veteran Cantillon, knowing how slim the chances that Johnson was even a bona fide major-league pitcher, to make light of the reports. "If this fellow is what they say he is," he joked, "we won't have to use but two men in a game, a catcher and Johnson. He strikes out most of the men, so why have an infield and an outfield? I shall give all the boys but the catchers days off when Johnson pitches."[14] Veteran pitcher Long Tom Hughes was openly scornful: "Strike out 166 men in eleven games? Well, that's rich. What kind of bats do you suppose they use in that Idaho State League? They must have the lead pencil special up there."[15]

Blankenship rejoined the Nationals in Chicago on July 12 and told Cantillon that Johnson had a ticket to Cleveland for the series there beginning on the 20th. The manager couldn't have been pleased that Blankenship, instead of bringing the boy with him as instructed, had permitted him to stay in Weiser until the end of the Idaho season. The "phenom" wasn't under contract, after all, and days passed with no word or sign of him. In addition, after the initial excitement subsided the realities set in regarding what Cantillon himself admitted was "something of a blind chance." From the start the ballplayers treated it as something of a joke; whenever a pitcher was hit hard they would tell him he had "better brace up, Johnson's coming."[16] Finally, a telegram arrived on the 22nd— Johnson was on his way. He wired that he thought he could make the last game of the road trip in Cleveland, but Cantillon told him to keep going east instead.

The Walter Johnson era in Washington began inauspiciously enough on Friday evening, July 26, 1907, when he arrived at Union Station stiff, sore, and covered with cinders from an exhausting four-day train ride. Taking the streetcar down Pennsylvania Avenue, the capital's historic "Avenue of the Presidents," Johnson got off at 15th Street, just short of the White House. Sitting on the porch of the Regent Hotel, hoping to catch a breeze on this typically sweltering Washington July night were Joe Cantillon and umpires Billy Evans and Jack Sheridan.

Evans was only 23 years old but already making a name for himself in his twin careers as one of the American League's new breed of gentleman arbiters and as the author of a syndicated sports column. In those capacities and others his career would be connected to Walter Johnson's for the next 30 years, during which they became good friends. Behind the plate for many of the pitcher's outstanding and historic performances, Evans the writer drew often on his own experiences on the diamond to acquaint the public with the character and personality traits he so admired in Johnson. Evans described their first encounter:

I saw a tall, gangling fellow approaching with a brand new suitcase swinging from his right hand as if it contained no excess baggage. I decided he was either a very strong young man or was traveling light.

"Is this the hotel where the Washington ballplayers stop?," he asked. "Only the good ones," replied Cantillon, who was keen for a joke no matter who suffered.

"Then I guess this is no place for me." The youngster had set his suitcase down as he talked to Cantillon. I could see he was well over six feet despite the fact that there was a bit of a stoop at the shoulders. His features were clean cut as if chiseled. His arms were tremendously long. He was in perfect condition. There wasn't an ounce of fat on his giant physique. He stepped over to where he had dropped his suitcase, picked it up and was about to start on his way when Cantillon asked:

"And who might you be?"

"My name is Walter Johnson."

Cantillon jumped to his feet and greeted the youngster like a long lost brother, asked where he had been, told how he had been watching every train for the last two days, and a lot of other things that made Mr. Johnson immediately feel at home.[17] He answered all of Cantillon's questions in a few words, and when asked about some of the bush feats credited to him only smiled and said anyone could have done the same against the teams he played against. It's safe to say that no more unassuming fellow ever broke into fast company.[18]

Johnson immediately became the center of attention at the hotel as players, newspapermen, and others gathered around to get their first look at the long-awaited phenom.[19] They might have been surprised, in light of the ballyhoo preceding him, how little of it there was in the youngster himself.

"I realize that an experience of only three years is pretty short," he told them, "and I know that it is pretty hard pitching in the American League. I have never received any coaching and I suppose that will be a big handicap, but I am willing to take a try."[20] Cantillon, more concerned with the new arrival's pitching abilities than his modesty, got an inkling of both when he asked, "How is your control, Johnson?" "I don't know, sir," the boy answered. "I never used any where I was."[21]

The team to whose fortunes Walter Johnson bound his own possessed a lamentable record of 26 wins and 55 losses to that point in the season, 5½ games behind the seventh-place Red Sox and sinking fast. Only shortstop Dave Altizer (whom Johnson knew from California) and right fielder Bob Ganley played the same positions every day, as Cantillon platooned and shuffled the rest in response to injuries and poor performance. None of this was apparent on Saturday as they beat St. Louis, 8–1, with Johnson watching his first major-league game in street clothes after resting up from the long trip. Donning a Washington uniform for the first time on Sunday, he got to throw only briefly before rain cancelled a game with the Chicago White Sox. A *Washington Star* writer found him to be "not unlike Rube Waddell in appearance and action. . . . [He] has the same careless movement of 'Rube' and, if anything, more speed." Continuing its comparison to the famed Athletics fireballer, who was en route to his fifth straight major-league strikeout crown, the paper reported: "The players and spectators who saw [Johnson] in action commented on the resemblance, and all expressed the wish that he would turn out as well as the eccentric one without his flaws."[22] The next day's game was also washed out, the team never leaving the hotel this time. On Tuesday, the last day of July, the Nationals split a doubleheader with the White Sox.

Cliff Blankenship was given the responsibility of looking after the new recruit and determining when he was ready to be tried out. Several teammates kidded the catcher about his find, but Blankenship insisted he would fool them all. Johnson, he said, "has everything a good twirler should have, and if I can instill confidence in him he will be a success from the start."[23] Blankenship backed up his words by offering Cantillon $500 for Johnson's contract should the Nationals' skipper conclude otherwise.[24] There was a big laugh on the Washington bench one day when Johnson asked Altizer, "When'll they let me start to pitch?", after which they assured him of all the pitching he wanted on the ragged, sore-armed staff.[25] The *Washington Post* noted that "Johnson is showing rare speed and curves in his daily workouts," and Cantillon decided it was time to check the boy out against major-league hitters, arranging for him to pitch batting practice on Wednesday against both teams.[26] Billy Evans was again on hand.

"Learning from Cantillon that he intended to have Johnson pitch to the boys in practice," Evans wrote, "I went out to the grounds early that afternoon and took a seat high in the grandstand. Knowing that Johnson hadn't done any pitching for about two weeks, Cantillon told him to be careful, take things easy and not to use too much speed. The first ball Johnson sent up in practice looked like a small pea, and the more he pitched the smaller it seemed to get. Most of the players had to take a couple of swings before they connected, and as each walked away from the plate he began to say things to the other players. It was evident that Mr. Johnson had something on the ball, for the best hitters on both teams were having their troubles in locating it. Throughout the batting practice Cantillon wore a happy smile."[27]

Second baseman Jim Delahanty, Washington's most consistent hitter, was the first man to face Johnson. A six-year veteran and one of five brothers to play in the major leagues, Delahanty watched as the youngster took a short windup and let go. "I never had time to take the bat off my shoulder," he said later. "That ball shot right by me, right in the groove and was in the catcher's glove before I knew it had left the rookie's hand. And when he came back with another in the same spot, I laid my bat down and walking over to manager Joe Cantillon, said, 'I'm through.'

'What's he got?', asked Cantillon. 'Has he got a fast one?'

'Fast one? No human ever threw a ball so fast before.'

'Has he got a curve?,' queried Cantillon.

'I don't know and I don't care. What's more, I am not going back to find out until I know how good his control is.'"[28]

Delahanty asked Cantillon when he planned to start "this blizzard," as he called Johnson. As soon as he looked ready, the manager told him. "If ever there was a pitcher in baseball that was ready," Delahanty shot back, "that rube out there is the guy!"[29]

"Walter Johnson pitched from the rubber before the game yesterday, but he afforded little batting practice for the players of both teams, as his fast ball seemed unhittable," the *Post* reported.[30] It wasn't long before Joe Cantillon had seen enough. "I knew I had a great pitcher after looking over Johnson's stuff for about ten minutes," he recalled. "I never saw a hurler with such terrific speed and perfect control."[31] He told Johnson, "Be ready to pitch tomorrow."[32] Cantillon gathered the local baseball writers together to inform them that the youngster would start one of the games of the next day's doubleheader with Detroit.[33] Later that afternoon while the great spitball pitcher, Ed Walsh, was shutting out Washington in the finale with the White Sox, One-Arm Phillips, the Nationals' pioneering megaphone man, delivered the news to the crowd, an announcement received "with great enthusiasm," it was reported.[34]

He was a nice guy, Joe [Cantillon] was, always kidding. Before the game, Joe came over to the Detroit bench and said, "Well, boys, I've got a great, big appleknocker I'm going to pitch against you guys today. Better watch out, he's plenty fast. He's got a swift." He told us that, you know. And here comes Walter, just a string of a kid, only about 18 or 19 years old. Tall, lanky, from Idaho or somewhere. Yes, Joe Cantillon was a kidder, but he wasn't kidding that day. He had such an easy motion, it looked like he was just playing catch. He threw so nice and easy—and then "swoosh," and it was by you.[35]

SAM CRAWFORD

The first time I faced him, I watched him take that easy windup—and then something went past me that made me flinch. I hardly saw the pitch, but I heard it. The thing just hissed *with danger. Every one of us knew we'd met the most powerful arm ever turned loose in a ballpark.*[36]

TY COBB

In all the world Walter Johnson couldn't have found a tougher opponent for his major-league debut on August 2, 1907. The Detroit team chosen by Joe Cantillon for his rookie's first test was the hardest-hitting crew in baseball, in the process of slugging its way to the first of three straight American League pennants. "An aggregation of the most aggressive players now playing ball," the *Washington Star* called them.[37] The peerless Ty Cobb, already the Tigers' unquestioned leader at the age of 20, was enjoying the first great season of his long and fabulous career. Between them, Cobb and Wahoo Sam Crawford would dominate the league's offensive categories for most of the next decade. With leadoff hitter Davy Jones they made up one of the finest outfields ever. (The trio finished 1–2–3 in runs scored this year.) If that wasn't challenge enough for a new pitcher in his first outing, Billy Evans remembered the 1907 Tigers as "a club that liked nothing better than fastball pitching"—the only kind that Johnson threw.[38]

Cantillon had meant to acclimate Johnson to his new surroundings more gradually, but two front-line pitchers were struggling with injuries and most of the others suffered from an acute shortage of major-league ability. Mounting evidence that the boy was a "prize package," as the desperate manager called Johnson, made the temptation to use him right away overwhelming.[39] Undoubtedly there was consideration also for the large crowd sure to turn out for the debut of the "Idaho Wonder." Indeed, a standing-room-only crowd of 11,000 or so packed the ballpark to overflowing.[40]

This was just fine with the Tigers, tangled up as they were in a fierce four-way battle with Philadelphia, Chicago, and Cleveland for the pennant. After the game, shortstop Charley O'Leary admitted: "When I was moseying around before the game I saw there was a new man in uniform and began hoping Cantillon would pitch him, for we need every game we can get, and the importations from the sage country are a big help. When the cub's name was announced, I took it as a big gift."[41] Cobb remembered, "He was only a rookie, and we licked our lips as we warmed up. Evidently, manager Pongo Joe Cantillon had picked a rube out of the corn fields of the deepest bushes to pitch against us."

The Tigers did everything they could to make the youngster's initial experience as unpleasant as possible. "We began to ride him as the game opened," Cobb recalled. "One of the Tigers imitated a cow mooing and we hollered at Cantillon: 'Get the pitchfork ready, Joe—your hayseed's on his way back to the barn!' "[42] But the Washington crowd greeted Johnson's walk to the mound with tremendous applause, and to the Tigers' dismay he paid no attention at all to the caterwauling coming from their dugout.[43] Johnson's first pitch to leadoff batter Davy Jones was a called strike—"the fastest ball I ever saw," Jones would call it.[44] The first inning was a breeze, two grounders to third and Crawford's pop to short sending Detroit back in order.

"We were most respectful now—in fact, awed—and there was only one answer left to his incredible, overpowering speed," Cobb recalled.[45] Leading off the second inning he laid down a perfect drag bunt past Johnson. Delahanty, who was playing first base for this game, fielded it too late to make a play. Tigers first baseman Claude Rossman followed with a carbon copy of Cobb's bunt, Delahanty this time making a futile toss to second baseman Rabbit Nill covering first. Charging around second, Cobb never broke stride as the stunned Nill stared in horror and then hurried a throw too late and wide of the bag at third. Detroit second baseman Red Downs flied to left, Cobb tagged up, and the Tigers had a 1–0 lead. The inning ended with no further damage, however, and Detroit catcher Boss Schmidt became the first Johnson strikeout victim.

After the Tigers went down in order in the third inning, Johnson struck out in his first major-league at bat. Cobb tried to wreak havoc again in the fourth, reaching base on a throwing error and stealing second and third on consecutive pitches with two outs before Johnson ended the threat with his second strikeout. O'Leary got the Tigers' first solid hit, a single in the fifth, but that was the only trouble until the seventh, when back-to-back singles put runners on the corners with two outs. O'Leary stole second while Johnson held the ball, frozen with uncertainty. "Every effort was made to send Johnson into the air," the *Star* reported, "but he refused to take the journey. Instead, he put on more steam and struck out [pitcher Ed] Siever to the mighty shouts of the multitude."

The Nationals had added to the excitement with a run of their own in the sixth inning to even the score at 1–1. With two down in the eighth Sam Crawford smashed a terrific line drive to the scoreboard in deep left, circling the bases for an inside-the-park home run and a 2–1 Detroit lead. In the bottom half, with two on and none out, Cliff Blankenship pinch-hit for Johnson, but the hapless Nationals couldn't push over a run. Each team scored once in the last inning for a 3–2 Tigers victory, and Walter Johnson lost his debut. He had nonetheless acquitted himself well, allowing the hard-hitting Detroit outfit six hits (only three of them out of the infield) and a walk in his eight innings on the mound.

But the star of this game, as in so many during his 24-year career, was the redoubtable Cobb. Here was a textbook illustration of his ability to dominate a game, even one in which he managed only a bunt single in four trips to the plate. But on the basepaths and in the field, Cobb was a force. Having created the Tigers' first run on daring alone, he almost did it again the next time up with his consecutive steals. Cobb threw out three Washington baserunners from right field, two of them at home (the only time he ever did that twice in a game) to shut off runs that would have changed the outcome of the game. His one-man exhibition continued into the second game of the doubleheader as he stormed all the way home from first base on a single, prompting manic Tigers' skipper Hughie "Ee-Yah" Jennings to turn to the grandstand from his third-base coaching box and holler: "Good boy, Ty. Gentlemen, *that* is the only way to play winning baseball!"[46] The doubleheader sweep vaulted Detroit into the American League lead by a narrow margin.

For the local sporting press and fans neither Cobb's performance nor the loss of another two games received much attention amid the surprise and amazement at finding the new pitcher to be everything claimed for him. "Idaho Wonder Justifies Blankenship's Boosting," "Johnson a Wizard," "Johnson a Real Phenom," Friday's headlines proclaimed.[47] "A jewel worth $10,000"; "The pitching find of the season"; "One of the biggest sensations of the American League season," the sportswriters called him. The praise lavished on Johnson might well have been viewed as simply an effort to boost the spirits of a beleaguered local fandom if not for the corroboration of others whose credibility on the subject was beyond question. Wild Bill Donovan, the ace of the Tigers' staff (25–4 in 1907), was one:

"It is no wonder to me that Johnson pitched 85 innings without allowing a run and struck out 166 men in twelve games up in Idaho," he said. "It is only a wonder to me that he didn't strike out every one of those bushers up there. He has remarkable speed and a great shoot on his fast ball, and to tell you the truth, he is the best raw pitcher I have ever seen. If nothing happens to that fellow, he will be a greater pitcher in two years than Mathewson ever dared to be. Mark that prediction. Look at that build. Nineteen years old. Well, I guess that fellow won't improve within a year or two."[48]

Several of the Tigers went to Frank Navin, the team's president, urging him to buy Johnson at once. "Even if he costs you $25,000, get him," Cobb told Navin, but the frugal ex-accountant just looked at his star as though he were crazy.[49] It's doubtful the Nationals would have let their prize discovery go for any price. Joe Cantillon was in a happy frame of mind for a manager who had just lost a doubleheader: "I was surprised the way [Johnson] went through that game," he said. "He was as cool as a cucumber at all stages, and he should have won his game in a walk. I believe we have the makings of a great pitcher."[50]

The phenom himself was a bit dazed by it all. After the game he remained on the bench while fans and ballplayers made their way out of the park toward their homes. (The clubhouse had burned to the ground during the road trip.) He was still there after the team bus had left for the hotel. "The scene comes back like a picture," Johnson wrote in 1924:

I was still sitting on the bench, all alone. Several fans walking nearby asked if I was going to sleep all night in the park. I was embarrassed and pretended to be looking for my glove. When in the excitement I did get started, I followed the crowd through the gate. Some of the fans noticed me and made a few wise remarks. But I kept right on hiking. And to tell the truth, I didn't have a very good idea just where I was hiking to.

"Hey, kid," someone shouted, "some guy wants you back there." I looked around and here came Joe Cantillon.

"Where you going, Johnson?" he asked, half smiling and half frightened.

"The hotel," I answered, in a doubtful tone of voice.

"Hotel? Hell!" he shot back, "You're already five blocks in the wrong direction."[51]

Any notions that Johnson's strong first effort might be a fluke were dispelled in his next appearance five days later as he picked up his first victory, 7–2, at the expense of a powerful Cleveland club that was itself in the thick of the pennant fight. Putting a brake to the Nationals' seven-game losing streak, Johnson had an easy time of it with the hard-hitting "Naps" as they were known in honor of their great second baseman and manager, Napoleon Lajoie. A pair of hits in each of the first and last innings was the extent of the Cleveland offense, and five times they were retired in order. Former batting champion Elmer Flick, a perennial .300 hitter and one of the hardest men in the league to strike out, went down swinging twice. The *Star* described their difficulties in detail:

"The ball that bothered the Naps most yesterday from Johnson's delivery was a fast high inshoot that broke just in front of the plate. He had all the Cleveland batsmen guessing on this ball. If it failed to break, it cut the plate at about the height of the batsman's breast letters. When they swung at it, however, it seemed to lift over the handle of the bat. This ball, breaking properly, is practically impossible to hit squarely, and it will fool the cleverest stick artist in the business. Johnson's speed, of course, is a factor in all of his work, his curves taking their swing viciously just before reaching the batting area."[52]

"He was complete master of the situation," Thomas Rice of the *Washington Times* wrote, "and last night the Naps were unanimous in declaring the Idaho recruit the greatest phenom that has been sprung in the league this season. The Cleveland players have long been noted for their slugging abilities, but yesterday they were helpless before the Idaho twirler. Lajoie was enthusiastic about Johnson, and said this morning, 'Joe Cantillon certainly slipped one over on the rest of the American League when he landed that fellow. Why, he's got speed and breaks that make you wonder what's wrong with your batting lamps when he lets out a kink, and if you do happen to land, you don't know where the ball is going.'"[53] Cleveland's own ace, Addie Joss, said that he was "very much impressed. . . . That young fellow is another Cy Young. I never saw a kid with more than he displayed. Of course, he is still green, but when he has a little more experience he should be one of the greatest pitchers that ever broke into the game."[54]

Washington fans were no less enthusiastic about the rookie's performance. When the game ended, a crowd rushed from the stands to the players' bench and surrounded him, all the while trying to shake his hand and pat him on the back. As the team made its way to the automobiles waiting to take them back to the hotel, the mob followed, and in fear for Johnson's safety Cantillon and a group of players formed a cordon to protect him from his new friends. They reached the transports only to find them blocked in by an estimated three or four hundred fans, and when the vehicles finally got underway they were followed for blocks by a cheering human stream.[55] In a letter written that night to Weiser teammate Tommy Higgins, Johnson said: "I am glad I came here, not only because I made good, but because I like this city. They are just as crazy over baseball here as they are there." Of his major-league pitching experience so far, Johnson had only this to say: "It's just as easy to pitch here as down there, only you have to put them over."[56]

Although he had already pitched two games for them, Washington still did not have Johnson under contract—an astonishing situation in light of the sensation he was causing. Cantillon offered a salary of $350 per month for the rest of the season, but the unproven pitcher held out from the start for $450. Johnson's sweet disposition would come to be nearly as well known as his prowess on the mound, but he was never unaware of his value as a pitcher or backward about seeking fair compensation for it. Even so, it is surprising to find him negotiating for a higher salary at the very start of his career. Perhaps Tacoma's offer of $350 per month made Washington's seem low, or maybe Johnson had in mind the $150 Blankenship apparently pocketed in Weiser. Whatever his reasoning, though, he was adamant and Cantillon caved in after the Cleveland game, no doubt concerned to get his phenom under legal contract without delay. When Johnson finally signed on August 8 Cantillon conceded, "If you make good with our ballclub, you are worth $450."[57]

Any reservations Pongo Joe might have had along those lines vanished with Johnson's next start in St. Louis on August 14, the first of 26 heartbreaking 1–0 losses in his career. After the game Cantillon consoled him in the hotel lobby: "That was a hard game to lose, Walter. You deserved to win, but that's impossible if your teammates don't get you any runs. From now on, you can expect to take your regular turn in the box." Johnson recalled that "For the first time, I realized that I was a sure-enough big leaguer."[58]

Cantillon was bringing new players in and trying them out at a dizzying pace, with no effect on the club's stranglehold on the bottom of the league. The Nationals bought the contract of catcher Charles "Gabby" Street from San Francisco of the Pacific Coast League, and purchased veteran shortstop George McBride from Kansas City of the American Association, both for delivery in 1908. Clyde Milan joined the team in Cleveland on August 19 after leading Wichita to the Western Association pennant. For exactly one inning Cantillon resisted the temptation to put young Milan to the test, sending him into right field in the second inning on the day of his arrival. Two days later Milan started in center field and ran three-year regular Charlie Jones out of the lineup. The job would be Milan's for the next fifteen years. In a span of three weeks Joe Cantillon had picked up the four brightest lights in the Washington baseball constellation for years to come.

Jesse Clyde Milan was born and raised deep in the Smoky Mountains of Tennessee, in the little town of Linden where his father was the blacksmith. The son never did like his first name, choosing to go by the middle one instead. During his short time in the minor leagues he picked up the nickname "Zeb," and it stuck. Milan's talent for spinning tales and folklore of the mountains around Reelfoot Lake where he grew up was matched only by his ability to keep a straight face throughout the most outlandish of yarns. "Zeb outshines [Baron von] Munchhausen when it comes to telling tales," wrote Ed Grillo of the *Post*. "One of Milan's favorite stories is about the creek near Linden where the fish are so plentiful that it's not uncommon to see a boy dive into the water and come up with five fish—one in either hand, one under each arm, and one in his mouth. Milan claims there is an 80-year-old man there who goes out in the morning with a basket containing 20 walnuts and returns with 18 or 19 squirrels that he killed by hitting them between the eyes with the nuts."[59]

Milan would tell about the wonderful pointer dog, without equal in the area. One day he and a friend were out hunting when a bird they had shot fluttered down by the edge of the lake. When they went over, the dog was standing on the shore pointing out toward the water. They couldn't understand it, because there was no bird there and the dog had never failed them before. Then Milan spotted a large bass relaxing in the shallows, and reached down and grabbed it. When they got the fish home and cleaned it, there in its stomach was the bird, he declared.[60]

Walter Johnson and Clyde Milan were both 19-year-old country boys new to the East and the major leagues. They had personality traits in common also, both being modest, reserved, and quiet, preferring to avoid the limelight and the fast life open to young, single ballplayers. The two compared notes, exchanged confidences, and became best friends, virtually inseparable during the baseball seasons before their marriages. It was a friendship that would last for the rest of their lives.[61] "We bought a car together and roomed together on the road and at home until I was married," Milan recalled. "In the 14 years I roomed with Walter, I doubt if there were 10 nights when we didn't go to our room together. When we were young, Walter liked to take in a burlesque show occasionally, and I wouldn't go with him. He went a few times, then came in one night and said, 'You're right, Clyde. I'm not going any more.'"[62]

Milan was a worrier, more cautious about the ways of the world than the friendly, easygoing Johnson, and had to watch over his roommate on occasion. "This diamond salesman used to give the boys rings, studs and pins on approval," Milan remembered. "If the boys liked them, they would buy them. Sometimes one of their girls would talk them into it. One day he stuck one in Walter's tie, and walked away without saying anything. I forgot about it until one day I was going through Walter's dresser drawer—probably to swipe a necktie—when I found this diamond, probably worth $500, just laying there. I asked Walter about it and he said he had meant to give it to the hotel maid but had forgotten it. 'Maid?' I said, 'This thing is worth about $500.' Walter wouldn't believe me for a long time, but when I got him convinced he grabbed the diamond, ran down the stairs, and I didn't see him again until he found the salesman and gave it back. He had thought it was just a piece of glass."[63] The Damon and Pythias of the game, Denman Thompson of the *Star* called the two of them. Another expression, "the Gold Dust Twins", referred to their 16 seasons together as major stars on otherwise lackluster Washington ballclubs.[64]

For the second game in a row Johnson's mates failed to produce any runs for him in a 3–0 loss at Cleveland on August 20. (He would suffer that unfortunate fate, which made victory a statistical impossibility, 66 times in his career.)[65] But though he lacked scoring support from the Nationals, he did have the visible and vocal backing of the Cleveland fans, an unusual phenomenon that was to become routine in ballparks around the American League when Walter Johnson was on the mound for Washington. "The crowd took a great fancy to young Johnson and gave him a fine ovation after he had fanned [Bob] Rhoads and Flick in the fifth," the *Star* noted. Cantillon used him in relief for the first time on the 26th in Detroit, and again the next day, and he lost both games. Although striking out five batters in as many innings in the first game, he also gave up four runs, with Cobb once again stealing two bases off him. On the 27th he came in with one out in the bottom of the ninth of a 3–3 tie, retiring one batter before giving up a hit that brought in the winning run.

Johnson's weakness in fielding his position had been exposed in the debut against the Tigers. Determined to improve that aspect of his game, he enlisted the help of several veterans on the team, including Jim Delahanty, (who would play every infield position during his career), Cliff Blankenship, a first baseman when not catching, and outfielder Bob Ganley.[66] The work paid off. "Things were different the next time Walter pitched against us," a grinning Ty Cobb remembered. "My first time up I bunted again. Johnson bolted off the mound like a shot, fielded the ball expertly, and I was out. Just as simple as that. That's the last time we tried to bunt on him."[67]

Helpful in ironing out the rough spots in Johnson's pitching were the Washington catchers, all longtime veterans of the game. Jack Warner, 35 years old and a 13-year major-leaguer, had caught Christy Mathewson during some of his greatest seasons with the Giants. Cantillon gave Warner the assignment of coaching Johnson when he first came to the team. He had also been scheduled to catch the rookie's debut until an injury sidelined him the day before, so that honor went instead to Mike Heydon, a seven-year backup catcher with a .179 lifetime average who was fated to pick up a bit of reflected glory now in the twilight of his career. Heydon caught Johnson's first three games before well-traveled veteran Mike Kahoe took over for the next three until Warner was healthy enough to finish the season behind the plate.

When Warner first took Johnson to the bullpen to check him out, he told the rookie flatly, "You can't get by in this league with only speed." Warner suggested he learn the spitball, a pitch gaining prominence with the great success of Ed Walsh. Johnson practiced moistening the ball for a while but never got it to break an inch.[68] One morning a week before the end of the season Cantillon and Kahoe took Johnson aside to teach him the change of pace. They were amazed at how quickly he mastered the pitch, which took some rookies an entire season to learn. As a test Johnson was put in to pitch batting practice. Mixing his new slow one with the fastball he was virtually unhittable, according to reports. "Johnson is the most apt youngster that ever broke into the game," Cantillon told a reporter afterwards. "He learns quicker than any player I have ever come across. He mastered the slow ball in less than half an hour."[69]

The losses in Detroit had left Johnson with a four-game losing streak and a distinctly unphenom-like 1–5 record as the Nationals came home briefly from their disastrous road trip for a series with the Red Sox. But Cantillon was unapologetic about his rookie. "Johnson pitches better ball every time he walks to the rubber," he said, "and he is now conceded to be the best young pitcher in the country." Mike Kahoe, who had been behind the plate for Johnson's last three outings, was equally enthusiastic:

> Greatest ever, that kid. I have seen them all, but I have never seen a raw recruit get into the big league and show so much class. He can do more with a ball right now than nine-tenths of the pitchers who have been in the big leagues for years. I can hold my glove wherever I want to and Johnson can put the ball in the center of it at full speed. He has more speed on his ball than any pitcher I have ever caught, and while he is not finished, because he lacks experience, I make the prediction now that he will develop into a wonder. He has not had a single ball hit hard off him since I have been with the club. It is next to impossible to hit him.[70]

Cantillon chose Johnson to open the series against Boston, an honor usually reserved for a team's top pitcher, and he responded with a tight 2–1 victory. In Philadelphia on September 2 he lost a 3–2 duel with A's ace Eddie Plank by throwing a bunt into left field in the bottom of the ninth. In the morning half of the doubleheader Johnson had watched Rube Waddell come in to save the game for the A's with five strikeouts in three innings. (Waddell would be Johnson's pick as the best pitcher he ever saw.)[71] In his next start, at Boston on September 7, Johnson turned in his top performance of the year, a 1–0 beauty—the first of 38 career 1–0 wins.[72] A second straight shutout, 2–0, followed five days later in New York.

If praise for the Washington rookie had been extravagant earlier, though based on little more than potential, the reporting now was sensational. "The prediction is not amiss that he is the greatest of all pitchers the game has ever developed," Ed Grillo asserted, with a large headline to that effect in the Sunday edition of the *Post*.[73] Unfortunately for Grillo's credibility, Johnson lost his next three games, all of them in a long home stand that ended the season. That might have had some reevaluating their opinions of him, but Johnson came back on October 4 with a thrilling extra-inning 2–1 win over Plank and the Athletics to quash the A's pennant hopes as Detroit was beating St. Louis.

The game also brought an end to Walter Johnson's first season in the major leagues. An unimpressive 5–9 won-lost record masked a solid start for the 19-year-old, reflecting instead the failures of his team. Five of the losses were by one run. (The 49–102 Nationals had only one pitcher with more than 10 wins—Case Patten with 12—while others had 20, 17 and 16 losses.) In twelve starts Johnson failed to complete just one—the debut. His 1.88 earned run average was fourth-best in the league, his 5.53 strikeouts-per-game second only to Waddell.

On October 5, the day after his last game, Johnson left for California confident that a bright future in baseball lay ahead of him.[74] He was hardly alone in that assessment. Shortly after the end of the season *The Sporting News* ("Baseball's Bible") profiled the 19-year-old under the headline, "Sure to Be a Star":

> This young man is going to be a real star. This boy, notwithstanding his great success in big league cities, went home the same unassuming, quiet, retiring youth that he was when he came here. That he was not spoiled by the fulsome praise and many flowery notices showered on him is as great a wonder as his pitching ability.[75]

CHAPTER 4

Labor Day

"Johnson's Jingles"

Some pitchers have to hurl the bulb but once or twice a week,
But every day is labor day for me.
Some pitchers get a walloping then turn the other cheek,
But every day is labor day for me.
This morning when I left the hay, and gazed into the street,
And saw the holiday parade, and heard the marching feet
Of fifty thousand happy men, I longed to join the fleet,
But every day is labor day for me.

WILLIAM F. KIRK, NEW YORK AMERICAN
SEPTEMBER 8, 1908

The *Anaheim Gazette* reported Walter Johnson's return to Olinda in the fall of 1907 "loaded with laurels from Eastern baseball centers." Even so, it pointed out, "He wears the same sized hats."[1] Johnson joined up with Santa Ana in the new 10-team California Winter League at a salary of five dollars per game, and the season kicked off with an exhibition doubleheader against Huntington Beach on October 27.[2] Johnson played center field in the opener, hitting his first home run ever and unleashing a throw that was still clear in the mind of Santa Ana left fielder Lester Slaback 50 years later:

The other team had a man on third base with one out. The batter hit a line single to center. The ball hit in front of Johnson and he fielded it on the first hop. Walter threw the ball to the plate like a shot out of a gun. Guy Meats was catching, and Johnson's peg bulleted into his glove, ankle high, just in time to nail the baserunner. That's the only time I ever have seen a man thrown out at home [from third] on a clean base hit. Walter's throwing ability was unbelievable.[3]

With the winter league not formally getting underway for another two weeks Johnson went 100 miles south to pitch for the San Diego Pickwicks in a series against the Los Angeles Angels. With the Pickwicks winners of the semipro Southern State League and the Angels champions of the Pacific Coast League, the best-of-five set between them was being billed as the "Coast Championship." It began on November 7, the day after Johnson's 20th birthday, and he celebrated by outdueling future Washington teammate Sleepy Bill Burns, 1–0. Sixteen Angels went down on strikes, three hits and a walk the sum of their meager offensive output. Catcher Jack "Chief" Meyers was the Pickwicks' other star, banging out three of their five hits and throwing out three runners. The motivation for Johnson's appearance in the series was explained by the *San Diego Union* under the headline "Dillon Goes Into Trance Over Result":

If ever there was a surprised bunch of champions, it was this Los Angeles crowd yesterday afternoon. After the last man had gone out in the last inning, it took them nearly five minutes to recover from the catastrophe. Captain Dillon was so surprised he could hardly speak, and his faithful minions did not have the heart to bring him out of the trance. "There's the boy you turned down last season!" This was the cry that greeted Dillon when Walter Johnson stepped out on the diamond for the first time. And at regular and frequent intervals during the entire nine innings of play the cry was repeated, that Dillon might not have the opportunity to forget the chance that was once his. There is no one who realizes his mistake more than Dillon himself, and he has been well aware of his error for several months. But the crowd delighted in rubbing it in, and it galled him to stand on the coaching line near first base and watch man after man, including the heaviest hitters on the nine, step to the pan, nearly wrench their vertebrae out of joint in wild and ineffectual attempts to connect with the leather as propelled by the good right arm of Johnson, and then retire with more or less bad grace to the bench.

Unfortunately for San Diego fans thrilled by the possibility of beating the Angels, the Pickwicks had only one Walter Johnson and lost an exciting series, three games to two.

Johnson's 1907–08 California Winter League season was most impressive, even if expected now of one of the bright prospects of the major leagues. In 102 innings he gave up just four earned runs on 35 hits and five walks while ringing up 152 strikeouts. His last two appearances were a 22-strikeout, 12-inning 0–0 tie with San Pedro on January 5th and a no-hit, no-walk game against the Hoegees two weeks later. "I never let it out too much, but just toss the ball over," Johnson professed in a letter to a friend back in Washington. He was prouder of his improved hitting, a .372 average with two over-the-fence home runs and five doubles.[4] "You ought to see me bat," Johnson boasted, "I bat better than any man in the league, and there are some good hitters and pitchers out here. I don't pull away like I used to back there."[5]

Two months in the American League had also smoothed rough edges from other aspects of Johnson's game, as Bob Isbell remembered years later: "What a change a few months in the big leagues made in his throw to the bases! When he played with us as a kid, he made a few false motions before he got the ball to a base. But when he returned at the end of the season, he got his throws there faster and straighter than anyone before or since. It was suicide to try to steal a base on him."[6]

Shortly into the new year of 1908 Johnson developed an infection of the mastoid area behind his right ear and was out of action for 10 days before returning to pitch the no-hitter on January 19. When the infection became acute, doctors urged him to undergo an operation to remove the abscess. But fearing that the recovery period would cause him to miss his first spring training, Johnson resisted until he couldn't get out of bed, and even then put the operation off for another two weeks hoping the problem would disappear. Instead of healing, however, the infection spread, and on February 27 Johnson went under the knife at Fullerton Hospital.

The operation, involving permanent removal of a section of bone from behind his right ear, was serious. John Perry wrote to relatives in Kansas that his grandson's life "was despaired of," and newspapers reported him in critical condition.[7] Johnson was in considerable pain for several weeks, and his disappointment at missing the Nationals' spring training was sharpened by the newspaper accounts of the White Sox camp in nearby Los Angeles. But relatives looked after him constantly even though he could barely move his jaw to talk to them, and "The administration of opiates to the wound relieves him," the *Los Angeles Times* reported.[8]

His recuperation was supposed to have taken three weeks to a month, but Johnson went home to Olinda two weeks after the operation, wiring Joe Cantillon of his intention to join Washington for their exhibition swing north from the spring camp at Galveston, Texas.[9] A second telegram several days later backed off from that optimistic prediction while still assuring that he was "doing fine and will be in fighting trim by April 14, depend on it."[10] Within the week Johnson was back in the hospital, however, and this time for a much longer stay. His attempt at a premature escape had backfired, and not until late in May would he be well enough to resume normal activities.[11] In addition to ruining his chance for a first full season in the major leagues, the surgery and extended hospital stay cost Johnson $700 of the $1,100 he had brought back to California that fall.[12]

Johnson finally hooked up with the Nationals in Chicago on June 6, almost two months into the season. Slightly underweight but in excellent health otherwise, he was ready to pitch except for a lack of "wind," tiring easily from even minimal effort after the prolonged inactivity. His arm felt strong, though, and his spirits were lifted just being out on a baseball field again. "I tell you it feels good to get a uniform on again after having been forced to sit around the house for months," he said.[13]

Needing several weeks to round into shape, Johnson got several days instead. Trying to halt a long Nationals losing streak, Cantillon started him in St. Louis on June 11. For three innings he was fine before getting hammered by the Browns and taken out in the fourth. Control problems had forced him to "aim" the ball, according to the *Post.* After this debacle, the Washington skipper allowed Johnson almost two weeks to work into condition before his next start. In Boston on June 23 he went 8 innings of a 2–2 tie against Red Sox rookie Ed Cicotte, and on the 29th in Philadelphia he had five strikeouts in the first three innings before tiring, taken out after seven innings of a 4–0 loss. His first victory and complete game came on Independence Day in Washington, a 6–2 win over the New York Highlanders. Clark Griffith, recently fired as manager of the Highlanders, watched the game from the stands and expressed to the *Post* his wonderment at Johnson's natural abilities: "Don't overlook the fact that that is only a 20-year-old boy out there," said Griffith, himself one of the great pitchers in the game's history. "He is not through developing yet. But for his illness he would have been a marvel this year, and he will be a wonder this fall. But next year he will be in a class by himself. There are several things about pitching that he still has to learn, but with such speed and perfect control he is sure to become one of the game's greatest stars among twirlers."

But after a string of inconsistent performances and woeful hitting support led to five losses in a row, Johnson's 1–6 record must have started some to wondering whether he was just another flash-in-the-pan. Then in St. Louis on July 28 came one of the great games of his career, a stirring contest that went into the 15th inning a scoreless tie. Striking out 15 Browns as the Nationals pulled out a 2–1 victory in 16 innings, it would stand as Johnson's highest strikeout total and his third-longest game in innings. Why Cantillon would allow his prize youngster, having just recovered full strength, to go the distance in this game is puzzling, but no ill effects were visible in his four-hit, complete-game win over Big Ed Walsh and the White Sox four days later.

Johnson went on a streak of 11 wins in 13 decisions, in fact, including a 1–0 two-hitter over Chicago on August 14 in which his no-hitter was broken up by opposing pitcher Doc White's single in the ninth.

Behind the plate in 1908 was Johnson's first great catcher, Charles "Gabby" Street, a National League veteran with Cincinnati and Boston in 1904–05 who caught 179 games (a "world record" according to *The Sporting News*) for San Francisco of the PCL in 1907. Surprisingly quick for a man of his stocky build, and blessed with a powerful arm, Street would be called by Johnson "the best all-around catcher I ever watched."[14]

"What a catcher he was," Johnson said, "a big fellow, a perfect target, great arm, spry as a cat back of the plate, always talking, always hustling, full of pep and fight. Gabby was always jabberin', and never let a pitcher take his mind off the game. When we got in a tight spot Gabby was right out there to talk it over with me. He never let me forget a batter's weakness. If he called one wrong and it cost the ball game, he took the blame for the loss. Gabby had a great arm, and he was pretty proud of it. I'd be tossing to first to try to keep a man close to the bag, and you could hear Gabby chattering all over the park: 'Let 'em run, Gabby'll get 'em.' He would, too. He'd throw anyone out at second. I've seen him make Ty Cobb quit many a time. Ty would get a lead, Gabby would throw and Ty would be glad to scramble back to first."[15]

It was this gift of gab, of course, that gave Street his nickname. "He always kept the pitcher in good spirits with a continual chatter of sense and nonsense," Johnson recalled. "'Ease up on this fellow, Walter, he has a wife and two children,' he would call jokingly when some batter was hugging the plate and getting a toehold for a crack at one of my fast ones. 'This fellow hasn't made a hit off you since you joined the league,' might be his next remark. And so on throughout the game."[16] Particularly disconcerting to hitters were Street's entreaties for more speed from Johnson. "What's the matter, Walter," he'd shout while Johnson's fastballs exploded into his mitt with the crack of rifle-fire, "is your arm lame? A little more speed, a little more speed."[17]

Gabby Street gained fame first as "Walter Johnson's catcher," later for managing the St. Louis Cardinals to back-to-back pennants and a World Championship, and finally as a radio broadcaster. But he was destined to be remembered mostly for an offbeat stunt performed in the capital on the morning of August 21, 1908. Prompted by a bet between two local sportsmen, Street won a $500 prize and world-wide publicity by catching a baseball thrown from the top of the 550-foot-high Washington Monument. Though "considerably jarred by the impact" of the ball as it landed in his glove, it wasn't enough to keep him from catching Walter Johnson's 3–1 victory over Detroit that afternoon.

Street's experience on the receiving end of Johnson's "cannonballs," it was said, had uniquely prepared him to accomplish the feat at the monument.[18]

Also new to Washington in 1908 was George McBride, another well-traveled National League and minor-league veteran who had played briefly with Milwaukee in the first American League season of 1901. With the Nationals he found a home, taking over at shortstop for the next dozen years. The gentlemanly, dependable (150 or more games for the next seven seasons) McBride was a wizard at the position, and with Street behind the plate and the fleet Milan patrolling center field Washington was now rock-solid up the middle, a situation to gladden the heart of any pitcher. Unfortunately, until Milan blossomed at the plate several years hence none of them provided much offensive support. McBride still holds the record for lowest career batting (.218) and slugging (.264) averages of any player with more than 5,000 at-bats.[19] Street, with his .208 lifetime average and grand total of two home runs in an eight-year career, avoided the distinction only by not playing as much.

The weeks following Street's feat at the monument provided the first real demonstration of Walter Johnson's extraordinary powers of pitching endurance. The day after his win over Detroit Cantillon sent him in for two innings of relief. After a rest of one day, Johnson pitched another complete game on the 24th, this time losing to the Tigers, 1–0. An 8–0 shutout of Cleveland on August 28 and a 5-inning relief job against Boston (the first of two appearances opposite the legendary Cy Young) on the last day of the month preceded one of the great stretches of pitching fortitude in baseball history.

In New York for a four-game series with the Highlanders at Hilltop Park, Cantillon called Johnson aside. "Walter, I may want you to pitch the next three games," he said. "The boys are in pretty bad shape. You go ahead and pitch this first game today and then let me know how you feel." With three days' rest (the preferred break until late in his career) behind him Johnson bested New York ace Jack Chesbro, 3–0, on six hits in the opener on Friday, September 4. After the game Cantillon quizzed Johnson about his arm and was told it felt all right. "Are you ready to pitch tomorrow, Walter, if we need you?," the manager asked. "We want to win all the games we can, but I don't want to work you to death unless you can stand it." He would do his best, Johnson replied.[20] The next day, allowing only four hits this time, Johnson blanked the Highlanders again, 6–0. Although Cantillon's use of Johnson in this incredible series has often been described as spontaneous, it was actually planned, more or less. The Nationals' staff was completely shot with sore arms and other maladies, and only three pitchers—Johnson, Long Tom Hughes, and Burt Keeley—had made the trip.[21] Sunday baseball wouldn't be legal in New York for another ten years, and Cantillon told Johnson that his back-to-back wins had earned him a rest on Monday also; Keeley and Hughes would pitch the Labor Day doubleheader. But Keeley came down with a sore throat Monday morning and Hughes had returned to Washington to be with his wife, who was also ill, although he was expected back for the second game. Johnson would later say that he felt "quite proud" to be asked to pitch the team's third straight game.[22] Before a Labor Day crowd of 12,000 he did his team and himself proud, shutting out New York and Chesbro once more, 4–0, on a mere two hits this time. "It was not a partisan crowd," reported the *Star*. "When Johnson, Cantillon's splendid young pitcher of shutout fame, trotted from the field after his well-won game was over, he got an ovation as has seldom been heard in the coliseum on the heights."

Despite taking one of Chesbro's "inshoots" (spitballs) squarely in the ribs in the third inning, Johnson had gone on to pitch his best game of the series. He gave up the fewest hits, had the most strikeouts, and didn't walk a man in facing just 30 batters. In the three games only one New York runner had reached third base, only three making it to second. Johnson actually improved as he went along, giving up two fewer hits each time and no walks at all over the last two games. When the team returned to Washington on Tuesday, Gabby Street told the *Star:* "It was the best pitched three games of ball I have ever caught. Walter's speed was terrific. He was faster and his curve broke better in the last game than in any of the others. Why, he could have pitched the last game of the doubleheader."

Johnson might have done just that if he hadn't stayed in the clubhouse, avoiding Cantillon, until the second game was underway. As he walked to the bench after his victory, Jim Delahanty had told him to change shirts because he was starting the second game also. "I changed my shirt alright," Johnson recalled, "but I didn't put on my uniform until the second game had started. I thought Delahanty was in earnest and figured Cantillon might send orders for me to work again."[23] Indeed, the possibility hadn't been ruled out, according to Cantillon: "When we went out for the fourth game, Kid Elberfeld, shortstop [and manager] for the Highlanders, came over to our bench. 'Who you going to pitch, Joe?,' asked the Kid. 'I don't know,' I said, 'I haven't talked to Walter. He hasn't come out yet.'"[24]

On the heels of this performance, and with the Nationals climbing toward their best record in many years, Joe Cantillon put the durability of his young pitching wonder to the maximum test over the last month of the season. The Athletics came into Washington on September 11 for a critical five-game series, and with Johnson regaining his form the Nationals saw a chance to pass them into sixth place. He took the opener, a 2–1 duel with Eddie Plank in which Johnson faced for the first time the man he regarded "the greatest natural hitter I ever saw"—Joe Jackson.[25] Playing his second game in the major leagues, Jackson had a single in five trips to the plate. Touched for nine hits, Johnson lacked his usual "stuff" and by his own assessment was lucky to come away with a win. To Ed Grillo of the *Post,* the pitcher's honest evaluation of his performance was as much of a story as the game itself:

It is not often that a ballplayer will admit that luck has favored him in anything he accomplishes. He may know that his work did not deserve success, but he is usually willing to take the credit, whether it is due him or not. It was, therefore, out of the ordinary to hear Walter Johnson say, after winning the game yesterday, that he did not think he deserved the victory. He considered himself lucky to have won it, because he did not have what he usually has when he pitches. There are, however, a lot of pitchers who would consider themselves in fine fettle if they could show as much as Johnson did yesterday. There is something about this boy, aside from his ability as a pitcher, that makes him popular with the patrons of the game. He is absolutely honest in everything he does. He never complains of the umpires' decisions and is modest to a fault, believing that his teammates, more than himself, are entitled to the credit for what the team accomplishes when he is pitching.[26]

The day after this "lucky" win Cantillon found himself without a single healthy hurler other than his phenom. It was sore-armed Charley Smith's turn in the rotation, and although one look at his warm-up tosses made it clear that Smith was in no condition to pitch, Cantillon had no choice until Johnson "volunteered" to take his place, as reported by the *Post* under the headline, "Walter Johnson With His Arm of Steel Again Defeats Mack's Team":

When Smith warmed up, Walter Johnson picked up a ball, gave Mike Kahoe a wink, and the pair strolled out to the field.

"Let me try my arm, Mike," said Johnson, and he began to warm up. After ten minutes, Johnson remarked, "Well, she's better than she was yesterday," and slowly meandered to the players' bench. When the preliminary practice was over, Cantillon said to Smith,

"Charley, I'll have to ask you to go in, sore arm and all. We haven't anybody else."

"I tried my arm out, Joe, and she feels pretty strong," put in Johnson.

"Well, Walter, if you think you can work, it will be a big favor to me and the other pitchers," explained Cantillon.

"I'll try and tackle her," drawled Johnson, picking up his mitt and walking to the pitchers' mound.

Nine innings later Johnson had claimed his fifth complete-game victory in nine days.

This amazing stretch in the last month of the 1908 season was the outstanding example of his (and probably any other pitcher's) physical stamina, but endurance was to be a characteristic throughout Johnson's long career. A graceful, fluid delivery—"effortless," it was often described—gave his long arm tremendous leverage while spreading much of the effort to his back and legs, putting little strain on the arm and shoulder. Mike Martin, the Nationals' longtime trainer, said of Johnson's style: "For him, throwing a ball involves no more labor than snapping your fingers does for you, and as far as his wing is concerned, he will be able to pitch when he is 60."[27]

Johnson understood full well that every pitcher's approach was different: "Pitchers are born and their style comes with them," he said.[28] At the same time it was always a mystery to him that more pitchers didn't throw from the side and that more coaches and managers didn't encourage them to try it.[29] There were others, including Grover Cleveland Alexander, Addie Joss, Iron Man McGinnity, and to some extent Cy Young, who also found great success using a similar sweeping sidearm delivery. Of Red Sox pitcher Joe Wood, who threw with the more common direct overhand motion, Johnson said: "When I used to see Wood pitch, although I admired his speed and control, it made my own shoulders ache to watch his delivery. That pitching with the arm alone, that wrenching of the muscles in the shoulder, would wear out my arm, I am sure, much quicker than the easy, swinging motion I always aim to use."[30] To demonstrate his point Johnson said, "Try it without a ball. Hold your left hand on your right shoulder and try both ways. See how many more muscles seem to be put into severe play overhand as against sidearm."[31]

After taking ballots for several weeks, on September 13 the *Washington Post* announced the winner of its Nationals' popularity contest. Edging out Milan with 141,200 votes to 113,670, Walter Johnson picked up his first award, a large silver loving cup that would be prominently displayed in the department store window in Fullerton over the winter. With two days' rest following the back-to-back wins over Philadelphia, Cantillon put him in for three innings to save the last game of the series. In Chicago on the 18th Ed Walsh stopped Johnson's winning streak at six in a 1–0 heartbreaker in which the White Sox made only three hits. Another close defeat came two days later when the Browns scored with one out in the tenth inning to take a 2–1 thriller. Johnson's nine strikeouts in the game were dwarfed by the 17 rung up by Rube Waddell in one of his last great performances, in part the result of a remark by Nationals' catcher Mike Kahoe.

"We hit him (Waddell) hard in the first inning and scored a run," Johnson related. "He was a hard fellow to beat, but once on the run, he would look for a reason to get out of the game. As soon as the inning was over, he started for the bench with a decided limp that had not been noticed before we scored.

'You'd better limp,' said Mike Kahoe, standing in the coaching box, 'and before we finish, you'll have a sore arm, too.' He stopped limping immediately. Instead, he came back the next inning with blood in his eyes, and from then on he gave the greatest exhibition of all-round speed and unhittable curves that I ever looked at. Most of the time we were choking up on the bat and just trying to keep from getting struck out. But Rube burned them past in spite of everything." Johnson struck out four straight times himself in this game. Later, when asked his pick for greatest pitcher, the choice was Waddell. "Waddell had more sheer pitching ability than any man I ever saw," he said. "He had everything the ideal pitcher requires except, of course, his one great failing—discipline. He had a real curve and a real fast ball. And speed—no man ever lived with greater speed."[32]

The loss to Waddell gave Johnson seven complete games and a save within a span of 17 days, and Cantillon didn't spare him in the waning days of the campaign in a futile attempt to give Washington its highest finish since 1902. Johnson was used in both games of doubleheaders on September 29 and October 3 with a complete-game sandwiched in between. Then with three days' rest he pitched an 11-inning 1–0 gem over the Highlanders on October 7, the last day of the season.

Although posting their best record in years, 67 wins and 85 losses, the Nationals moved up only to seventh place, a half-game behind the A's and 22½ games behind repeat winners Detroit in the tight American League standings. Johnson finished with 14 wins and 14 losses, his 1.65 earned run average the fourth best in the league for the second year in a row. Despite missing the first 2½ months of the season, he put in what would be almost a full year for most pitchers: 36 games, 30 starts, 23 complete games, 256 innings, 160 strikeouts (fifth in the A.L.), and 6 shutouts. 1908 was a pitcher's year, with only three batting averages over .300 in the league and great seasons by Ed Walsh (40–15, 464 IP, 11 shutouts) and Addie Joss (24–11, 1.16 ERA, 9 shutouts). Christy Mathewson had his best year ever, 37–11, leading the National League in virtually every pitching category.

With the season over, Johnson and eight other Nationals accompanied Joe Cantillon to Chicago to pick up some extra money in a series of exhibitions against the outlaw Logan Square Club. This innocent gesture almost split the game into warring factions when American League president Ban Johnson, in his capacity as head of the National Commission (the governing body of organized baseball), fined each of the participants $100 and threatened to banish them from organized baseball for violation of the rule prohibiting participation in games with ineligible players.[33] Joe Cantillon and his brother Mike (owner of the Minneapolis American Association team), the organizers of the exhibitions, vowed to fight the fines in court if necessary. "One of the worst tangles in the history of baseball will eventuate if the belligerents make good the threats," predicted the *Chicago Tribune.*[34] The *Post* printed rumors that the players involved, including Walter Johnson, were organizing a movement to overthrow the National Commission.[35]

In the end it turned out to be just another of a series of skirmishes between ballplayers resentful of the Commission and its rules (particularly the hated reserve clause), and the imperious Ban Johnson, who was suspicious of any activity suggesting the spirit of independence he had epitomized himself a few years earlier in breaking the National League monopoly. The situation was defused when the players dispersed to their winter homes and the Commission, anxious to avoid judicial interpretation of its practices, backed off from its threat to bar them from the game. But Joe Cantillon would eventually pay a price for supporting the players in their stand against his old boss's dictatorial ways.

At the same time the Logan Square series was being played in Chicago, the World Series between Detroit and the Chicago Cubs was also taking place there, and the town became the center of the baseball world. One of the celebrities attracting the most attention was Walter Johnson. "Walter Johnson's fame seems to have spread from coast to coast," Ed Grillo reported from the Windy City. "Everyone who has not seen him pitch is anxious to hear about the great youngster, and when he strolled into one of the hotels during the World Series in Chicago, he was the center of attraction, and numerous requests were made for introductions. Ballplayers on other teams have given Johnson his reputation among those who have not had an opportunity to see him pitch. The players all agree he is the best young pitcher in the country today, and many are the predictions that he will lead all the twirlers in a year or two."[36]

Johnson's strong finish renewed the kind of praise accompanying his emergence a year earlier. "With a few years more of development and experience he will be the greatest twirler the game has ever known—barring neither Radbourne nor Rusie nor Mathewson nor any other boxman, past or present," declared the *Atlanta Journal.*[37] Billy Evans, who had umpired the shutout series in New York, wrote:

> That Johnson is a pitching wonder there is no doubt. It may be 50 years before another twirler is picked up like him and meets with the same success. He has a free, easy delivery and puts little strain on his arm when he throws. He is only 21 years old, leads a model life, and looks as if he might prove a rival to Cy Young for endurance honors. It's a good bet that no amount of money would buy this youngster who a year ago was unknown.[38]

Famed evangelist and former major-leaguer Billy Sunday picked Johnson for his annual All-American team, along with Mathewson, Walsh, Waddell, Joss, and Mordecai "Three-Finger" Brown. "I choose Johnson," Sunday wrote, "because he is young and has shown himself a wonder, and I believe him destined to be a great pitcher."[39]

⚾ ⚾ ⚾ ⚾ ⚾

Around the circuit they are keeping their eyes on Walter Johnson. They regard him now as Tyrus Cobb was regarded two years ago. And Joe Cantillon believes that Johnson will be to the list of American League pitchers what Ty was to the baserunners and hitters. "He is young and he is strong. Look at him there—big, strong, husky fellow, just 20 years old, I'm telling you, and good for 20 more. Just to show you how Johnson is regarded in the American League, I can get more for Johnson right now than any other manager can get for any other pitcher in the league. If he was put on the market he would bring the record price."

WASHINGTON POST, APRIL 4, 1909

Johnson signed up for another California Winter League season with Santa Ana, now called the "Yellow Sox" for the bright yellow striping on the socks of their new green uniforms. But first he went to Los Angeles to pitch for the Olive club against the Los Angeles Giants, called "the champion colored team" by the *Los Angeles Herald.*[40] Despite striking out 20, Johnson lost in 11 innings, the defeat of Walter Johnson elevating the Giants to a brief prominence in Southern California baseball, bringing challenges from the winter league champion San Diego Pickwicks and the PCL champion Los Angeles Angels.[41] This winter-league season wasn't one of Johnson's best, but he did finish with a flourish, shutting out the Pickwicks on two hits on February 22 and striking out 15 Hoegees in a 2–0 win on the 27th before heading off to Galveston, Texas, and his first spring training with the Nationals.

His 1909 contract called for a raise to $3,500 from the 1908 salary of $2,700 (the same $450 per month as in 1907), and just three days after his arrival in Galveston on March 4 he was earning his pay with a complete-game 2–0 two-hitter with 14 strikeouts against the minor-league Houston club. And when the Nationals' regular schedule of exhibitions began in the middle of the month Cantillon had Johnson pitching in all of them, typically for three innings at the start of the game. Facing the Detroit Tigers at their San Antonio camp on the 20th, Johnson went 11 innings only to lose, 3–2. After two days' rest he threw three perfect innings at minor-league Dallas on the 23rd followed by another six perfect innings against them the next day. "The Texans stood aghast" at Johnson's pitching, reported the *Post.*

As the Nationals played their way through minor-league towns in Texas, Kansas, and Nebraska, Johnson was the big attraction advertised to pull fans into the ballparks and defray training expenses. A solid 203 pounds now, the 21-year-old looked strong and was practically unhittable, so Cantillon kept the crowds happy by working Johnson every day. From March 23 through the 29th, seven days in a row, he appeared for at least three innings in every game.

This scheme worked all right in the warm Southern climate, but as the Nationals made their way north the weather turned. They pulled into bitter cold in Topeka on the 29th, but that didn't stop Cantillon from playing the game or from pitching Johnson for the seventh straight day. According to the *Post* a meager "16 fans, 4 or 5 of whom paid admission, braved the blasts of Borea . . . the players went through the motions of a game in a purely perfunctory way. The pitchers lobbed them over, the batters hit them anywhere they wanted to. Neither side made any attempt to play the game. A detailed record of the play would represent only the desire of the players to get back to town and a red hot stove." After that Johnson was granted a day off, finally, but was back on the mound in Omaha for his usual three innings on both the last day of March and the first of April for fans who "shivered while the wind blew in from the north a stiff gale."

That marked the end of Johnson's exhibition season. The rest of the tour he spent on the train or in hotels suffering from a terrible cold as the team continued north through Kansas City to Cincinnati, passing through snow and hailstorms along the way. When they pulled into Washington on April 7 most of the team had colds or fevers or both. "It's a wonder we didn't all die from pneumonia," an unhappy Johnson told the *Post.* He had lost 18 pounds—and the prized opening-day assignment—although once comfortably ensconced in his room at the Regent Hotel he made a rapid recovery. "Walter Johnson was able to sit up and read the *Ladies Home Journal,*" the *Washington Herald* reported two days later. "Outside of that, Walter is all right." He was well enough to travel to New York on the 11th and watch from the grandstand as Charley Smith beat the Highlanders in the season opener, and on the 17th he was in uniform for the first time in 2½ weeks.

Johnson was back in time to share in the excitement on April 19 when President Taft and Vice President Sherman walked into the ballpark at the start of the second inning. "The game was interrupted by the cheering, which spread in a great wave from the grandstand to the bleachers as the crowd recognized the President," the *Post* described. "He shared a 5-cent bag of peanuts with

Vice President Sherman, who kept score and kept Taft informed of vital statistics. No one in Washington could recall yesterday just when it was that a President of the United States last attended a ball game in this city." (It was Benjamin Harrison in 1892.) The *Post* added, with a hint of sarcasm, that "With all of his love for outdoor life and sports, Mr. Roosevelt did not go within the ball grounds during his seven years in the White House."

Johnson's first appearance of the season on April 24 in New York showed the effects of his layoff. "Johnson couldn't find the plate, try how hard he would," reported the *Washington Star.* He walked six, hit a batter, and was touched for six runs by the Highlanders before being mercifully taken out with the bases loaded and none out in the third inning. Those succeeding him had no better luck in one of the most lopsided beatings in Nationals history, 17–0, by the lowly New Yorkers, an early clue that the Highlanders had been supplanted this year as the worst team in the league.

Still recovering from the illness, Johnson's next appearance didn't come until ten days later, and again he failed to last the distance, giving up four runs in six innings in a 7–1 loss to the Red Sox on May 3. His old form surfaced in Philadelphia on the 7th despite losing in the bottom of the ninth to Jack Coombs, 1–0, after striking out nine A's. With two days' rest he put on another outstanding performance but dropped a second straight 1–0 heartbreaker to Chicago in the bottom of the 11th. It was a record third 1–0 defeat in a row for the team. "[Gabby Street] was so sore at losing that he walked out of the park in his stocking feet, throwing his shoes ahead of him and muttering savage words of revenge," the *Post* noted.

As soon as it became obvious that Johnson had gained back his strength, Cantillon reverted to pushing the limits of the youngster's powers. With one day off after the 11-inning loss, Johnson was back on the mound in Chicago, picking up a save in two innings of relief. The next day he started against the White Sox, pitching creditably before running out of gas in the seventh frame of a 17-inning 1–1 marathon. On two days' rest Johnson took another close complete-game loss in St. Louis, 4–3.

His record stood at no wins and five defeats, the third bad start in his three years in the major leagues. Given a break of three full days Johnson claimed his first victory on May 20, a 10-inning 3–2 duel with Addie Joss at Cleveland in which he struck out 10 and drove in the winning run. The irony of Johnson winning his own game at the plate after the Nationals had scored a paltry two runs in his first five starts was not lost on the *Post.* "Walter has been in as good form as he was yesterday," it noted, "but his team simply has not given him support in the field or at bat. It is a wonder that a pitcher of such unusual ability as Johnson does not lose heart entirely when he sees himself chalked up a loser again and again after he has pitched winning ball."

Johnson was rested for a day before starting again at Cleveland on the 22nd, but this time he had been pushed beyond the limit. After three innings his arm hurt. A concerned Cantillon gave his phenom a full week between each of his next three starts, the first two of them lackluster losses to New York and Cleveland. On June 11 Johnson tossed a 1–0 four-hitter at the champion Tigers, a return to form that continued through a five-game winning streak over the next two weeks. After his second victory in a row over Detroit on the 15th, the *Detroit Press* quoted "one of the star Tigers" as remarking: "If Johnson was pitching for us he wouldn't lose a game." Four days later in New York Johnson had one of his occasional games with too much "stuff." In a 7–4 win over the Highlanders he allowed only three hits and struck out ten, but also gave up seven walks, hit a batter, and threw *five* wild pitches.

"Walter Johnson had more stuff on the ball yesterday than he has ever had since I have been handling his delivery," Gabby Street told the *Post*. "He was so fast that his fastball took all sorts of shoots, and this made him wild. When he did get the ball over the plate it was next to impossible to hit it." The paper described Street's "treatment" to cure the problem: "The funny part of the game took place in the ninth inning. Johnson was wilder than he had been before. Street kept shaking his head and beckoning to Cantillon to send out another pitcher, but the manager was obdurate and refused to do so. Finally, Street grabbed the broom used by the umpires, swept off the plate and drew a line behind it so that Johnson could see it. From that time on until the finish Johnson did nothing but pitch strikes."

A 3–1 victory at New York on June 29 evened Johnson's record at eight wins and eight losses. During this series Highlanders manager George Stallings offered Washington $30,000—"a fortune," the *Post* called it—for Walter Johnson and Gabby Street. "Cantillon," it reported, "in turning the offer down said that he might just as well sell his whole team as part with those two men, and he was about right." Street's teammates had a lot of fun with him about it. "Yeh, $29,000 for Johnson, $1,000 for old Gabby," they kidded him.[42]

Johnson's resurrection helped the Nationals move out of the American League cellar for the first time since early May, passing the slumping Browns into seventh place, a lofty position they could hold onto only briefly before sinking to the bottom for the rest of the season. Johnson suffered through an eight-game losing streak, the longest of his career, the last of them a Rube Waddell shutout in St. Louis on July 25. With the Nationals piling loss on top of loss, Cantillon scheduled less time off between Johnson's starts, two days the norm now and often just one. A three-day break became a rarity. When

Johnson did get a decent rest he usually responded, as in a 1–0 gem against Addie Joss on August 4. But no matter how tired or overworked, Johnson always looked better to Cantillon than the alternatives, and he was always capable of brilliance. After giving up six runs in five innings to the A's on August 16, Johnson came back the next day with a 12-inning 1–0 four-hitter over Chief Bender. That performance seemed to take a lot out of him, though, as he was slammed for 12 and 15 hits in his next two starts.

Walter Johnson was human after all, and on August 29 in Chicago he reached the breaking point. "Johnson May Never Pitch Again," read the shocking headline in the *Post.* The pitcher himself explained:

It was during the game I pitched in Cleveland that something began to ache on the top of the shoulder, but I did not give it a thought. The next day my arm was awfully sore, and when Cantillon told me to warm up on Sunday [the 29th] I did so, but told him that my arm was not right. He told me to go in and see if I could work it out. Well, the Sox did nothing with me and only got one run, and so I stuck it out, but I am very much afraid that I have ruined my arm. I don't know how it happened, but I can't throw a ball across the room. Coming over from Chicago I lay awake all night, my arm pained me so. It does not hurt me any more now, but I seem to have lost the use of it.

"[Johnson's] arm hung limp by his side, and ached like an ulcerated tooth," the *Post* sadly reported. "It is feared that the injury is a permanent one, because of the location on the top of the shoulder, the spot where the pain is always located when a ballplayer loses his throwing arm."[43] But instead of going home to rest his arm, the only prudent course with Washington's season a lost cause, Johnson stayed with the team and by September 9 was throwing again in practice, less than two weeks after the injury. A week later he wrote Ed Crolic, manager of the Santa Ana winter-league club, that his arm was "OK."[44] And by September 21 it clearly was as he shut out Detroit, 2–0, in his first appearance in more than three weeks. "There is nothing wrong with Walter Johnson's arm," reported the *Post.* "Johnson was at his best yesterday. He had terrific speed, and relied entirely on this." His last two starts of the season were well spaced, and although he lost both of them there were no lingering effects of the injury.

Johnson finished with 13 wins and a whopping 25 losses (avoiding a league record by virtue of teammate Bob Groom's 26). This season would be the only one of his first 10 averaging more than two earned runs a game, at 2.22. But despite missing six weeks with the cold and sore arm Johnson was second in the league with 164 strikeouts, third with 296 innings, and fourth with 27 complete games. *Baseball Magazine* named him to its All-American team along with Mathewson, Walsh, Plank, Brown, and Pirates ace Babe Adams. The futility of the season is reflected in Johnson's league record for shutouts lost in a season (10), and his major-league records for shutouts lost in a month (5, in July) and to one team (5, to Chicago); Johnson's 13–25 record was the best on the staff, with Groom at 7–26, Dolly Gray 5–19, and Charley Smith 3–12. The wretched 1909 Nationals still hold the league records for fewest runs scored (380) and the most times shut out (29), and the major-league record for losses in a month (29, in July). Their miserable won-lost mark of 42–110 (.272) left them 56 games behind Detroit and a full 20 games below the seventh-place Browns.

After a performance like that, the announcement in late September that Joe Cantillon had been fired didn't come as much of a surprise. The Nationals' board of directors had favored keeping him, nonetheless, until the arrival of a telegram from Ban Johnson in the middle of their meeting instructing Tom Noyes to take no action on the matter until the two of them could talk. When they did, Johnson told Noyes that he "didn't consider Cantillon a desirable man for the league, and it would be against the best interests of the club to reappoint him"—a thinly veiled threat of revocation of the shaky Nationals franchise.[45] Cantillon and the Washington ballclub had both been in Johnson's doghouse, in fact, from the day Cantillon hired on as manager. Johnson had planned for Cantillon to take over the Boston Red Sox in 1907, and resented that he hadn't been consulted before Pongo Joe took the Nationals job instead. After the Logan Square incident in the fall of 1908, and the Cantillons' threatened defiance of the National Commission, rumor had it that Johnson was plotting to force Cantillon out of the league on a charge of bias toward Detroit in the waning days of the tight 1908 American League pennant race. Clark Griffith, recently fired at New York, was to be given the Washington job.[46]

Now Johnson asked Noyes to dump Cantillon and hire Jimmy McAleer, and the Nationals owner reluctantly agreed. A great defensive outfielder in the National League in the 1890s, McAleer had been canned by St. Louis after eight undistinguished seasons managing the Browns. One of the small original group of renegade National Leaguers (with Cantillon and Griffith) without whose help Johnson's new league would never have gotten off the ground, McAleer remained an important ally in American League affairs.[47] The imperious Johnson wanted his friend to stay in the league, and he wanted Joe Cantillon out. For his part Cantillon, resentful of Johnson's charges that he was disloyal to the American League, fired off a bitter letter to him: "You know I was with the American League when it was born," he wrote, "and I have been with it heart and soul ever since, and to say I am disloyal hurts."[48]

Cantillon would move on to be a successful co-owner, with brother Mike, of the Minneapolis Millers, managing them to American Association pennants from 1910–1912 and again in 1915.[49]

Walter Johnson was undoubtedly sorry to see Cantillon leave the Nationals. The avuncular Pongo Joe was in many respects a good first manager for the teenaged Johnson, unaccustomed to big-city ways and far from home and family. Cantillon took enormous pride in his discovery, of course, but he was also extremely fond of the youngster personally, and the feeling was mutual. The two remained good friends and there would be many happy reunions between them in the years to come. At the same time, their parting at this juncture in Johnson's career was probably the best thing for him professionally. Another year or two of overuse could have ruined his career, or at least shortened it considerably, a fate befalling such great pitchers as Toad Ramsey, Amos Rusie, Jack Chesbro, Iron Man McGinnity, and Big Ed Walsh.

In Cantillon's defense, after some of the stunts performed by his phenom he could be excused for wondering if the normal rules of physiology even applied to Johnson at all. During that astonishing stretch in September 1908, Ed Grillo wrote that "Manager Cantillon keeps a close watch on Johnson. He does not allow him to do any practice pitching. [Said Cantillon]: 'The only trouble Johnson gives me is to keep him from fooling with a ball whenever he gets into a uniform. He is always wanting to pitch.'" In the same article Grillo quotes Johnson: "Sure, I'll pitch both games [of a doubleheader with the A's that day, September 11] if Joe wants me to. It makes no difference to me. I'd just as soon pitch both games as one. It's not hard work, now that the weather's cool."[50]

After looking over his staff of stumblebums to choose a starter or send in a reliever, Cantillon must have been overwhelmed often by the temptation to send in his young wonder. Years later, Johnson described a bit of psychology used by the veteran manager: "Joe had a great system in those days to get me to work out of turn. I'd ask for an extra pass and he'd surprise me with half a dozen. A little later he'd say, 'Walter, you're looking pretty good today. We'd like to have you pitch.' And I'd generally pitch, because my friends were always after passes."[51]

As the 1909 season ended there was no indication of concern about his arm as Johnson signed up with Connie Mack's ambitious postseason barnstorming tour. After being nosed out by the Tigers for the pennant, Mack's quickly improving Athletics were scheduled to play for the next two months against an aggregation led by old-timer Frank Bancroft, a veteran manager of the 1880s and '90s. The "All-Nationals," as they were called, consisted of players from both leagues looking to pick up extra cash on their way to homes on the West Coast, including Rube Marquard, Chief Meyers, Fred Snodgrass and Larry Doyle from the Giants, Johnson and Dolly Gray from the Senators, and Rube Ellis from the Cardinals. A 50-game loop through the West, starting in Chicago on October 19 and ending in New Orleans in December, had been planned.

Johnson passed up the first week of exhibitions, going home to see his family instead. After stopping off at Weiser, Idaho, for a few days of fishing with old pals there, he hooked up with the tour in Seattle on October 27.[52] Chief Meyers, coming off his first season as Christy Mathewson's favorite receiver, was behind the plate for Johnson's 5–3 loss to the A's. Fred Snodgrass would catch him for the rest of the tour, the high points of which were two easy victories at Chutes Park over the Los Angeles Angels. The second of these, a week after his 22nd birthday on November 15, was billed as a homecoming. "Sunday will be Johnson Day at Chutes Park," the *Los Angeles Herald* advertised. "The wonderful Washington twirler will be greeted not only by a large delegation of fans from Fullerton, his home town, but in all probability by every devotee of the game who remembers Walter as a busher."

The end of the tour for Johnson and the other California natives came in Los Angeles again, on December 12, facing the Athletics this time in what the *Herald* claimed to be "the first contest between major league teams ever played in Los Angeles." Despite pitching well, Johnson lost a 4–3 contest when the A's scored all of their runs in the eighth inning, three of them on errors. The once-ambitious tour had been a dismal failure, with only 25 of the 50 scheduled games taking place and some of those to empty stands. The rest were cancelled because of rain, snow, or cold. According to the players, only the capable leadership of Mack and Bancroft prevented an even worse disaster.[53]

The California Winter League was already well under way when Johnson joined up with Santa Ana for the third time—and his final season of baseball on the Coast. Taking advantage of publicity generated by the barnstorming games, the Yellow Sox made December 26 another "Johnson Day," giving away 2,000 photo portraits of their star. And it was his day, indeed, thrilling the large crowd by no-hitting a Salt Lake City team. Santa Ana was bolstered after the New Year by the addition of Rube Ellis and a big 20-year-old second baseman named Charles Arnold Gandil, known as "Chick" at Ed Crolic's pool hall where he worked as a "house man." With Ellis and Gandil in the lineup and Johnson in top form, the Yellow Sox didn't lose a game the rest of the season. Johnson had a perfect 9–0 record, giving up a sparse five runs, 21 hits, and three walks in nine complete games. An interested spectator at one of Johnson's best performances, a one-hit shutout on January 9, was the new manager of the Washington Nationals, Jimmy McAleer.

On March 10, 1910, the *Fullerton Tribune* announced that "Mr. and Mrs. F.E. Johnson, accompanied by their son, Walter, left for Coffeyville, Kansas." Frank Johnson had recently returned from Kansas after buying a large farm there, and the family now reversed the move of eight years earlier. Walter Johnson had never gotten completely acclimated to the constant weather of Southern California,[54] and the development of the oil leases around Olinda had taken on an increasingly furious pace.[55] The Johnson family had missed Kansas and their roots there, and they missed farming, and after three years of major-league salaries they were in a position to do something about it.

CHAPTER 5

Formidable

Another instance which shows the character of the great pitcher occurred in Boston one day when McAleer had the club. Walter was pitching brilliantly against the Red Sox in a very close game when a couple of errors and a base on balls filled the bases with no one out. It looked as if the game would be lost at this stage and the crowd went wild. But Johnson buckled down to business and struck out Hooper, Speaker and Lewis, Boston's big guns, and then with his head down walked to the bench. I was sitting with McAleer at the time, and as Johnson walked from the mound, McAleer poked me in the ribs and shouted, "Look! Look! He's ashamed he did it."[1]

ED GRILLO

The first major change for Walter Johnson under the Nationals' new management took place even before the start of spring training in 1910: permission from Jimmy McAleer to skip the training camp altogether. Before going home at the end of the previous season Johnson had told the *Post:* "I shall propose to manager McAleer not to ask me to report for the training trip. It seems absurd to take me out of the finest climate in the world to snow and rainstorms. I can get into perfect condition out home. I could get myself ready to work out there and report to the team a few days before the season starts."[2]

To many in the game it must have seemed unusual that Johnson be allowed to forgo all formal preparation for the coming season. But viewing Johnson's performance as key to his team's improvement, the new manager had puzzled over how the youngster might finally achieve the success predicted for him. The answer, he decided, was simply to stop working Johnson to the point of exhaustion. Relief appearances would be rare and normal rest between starts common during McAleer's tenure. He also had a theory about Johnson's pitch selection. Barely a month after taking over at Washington, McAleer outlined his approach:

"With everyone who has ever seen him work considering Walter Johnson one of the greatest pitchers that ever faced a batsman, it seems strange that he has not made a better showing. There must be something materially wrong in the way he works, and I think I know what the trouble is and will correct it. Johnson ought to use very few curve balls in a game. We always figured when he worked against us that if he began to curve we had a chance to beat him, but when he relied on his fast ball almost entirely we did not figure to have a look-in. He has so much on his fast one that he should seldom use a curve. I expect to make a big improvement in Johnson."[3]

One of the strategems tried by desperate batters throughout Johnson's career was to "take two strikes and wait for the curve ball." Eventually he developed an effective curve, but at first it didn't have much of a break—a fact that didn't discourage him in the least from throwing it. "Johnson would throw you two fastballs that scorched your uniform for two strikes," Ty Cobb related, "and then would want to throw his 'curve' just for the variety of it. It had just a wrinkle on it. Batters would wait for that one—it was just about their sole chance to touch the Big Train."[4]

In mid-March the Johnsons arrived at their new home four miles southeast of Coffeyville, Kansas. The property was about the same size, 160 acres or so, as the old Humboldt place, but with a much nicer house and barns. "It's one of the finest farms I've ever seen," Johnson told the *Washington Herald.* "Fruit trees all over, and all as healthy as can be."[5] The $6,400 purchase was intended to be more than just a home for him and his family. "I hope to realize on it handsomely," Johnson said in a letter to William Peet, sports editor of the *Herald.* He also told Peet, "I have been laid up in bed with a severe attack of the grip[pe]," which he presumably picked up on the trip from California.[6]

Johnson was in fine shape by the time he reached Washington on March 28. After a two-day holdout ("There is a slight difference between Jimmy and myself") and a meeting with Tom Noyes, his salary was raised another $1,000 to $4,500. Ed Walsh was the only American League pitcher making more.[7] It didn't take Johnson long to get into action, going three innings in an exhibition game against the Philadelphia Phillies later that day. With his only preparation a brief workout the day before, Johnson wasn't expected to pitch. But after warming up he told McAleer that a few innings wouldn't do any harm, and the manager acceded. Johnson gave up a run but also "displayed all the terrific speed which makes him a pitching wonder," according to the *Post,* "and without throwing a curve he struck out three of the four men who faced him in the first inning. It was just a nice workout for the big fellow."

Three innings against Cornell on April 2 completed Johnson's scant competition before the start of the season two weeks later. McAleer was intent on seeing the young pitcher well-rested if nothing else, and the effect was obvious. "Johnson is looking better than he ever has upon his arrival here," reported the *Herald.* "He is brown as a berry, and says he is feeling fine." With no mound exploits to detail, the biggest news about Johnson was the change in "his once admired crop of blond hair . . . the peerless one is now sporting what can be called a dark crown."[8]

April 14, 1910, was one of those lovely spring days when Washington, D.C., with its parks bursting with flowers and its gleaming white government buildings and monuments, can be as beautiful as any city in the world. The ideal weather brought out the capital's largest baseball crowd ever for the opening game of the season between the Nationals and the Philadelphia Athletics. In addition to a great game, these fortunate fans were treated to a bit of baseball history when President and Mrs. Taft, Vice President and Mrs. Sherman, and a number of Cabinet officers and other dignitaries showed up at the ballpark unannounced and unanticipated. Taft had sweated through a rough reception earlier in the day from the 42nd annual Suffragist convention, which hadn't taken kindly to his suggestion that "Power might be exercised by the least desirable persons" should women be allowed to vote. "This did not please the Suffragists," reported the *Post,* "and although President Taft was their guest, his speech was interrupted by an outburst of hisses from all over the hall. With the hisses were half-suppressed 'catcalls.'" After that "trying moment," Taft suggested to Sherman that they take in the game.

The appearance of the president's party took Nationals officials by surprise, but they provided whatever red-carpet treatment could be quickly arranged, including a large armchair to contain the 300-pound president's enormous bulk. It was Jimmy McAleer's idea for Taft to throw out the ball to start the game, and it was his idea, too, that Johnson should catch it—an honor the pitcher tried to sidestep but for which fate had destined him anyway.[9]

"McAleer kept insisting that I go over toward the President's box and catch the ball he would throw out," Johnson recalled. "But I told him Mr. Taft had come out to see a ball game and not to play catch with me. Before game time Billy Evans made his way toward the President's box, where he presented a brand new ball to Mr. Taft. He asked him to pitch the ball to a Washington player and the President agreed, immediately removing his gloves. In the meantime, Evans passed the ball to Mrs. Taft, who examined it carefully and expressed surprise at its weight. As the bell rang to start the game, the President rose in the grandstand and prepared to throw. Gabby Street was standing at homeplate, waiting for the throw, but suddenly the President shifted his position and aimed at me—and his aim was very good. I caught the ball and stuck it right in my pocket. A newspaperman sitting near the Presidential box told me later that just as the President was going to throw the ball to Street, a member of his party, who had overheard my remark to McAleer, repeated it to Mr. Taft as follows: 'Johnson is a shy fellow. He told McAleer there was no use being out there as you didn't come to play catch with him.' The President laughed aloud and asked where I was standing. He threw the ball and I caught it."[10]

The crowd applauded heartily and Johnson turned to walk out to the mound. But Billy Evans called him back, took the ball, and gave him another to start the game. Then Johnson put on a show for the president and the other fans, pitching one of the great games of his career, a 3–0 gem over Athletics ace Eddie Plank. Connie Mack's team would be crowned world champions by year's end, but on this day they could manage only a single hit off Johnson's offerings. It was the overflow crowd, and a rope strung around the outfield to accommodate it, that cost him a no-hitter. In the seventh inning, Frank "Home Run" Baker lifted a pop fly that would ordinarily have been an easy out. But as he was about to make the catch near the rope, right fielder Doc Gessler tripped over an encroaching fan (described variously as a "boy" and a "cripple") who couldn't scramble out of the way in time. Gessler was heartbroken, feeling that he had cost Johnson the no-hitter, and afterwards apologized profusely when the two met at the hotel. Johnson, according to the *Post's* account of the conversation, assured Gessler there was no reason to feel bad. "That's all right, Doc," he told him, "We won, didn't we? Well, that is good enough."

After the game Mack, whose own big-league career had started with Washington 25 years earlier, became the first to call Johnson unequivocally the fastest pitcher ever. "Until Walter Johnson broke into baseball," the *Post* reported, "it was generally conceded that Amos Rusie had more speed than any other pitcher, but there is some doubt to that now, for there are those who believe that Johnson has more speed than Rusie ever possessed. Among those who are of that opinion is Connie Mack, a man who has spent almost his entire life in baseball, a good judge, and a very conservative one: 'Johnson's pitching yesterday was marvelous, and his speed was the greatest I ever saw. My players tell me that they had no trouble seeing the ball after it left his hand, but that it seemed to jump at them before they could get their bats into motion. Yes, Rusie never had more speed, and I don't believe as much, as this young fellow.'"[11]

The next morning a friend of Johnson's who worked at the Capitol took the ball tossed by Taft to the White House along with a note from Johnson asking the President to sign it. Several hours later, a messenger arrived at the ballpark bearing the ball and a letter from President Taft: "I have yours of April 15 asking me to autograph the ball with which the game of yesterday, the 14th, was opened. I have great pleasure in doing so, and transmit the ball herewith. Sincerely Yours, William H. Taft." Johnson proudly showed off the treasures to teammates and Philadelphia players. On the ball itself, before his signature, the President had written: "To Walter Johnson, with the hope that he may continue to be as formidable as in yesterday's game."[12]

In the first half of the 1910 season Johnson was sometimes formidable and sometimes not. Anemic batting support cost him three low-scoring games early on, but he also won one of those against Boston on April 28, a strange 12-inning 2–1 squeaker in which he struck out 12 but also gave up 16 hits. He allowed 15 hits on May 6 in a 4–3 loss at Philadelphia and four days later gave up seven runs in five innings of a 10–3 blowout by Chicago. His record stood at two wins and five losses, his fourth straight bad start. Johnson was even forced to deny insinuations that he was pitching poorly on purpose to force the Nationals to trade him to a better team.[13] The sports editor of the *Post,* H.T. Brewer, had had enough of Johnson's inconsistency and failure to live up to his promise:

> In view of the poor showing made by Walter Johnson, our pitcher ideal, both this year and last year, don't you think it would be very advisable for manager McAleer to trade this phenom for a couple of good fielders? From past performances by Johnson, it is clear that he cannot win games for Washington, despite the fact that he is touted as being one of the greatest pitchers in the game. Such a man would make good trading material, and with an eye to business Mr. McAleer should be greatly benefited by releasing him.[14]

All such talk ended with shutouts in his next two games and a string of four wins in a row. A 1–0 beauty over Cleveland on May 14 was Johnson's final duel with the ill-fated Addie Joss in one of his last appearances before being stopped by the illness that would take his life a year later. On June 4 Johnson picked up an 8–2 win in his only start against Cy Young.

A 12–3 victory over St. Louis on July 8 provided an outstanding example of what was sometimes referred to as Johnson's "artful loafing." His first seven outs of the game and eight of the first nine were strikeouts, but after the Nationals scored ten runs in the fifth inning he didn't notch another. It wasn't really loafing at all, but a strategy eventually adopted by all smart pitchers. "Johnson has entirely changed his style of pitching," wrote Ed Grillo, who had moved over to the *Star* as sports editor. "It used to be that he would go at top speed from the first inning to the last as long as his strength would hold out. Now he has adopted an entirely different policy. Johnson loafs in his games now until he finds himself in a pinch, when he lets himself out to the fullest extent. The result of this system is that he always has something in reserve and is as good in the final inning as he is in the first. Whether Johnson has copied this style from Mathewson or not is not known, but that is the system the great New York pitcher has followed for years."[15]

The turning point in Johnson's season came after his worst outing of the year, a 7–5 loss in Philadelphia on July 30. Gabby Street was out with an injury and McAleer had revamped the Nationals' catching corps, releasing backups Blankenship and Kahoe (who stayed on as a scout), buying Heinie Beckendorf from the Tigers, and signing John Henry out of Amherst College. Beckendorf was with the Nationals for just a few games, Bull Henry (6 feet, 190 pounds) for eight years, but neither would catch Walter Johnson much. The *Post's* account of the loss to Philadelphia explains why:

> Never in recent years has a pitcher showed up his catchers as Walter Johnson did Beckendorf and Henry. This marvelous pitcher put Beckendorf out of commission on about six pitched balls, and Henry would never have lasted the game had Johnson not stopped hurling smoke balls over. Street, who is one of the best maskmen in the country, is the only backstop on the team who can hold Johnson, and he himself is disabled as a result of handling Johnson's terrific shoots. Manager McAleer might as well keep Johnson on the bench until Street is ready to catch him. Right now Johnson would win the pennant for any of the four clubs in the first division at present. He wouldn't lose more than one game out of ten were he playing with the Athletics, New York, Boston or Detroit. He is truly the master pitcher of the American League. Pretty tough when a manager has one of the greatest pitchers of modern times but cannot use him for fear of crippling his catchers.

Johnson's record stood at 13 wins and 14 losses, but without another bad performance for the rest of the year he closed with 12 wins in 15 decisions. A five-game winning streak was stopped on August 23 by a 1–0 loss to Walsh (his third straight 1–0 victory over Johnson) in which Johnson struck out twelve White Sox. He notched another dozen strikeouts against Detroit in his next game, then sent down 14 Browns in an 8–0 win on the last day of August—a total of 38 strikeouts in three games, the major-league record for 64 years.[16] In a 3–1 win over Chief Bender on September 3, the A's sent up pinch-hitters Jack Lapp, Topsy Hartsel, and Ben Houser, all lefthanded hitters, and Johnson struck them out on ten pitches. (Lapp managed a foul.)

Rookie Eddie Ainsmith was sent in to catch Johnson for the first time on September 7. "The young catcher seemed fully competent," the *Post* reported, noting that at first "Johnson slackened his speed, pitching a game entirely different from that he had shown when Beck was working. He did not know just how Ainsmith would handle him." On September 25 in St. Louis Johnson pitched one of his great games, another near no-hitter in which he struck out 11 and allowed only one baserunner (a much rarer achievement than a no-hitter). The season ended October 6 with Johnson, in only his third relief appearance of the year, saving a victory over Boston in a duel with Smoky Joe Wood.

McAleer's new protocol had worked wonders. With regular starts and regular rest, not only was Johnson's effectiveness improved but he was capable of pitching more, leading the American League in games (45), starts (42), complete games (38), and innings pitched (370). His 313 strikeouts were the most by far in the major leagues in 1910 and the second-highest total to that point. (There was a brief flurry of excitement when it was heralded across the country as a new record until it was recalled that Rube Waddell had struck out 349 in 1904.) Johnson's 1.36 earned run average placed third in the league, his eight shutouts second. His turnaround from 25 losses to 25 wins—the only time that's ever been done—improved the Nationals' record by 24½ games to 66–85, but they moved up only one spot to seventh place, a game behind the White Sox. As usual the problem was hitting, with Clyde Milan's .279 batting average tops on the team. Milan's paltry 16 RBIs in 531 at-bats was indicative of the Nationals' anemic attack.

The generation of pitchers who had dominated the American League during the first decade of the modern era of baseball was now passing from the scene. The shift had begun in 1909 as Jack Chesbro, Bill Dinneen, Nick Altrock and Jesse Tannehill faded out of the big leagues; 1910 was the last year for Addie Joss, Rube Waddell, and Ed Killian; Cy Young and Bill Donovan would call it quits in 1911, and 1912 would be the last hurrah for Chicago's great tandem of Ed Walsh and Doc White. Only Eddie Plank and Chief Bender continued into the second decade with effectiveness. Foremost among the generation taking their place was Walter Johnson, but there were also Smoky Joe Wood, Eddie Cicotte, Jack Quinn, Jack Coombs, Russ Ford, Herb Pennock, Vean Gregg, Ray Caldwell, Red Faber, and Harry Coveleski.

The American League season ended a week before the National League's. Seeking to keep Philadelphia sharp for the coming World Series against the Cubs, Connie Mack asked old friend Jimmy McAleer to assemble a team for a string of exhibitions with the A's.[17] A lineup was put together of Milan, Street, McBride, and Kid Elberfeld from the Nationals; Tris Speaker, Harry Lord, and Jake Stahl from the Red Sox; and Ty Cobb from the Tigers. Cobb, Speaker, and Milan, the cream of the center field crop in baseball, made up the outfield. The pitching staff consisted of Walsh and White from the White Sox, and Walter Johnson. The powerful Athletics, American League pennant-winners four of the next five years, got more than a workout from this "All-Star team," losing the first four games before taking the finale. Johnson bested Bender, Plank, and Coombs, 8–3, on October 11, then held the A's scoreless for the first eight innings of a 4–1 win three days later. After sweeping the first three games of the World Series and beating the Cubs four games to one, Mack credited the exhibitions: "Those games with the American League All-Stars were the making of our team in its battle in the world series with the Cubs," he claimed. "Those games, more than anything else, put the Athletics in a condition to outclass the National League champions."[18]

Another confrontation with Ban Johnson and the National Commission flared up when an exhibition series of 12 games was arranged with some of the best players in the game (Johnson, Cobb, Speaker, Eddie Collins, and Three-Finger Brown among them) to be managed by John McGraw and Hughie Jennings. When the Commission peremptorily banned the tour, promoter Daniel Fletcher tried to parlay the players' resentment into a third major league, actually signing some, including Johnson, Cobb, Street, and Russ Ford to options on contracts calling for $10,000 signing bonuses and big salaries, but failed to find the financial backing needed to go further. Within a couple of months Fletcher faded from the scene completely, but not without stirring up considerable commotion in the meantime.[19]

On October 26 the *Post's* sports section headlined a rumored Ty Cobb-for-Walter Johnson trade, consideration of which was flatly denied the next day by Detroit President Frank Navin. Washington would never entertain any offer for their star, scoffed Navin, who called Johnson "in my opinion the best pitcher in the country, and doubly valuable because he is so young."[20]

Johnson had to go only about half as far now to get home at season's end. Coffeyville, Kansas, is in the southeast corner of the state on the Oklahoma border and not far from Missouri and Arkansas. The town was named for Colonel James Coffey, the founder also of Humboldt 60 miles to the north. With the huge Osage Indian Reservation only 25 miles to the southwest, and in the middle of the Kansas-Missouri border-war bloodletting of the Civil War period, the area had already witnessed its share of history before October 5, 1892 (just 18 years before the Johnsons moved there), when Coffeyville attained a special place in the saga of the Wild West. That was the day of the Dalton Gang raid, the last big shootout between the law and the famed original outlaws of the Southwest.[21] Cousins of Cole Younger and his brothers (original members of the James gang), the four Dalton boys had grown up outside of Coffeyville before turning to a life of robbing trains and banks.

When they attempted to rob two banks in their hometown simultaneously, three of the brothers and another confederate were gunned down.[22]

Despite a sometimes lurid history, the area also had its share of productive, law-abiding citizens. The rolling prairies of southern Kansas contained some of the richest soil in the world, along with healthy deposits of oil. The Johnson spread of 160 acres lay across the Verdigris River four miles southeast of Coffeyville, a prosperous town of 18,000 residents. This was by no means the subsistence farming of the family's Humboldt days. Rather, they took to raising blooded dairy stock. "No ordinary cow can find a welcome on the Johnson estate," wrote *Baseball Magazine* editor F.C. Lane after a visit there in 1915. At an initial cost of $300-$600 each, a herd of Holstein-Freisian cattle, "The most celebrated milk breed Holland has produced," according to Johnson, was built up. (One of their cows produced a whopping 457 pounds of milk and 19 pounds of butter in a week.) He developed an interest in the science of breeding and raising cattle, reading a half-dozen dairy magazines with the latest theories. Johnson also began a lifelong hobby of raising thoroughbred birds, winning contests at county fairs and shows in the area with his White Orpington chickens and other prize specimens.[23]

"While I may be a ballplayer by profession, still I am a farmer at heart," Johnson said of his off-season life at Coffeyville. "I am perfectly happy when I get home in the fall, and can put on some overalls, a soft shirt, a pair of boots and then get out, tramp through the fields, and breathe the good fresh air. It surely is a treat after being shut up in the cities all summer, and I always feel like a bird that has been let out of a cage."[24]

I'm not boasting about my first experience with Johnson though. They can't never tell me he throws them balls with his arm. He's got a gun concealed about his person and he shoots 'em up there. I was leading off in Murphy's place and the game was a little delayed in startin' because I'd watched the big guy warm up and wasn't in no hurry to get to that plate. Before I left the bench, Connie says:

"Don't try to take no healthy swing. Just meet 'em and you'll get along better."

So I tried to just meet the first one he throwed; but when I stuck out my bat Henry was throwin' the pill back to Johnson. Then I thought: Maybe if I start swingin' now at the second one I'll hit the third one. So I let the second one come over and the ump guessed it was another strike, though I'll bet a thousand bucks he couldn't see it no more'n I could. While Johnson was still windin' up to pitch again I started to swing—and the big cuss crosses me with a slow one. I lunged at it twice and missed it both times, and the force o' my wallop throwed me clean back to the bench. The Ath-a-letics was all laughin' at me and I laughed too, because I was glad that much of it was over. McInnes gets a base hit off him in the second innin' and I ast him how he done it.

"He's a friend o' mine," says Jack, "and he lets up when he pitches to me."

I made up my mind right there that if I was goin' to be in the league next year I'd go out and visit Johnson this winter and get acquainted.[25]

FROM "HORSESHOES" BY RING LARDNER

Hoping to end his tradition of bad starts, perhaps, Walter Johnson decided to go to spring training in 1911. First he put in a couple of weeks at Hot Springs, Arkansas, where many major-league stars "took the baths," played golf, and soaked up the resort's hospitality before heading off to join their teams. Sometimes they even played a little baseball, and Johnson was in right field for three pickup games, the "All-Americans" against the "All-Nationals," hitting home runs in the first two. At the Nationals' camp in Atlanta he pitched in a handful of games, getting plenty of rest in between. Washington shared the Atlanta ballpark with the New York Giants, and on March 29 Walter Johnson was introduced to Christy Mathewson for the first time. "Matty has never seen Johnson pitch a game," the *Post* reported, "and asked interestedly when he would work, that he might go out to watch the Washington star." Johnson pitched four innings of an intrasquad game the next day and it's likely that Mathewson and the other Giants, waiting to take the field after the Nationals, saw him in action.[26]

Looming in the background throughout the training period was Johnson's refusal to sign a contract. McAleer had offered, and Johnson immediately rejected, a salary of $6,000, the pitcher asking for $7,500 while insisting that under no circumstances would he accept less than $7,000. Eventually President Noyes was sent for, but he had no better luck in his meeting with Johnson. Particularly upsetting to Noyes was the pitcher's statement that if he had another season like the last one he would be looking for a long-term deal at $9,000 per year. Noyes waited several days for a call from Johnson before returning to Washington.

For a month management and player sniped at each other sporadically through the press. Johnson insinuated that promises made to him in the past had gone unfulfilled, while Noyes and McAleer charged that during the exhibition series with the Athletics Ty Cobb had urged Johnson to hold out for a contract similar to his deal with the Tigers, three years at $9,000 per year, tops in the American League. Trying to connect Johnson's demands with Fletcher's ill-fated third-league attempt, they claimed that Cobb was a lieutenant of Fletcher's and an agitator in both instances. Noyes also argued publicly that although Johnson was indeed as much of an attraction as Cobb when he started a game, the fact that Cobb started four times as often rendered any comparison of their values invalid.[27]

The standoff came to a head on April 6 when McAleer ordered Johnson to leave the training camp for refusing to sign a contract. McAleer insisted that outsiders had to be using Johnson, inducing him to take this stand, because he knew Johnson to be such a "sensible fellow and such a willing worker," he told the *Post.* "He's one of the finest fellows in the world in every way," said McAleer. "You couldn't have an argument with him on any question except this salary matter." Shocked and hurt by McAleer's action, Johnson requested to go to Washington for another meeting with Noyes, but was refused. After bidding a sad farewell to Milan and his other teammates, Johnson boarded a train for Coffeyville. In his *Washington Star* column Ed Grillo issued a warning to the Nationals:

> If it were any other player but Johnson, the chances are that he would crawl into the fold within a week or two, but anyone who knows Johnson knows that this is not in his makeup. Nor can he be charged with suffering from an exaggerated ego, for there is nothing in his demeanor, either on or off the field, to justify this belief. But he has peculiar ideas about money matters, and these he is not apt to change even though he does not earn a cent from baseball this season.

When he got to Coffeyville Johnson was upset and determined to hold out for the full $7,500. But after discussing the matter with his parents for most of an afternoon, they advised him to avoid staying out of the game for an entire season, to take the best offer he could get. A flurry of telegrams between Coffeyville and Washington ensued, a three-year deal at $7,000 per year was struck, and after one day in Kansas Johnson was off for the capital. For all of the Nationals' wailing and accusations of highway robbery, the three years Johnson was to give them under the contract made it the baseball bargain of the century.

Johnson's holdout cost him the opening-day assignment, and on April 12 it was Dolly Gray on the other end of President Taft's toss instead. But Johnson wasn't alone in not being entirely prepared for the game. Eighteen days earlier while the team trained in Atlanta, the Nationals' old wooden ballpark had burned to the ground except for a small section of bleachers. A new one, larger and in the modern mode of steel and concrete, was immediately put under construction and somehow made ready for the first game as scheduled, despite wooden forms still protecting much of the drying concrete and no second tier, roof, or box seats (except for the presidential box).[28]

Although losing his first two games in 1911, allowing 11 hits in each, Johnson finally managed to avoid the bad start plaguing his previous seasons. His debut was a 6–2 defeat by the Red Sox, the redeeming feature of which occurred in the fifth inning when he became the first American League pitcher to strike out four men in an inning. After Boston pitcher Ray Collins went down swinging, a third strike to Larry Gardner got away from Eddie Ainsmith and Gardner reached first base. Harry Hooper struck out, but Gardner stole second and scored on Speaker's double. Duffy Lewis then became the fourth victim. McAleer held Johnson back for nine days, a layoff that seems to have done more harm than good as he walked four batters and hit one, threw two wild pitches, and gave up four triples, two doubles, and 11 hits in a 5–3 loss to Jack Quinn in New York. "The high-priced Johnson was unruly and wild," quipped the *New York Times*.

Johnson's first victory came on April 28 in Philadelphia, 2–1, the Athletics' only run the result of the first ball ever hit over the fence against him. The feat was accomplished, appropriately, by Frank "Home Run" Baker. Always a tough out for Johnson, Baker would hit five homers off him in his career, second only to Babe Ruth's ten. On the Nationals' first swing through the West Johnson came down with the grippe in Chicago and was sidelined for two weeks. While the team played a series in St. Louis, Johnson, as he would do many times in the coming years, took the "Katy" train (Kansas, Arkansas, & Texas Railroad) to Coffeyville to visit his family, and in this instance to recuperate.

While he didn't get off to a bad start this year, it wasn't a particularly good one either. After a 13–8 pounding (the most runs he ever gave up in a game) by the Athletics on July 1, Johnson had a losing record, seven wins and eight losses, almost midway through the season. After a defeat at Cleveland on the 13th, Johnson was at .500 with nine wins and losses, having allowed 28 runs and 44 hits in his last four games. The most notable achievement in the first half was another freakish one, retiring the side on the minimum three pitches at New York on June 27, the first of four times that happened in his career.[29] But a 3–0 victory at Chicago on July 17 was a turning point, the first of 16 wins in 20 decisions, including ten in a row at one point, to the end of the year.

The American League paused on July 24 to pay tribute to Addie Joss, dead of tubercular meningitis in April at the age of 31, and an exhibition to benefit Joss's family was played in Cleveland between the Naps and an American

League All-Star team. The lineup for the All-Stars was Tris Speaker, Eddie Collins, Ty Cobb, Sam Crawford, Hal Chase, Bobby Wallace, Gabby Street, and Joe Wood. The Naps made up a virtual all-star team of their own, with Joe Jackson, Napoleon Lajoie, Terry Turner, and starting pitcher Cy Young, who had one more game in the American League (against Washington on July 29) before going to the Boston Braves briefly to end his magnificent career. The game raised $13,000, as a crowd of 15,000 saw the All-Stars win, 5–3. Clyde Milan replaced Speaker in center field midway through the game, and Walter Johnson blanked the Naps on one hit in three innings in relief of Wood.

On August 4 Johnson shut out the White Sox in 11 innings, 1–0, in the strangest contest by far of his long career. Famed Chicago sportswriter Hugh Fullerton called it "the greatest game of baseball ever played from the standpoint of unusual and sensational happenings. As much happened in that game as usually happens in a season, and two things that never happened in any other game." The first of those took place in the Nationals' fourth inning with Johnson at bat. It was one of those steaming late-summer Washington days, and although the players couldn't see it yet, a huge black thundercloud was rolling in toward the ballpark from beyond the outfield. Spectators in the upper deck and writers in the press box spotted it first and quickly scampered for cover, while at the plate Johnson clobbered a Doc White fastball, sending it toward center field destined to clear the fence easily. Center fielder Ping Bodie turned and raced back at the crack of the bat.

The ball was still rising when the storm hit full force. A wall of wind blew in suddenly, catching the ball as it was about to sail high over the fence—and stopped it dead. For a moment the ball fell straight down before the gale caught it and sent it hurtling back toward the infield as Bodie reversed himself and started racing in the opposite direction. With a tremendous effort he caught the ball barely off the ground. Gabby Street had gone all the way from first base to third in the meantime, and was easily doubled up. The amazed crowd stopped laughing and cheering only when a deluge of rain followed on the heels of the wind, sending everyone for shelter.

The storm passed quickly, and in ten minutes the sun was shining. A few small lakes had been created in the outfield, but the game was resumed and the crowd immediately treated to another freak play. Rollie Zeider of Chicago hit a high fly to short center. Nationals outfielder Tilly Walker came running in for the catch, but between Walker and the spot where the ball was coming down was the largest puddle, and instead of going through it he decided to go around. When he reached the other side, however, he saw the ball going farther than anticipated and with an acrobatic backward leap made a breathtaking catch before falling into the middle of the water with a tremendous splash.

"There may have been more desperate and brilliant baseball played than that which marked the next five innings," Fullerton wrote, "but in 40 years of watching the game I have never seen it. White and Johnson were pitching superbly, and the teams were straining every nerve and muscle to score. Brilliant fielding feats followed each other in steady succession. I never have seen players take more desperate chances." ("Five double plays, all of them on chances that would have decided the game if they had not been handled," the *Star* reported, "tells of the thrills that the crowd experienced.")

All of that was merely prelude to the most bizarre play of all, though, which took place in the bottom of the ninth inning of the scoreless struggle. Milan opened with a double. Nationals first baseman Germany Schaefer bunted back to White, who turned and threw to third hoping to trap Milan. With a wild, sprawling slide Milan avoided the tag and the Nationals had runners on the corners. Elberfeld popped out and Schaefer stole second, hoping to draw a throw so Milan could sneak home, but Chicago catcher Fred Payne wouldn't bite. Gessler struck out and Walker, who had been an easy out for White all day, stepped up to the plate. Schaefer danced off second trying unsuccessfully to tempt White or Payne into a pick-off attempt. Then he came up with one of the most imaginative and legendary plays in the history of the sport.

As White pitched, Schaefer "stole" from second base back to first. White, apparently rattled in the middle of his motion by the sight of the runner heading in a reverse direction, heaved the ball in to Payne but far away from Walker. Schaefer danced off first, hollering taunts to the White Sox, and Payne finally tossed the ball there, whereupon Schaefer took off for second. This was Milan's cue and he dashed for the plate, but the ball was hustled in to Payne in time to block the plate. Umpire Tommy Connolly called Milan out. But during the play White Sox manager Hugh Duffy had rushed out of the dugout to protest Schaefer's move to the other umpire, and now it was Washington's turn to complain about Duffy's presence in the middle of the field while Milan was being tagged out. But the play was allowed to stand and the game resumed under the Nationals' formal protest, which became moot when they pushed over a run after several more thrilling plays to win the game in the bottom of the 11th. Schaefer's gambit "was as amusing as baffling to the spectators," the *Star* reported. And although the White Sox had defensed the move perfectly, in 1920 a rule was instituted to prohibit running the bases in reverse order "for the purpose of confusing the fielders or making a travesty of the game." (It's hard to imagine any other reason for doing it.)[30]

Jimmy McAleer announced his resignation on September 15, making him the first Washington manager to leave of his own volition. Another year remained on a contract paying him $10,000 a year, but McAleer had endured enough of the club's inept administration and inadequate financial resources.[31] Ban Johnson arranged for McAleer and American League secretary Robert McElroy to purchase a half-interest in the Red Sox. The 1911 Nationals finished seventh again, with 64 wins and 90 losses, hardly a cause for much sadness over McAleer's departure.

Once again Walter Johnson had a fine season in spite of his team, winning 25 games and losing 13. He led the league in complete games (36) and shutouts (6), was second in earned run average (1.90) and third in wins, strikeouts (207), and innings pitched (322). The biggest improvement was in Johnson's hitting as he raised his average 60 points to .234. The team as a whole showed more life at the plate in 1911, paced by Germany Schaefer's .334 mark. Milan topped .300 for the first time, at .315, and led the American League with 616 at-bats. He also established himself as one of the top base thieves in the game with 58 steals, second only to Ty Cobb's 83.

Several weeks after leaving the Nationals, Jimmy McAleer was asked how Walter Johnson compared to other pitchers, past and present. "The greatest pitcher I ever saw," was his unequivocal answer. "I guess that I have seen all of them. I've batted against Rusie, Meekin, Breitenstein, Clarkson, and a lot of them who were considered the last word in pitching. I've managed the club that had Rube Waddell. I have watched Chesbro, Young, Joss, Mathewson, and Brown, but I've never seen the man I'd for a moment consider Walter Johnson's equal. Some year he will have his share of luck in health and support. When he does he will set a season's record they will all be shooting at for many a year."[32]

Johnson again helped the Athletics prepare for their upcoming World Series, this year against the New York Giants. The "All-Star" squad this year consisted mostly of Washington players along with Cobb, Hal Chase, and Larry Gardner, and the games were played in the capital. The $275 each player received from the Athletics was considerably less than the year before and the unhappy All-Stars made up some of the difference with a side game in Baltimore against the International League Orioles. Johnson then went to New York and saw his first World Series game, the October 14 opener in which Christy Mathewson bested Chief Bender in a stirring pitcher's duel.

The following day Johnson received $600 and Gabby Street $300 for an October 15 exhibition game in New York. When they arrived at Olympic Field in New York, Street, a Huntsville, Alabama, native, wasn't thrilled to discover that their opposition was the greatest black team of the time, the fabled Lincoln Giants.[33] Boasting four .400 hitters, the Giants had a 1911 record of 105 wins and 17 losses, mostly against white semipro teams. But the money—and perhaps some urging from Johnson—prevailed over Street's reservations (many white players refused to play against blacks at the time), and they made up the battery for the "All-Leaguers," an aggregation of major- and minor- leaguers that included the legendary Honus Wagner at shortstop.

It was the only time Johnson ever appeared in a game with Wagner, and what made it even more special was the presence in the Giants' lineup of John Henry "Pop" Lloyd, "the black Wagner" as he was called by some. Dick McClelland, the diminutive hero of the black World Series of 1903, was on the mound for the Giants. Despite having gone the route for the All-Stars against Baltimore two days earlier, Johnson notched 14 strikeouts in a 5–3 victory. Both Lloyd and Louis Santop, the Giants' slugging catcher, went 0 for 4 as Johnson gave up 6 hits and no walks.[34] "But for errors behind him, Johnson would have shut out [the Giants]," reported the *Washington Times*. "Johnson had perfect control and his speed was terrific." In addition, he smashed two doubles and scored three runs himself against McClelland.

Johnson attended the rest of the World Series except for the last game and arrived back in Coffeyville on October 27. That same day Clark Griffith's appointment as the Nationals' manager was announced, an event probably eliciting little more than shrugs from his new ballplayers. Griffith's record over the past few years was hardly more distinguished than McAleer's, and his sixth-place finish with the 1911 Cincinnati Reds not much of a recommendation. At the time, neither Walter Johnson nor anybody else—certainly not the poor Washington fans who had suffered through nine straight last or second-to-last-place finishes—could have imagined that Clark Griffith was to be their baseball Moses, come to lead them from the wilderness of the bottom of the American League.

CHAPTER 6

Griff

When I came in the old days and sunk my meager capital in the town, I was called a fool. But I have always had Walter Johnson to lean on.[1]

CLARK GRIFFITH

Clark Calvin Griffith was born in 1869 in Vernon County, Missouri, the same part of the state to which John Perry moved his family at about the same time, and close by the border with Kansas where Walter Johnson would be born 18 years later. The circumstances of Griffith's early life were even more primitive than those of the Johnsons and Perrys. In 1867, Isaiah and Sarah Griffith brought their four children from Illinois in a prairie schooner, one of a long wagon train. Staking out a 40-acre claim, they built a log cabin and tried to establish a farm, but it was mostly Isaiah's hunting and trapping that kept the family fed. And it was while doing this that the 33-year-old father of five was accidentally shot and killed by another hunter in 1872.

Pregnant with her fifth child at the time, Sarah Griffith carried on nonetheless with considerable help from neighbors at plowing and harvest time. But it was still mostly up to the family to provide for themselves in the wilderness country, so 10-year-old Earl Griffith went out with his father's heavy musket to bring in wild turkey and other game. At an even younger age Clark became an expert trapper, catching raccoons, possums, and "polecats" (skunks) to sell the skins at Nevada, Missouri, a 12-mile haul. But at the age of 11 Clark began suffering from persistent chills and fever. A small but sturdy child until then, he became frail and his health precarious, forcing him to bed for long periods of recuperation. After two years of infirmity Clark was finally diagnosed with malarial fever, the dreaded "ague" of the Missouri lowlands, and his mother was warned that unless her son was moved out of the area, he would probably die of the disease.

Sarah Griffith put her property up for sale and took her family to Bloomington, Illinois, where she had relatives. Soon 13-year-old Clark was restored to good health. He played baseball for the first time, and though judged too small for his high school team, developed a reputation as a good pitcher in sandlot games around Bloomington. He had the good fortune to come under the tutelage of the greatest big-league pitcher of the era, Charles "Old Hoss" Radbourne, who made his home there. By the age of 16 Griffith was earning money playing baseball, and in 1888 signed his first professional contract with Bloomington of the Interstate League (later the Three-Eye League). With Bloomington Griffith won 10 of 14 decisions and so impressed the Milwaukee Western Association club in an exhibition game that they bought his contract and signed him for $225 a month. Milwaukee's leadoff hitter was Jimmy McAleer.

After a 27–7 season with Milwaukee in 1890, Griffith jumped to the big leagues with the St. Louis Browns of the American Association at the behest of Browns manager and first baseman Charlie Comiskey. After going 14–6 for St. Louis, toward the end of the 1891 season he was traded to league champion Boston, where his teammates included Hugh Duffy, Dan Brouthers, and Mike "King" Kelly (all of whom would be inducted into the Hall of Fame in 1945, a year before Griffith himself). The American Association disbanded before the start of the 1892 season, however, and Griffith found himself back in the minor leagues, with Tacoma in the Northern Pacific League, which itself collapsed in August. Griffith was in the same position, ironically, as Walter Johnson would be 14 years later—stranded in Tacoma—and was rescued in the same manner, by a telegram from a small town in a nearby state. In Griffith's case the message was an offer to play for the wild mining town of Missoula in the semipro Montana State League.

In 1893 Griffith was the top pitcher in the California League, his 30–17 record boosting the Oakland team to the top when that league, too, folded in August, the third circuit in three years to crumple beneath him. (The early 1890s were the worst depression years until the 1930s.) Stranded and broke once again, Griffith drifted with his Oakland teammate and pal Joe Cantillon over to San Francisco and California's infamous Barbary Coast. They found work in a music hall honky-tonk, performing a skit several times a night in which Griffith, using native yells he had picked up in Missouri, played a marauding Indian gunned down by a cowboy, Cantillon. Griffith was rescued from this theatrical indignity by James Hart, his old manager at Milwaukee who was now president of the Chicago Colts of the National

League. Learning of the California League's demise, Hart wired for Griffith to come to Chicago.

With the Colts, owned by baseball pioneer Albert Spalding and managed by the legendary Cap Anson, Griffith came into his glory, winning more than 20 games six years in a row beginning in 1894. Not blessed with an overpowering fastball, the bantam (5-foot-6-inch) pitcher instead used his knowledge of batters' weaknesses and a bewildering array of other pitches, including the screwball, which he later claimed to have invented. Several of the other pitches in his arsenal were derived from various illegal methods of tampering with the ball. While still in his twenties, Griffith picked up the epithet "the Old Fox" for the ability to win games with his brain as much as his arm.

In September of 1900, Griffith, along with Ban Johnson, the president of the minor Western League, and Charles Comiskey, manager of its St. Paul team, conspired to elevate the circuit into a second major league—the American League. As one of the biggest stars in the National League and Vice-President of the Ballplayers Protective Association, to Griffith fell the task of providing players for the new league. After announcing his defection from the National League, he spent the winter traveling around the country convincing others to do the same. With his prestige and powers of persuasion, not to mention the higher salaries and other benefits promised, Griffith was tremendously successful. Of 40 National Leaguers "drafted" by teams in the new league, he failed to talk only one, Honus Wagner of the Pittsburgh Pirates, into making the jump.[2]

Griffith's reward was appointment as manager of Comiskey's Chicago White Sox, and he led them to the first American League pennant in 1901. It helped that his team had one of the top pitchers in the league—Clark Griffith—enjoying one of his finest years, with 24 wins and 7 losses. Those successes were not to be repeated, although he came close to pennants with the New York Highlanders (where Ban Johnson sent him in 1903 to compete with McGraw's Giants) in 1904 and 1906. In the last five years Griffith had brought his teams into the first division only once, a fourth-place finish with Cincinnati in 1909.

In the course of the 1911 World Series, Edward Walsh, a director of the Washington Nationals, approached Clark Griffith about becoming the club's manager. The cost of rebuilding its burned-out ballpark had forced the franchise to double its capital to $200,000, creating an opportunity for Griffith to buy stock in the club. Of the three men most responsible for the existence and success of the American League, only Griffith hadn't benefited to a commensurate degree. Ban Johnson paid himself an enormous salary as league president, and Charlie Comiskey was amassing a fortune with his White Sox;

now Jimmy McAleer was moving up to the ownership class with the Red Sox. It seems likely that Griffith would have taken the job in any case; the Reds had declined steadily during his three years in Cincinnati, making his situation there tenuous. And as one of the founding fathers of the American League, Griffith was never entirely comfortable in the rival National League. He was most receptive to the idea of buying into the Washington franchise, but where would the money come from?

There would be no support, financial or otherwise, from his former fellow conspirators. Ban Johnson had promised Griffith a $10,000 loan to help buy into a franchise, but turned him down flat now when asked for the money. Comiskey said he was crazy to invest in "that baseball graveyard" at Washington. But determined not to let the opportunity pass him by, with $7,000 in cash and a $20,000 mortgage on his 6,000-acre Montana cattle ranch, Griffith purchased a 10% share in the Nationals, becoming the team's largest single stockholder.[3] As he took over the pathetic Washington ballclub, it might have seemed merely the last hurrah of a once-great warrior. Instead, Clark Griffith was just beginning a 44-year chapter of his career that brought the city and its team greater glories than anyone could have imagined.

Griffith didn't waste any time putting his imprint on the Washington team. He tore into the Nationals roster, embarking on a youth movement that saw ten players departing for other venues. He caused a sensation with his very first move when Gabby Street was traded to New York. "Who'll catch Walter Johnson?" protested Tom Noyes. Eddie Ainsmith and John Henry were both good enough to catch Johnson, Griffith told him, "and if not, I'll catch him myself."[4] Ainsmith was in the Street mold: stocky and strong, an excellent defensive catcher, but eight years younger. He would be "Walter Johnson's catcher" for the next seven years. John Henry would be the Nationals' regular backstop, but when Johnson pitched, Ainsmith was behind the plate, even taking over for Henry when Johnson came in to relieve. "There really wasn't any other catcher who could hold me when I opened up with full speed," Johnson said.[5]

Washington sportswriter Vincent Flaherty described Eddie Ainsmith as "one of the nicest fellows in the game," but he was also one of the toughest.[6] An early proponent of strength conditioning, Ainsmith carried 180 pounds of solid muscle, and runners trying to get through him to the plate "fairly bounced off that fellow," Clark Griffith said.[7] Ainsmith had large, strong hands, and as a joke would occasionally reach up to grab one of Walter Johnson's high fastballs with his bare hand. He preferred light padding in his mitt, and would let Johnson's warm-up pitches smack into the middle of it like rifle shots, then rock back on his heels as if the pitches were almost knocking him

Top: Walter Johnson's birthplace and home for 14 years, near Humboldt, Kansas.

Above: Family and relatives at the Johnson place in Olinda, California, c. 1907. Minnie, Frank, and Chester Johnson behind fence second, third, and fourth from left. Blanche Johnson last girl in front on right; Effie Johnson Tongier and husband Russell last on right behind fence. The rest are Walter's aunts, uncles, and cousins. (George Key Ranch and Museum)

Above: Fullerton Union High School, 1905. Seventeen-year-old Walter Johnson is fifth from left behind wall.

WALTER JOHNSON "THE WEISER WONDER."

Top: The Weiser "Kids," 1907. Johnson in sweater. Clair Head, the Olinda teammate whose telegram brought Johnson to Idaho, is seated second from the left. On his left is Guy Meats, Johnson's catcher for five years in California and at Weiser.

Above: San Diego Pickwicks, November 1907. Johnson at left, Jack "Chief" Meyers third from left. (San Diego Historical Society)

Above: Santa Ana Yellow Sox, November 1908. Johnson at top left.

Above: Shortly after arriving in Washington, 1907.

Above: In Cleveland, on August 20, 1907, during his first road trip. (National Baseball Library)

Above: Portrait of a 19-year-old rookie, 1907.

Above: August, 1912. The arm band is for Nationals president Tom Noyes, who died several days earlier.

Above: "The finest motion in the game," Grantland Rice called Walter Johnson's distinctive sidearm delivery. (National Baseball Library)

Above: "He had such an easy motion, it looked like he was just playing catch," said Detroit outfielder Sam Crawford. "That's what threw you off. He threw so nice and easy—and then swoosh, and it was by you. Easily the greatest pitcher I ever saw." (National Baseball Library)

(National Baseball Library)

Top: With Clyde Milan, 1911. Coming to Washington within three weeks of each other in 1907, the two 19-year-old rookies became best friends. "The Gold Dust Twins," one writer called them as the only stars on otherwise lackluster teams. (Culver Pictures)

Above: With Clyde and Margaret Milan at Great Falls, Maryland, spring, 1914. Picture taken by Hazel Lee Roberts.

Top: Meeting Christy Mathewson for the first time. Atlanta, Georgia, March, 1911.

Left: With Mathewson in Joplin, Missouri, October 27, 1913. The next day in Tulsa, Oklahoma, they pitched against each other for the only time, a game won by Johnson, 6–0.

Above: With Joe Wood at new Fenway Park in Boston, September 6, 1912, before their famous "match" game. Red Sox outfielder Harry Hooper, who played in four World Series during his career, called it "the most exciting game I ever played in or saw."

Top: With The Old Fox, Clark Griffith, in 1912, their first year together.

Above: With Joe Engel, c. 1913. Throughout Engel's long career with Washington as pitcher, scout, and minor-league team owner, the two were the best of friends.(Bob Engel)

Above: American League All-Star team for the Addie Joss benefit game in Cleveland on July 24, 1911. They beat a Cleveland team with some all-stars of their own: Joe Jackson, Napoleon Lajoie, Terry Turner, and Cy Young, in the last year of his monumental career.

over. Fans loved these displays, but the intended audience was batters waiting nervously in the on-deck circle.[8]

"Eddie Ainsmith was a real sportsman," Walter Johnson recalled. "Many's the time I've seen him actually bleeding from spike cuts, but you couldn't persuade him to let anyone substitute for him. 'No,' he'd say, 'this doesn't amount to anything.' The trainer would say, 'Let me dress that wound, Eddie, let me bandage it up.' Ainsmith would reply, pushing him away good-humoredly, 'Say, what do you think I am? I'm not hurt. What's a little blood?' "[9]

The great Athletics second baseman, Eddie Collins, told how Ainsmith's rippling muscles almost worked against the Nationals on one occasion:

> One day in Washington, Bender coached first all afternoon. Ainsmith was catching, and it was infernally hot. About the fifth inning, Ainsmith hit a home run and when he returned to the bench he was so nearly melted that he went into the clubhouse and took off his long-sleeved flannel undershirt. A close observer like the "Chief" couldn't avoid looking at Ainsmith's muscular arms that had seldom been displayed before. Bender quickly noticed that on some signals the muscles were relaxed. He decided that when the muscles of the arm moved, Walter was to throw a curve and the rest of the time the fast one. After one inning, he knew he was right, so he began to tip us off and we had a little better luck. Ainsmith, noticing the change but not guessing why, decided to switch the signal just as [Jack] Barry went to bat. On the pitch, Bender gave Barry the tip and Jack stepped in to take a cut at the curve. The ball was not only fast but high, and it hit the side of the peak of Barry's cap and turned the cap halfway around. He got his base for being hit with a pitched ball. Jack's face was as white as milk, partly with anger, as he went to first. When he reached there he spoke a piece to Bender, which the Chief still recalls as a grim smile spreads over his face.[10]

Griffith assembled the 1912 Nationals in his own image: small, but smart and quick. There wasn't much hitting, and no power, but defense, baserunning, and pitching almost took them all the way. "My Little Ballclub," Griffith fondly called this team in later years.[11] Milan and McBride were already in place, but every other position was turned over. Eddie "Kid" Foster was bought from Rochester to play third base. A defensive whiz and solid hitter and base-stealer, Foster was also durable, playing every game in five different seasons and leading the league in at-bats four times. He also showed less power than any man in baseball history, his six career home runs the fewest of any player with more than 5,000 trips to the plate. (McBride is third with 7.)[12] But Foster, according to Griffith, controlled a bat better than even Willie "Hit 'em where they ain't" Keeler, a talent that reportedly led Griffith to invent the "run-and-hit" play, whereby a runner could go at will with the confidence that Foster would make contact.[13]

Coming with Foster from Rochester was outfielder Danny Moeller, a speedster who made up a base-stealing tandem with Milan to rival Ty Cobb and Donie Bush at Detroit. Howard Shanks, a versatile 21-year-old, would be a Washington regular for the next 11 years. Ray Morgan, 22, came to the Nationals late in 1911 and played a solid second base for seven years. The last piece of the puzzle moved into place with the arrival of first baseman Chick Gandil in June. The lineup of Henry (or Ainsmith), Gandil, Morgan, McBride, Foster, Moeller, Milan, and Shanks held together for the next four years, a remarkable record of consistency.[14] The pitching staff wouldn't undergo renovation for another year, with the veterans Johnson, Hughes, and Groom still the front line. But Dolly Gray, loser of 19 games in two of his three years with the Nationals, was allowed to move on. The most notable addition to the staff was Joe Engel, who was discovered in a saloon.

Clark Griffith sometimes quaffed a beer or two at Engel's Beer Garden on E Street in Washington, a favorite haunt of local notables including writers from the *Washington Post* next door. One day the proprietor brought his son over and introduced him to the new Nationals manager. "He's a ballplayer, my poy Choe," the elder Engel said in his heavy German accent. One look at the hulking 18-year-old, 6-feet-2-inches tall and nearly 200 pounds, and Griffith invited him to training camp. Joe Engel had already had something of a career with the Nationals, as it happened, having been a batboy during Cantillon's three-year reign. He had gone on to become a hard-throwing pitcher at Mount St. Mary's College, and the Nationals gave him four years in the major leagues to learn where the ball was going once it left his hand, with little success. Joe Engel was to carve a fascinating niche for himself in baseball history during his 50-year association with the Nationals, but not as a pitcher.[15]

Coming with Griffith to the Nationals was Mike Martin, 27, a physical trainer who had been with the manager at New York and Cincinnati as one of the first full-time trainers in baseball. Martin learned his craft at the famous New York Athletic Club and had also tutored under Mike Murphy, renowned trainer at the University of Pennsylvania. He had worked on Marcus Hurley, world-champion bicycle racer, and boxing champion Terry McGovern. Martin was the trainer at Columbia University when Griffith came to New York to manage the Highlanders. A baseball fan, he approached Griffith one day at the ballpark and told him that if any of his players had sore arms or bruises, he could cure them. Griffith gave Martin a trial and must have been pleased with the results, for the two were together for 48 years. In 1915 he began marketing

"Mike Martin's Liniment", an ointment that sold for many years with the endorsement of Walter Johnson and other big-league stars. "Mike's stump juice," the Washington players called it.[16] In spite of the rough-and-tumble atmosphere in which he did his work, Martin himself was a real gentleman: modest, quiet, and friendly. In addition to his professional admiration for Walter Johnson's wonderful physical attributes, the two became good friends.

Griffith breathed fire into his youthful aggregation, seeking to dispel the idea that Washington teams were destined for failure. At training camp he held a mandatory meeting each morning at nine o' clock, with a box of his favorite cigars the fine for those who showed up late. These assemblies often took on the flavor of pep rallies, and the tradition continued into the season. To close the meetings before ballgames Griffith would ask them, "What pitcher do we fear most?," and his boys would shout back, "There ain't none!"

To save money the Nationals went "south" only as far as the University of Virginia at Charlottesville in 1912. That seemed a mistake when it snowed almost constantly during their first two weeks of spring training there. But the spirit of camaraderie and loyalty Griffith wanted to instill in the team was actually fostered by their time together in the fraternity house where they were quartered when not out shoveling snow off the field. For a while he was more a cook and general factotum than manager.[17]

As the new man in charge, Griffith, the craftiest of pitchers in his day, was not averse to trying to change even Walter Johnson, despite his 25 wins in each of the last two seasons. "Although I'd been with Washington five years," Johnson recalled, "he didn't entirely approve of my style of pitching. 'You've got to learn some trick deliveries,' he would tell me during practice. And if any pitcher in baseball ever had a full bag of tricks it was Clark Griffith. They say as a pitcher he never had much 'stuff' but he was as smart as a whip and always kept the batter puzzled. 'Griff,' I used to say, 'there's only one way I can pitch—and that's in my own style.' Gradually he became discouraged and left me alone."[18]

Johnson pitched only briefly in the cold of Charlottesville, but as the weather warmed up and the team moved back to Washington, he appeared in several exhibitions against National League teams. In a rain-shortened game with the Phillies on March 29 he dueled for three innings against Grover Cleveland Alexander, who was coming off his phenomenal 28-win rookie year, for the first of several matchups in their careers. (Alexander would place second to Waddell on Johnson's list of the best pitchers he saw). On April 2 Johnson was scheduled to pitch against his third choice, Christy Mathewson, and the New York Giants, but Mathewson was scratched and Rube Marquard, who had put together *his* first great year in 1911, pitched instead. Johnson struck out six Giants in five innings. Years later John McGraw described how one of his players, Josh Devore, reacted to facing Johnson on this occasion:

> I shall never forget when we went to Washington to play an exhibition game with the Senators and Josh Devore, for the first time, saw the great Johnson. There had been much talk among the players as to whether Walter really had so much smoke or if it was just fan talk. Devore, a whimsical little fellow, walked up to the bat and set himself. Immediately Johnson whipped one by him so fast that he didn't even see the ball. He looked around sort of dazed, and as he did so Johnson whipped over another. By this time Devore was staring in wonder. Then Johnson popped one into the catcher's hands so quickly that Devore didn't get a chance to draw back his bat. "Say," he said, coming back to the bench, shaking his head. "You know, that's so, what them fellows've been saying about that guy. He's got it."[19]

Johnson bought his first automobile, a new Cole Eight, and the event brought him the nickname by which teammates and friends, and later the general public, would affectionately know him—"Barney." "I once owned an old-fashioned two-cylinder motor car," Johnson remembered. "The first day I took possession, Clyde Milan and Germany Schaefer were along. The salesman insisted on giving me complicated directions, but I just took hold of the wheel and stepped on the gas. We'd only gone two blocks when a motor cop picked us up for speeding. 'This is Barney Oldfield,' [famous race car driver of the day] said Schaefer to the officer. The officer, believing him, released us. In a game at Washington shortly thereafter, I had struck out nine batters using nothing but my fastball. As the 10th batter fell victim to the speed, Schaefer shouted, 'Barney Oldfield's got nothing on him for speed.' That's how my nickname started."[20]

Johnson opened the Nationals' season in Philadelphia on April 11. Jack Coombs and the World Champion Athletics beat him, 4–2, and it looked like he might be handicapped by a poor start yet again. But Jack Quinn was bested, 1–0, in New York on the 15th, beginning a five-game win streak that included three shutouts. Busy with details of the tragic loss of the luxury liner *Titanic* four days earlier, President Taft skipped Washington's home opener on the 19th. Taft's aide and close friend Archie Butt was among the 1,595 going down with the "unsinkable" ship, and Taft was in no mood for a ballgame.[21] Vice President Sherman threw out the first ball to Johnson, who continued his opening-day mastery of the World Champion Athletics, 6–0.

Ed Walsh and the White Sox stopped Johnson's streak on May 8 with a 7–6 pounding in which a Johnson fastball ended the career of Chicago third baseman Lee Tannehill. The 10-year veteran's arm was broken near the wrist and his throwing ability permanently impaired. Although Tannehill, 31 years old at the time, paid the most drastic price for being hit by a Johnson pitch, there are other examples of the cost to human flesh and bone of stopping one of his fastballs. Only two weeks later on May 25, New York shortstop Jack Martin sustained the most grievous injury from such an event when his jaw was shattered. It was the third time in the game Johnson had hit a batter and the second for Martin, who lost several teeth but was back in the lineup to face Johnson again five weeks later.[22] In 1910, Red Sox captain and third baseman Harry Lord's finger was jammed against the bat and broken by a pitch from Johnson. His substitute, Clyde Engle, played so well that Lord lost his starting position, became disgruntled and was traded to the White Sox.[23] And earlier that same year a real tragedy was narrowly avoided when Highlanders outfielder Birdie Cree turned away just in time to miss taking a pitch squarely in the temple. Cree was hit in the back of the head and "felled like a log," according to the *Washington Post.* He was unconscious for five minutes, but recovered to play the next day.[24]

One of the great ironies of Walter Johnson's career is his major-league record of 205 hit batsmen despite overwhelming anecdotal evidence that he was one of the few pitchers of his era who worried at all about batters' safety. "You can count on two fingers the guys who wouldn't throw at anybody in those days," Lefty Grove said. "Walter Johnson was one and Herb Pennock was the other."[25] Similar observations are legion among Johnson's contemporaries. "Walter was so damned careful," recalled Browns third baseman Jimmy Austin. "He was too good a guy, scared stiff he'd hit somebody."[26] The argument was sometimes carried a step further to imagine the effect if Johnson had adopted the prevailing attitude. Grantland Rice devoted a column to it in 1915:

> A bunch of ballplayers the other night were discussing the case of Walter Johnson as a pitcher. It was agreed that Johnson would be almost unhittable, beyond all range, if he ever adopted the tactics used by most successful slabmen—that is, the policy of shooting a stray shot at the batsman's onion once in a while. This system has kept many pitchers up in the winning ranks, as it has a decided tendency to drive the athlete back from the plate and work upon his nerves. But Johnson never uses it, and mainly for the reason that the batsman would have only an outside chance of ducking the shot as propelled by Walter's arm, and if the shot landed squarely Johnson would have the ghost of a dead man stalking his sleep.[27]

It was Johnson's nerves instead that were frequently shaken when one of his pitches crashed into a batter. After Jack Martin was carried from the field on a stretcher Johnson, who had a shutout going, "went bad immediately," the *Washington Post* reported. "The incident seemed to unnerve the Washington pitcher. Nobody could have shown more regret than the author of the injury."[28] Although becoming ineffective, Johnson did finish the game, losing by 6–3. There were other instances when Johnson was unable to continue at all after such an incident. As for why he hit so many batters over the course of his career despite possessing such great control, part of the answer lies in the sheer volume of his pitching; there are many pitchers whose frequency of hit batsmen is higher.[29] Other factors might include a shorter reaction time due to Johnson's speed; unpredictable movements of the ball caused by the other pitcher's tampering with it, not uncommon in those days; and batters trying to get on base against Johnson by any method.

Two days after Tannehill's injury Johnson came back on May 11 with a sparkling 8–0 win over Cleveland, striking out Joe Jackson twice among 11 victims. A 13-strikeout, 5–0 win at Boston on Memorial Day (his third complete game in six days) proved to be the turning point of the season for the Nationals, who the day before had lost both ends of a doubleheader in which Boston scored 33 runs. After dropping the first game of the holiday twin-bill on May 30, Washington had fallen into the second division with 17 wins and 21 losses. Despite Griffith's changes and his attempts to imbue the squad with confidence and a fighting attitude, the familiar curses of weak hitting and inconsistent pitching seemed to be settling over the Nationals again this year.

Already judged a flop by some, Griffith made one more, very expensive, move. For $12,000 and two players Griffith acquired Chick Gandil, a big 24-year-old first baseman from Montreal. Gandil had followed his stint with Santa Ana in 1910 with a disastrous half-season with the White Sox, where he hit .193. But this year he was tearing up the International League, and with first base the Nationals' weakest position Griffith went to Canada and brought Gandil back with him. The youngster was hustled into the lineup for the Decoration Day games and his slick fielding and solid hitting gave the club an immediate boost. It would be three weeks before they lost another game.[30]

The team's spirits might have gotten a lift also from the support given Johnson by the large holiday crowd at Boston's new Fenway Park, this despite the Red Sox standing a mere two games off the league lead. "No place in the circuit is Walter Johnson as big a favorite as in Boston," reported the *Star*. "After every one of his good innings yesterday the people in the stands arose and applauded him, and his praise could be heard on all sides." "Though he was beating the home club, local fans went wild over the great exhibition of pitching," said the *Post*. "He seemed to be able to strike out a batter any time that he needed to."

If he'd had the club behind him that I had behind me, he never would have lost a game. That's the unfortunate part of Walter's pitching—he had a bad club behind him all the time. Walter . . . my God . . . he was the only pitcher I ever hit against that I didn't know whether I swung under the ball or over the ball, I just missed it, that's all, and I don't know how.[31]

JOE WOOD

From Boston the Nationals swung out on the western part of their road trip, 15 games in St. Louis, Chicago, Detroit, and Cleveland—and won them all. From May 28 through June 12 Johnson rang up six straight victories and a save. Sensing an opportunity as the team gathered momentum, Griffith had radically changed the way Johnson was used. For the first two months of the season he had pitched only in a regular rotation as under McAleer, but now Griffith sent him in to relieve whenever a game was on the line. Johnson had made 19 relief appearances in his first five years with the Nationals, but for the last two-thirds of the 1912 season alone Griffith inserted him 13 times. In 51 relief innings Johnson allowed just two earned runs, and for the next dozen years Johnson's schedule would always be subject to change depending on circumstances. Somehow Griffith, the shrewd former pitcher, and Johnson, at the peak of his physical powers, made this "system" work. After the first relief job of the year, a four-inning stint to beat Chicago on June 6, Ed Grillo described how Johnson's mere availability became a weapon in Griffith's arsenal:

Having Walter Johnson ready to relieve one of the other pitchers is of great help to the team. The moral effect of sending Johnson out to warm up when one of the other pitchers happens to be going poorly cannot be estimated. It has a smothering effect on the opposing batsmen when they realize that another base hit means the coming in of Johnson, and they usually give up under such conditions.[32]

Johnson never liked relief pitching—a "disagreeable experience for any pitcher," he called it, "to sit on the bench not really expecting to work, and then to have to hustle out to the bullpen for a few minutes of practice and then rush into the game perhaps half warmed up and in no shape to do your best. Usually there are men on base and the score is so close you can't safely allow these men to advance. In most cases it is as hard to go in and relieve another pitcher for two or three innings as it is to work through the whole game. Sometimes it's very much harder. In my own case I well know which I prefer."[33] But rather than complain, or refuse, "Johnson was always willing to step in," Nick Altrock recalled years later, "and never squawked because he felt he was carrying too heavy a burden."[34]

After 16 straight road wins (the league record until 1984), the Nationals returned to Washington on June 17 in second place behind the Red Sox, who were running away with the pennant race. They were given a heroes' welcome by thousands of fans at Union Station, who then caused bedlam on Pennsylvania Avenue by escorting the team to the ballpark. The next day the town took an impromptu holiday as 15,516 fans jammed American League Park to see the Nationals win their 17th in a row, a 5–4 thriller over the Athletics. President Taft threw out a belated "opening-day" ball and Vice President Sherman threw his hat into the air when the winning run scored. Also in attendance were Speaker of the House Champ Clark and "members of the United States Supreme Court, senators, representatives, government officials . . . and many beautifully gowned society women," according to the *Washington Post.*

Witnessing the affair in civilian clothes, despite suffering from a bad cold and tonsillitis that kept him out of action for two weeks during this time, was Walter Johnson. Midway through the Nationals' streak, Ed Grillo gave Johnson much of the credit for the surge, and not for his pitching feats alone. "There never has been a ball club which works together better than the Nationals," he wrote. "The best of feeling exists, and there are no swelled heads in the party. To a large extent Walter Johnson is responsible for this encouraging condition for, though an acknowledged star, Johnson is modesty personified and he thereby sets a good example for his teammates, especially the youngsters."[35]

On the field it was Griffith's fighting spirit they took for a model. "One thing about Griff as a manager—the Washington ballplayer was always right," Johnson recalled. "No matter what the argument, he stood behind his players. In a row with the umpire, Griff was the first man in a Washington uniform to come to his player's support."[36] Clyde Milan in particular was playing as though possessed, batting .350 and running wild on the basepaths. In the Nationals' 14th straight win in Cleveland on June 14 Milan stole five bases, including home, in a span of three innings.

The bubble burst with a loud bang when the A's, taking revenge for their loss in front of the president, swept back-to-back doubleheaders on June 19 and 20. Home Run Baker personally demolished the Nationals, going 9 for 15 and driving in the winning runs in three of the games. Washington's momentum was stopped cold by the multiple defeats. Ten days later, after another string of losses to Philadelphia, the Nationals had been shoved back down to fourth place. Baker was again the tormentor in Johnson's tough 2–1 loss on the 29th. But instead of folding up, Griffith's club embarked on another winning tear, a ten-game run this time. As for Johnson, it would be two months before he lost again.

Johnson's previous winning streaks in 1912 had lasted five and six games each. This one went a league record 16, starting with a 10–2 victory over the Highlanders on July 3. Johnson was lifted after six innings when the Nationals ran up a big lead, then after a day's rest came back against them with the longest and best relief effort of his career. He took over for Joe Engel in the fourth inning with one out and two on before a rare McBride misplay let the runners score, tying the game at 5–5. Not until the bottom of the 16th did the Nationals push over a run to take the game, during which Johnson had gone 12⅔ innings without allowing a run of his own, parcelling out a scant three hits to the New Yorkers along the way. The victory returned Washington to second place.

Nick Altrock joined the team in mid-July, and it was nearly fifty years before he left. Altrock had been released by Kansas City of the American Association, the last stop of a pitching career that began in the major leagues in 1898 at Louisville, where his teammates included Honus Wagner, Rube Waddell, and Fred Clarke. Altrock won 19, 23, and 20 games for the White Sox of 1904–06, the last of those teams famous as the "Hitless Wonders." His strengths on the mound were cunning and control, and he was one of the best fielding pitchers of all time, still holding a handful of major league records. Altrock's deadly pickoff move brought him one of the oddest records when he won a game in 1906 without throwing a pitch. Coming in with two out in the top of the ninth inning, his first throw was a successful pickoff for the third out. The White Sox then scored two runs in the bottom half for the victory. But Altrock's playing career was just a preamble to his record 46 years as a coach at Washington. He holds the distinction of wearing a major-league uniform for more years, 55 (officially), than anyone else, and on October 1, 1933, he became the oldest player in a game when he pinch-hit at the age of 57.

It wasn't as pitcher or coach that Nick Altrock achieved his greatest fame and reputation, however, nor was it for those abilities that Clark Griffith summoned him from Kansas City. Altrock was a talented comedian, and what Griffith, always a shrewd promoter ("The heart of a showman," Fred Lieb said), had in mind was teaming him with Germany Schaefer, the pioneer of the art of baseball clowning.[37] Schaefer was a jovial comic who for years, first with Detroit and then Washington, delighted fans with his spontaneous antics. Legend has it that Schaefer got a reluctant umpire to call a game being played in pouring rain by trotting out to his second-base position wearing rubber boots and carrying an umbrella.[38] With both of them endowed with large, clownlike faces and a mutual penchant for mischief, Altrock and Schaefer were a natural pairing. Altrock's specialties were pantomime and juggling, at which he was expert. A crowd favorite, but not so funny to the umpires, was Altrock's exact mimicry from his coaching box of their every move, from swatting away a fly to calling runners out.

It wasn't for their comedic talents alone that Griffith wanted these two. The Old Fox made it a tradition to have baseball clowns on his teams, but he didn't suffer fools lightly. Stanley Milliken of the *Post* outlined their wider role: "Many of the fans who see this pair at home and abroad have the idea that Griffith carries them simply because of their funny antics on the field. It is true that they are baseball's greatest comedians, and that they aid in swelling the attendance at games. But do you know that they are Nationals today for another reason? Altrock and Schaefer are wonderful exponents of the national game, and many a tip has been handed manager Griffith during a close contest by one of these veterans. A better pair of coaches with men on the bases cannot be found. They are keen judges of ballplayers. Altrock is a great tutor for the young pitcher, and is practically in charge of the young slabbists in camp. Altrock was a wonderful pitcher in his day and knows all the tricks of the trade."[39]

On July 22 Johnson struck out the first five batters to face him in a game with Detroit. Davy Jones, Donie Bush, Ty Cobb, Sam Crawford, and Charlie Deal went down before George Moriarty doubled to break the string, after which Baldy Louden became Johnson's sixth strikeout in the first two innings. On August 16, after picking up a relief win over Ed Walsh and the White Sox the day before, Johnson faced only 29 batters for the second time in 1912 in a 4–0 one-hitter over Chicago. After a third-inning single, the last 19 batters went out in a row, with just two balls making it to the outfield during the game. An 8⅔-inning relief victory over Cleveland on August 20 was Johnson's 15th in a row, breaking Jack Chesbro's record.

The Nationals' sudden success had turned the attention of the baseball world in their direction, and Johnson's record winning streak thrust him into full national prominence for the first time.[40] The August 1912 issue of *Baseball Magazine* featured his autobiographical piece, "My Life So Far," followed in September by editor F.C. Lane's lengthy profile, "The Greatest Pitcher On The Diamond Today." Ed Grillo, a Johnson champion from the beginning, described the combination of skill and winning personality that made him a star of the first rank:

Speaking of popularity on the field, it is doubtful if there is a player in either league so universally admired as Walter Johnson. When his name is announced as the Washington pitcher the crowds [on the road] always applaud, and when he gives an exhibition of his marvelous skill by striking out some noted batter in a pinch, applause always greets him. The umpires have done much to acquaint the public with the splendid disposition of Johnson. The fact that he never questions a decision on balls and strikes forces the umpire to boost him and they never overlook an opportunity to break into print with praise for the Washington pitcher.[41]

On August 23, 51 days into his streak, Johnson beat the Tigers for his 16th straight victory. He now had 29 wins against 7 losses. But against St. Louis on the 26th both the consecutive-win streak and a run of 15 in a row over the Browns came to a halt. Griffith sent Johnson in to relieve Tom Hughes with runners on first and second and one out in the seventh inning of a 2–2 tie. The first batter struck out, but the runners moved up on a wild pitch before St. Louis right fielder Pete Compton grounded a single through the infield, scoring both. A Nationals rally fell short and the game was lost, 4–3. Ban Johnson, who as league president decided such matters, ruled that Johnson, not Hughes, be charged with the defeat for giving up the hit that brought in the winning runs.

Cries of protest erupted from Washington fans, press, and players, all disappointed to see Johnson denied the chance at Rube Marquard's major-league record of 19 straight, set earlier in the year. Ed Grillo wrote to National League President John Heydler, printing the reply that in Heydler's league Hughes would have taken the loss for putting the runners on. After the season, the American League changed its rule to conform with the National's, but the irascible Ban Johnson denied that this had anything to do with the Walter Johnson case, but was done merely to simplify the compilation of his league's new earned-run-average statistic.[42] For the man who suffered most from the decision, there was no controversy at all. "I lost the game," Walter Johnson declared. "It would be unfair to charge Tom Hughes with the defeat, just to keep my record clean. He didn't make that wild pitch or allow the single that scored the two runs. I lost the game, so what's the use worrying and fussing over it."[43]

The furor abated when Johnson lost his next game, 3–2, to St. Louis on the 28th, despite striking out a dozen Browns. But no sooner had his record gone into the books than a threat to it appeared on the horizon. Red Sox pitcher Smoky Joe Wood, in his one fabulous year in a career cut short by injury, was almost unbeatable in 1912. He had put together a string of 13 straight wins, and as the Nationals were about to go to Boston for the first leg of a month-long road trip to end the season, Clark Griffith—ever the opportunist—turned an ordinary ballgame into a storied and profitable affair. First he implied through the press that Wood was being given easy assignments by Red Sox manager Jake Stahl to keep his streak alive. Then as the Nationals-Red Sox series began, Griffith announced he was holding Walter Johnson back until Joe Wood pitched so Wood would have to earn the record against Johnson himself. "Tell Wood that we will consider him a coward if he doesn't pitch against Johnson," Griffith challenged. Stahl announced that Wood was being moved up a day to accommodate Johnson's scheduled start of Friday, September 6. "We intend to defeat the Senators with Johnson pitching for them," Stahl said.[44] The stage was set for a "challenge match" between the two greatest pitchers in baseball: Johnson, with his 29–9 record and 16 wins in a row, versus Wood, 29–4 with 13 straight and counting.

"The newspapers publicized us like prizefighters," Joe Wood remembered, "comparing our height, weight, biceps, triceps, arm span, and whatnot. Fenway Park must have contained twice as many people as its seating capacity that day. I never saw so many people in one place in my life. In fact, the fans were put on the field an hour before the game started, and it was so crowded down there I hardly had room to warm up. The fans were sitting practically along the first-base and third-base lines. We were sitting on chairs right up against the foul lines, and the fans were right behind us."[45]

Surprisingly, the game itself—and the pitching—lived up to the advance billing. "That was probably the most exciting game I ever played in or saw," Boston right fielder Harry Hooper, who was in four World Series during his 17-year Hall-of-Fame career, said of it later.[46] The final score was, appropriately, 1–0, the Red Sox prevailing as Stahl predicted. The Great Pitching Duel came out about even, with Wood giving up more hits, six to five, and walks, three to one, but ringing up nine strikeouts to Johnson's five. Wood actually had a harder time of it, pitching out of trouble in the third (striking out Moeller with the bases loaded), sixth, eighth, and ninth innings. Johnson breezed along most of the way, in contrast, until done in by back-to-back doubles from Tris Speaker and Duffy Lewis in the sixth. Speaker's was an opposite-field, ground-rule number into the roped-off crowd in left field that would have been an easy out any other day and Lewis shanked a pop fly into right field that trickled off Danny Moeller's glove after his long sprint to the foul line.[47] Despite the defeat, Griffith picked up a substantial visitors check from the sold-out contest and handed the losing pitcher a $500 bonus for his effort.[48] Johnson's American League consecutive-win mark of 16 stands to this day, although in one of those quirks of the record book it has been tied three times since—beginning with Joe Wood in 1912.

Another close loss at Cleveland on September 11 was Johnson's fifth in a row, part of a Washington slump that allowed the Athletics to move ahead of them for the first time in more than two months. But for the third time that year the Nationals defied expectations of a collapse, rallying once again to move back in behind the Red Sox. The last week of the season began in

Philadelphia with a three-game series likely to decide the battle for second place. When the first game, scheduled for September 25, was rained out, the last two became even more crucial. On the 26th Johnson relieved Tom Hughes in the seventh inning with one out and two on and Washington ahead, 3–1, but the lead evaporated quickly when an error and wild pitch allowed the runners to score and tie the game. With Ainsmith out with a broken finger, third-stringer Rip Williams was catching—or at least trying to. The day was overcast, and the "wild pitch" was simply a high fastball that Williams hadn't seen in time as it went on a line, untouched, to the grandstand. "Williams had a tough time with Johnson," reported the *Post.* "Johnson was extremely fast, but he was also wild. All through the last three innings the light was bad, and it was hard to see the ball. Any man who went to the plate took a chance on being killed. McInnis plainly was frightened, and took a wild swing at a ball a foot over his head as a third strike." Umpire Billy Evans hadn't said anything after the first wild pitch, but in the bottom of the ninth another one glanced off Williams's mitt and whizzed by the umpire's ear. "Did you see it?" he asked Williams, who answered in the negative. "Neither did I," said Evans, "game called."[49] There was plenty of daylight left, the *Post* noted, but "The game was called by umpire Evans out of mercy for the Athletics and with some consideration for himself and his family."

The next day's game was also tied after nine innings, 4–4, when Johnson took over for Bob Groom. The Nationals finally pushed over a run in the 19th inning, and Johnson finished off the A's in the bottom half to complete 10 innings of scoreless relief. "I believe he was never better in his life than he was that evening," Eddie Collins recalled later. "We didn't have a good look at the ball during the last five innings. We would see that easy swing and then chug, in the catcher's mitt and we were out."[50] It was around that time, in fact, that the expression "You can't hit what you can't see" began to be commonly used in reference to Johnson.[51]

Johnson's 4–3 win at New York in the last game of the season on October 3 clinched second place for the Nationals, 14 games behind the Red Sox and a game ahead of Philadelphia. The magnitude of their accomplishment in beating out the two-time world champion Athletics would become even clearer when the A's regained the American League flag in 1913 (winning another World Series) and 1914. Without Smoky Joe Wood's phenomenal 34–5 season there would have been a three-way struggle for the pennant with Washington in the thick of it. Sadly, Tom Noyes, who had suffered through eight years of the team's misery, wasn't around to enjoy the success. After a short illness he had died suddenly of pneumonia on August 21 at the age of 44. Noyes's prominence in the capital was demonstrated by the presence of President

Taft among the hundreds attending the funeral. Clark Griffith, who had received great support from Noyes in rebuilding the ballclub, was among the legion mourning his passing. With new Nationals president Benjamin Minor, Griffith would struggle for everything.

Walter Johnson's 33–12 record didn't have the glitter of Joe Wood's, but there was little to choose between them in 1912. Johnson's earned run average (1.39) and strikeouts (303) were better, while Wood led in shutouts (10) and complete games (35). Johnson's .264 batting average and .403 slugging average signaled an end to his days as a liability at the plate. Included in his hits were a pair of home runs, four triples, and six doubles. He would be called on to pinch-hit 110 times in his career. Johnson finished third (and Clyde Milan fourth) behind Tris Speaker and Ed Walsh in the voting for the Chalmers Award as the league's most valuable player. In Billy Evans's poll of umpires for his All-American League team, Johnson, not Wood or Walsh, was the choice for pitcher,[52] as he was also for Grantland Rice's All-Major League team.

Johnson wasn't the only major star on the team now, however. He had to share some of the spotlight with his roommate and best friend, Clyde Milan, who had broken Ty Cobb's major-league record for stolen bases on September 22 and finished the season with 88 thefts, 25 more than runner-up Eddie Collins. Possibly the fastest man in the league (Chief Bender dubbed him "Deerfoot"), Milan had reached his full potential under Griffith's aggressive style of attack, which had also brought out the best in Bob Bescher, the National League stolen-base champion in each of their three years together at Cincinnati. But it wasn't only on the basepaths that Milan stood out, for he had also moved into the elite class, alongside Ty Cobb and Tris Speaker, as an outfielder.[53] Jimmy McAleer, perhaps the greatest center fielder of the 1890s, had made Milan his pet project, teaching him how to play even shallower than Speaker, who routinely snuck in behind second base to take pickoff throws.[54] And Milan was durable, appearing in a record 511 straight games in the outfield from 1910–13. His .306 average led the Nationals in 1912. All of which made Milan the ideal ballplayer, in Griffith's estimation: "[Milan] is one of the most valuable men in baseball. He is quiet, popular, loyal and always attends to business. No manager has had any trouble with him and he is a player that any manager would be glad to get."[55]

On October 6 Johnson went from New York to Bridgeport, Connecticut, and the Remington Arms Company's bullet-testing range, for an attempt to gauge the velocity of his pitches. The frequent discussions about Johnson's speed prompted *Baseball Magazine* editor F.C. Lane to put it to a scientific test, after first clearing the idea with Griffith. Also to be clocked was

Brooklyn's Nap Rucker, said to be the fastest pitcher in the National League. The rudimentary testing apparatus consisted of a tunnel of fine wires ending at a steel plate. A projectile tripped the wires as it passed through, registering the time, which was then compared to the time of arrival at the steel plate to gauge the speed.

After a few warm-up tosses against the steel plate, and still in street clothes, Johnson stepped in, but the tunnel was at shoulder height to measure bullets fired from a standing position and at first Johnson couldn't get his sidearm throws to go straight through to the plate. "At length, however," it was reported, "after some effort and with a consequent loss of speed in an attempt to place the ball accurately, the sphere was successfully hurled in the proper direction, broke one of the fine wires in its transit and collided with a heavy thud against the steel plate." Johnson's best throw was clocked at 122 feet per second (82 m.p.h.), Rucker's at 113, both on their third and last tries.[56] Despite the flawed procedure, it does allow for some comparison. In June, 1933, Van Lingle Mungo of the Dodgers and Lefty Gomez of the Yankees, two of the fastest pitchers of their era, were tested at West Point's department of ballistics and mathematics, presumably with more sophisticated equipment. Mungo registered 113 feet per second and Gomez 111 on their best throws.[57]

Rucker was most impressed with his first look at Walter Johnson. According to F.C. Lane, "During the proceedings Napoleon Rucker was perhaps the most interested of the spectators. He watched the tremendous speed of Johnson with unalloyed admiration. The Brooklyn star had never seen the Idaho Wonder pitch before and the episode was a revelation. 'I never saw anything like it,' he said to me as we stood on the side of the shed dodging the ball as it rebounded from the steel plate and shot past us. 'I didn't think there was a man in the world who had so much speed. I have heard a good deal about Johnson's speed, but now I know. There isn't a man in the world who can touch him. He is in a class by himself.'"[58]

Johnson returned to New York to cover the 1912 Giants-Red Sox World Series for the *Boston Herald,* which was paying him $300 to "write" articles after each game that were then syndicated under his picture and byline to a dozen newspapers around the country.[59] Like other stars such as Young, Mathewson, Wood, Speaker, Cobb, and McGraw, being paid to cover the Series, Johnson had a "ghostwriter" (in his case a Boston newspaperman) to do the actual reporting and writing. (One day a Washington reporter encountered Johnson buying a paper. As he opened it, the pitcher said sheepishly, "Let me see if I have been quoted correctly.")[60] Although decrying the ghostwriting practice, the *Washington Post* noted: "In fairness to Johnson, it must be said that he at least read the stuff before it was put on the wires, and often made alterations when statements were too strong."[61] His articles were carried in the capital by the *Washington Times,* but Johnson's credibility was given a boost when the *Post* trumpeted his statement from the press box before the start of the first game that conditions were ideal for Joe Wood and the Giants would be unable to hit him to any extent. "Johnson Predicted That Wood Would Win Game," headlined the *Post* after Wood's thrilling victory.

Johnson's job gave him a front-row seat at the greatest Series yet played, one not topped for drama and excitement for another dozen years. The Giants and their hero, Christy Mathewson, went down in extra innings in the last game, and Joe Wood capped his amazing year with three World Series wins. Although his candle was to burn out before too long, no pitcher's ever burned brighter than Wood's in 1912. "I have seen Joe Wood pitch some days when I thought that he was faster than I," Walter Johnson said at the time, "and I believe that for two or three innings he has as much swiftness. But he could not hold it during the game. He has a jerky motion, and it is this motion that weakens him."[62]

When the Series was over Johnson went to Woonsocket, Rhode Island, to pick up a quick $250 for pitching neighboring Whitinsville, Massachusetts, to victory in the last game of a series "for which both teams have loaded up," and "on which all kinds of money has been bet," according to the *Post.*[63] Throughout his career Johnson routinely earned an extra $1,000 or more in exhibition games at the end of the season.[64] Most years he would pitch a game or two in the Northeast before returning to Coffeyville for a handful of games in the four-state area of Kansas, Missouri, Arkansas, and Oklahoma. The rare chance to see Walter Johnson and other big-league players made these contests big events, often reminiscent of the overheated "town ball" contests of Johnson's youth. Some of the most exciting and interesting games he ever pitched took place under these circumstances.

In 1912, Johnson began a tradition of pitching a charity game each year for both Coffeyville and Humboldt. The towns virtually closed down for "Walter Johnson Day" celebrations, with several thousand people coming from many miles around. Another major-leaguer usually pitched against him, with major- and minor-leaguers from the area playing alongside local semipros. The first of these contests drew 3,000 people to Forest Park in Coffeyville on October 27, and Johnson gave them what they had come to see, striking out 13 of 16 batters faced in the five innings he worked.

"Not once did Johnson exert himself," the *Coffeyville Journal* reported. "He merely cranked up and tossed his arm in the general direction of the plate. There was a streak and a 'wop' as the ball collided with the catcher's glove, while the batter grinned sheepishly and shook his head. 'Did you see that ball jump?' or 'I never saw one of those three strikes,' were typical comments." Johnson was relieved by Larry Cheney, winner of 26 games for the Chicago Cubs that year, and playing center field for Coffeyville was Kansas City native Charles "Dutch" Stengel (later known as "Casey"). The other big news in Coffeyville was the arrival of Johnson's new touring car, which had been shipped from Washington by train. "Neighbor Kids Ride in Johnson's New Machine," the *Journal* headlined. "He drove it to the farm and showed Mrs. Johnson and the children how it worked on a trial spin. Walter picked up all the neighborhood boys he passed and promised them more rides later."[65]

On November 7 he went up to Humboldt for the first "Walter Johnson Day" there. Again he gave the fans what they wanted, sending the first nine Iola batters back on strikes. Johnson's catcher, as he would be each year in the Humboldt game, was none other than childhood pal Dave Woods. "I was scared to death to catch him when he returned for his first game after becoming so famous," Woods recalled.[66] Like so many of Johnson's catchers, however, Woods discovered to his great relief that "Walter had a blazing fastball, but he was easy to catch. He had such marvelous control. I'd just make a target for him with my glove and he'd hit it every time."[67]

I will always remember a little incident in a game between Philadelphia and Washington several years ago, when both clubs had a chance for the pennant. Washington had been the sensation of the American League that year. The game was played at Washington. Late in the game, with two out, a runner on third, and the score tied, a Philadelphia player hit a soft grounder to Chick Gandil, playing first base for Washington, making it necessary for Johnson to cover the bag. Gandil and Johnson both made beautiful plays on the ball and would have registered an out had not Johnson overstrided a bit and missed first base by a few inches. It was evident Johnson had beaten the runner to the base, and there was a loud wail from the Washington players when I ruled the runner safe and the winning run crossed the plate. It was an embarrassing situation for me. My decision was correct, yet it looked like a poor one. Some stars would have been content to use me as an alibi, but not Johnson. Almost before the players had gotten underway with their protest, Johnson broke up the squabble by remarking, "Ride me, not Evans. I didn't touch the base".[68]

BILLY EVANS

CHAPTER 7

Hazel

Tell you about Walter? I can tell you this. If I were manager of a team that had one game to play—the one most important game in all the world to play—and if the good Lord called down and said, 'Milan, you choose your own pitcher for this. Just tell us what you want and we'll make up a pitcher to fit your specifications. He can have Matty's curve, or Rusie's speed, or Griffith's shrewdness, and anything else you want. Well, if that happened, I'd say, "Never mind the specifications. Don't make me up anything fancy. Just send me Walter Johnson when he was about 26 years old, and you don't have to add even one little item. He'll do for me, thank you kindly." I'm saying that, son, after hitting against all the good pitchers that ever put on a spiked shoe. I was up there against them all a good many times, and I got along pretty good. And not a day went by that I didn't thank the Lord that I didn't have to bat against Walter except in practice.[1]

CLYDE MILAN

Spring training, 1913, went smoothly for the Washington Nationals and for Walter Johnson, a good omen for both. There were no disruptions, no illness or injury, no salary disputes. Even the weather cooperated, with balmy mid-March temperatures bringing a premature end to winter. Months of work on the farm had Johnson in top shape. "I feel as strong as an ox," he said upon reporting to camp.[2] Griffith used him sparingly in exhibition games, just enough to be primed for the start of the season, and his most notable appearance was not on the mound but pinch-hitting against Christy Mathewson in Washington on April 7. The situation called for a sacrifice bunt, which Johnson executed perfectly, so his chance to swing away against the great Matty would have to wait.

A bond developed between Walter Johnson and Clark Griffith over the years that was part father-son relationship, part mutual professional admiration, and the rest genuine friendship. An 18-year age gap and their different roles on the team prevented a closeness of the kind Johnson shared with Milan, but the respect and affection each had for the other was nonetheless profound. Griffith had known Johnson since his entry into the league in 1907, but it was an incident at the Charlottesville camp in 1913, he remembered, "when Walter showed the real stuff he was made of":

He and Germany Schaefer wanted to go fox-hunting, but I put my foot down and said no. He was our biggest asset, and if he fell off a horse and hurt himself we would have been in a terrible fix. But the folks down that way put a lot of pressure on him and he wanted to go badly, so he and Schaefer slipped off and went. I was waiting for them at the fraternity house when they came in that night. "I'll see you boys in the morning," I told them. We had a sort of a court where the rest of the players tried those who broke training rules, so we called a meeting the next morning, and while Johnson and Schaefer waited outside I explained the circumstances to the rest of the team. Now don't forget, Johnson was the biggest star in baseball at the time and could have told us where to get off if he didn't like it. But we went through the motions of a trial and the jury decided the two of them would have to shag flies all day—just the two of them, mind you. And we had two sessions lasting about two hours.

Well, Zeb Milan was knocking the ball to them and he'd hit one over third base and the next one over first. He ran 'em ragged, and when lunchtime came their tongues were hanging out. They were so tired they just called us to bring them something to eat. We brought 'em a sandwich and a glass of milk apiece and after lunch we started the same thing all over again. Johnson took it like a major. He never uttered a word of complaint, but that was the way he took everything. Some other players might have balked, especially one as big as Walter, but not he.[3]

The new president of the United States, Woodrow Wilson, did the honors on Opening Day, April 10, 1913. As the second president to grace the inaugural, Wilson made the practice more or less "official" and Griffith, the great promoter, did everything in his power to make it a firm tradition in the years to come. Eventually he persuaded the baseball powers to schedule the first game in Washington each year to highlight the president's anointing of the "national game."[4] Accompanying Wilson were his daughter, Eleanor, and Vice President Thomas Marshall, along with the usual assemblage of official Washington among the 16,000 spectators. "Every neck was craned to glimpse the 'First American' as he rose to toss the ball to Walter Johnson, by every true Washingtonian thought to be the 'First Pitcher'," reported the *Post*. "Johnson had already received several ovations, but as he caught the ball from the President's hand, men and women arose that they might make more vociferous their tribute to the hero of the diamond." Griffith later took the ball over to the presidential box to get it autographed, "which request was granted with a smile," according to the *Star*. It was the second such prize for Johnson's collection. Wilson, like Taft a true baseball fan, stayed for the entire game but was criticized for ignoring the seventh-inning stretch. "While the throngs around him stood shouting encouragement to their team," the *Post* noted, "he sat smiling at the demonstration."

In 1913 Walter Johnson limited his usual bad start to one inning. He allowed the New York Yankees [as they were called now] a run in the top of the first, then shut them down the rest of the way for a 2–1 victory. More than a month passed, through eight games and 56 straight innings, before he was scored on again, and it was almost six weeks before he took his first defeat. It wasn't just Johnson's best start ever—it was anyone's best start ever. The scoreless stretch contained four complete-game shutouts, two of them two-hitters. Typical of his pitching strategy now was the sixth inning of a 3–0 victory at New York on April 19. The Yankees opened with a single and double, putting men on second and third with no outs. Johnson then struck out the side. "He toyed with his opponents until they threatened, then came that terrific speed which the human eye cannot gauge," the *Star* reported. As he walked back to the bench, 18,000 New Yorkers rose in a standing ovation.

The Nationals went north at the end of April for the first leg of a month-long road trip, and as Johnson's scoreless streak mounted with each appearance, his soaring popularity kept pace. On May 5 in Boston Johnson shut down the Red Sox for the last five innings of a 12-inning, 5–3 Washington triumph. "When Griffith ordered Johnson to warm up after the Nationals had tied the score," the *Star* reported, "the crowd went into an uproar, cheering and applauding. Though the coming into the game of Johnson made the Red Sox chances of victory look rather slim, the fans were so pleased at the chance of seeing Johnson pitch that they actually went into ecstasy. In every city the Nationals visit, Johnson is the center of attraction. His mere walking across the field on days when he is not pitching brings forth ripples of applause, and whenever he is announced as working he is given an ovation." A pinch-hitting appearance in another game of the series with Boston was the occasion for a standing ovation. "It is doubtful if there is a more idolized player in the game today than Walter Johnson," wrote Ed Grillo. "His very appearance on the field in any city of the circuit wins him applause. Johnson is not only noted for his remarkable ability, but he has made many friends by his modest demeanor. Unlike most of the other stars in the game, Johnson does not push himself into the limelight. He never does anything to attract attention to himself."

The limelight is no respecter of wishes or intentions, however, and now Walter Johnson was caught full in its glare, never again able to completely escape. But the same patience, understanding, and graciousness that characterized his approach to life generally became his method of dealing with fame also. By all accounts he remained entirely unchanged by his enormous celebrity, something that amazed observers almost as much as his athletic prowess. "Johnson is one of those that can 'walk with kings nor lose the common touch,'" one wrote in 1924, borrowing from Kipling. "He is the hero that never struts; the star that never brags. Throughout as brilliant a career as any athlete ever had, he has remained modest and simple and sportsmanlike. He is sophisticated enough so that nobody would mistake him for a probable purchaser of green goods, but sophistication hasn't spoiled him."[5] He was receiving up to 60 letters a day now, and answering them all. "Folks who are interested enough in the game and me to take the time to write are entitled to a reply," Johnson said simply.[6]

One of the pitfalls of renown was brought home to him on the morning of May 8, when he and several teammates went to a Chicago courthouse to see another Johnson, of equal prominence in the sporting world—heavyweight champion Jack Johnson, who was on trial for violation of the Mann ("White Slave") Act. "As soon as the pugilist recognized his namesake," the *Post* reported, "he rushed over and said, loud enough for the jury to hear, 'Why, Mr. Johnson, I'm delighted to see you. This is worth a fortune.' Walter's greeting was not so profuse, and after listening to the testimony for a few minutes, the ballplayers left the court in disgust."[7] Nonetheless, boxing champion Johnson (who had played pro baseball himself with the Philadelphia Black Giants) returned the favor two days later, appearing at Comiskey Park to see pitcher Johnson throw a 1–0 two-hitter at the White Sox.

Of all the great streaks and records in his career, Johnson was proudest of his 56 consecutive scoreless innings, a record set in St. Louis on May 14 in a 10–5 win over the Browns.[8] Although normally paying records and statistics little heed, he bore down from the start on this occasion, when just two outs were needed to break Jack Coombs's standard of 53 straight innings without giving up a run. A strikeout of the first batter tied the record before a flyout to center field (by Pete Compton, who had also ended Johnson's 16-game win streak) broke it. Johnson added three more innings to the record, six of the nine outs coming by strikeout. With one out in the fourth, Browns right fielder Gus Williams doubled. Del Pratt singled him home, and the streak was over. Clark Griffith had seen it coming. "He had St. Louis shut out," he recalled later, "but then we scored six runs and I said to myself, 'Good night, here it goes.' I knew he'd coast on that lead, and I'd advertised him in Detroit, where we were going next, and Cobb had been promising to score on him and I knew we'd get a crowd up there. Sure enough, he threw a nothing ball to Williams."[9] But the mark had been set, and it would hold up for 55 years.

Griffith got his crowd anyway, a Detroit record of nearly 25,000 on Sunday, May 18. The *Detroit Free Press* had reported several days earlier that "fans from all parts of the state, neighboring Canada and even as far away as northern Ohio points have written to the Detroit management asking when the Great Walter is to appear, so that they may time their visits to this city." The Great Walter didn't disappoint them, either, in a 2–1 Nationals' victory, and the Great Cobb fulfilled his promise also, stealing home with the lone Detroit run. In his next appearance against the Tigers on June 10 in Washington, Johnson faced only 27 batters in a nine-inning game, the first of two such minimal efforts in his career. He gave up two hits and a walk, but double plays wiped out all of the baserunners.

Johnson took his first loss in Cleveland on May 22, after ten straight victories. He split the next ten decisions, but a 2–0 three-hitter over the Athletics on June 27 propelled him into an even longer win streak, this one stretching 14 games over more than two months. In Boston on July 3 Johnson gave an extreme demonstration of his "artful loafing" in a 1–0 shutout in which 15 Red Sox hits (still the record for hits in a shutout) were spread over as many innings. He retired the side in order just once, and in only two innings did Boston fail to get a hit. "Hitting Johnson when there is no danger of getting runs and doing it when there is danger are two different propositions," the *Star* observed. Fifteen was again the significant number on July 25 in Washington, this being the number of batters struck out by Johnson in 11⅔ innings of relief in a 15-inning tie with St. Louis. (The 15 strikeouts in relief is also a record.) Nationals pitchers struck out 19 Browns, and St. Louis pitcher Carl Weilman was a strikeout victim himself six times (yet another record). Johnson's ankle was badly spiked in the 13th inning covering first base on a ground out. Mike Martin washed the wound, which went to the bone, but Johnson insisted on staying in the game despite a bad limp. That night 7,000 people showed up at Glen Echo Park outside of Washington for a Walter Johnson testimonial sponsored by the *Times*. Johnson "spent most of the time lounging in his automobile, and was the object of admiration both with the kidlet and the sage," it was reported. "He expressed himself as being tremendously gratified, but bashfully refused to make a speech."[10]

August 2, marking the sixth anniversary of Johnson's debut, was celebrated with "Walter Johnson Day" at the ballpark, where he received a huge sterling silver loving cup stuffed with $674 in cash. Johnson "modestly accepted the beautiful cup and its contents with a pair of flushed cheeks and a pleasant smile," reported the *Star.* The crowd of over 17,000 was the largest so far to attend a ballgame in Washington, and the *Star* noted that the "remarkable feature of the attendance was in the fact that nearly 50% represented the fair sex." Lending his prestige to the occasion was President Wilson, who, it was reported, "joined heartily in the ceremonies, cheering and applauding as loudly as any of the spectators. He gave the pitcher a great hand when he entered the box."[11] Johnson's ankle injury, which had sidelined him for a week, was still quite painful, but not wanting to disappoint the huge crowd and the President of the United States, he went the distance against Detroit. Only the great pair of Cobb and Crawford were left from the team Johnson faced at the dawn of his career six years earlier, but the score was the same, 3–2. This time he came away with a victory, his 24th of the season.

The appearance at Johnson's anniversary game of a large contingent of feminine fans, unusual for that era, was easily explained. Twenty-five years old and unmarried, he was one of Washington's most eligible bachelors. Handsome, with an easy smile and warm, friendly manner; genuinely modest and unassuming; one of the greatest stars in baseball and unequalled as a local celebrity; earning a salary twice that of the average bank president. The term "prize catch" seems hardly adequate to describe how Johnson must have been viewed by many single young women in those days. That he had managed to avoid matrimony this long can only be attributed to his cautious approach to life generally. Opportunities for romance must have presented themselves many times, and there is evidence that he hadn't always failed to take advantage of them.

The earliest known example of this was at Weiser, where Johnson "went with a girl," as he put it years later.[12] Unfortunately, that's all that's known about the relationship. Then on August 23, 1911, the *Washington Post* carried a startling announcement: "Walter Johnson to Wed California Girl in Fall." According to the story he was to go to Los Angeles at the end of the season to marry Mildred Taylor, an Eastern girl who had been in California for several years whom Johnson had met while playing for Olinda. Frank J. Perkins, "a prominent Southern California baseball magnate," made the announcement of Johnson's intentions, which allegedly were told to him by Miss Taylor. There is no recorded reaction to the story by the supposed suitor, and no way to know what there was, if anything, between the two. Late in April, 1913, a similar engagement announcement came out of Cambridge, Massachusetts, but this time Johnson was quick to set the record straight about his involvement with 19-year-old Anna Scully. "Me engaged to be married—and to a Boston girl?" he exclaimed. "Well, I should say not. I hope to be spliced some day, but the right girl hasn't appeared yet. I know Miss Scully, and called upon her when the club was in Boston last summer, but only saw her once or twice and certainly never made love to her to my knowledge. Far be it from me to contradict a lady, but if she declares we are engaged to be married, I shall have to be ungallant enough to say that the young lady is crazy."[13]

Whatever the extent of Johnson's involvement with the opposite sex to this point (and to take Clyde Milan's word for it, there wasn't much) it's clear that with all he had going for him it wouldn't be long before the "right girl" appeared. And sometime during the three-week home stand of which Johnson's anniversary day, August 2, was the midpoint, that's exactly what happened.

Clyde Milan met her first in the summer of 1913 when he and Walter were rooming at the Hotel Dewey. She was so beautiful in her evening gown when Milan was introduced at a small dance at the Dewey that the usually suave little outfielder was a bit skittish at first. She was as tall as Milan, perfectly proportioned, rich brown hair coiled gracefully on her proud head. Her eyes were large, wide and blue as the summer sky. She danced beautifully and was one of the most popular partners at the many affairs that took place in Washington's highly glamorous society. Milan danced with her several times that evening, and she was soon discovering that a baseball player was not necessarily a lout. This one was quiet, gentlemanly, and treated her with considerably more respect than some of the tail-coated partners who made her life miserable at the diplomatic parties to which her father often took her. She knew vaguely that Clyde Milan was quite somebody in the baseball world and she had seen him often with the tall, gentle-looking man named "Walter" something, who seemed to be so popular with all the men—and many of the women. That "Walter" had always intrigued her with his smile, and once, when he had turned quickly to find her watching him, he had started to smile, then blushed deeply and hurried out of the elevator. That had amazed her.

ROGER TREAT

WALTER JOHNSON, KING OF THE PITCHERS

Her name was Hazel Lee Roberts. She was 19 years old, a lithe beauty with an effervescent personality and a wonderfully happy, girlish smile. The daughter of Nevada's only congressman, Edwin E. Roberts, she was a debutante in the Washington social scene, prominent at the teas and formal balls of the congressional set. Within months of coming to Washington with her parents in 1911 she attended one of the grand events in Washington social history, President and Mrs. Taft's silver wedding jubilee at the White House. "Nobody enjoyed the affair more than Mrs. and Miss Roberts," it was reported. "They promenaded through the White House grounds and the building itself, enjoying the Marine Band music, the floral decorations, the supper, the singing concert and other features of the entertainment, which they voted a great success."[14]

Born on February 8, 1894, in Hollister, California, Hazel Roberts was the grandchild of original "'49ers" who had come West in the Gold Rush. In 1896 her father traveled over the Sierra Mountains to Carson City, Nevada, for the Corbett-Fitzsimmons heavyweight championship fight, and was so taken with the area that he moved his family and started his law practice there. Hazel was something of an athlete herself, a member of the Carson City High School girls' basketball team, Nevada state champions in 1909. The next year she captained the team. After her father was elected to Congress Hazel spent the 1911–12 academic year at Mrs. Scoville's School for Girls on Fifth Avenue in New York before completing her education at Martha Washington College, a finishing school in Washington. She played Octavian in her high school production of *Julius Caesar,* sketched, and wrote poetry.[15] Active in the suffragist movement, she played a prominent, though mostly theatrical, role in the big demonstration for women's voting rights in Washington in 1913. "Miss Roberts was the central figure posing as 'Today' in the suffragette parade on March 3," it was reported, "and was surrounded by a bevy of thirty young women from the District of Columbia and the various states."[16]

The Dewey Hotel at 13th and L streets in the Northwest section of Washington, D.C., was a first-class apartment-hotel that included a number of congressional families among its tenants. Just a few blocks southwest of the ballpark, the Dewey also was home to several of the Nationals, including Johnson, Milan, and Ainsmith. The mix of young, energetic ballplayers sharing the lobby and hallways with staid members of the country's political establishment must have made for some unusual occasions there, but none could have been more interesting (certainly not to them) than when Walter Johnson and Hazel Lee Roberts were introduced at the Dewey by Clyde Milan. By all accounts they were instantly smitten with each other. And although much would be made of their divergent backgrounds, in many ways it was a match made in heaven.

The congressman got things rolling by extending the famous ballplayer an invitation for dinner at the Roberts's apartment.[17] Johnson quickly reciprocated with passes to the ballpark. (Perhaps to the Walter Johnson Day game—what girl wouldn't be impressed to see the president cheering for him?) Soon the entire Roberts family, which had known little of the game previously, became great fans. "I had never seen a ball game," Hazel recalled some years later. "I went to the game, but I didn't have the slightest idea what it was all about. I don't know to this day whether Walter won or lost—though I think he probably won—but I do know I enjoyed watching him. After that I went to see every game he pitched, and it wasn't long until I became a rabid fan."[18] When the Nationals left on their final road trip of the year, Johnson wasted no time in letting Miss Roberts know he was thinking of her. "I couldn't get a card on the train so I am doing the next best," he wrote on a Detroit hotel postcard. "Was real cold last night but warm today. I hope this finds you the same as when we left. I am yours, Walter J."[19]

While the Nationals were in Detroit, Clark Griffith wrote a little note of his own—a check to the Tigers in the amount of $100,000. All he wanted in return was Ty Cobb. The Athletics had settled the American League race by July, and second-place Cleveland had put a healthy distance between themselves and the rest of the pack. The Nationals appeared relegated to a struggle for third with Chicago and the defending world champion Red Sox. But with Johnson winning every time out, they put those two teams behind them and were closing in on the slumping Naps. Griffith figured that Cobb, with his gaudy .420 and .410 batting averages the last two years, would assure Washington of a second-place finish and might even improve them enough to challenge the A's for the pennant. Griffith was also mindful of Cobb's impact on box-office receipts, no doubt.

To show Frank Navin he was serious, Griffith signed the check and handed it over. Looking at the enormous figure, an unprecedented amount for the sale of a ballplayer, Navin agreed to think it over but expressed surprise that he had that kind of money at hand. "You'll have to give me a little time to work on that check, Frank," Griffith told him, "but I'll make it good, if it buys Cobb. Give me two weeks." Navin agreed to consider the deal, but when the sensational news got back to Washington, the Nationals' board of directors thought Griffith had lost his mind. He wasn't authorized to spend that kind of money, and they didn't have it anyway. But Griffith's plan didn't require any of the club's funds. He was going to sell 100,000 one-dollar tickets good for any future game, urging Washington fans to buy them if they wanted Cobb and a pennant. The unique scheme was never put to the test, though, as Navin decided Cobb was not for sale.[20]

With the Nationals out of the pennant race, Griffith made it a point not to overwork Johnson over the last two months of the season. "I am going to win a pennant some day with Johnson," Griffith told Ed Grillo, "and I am going to keep him in form until the time comes."[21] Relief appearances were rare, and there was plenty of rest between starts. Griffith even prohibited Johnson from hitting fungoes during practice for fear he might injure himself in the process, a great disappointment to the big pitcher, who was one of the strongest fungo-hitters in baseball and on the days between starts enjoyed sending fly balls soaring high and deep over the field.[22]

Johnson won his 14th straight on August 24, a dramatic 2–1 squeaker in Chicago. "From the moment he stepped on the mound there was continuous hand clapping and applauding," the *Post* reported. "When he fanned Lord, Chase and Bodie, the Sox heavy artillery, in succession in the eighth, the 28,000 spectators cheered him for fully five minutes. This also occurred in the ninth when, with two out and two on, Johnson struck out Collins on three pitched balls." The Nationals were now the best draw in the league. The comedy team of Schaefer and Altrock was a fan favorite everywhere around the circuit, but the team also attracted large crowds with their scrappy, heads-up style of play. "The greatest card, of course, has been Walter Johnson," Ed Grillo observed. "The very announcement in any city that he is going to pitch means a 100% increase in attendance. Johnson is today the idol of the baseball world. This is demonstrated when the crowds in other cities pull for him to win his games."[23]

Johnson's winning streak ended in Boston on August 28th with one of his greatest performances, ironically—the best yet, by his own estimation.[24] Red Sox second baseman Steve Yerkes, with a single in the second inning, was Boston's only baserunner in the first ten innings as Johnson and Ray Collins dueled into the 11th inning of a scoreless tie. After 26 Red Sox had gone down in a row, Yerkes singled again, drilling a ball sharply to center field that Milan, in a rare lapse, let roll through his legs, and Yerkes made it to third base. On Heinie Wagner's grounder Yerkes was trapped on a fielder's choice, but Wagner reached second on the play and Bill Carrigan singled him home with the winning run. In this losing effort Johnson gave up just three hits and no walks in 10⅓ innings, while striking out ten. Harry Hooper, one of the toughest men in the league to strike out, went that way three times, as did five Red Sox in a row. When Johnson reached the dressing room, Tris Speaker burst in and shook his hand.

"Walter, I am glad we won," he said, "but I am awfully sorry you lost. It was the greatest exhibition of pitching that I have ever seen in my life, and you deserved to win."[25]

After the game, Milan "had a grouch on," according to the *Post*. "No one could get within yards of him tonight and get a civil answer to questions. He has taken the whole matter to heart much worse than Johnson or the other members of the team." But even the normally unperturbable Johnson was affected by this heartbreaking loss. "Whether the tide of battle swings his way or not, the big pitcher never mentions his defeat or victory," noted the *Post*. "Tonight it was different. When some friends of his talked of the game, tears actually came to his eyes." As happened often during his career with Washington, however, defeat—or more accurately, his reaction to it—added another tale to the Johnson legend. Clark Griffith would often cite this game to describe the kind of man Johnson was, relating how a teammate came over in the locker room to console him about losing such a game on an error. Johnson looked up at his teammate and said quietly, "Well, you know Zeb doesn't do that very often."[26]

After another extra-inning loss in Philadelphia on September 1, Johnson embarked on his third winning streak of the year, this time seven in a row starting with a 1–0 beauty in New York on the 5th. A walk in the first inning of this game was his first in 37 innings and one of only three passes in an 80-inning stretch. Cleveland slumped badly, and the Nationals' five-game sweep against them in mid-September decided the battle for the American League runner-up spot. With second place suddenly within reach, Griffith made full use of his ace. Johnson contributed four complete-game wins and a save in an 11-day span, ending his season in style on the 29th with another 1–0 gem over the league-champion Athletics in Washington.

With the Nationals guaranteed second place, Griffith made the last game of the season against Boston on October 4 a "joke" game, something Griffith often did in the season finale when it couldn't affect the standings. Johnson played center field, the first time in his big-league career at another position, and had two hits and two stolen bases. "From beginning to end, the contest was a joke," reported the *Post*, "but it served to amuse the crowd more than any other engagement staged here this year.

"About half the time neither team knew whether there were one out or six. It often happened that four men were retired before the other team took its turn at bat. The umpires, Dinneen and Connolly, were so overcome with laughter that they, too, fell in with the rest of the company. During most of the day, the Nationals were minus a right gardener. Schaefer was supposed to play this position, but instead he cavorted around the infield most of the time. At times he would perch himself on the Bull [Durham] sign in right field, and then again lie down apparently asleep." At the end of eight innings Washington led 10–3, so Griffith pulled out all the stops.

At the demand of 1,000 cavalry soldiers attending the game as guests of the Nationals, Johnson was sent in to pitch. His catcher was Jack Ryan, a 43-year-old coach who, except for a similar joke game the year before, hadn't played in the major leagues since 1903. Lobbing pitches over, Johnson was touched for two quick hits before going back to center field in mock disgrace. His replacements on the mound were Eddie Ainsmith, who gave up two more hits to score Johnson's runners, infielders Germany Schaefer and Joe Gedeon, and finally another pitcher—Clark Griffith—who managed to retire the side in time for a 10–9 Washington victory. What nobody knew at the time was that the innocent buffoonery would cost Walter Johnson the major-league record for lowest earned-run average in a season (300+ innings). His 1913 ERA was listed for many years at 1.09 until the two runs in the joke game were added, raising it to 1.14. This slight difference would have been of little consequence, of course, had Bob Gibson not registered a 1.12 ERA in 1968.

Record or no, Johnson's 1913 performance is always prominent in discussions about the best season ever by a pitcher. He won 36 games and lost only 7, leading the major leagues in wins, winning percentage (.837), earned run average, complete games (29), innings (346), strikeouts (243), and shutouts (11); American League batters averaged a meager .187 against him, and he walked only 38 of them—less than one per nine innings; he had winning streaks of 14, 10, and 7 games; five wins were by 1–0, six by 2–1, 15 by one run and six by two; he was a perfect 7–0 in relief and an astonishing 20–3 on the road; he batted .261 with a .433 slugging average; he was perfect in the field, handling 103 chances without error (the major-league record for pitchers until 1976, and still the American League standard).

The Nationals were runners-up in the league for the second straight year, shattering any notion that their 1912 accomplishments had been a fluke. Although their 90–64 record was slightly worse than the year before, the gap of only 6½ games between them and the champion Athletics makes the 1913 race appear much closer than it was. Philadelphia maintained a comfortable double-digit lead until the last week, when their slump and the Nationals' surge narrowed the margin. Washington stole 291 bases on the year (a league record until 1976), with Milan again leading the circuit in thefts with 75 and Danny Moeller second with 62. Even Eddie Ainsmith got in on the base-stealing act with 17, including a theft of second, third, and home in the same inning.

Walter Johnson's wonderful season was recognized officially with the Chalmers Award as the Most Valuable Player in the American League. Joe Jackson, runner-up to Cobb for the league batting title for the third straight year despite averages of .408, .395, and .373, finished second in the MVP balloting also. Johnson accepted the award, a Chalmers luxury sedan, in Philadelphia before the second game of the World Series between the Athletics and Giants. The car was presented by its manufacturer, Hugh Chalmers, and to the great cheers of the fans they took it for a ride around Shibe Park. The game itself was one of the great pitching duels in World Series history, Mathewson and Plank battling to a scoreless tie after nine innings before the Giants won it in the tenth.

Johnson had received several offers from newspaper syndicates (as much as $1,000, according to reports) to again lend his name to ghostwritten accounts of the Series, but on September 24 Ban Johnson had the National Commission step in to prohibit such practices. Ostensibly protecting the public from fraud, the action was taken at the behest of the newly-formed Baseball Writers Association, some of whose members were upset by the ballplayers' usurpation of their bylines. The American League president, a former sportswriter himself, proclaimed that any article appearing under a player's name would be minutely examined for "faking" and forbade players actively involved in the Series from writing about it at all. Players Fraternity president David Fultz announced the union's legal support for any players or writers with a ghostwriting arrangement, raising once again the possibility of warfare between the players and the baseball establishment over a minor issue. When the Commission threatened cancellation of the World Series if their decree was ignored, the ghostwriting deals were called off.[27]

Walter Johnson attended the World Series anyway, accompanied by Milan and several other Nationals, and apparently made money on it despite the Commission's edict. According to the *Washington Times,* the capital contingent "cleaned up" by laying heavy bets on the A's to take the Series. "Walter Johnson, George McBride and Herman Schaefer made $5,000 among them backing the Athletics against the Giants, and smiles covered their faces when they left the Polo Grounds [after the last game of the Series]," it was reported.[28]

Before going to New York City for the start of the Series, Johnson first went to Schenectady on October 5 to pick up $500 for an exhibition against the black Mohawk Giants. Pitching for the Giants was their star, Frank Wickware, nicknamed "the Red Ant," who had been born in Coffeyville, Kansas, coincidentally. An estimated 7,000 fans showed up for the contest, which almost turned into a riot. The Giants' manager, a white promoter named Bill Wernecke, apparently owed his players $921 in back pay. Giants players, seeing this as their last chance to collect, appeared at the box office demanding to be paid even as patrons bought tickets and streamed into the ballpark, which sat on an island in the middle of a lake. When a police patrol was called out, several hundred fans, thinking the game would be cancelled, rushed back over the pontoon bridge between the ballpark and the ticket office to get a refund. With the bridge about to collapse, the sheriff ordered the game to begin.

"The scene was disgraceful in many respects," the *Schenectady Union-Star* reported. "Wickware, in an ugly mood, used his tongue too freely as he strode about the crowd, swinging a bat dangerously near to the spectators and muttering threats against Wernecke." Nonetheless, the game turned out to be the thrilling pitching duel everyone had come to see in the first place, called for darkness (the ruckus had delayed the start by two hours) after the top of the sixth inning with the Giants ahead, 1–0. Back-to-back ground-rule doubles into the fenced-off overflow crowd in left field were Johnson's undoing, and in spite of the loss he had outpitched Wickware by a considerable margin. In five innings Johnson gave up two hits, no walks, struck out 11, and had two doubles himself off Wickware. The Red Ant, whose main weapon also was a blazing fastball, gave up six hits in as many innings, walked three, hit a batter, and set four down on strikes. Meanwhile, "manager Wernecke quietly disappeared with the 'strong satchel' [the money] to safety," according to the *Union-Star*.

The same day, by an interesting coincidence, Cyclone Joe Williams [also known as Smokey Joe] was beating Grover Cleveland Alexander and the Phillies in New York. These two victories of black teams over the best pitchers in white baseball "set the fans to arguing as to the relative strength of some of our colored baseball teams as compared with the big league teams," the *New York Age* noted, begging the question that could never be answered satisfactorily.[29] Similarly, comparisons of individual players, normally grounded in records and statistics achieved under more or less uniform conditions, are likewise impossible. An intelligent discussion can be mounted about whether Cy Young was as good as Walter Johnson, or if Bob Gibson was better than both of them. But was Walter Johnson as good as Satchel Paige? Was Joe Williams as fast as Walter Johnson? Unfortunately, we'll never have the information even to hazard a guess. In Johnson's case there are the handful of games he pitched against the finest black teams and players of his day, and from these one thing is clear, at least: Walter Johnson was just as great against them as he was against everybody else.[30]

Meanwhile, the Nationals had stayed together after the season for exhibitions in New York and Connecticut that were to be followed by a month-long tour of Cuba. Johnson pitched for them in Hartford on October 6, the day after the game with the Mohawk Giants, but declined to participate in the Cuban venture, which was then cancelled when the promoters on the island learned he wouldn't be along. According to *The Sporting News* this didn't sit well with some of Johnson's teammates, who had stood to make $500 each from the trip and were said to be "somewhat peeved" by his decision not to go.[31] After playing in a semipro game in New York City on October 12, the day after the World Series ended there, Johnson headed home to Coffeyville.

In the annual homecoming game at Humboldt, Johnson struck out 24 Iola batters, his second-highest total ever, in a ten-inning scoreless duel with Ad Brennan of the Phillies. Both pitchers gave up only two hits and walked none, and Brennan fanned 17 himself. Johnson almost didn't make it to the game when he missed the train in Coffeyville, but Santa Fe Railroad officials were called and a special train was dispatched to take him the 60 miles to Humboldt.

A game of much greater historical note took place on October 28 in Tulsa, Oklahoma. Walter Johnson and Christy Mathewson, often called the greatest pitchers in the history of the game, took the mound against each other for the only time. The Giants-White Sox World Tour, the first since Cap Anson's in 1888–89, was playing its way across the U.S. on the way to Japan (where it would introduce baseball), Australia, and Europe. Johnson offered his services free of charge to the White Sox for the chance to pitch against the great Matty, and it was arranged for them to face each other at Joplin, Missouri on October 27. But Mathewson, appearing frequently as the tour's greatest attraction, and having pitched a complete game on the 25th, begged off from exhaustion. Not wanting to disappoint the crowd completely, Johnson went the first three innings for the White Sox, giving up two runs and six hits in a 13–12 slugfest won by the Giants. The next day the tour moved to Tulsa, and Mathewson felt well enough to start. But the historic matchup was delayed further when just before the game was to begin, the crowd of 5,000 overwhelmed rickety wooden stands and a large section crumpled under the weight, burying 700 people in the rubble. One fan was killed and 52 seriously injured. Among those escaping injury was the governor of Oklahoma.

Incredibly, after two hours of pulling people out of the debris the game went on. "Sorrowed by the sad accident, and chilled by a north wind that threatened to break into snow at any minute, the crowd greeted the big league favorites with enthusiasm but did not give the rousing welcome they would have accorded under more auspicious circumstances," the *Tulsa World* reported. "When umpire [Bill] Klem announced the batteries as Mathewson and Meyers and Johnson and Schalk, a great roar of approval went up from the stands." The biggest applause, however, was reserved for the Giants' Jim Thorpe, a native of the Osage Reservation not far from Tulsa, and Chief Meyers. The game itself was anticlimactic (as it would have been no matter what happened on the field), an easy 6–0 White Sox victory over the three-time National League champions. Mathewson gave up two runs in four innings before being relieved in the fifth inning by Hooks Wiltse. Johnson, with a team including Tris Speaker, Sam Crawford, Buck Weaver (five for five on the day), Ray Schalk, and Germany Schaefer, went the distance for the Sox, allowing eight hits and one walk while striking out eight.

The outcome of this lone Mathewson-Johnson match is meaningless in itself, and Big Six still had one last great season left in his arm. But the temptation is irresistible nonetheless to see in this game a passing of the torch. The previous year, when picking Johnson as the pitcher for his 1912 All-Major League team, Grantland Rice had already heralded the transition. "Johnson," wrote Rice, "steps forth where Mathewson left off as the grandest pitcher in the game. The Washington pitcher stands alone as the premier of the firing line, a worthy companion to Christy Mathewson before time and taxing service called for their relentless pay."[32]

CHAPTER 8

King of the Pitchers

When he first came up, he was so fast that he made me blink when I worked back of the plate even though the catcher was in front of me and I was wearing my mask. I thought he was going to be hard to work with, but the batters took all the worry off my chest when they started asking me what Walter was pitching.

"What was that one, Billy," the batters would say, "a fast one or a curve?" When they asked me that I knew that umpiring back of Johnson was going to be a cinch.[1]

BILLY EVANS

Undocumented but always well received is the story of the day Eddie Ainsmith cooked up the hoax with two strikes on the hitter and darkness threatening to call the game. Walking out to the mound, Ainsmith said to Johnson, "This guy'll swing at anything, so you wind up but don't throw the ball. I'll pound my glove and it's so dark maybe the ump will think he didn't see it either." Johnson went through his motion, but held the ball and Ainsmith pounded his mitt to simulate the pitch striking it.

"Strike three," yelled the umpire.

"That was no strike," yelled the batter. "It was a foot wide."[2]

SHIRLEY POVICH

Johnson's three-year contract with the Nationals had run out, and his stellar work was rewarded with a $5,000 raise to $12,000 for 1914,[3] equal to Ty Cobb's 1913 salary with Detroit. (Cobb moved up to $15,000 this year after his seventh straight batting title.)[4] Johnson was now in complete charge of his own conditioning and preparation in training camp, deciding each day what and how much to do. He pitched in only four exhibition games in 1914, a total of 18 innings spaced over three weeks, tuning up for the season opener with a win on April 10 over the Boston Braves, soon to be known as the "Miracle Braves" for their amazing last-to-first rush in the second half of the National League pennant race.

Four days later Johnson picked up where he left off the year before, shutting out the Red Sox 3–0 in the inaugural game at Boston. "So effective was the work of Johnson," the *Post* reported, "that the 24,741 fans who passed the turnstiles to cheer for the Red Sox began to pull instead for the big pitcher, and when Carrigan crashed into the base hit column in the sixth for Boston's first safety, a groan of disappointment arose, that Johnson could not achieve a no-hit game." He won again in New York 4–1, but the Red Sox turned the tables on him in the Washington opener on April 23 with a 5–0 thrashing. President Wilson wasn't present for the humiliation, kept from the game by his wife's illness (which would take her life in August).

After an inconsistent start splitting his first six decisions, Johnson on May 8 made the worst relief effort of his career. He had to be relieved himself after allowing six runs in three innings of a ten-inning 9–9 tie with the A's in Washington, the other notable feature of which was a pitch Johnson threw at Frank Baker, the only beanball of his career. Home Run Baker had always done great damage to the Nationals, and was a particular "hoodoo" for Walter Johnson. "The most dangerous batter that I ever faced," Johnson called him.[5] Washington pitchers started throwing at Baker to drive him off the plate. "Frank Baker's head is the target for every pitcher used by the Nationals," the *Post* reported, "with the exception of Walter Johnson, who never throws at anyone's head."[6]

In this game Johnson did just that, however, reportedly at the urging of Mike Martin.[7] He "let fly a wild fast one which almost put the home-run king into a state of dreamless slumber," the *Post* poetically described.[8] Baker dropped to the ground quickly enough to avoid the ball, to Johnson's everlasting relief. "The moment I threw the pitch," he said later, "I wished I had it back."[9] Baker dodged more beanballs from Doc Ayers and Joe Engel during the game, but "had no more trouble as long as Johnson stayed in," according to the *Post.* Johnson's pitching became ineffectual, and he was soon driven out of the game, unnerved and chastened by the episode. "I have pitched only one beanball in my life and I always regretted that," he wrote later. "I made up my mind never to throw another."[10] Coincidence or not, Baker's days as Johnson's nemesis were over. In the preceding four seasons Baker had hit .385 against him, with four home runs, three triples, and six doubles. In the nine years starting in 1914, by contrast, Baker averaged just .207 facing Johnson, with a home run and double the only extra-base hits in 111 at-bats.

Baseball was hardly the only thing on Walter Johnson's mind in the spring of 1914, as he quickly renewed his acquaintance with Hazel Roberts. Clyde

Milan had married his longtime sweetheart, Margaret Bowers, in November, and the two couples became almost as inseparable as the teammates had been. The women, in fact, became best friends themselves. "The first time Hazel and I met we seemed to 'click.' We loved being together," Margaret Milan wrote many years later.[11] A series of snapshots documents a happy picnic the four of them took at a park overlooking the Potomac River just outside of Washington,[12] and according to one account it was on another outing here that Walter Johnson first professed his love to Hazel Roberts.[13]

Whatever the exact circumstances of their "engagement," which never was officially announced, her presence at the ballpark could be counted on now when Johnson was scheduled to take the mound, and the romance was an open secret. "Their devotion to each other has attracted much attention and comment among their friends," noted the *Times.* "Both have, however, persistently refused to admit any engagement or marriage plans."[14] When the *Herald* broke an "exclusive" in mid-June that a wedding was imminent, Hazel was curiously adamant in her denial. "What? I marry Walter Johnson? It's not so," she was reported as exclaiming. "Please deny it. Nothing like that is going to take place."[15]

Nothing like that could take place, anyway, until the Nationals returned from a month-long road trip on June 24th. Their first day back, Johnson was on his way to a 2–1 victory over the Athletics when newsboys suddenly came running through the aisles of the ballpark waving their papers and shouting out the headline of the *Times'* 5:30 edition. "Walter Johnson Will Be Wed Tonight," they hollered over and over, the commotion momentarily stopping the game. Someone yelled out, 'There she is,' and pointed to a pretty girl in a box near the front of the stands. Every neck in the park craned for a look at the baseball idol's fiancee. "But the funny part of it was that I wasn't the girl in the box at all," Hazel Johnson recalled later. "I was sitting in the very last row and no one even looked my way. After the game, I slipped away unnoticed while everyone was staring at the girl in the box."[16]

The marriage was performed that evening by the Chaplain of the Senate, Reverend F.J. Prettyman, at the Roberts's new apartment on Monroe Street. The event was described by the *Herald:*

> Walter, breathlessly excited, rushed into the bride's apartment at 8:15, the hour set for the wedding, giving hurried explanations about a breakdown with his automobile and that he hoped he had not kept Hazel "watchfully waiting." The reporters, who had wormed themselves into the apartment, were then gently put out in the hall, but took turns witnessing the ceremony through a key hole. The bride, in a low, sweet voice, promised to obey the great and only Walter who, in return, declared

that all his worldly possessions were hers. Representative Roberts gave his daughter away with all the assurance betokening his utmost satisfaction, but the mother had almost a tearful tone when she kissed the bridegroom and bade him to be good to her only child. The bride is an attractively pretty girl of twenty summers, with large blue eyes and light brown hair and a manner that is both magnetic and girlishly sweet. She was gowned in white taffeta and lace, and wore a most unique white hat, made entirely of feathers with a large white bird directly in front. The bridegroom wore a blue serge suit with a white buttonaire.

The plan was to spend the night at an apartment they had taken on Biltmore Street, then drive to Atlantic City for a two-day honeymoon. They would join up with the Nationals in Philadelphia, where Johnson was scheduled to pitch three days later. But car problems, which had almost caused him to be late for the wedding, now delayed the newlyweds' departure. This incident, too, was reported in detail:

Peerless Pitcher Peeved by Prank

At 9 o'clock, Mr. Johnson and his pretty bride descended the steps of the Raymond. A good-sized crowd of youngsters had gathered around the car by this time. All along Monroe Street necks were craned in an effort to get a glimpse of the pair. Mrs. Johnson was placed in the machine, and the famous Walter, king of all baseball pitchers, bent to crank the motor. Three or four turns of the mighty arm spun the motor over. Five or six more violent jerks failed to get a sign of an explosion. The famous pitcher stood up for a second to get his breath and again assaulted the unwilling machinery. Eight turns failed to do the work. "Just a moment," said the peerless pitcher to the blushing bride. With an encouraging smile Walter took several more turns at the crank. By this time some of the more venturesome youngsters began to give advice. "Keep right after it, Walter," said one. "He can spin it, too. That's some arm," said another admirer. Mrs. Johnson said nothing. "Say, you'll never be able to pitch if you don't cut that out," advised another as the perspiring bridegroom manfully stuck to his task. "38, 39, 40," counted the kids as the crank spun around and around. Gone was the collar, wilted to the neckband under the furious cranking. Eighteen minutes Johnson worked. It was discovered that the electric light was out and then Johnson gave it up. A neighbor offered the use of a machine and bore off the happy pair down Monroe to Fourteenth. There were cheers along the row of houses on either side of Monroe Street. "Hooray for Walter," shouted the youngsters, "hooray, hooray," and then a second later, "Hooray for Mrs. Johnson."

It was also reported that two single members of the ballclub had been spotted near the Chalmers while the wedding was taking place inside, and when the car was later taken to a garage, two neatly severed wires were found to be the problem. This was easily fixed and the Johnsons took off for Atlantic City as scheduled.[17]

The high point of the Nationals' season came on June 7 when they slipped into first place for a day, sparked by five Johnson wins in a row after the "Baker beanball" incident. But then Chick Gandil slumped badly, and on July 17 Clyde Milan's jaw was broken in two places in an outfield collision with Danny Moeller. Milan was out for 40 games, effectively dooming the team's pennant chances. Johnson had his own difficulties, including the worst start of his career on September 8, when the A's got seven runs on 13 hits in only 3⅓ innings. A lack of hitting support produced many low-scoring losses in 1914, preventing the momentum of long winning streaks that had characterized his MVP year. There were control problems, too, that didn't exist the year before, as Johnson's walks jumped from 38 to 74. (Although his per-game average almost doubled, it was still second-lowest in the league.) On September 21 he had one of the worst momentary lapses of control in baseball history, throwing four wild pitches in the fourth inning of a game in Chicago. Oddly, this occurred in the course of an otherwise fine performance, Johnson dueling Red Faber for 13 innings and striking out 12 (his high for the year) before the Nationals broke the game open for a 6–1 win.

Billy Evans attributed Johnson's problems to overuse of the curve ball, which the umpire felt diminished his speed in a game. Evans wrote that in previous years Johnson seldom threw as many as a dozen curves in a game, but in one game in 1914 Eddie Collins got eight curves in a row before finally hitting one safely.[18] Collins called Johnson's curve "an awful thing to hit. [It] travels almost as fast as his straight one, only instead of coming across the plate with a good hop on it, it hooks across at an angle."[19] After the season, Johnson himself estimated that on average four out of 10 pitches were curves. "No doubt I carried curve pitching too far last summer," he admitted.[20]

A strong finish, in which he won five of six decisions in the last month of the season, helped the Nationals prevail in a fierce struggle with the Tigers for third place. Connie Mack's awesome Athletics once again left the rest of the league behind by midseason on the way to their fourth pennant in five years. Boston, which had slumped to fourth place in 1913, rebounded to a respectable second. The Red Sox were just one player away from replacing Philadelphia as the dominant power in the American League for the next few years, and in Johnson's last game of the year, a 9–3 win in Boston on October 5th, he faced that player for the first time. George Herman "Babe" Ruth, called up to the majors for the second time after pitching Providence to the International League title, pinch-hit in the course of Johnson's 28th victory of the year—the first time Ruth was used for his hitting.

"I had seen Ruth around for quite a while before I ever pitched to him," Johnson recalled. "He worked in a number of games but not on days that I happened to pitch. One afternoon he was sent up as a pinch hitter and I got my first good look at the boy who was just starting to attract national attention. Three fast balls across the center of the plate and Babe was through. Afterward he said, 'Gosh, I'd sure like to get ahold of one of those fast balls.'"[21] Two days later Ruth pitched three innings of relief and banged out a single, his first major-league hit. It came in another of Griffith's season-ending joke games, in which the Old Fox made the last appearance of his 240-win pitching career and Tris Speaker took to the mound for the only time in his 22 years in the big leagues.

Though it lacked the sheer brilliance of the previous year, Johnson's 1914 season was fabulous nonetheless. He won 28 games and lost 18 with a 1.72 earned run average, leading the league in wins, games (51), starts (40), complete games (33), innings pitched (372, his most ever), strikeouts (225), and shutouts (9). The lack of hitting support for the pitching staff is reflected in the record 11 1–0 wins they were forced to struggle through, three of them by Walter Johnson.

⚾ ⚾ ⚾ ⚾ ⚾

From the first, I was always impressed with the Federal League. They looked to me like a game crowd, and I admired their courage. I do not see how anyone who has seen how they have fought against the greatest odds can fail to be impressed with their courage. I always hoped they would succeed, for I thought their success was a good thing for the ballplayer, and a good thing for the public.[22]

WALTER JOHNSON, 1915

Like all professional ballplayers, Johnson sympathized with the Federal League in its attempt to break the major-league monopoly over the game. Every one of them had felt the yoke of the National Agreement and the take-it-or-leave-it attitude of the owners. But it was the big stars, whose effect on club attendance and revenue was most obvious, and who were constantly reminded by the press of their importance, who chafed hardest at the lack of options. Their only real leverage was the threat that an egregiously unfair contract might cause them to malinger, to play poorly and force a trade to another team. But pride in their skills and accomplishments kept most of the great players from employing the tactic. The contract process for superstars usually followed a predictable pattern, with the owners offering the least they thought they could get away with, and the players holding out until it was obvious that it was all they would get. Walter Johnson described the process colorfully in a July 1911 *Baseball Magazine* article entitled "Baseball Slavery: The Great American Principle of Dog Eat Dog." "The employer tries to starve out the laborer," he wrote, "and the laborer tries to ruin the employer's business. They quarrel over a bone and rend each other like coyotes."

That changed during the brief existence of the Federal League. A six-team circuit independent of the National Agreement, the Federals weren't of much consequence to the established leagues when starting out in 1913, just another outlaw outfit that would fold up after a while or come into the family of organized baseball as a minor league. But in 1914 the Federal League attracted a handful of wealthy investors and expanded to eight cities, four of them existing major-league venues, and began raiding American and National League clubs for playing talent. The biggest star corraled was Joe Tinker, shortstop on the famous "Tinker-to-Evers-to-Chance" Chicago Cubs dynasty of several years earlier. Tinker jumped from the Cincinnati Reds, where he was player-manager, to assume the same position with the Chicago Federal League team, the "Chifeds."

On Sunday, May 24, Tinker brought his club to Washington for an exhibition game against local amateurs, taking advantage of the Nationals' refusal to play on Sundays. (This despite a recent court ruling striking down "blue laws" prohibiting Sunday baseball in the capital; these exhibition incursions by the Feds would hasten the start of Sunday ball in the District.)[23] That evening Tinker asked Walter Johnson to come to his hotel to talk about the Federal League, and in their two-hour meeting found the pitcher more receptive to the idea of jumping than Tinker could have imagined. Johnson was quoted afterward to the effect that Tinker would offer him a contract when the season was over, and that if it contained the salary mentioned (reportedly $25,000 per year), he would accept—unless the Nationals matched the offer, in which case he would stay with them. Johnson stated that two other Federal League clubs had also made offers. "I will pitch for the one that gives me the most money," he said, according to the *Post.* Clark Griffith seemed surprisingly calm when faced with such startling news. "I am not worried," he said. "When the time comes, Johnson will do the right thing."[24]

Griffith was less sanguine about a second meeting between Johnson and representatives of the Federal League on June 3, when the Nationals were in New York. The pitcher was picked up at his hotel by Jim Bradley, manager of the Brooklyn Federals, and old teammate Jim Delahanty, their second baseman, and driven to the mansion of bakery magnate Robert Ward, the Brookfeds' owner and one of the principal backers of the third-league venture. Getting wind of the meeting, Griffith quickly arranged for a conference with Johnson at which he made a preemptive proposition for a five-year contract at $16,000 per year, or one or two years at $18,000. Johnson then went off to his meeting with Ward, during which a three-year deal for $25,000 a year was reportedly offered. Griffith expressed confidence he would re-sign his ace to a long-term contract, but noted that Johnson would be breaking his current contract if he signed with the Feds, invoking for the first time the threat of the "reserve clause."[25]

For many years, organized baseball claimed for its teams a permanent legal right to their players. The standard contract was structured so that 25% of the salary was said to be consideration for the player's agreement to this principle, which in effect made him the club's property. But in the case of Red Killefer, the Phillies catcher who had jumped to the Chifeds, a federal court of appeals called into question the legal soundness of this formulation, although it did uphold Philadelphia's claim to Killefer on "moral grounds".[26] Contracts for 1914 were then written specifying an amount for the reserve feature. In Walter Johnson's case, $2,000 of his $12,000 salary was said to be for an option on his services the following year also, and at the same rate. Johnson probably wasn't aware of this new feature when he signed a new one-year deal at the end of the 1913 season, but shortly thereafter the fledgling Players Fraternity was warning others about signing such contracts.

Johnson was open and honest from the beginning about his dealings with the Federal League, and the forthrightness with which he discussed his financial situation made him look starkly mercenary. "It is true," he told Ed Grillo, "that the Federal League has made me a proposition which, if carried out, will make me wealthy in a few years. I am naturally out for the money. I want to make all I can while I can, but I am no hog. I am a loyal ballplayer. I have been treated well by Griffith in the past and I am sure will be treated similarly in the future. I am not in the market for the highest bidder. I know Griffith will pay me what I'm worth, and I don't believe we will have any trouble coming to terms. I have had offers, but I have not committed myself, and I resent the insinuation that I am not loyal to my club."[27] Shortly after his interview with Robert Ward and the Brookfeds, Johnson received a check from Ban Johnson for $50, a refund of the fine for playing against the outlaw Logan Squares *six* years earlier.[28]

This is where things stood as the season ended and Johnson's contract with the Nationals expired. Griffith approached him several times over the summer to try to firm up a deal, but Johnson kept his options open, telling his boss he didn't want to rush things.[29] Rumors swirled around the World

Series in Philadelphia that the St. Louis and Chicago Federals were both after Johnson and offering a $25,000 bonus for signing. Johnson said only that he hadn't signed with anybody yet, but added, "Griffith and I are the best of friends and there is no manager in baseball I would rather work for."[30]

Johnson and his bride were in Philadelphia for her first World Series, and a delayed honeymoon. Hazel was by now a great baseball fan, turning her back on the capital's social scene for afternoons at the ballpark. Only rarely did she miss one of his games, and she was always eager to hear all about the road trips. Hazel even went on a road trip herself, with Margaret Milan and Mrs. Ainsmith also along. But in an interview a month after their marriage she expressed frustration at her husband's lack of cooperation in her attempts to learn the game. "Walter does not talk to me very much about [baseball]," she laughed, "because, he says, I don't know any too much about it yet. And I suppose I don't, from his standpoint. Besides, he hears nothing but baseball from morning until night. If he meets new people, the first thing they want to discuss is baseball, while his friends are always talking about it, too."[31] They apparently did talk about one of her interests: women's suffrage. "She has converted me," Johnson declared. "Mrs. Johnson is a Nevadan and has all the open-minded spirit of the west. I firmly believe in the ballot for women."[32]

Toward the end of October rumors heated up again about huge enticements dangled in front of Johnson by the Federals, Griffith dismissing them still on the grounds that the reserve clause held him to Washington. The Nationals seemed curiously passive about re-signing their star. But Ed Grillo, for one, was taking seriously the possibility of a defection. "There are going to be a lot of disappointed fans if Walter Johnson should jump to the Federal League," he wrote, hoping perhaps the column would make its way to Coffeyville. "Never before in the history of the game has a ballplayer been idolized as has Johnson. His reputation for honesty and his recognized modesty made him the most popular ballplayer in the game. It was his reputation as a man which made him the drawing card he has proved, as much as his ability as a pitcher. But his reputation among the patrons of baseball will be shattered if he takes the leap to the outlaws. No player ever received better treatment at the hands of the fans of his town than Johnson has here. He has been shown every consideration. While Johnson has always proved himself a good businessman in making his contracts, he has been fair and above board in his dealings, and it is hard to believe that he is apt to undergo any change of character."[33]

On October 29 Johnson took a train from Coffeyville to Fort Smith, Arkansas, for a three-day, three-game exhibition series between the "Arkansas

All-Stars" and "Johnson's Kansas All-Stars," teams made up of major- and minor-leaguers from those states. Riding with him was Fielder Jones, former outfielder-manager of the White Sox and now boss of the St. Louis Federals, who had called Johnson requesting a meeting. Jones made a firm offer of $20,000 a year for three years, $10,000 up front, but was told by the pitcher that he expected to re-sign with Washington for something less than that. While in Fort Smith Johnson was shown a news dispatch from Chicago in which Ban Johnson declared that the Nationals' star wouldn't sign away from Washington under any circumstances. "That's about as much sense as [Ban] Johnson usually displays," player Johnson responded testily.[34]

Johnson probably enjoyed his position for a time. It must have been refreshing to have leverage for once. But what he wanted now was a formal offer from the Nationals that he could sign and be done with the whole matter. One hadn't been forthcoming, though, and it is as difficult now as it must have been to him then to understand why they were willing to leave him to the attentions of the Federals for so long. All the bluster about the reserve clause didn't change its shaky legal foundation. Organized baseball's own lawyer had cautioned them not to take to the courts a case in which the jumper's contract had expired.[35] The behind-the-scenes maneuvering on both sides of the baseball war must have been tremendous at this stage, with much of it centered on Walter Johnson. The existing leagues had already felt the effects of competition on their salary structure, and knew that the Federals had to be feeling the weight of the jumpers' contracts in addition to the other problems of starting a new league. Organized baseball was on a death watch, looking anxiously for signs of the imminent demise of the upstart Federals and a return to its monopoly position over the players. There was no mystery about Walter Johnson's plan: use the Feds to extract a long-term deal at a sizable salary from Washington. Indeed, he had perhaps made his strategy too obvious with numerous statements affirming his desire and intention to stay with the Nationals.

With no communication from Washington, Johnson wrote Griffith on November 13 asking for $16,000 a year for three years, and a $6,000 bonus. There was no reply. He wrote again, and still there was no answer.[36] On the 23rd, Federal League President James Gilmore declared that his league was no longer going after high-priced stars but would concentrate on upgrading the general level of play instead. Walter Johnson was specifically mentioned as one of those in whom the Federals had no interest now. Several days later, Johnson finally heard from the Nationals. A letter from President Minor, dated November 28, contained an offer of one, two, or three years at $12,500, "stretching to the utmost our facilities for payment," Minor claimed. Johnson was informed that if the offer wasn't accepted the club would invoke the reserve clause in his old contract, obligating him to play for last year's salary of $12,000.[37] A few months later Johnson would offer an explanation for Minor's letter and his reaction to it.

"About this time there was a general rumor that the Federal League would go under," he said. "[Minor] thought I had no chance to play anywhere else, and that he had me where he could dictate terms. Now I don't mind saying that nobody ever had me where they could dictate terms, and I don't think they ever will. I can make a living if I never play any more baseball. It might be said that I ought to have been satisfied with $12,500, and that lots of people would have been glad to get that much money. I was myself, when I got it, but I had just turned down an offer for $20,000 and had a previous offer from Washington for $16,000 and a good hope of getting $18,000. So, in my situation, coming so suddenly and unexpectedly, the letter made me sore, and I resented it."[38] The letter was mild, though, compared to what Minor reportedly told Griffith, who was desperately trying to keep him from driving Johnson over to the Federals. "Johnson had a bad season this year," Minor said. "He only won 28 games. That doesn't warrant the $12,000 we're paying him now."[39]

The St. Louis Federals, meanwhile, had heard nothing from Johnson regarding their offer. After almost a month they wired him asking for a yes or no answer, but received no reply and decided to end all efforts to sign him. At the Federal League meeting in Chicago on November 28, Chifeds owner Charles Weeghman got the okay from his St. Louis counterpart, Phil Ball, to talk to Johnson. Weeghman contacted Johnson after Minor's letter and found him agreeable to talking to the Chifeds.[40] Joe Tinker was sent to Coffeyville, and on December 3, after only 20 minutes of discussion, Johnson signed a three-year contract with the Chifeds for $17,500 a year and a $6,000 bonus. Later in the day a letter arrived from Griffith telling Johnson not to worry about Minor, that the two of them could work things out and that Griffith was coming to Coffeyville to talk it over. Johnson said later that if he had received the letter before Tinker arrived, he would have put off signing until he had talked to Griffith. "But as things were," Johnson said, "they were settled, I thought, so far as I was concerned."[41]

As far as Clark Griffith was concerned, they were anything but settled. The news that Johnson had actually signed with the Feds came as a tremendous shock to him, having heard only recently from Clyde Milan that Johnson was ready to do business with the Nationals.[42] At first Griffith lashed out in anger, ironic in light of his own jump to the American League and his raids on National League teams 14 years earlier. "Nationals Manager Raves Wildly and Accuses Star Hurler of Avarice, Ingratitude and Other Things," headlined one report of Griffith's outburst:

Johnson tried to hold up the Washington ball club, and I wouldn't stand for it; that's about the whole story. The closer one gets with Johnson, the more he realizes his love of money. His ingratitude for all the kindness he had received from the Washington public and the ballclub has never been equalled in all my career in baseball. Way back last summer we could see that the fans were getting away from him. His popularity was waning fast. Indeed, I was surprised that he was such a poor drawing card during our last home stay. All those stories about his hobnobbing with the outlaws were turning his friends away from him. He never denied any of them and the fans ate them up. But he'll never be drawing for the Feds. He will never play a game with the outlaws.[43]

Johnson had violated the club's option on his services, Griffith told the Associated Press, and Washington would "sue him to the end of the earth." Ban Johnson added the ludicrous assertion that Johnson had lost his value to the Nationals anyway. "I was not surprised when I learned that Walter Johnson had jumped to the Federals," the league president claimed. "He is a great pitcher, but to the Washington club he was 'damaged goods.' The people of Washington had lost confidence in him, and had he remained in the American League he would have been traded by the Washington management to some other club."[44]

As soon as they had recovered from the initial jolt of the defection, however, the two veterans of the baseball wars set about dealing with it. Ban Johnson quickly arranged for Connie Mack to sell his biggest star, Eddie Collins, to the White Sox for a record $50,000 to counter Walter Johnson's gate appeal with the Chifeds. Despite the recent success of his Athletics, Mack was unwilling to try to hold his players in a salary war with the Federals, deciding instead to dismantle his team and get as much cash for the players as he could. He pulled in $180,000 that way, but Mack (and Philadelphia) paid a heavy price in baseball terms as the A's went from first in 1914 to last in 1915. For seven years they would remain in the American League cellar.[45]

Clark Griffith decided to take the opposite approach. He would fight. After conferring with Ban Johnson and Charles Comiskey at the major league meetings in New York on December 8, a flint-eyed Griffith emerged ready for battle. "The American League is going to make a fight for Walter Johnson," the *Times* reported the next day, greatly overstating the league's determination. It was Griffith, virtually alone and by the sheer force of his grit and cunning, who was going to bring Johnson back. He knew that without Johnson the Nationals, and his $27,000 investment in them—maybe even his future in the game—were all but finished. At a meeting of the team's board of directors, Griffith tried to make them understand that Johnson was the biggest single asset in all of baseball. He asked for approval to make a better offer, but the Minor faction wouldn't budge.[46] That would have ended the matter for most men, but Griffith refused to give up. He wired an old friend, Pittsburgh Pirates manager Fred Clarke, at his farm near Independence, Kansas, not far from Coffeyville. Griffith asked Clarke if he would visit Johnson and try to talk him away from the Federal League, then get Johnson to agree to meet with Griffith. Clarke thought there was little chance of the pitcher changing his mind, but agreed to try.

Johnson welcomed Clarke heartily into his home and introduced him to the rest of the family. They sat down by the fireside and chatted pleasantly, then Clarke explained the purpose of his visit. Johnson asked the family to excuse the two of them while they talked business, but the crafty Clarke wanted them to hear his plea, saying: "There is nothing we need to talk over in private." He then proceeded to remind Johnson of his obligation to Washington fans and to baseball, telling him there was only one right thing to do and it was up to him to do it. By the time he finished, according to Clarke, Johnson was in tears. A meeting with Griffith was arranged.[47]

On December 19 Johnson drove with Hazel to Kansas City to meet with Griffith at the Coates Hotel. The Nationals manager knew Johnson well enough not to get into an argument over the legal or financial specifics of the situation. Instead, his appeal was directed straight to the pitcher's heart. "Griffith showed me where I had not done right by him and the club," Johnson summarized the discussion a few months later. "He had invested all his money in trying to make Washington a winner. He told me my leaving wrecked his pitching staff and put the club that he hoped might be a pennant winner into the second division. He said that he didn't deserve any such treatment from me, as he had always done well by me."[48] A few days later Griffith would tell a gathering of fans that Johnson, tears in his eyes, said, "Griff, I never wanted to leave you or Washington."[49] Griffith convinced Johnson to accept Minor's offer of $12,500 for 1915, assuring him that he would do everything in his power to secure a long-term contract with a big raise after that. Griffith was true to his word, and the next year Johnson signed a five-year deal at $16,000 per year.[50]

But Griffith's problems weren't completely over yet. There was the matter of the $6,000 bonus from the Chifeds, which Johnson had given to his brother Leslie to buy a garage in Coffeyville. Without authority from the team, Griffith had agreed to cover repayment of the bonus. Shirley Povich (whose source presumably was Griffith himself) later reconstructed Griffith's finessing of the dilemma:

Telephoning the American League headquarters at Chicago, Griffith inquired for league president Ban Johnson. He learned that Johnson was taking the baths at West Baden, Indiana, with Charles Comiskey, owner of the White Sox.

"I need [$6,000] to retake Walter Johnson from the Federal League," Griff told Johnson.

"What do you want me to do about it?" asked Johnson.

"I want you to give it to me from the league funds," said Griffith.

"It can't be done," declared Johnson. Then Griff pointed out that the American League boasted of a $450,000 reserve fund which had always been used for such emergencies. But Johnson was adamant. The Washington club would have to fight its own battles, the league wouldn't help.

"Let me talk to Comiskey, then," Griff shouted. Getting Comiskey on the phone, Griff said, "I want [$6,000] from you."

"For what?"

"To pry Walter Johnson away from the Federal League."

"That's your problem, not mine," said Comiskey, laughing.

"Oh, no, it's your problem, too," said Griff.

"How do you figure that?"

"The Federal League is giving you some competition over there on the north side, isn't it, Commy?"

"Yes."

"Well, then, how would you like to have Walter Johnson playing for the Chifeds next season and drawing all those fans away from the White Sox?"

"Holy smokes!" said Comiskey, "How much did you say you wanted?"[51]

Thus, according to the story, the Old Fox pried $6,000 out of the miserly "Old Roman," the biggest tightwad in baseball.

Walter Johnson issued a brief statement, probably written by Griffith, announcing his jump back to the American League. The reserve clause, which there was little reason to fear if his decision had been to stay with the Chifeds, now served as a convenient excuse for his reneging on his Federal League contract. "After a conference with manager Griffith and legal authorities," Johnson declared, "I am convinced the option in my last year's contract was binding, and I am going to return to the Washington ball club and fulfill my agreement and at the terms offered me by that club."

It was the Federals' turn to fulminate over the turn of events. "If Johnson pitches for any team besides the Chicago Feds next season," Phil Ball said, "it will be in Leavenworth, Kansas, and his identity will be hidden behind a number."[52] Right up to the start of spring training the Federals were still issuing threats of legal action against Johnson if he played for Washington, but none was taken. Nor did dire warnings in the press that Johnson's "double flop" would ruin his reputation with the baseball public come true in the slightest. Johnson, in fact, had his defenders as well as detractors. "A year ago Johnson was offered a vaudeville contract calling for $15,000," wrote Grantland Rice in 1915. "There is no bunk about this. If he had been an entirely commercial soul he would have wrenched a kneecap jumping for this offer. But he turned it down without a quiver."[53]

Baseball Magazine (and its editor, F.C. Lane), which took pride in its independence from the baseball establishment, also helped Johnson's cause, covering the entire matter in great detail in the "Walter Johnson Issue" of April 1915. The Minor letter was reproduced in full, and Johnson himself was given ten pages to explain "Why I Signed With The Federal League" and, more importantly, why he flopped back to the Nationals. "Whichever way I turned I was wrong," Johnson wrote. "I didn't treat the Federal League right. I broke my contract with them. But I did so only because I was convinced that by not doing so I would be doing an even greater injury to Washington. It is a humiliating position to be in."

Above and Previous Page: Great Falls, Maryland, Spring 1914. It might have been on this outing that Johnson proposed to Hazel Lee Roberts.

Right: Hazel Johnson and Walter, Jr., 1916. "Heir is born to King of Pitchers" was the headline upon his birth.

Left: Three generations, c. 1917.

Below: Frank and Minnie Johnson's family at Coffeyville, Kansas, March, 1916: Blanche, Effie, Walter, Chester, Frank, Leslie, Minnie, and Earl.

Right: At the new house in Coffeyville, c. 1918, with Hazel's father, Congressman E.E. Roberts, grandmother Anna Roberts, Walter, Jr., and Eddie.

Below: With Walter, Jr., Eddie, and Elinor.

Above: May 19, 1917. (Boston Public Library)

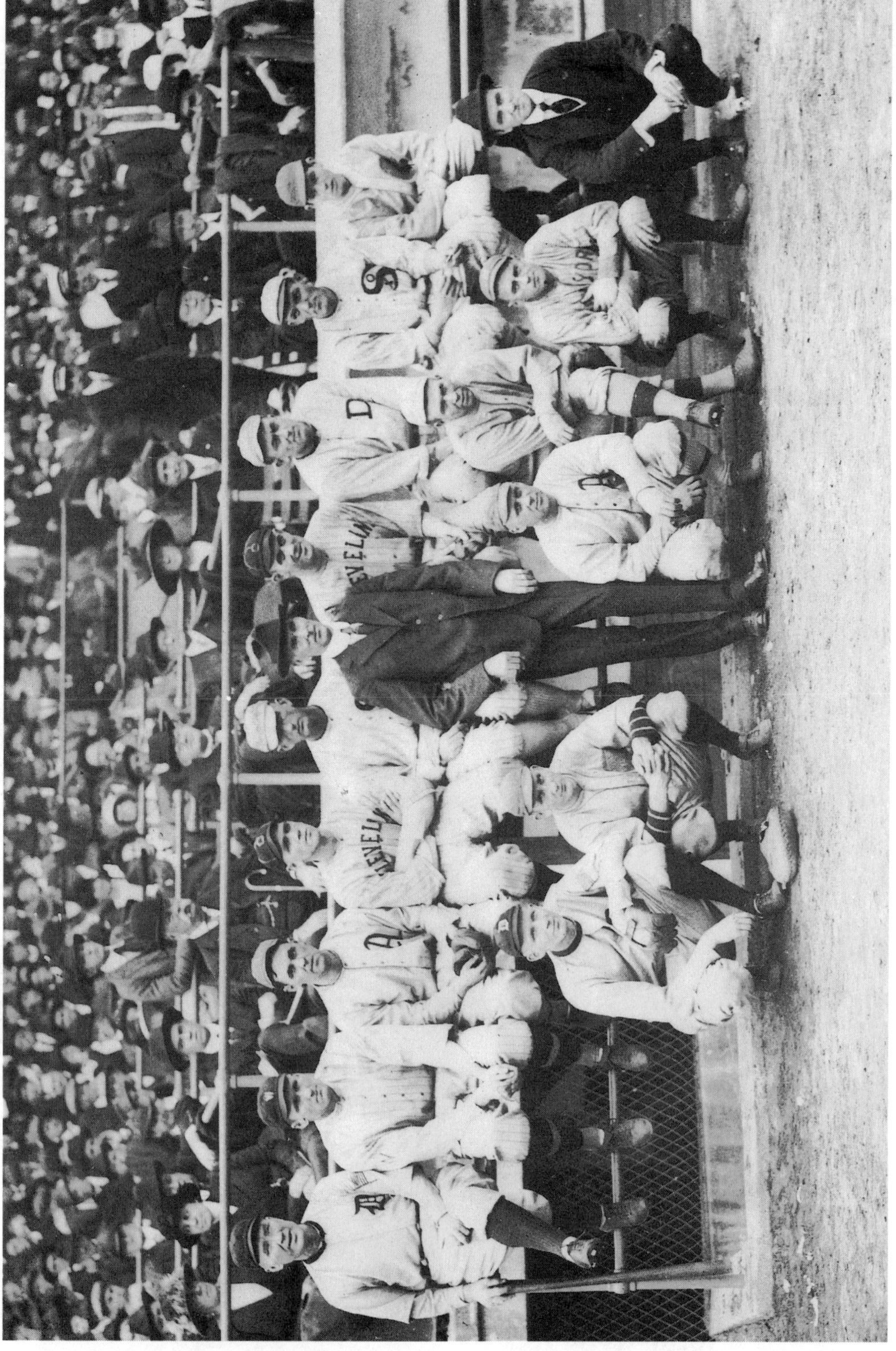

Opposite: Boston, September 27, 1917. American League All-Star team for game to benefit the family of sportswriter Tim Murnane. On rail: Hughie Jennings, Walter Johnson, Stuffy McInnis, Steve O'Neill, Joe Jackson, Ray Chapman, Ty Cobb, Buck Weaver.Kneeling: Howard Ehmke, Rabbit Maranville, Connie Mack, Wally Schang, Tris Speaker. This team was beaten 2–0 by young Red Sox lefthander Babe Ruth.

Above: Two generations of Johnson automobiles, c. 1912, and below, 1924.

Opposite Top: Walter, Jr., watching the game with President and Mrs. Harding on Opening Day, April 12, 1922. "That's a mighty fine boy you have there," the President told the proud father.

Opposite Bottom: With Harding and Washington manager Donie Bush at brand-new Yankee Stadium, April 22, 1923. The President wouldn't live out the summer.

Above: With father-in-law E.E. Roberts and The Reverend Brewster Adams.

Above: Mayor Roberts in his office on Virginia Street, Reno, Nevada. As a lawyer specializing in divorce cases, he won over 2,000 of them—and lost only one. "My client lied to me," Roberts explained. "The chump didn't tell me that he had another wife living, and I didn't find out until she showed up in court."

Opposite: Ty Cobb's career covered the entire 21 years of Johnson's, during which Cobb spent a full two-thirds of a season, 368 at-bats, facing him. He had a tough time of it until seeing Johnson fall apart after beaning Ossie Vitt in 1915, after which Cobb turned Johnson's fearing of killing a batter into the edge he needed. Johnson, who never had an enemy in baseball, was probably the closest thing to a friend Cobb had in the game.

W
D

Above: Children's Hospital, San Francisco, California, January, 1923.

Right: Newark, 1928.

Opposite Top: Nick Altrock entertaining Milan, Johnson, and trainer Mike Martin, 1922. "[Johnson] had those long arms," Detroit outfielder Davy Jones told writer Lawrence Ritter, "absolutely the longest arms I ever saw. They were like whips, that's what they were. He'd just whip that ball in there."

Above: Al Schacht and Altrock mugging for the camera. Their comedy routines made them famous from ballparks to vaudeville, but the two didn't speak to each other for years.

Opposite Top: With Bucky Harris. "I never saw a competitive spirit the equal of his, not even Cobb's," recalled Clark Griffith. "He was the gamest ballplayer I ever saw in 50 years of baseball."

Opposite Bottom: With Muddy Ruel. Johnson had several fine catchers during his career, but considered Ruel the best.

Above: 1924 Washington infield: Ossie Bluege, Roger Peckinpaugh, Bucky Harris, and Joe Judge. Doubleplays were a specialty—"When the ball is hit their way, everybody is out," Clark Griffith said of them.

Above: The pitching staff. Standing: Tom Zachary, Walter Johnson, George Mogridge, and Fred Marberry. Kneeling: Curly Ogden, Paul Zahniser, Byron Speece, and Joe Martina.

Right: The outfield: Earl McNeely, Nemo Leibold, Sam Rice, and Goose Goslin. Rice's speed and .322 lifetime average and Goslin's power and .316 took them both to the Hall of Fame.

CHAPTER 9

The Big Train

Clyde Milan once told me of an exhibition game the Senators played against the Braves. Johnny Evers, a cocky little cuss, doubled off Walter in his first time at bat. When the inning ended and Milan trotted past second base, Evers refused to keep his big trap shut.

"So that's the great Walter Johnson," he said to Milan. "Listen, we got a half dozen pitchers in our league who are faster than he is."

Milan sat alongside Johnson. "Walter," he said, "Evers just told me that there were half a dozen pitchers in his league faster than you are." But Johnson never said a word. A few innings later Evers came to bat again. Walter threw him three pitches and Johnny hasn't seen any of them yet. Evers was still pale and shaking when he met Milan at the inning's end.

"You big blabbermouth," he screamed. "You told Johnson what I said, didn't you?"[1]

STEVE O'NEILL

Walter Johnson walked into the Washington training camp at Charlottesville on March 8, ending all doubt about where he would be pitching in 1915. Clark Griffith and the other Nationals, worried since the day before when Johnson hadn't come in on the train as expected, didn't try to hide their elation. After all that had happened, to see Johnson in person was a tremendous relief to the team. The Federal League was still threatening legal action if he didn't report to the Chifeds (the "Whales" now), and Joe Tinker expressed confidence that Johnson would show up there. But Tinker knew Johnson well enough to realize that a hard approach to the matter had no chance at all, and took a conciliatory stance instead. "I think [Johnson] is the greatest young fellow in the country," Tinker told the press. "If he never comes anywhere near my ballclub and never speaks to me again, I'll still say that. Moreover, if he wants to he can come back to me tomorrow."[2] They would be expecting him at the Chifeds' camp, Tinker simply said in a letter to Johnson.[3]

In addition to creating momentary unease in the Nationals' camp, Johnson's late arrival became the inspiration for the nickname with which he would be most famously associated. "A storm prevented the 'Big Train' from reaching these parts on time," wrote T. Stanley "Bud" Milliken of the *Post* in the first use of this moniker.[4] Two weeks later Milliken applied it again, this time without the double meaning: "The 'big train' would not have been scored on but for an error," he wrote.[5] By the next year Milliken had the expression capitalized and without quotation marks: "The way the Big Train looked yesterday. . . . ," the form in which it was eventually picked up by other writers.[6] Curiously, it wasn't until the early 1920s, more than five years later, that the nickname would come into common usage.

The question of how Johnson would be received by Washington fans was answered even before the April 14 season-opener got underway. Raucous applause greeted his emergence onto the field to warm up. "The fans seemed determined to let the pitching king know they were more than happy to have him back," the *Post* reported, "and as the game progressed and the big fellow demonstrated that he is due for another big year, his popularity became more and more striking." It was a masterful performance indeed, a 7–0 two-hitter over the Yankees that was witnessed by President Wilson, Secretary of State William Jennings Bryan, and other cabinet members and assorted dignitaries.

1915 was a year of significant change in the American League, highlighted by the stunning decline of the Athletics and the emergence of the Red Sox as the dominant power. Rookie Babe Ruth was a pillar of the brilliant Boston pitching staff, winning 18 games, one of those a 4–3 victory over Walter Johnson in their first matchup on August 14. Ruth also went 2 for 3, drove in a run and scored the winner, a harbinger of things to come from the gifted youngster. Another Red Sox rookie pitching sensation, hard-throwing submariner Carl Mays, lost his debut to Johnson on April 19, 4–2, before moving to the bullpen for the rest of the year as the club's standout reliever.

Also making his entrance onto the major-league stage that year was George Sisler, who joined the St. Louis Browns after graduating from the University of Michigan. Sisler was the losing pitcher, 5–1, on Walter Johnson's eighth anniversary with the Nationals on August 2, but came back to beat Johnson—his boyhood idol—2–1 on the 29th.[7] The *Post* called Sisler "a baseball freak. Manager [Branch] Rickey does not know what to do with the Michigan boy. He plays him in the outfield and he makes sensational catches and throws out runners moving around the sacks. He plays him on first base, and he looks like Chase when Hal was the king of first sackers, and then on the hill he goes out and beats Johnson." Johnson was a 1–0 winner in the last mound decision of Sisler's career, on September 17, 1916, although "Gorgeous George" was already on his way to becoming one of the game's great first basemen. Also debuting in St. Louis in 1915 was 19-year-old Rogers Hornsby of the Cardinals, destined to be the premier hitter in National League history. Between them, Sisler and Hornsby would hit better than .400 five times.

The Nationals added two terrific young players of their own, Sam Rice and Joe Judge, both of whom were to loom large in the team's future. They would be teammates at Washington for a record 18 seasons, breaking a mark set by Johnson and Milan.[8] Edgar "Sam" Rice became the greatest hitter in franchise history, but like Ruth and Sisler started his big-league career as a pitcher. He was 25 years old when he joined Washington, a late start for which there was an astonishing explanation that wouldn't surface for 70 years. In April, 1912, Rice went to try out for the Galesburg, Illinois, Central Association League team, leaving his wife and two small children at home in Indiana. A few days later they went to visit his parents at their farm near Morocco, Indiana, and one evening a devastating tornado hit the farm, killing all of them. Rice's wife, children, parents, and sisters were gone in one blow.[9]

His world shattered, Edgar Rice became a drifter, working odd jobs in various parts of the country until joining the Navy in 1913. On the battleship USS *New Hampshire* he became the star pitcher of the ship's baseball team, pitching three games in three days in a losing effort in the Navy championships at Annapolis. In 1914 the *New Hampshire* was dispatched to Mexico in the U.S. effort to quell the uprising that followed the assassination of President Madero, and Rice was among the troops going ashore at Vera Cruz. "Bullets were flying all over the place," he recalled later. When the ship returned to its home berth at Portsmouth, Virginia, Rice pitched for Petersburg in the Virginia League during furloughs.[10] He did so well that the owner of the team bought him out of the Navy, and when the Virginia League went under in 1915 Rice was sent to the Nationals to pay a debt the Petersburg owner owed Clark Griffith.[11]

Rice made his big-league debut on August 7, 1915, relieving starter Jim Shaw in a 6–2 loss to Chicago. Backing him up that day in right field, where Rice was to star for so many years, was Walter Johnson, filling in for the injured Danny Moeller. Rice appeared on the mound only nine times before giving up the idea of a pitching career. The breaking point reportedly came in Detroit when Tigers pitcher Hooks Dauss tripled home the winning runs. Returning to the dugout, a disgusted Rice tore the toeplate from his shoe.

"That's enough," he declared. "If that guy can hit me for a triple, I'm no pitcher."[12]

Perhaps not, but in Griffith's opinion Rice did become "the best all-around ballplayer we ever had."[13] A lifetime .322 hitter, Rice had more than 200 hits in six seasons, and despite the late start ended his career just 13 hits shy of 3,000. With his level swing producing screaming line drives, Rice didn't get the loft necessary for home runs, hitting only 34 in 20 years. (In 19 years playing in Washington, Rice never hit a ball over the fence. All nine of his home runs there were inside-the-park.)[14] But he had plenty of doubles and triples, and still holds several records for singles. He was one of the hardest men to strike out in the history of the game. Dubbed "Man O' War" after the famous racehorse of the time, Rice was a prolific base-stealer with tremendous range in the outfield, known for his spectacular running catches. As for the name "Sam," a Griffith memory lapse was responsible for that. Calling a local paper with the news of his latest acquisition, Griffith was asked the recruit's first name. "It's Sam, I think," he muttered.[15]

Joe Judge grew up in a tough section of New York City, the son of Irish immigrants. Dropping out of school after the eighth grade, he was making money playing semipro baseball in Brooklyn by the age of sixteen. In 1915 Griffith went to Rochester to look at Charlie Jamieson, an outfielder with the International League Buffalo Bison, but it was the first baseman, Judge, who got Griffith's heart pounding. The Old Fox talked Buffalo into throwing him into the Jamieson deal for an extra $500.[16] "It took only a few minutes for me to get a line on this player," he told the *Post* upon his return. "He can hit with the best of them. Judge is a natural ballplayer." Griffith declared Judge a better first baseman than Hal Chase when Chase first reported to Griffith's Highlanders in 1905—high praise indeed, as "Prince Hal" was generally regarded the finest first sacker in the game.[17]

As usual, Griffith's assessment was on the money. Judge averaged just below .300 in a 20-year career, topping that mark in nine seasons. Considered by his peers the equal of Chase and Sisler at first base, he set a number of American League fielding records, and his incredible lifetime fielding percentage of .993 was the major-league standard for more than 30 years. Judge was small for the position, standing only 5 feet 8 inches, but had great stretching ability and was deadly at the 3–6–3 doubleplay. "A genius around that bag," was how teammate Ossie Bluege, himself one of the finest infielders ever, described Judge's play at first base.[18] Judge got into a mere dozen games before the season ended, but Griffith knew he had found a replacement for the talented but increasingly unreliable Chick Gandil, who was sold to Cleveland over the winter.

At the same time those young stars were coming onto the scene, some of the early greats were fading from it. Such legendary names as Lajoie, Walsh, Mathewson, Wagner, Crawford, Plank, and Bender would soon be gone from the box scores. But the American League still had a handful of its all-time greatest players in the prime of their fabulous careers: Johnson, Cobb, Speaker, Jackson, Collins, and Baker. These names resonate down through the ages, but in 1915 they were fixtures at ballparks around the circuit. For 21 seasons fans in any American League city could see Walter Johnson and Ty Cobb in action several times a year. Those two faced each other more than any other pitcher and batter in American League history, and over the course of his career Cobb spent an amazing two-thirds of a season, 368 appearances, against Johnson alone.

In their first eight seasons battling each other, Johnson dominated "the Georgia Peach," the American League batting champion in every one of those years. In 131 at-bats Cobb had 36 hits (six for extra bases) for a .275 average. In the seasons of 1913–14 Johnson's mastery of Cobb was virtually complete, the fiery Georgian managing only three hits in 26 trips to the plate. Johnson had learned in his first game in the major leagues what could happen when Cobb got on base. "I always gave him everything I had, plus a little I kept in reserve for the good hitters," Johnson said later. "Not a soft pitch did Ty ever get from me. I always believed that if you could keep Cobb off the bases, you could keep out of a lot of trouble."[19] A steady diet of chest-high fastballs, difficult for Cobb to bunt or place-hit, did the trick early on.[20] Billy Evans recalled Cobb grumbling as he stepped in to hit, "Watch the big Swede go into high as I come up."[21] Asked one time to describe his most embarrassing experience in baseball, Cobb answered, "Washington on any dark afternoon with Walter Johnson pitching."[22]

For a time Cobb was upset with Johnson, convinced that the pitcher had favored Joe Jackson during one of their epic battles for the hitting title.[23] (In his peak seasons of 1911–13, Jackson was indeed a tough out for Johnson, hitting .346 with great power. But from 1914–20 he became much easier, hitting .256 with few extra-base hits. His career average against Johnson was .270.) It also galled Cobb that teammate Sam Crawford enjoyed great success facing Johnson. (From 1907–12, Crawford hit .408 against him, with power.) Many years later, Crawford offered an explanation:

> One thing that really used to get Ty's goat was when I'd have a good day and he didn't. Oh, would he ever moan then. Walter Johnson and I were very good friends, and once in a while Walter would sort of "give" me a hit or two, just for old times sake. But when Ty came up there, Walter always bore down all the harder. There was nothing

he enjoyed more than fanning Ty Cobb. You see, Walter liked my model bat. Somehow he got the idea that my bats were lucky for him. So very often when the Senators came to Detroit Walter would come into our clubhouse and quietly ask me if I could spare a bat for him. "Sure, Walter," I'd say, "go and take any one you want." He'd go over to my locker, look them over, pick one out, and quietly leave. Well, whenever the occasion arose when it wouldn't affect a game, Walter would let up a bit on me and I'd have a picnic at the plate—like, if Washington had a good lead and it was late in the game. I'd come up to bat and Gabby Street, Walter's catcher, would whisper, "Walter likes you today, Sam." That was the cue that the next pitch would be a nice half-speed fast ball. So I'd dig in and belt it. Of course, if it was a close game all that was out the window. The friendship deal was off then. Cobb never did figure out why I did so well against Walter, while he couldn't hit him with a ten-foot pole.[24]

That situation changed dramatically on August 10, 1915. Pitching at home against Detroit, Johnson hit Tiger third baseman Ossie Vitt in the forehead with a curveball. Vitt fell, unmoving, and didn't open his eyes for several minutes. Johnson rushed in and stood over him at the plate, his face white as a sheet.[25] "The world stopped moving for awhile when that ball connected with my cranium," Vitt remembered. "Johnson thought I was killed and I guess I thought so myself so far as I was able to think at all."[26] Vitt had to leave the game, incurring only a slight concussion and severe headache. "It is a good thing that the ball was a curve instead of a fast one," commented the *Post,* "or there might be a real sad story to tell." For the rest of his life Vitt bragged about how he took a Walter Johnson pitch in the head and lived to tell about it.[27]

Shaken by the incident, Johnson became ineffective. As Milliken of the *Post* put it the next day, "When Walter Johnson hits a batter, both are usually through for the day." The game turned into his worst outing of the season by far, giving up four runs in that first inning and four more over the next five frames before being relieved by Rice. Watching all of this with keen interest was Ty Cobb. As Johnson fell apart after the beaning, Cobb realized that here was the edge he had been looking for.

"[Johnson] was so frightened of his own speed—the fact that he'd almost killed Vitt—that he had to take himself out of the game," Cobb recalled. "Well, wasn't that provocative. I thought about it, and realized that Johnson was so nice a guy that he never dusted off a batter. He had pinpoint control, along with his speed, and took good care not to split anyone's skull. Very considerate of him. And yet a weakness that could be exploited. Gradually, I began to crowd the plate on Johnson. From 10 inches or so back of the plate, I moved in until at last I was standing right against it, and even out over the plate with my bent knees and arms. With the plate tucked in under me, I was giving Johnson only a few inches of target. It was cheating, if you will, but also strategy. I was gambling that Johnson would be so afraid of hitting me that he'd work to the outside corner, and that he did. Now, Johnson wouldn't be wide of the plate by much—he had such great control. But he'd miss the corner a fraction, get behind in the count, two balls and no strikes, and that's when I'd resume my regular stance and whack the cripple that had to come down the middle. I'd never in a million years expected to dominate Walter Johnson, and yet in a way that's what happened."[28]

Who else but Cobb, after seeing a teammate nearly killed by a Johnson pitch, would move closer to the plate? "I had to do something to get base hits against Johnson," he told Shirley Povich in 1940, "he was making it too tough for me."[29] The strategy worked so well that it completely reversed the situation between the two. In seven prior seasons, Cobb hit better than .222 only once against Johnson. But for the years 1915–26 his worst year was .276 as he averaged .435 against Johnson during that time. Overall, Cobb finished with a .370 average facing Johnson, three points higher than his career figure.[30]

Despite their intense rivalry on the ballfield and disparate temperaments, the two baseball titans got along well personally. "We were friends at all times—on the diamond or across a poker table," Cobb remembered,[31] a sentiment expressed also by Johnson. "In 18 years, I have never had an unfriendly word with Cobb. I consider him one of my best friends. Even when I landed from the wilds of Idaho, a raw and frightened kid, Cobb treated me right." They both liked to tell the story of a run-in with the law they had together. Johnson wrote in 1924:

> We were playing a series in Detroit some years ago and Ty asked me to take a spin in his new automobile. Driving out over the Grand Boulevard, the temptation to speed was strong and Cobb stepped on the gas. A motor cop soon flagged us and filled out one of those unwelcome invitations to meet the traffic judge. Cobb took it like a good sport and just as we were starting up, yelled at the officer "Here, you were pretty decent about it, even if you did give us a ticket. Take these," and he handed the officer two tickets for that day's game. Thus surprised and embarrassed, the policeman said that on second thought, he would tear up the court summons. "You go out there and knock two home runs this afternoon and we'll call it square," was his final warning.
>
> When the game started, I saw the motor cop sitting in a grandstand box, apparently with his best girl. Along about the sixth inning, Washington was ahead and I hollered to Cobb: "That cop's up there waiting for those home runs. Better hurry or he'll pinch you again." Cobb came through all right and drove the ball out of the park in the seventh inning. When he came up again in the ninth he looked over toward

me and pointed toward the traffic officer. Then he shouted, so everybody in the grandstand heard: "If I don't get another one, you can phone for the wagon." No one but the cop and myself appreciated Ty's remark, but just the same, he caught hold of the first ball pitched and planted it up in the right field bleachers for his second home run of the day.[32]

Johnson must have seen his share of Cobb's notorious darker side, of course. He was the winning pitcher in a game on September 24, 1921, that led to a famous fight in the dressing room at Griffith Stadium between Cobb and umpire Billy Evans, an altercation Johnson tried to prevent, according to Cobb's "as told to" biographer, Al Stump.[33] On another occasion Johnson was having dinner (along with Clark Griffith) at Cobb's house in Detroit in June 1914, when the host rushed off from the table to physically settle a dispute with a butcher.[34] Nevertheless, Johnson insisted that the fiery Georgian was largely misunderstood by the public, that he was a hard fighter but a clean one. "He was always willing to fight to win," Johnson said, "but I don't believe Cobb ever picked a fight just for the sake of a row. Leave him alone and treat him right and he is all you expect to find in a well-mannered Southern gentleman. But start something unfair and you'll get a fight—whether you're a ballplayer or a taxicab driver! It didn't take me long to size him up as a hot-headed young fellow who didn't mean half the things he said."

Nor did Cobb ever go into a base with the intention to do harm, according to Johnson. "The rules of baseball say that the runner has the right-of-way going to a base and Cobb demanded that right in its fullest sense," he said.[35] Agreeing with that assessment was George McBride, who as a long-time American League shortstop and then a coach for Cobb at Detroit would know better than most. "Some say he was a dirty ballplayer," McBride said years later, "but I say he was a good, hard ballplayer. There are some players who didn't like him, but you know he was a ballplayer's ballplayer. I never had any trouble with Cobb and those spikes of his."[36] Despite their base-stealing rivalry, Clyde Milan was also friendly with Cobb, the two Southerners often getting together to talk hunting.[37]

The high point of the 1915 season for Walter Johnson came on July 1, but it had nothing to do with baseball. Hazel gave birth to Walter Johnson, Jr. that morning, after Senior had taken the midnight train from New York. "Heir is Born to King of Pitchers," heralded the *Post.* The Milans had a daughter, which drew the two new mothers even closer. "Hazel and I were so happy together with our first babies," Margaret Milan recalled.[38]

The baseball news that year wasn't as happy, despite a surge in the last two months of the season that gave the Nationals a creditable 85 wins against

68 losses. Although several games better than 1914, it was good enough only for fourth place behind the Red Sox, Tigers, and White Sox. For the first time in four years the team at no point in the season threatened for the top. A finish of seven straight wins helped Johnson to a fine record of 27 wins and 13 losses, the league leader in wins, starts (39), complete games (35), innings (337), strikeouts (203), shutouts (7), and fewest walks-per-game. His problems this year came almost entirely on the road, the home mark of 17–2 a career best. One of the oddest events of the season came in the second inning of an 8–1 win at Detroit on August 22. The Nationals managed to score a run without an official at-bat in the inning—the only time that's ever been done in the major leagues. Chick Gandil and Merito Acosta walked and moved up on Rip Williams's sacrifice bunt; McBride's sacrifice fly scored Gandil, and Acosta was picked off second.

Casey Stengel tells a story about his first and only appearance at bat against the "fireball king" in an exhibition game one Fall. "I walked up to the plate," said Casey, "and stood ready with my trusty bludgeon. Johnson made a pitching motion, the ump called a strike and I stood there. The same thing happened on strike two. When Walter cocked his arm again, I threw my bat down and went back to the bench."

"Come back here, you blind fathead," the ump yelled. "He threw that last ball to first base."

"That's all right" I yelled from the bench. "I didn't see the other two either."[39]

AL DEMAREE

Ray Chapman was the hitter for the Cleveland Indians on a day in 1915. First one, then another blurred streak of white hissed past Chapman's cocked but motionless bat and pounded into the mitt of catcher Eddie Ainsmith.

"Strike two," intoned umpire Billy Evans. Suddenly, Chapman tossed the bat away and started toward the Cleveland bench.

"That's only strike two," yelled Evans. Chapman didn't even break stride as he said to Evans over his shoulder,

"I know it. You can have the next one. It won't do me any good."[40]

SHIRLEY POVICH

Although still at the top of his game, for the next two years of 1916–17 Walter Johnson no longer stood alone, unchallenged, as the best pitcher in the American League. Joining him now in the top echelon of hurlers was the precocious Boston left-hander, Babe Ruth, as he followed an impressive 18-win rookie year with a 1916 record of 23 wins against 12 losses, leading the league in earned run average, starts, and shutouts (nine, still the American League record for lefties). The next season brought 24 victories and a league-best 35 complete games, and Ruth's mastery over Johnson in their direct matchups was even more striking. He was the victor in the first six games in which they both took decisions, three of them 1–0 duels (including a 13-inning epic), one 2–1, and another 4–3. Ruth came within one out of a fourth 1–0 win but the Nationals rallied, he was relieved, and Johnson took a ten-inning, 4–3 victory. On October 3, 1917, in his last game of the season, Johnson finally defeated Ruth 6–0, providing much of his own support with a bases-loaded double.

The Nationals' fortunes continued to decline, meanwhile. In 1916, despite finishing just shy of .500 and only 14½ games behind the repeating champion Red Sox, they slipped to seventh place, an astonishing 40 games ahead of Philadelphia with its egregious 36–117 record. Johnson won 25 games—his seventh straight season with 25 or more victories—but also lost 20 for the second time in his career. Thirteen defeats came by one run, four of them 1–0 heartbreakers. His 1.90 earned run average placed third in the league, and he was the leader in wins, complete games (36), strikeouts (228), and innings (370). 1916 was one of three seasons in which Johnson didn't give up a home run, and it is still the record for most innings pitched without allowing one. The Nationals' hitting was even worse than usual, their .242 average the lowest in the league.

An exhibition in Kansas City on November 29 gave Johnson his first opportunity to pitch a full game against his National League counterpart, Grover Cleveland Alexander. Like Johnson, Pete Alexander threw sidearm with great control. He didn't have the Washington ace's overwhelming speed, but mixed a good fastball with an effective curve, a master at keeping the ball low in the strike zone.[41] 1916 was the second of three straight 30-win seasons for Alexander, and his 16 shutouts that year is still the record. The "Johnsons" vs. "Alexanders" game at Kansas City consisted entirely of professional players, including the great Brooklyn outfielder Zack Wheat for the Johnsons and Hal Chase, Casey Stengel, and Max Carey, the Pirates' base-stealing champion, for the Alexanders. As might have been predicted it was a pitchers' duel, the Johnsons eking out a 3–2 victory.

Like everything else in America, baseball went into 1917 in the shadow of war. Until then the three years of bloody conflict devastating Europe had made little impact on the United States, but the sinking of American vessels by German submarines precipitated a declaration of war on April 6. "The world must be made safe for democracy," said President Wilson. A "military census" was instituted requiring adult males to register with draft boards, and single men between 21 and 30 years old whose numbers were picked early in the draft lottery would soon be in uniform. The potential impact on baseball was enormous, including the possibility of a complete shutdown, so the game was careful to appear patriotic and supportive of the war effort. Ban Johnson set up a program for teams to receive instruction in military drill from Army sergeants throughout the season, culminating with a competition for cash prizes in August. As it turned out, baseball had little to fear in 1917. Only one name player, Braves catcher Hank Gowdy, switched to a military uniform, and his enlistment was voluntary. Gowdy fought in the trenches and returned a much-decorated war hero.[42]

At the Nationals' home opener on April 21, the flags of England and France flew over the grandstand of American League Park in a display of the game's solidarity with America's new allies, and the Nationals staged an infantry drill on the field before the game, hoisting bats instead of rifles. Assistant Secretary of the Navy Franklin D. Roosevelt led them and a marching band "in more or less military cadence" to the flagpole in center field for the flag-raising. President Wilson, who had presided at Washington's home opener three times in four years, was absent "because of the pressures of state affairs." Vice President Thomas Marshall officiated and saw the Nationals, with Walter Johnson on the mound, crush the Athletics, 11–6. Johnson had opened the Nationals' season in Philadelphia 10 days earlier with a more artistic 3–0 whitewash of the hapless A's.

The team improved two places in the standings to fifth in 1917. Johnson got off to his worst start in years, his 7–13 record at midseason mirroring a woeful first half for the team. But from that point he went a sparkling 16–3, including a nine-game winning streak in less than a month (July 24–August 22), to help the Nationals pull to within five games of .500 by season's end. Sam Rice was their first .300 hitter in four years at .302 in his first full season. The team moved up to seventh in the league in batting, and hit only *four* home runs on the year.

If the 1917 race was a washout for Washington pennant hopes, the season didn't lack for notable events. In the first game of a doubleheader in Boston on June 23, Babe Ruth walked leadoff hitter Ray Morgan. When Ruth stormed down from the mound to argue the call, umpire Brick Owens warned him to go back or risk being tossed from the game. "If you chase me, I'll punch your face," Ruth declared, whereupon Owens retorted, "You're through now," and waved him off the field. Ruth rushed Owens and landed a glancing punch to the umpire's ear. Owens balled his fist to retaliate, but held his temper as Ruth made a retreat to the bench. "Brick has the reputation of being able to lick his weight in wildcats, and had he mixed with Ruth there is little question but what the pitcher would have come in second," the *Post* declared.[43] But that was just a preliminary to the main event as Ernie Shore, coming in to pitch for Boston without notice, picked off Morgan and then retired the next 26 Nationals in order.

On August 6, four days after his 10th anniversary with Washington, Johnson pitched his best game of the year, an 11-inning, 1–0 thriller over 41-year-old veteran Eddie Plank and the Browns. It was to be the last game of Plank's brilliant career, which had begun with the American League in 1901. Ironically, Johnson would go on to break Plank's league career records in virtually every category. Though clearly still effective, Plank would retire officially a week later, citing stomach problems. In reality, the decision was precipitated by his disgust with the Browns, who, despite the addition of George Sisler, had nearly wrested last place from the awful A's. (Plank's 1.79 earned run average earned him a 5–6 record.) It appears that Plank knew it was his last game, for in spite of the tight contest in which they were engaged, "Plank and Johnson had plenty of fun kidding each other," the *Post* reported. "Zeb Milan and the Brown twirler also engaged in some friendly repartee."

Johnson played in his last great "All-Star" game on September 27 at Fenway Park, an exhibition to benefit the family of late Boston sportswriter Tim Murnane. Babe Ruth and Rube Foster combined for a 2–0 Red Sox victory over Connie Mack's American League aggregation of Cobb, Jackson, and Speaker in the outfield, along with Buck Weaver, Rabbit Maranville, Ray Chapman, Stuffy McInnis, and Steve O'Neill. Urban Shocker and Howard Ehmke held Boston scoreless for the first six innings before Duffy Lewis drove in the winning runs off Johnson in the eighth. A crowd of 17,000 raised $13,000 for the cause and was treated in return to a spectacular show. Will Rogers performed his famous "rope work and other range stunts," one of them a 30-foot loop around both teams. Female members of the Ziegfeld Follies, including legendary songstress Fanny Brice, sold scorecards, and former heavyweight champion John L. Sullivan was in the coaching box for the Red Sox. Babe Ruth won a fungo-hitting contest at 402 feet (Johnson was third at 360), and Joe Jackson took the throwing prize with a toss of 396 feet.[44]

The second and last matchup between Walter Johnson and Grover Cleveland Alexander took place on November 21 in Kansas City. Johnson had the Wheat brothers, Zack and Mack, and George Sisler and Del Pratt of the Browns, while Alexander's lineup included Carey, Chase, Stengel, and 21-

year-old Rogers Hornsby. After eight innings Johnson hadn't allowed a man to reach second base for a 3–0 lead. Two singles opened the ninth before Carey struck out, but the ball got away from catcher Mack Wheat and the runners moved up. Stengel singled them in, and up came Hornsby, who had struck out twice. What happened next was still vivid in Hornsby's mind 45 years later: "Johnson had two strikes on me. He threw me a real fast ball and I knocked it straight for the fence. The ball hit the Bull Durham sign and happened to hit on a knot. The ball knocked out the knot and went through the fence for a home run and we won, 4–3. The hole, I admit, was one of the biggest cases of pure luck I ever heard of. I'm convinced he absolutely had the best fastball of anyone who ever played baseball."[45]

By now Walter, Jr. had a brother, Edwin Roberts Johnson, born in September 1917, and the apartments the family had lived in were no longer adequate for the growing brood. They bought their first house in Washington, a spacious stone and brick four-bedroom townhouse on a hillside overlooking the wild and beautiful Rock Creek Park. The most distinctive feature of the location was the roar of the lions at the National Zoo a short distance across the park.

Johnson also bought a parcel of land a mile outside of Coffeyville on which they had an off-season home built. In the last several years he had developed a passion for hunting during the off-season, especially for raccoons and coyotes, which were considered pests by farmers in the area. Soon the family was sharing their domicile with a motley assortment of hunting dogs, and when they were looking for a name for the place, someone suggested "The Home For Ancient and Crippled Hounds." "Some of them have been wished on me," Johnson explained, "some I have bought, some I have borrowed, and the rest have just strayed in." He even kept a greyhound for chasing jackrabbits on the open plains of nearby Oklahoma. But it was going after the elusive coon that provided the most excitement. "The finest sport in the world," Johnson declared it, providing a vivid description of the adventure:

> There are usually four or five in our crowd when we start off for a hunt. We drive in a machine, with the dogs, lanterns, axes, etc., all piled in, about 15 miles down in Oklahoma where we follow along the Verdigris River. We leave the car along the road somewhere and turn the hounds loose, and generally they hit a trail before long. Sometimes it proves to be an opossum and once in a while a house cat, but we know the difference in the way they trail. But the opossum is a stupid animal and easily caught, and doesn't put up a fight at all, whereas a coon is just the opposite. They are the smartest wild animal that I ever saw, and are the gamest fighters, too. Believe

me, they can give the dogs a chase. We have run them all night long, only to have them lick the dogs and escape. It is worth running all night to see the fight. No one but a coon hunter can appreciate what great sport it is, to follow the constant yelp of the hounds on a hot trail through the woods, across streams, and then hear the dogs bark "treed." The bark of a hound when trailing, and when he trees his object, is entirely different, and easily distinguished. But the best time of all is after the hunt, when we build a big bonfire and sit around and get warm, and eat our lunch. My wife is always afraid that we will get lost in the woods or have a breakdown, and she sends along enough lunch to last us several days. Sometimes we lie down and sleep till daylight, when we start home.

One such expedition in February, 1917, nearly cost Johnson his life:

We had been having very cold weather, and the first warm night we went off on a hunt, as the coons always come out after a cold spell looking for food. The river was apparently frozen solid and we were on a hot trail and were crossing on the ice. I was in the middle of the river when the ice gave way without any warning and under I went, my lantern with me, and it was pitch dark. The water was over my head and I had a good stiff fight getting out as the ice kept breaking away as soon as I bore the weight of my arms on it. I had about decided that my coon hunting days were over when my brother-in-law (Effie's husband, Russell Tongier), who was the only member of our party that crossed with me, managed to get a limb of a tree to me, and by using it I got out, numbed to the bone and a little wiser about crossing rivers.[46]

CHAPTER 10

Sir Walter

How do they know what Johnson's got?
Whether he used a curve or not?
Whether his break is set?
How can they tell how his outshoots fall?
Whether his incurve's big or small?
How can they tell what he's got on the ball?
Nobody's seen it yet.

GRANTLAND RICE

The first year of America's direct involvement in the Great War left baseball more or less unscathed, but as the 1918 season rolled around the question in the minds of baseball men was not whether the game would be affected, but how great the damage would be. Mobilization of the civilian population in support of the war effort, just getting under way a year earlier, was now in full swing. Many ballplayers had volunteered or been drafted, and in the early months of the season the loss of personnel accelerated. Grover Cleveland Alexander, Joe Jackson, Red Faber and Rabbit Maranville were among those now practicing on a different kind of field.[1] Despite his previous Navy service, Sam Rice was drafted into the Army and lost to the Nationals except for a few games during furloughs.[2]

The best the Nationals could do for the ceremonial season-opening toss on April 15 was a District of Columbia Commissioner. The game was equally uninspiring, with Johnson suffering through the worst opening day of his career in a 6–3 loss to the Yankees. He lost his first three games in 1918 before a 5–0 victory over Carl Mays in Boston on May 1, the first of three wins in nine days over the Red Sox, boosted Johnson to the .500 mark and put him on track for another terrific year. The last two of those games happened to coincide with Babe Ruth's transition from marvelous pitcher to devastating slugger, the move that made him the transcendent figure in baseball—and changed the game itself.

Ruth's home run (the first of 10 off Johnson), a tremendous blast over the right-field wall into a Washington resident's "war garden," was the only scoring for the Red Sox in a 7–2 loss on May 7. It was the third homer in as many games for Ruth, who was playing a position other than pitcher and not batting ninth for only the second time in his career. At the urging of Red Sox captain Harry Hooper, Boston manager Ed Barrow had started the big youngster at first base two days earlier, and he wasted little time demonstrating what he could do as an everyday player. On May 9 Johnson picked up another win over the Red Sox, coming in to pitch the 10th inning of a 4–3 victory. Ruth went all the way on the mound for Boston, losing his second game to Johnson (against six wins) in their last official pitching matchup, and getting the only Red Sox hit off Johnson, a double—Ruth's fifth hit of the game, four of them for extra bases.[3]

A brilliant stretch of three shutouts in a row gave Johnson five straight wins, all at home. Cleveland's Jim Bagby was bested 1–0 on May 11, followed by a second straight 1–0 victory four days later against the world-champion White Sox. Chicago, which had lost Joe Jackson and Red Faber to the service, would be the team hit hardest by the war, falling to sixth this year between pennants in 1917 and 1919. But the fact that the White Sox lineup wasn't at full strength hardly dims the luster of Johnson's remarkable performance in the game, as he pitched the equivalent of *two* games, 18 innings, the longest shutout ever in the major leagues.[4] Chicago's Lefty Williams also went the distance in this unusual contest in which the 18 starters played the entire game without substitution or error.

The war-shortened season of 1918 is notable, in fact, for Johnson's extraordinary number of extra-inning games. Of 88 career decisions in extended contests, an amazing 15 took place that year, including nine complete games, five of them going 13 innings or more. Another long 1–0 victory, this one 15 innings, came in St. Louis on July 25, and on August 4 Johnson pitched his second-longest game ever, 17⅓ innings, in an odd 7–6 loss to the Tigers in which he allowed 16 hits, 8 walks, and faced a career-high 64 batters. On a brutally hot day in Detroit, Johnson had been roughed up and was just about finished after a hit by Ty Cobb tied the game at 6–6 in the 7th inning. But a second wind came over him and it wasn't until the 18th inning that Detroit pushed over another run, the game-winner, once again driven in by Cobb.

On May 23 baseball was dealt the first of a series of blows that would eventually bring a premature end to the season. Secretary of War Baker and Advocate General Crowder had responded to the war hysteria by issuing a "Work or Fight" order requiring all able-bodied men of draft age to either enlist or take a job in an industry deemed necessary to the war effort. Baseball was not one of those, and the game was losing players at an increasing pace as draft boards began enforcing the edict. (Many ballplayers simply switched baseball uniforms, performing their "essential" work for factories, mills, and shipyards fielding semipro teams.)

Eddie Ainsmith had been granted an earlier deferment, but was now ordered by his draft board to "work or fight." Clark Griffith and the Washington ballclub appealed the ruling to the Secretary of War, hoping to secure the same exemption given actors on the grounds that public entertainment provided relief for weary war workers.[5] Ainsmith became the test case on which the fate of all players eligible for the draft, and indeed of the game itself, rested, and there was a tremendous disappointment when Baker ruled on July 19 that playing ball was not essential work.

Dismay turned to shock for American League owners when Ban Johnson, in a sudden and unnecessary display of patriotism, announced the immediate shutdown of the league. The games of Sunday, July 21, would be the last, he declared. But this time the owners were having none of Johnson's autocratic decrees—and said so publicly and to his face. Under pressure to recant, Johnson declared that the American League, like the National, would continue play pending further developments. On July 24th a meeting was held in Washington between Secretary Baker and General Crowder and a dozen baseball officials, including Griffith and Minor of the Nationals. A compromise was struck in which baseball was allowed to continue, and players exempted from work-or-fight, until September 1, with the pennant-winners granted another two weeks to play the World Series.[6]

Smarting over a loss of authority within his own league and jealous over the role played by National Commission head Garry Herrmann in arranging the deal with the government, Ban Johnson now proclaimed that the American League would close down on August 20, ten days earlier than required by the agreement, and if it was up to him there would be no World Series. When he argued publicly that baseball should cancel its plans for a 1919 season, however, any remaining credibility Johnson had with the owners evaporated. Ignoring his declarations, they banded together to arrange for an orderly end to the season themselves. It was a stunning loss of power from which Johnson never recovered, his mishandling of the war issues having rendered the one-time "czar of baseball" practically impotent within the higher councils of the game.

Among those stepping in to fill the void was Clark Griffith. The Old Fox's forcefulness on war matters, and the help of his influential friends in Washington had prevented a financial catastrophe in the game.[7] Griffith had recognized early the threat to the game posed by America's entrance into the war and the difficulties of countering it without seeming unpatriotic. A stroke of particular public-relations genius was his hugely successful "Clark Griffith Ball and Bat Fund," started in 1917 with the goal of raising enough money to stock every U.S. Army company overseas with the equipment to field a baseball team.[8]

For the first six weeks of the 1918 season virtually the only bright spot for the Nationals was Walter Johnson. June found them struggling with the Tigers for seventh place, barely ahead of the perennial cellar-dwelling Athletics. But from that point they took off on a hot streak lasting, except for a two-week slump in July, for the rest of the year, and leaving the Tigers and everyone but Boston and Cleveland in the dust. Washington finished a mere four games back of the champion Red Sox, the franchise's best showing ever, and their 72–56 record for the abbreviated season was an improvement over 1917 of more than 20 games.

Walter Johnson, with two children, was exempt from the draft, and the rest of the front-line pitching staff was also largely unaffected. The availability of backups became so precarious, however, that even "Uncle Nick" Altrock, almost 42 years old and nine years past his last serious big-league appearance, got called into action for five games, including three starting assignments. The aging clown-coach somehow managed to hit a home run, his first since 1904. But most amazing of all was Altrock's complete-game victory at Detroit, a performance that gave rise to the following story, as Shirley Povich tells it:

> He beat the Tigers that day, and at the end of his afternoon's labors repaired to his favorite Detroit saloon to drink a dozen beers or so, as was his habit. Suffused with the beer and his triumph of the day, he sought to talk with the only other customer at the bar. Fishing for a compliment, Nick pointed to the score by innings posted behind the bar and said, preparatory to taking a bow, "I see where Altrock beat the Tigers today with six hits." His new companion squinted at the score and said, "Altrock? I never knew that old guzzler had a son pitching in the big leagues."[9]

The Nationals' surprising finish in the American League race was largely the result of Walter Johnson's best year since 1913. In a 128-game season Johnson won 23 and lost 13. His 1.27 earned run average hasn't been equalled in the American League since, and he was the league leader in wins, ERA, strikeouts (162), and shutouts (8). Johnson finished every game he pitched, all 29 starts and 10 relief appearances. A .267 batting average was his best so far, and Griffith pinch-hit him 20 times (five hits) and played him four games in the outfield.

The Nationals' season ended against the Athletics on September 2, perhaps the last game for many years as far as anyone knew. The devastating effects of the war were in full and poignant evidence that day in the presence of thousands of wounded soldiers from Walter Reed Army Hospital. Johnson played center field until the ninth inning, when Griffith put him in to pitch at the demand of the soldiers. Army Chief of Staff General P.C. March threw Johnson a ceremonial toss to open the last inning.

With no plans for a 1919 season, the outlook was bleak indeed. But little more than two months later, on November 11, peace was declared and the pessimism evaporated overnight.[10] Although 124 American League and 103 National League players had served during the war, incredibly—and perhaps owing to baseball's exemption from the work-or-fight order until September—not a single active major-league player was lost in the war.[11]

The great killer in the United States in 1918 was an influenza epidemic that claimed a half-million lives. Walter Johnson came down with two attacks of the flu himself that winter, but reported healthy and fit to the Nationals' 1919 training camp at Augusta, Georgia. According to Johnson's own candid assessment, however, his 31-year-old pitching arm was not quite the same methodical machine now as in the bloom of youth.

> I can no longer depend on my speed as I once could. Some days I believe I am as fast as I ever was. But there are other days, and they will probably grow more frequent as time passes, when I can no longer burn the ball across the platter as I could when my arm was a little younger and I had more reserve strength. Barring accidents or sickness, I know that I can do good work for several years. But the fact remains that I am on the downgrade, and I know it. I do not believe that the use of speed has worn me out. In my younger days, it was no exertion for me to pitch a fast ball, and I rather liked to baffle the batter. When I became a more experienced pitcher, my strikeout record declined, for I learned to pitch to each batter's weakness and to depend upon my fielders. Only in a pinch would I try deliberately to strike out the batter. There were times when I was younger, and maybe a little overconfident, when I felt that I could use so much sheer speed that a batter could not hit the ball. I have developed what I consider a pretty good curve ball. It has proved serviceable to me. Many days now when my fast ball is not quite as good as it used to be, I fall back on my curve. Probably I shall depend more and more on my curve as time goes on.[12]

Even so, as Grantland Rice observed: "Johnson seems to have slowed up in the same way that John D. [Rockefeller] has gone broke—both have lost something, but they still have enough."[13] Nowhere was this more evident than in the opening game of the season in Washington on April 23, a victorious 13-inning, 1–0 duel with Scott Perry of the Athletics. With President Wilson otherwise engaged in Europe, Army Chief of Staff March threw out the opening ball. Franklin D. Roosevelt was once again among those representing official Washington in the president's absence.

On May 11 Johnson pitched one of his greatest games, a 12-inning 0–0 battle with Jack Quinn on a gloomy, overcast Sunday in New York. From Roger Peckinpaugh's single in the first inning to Frank Baker's walk in the 10th, Johnson retired 28 batters in a row. Giving up only two hits and a walk, he faced 37 batters—one over the minimum—as two of the three baserunners were thrown out trying to steal. It was the first legal Sunday baseball game in New York, halted at 6 P.M. with plenty of daylight left by Yankees owner Jacob Ruppert because of his misunderstanding of the new law.[14] In a 1–0 win over the Athletics in Washington on July 24, Johnson had his best inning ever when he struck out the side (Kopp, Thomas, and Walker) on 9 pitches.[15]

Midway through the 1919 season, Griffith brought Joe Engel back to the Nationals, but not as a pitcher. After a brief trial with Cleveland earlier in the year, Engel finally gave up the eight-year struggle to get control of his fastball. Griffith had always been impressed with Engel's baseball acumen, even as a youngster, and hired him now to be the Nationals' first full-time scout. Even as scouting became an increasingly sophisticated operation, with most clubs employing a corps of them along with numerous paid stringers, Engel made his legend as the "Lone Wolf of the Bushes," almost singlehandedly stocking the Washington ballclub with talent that made it one of the most successful in baseball over the next 15 years.

Engel's first scouting assignment had come four years earlier, in 1915, when he was farmed out to Joe Cantillon's Minneapolis club. He was instructed to secure from Cantillon a couple of players for the Nationals in return, Griffith in effect asking Engel to complete the trade for himself. The 22-year-old pitcher somehow talked cagey old Pongo Joe out of Pat Gharrity, who would move Eddie Ainsmith out as the Nationals' regular catcher. In addition, Engel got Cantillon to throw in pitcher George Dumont, who gave the Nationals four years of the same kind of mediocrity as Engel had, making Gharrity practically a bonus in the deal. Engel's clever bargaining had impressed Griffith, and with the Nationals needing a full-time scout to compete with the other clubs, he got the job.[16]

Joe Engel was a "rollicking, good-humored man," in the words of one writer who knew him well.[17] His friendly, outgoing nature and lively personality were perfectly suited to the job. "Naturally a fellow will do more for a friend than for a stranger," Engel reasoned, "and so I cultivate whole families and always remember to take the kiddies presents and in that way stand in with their dads. This not only makes it easier for me to drive a good bargain but, being friends of mine, they don't try to sell me any cripples." As for his ability to distinguish the wheat from the chaff among raw, crude prospects—that was simply a "gift," more or less, in Engel's opinion.[18] Like Griffith, whom Engel considered the smartest baseball man he ever knew,[19] his judgments were made quickly and based on what he saw ("the way a player handles himself"), not on statistics or recommendation by others. Griffith's regard for Engel came to be such that almost alone among big-league scouts, Engel spoke with the authority of his boss, a tremendous advantage on occasion. "There are times when a scout has to close a deal at once or lose his man," Engel explained. "While some have been trying to get in touch with their office, I have often stepped up and landed a player, for throughout the minors the owners know that Griffith will go through with any deal I make."[20]

Engel, who had idolized Walter Johnson while serving as batboy during Cantillon's reign, then became his teammate and fellow pitcher, developed into one of Johnson's closest friends over the next few years. They both loved to hunt and were particularly interested in the dogs that were such an integral part of the sport. Eventually they owned a kennel together, raising purebred hounds that won prizes at field trials all over Maryland and Virginia. "People used to wonder at our close friendship—said we were so different," Engel reminisced many years later. "Walter didn't drink or smoke and was more or less on the serious side. I liked my fun and as a youngster was something of a hell-raiser. But we just clicked. I spent many happy hours in his company, especially when we'd go on hunting trips at the end of the season. We both were proud of our packs of fox hounds. And after the hunts we'd sit around the fire, talking of Johnson's early years in the American League and the personalities on the Washington clubs who played for Cantillon, McAleer and Griffith."[21]

Of the hundreds of acquisitions Engel would make for Washington over the years, the most important was his very first, and that one came about purely through coincidence. Griffith sent him to Binghamton, New York, to look over pitcher Pat Martin, scheduled to work against Buffalo. Engel didn't think much of Martin, but early in the game a fight broke out between the Buffalo second baseman and a runner who looked to be about twice as big. The little second baseman not only held his own, but shouted defiantly at the larger man the whole time. For the rest of the game Engel watched the kid and saw that he played with the same nerve and aggressive spirit.

The scout phoned back to Washington, but when Griffith heard the name—Stanley Harris—he wasn't impressed. Joe Judge had played with Harris on a Baltimore shipyard team the year before and had mentioned him, but there was no evidence that the boy was much of a hitter. Although just 26 years old himself and new to his job, Engel was so persistent that Griffith finally agreed to take the train up and see for himself.

With Engel and Griffith in the stands for a doubleheader in Buffalo, Harris had six hits, walked, and was hit by a pitch in eight trips to the plate. The clincher came when Griffith walked into the dressing room after the game and found the boy unwrapping two fingers he had taped together. Harris had broken a finger, perhaps in the fight at Binghamton, but wasn't going to let it force him out of the games, not with big-league scouts looking on. That was Griffith's kind of player. Ironically, in light of events several years later, John McGraw passed on Harris twice that year, first snubbing him in a tryout at the Polo Grounds and then choosing pitcher Rosy Ryan to satisfy the Giants' option on a Buffalo player. Griffith got Harris for $2,500 and light-hitting utility infielder Hal Janvrin.[22] For his part Harris was glad not to be going to the Giants, who were grooming Frankie Frisch to take over at second base.[23] And as he would later recall his Buffalo teammates telling him, he was "lucky in getting with a club where I wouldn't have to bat against Walter Johnson."[24]

Stanley Harris picked up the nickname "Bucky" at the age of 12 working as a coal mine "breaker boy" (separating slate from coal as it came down the chutes) in his hometown of Pittston, Pennsylvania, and the name stuck through a long baseball career that ended at the Hall of Fame. Harris would be the Nationals' second baseman for the next decade, one of the best in the game.[25] His hustle and instincts gave him tremendous range at the position, and he "had no peer" at pivoting for the doubleplay, according to Walter Johnson.[26] The handsome Harris (who bore a resemblance to '20s crooning sensation and movie star Rudy Vallee) made himself into a better hitter in the big leagues than he had been in the minors, averaging around .300 most years. He supplemented his base hits with an adeptness at getting hit by pitches, leading the league in that category his first three years.[27]

A better-than-average bunter and base-stealer, Harris was always at his best in the clutch. But what distinguished him most, and proved of most value to the ballclub, was his aggressive attitude, always looking to make things happen for his team and make opponents pay for lapses and mistakes. He exuded a self-confidence that bordered on cockiness. "I never saw a competitive spirit the equal of his, not even Cobb's," Clark Griffith said of Harris years later. "He was the gamest ballplayer I ever saw in 50 years of baseball. He was the smartest player I ever had."[28]

The day after Harris arrived, damaged finger and all, Griffith had him in the lineup. His first game, in New York on August 28, gave the 22-year-old quite an introduction to the major leagues, and to Walter Johnson. The Nationals' ace had been fighting a cold for 11 days, pitching just two innings in relief during that time, and was hardly at the top of his game. He gave up 19 hits (the most ever in his career) in a game lost in the 14th inning, 5–4, and it was Harris who cost him the game. On a high fly to short center field, a ball Harris should have waved the others away from, Milan, Rice, and Harris all stopped short as the ball fell safely to win the game for the Yankees. Harris was surprised when no one, not Griffith, not Johnson, none of his new teammates criticized him for the error, even though it had lost the game. Griffith just told him to take charge of the play next time. Another surprise was the great applause given Johnson by the large New York crowd as he walked off the mound. Harris thought to himself what great sportsmanship there was in the major leagues for the crowd to treat the visiting pitcher like that. "From the cheers one would have thought him the winner," he wrote several years later. "I didn't know that Johnson was the idol of American League fans the circuit over."[29]

Another significant acquisition for Washington late in 1919 was 23-year-old Tom Zachary, a tall, loose-limbed pitcher who would win 15 or more games for the Nationals four out of the next five years. Zachary, a Quaker, was a quiet, gentle man, a college graduate and avid reader. He had the face of a village parson but was actually a tobacco farmer in his native North Carolina when not baffling hitters with his assortment of knuckle-curves and screwballs.[30]

Baseball owners had reacted to low attendance in 1918 by shortening the 1919 schedule to 140 games, which saved them two weeks' payrolls. But with the end of the war crowds rebounded and the short-sighted moguls instead lost 14 games of gate receipts.[31] Out of the pennant chase from the start, the Nationals fell to seventh place, 32 games back of the champion White Sox and a full 11 games out of sixth place.

Johnson's fortunes initially followed the team's, but a 15–7 run at the end of the season gave him his tenth straight year of 20 or more wins, a respectable 20–14 mark. Eleven of the losses had been by one run. In a year of greatly increased hitting (the league ERA shot up from 2.77 to 3.21, home runs from 98 to 241), Johnson's 1.49 earned run average stands out in particular—almost two runs under the league average—as do his seven shutouts, five of them by 1–0. For the eighth year in a row he was the American League strikeout leader. But the high point of this season didn't take place on a ballfield. On August 11 Elinor Lee Johnson was born. She had blond, curly hair, Hazel's big blue eyes, and was solid like her dad, entering the world at a robust 10 pounds.

For some time Clark Griffith had been fed up with the penny-pinching, shoestring administration of the ballclub, and wanted to gain control over its affairs. In 1917 Griffith was promised the financial backing to do just that by John Wilkins, a wealthy Washington coffee magnate, but the U.S. declaration of war had scotched the deal. In the fall of 1919, following the team's worst season by far under Griffith's management, the directors weren't much fonder of him than he was of them. But just when it looked as though Griffith's position might be getting precarious, old friend Connie Mack came to the rescue, introducing Griffith to William M. Richardson, a wealthy Philadelphia grain dealer and business partner of the Athletics' financial "angel," Tom Shibe.

Richardson agreed to back Griffith if they could buy enough stock to control the club. Griffith already held 2,700 of the 20,000 shares, and after several lean years most of the other stockholders were more than willing to sell their interests for $15 a share—a steal for Griffith and Richardson, as things turned out.[32] They ended up splitting 15,702 shares.[33] Griffith repaid Richardson with an $87,000 loan from the Metropolitan Bank of Washington based on nothing more than the banker's high personal and professional regard for Griffith. Richardson wanted no involvement in the day-to-day running of the club, signing his voting rights over to Griffith.[34] A perfect partnership, apparently unmarred by a single dispute in 27 years before Richardson's death in 1946, was formed: Richardson stayed out of the way and let Griffith develop one of the best clubs in baseball, making lots of money for both of them along the way.[35] E.B. "Eddie" Eynon, a Washington amateur golf champion who had impressed Griffith with his chairmanship of the local Liberty Loan drive during the war, was hired to manage the club's business affairs.[36]

The Old Fox had reached his final destiny as owner and president of the Washington Nationals. Shedding his uniform as field boss after the 1920 season, Griffith embarked on the longest and most satisfying phase of his monumental 70-year career in baseball. A seemingly effortless transition saw him transformed from fiery, fighting, manager into a soft-spoken, distinguished, white-haired gentleman and pillar of the community. Revered by several generations of ordinary Washingtonians, Griffith was at the same time personal friends with many of the most powerful men in the country, including a long succession of U.S. presidents. The donning of a new outfit—three-piece suits and his ever-present cigar—seemed to bring about a change even in Griffith's countenance, the furrowed brow and piercing eyes replaced now by a gracious, grandfatherly smile. Indeed, he ran his ballclub like a big family. "He was a wonderful man, always helpful and kind," Goose Goslin recalled. "He wasn't like a boss, more like a father."[37]

This sentiment was expressed often by Griffith's former players, employees, and associates, although he was known to be a tough negotiator when it came to business matters. ("He had to be economical," explained Al Schacht. "He didn't have any great wealth of his own.")[38] The stories of his generosity and kindness are legion. One of them has to do with Washington Redskins owner George Preston Marshall, who rented the ballpark from Griffith for football games. One day Marshall came to his landlord with a complaint. Shirley Povich wrote of the incident:

It concerned the gatemen at Griffith Stadium. You've seen them, white-haired old fellows for the most part, some of them old-time ballplaying pals of Griffith. The old ballplayer always gets a job from the Nats owner. The pay isn't much, but they like their work, and Griffith likes to call them in for a game of pinochle on rainy days. His is an organization in which the president is one with the lowliest employee. Well, one day [Marshall] went into Griffith's office, screaming. The old gatemen weren't moving fans into the park fast enough. They moved too slowly "and we've got to have younger men on the gates," demanded the football boss. Griffith simply shook his head.

"Those old fellows are my friends," he said, "they'll have to stay on their jobs. They need the money."

"But I'll pay for the extra help," said the football man, "and it won't cost your old friends anything. After all, I've got some rights. I'm renting this park." Griffith was adamant.

"Those old friends of mine will have to stay on their jobs," he said. "Nobody is going to tell them they are through. Don't you see, it would break their hearts."[39]

J is for Johnson.
The Big Train in his prime,
Was so fast he could throw
Three strikes at a time.[40]

OGDEN NASH

Walter Johnson's "prime" lasted ten years, from 1910 through 1919, coinciding neatly with the second decade of the century. He won 265 games, an astonishing 35% of the Nationals' 755 wins during that time; he led the American League in strikeouts nine times; shutouts and complete games, six times; wins and innings pitched, five times; earned run average, four times. Although Johnson himself admitted to a diminution of his powers, after fifteen years of slinging the fastest pitches on the planet one could search the record in vain for the slightest evidence of it. The shortened seasons of 1918 and 1919 had been two of his finest in every respect.

Johnson began the 1920s, however, with the same kind of rocky start that had characterized his last bad season back in 1909. After spring training in Tampa, Florida, the Nationals broke camp in late March for a barnstorming tour north with the world champion Reds, 13 games in as many days, ending in Cincinnati. Thirteen straight nights on a "sleeper" [Pullman train], jumping from the hot Florida sunshine into a cold and damp early spring in the North, laid Johnson low with a heavy cold. Waking up in Clarksburg, West Virginia, one morning, he couldn't raise his arm to tie his necktie. "[The cold] seemed to settle in my arm," he said.[41] A 10-day layoff seemed to have taken care of the problem as he pitched four shutout innings against the Reds in Roanoke, Virginia, and creditably again in Cincinnati on April 11 in his last exhibition tuneup.

The cold and sore arm continued to dog Johnson all spring, which was unusually wet and cold in the East.[42] He clearly wasn't ready for the season opener in Boston on the 15th, leaving the game after two innings having given up five runs in a 7–6 defeat. Massachusetts Governor Calvin Coolidge threw out the first ball, which on a beautiful spring day drew only 7,000 fans to Fenway Park—the fans' reaction to Red Sox owner Harry Frazee's sale of Babe Ruth and other star players to the New York Yankees. After breaking the home-run record with 29 despite the short 1919 season and putting in 15 starts on the mound, Ruth had been sold for the astounding price of $100,000 and a $300,000 loan to Frazee from the Yankees owner, beer magnate Jacob Ruppert. But Ruth was just one of many going from Boston to New York in a virtual franchise shift that also involved Duffy Lewis, Carl Mays, Dutch Leonard, and Ernie Shore. (Oddly, although the deals clearly favored the Yankees, Boston moved up a place in the standings in 1920 with about the same record.)

Johnson was out of action for another ten days following his abortive stint in the opener and didn't pitch the Nationals' home opener for the first time since 1911. President Wilson, incapacitated by a recent stroke, also missed the game. As Edith Wilson filled in for her husband at the White House, Vice President Marshall did the honors at the ballpark. Johnson came back on April 25th with a 2–0 shutout of the Red Sox, and the pattern was set for the season: good and bad performances alternating with no apparent reason, perhaps due to fluctuations in his health. Scratched from a start against Cleveland on May 26 because of a sore arm, he came back in Philadelphia three days later with a 5–0 gem.

The start of the game gave no clue that it was to be a brilliant performance when Johnson hit the first two batters. Jimmy Dykes, the Athletics' 22-year-old second baseman in the first full season of a long and distinguished playing career (followed by many more as a manager), was the leadoff hitter, and the experience was still clear in his mind many years later:

I still remember the first time I faced Walter Johnson. He rears back and whizzes two strikes past me so fast I didn't have time to figure out what to do. They talk about a batter being slow to get his bat off his shoulder. I didn't have time to even think about swinging. Johnson winds up again and wham, another one zips past me. I didn't know what it was or where it was, high or low, inside or outside. I look back at the umpire to see if I'm out on strikes.

"Take your base," he says. I don't know what he's talking about.

"What for?," I ask.

"He hit you with that last pitch," says the umpire. I look so puzzled he takes pity on me.

"So you don't think he hit you," he says. "Well, tell me this: do you always wear your cap the way you're wearing it now?" I reach up and feel for my cap. The bill is turned clear around on the side where Johnson's last pitch had clipped it.[43]

The second man up, Fred Thomas, was also hit, the pitch skimming his shirt. The next two hitters struck out. "For the rest of the game [Johnson] had the batters virtually taking their cuts from the dugout," Al Schacht remembered.[44]

Griffith had Johnson back on the mound in New York just two days later, May 31, for 4⅔ ineffective innings of relief in a 10–7 slugfest won by the Yankees. Over 38,000 fans packed the Polo Grounds for the afternoon game of a doubleheader, the largest crowd yet recorded in the major leagues. Another 5,000 were turned away at the gate. The attraction was Babe Ruth, in the middle of a year judged by one analyst "the best season any mortal ever had."[45] Ruth's home runs were a sensation, his 54 that year nearly doubling his own record and more than 14 *teams* hit in 1920. He didn't disappoint the crowd in this game, either, sending a tremendous blast slamming with great force into the facade above the upper deck in right field, the first of eight Ruth homers as a Yankee off Johnson.

On June 27 in Washington Walter Johnson had his best game of the season up to that point, a three-hit, no-walk, 7–0 beauty over the Athletics. It was the most efficient game of his career, requiring just 72 pitches (69, by one writer's count) and a mere hour and 18 minutes to play. The 18th consecutive loss for the A's, it was the seventh straight win for the Nationals, moving them past the Red Sox into fourth place. As the team went up to Boston for a one-series road trip, Johnson stayed in Washington to help Hazel look after Walter, Jr., and

Eddie, both of whom were sick. He took a night train to make his scheduled start on July 1. Still trying to shake off his own continuing illness (the grippe), Johnson at first didn't feel well enough to play, but told Griffith he would pitch the first inning and see how it went. After setting the Red Sox down in order he told the manager he would go another inning.[46] Johnson was surprised by his own speed, and with his curve breaking sharply and an occasional slow ball keeping the batters off balance he breezed along, not a man reaching base in the first six innings.[47] A terrific pitching duel developed between Johnson and Harry Harper, a close friend during Harper's seven-year stint with the Nationals from 1913 to 1919.

Leading off the seventh inning for the Red Sox, left fielder Harry Hooper hit an easy chance to Bucky Harris at second. Harris, who had driven in the only run of the game in the top of the inning, muffed the ball, allowing Hooper to reach first to end Johnson's perfect game. But the rest of the side was retired in order, and in the eighth inning it dawned on everyone, including Johnson, that there were only a few batters between him and a no-hitter, a feat that had thus far eluded him. "Walter, seeing a long-deferred record in sight, cut loose with everything he had," Harris wrote several years later. "It was almost impossible for the Boston batters to see his fast ball. His control was well-nigh perfect. His curve ball was breaking beautifully."[48]

With the score still 1–0, Boston sent up two left-handed pinch-hitters to start the 9th inning, but Johnson struck them out. That brought up Hooper, who was not feeling at all sentimental about the prospect of a Johnson no-hitter. "Tell Walter he's got to pitch to me," Hooper said to catcher Val Picinich. "I'm going to bust one out of the park if I can." Hooper drove a hot grounder down the first-base line. Bounding over the bag and hooking (by one estimate 15 feet) into foul territory, the ball was intercepted by Joe Judge from his position deep behind the bag. On the dead run Judge speared it in his glove, then stopped on a dime and tossed to Johnson to beat the sprinting Hooper by an eyelash. Judge went into a war-dance, rushing over to shake the pitcher's hand. Hooper was next, telling Johnson, "I'm glad to lose that hit for your no-hit game." Boston fans, who had been pulling openly for the no-hitter, poured onto the field, crowding around Johnson and patting him on the back. In the happy Washington clubhouse, congratulations were being offered all around when someone yelled, "Speech!" Typically, the full extent of Johnson's oration was: "Goodness gracious sakes alive, wasn't I lucky!"[49] A telegram arrived shortly with more congratulations, along with some good news: "Eddie doing fine today. Hooray for your no-hit game. Hazel."[50] Walter, Jr., was also on their minds. It was his fifth birthday.

In this near-perfect (one-runner) game, the second of his career, Johnson struck out ten Red Sox and got six others on foul pops, four of them caught by Picinich behind the plate. It was the first no-hitter in the history of Washington's professional teams going back to 1884, and the only one in the major leagues in the "lively ball" years of 1920–21. A scant 3,000 lucky witnesses were on hand to see the high point of Johnson's career to date, the Boston fans still, as one Washington newspaper put it, "giving the Red Sox the absent treatment since the sale of Babe Ruth."[51]

Johnson took the train back to Washington ahead of the team to rest up for his next appearance, which Griffith was already touting to the press. It was to be the concluding game of a Sunday doubleheader against Babe Ruth and the Yankees on July 5, and Griffith was hoping to use the excitement over Johnson's no-hitter to bring out a large crowd. As fans started wiring for tickets from all over the area and beyond, it became clear that that's exactly what was going to happen. The paid attendance for the afternoon game was 18,821, demolishing the previous record of 16,340 set on opening day, 1911.[52] The only problem was that Walter Johnson was in no shape to pitch. His arm had bothered him ever since Boston, and adding to his misery was a pulled leg muscle incurred during practice the morning of the big doubleheader. With Griffith in a real spot, salvation came from a most unlikely source—27-year-old rookie pitcher Al Schacht, who would turn this game into the big break of a long and colorful career. In his autobiography, Schacht told the story:

About an hour before game time, Griff called the team in the clubhouse for a meeting, and he looked grim.

"Johnson can't pitch," he said sadly. "Not only is his arm bothering him, but he strained a muscle in his groin. Five years ago I advertised Johnson would pitch, just like today, and almost the same thing happened. The fans stormed the box office demanding their money back, and we've got a bigger crowd today," he groaned, pacing back and forth. "Men, I'm in a desperate spot," he gazed slowly around the room, "and so is the pitcher who has to take Johnson's place . . . it's between Ericson, Courtney, Shaw, and Schacht—who wants the ball?" The dressing room was silent for half a minute. Nobody stirred. Just the breathing. Then a voice shattered the stillness.

"I'll pitch it, Griff." The voice was mine. It startled everybody, including myself. Griff stared at me—then came over and handed me the ball. Gripping my shoulder, he said:

"If you win this game today, Al, as long as I have anything to say about this ball club you'll have a job with me. I mean it. I don't care if you don't win another game this season—you've got to win this one!"[53]

Schacht did win the game, 9–3, striking out Babe Ruth with the bases loaded at one point. The Nationals swept the doubleheader, raising themselves several games over .500 and dealing New York a blow in their neck-and-neck struggle with Cleveland for the league lead. What might have been a much more costly setback for the Yankees was narrowly avoided when Ruth, driving his big touring car from Washington to Philadelphia, went off the road and rolled it. Luckily, neither Ruth, his wife Helen, nor any of the three teammates riding with them were seriously hurt, although there were premature reports of the slugger's demise in the accident.[54]

It wasn't until 10 days after his no-hitter that Johnson pitched again. But, as one report put it, "if his leg was in good condition, his arm was not," and he was taken out after giving up ten hits in seven innings of a 4–0 loss to Cleveland. In the past, minor problems with his arm had cleared up with rest followed by a gradual return to a regular schedule, and that was the course followed now. But Johnson's arm didn't respond this time, and his attempts to pitch through the injury only made it worse.[55] He managed to go the route on July 16 in a 4–1 loss to Red Faber and the White Sox, but afterwards couldn't throw even lightly in practice without "pronounced pain" in his arm. It was decided to give his arm an extended rest. But when the pain persisted after two weeks of inactivity, Johnson was sent to Rochester, New York, and put under the ministrations of Dr. "Bonesetter" Knight.

Traveling with Johnson to Rochester was Al Schacht, who had injured his shoulder sliding into second base in his first start after beating the Yankees. A natural comedian, Schacht clowned around trying to cheer up the dejected Johnson, who was concerned about the first serious injury to his "salary whip," as the writers called a pitcher's throwing arm. The tables were turned when Knight relieved Johnson of his worst fear; the injury wasn't permanent and he would definitely pitch again, the Bonesetter told him.[56] But for Schacht, with a long history of arm problems, the news wasn't so good, and now it was Johnson's turn to encourage him.[57] This was the beginning of a friendship between the two, in spite of their quite different personalities. They would be roommates on the road for seven seasons, and their battles over Johnson's favorite card game, casino, were legendary on the team.[58] A master of pantomime, Schacht would imitate Johnson's Will Rogers-like "aw-shucks" mannerisms for audiences in the lobby of the Tampa Hotel during spring training, to the great amusement of the subject also. Johnson would get revenge by calling Schacht "Jack Keefe" after the self-deluded, no-talent pitcher in Ring Lardner's classic, *You Know Me Al*.[59]

After three days of little more than massage and heat treatments in Rochester, a restless Johnson took the train back to Washington.[60] Given a prescription of complete rest for his arm, he went to Coffeyville to visit the family for a month, and engaged in nothing more strenuous than helping his father win election as a county commissioner. Rejoining the Nationals in St. Louis on September 9, Johnson saw limited action as a pinch-hitter over the next two weeks, pitching only in light workouts. His arm was stiff after throwing, but the pain was gone and Griffith claimed that his star was "just as good as ever."[61] Johnson knew differently. In a letter to *Baseball Magazine* editor F.C. Lane several years later, he described his feelings after the injury. "No one knows what a sore arm is unless he has had one," Johnson wrote, "and it sure was hard on me as I never knew what a bad arm was. Most people said, 'Well, he was a good pitcher, but he is through now.'"[62] Not sure that they weren't right, Johnson seriously considered retiring, but Griffith and Mike Martin talked him out of it. Griffith had his own stake in the matter, of course, but Martin was convinced Johnson wasn't finished. "You've got several good years in your system yet, Walter," Martin told him. "Leave it to me and you'll never be sorry."[63]

CHAPTER 11

These Things Come

If any youngster, breaking into the ranks of professional baseball, is looking for a model, he can find no more wonderful one than Walter Johnson of the Senators. In all baseball history, no pitcher ever has achieved greater fame than Johnson; none has lived finer or cleaner; none has been a greater credit to the game. Johnson has been in the big league show for something like 15 seasons. Never in all that time has he been guilty of rowdyism; never has he been put off a ball field; never has one taint of scandal or criticism been found upon his record. Fame has not turned Johnson's head. He is today just as modest, quiet and unassuming as he was in the long ago when, as a tall, raw-boned youngster, he came from Idaho and made his big league debut.[1]

JAMES J. CORBETT

Returning to the tranquility and stability of Coffeyville, Walter Johnson must have wondered about his future in baseball. He would be 33 years old at the start of the next campaign and on the downhill side of his career physically, as he was the first to admit. That would have been the scenario in any case, but the injury added a more worrisome element of doubt, and it would be six months before his arm could be tested. And during this time of uncertainty about Johnson's personal situation, it so happened that the game itself was undergoing the greatest turmoil, on and off the field, since the beginning of the modern era at the turn of the century.

On the same day Johnson had called it quits for the season, September 27, 1920, a Philadelphia newspaper broke the shocking story that eight Chicago White Sox players (immediately tagged the "Black Sox") had accepted bribes to throw the 1919 World Series to Cincinnati. Of particular interest to Johnson must have been the participation of two former teammates.

Sleepy Bill Burns, a pitcher with the Nationals in 1908–09 and briefly Johnson's roommate,[2] had been the agent between players and gambling interests. Chick Gandil, the ringleader of the crooked faction on the team, had played with Johnson at Santa Ana and Washington. Years later, Gandil cited his association with the Nationals' pitching star as having led to his involvement with big-time gamblers. As early as Gandil's rookie year of 1912 Boston gambler Joe "Sport" Sullivan was paying him for tips about Johnson's pitching schedule, the state of his health, anything that might help beat the odds.[3] The success of Sullivan's baseball wagers had elevated him into the higher echelons of his profession and led to his involvement as one of the principals in the Black Sox affair.[4]

As it cast a stain of corruption and dishonesty over organized baseball, the scandal was terribly disheartening for everyone in the game. But for those whose integrity was absolute, such as Walter Johnson, the hurt must have been especially profound. Just a few years earlier, ironically, Johnson had dismissed the possibility of such a widespread conspiracy in baseball. "I do not think [gambling] will ever seriously threaten the game," he declared. "Under present conditions the only way anything could become a real menace to the game would be through the cooperation of the players not only individually but as a team . . . and it would be manifestly impossible for any group of players to enter into such an agreement."[5] Organized baseball, which had exploded in popularity since the end of the war, was shaken severely by the revelations, and could have been destroyed. To save themselves and their game, league presidents Ban Johnson and John Heydler, along with the team owners, reluctantly gave Federal Judge Kenesaw Mountain Landis a 25-year contract with practically unlimited authority as the commissioner of baseball. Landis acted quickly and decisively to restore the game's reputation, imposing a lifetime ban on the eight Black Sox and several other players charged with gambling improprieties.

"There is no place for such fellows in baseball," agreed Walter Johnson, who had sympathy only for Joe Jackson.[6] "Poor Joe . . . I feel sorry for him. Others were guilty; Joe was merely foolish," Johnson claimed.[7] And although Babe Ruth and his home runs have been credited with saving baseball by restoring its popularity after the Black Sox scandal, of much greater importance no doubt was the presence in the game of those players the public regarded as incorruptible, men who wouldn't be associated with something not "on the square." It hardly seems likely that fans would have had much interest in games they thought fixed from the outset, no matter what took place in them. Following another, more minor, scandal four years later, the *New York Evening World* editorialized: "When scandals now and then blacken the record of the diamond, it will always be consoling to reflect that there are Walter Johnsons in the game."[8]

Momentous changes were also taking place in the way the game was played on the field, the cumulative effects of which altered the balance between pitching and hitting that had held relatively constant for almost 30 years. Between 1917, the last full year of the so-called "dead-ball era," and 1921, American League batting rose from .248 to .292; ERA soared from 2.66 to 4.28; extra-base hits jumped from 2,143 to 3,211; and most remarkably of all, home runs exploded from 136 to 477. Controversy raged at the time, and continues to this day, about whether the construction of the baseball had changed. Officials of the game and of the A.J. Reach Company, which manufactured major league baseballs, vehemently denied the charge, claiming that the introduction of the cork center in 1910 had been the last major change. But a different type of yarn in use since the end of the war seemed to show more spring, perhaps from being wound more tightly around the core.[9]

There was no doubt in Walter Johnson's mind. He spoke matter-of-factly at the time about the "lively ball."[10] And in 1927, he said: "I know it has been denied by some that the ball was changed, but I also know there was a great difference between the ball that was in use when I broke in and the rabbit ball that was handed us a few seasons ago. This ball traveled with much more speed than the old one when hit."[11]

Also contributing to the increased hitting of the 1920s, although of less direct significance to Johnson, was the banning of the spitball and other so-called "freak" pitches. A number of great pitching careers had been built on the freedom to tamper with the ball and the ability to control the sometimes bizarre movement caused by the alterations: the spitball took Ed Walsh, Red Faber, Burleigh Grimes, Stan Coveleski, and others into the Hall of Fame; Russell Ford was on top of the pitching world for a while with his "emery ball" (scuffed with an emery board); Eddie Cicotte's career took off when he perfected the "shine ball" (using paraffin wax). The initial restriction, in effect for 1920, limited each team to two spitballers, but the following year the practice was outlawed altogether except for eight American League and nine National League pitchers permitted to continue using the technique until the end of their careers. (Grimes was the last sanctioned spitball pitcher, finishing his career in 1934.)

Perhaps the biggest change was the result of the worst tragedy in big-league history: the death of Cleveland shortstop Ray Chapman from a Carl Mays pitch on August 17, 1920. Walter Johnson's greatest fear—killing a batter with a pitch to the head—had come true for another pitcher, but it just as easily could have happened to him. Like most pitchers, Mays didn't hesitate to use the ball on occasion to make a statement to the batter, but on this terrible occasion the pitch that killed Chapman might actually have been a strike. The day was overcast and dark, the ball had been in play for some time, and Mays was a "submarine" pitcher who threw the ball practically from the ground, all factors reducing the visibility of the pitch. Chapman had frozen in a crouch over the plate, apparently not seeing the ball at all as it tailed into him.

Despite the demise of this fine ballplayer, organized baseball had no more luck curbing use of the beanball than it ever had, but it did order the umpires to keep a clean ball in play so batters could at least see it coming.[12] In the early days one baseball was often used the entire game, becoming lumpy, scuffed, discolored and difficult to see, traveling neither as fast nor as far when hit. Under the new order hitters had white baseballs to view against the normally dark background of stadium walls and stands, and air resistance was minimized with a clean surface. It's easy to imagine the difference, although as with the ban on freak pitches it didn't affect Johnson directly. He had always been the biggest stickler in the game for an unmarred ball to throw. Umpire Bill McGowan wrote: "It has been the custom in the American League that when Johnson is pitching and the batter wished the umpire to look at the ball, the umpire usually yells to Walter, 'How is the ball, Barney?' If the ball is satisfactory to Johnson's way of thinking, it is all right with the umpire and the batter."[13]

The cumulative effect of these physical changes—at the same time a cause and an effect of the new power game—was to alter the general strategy of play. When teams were scoring two or three runs a game on average, every run was viewed as the potential game-winner. The prevailing theory at that time was to get a runner on base and move him around with sacrifices, hit-and-runs, steals, etc., giving up outs along the way if necessary. Taking an extra base, drawing a throw that might go astray, hitting the ball to different parts of the field, and numerous other fine points of offensive play often proved the difference between victory and defeat. Sharp defensive work to limit the progress of runners was likewise valued. In that kind of game pitching was paramount, and strikeouts were the ultimate weapon—and the ultimate humiliation for a batter.

But with greater scoring, and the lightning threat of the home run everpresent, a different strategy was now called for. Except in the late innings of a close game, a single run was not worth giving up outs for. With five or six runs needed to win a game, an explosion of hits, preferably for extra bases, was desired, and that can happen even with two outs. A strikeout became just another out, the price paid for swinging away for those long hits. For the defense, runners—runs even—became secondary. Outs were the primary concern, so the infield and outfield played farther back, concerned less about allowing a baserunner or two than about covering more territory to make outs and cut off extra-base hits. "A certain looseness in defense," was how Walter Johnson characterized the new approach.[14]

Towering over this shifting landscape of the diamond, a promoter of these changes as well as the beneficiary of them, was the imposing figure of Babe Ruth. Whatever the factors contributing to greater hitting, especially extra-base hitting, beginning in 1919, Ruth was not the only one taking advantage of them. But it was his proclivity for blasting home runs out of the park that captured the public's imagination and set him apart. And as his salary zoomed from $10,000 in 1920 to $25,000 in 1921, then to $52,000 in 1922, it wasn't long before swinging for the fences became the vogue among hitters. The high-scoring style of play coincided with a post-war attendance boom, leading owners to adopt any measures they could think of to increase home runs in particular and scoring in general. Fences were brought in, pitching mounds lowered, grass trimmed, strike zones reduced, and so on. "Since I came in," Walter Johnson lamented toward the end of his career, "everything possible has been given to the batter and everything possible taken from the pitcher."[15]

If the new game, with its emphasis on pyrotechnics over the more subtle skills, attracted a wider audience, it also lost some who preferred the dead-ball days and a more suspenseful and cerebral style of play. "Well, friends," Ring Lardner wrote in 1921, "may as well admit that I have kind of lose interest in the old game, or rather it ain't the old game which I have lose interest in, but it is the game which the magnates has fixed up to please the public with their usual good judgement." Upon John McGraw's retirement in 1932, Lardner told him: "Baseball hasn't meant much to us since the introduction of the TNT ball that robbed the game of the features I used to like best—features that gave you and Bill Carrigan and Fielder Jones and other really intelligent managers a deserved advantage, and smart ballplayers like Cobb and Jim Sheckard a chance to *do* things."[16]

It was into this changing milieu, then, that Walter Johnson entered his 15th season in the big leagues. With Eddie Cicotte banished for his role in the Black Sox scandal, Johnson became the veteran pitcher in the game, exceeded in length of service among all players by only Ty Cobb and Eddie Collins. Perhaps with an eye toward the inevitable end of his pitching days, he invested $5,000 in the New Haven club of the Eastern League, beginning a friendship with the team's 26-year-old owner, George Weiss. Johnson and Cobb, who also had a piece of the team, were named to the board of directors. A token $100 was also put into the new Coffeyville Southwestern League team, legally incorporated as the "Walter Johnson Baseball Association."[17]

There was yet another major change for Johnson as the 1921 season got underway: after 35 years in a baseball uniform, the last nine of them as manager of the Nationals, Clark Griffith decided to retire from the field to concentrate on the broader duties of team president. Replacing him was shortstop George McBride, captain of the team for the last six years and acting manager when Griffith was away. For Johnson, who got along famously with both men, the change meant little. Of greater importance to the team ultimately was the addition to the pitching staff of George Mogridge, a lanky, good-natured left-hander acquired from the Yankees. Although there wasn't much in his eight-year big-league record so far to predict a great contribution to the Nationals, he would average 16 wins a year for the next four seasons with an assortment of curves and off-speed stuff.

Before leaving for Hot Springs Johnson "tossed a few" to one of his brothers in Coffeyville, then engaged in a few light practices at the resort, without experiencing any of the pain that had brought his 1920 season to a halt.[18] In his first real test, a 79-pitch workout in Tampa on March 15, John Dugan of the *Herald* reported that "All the old pep was there and at regular intervals Gharrity's big mitt would resound with the mid-season smack." But he was wild in his first intersquad appearance on March 26, hitting three batters (including a glancing blow to Bucky Harris's head) and walking two others in three innings, during which he was touched for seven runs. "The comeback of Walter Johnson was not quite as impressive as manager McBride had hoped for," one paper understated the result.[19]

Opening Day on April 13 wasn't any more encouraging, as Johnson gave up nine hits and four runs in four innings of a 6–3 loss to the Red Sox. The new president, Warren Harding, made the inaugural toss, the first by a chief executive since 1916. After autographing the ball he threw it to Johnson, who put it aside for his growing collection. Vice President Calvin Coolidge and Secretary of Commerce Herbert Hoover were also in attendance.

Any notion that Walter Johnson was through, however, was quickly dispelled with victories in his next two starts. In a 3–1 win over the Athletics on the 17th, the *Herald* reported that "The smokeball king was just as fast as ever, his sharp-breaking curve had the Athletics hitters backing away from the plate, and his control was faultless." A 5–3 victory over Carl Mays in New York on April 25 was the 307th of Johnson's career, breaking Eddie Plank's American League record.

On May 7 Johnson was beaten by a mammoth Babe Ruth home run, said to be "undoubtedly the longest hit ever poled" at the Washington ballpark.[20] It sailed high over the large wall recently erected in center field, and was probably the same clout Johnson recalled for an interviewer in 1942: "[Ruth] was in a terrible slump once, and I struck him out three straight times. But the fourth time he came up . . . goodness, he hit that ball. It went over the fence into a big tree across an alley. Colored fans used to pay 25 cents to sit on the limbs of the tree, and it was packed this day. When Ruth's ball sailed into the tree, the fans fell out of it like apples."[21] Johnson was victimized for three of Ruth's record 59 homers in 1921. When asked years later to compare the length of Ruth's blasts to those of Jimmie Foxx and Hank Greenberg, Johnson replied, "All I can say is that the balls Ruth hit out of the park got smaller quicker than anybody else's."[22]

Among those witnessing the game was former President Woodrow Wilson, taking in his first baseball game since 1918. He sat in the presidential box behind the Nationals' dugout, but his failing health necessitated a different arrangement for the many games he would attend before passing away three years later. Griffith allowed Wilson's big sedan to pass through a gate in right field and park behind the Nationals' bullpen next to the foul line. The former president and his wife watched the games from there, guarded from foul balls by bullpen pitchers positioned on either side of the car. Although his deteriorating condition was obvious in a trembling right arm and whispering voice, Wilson was a real fan who always kept a scorecard and liked to talk baseball with the players. Al Schacht was his favorite, keeping the ex-president amused with his repertoire of stories.[23]

The spring of 1921 was a wintry one, which didn't help Johnson, never a good cold-weather pitcher, overcome the lingering effects of his injury. In conditions called "propitious only for Polar bears" in Detroit on May 15 he was taken out after giving up eight runs in four innings. McBride was harshly criticized for leaving Johnson in so long to be "killed off [by the weather] to please Detroit fans," 28,000 of whom showed up despite the freezing temperatures after heavy advertising of his appearance there.[24] Johnson caught a bad cold (the grippe again) that hung on for months, and although he was never knocked out of the rotation, his pitching was handicapped.[25] It wasn't until late June that the arm stopped hurting when he pitched, but even so there were good days as well as bad, and after a 9–2 win over the depleted White Sox on June 5, his record stood just short of .500 at 4–5.

In the course of Johnson's career there had been other bad starts, but usually the team had done even worse and no blame was placed on him. But in 1921 the Nationals got off to a fast start, solidly in third place by mid-June and trailing the Indians and Yankees by just a few games. Johnson's inconsistency was seen as a serious liability now, and when two of his worst performances of the season came back-to-back at home, the Washington crowds voiced their displeasure. On June 9 Johnson was driven out in the fifth inning of a 10–6 loss to the Tigers. A clearly shocked H.G. Salsinger of the *Detroit News* described the scene that unfolded in the fourth inning:

As his control faltered, there came the rumbling of discontent from the sun gods of the bleachers and soon, across the broad expanse of the Washington ball lot rolled the dreaded, "Take him out!" Johnson, shaky, started the fifth. Ehmke led off with a two-bagger and then, from bleachers and pavillions and grandstand arose the cry, "Take him out! Take him out!" At first a few, then a chorus, and soon it was the distressing yell of a mob. As Johnson, beaten, stood on the mound in the fifth his delivery constantly slowed down. Usually a fast worker, he took more and more time between each pitched ball. Once he rubbed his glove hand across his eyes. It may have been a speck of dust that bothered his vision; it probably was a tear.[26]

An editorial in the *News* two days later, possibly written by Salsinger, tore into the Washington fans as it was impractical for the local press to do:

The Washington baseball crowd, disowning the peerless Walter Johnson and hooting him, is the same as any such crowd. Yet it revives anew the pessimism in the heart of man and forces a sigh for that loyalty and remembrance we would have all men possess, and which so frequently it demonstrates that they do not. Washington is pennant crazy and, with the unaccustomed smell of battle in its nostrils, is ready to rend its own and devour those who, it thinks, hinder its progress. If it involved only the fame of some shooting star, an emblem of sudden fortune, whose quick day was done, the wound would not be so deep. But when one reviews a decade in baseball and ponders the indubitable fact that Walter Johnson was, himself and almost alone, Washington's link to major sports; when one meditates on the irking monotony of constant bafflement which any great pitcher must suffer with an also-ran team; and when one sums up those years of loyalty and service, the reflection presses that Johnson was very, very much greater than all the crowd, put together, which humiliated him. The Washington fans owe Johnson something more than a jeer. Virtue is none too conspicuous in professional sport. An upright player, true to the best traditions of his craft, who has spent himself in a forlorn cause, is entitled to a generous memory.[27]

There was worse to come. In his next appearance, a relief effort against Cleveland on June 13, Johnson faced five batters and gave up a double, a triple, two singles, and a walk in another 10–6 defeat. Frank Menke, writing for the King Features Syndicate, reported the crowd reaction in an article entitled "Hero Life in Baseball is Short, Sweet":

As Johnson, hero of nearly 500 diamond battles, walked across the field, a few "boos" were uttered a little timidly by those who weren't sure that they would get support in their "razzing" of a wonderful pitcher. In a second, however, others joined the chorus which instantly swelled to a thunder of sound. A mighty multitude practically arose to its feet that afternoon to attack with voice, for a single failure, the man who was a hero of heroes. Amazed, almost numbed by the surprising action of the rabble, Johnson's eyes swept up and down the hooting stands. Then he continued on his saddened journey while hisses and unintelligible jeers became intermingled with the "boos." A hero yesterday, a bum today.

Another observer called it "a painful study in the psychology of the crowd. Walter Johnson, the greatest pitcher who ever stepped on a mound, the hero of countless thousands, heard the thunderous roar of 'Take him out! Take him out!' The man who once fed on wild applause and encouraging greetings, even when he wasn't going good, heard only the words that must have pierced his heart to the quick. The Roman gladiators knew this human tragedy only too well."[28]

A much greater tragedy, this one of a deep personal nature, awaited Johnson when the team passed through St. Louis in early July. Just before a scheduled start on the 9th, word came to the ballpark that his father was seriously ill, so he left immediately for Coffeyville. Upon arriving there he learned that Frank Johnson, 59 years old, had died of a stroke. The father had seen his famous son pitch in the major leagues only once, in St. Louis in 1916, but had always followed his career closely through the newspapers. After two weeks of mourning and helping to arrange the family's affairs, Johnson returned to the team.

Not until September was there any evidence that Walter Johnson was capable of being more than just an average pitcher now, and an erratic one at that. But five wins in his last six starts, including several fine performances, provided some hope. His only shutout of the year came at home on September 14 against St. Louis, a 1–0 gem that was the second of two games in his career facing the minimum 27 batters. Three hits produced the only runners, but all were erased from the basepaths, two of them on a triple play started by George Sisler's line drive. Johnson's only ten-strikeout game of the season came in his last appearance, an October 2 win over the Athletics before 14,000 fans on "Clyde Milan Day" in Washington.

In a year marked by an explosion of hitting (Detroit finished sixth with a team batting average of .316), Johnson led the major leagues in strikeouts with 143, and his strikeouts-per-game average of 4.87 was also tops. His 3.51 earned run average, though far above that of his halcyon days, was still far below the American League ERA of 4.28. But despite a creditable 17–14 record, for the first time since he joined the Nationals Walter Johnson was not their top pitcher. That honor went to George Mogridge, who led in almost every category except strikeouts while compiling an 18–14 record. The team as a whole showed much improvement, moving up to fourth (within a half-game of third) under McBride's capable leadership. Unfortunately, in mid-August he took a ball in the face during a practice session and spent three weeks in the hospital. Suffering fainting attacks and vertigo, McBride went home before the end of the season to bring a sad end to his big-league career as player and manager. Clyde Milan ran the club through the end of the season and was given the job for 1922.

Johnson pitched Coffeyville to victory over neighboring Nowata on October 23, a date more notable for the birth of his third son, Robert Warren (for President Harding) Johnson. Three days later the annual game in Humboldt was part of larger festivities dedicating the Walter Johnson Athletic Field, built from the proceeds of the exhibitions over the years. With a crowd of several thousand on hand, a high school football game inaugurated the field after Johnson's ceremonial kickoff, his only recorded appearance on the gridiron. A report of the episode several years later, based on Johnson's account, noted that "as a football player, Walter was a great pitcher. They still point to the hole in the ground dug by Johnson's foot when it missed the ball."[29]

The bad luck plaguing him all year followed Johnson to Kansas, where most of the fall and early winter were taken up with the sad process of auctioning the considerable livestock and implements from Frank Johnson's farm, followed by the sale of the farm itself. Then, just before Christmas, came the most crushing blow of all: the death of 2½-year-old Elinor Johnson from influenza. Her father, stoic and brave under the most trying of circumstances, found it impossible to hide the pain brought on by this sudden and grievous loss. In a letter to F.C. Lane three weeks later, Johnson wrote: "I had a fine little family all my own, three boys and a little girl, and there was never a happier family. There never was a happier, healthier, sweeter baby than our little girl. She took sick and died just before Christmas. Only people who have had the same experience know what that means to a home."[30]

The anguish of Elinor's death, following closely upon his father's, was such that Johnson decided to move away from Coffeyville and its now-tragic associations.[31] In a letter to Hazel from spring training several months later, his undiminished grief is palpable.

"Time will make a big difference," he wrote, "but like you say the hurt will still be there and if we live to be several hundred we would always remember what a sweet child she was and how precious she was. These things come and no matter how hard it is we have to go on. We can look back and say and know we had a wonderful little girl, just as perfect as could be. You have been so brave and although you have suffered so much you are going right along to be the same mother to our dear boys. You have been such a good mother, have done so much to make our little family. You get out and ride as much as you can. We will just try and sell and get away from there, that's the way I feel."[32]

Hazel's sorrow was etched into a poem, *Just For a Little While* (A loving remembrance of Baby Elinor, who fell asleep December, 1921):

Beautiful memories soften our grief
As we tremblingly try to smile,
And thank the Good Father, who gave you to us
Just for a little while.[33]

I used to think every once in a while that I wanted to quit baseball. When you don't have to do something, [that option] sometimes looks attractive. But when you are brought up short, face to face, and given no chance, then the attractive features are likely to melt away. I doubt if any player who has been in the game as long as I have ever really wants to quit when the time comes. I used to say that I would finish while I was still good, that I would leave voluntarily instead of being forced out. But I am beginning to sympathize with the point of view of some of the old veterans that I have heard say they would quit only when they had their uniforms taken away by force.[34]

WALTER JOHNSON, FEBRUARY 1922

Misfortune continued into the winter. Walter, Hazel, and four-year-old Eddie all had bouts with the flu that hung on into the first part of the season. Hazel's weakened condition might have contributed to an infection of her right eye necessitating an operation in Tampa on March 27. The tragic losses and worries about his family's health produced a noticeable, if temporary, change in the big pitcher's disposition. "Johnson is unusually grave and quiet this year," noted one reporter during the training camp.[35] His illness prevented Johnson from working out much, and kept him out of exhibition games entirely.

Not ready for the start of the season on April 12, Johnson wasn't on the mound in the Nationals' opening game for the first time since 1911. He watched with the rest of the team as President Harding tossed the ball to George Mogridge. But that didn't mean that no Walter Johnson would receive attention from the President of the United States that day. Just before the start of the game, Harding noticed six-year-old Walter, Jr. playing in front of the Washington dugout all decked out in a miniature Nationals uniform. Calling

Junior over to the presidential box, the chief executive hoisted the boy over the fence and planted him squarely in the lap of power. That was Junior's vantage point for the first inning, during which he received more attention from the president and first lady than the game itself. The father, undoubtedly wondering what trouble his wandering boy had gotten himself into, emerged from the dugout at the end of the inning to relieve the president of his husky young burden. "That's a mighty fine boy you have there," Harding told him.[36]

In the first month of the 1922 season Johnson appeared in only four games, pitching only seven and one-third innings. Between April 18 and May 6 he pitched to a single batter, striking out Bing Miller of the Athletics with the bases loaded to help preserve a Nationals victory on April 29. But upon finally joining the rotation on May 10, Johnson reeled off five complete-game wins in a row. There were no masterpieces among them, but his arm felt okay. In mid-June Johnson hit his stride with three shutouts in a row, including 1–0 victories over Red Faber of the White Sox and the Yankees' young sensation, Waite Hoyt. In the latter game Johnson registered nine strikeouts against a powerful New York lineup of Babe Ruth, Frank Baker and the original "Murderers Row."

Johnson's record stood at 9–3. But with meager batting support costing him a number of close games and his own poor performance losing others, he finished with a 6–13 run for a losing record of 15 wins and 16 losses by season's end. His 2.99 earned run average was fifth best in the league and more than a run below the league's. With a better club Johnson could easily have won 20 games, but the 1922 Nationals were a sixth-place team, with the second-worst hitting in the league. Clyde Milan's stomach problems, which had bothered him for years, became exacerbated by the stresses of managing and precipitated his retirement. "He was too good a fellow to manage a ballclub," Walter Johnson told a reporter. "The fellows took advantage of his good nature and that hurt."[37]

True to his word about leaving Coffeyville, Johnson spent the winter at the Reno, Nevada, home of Hazel's parents, Edwin E. and Nora Roberts. "E.E." Roberts, as he was known in political circles ("Ed" to his friends), had moved to Reno after losing a close election in 1918 for the U.S. Senate. (His opposition to America's entrance into the war hadn't gone over well with Nevadans). He opened a law practice specializing in divorce cases, and within 10 years had won over 2,000 of them—while losing only one. "My client lied to me," Roberts explained. "The chump didn't tell me that he had another wife living, and I didn't find it out until she showed up in court."[38] He claimed a record in 1929 by securing five divorce decrees in 20 minutes.[39]

The most colorful chapter in the career of E.E. Roberts began in 1923 with his election as mayor of Reno, a city of some 15,000. Advocating a "liberal interpretation of the city ordinances," Roberts won by a 4 to 1 landslide and immediately went about fulfilling his campaign promises. When Reno's red-light district was shut down by a city order the previous year, the disenfranchised prostitutes simply scattered their business around town. Roberts established a "segregated district" on the edge of the city, watched over by police, that came to be known as the "stockade" (a precursor to the Mustang Ranch). Opposed to Prohibition, he instructed the sheriff to ignore liquor offenses unless federal agents specifically asked for their help.[40] With Roberts's strong support the Nevada legislature legalized gambling in 1931, and at the opening of Reno's casinos he outlined his libertarian philosophy: "It's all nonsense trying to regulate people's morals by law," he told the *New York Times*. "For eight years I've been trying to make Reno a place where everybody can do as they please, just so they don't interfere with other people's rights. Now we can do lawfully what Nevada has always done undercover."[41]

If E.E. Roberts's views were somewhat unorthodox, they were also immensely popular in Reno, leading to overwhelming re-election victories in 1927 and 1931. A consummate politician, he played the part to the hilt. "If there was anybody that looked like a congressman, it was Ed Roberts," recalled a reporter for the *Reno Journal*. "He always walked down the street in a big frock coat with a heavy gold chain draped across the front of his vest, and carried a cane, and wore a derby hat, which was quite a big deal in Reno because very few people ever saw derby hats there. He was quite a dandy."[42]

A reporter for the *Reno Gazette*, which opposed the Roberts platform editorially, remembered him as "one of those politicians, good ones, who never took personally those things that were said about him politically. We might carve him all to pieces in the paper and see him the next morning: 'Well [Roberts would say], why don't you come in and have a drink with me and open up the day?' He always opened up the day with a slug of whiskey and a glass of milk. He swore that was what kept him in good health."[43]

The mayor's office on Virginia Street reflected his love for Nevada and its diverse and flamboyant history. "Guns, pistols and derringers were placed so close together around the door and window frames that the wood was almost hidden," a visitor described. "Birdnests decorated the chandelier. On the walls were postcards, posters, handbills and photographs. A great heap of deer antlers occupied one corner. Piles of ore—gold, silver, copper—were massed under the window, together with Indian mortars and grinding stones. 'You see that pair of deuces over there?' [Roberts] said. 'Those little two-spots were worth $15,000 to the nervy man who held them in a game in Gold Hill in the '70s. And that pair of aces won $37,000 over a pair of jacks. Tex Rickard sat in that game, and Walter Mack.' "[44]

The change of scenery to Nevada's rugged wilderness was just the tonic Walter and Hazel needed to heal the wounds and soften painful memories of the past year. Johnson lost himself in the fabulous hunting found there, especially at his father-in-law's duck reserve in nearby Spanish Springs Valley. "I am out every day tramping around the mountains and sure enjoy it," he wrote F.C. Lane. "I shot a wild buck, the first wild one I ever saw, shot some fine pheasants and shoot ducks nearly every day. I have seen several wild horses, they run over the cliffs and mountains just like deer and are wilder. Anyone who enjoys being out in the open couldn't help but like this country, mountain streams and lakes full of fish, plenty of game and lots of room to turn around. My hunting partner is a preacher [Brewster Adams, a Roberts friend] so you see I keep good company."[45]

Toward the end of his stay in the West family concerns, happy and sad, once again predominated. A healthy Carolyn Ann was born on the last day of January 1923, but just a few days later 18-month-old Bobby developed a mastoid infection. When his situation turned serious in mid-February, Johnson took the boy to Children's Hospital in San Francisco, where he underwent an operation similar to that undergone by the father in 1908. Additional surgery became necessary, and it wasn't until a week or so later that Bobby's survival was assured. Joe Cantillon happened to be in San Francisco at the time, and when he heard that Walter Johnson was there the two had a joyful reunion, providing a bright moment during an otherwise dismal and worrisome month on the Coast.[46]

Having lost the first month of spring training looking after Bobby, Johnson made only a single exhibition appearance in 1923, a five-inning stint against the Braves on April 7. His vigorous activity in the off-season had put him in excellent condition, though, feeling fine and anticipating a good year.[47] Once again he was left to train himself by the Nationals' new manager, former Tigers shortstop Donie Bush. Johnson lost the season opener in Philadelphia on April 18, 3–1, but came back with three straight wins, two of them memorable performances against a New York club on the way to its third straight pennant.

A 4–3 victory over Bob Shawkey and Herb Pennock on April 22 was the first Sunday game in the spectacular new Yankee Stadium, and a capacity crowd of almost 70,000 turned out to watch Johnson hand the New Yorkers their first defeat there. Two days later President Harding was on hand to see the Babe smash a home run in "The House That Ruth Built," leading the Yankees to a 4–0 win over the Nationals in the first shutout there. The president sent for Johnson before the game, telling him casually as they shook hands, "Well, Walter, I came out to root for Washington."[48] (Harding died in San

Francisco ten weeks later.) On May 2 Johnson bested Shawkey again, blanking the Yankees on three hits, 3–0.

In St. Louis on May 20 Johnson injured his left knee striding to make a pitch, the beginning of leg problems that would nag him for most of the season. Washington coach George Gibson had sought to strengthen Johnson's legs by having him chase fungoes every day in practice, and Johnson, always a willing and enthusiastic worker, went along with the regimen. But when it became obvious to manager Bush that Gibson was only making the situation worse, he fired Gibson and replaced him with former pitching great Jack Chesbro.[49]

On the occasions when his legs were all right, and especially toward the end of the season when they finally felt strong again, Johnson showed flashes of the old brilliance. On September 17 in St. Louis he won both ends of a doubleheader (one in relief, one starting) for the only time in his career, and the old-time "smoke" was in evidence in a 1–0 win over the White Sox nine days later. In the last game of the year, an October 5 4–2 win over Boston, he struck out 12, best in the major leagues in 1923. Johnson's 130 strikeouts reclaimed his perennial league leadership in that category, and a strong finish boosted his record to a respectable 17–12 for the year.

Clark Griffith wasn't satisfied with Donie Bush's performance, however, the Nationals nudging the Browns out of fourth place at the last minute after languishing in the second division all season. The hope that the fiercely competitive Bush would light a fire under his charges had backfired, and he seems to have antagonized them instead. A September 3 shouting match with mild-mannered Sam Rice probably sealed Bush's fate. Rice drew a suspension from the manager but was immediately reinstated by Griffith, who had more use for the team's leading hitter than he had for Bush.[50] More than 30 years would pass before Griffith again reached outside the Nationals family for a manager.

Although the sixth-place finish in 1922 and lackluster performance the following year (much of which was spent one notch out of the cellar) offered little evidence of it to date, the worn-out parts from Griffith's original "little ballclub" were being gradually replaced and upgraded. With Joe Engel combing the bushes for talent and the Old Fox wheeling and dealing, free now to spend money when necessary, the team had been greatly improved everywhere but centerfield, where Milan's exceptional talents were sorely missed. The outstanding defensive play and solid hitting of Judge at first base, Harris at second, and Rice in right field had long since eliminated those positions as a source of concern, and the frontline pitching of Johnson, Zachary, and Mogridge made up a solid core, the Nationals' best in years.

Late in 1921, Griffith learned from an offhand remark by a golfing partner that Jack Dunn, the brilliant operator of Baltimore's International League club, was about to buy a 20-year-old outfielder from Columbia, South Carolina, of the South Atlantic ("Sally") League for $5,500. Griffith knew that if Dunn, the "discoverer" of Babe Ruth and many other major-league stars, was paying that kind of money for a class B ballplayer, he must know something. Tricking his informant into revealing the name of Dunn's find—Leon Goslin—Griffith quickly arranged to buy him for $6,000.[51]

The serendipitous tip brought to Washington the greatest left-handed power hitter in their history. The solidly-built Goslin, whose nickname "Turk" soon gave way to the predictable "Goose," was a line-drive hitter who sprayed doubles and triples around in great numbers, but who had such power that home runs also came his way with frequency. Three times he hit three in a game. Deadly in the clutch, Goslin was a prodigious run-producer, driving in 100 or more 11 times in an 18-year career and scoring at least 100 runs seven times. Along with a .316 lifetime batting average and .500 slugging percentage, these numbers gained him admittance into the Hall of Fame. Certain fielding idiosyncrasies—such as taking an occasional fly ball on the head—were smoothed out in time, and his shotgun arm was one of the most feared in the game.[52]

A devotee of the high life, the handsome, dapper Goslin was a manager's nightmare. A mere two weeks into his first spring camp in 1922 he was suspended and fined for breaking training rules. But with men on base and a crucial game on the line, there was no sweeter sight to a manager's eyes than that of Goslin swaggering up to the plate with his chest out, swinging his war-club back and forth, hardly able to wait to get his cuts at the ball.

For some time Griffith had been looking for the right man to replace the aging George McBride at shortstop. Eventually he set his sights on Roger Peckinpaugh, a main cog of the Yankees' 1921 pennant-winning club, who had always been a particular thorn in the Nationals' side.[53] In December of that year New York sent Peckinpaugh to Boston in a seven-player swap, reportedly due to Babe Ruth's dislike for Miller Huggins and his stated desire that Peckinpaugh be appointed manager instead.[54] Several weeks later Griffith engineered a three-way deal, shipping outfielder Bing Miller and $50,000 to the Athletics for third baseman "Jumping Joe" Dugan, then swapping Dugan to the Red Sox for Peckinpaugh. The price was high, but the wide-ranging, smooth-fielding veteran "Peck" was the premier shortstop in the game and could anchor the infield as McBride had done for so long. Peckinpaugh, Harris, and Judge formed one of the greatest double-play combinations ever. "When the ball is hit in their direction, everybody is out," Griffith said.[55]

But Peckinpaugh could also hit, and was particularly effective under pressure. A three-sport star at East Cleveland High School, Peckinpaugh was picked up by the Naps after his graduation in 1910 and started his career in a home-town series with the Nationals. "I broke in against Walter Johnson," he recalled. "The first time I went to bat he struck me out. The speed he had! I was pretty much cut up and showed it. It wasn't so easy to act like a big leaguer in your own town, where the folks knew you were just a green high school player. Jim McGuire, the old catcher who was managing Cleveland, noticed how I felt. 'Never mind that, kid,' he told me. 'They all do that against him.' His words made me feel a lot better. Later in the game I hit a couple of fly balls off Johnson. I thought, 'Well, that's pretty good.' "[56] At Washington, Peckinpaugh and Johnson became close friends.

To play alongside Peckinpaugh at third base, Engel found a 21-year-old former Chicago sandlot star at Peoria of the Three-Eye League. It would take Ossie Bluege a couple of years to prove he could hit in the big leagues, but there was never any doubt about his abilities at the "hot corner." During most of his 18-year career Bluege was regarded as the best in baseball at the position, and Bucky Harris considered him even superior to the latter-day third-base standard, Brooks Robinson.[57] Clark Griffith simply called Bluege "the greatest fielder I ever saw."[58] A quiet, modest man—"poker-faced with a golden glove," was Washington writer Joe Holman's characterization—Bluege had a theory about the position that led him to play it more shallow than any man in the league. The territory a third baseman had to cover was cone-shaped, he figured, widening as it moved out from the plate. Bluege played in as close to the narrow end of the cone as he safely could, cutting off countless hits with his catlike reflexes.[59] It also made him, according to Shirley Povich, a "devourer of bunts, with his dashing one-hand pickups and accurate off-balance throws to first."[60] Bluege claimed to have been the first to "shade" the third-base line with a one-run lead to prevent extra-base hits into the left field corner.[61]

For years Washington catchers had either been defensive specialists like Gabby Street, Eddie Ainsmith, and John Henry, or decent hitters like Pat Gharrity and Val Picinich, Walter Johnson's receivers from 1919 through 1922. Finally the team got both in the same man with the arrival in 1923 of Herold "Muddy" Ruel in a trade with Boston. A graduate of the University of St. Louis law school and a practicing attorney in the off-season, Ruel was said to be "the only big-league catcher certified to practice before the United States Supreme Court,"[62] as well as the originator of the term "tools of ignorance" to describe catchers' equipment.[63] Small for the position (5 feet 9 inches, 150 pounds) and not blessed with a great arm, Ruel fashioned a distinguished

19-year career on quickness, intelligence, and the ability to hit well in the pinches. He was a master at pitch-calling and handling pitchers.[64] Shortly before Miller Huggins's death in 1929, the Yankees skipper with a reputation for judging talent was asked if he had ever let a good player slip away. "Yes," he replied, "Muddy Ruel. I always had a personal liking for Muddy, believing him to be one of the finest young men I've ever known, but I could not see him as a catcher. So I let him go. It wasn't very long thereafter I realized how badly mistaken I had been. Now, every time I'm tempted to pass snap judgement on a youngster, I think of Muddy—and I wait a while!"[65]

Walter Johnson got along extremely well with the smiling, affable Ruel, and in the five years they were teammates it was a rare Johnson performance that didn't find Ruel behind the plate. As a boy growing up in St. Louis, Ruel had revered the great pitcher. "My one ambition in baseball from my earliest days was to catch the famous Walter Johnson," Ruel recalled in 1927, "but I never dared to expect that I would ever have the opportunity. 'Barney' always was my particular idol. My father used to take me to the games in St. Louis 15 or so years ago, and I never missed the days when Johnson was scheduled to work. He was my hero, up on a pedestal. Boys' dreams do come true sometimes in real life as well as in fiction, and on the spring day in 1923 when a Washington paper announced that I was scheduled to work with 'Barney' I was easily the happiest player in Tampa, Florida."[66]

Coming from Boston with Ruel was pitcher Allan Russell, whose specialty was loading the ball with a substance known as "slippery elm."[67] Russell was one of the first pitchers to make a career predominantly as a reliever. With the Nationals in 1923 he made 46 relief appearances and only six starts, the greatest degree of bullpen specialization to that time.

Coincidentally, the man with greatest claim to the title of relief-pitching pioneer—Fred Marberry—also came to the Nationals in 1923, late in the season. Joe Engel had found Marberry, nearly 25 years old, languishing at Little Rock in the Southern Association.[68] Dubbed "Firpo" (a nickname he didn't like) by sportswriters because of his size (6 feet 1 inch, 200 pounds) and facial resemblance to the huge Argentine heavyweight fighter Luis Firpo, Marberry had grown up on a cotton farm in Texas. With an angry attitude on the mound (perhaps because he hated the limited "fireman" role assigned to him), and a blazing fastball, he was the first of the great relief "intimidators." "Sometimes Bucky would go to the pitcher's mound just to talk to the pitcher, unsure about whether or not to take him out," Al Schacht recalled. "But he'd no sooner get to the mound, and there would be Marberry—out of the bullpen, coming in. He was that willing and that anxious."[69] Ossie Bluege said: "You should have seen Fred walk across the outfield when he was coming in to relieve. He moved just as fast as he could and just as determined and as confident as could be."[70] Marberry could warm up quickly with a half-dozen pitches, but once on the mound he would pick up dirt, paw the ground, fret and fume. Finally he would rear back with his leg high in the air, his shoe in the batter's face, and fire in a smoking fastball.

In a hotel or on a train Marberry was a peaceable, friendly soul who wasn't looking for trouble from anybody. On the diamond it was a different story altogether. Shirley Povich told of a game in New York in which the Yankees rode the big Texan mercilessly. As he passed by their bench on the way to the showers, Marberry stopped. "You, Ruth, can be first," he shouted to the great slugger, "and you'll need all the help you can round up." The Yankees just stared out at the hulking farmboy in silence.[71]

Nemo Leibold, yet another Red Sox alumnus, was picked up on waivers early in the 1923 season and installed as the team's center fielder. Sam Rice and Clyde Milan had switched positions in 1920 to reduce the territory Milan's aging legs had to cover, but Rice preferred right field and the acquisition of Leibold, who had played several years in center for Cleveland, allowed him to return there. Leibold was actually a natural right fielder too, having played that position for two American League champion Chicago clubs, including the 1919 Black Sox. One of three regulars on that team not on the take (Eddie Collins and Ray Schalk were the other "Clean Sox"), he suffered through the worst series of any of them, ironically, going 1 for 18. It was a subject he didn't like to talk about.[72] Leibold was a scrappy little fireplug, a slap hitter with good speed who hit .305 for Washington in 1923.

Attendance at Washington's American League Park had taken a dramatic turn upward since Clark Griffith assumed control of the club, soaring from 234,000 in 1919 to 359,000 the next year, then over 450,000 in 1921 and 1922. In 1923, with the team's horrendous start and only partial recovery, it fell back to 360,000.[73] Now Griffith took some of the profits to give his customers an enlarged and improved ballpark. Thirteen thousand seats were added with a new steel-and-concrete stand in left field, the peculiar feature of which was a roof higher than that covering the original pavilion. The wall in right field was raised to 30 feet and the field re-sodded, the infield grass imported from the greens of a local golf course. The *Post* called it the "million-dollar infield . . . said to be the best diamond in any of the major league parks."[74] The players got renovated clubhouses, and the improved and expanded structure got a new name: Clark Griffith Stadium.

In hindsight, it's easy to see that Griffith had put together a very good team, almost a great one, full of future Hall of Famers (Johnson, Goslin, Rice, Harris) and many other excellent players. But there were plenty of good ballclubs in the league, several of which had always managed to finish ahead of the Nationals in recent years. There was little real cause for optimism as the 1924 season approached. On the contrary, with the search on for a fifth manager in as many seasons the club might have been viewed as in a state of some disarray. For Washington fans, the only ones in either circuit never to have experienced a championship since the beginning of professional baseball nearly 50 years earlier, there was only the usual bromide to fall back on: "Wait 'til next year!", a cry growing fainter with each passing season. But this time the capital—and the baseball world—were in for a big surprise.

CHAPTER 12

Pulling For Walter

Several years ago when the Washington team visited Detroit, I witnessed an incident which was both humorous and pathetic. There is a young deaf and dumb fellow in that city who aspires to be a pitcher. On one occasion when we arrived in town, Walter Johnson received a note from this man, asking for an interview. They met in the hotel lobby, and neither was able to communicate with the other. A number of us were amused by seeing Johnson waving his hands to and fro, endeavoring to explain certain things to him. Johnson, while illustrating the kind of balls to throw, made motions and took exercise enough to pitch a couple of games. I laughed until I almost fell off my chair at the maneuvers of the two. The peculiar feature of it is that whenever we visit Detroit this young man always comes around and practices a few hours before each game while Johnson still takes as much time as ever in instructing him. Aside from the communication Walter received the first time, I don't think there has been a single line between the two for several years other than in the crude sign language.[1]

WILLIAM FOWLER, CLUB SECRETARY
WASHINGTON NATIONALS

By waiting until 1924 for Washington to achieve its first full measure of baseball glory, fate assured that the event would have a maximum impact on the rest of the nation. A transportation and communications revolution was knitting all parts of the country together for the first time into a larger social fabric. The Ford Model T was within almost every worker's reach at $260; a vast railroad network crisscrossed the country, passing through every section; the first nonstop coast-to-coast airplane flight took place in 1923, and on August 1 of that year WRC became Washington's first radio station in time to broadcast the World Series. The radio and phonograph were becoming standard fixtures in American homes. Movies (and their everpresent newsreels) were the most popular way to spend a night out. The printed word had hardly been rendered obsolete by the newer media, however. A proliferation of newspapers, magazines, books, and other written material of every conceivable format and theme took place simultaneously.

Taking up much of the pages, airwaves, grooves, and screens of the Jazz Age was a new cult of the celebrity. There had always been famous people, of course, but their renown had usually arisen out of great accomplishment, usually over a long period of time and in those fields emphasized by newspapers and magazines: war and diplomacy, politics, exploration, business, invention, literature, and the like. But the newer forms of communication were more immediate and direct. The public didn't just read about actors and musicians, they saw and heard them, and widespread fame was now possible overnight with a hit movie, radio show, or recording. Rudolph Valentino, Tom Mix, Will Rogers, Douglas Fairbanks, Mary Pickford, Clara Bow, Charlie Chaplin, Paul Whiteman, Al Jolson, and many others were as widely known in small hamlets as in the big cities.

Because of the large crowds and extensive print coverage it attracted, sports, and especially baseball, had for some time been one of the few avenues for national stardom. Now athletes could vault into the public awareness with a single momentous performance, while the consistently great ones were rewarded with previously unheard-of prominence and popularity. It's no coincidence that the hero-worshipping 1920s has been labeled "the Golden Age of Sports," with the media making giants out of Red Grange, Jack Dempsey, Bobby Jones, Bill Tilden, Johnny Weissmuller and many others. In baseball it was the one and only Babe Ruth commanding center stage, although for several years he would have to move over and share the spotlight with a rival—Walter Johnson—for his crown as king of the diamond.

Curiously, the new personality-worship and such other manifestations of the "Roaring Twenties" as wild new dances, elevated hemlines, and the omnipresent speakeasies with their bootleg whiskey and bathtub gin, all took place under the cautious and conservative administration of the new Republican President, Calvin Coolidge. Even as details of the Teapot Dome scandal (in which oil magnate E.L. Doheny had "loaned" $100,000 to President Harding's Secretary of the Interior Albert Fall to secure a favorable lease on the Elk Hills naval oil reserve in California) were coming to light in the fall and winter of 1923–24, Coolidge declared, "The chief business of the American people is business." Following a series of national traumas beginning with the war and ending with the death of President Harding and the unraveling of the scandal, this laissez-faire attitude struck just the right tenor for the times.

Going into business was exactly what Walter Johnson had in mind. Returning his signed contract in January 1924, Johnson notified Griffith of an intention to retire from the major leagues at the end of the season to buy a Pacific Coast League franchise.[2] The Vernon club of Los Angeles was the original subject of discussions (and perhaps negotiations), but when the press reported Johnson's interest in buying a minor-league team other propositions were presented. Oakland's PCL club soon became the focus of interest.[3] At some point George Weiss, in Tampa with his New Haven ballclub (and its manager, Clyde Milan), became involved with Johnson in the effort to buy a PCL team.[4] After the story broke, Johnson outlined his intentions:

> What I propose to do, if possible, is buy into one of the Pacific Coast League clubs. There are three or four that could be considered. I have friends who have assured me of all the financial support necessary to swing such a deal as I have in mind, and if my hopes are realized there will be someone [Weiss] to look after the business end as president of the club, while I will run the team and play some, too. The situation is that I know I am nearing the end of my string and it's up to me to look to the future. I probably could get by for a couple of years or so yet, but what after that? I do not intend to do nothing after my big league career is ended, and having been in the game for so long, baseball naturally is the only thing I know. As things are now, I have a home in Kansas, another in Washington, and spend most of my time in Nevada. I have a family, with two children of school age, and no permanent residence. It is an injustice to them to have to chase all around the country. I want to settle down in one place and make it my all-year-round home and I hope to do it on the Pacific coast.[5]

The confirmation that 1924 would be Johnson's last year with the Nationals was greeted with the expected surprise and disappointment by the team and its followers, but for his part there was only optimism and enthusiasm for the future. Johnson told *Post* writer Frank Young that if the Coast League propositions had come his way a bit earlier, he wouldn't be with Washington now.[6]

When Clark Griffith finally decided on a new manager (on February 9, the eve of spring training), no one was more surprised than the appointee himself—Bucky Harris. Many names had been floating around, but Harris's wasn't among them. Eddie Collins and Jack Barry both rejected offers from Griffith, and George McBride, Roger Peckinpaugh, and Walter Johnson were considered serious possibilities.[7] Harris was team captain in 1923, but no one believed he would be in line for the big job. Indeed, Harris had been asked to shift to third base should the Nationals get Collins to come over from the White

Sox as player-manager.[8] Then he got into hot water by playing pro basketball in the off-season in violation of a clause in his contract. Early in his career Harris had made extra money from the other sport before Griffith, worried about leg damage from pounding up and down the hardwood, forbade it.[9]

In Tampa getting ready for spring training, Harris received a letter from Griffith. His first thought might have been that he had been traded, and he certainly wasn't expecting an offer to manage the ballclub. But there it was: "If you want the job, it is yours," it said. According to Shirley Povich, when a poor phone connection prevented Harris from communicating his acceptance to Griffith, he gave a Western Union operator 20 dollars to send the same telegram every hour for four hours straight. "I'll take that job and win Washington's first American League pennant," it's supposed to have said with typical Harris bravado.[10]

Except for Goose Goslin, Harris was the youngest starter on the team. But exposure at an early age to the harsh realities of life in the Pennsylvania coal pits had matured him more quickly than most. The responsibilities and demands of the job held no fear for Harris, and his tough play at second base had long since earned him the respect of his teammates—his players now.[11] He was also smart enough to assuage any hard feelings among the older veterans who were passed over for the position, or merely perplexed by the choice.[12] Harris went to Johnson and Judge first and asked for their support. Not only were they behind him 100 percent, they told him, but would make sure that it went for the rest of the team also.[13] "The boys all like Harris and are going to work hard for him," Johnson declared shortly after arriving in Tampa.[14] For his part Harris expressed to the players his feeling that his success depended on them, not the other way around.[15] They appreciated his honor system with regard to training rules, eliminating bed checks and other restrictions. Harris was patient and understanding with his players, as might be expected considering he was still one himself, but when necessary he could also be firm.[16] Harris sat Goslin down for a chat one day at Tampa, and whatever was said between the two, there was no more trouble from the young slugger.[17] "[Harris] knew men and how to handle them," writer Joe Holman said.[18]

At Hot Springs, even before the formal start of spring training, a spirit of camaraderie developed among the regulars that "laid the foundation for the club spirit which helped carry us to success," Harris wrote in his book about the 1924 season, *Playing The Game.* They worked out together, took marathon hikes in the Arkansas hills, enjoyed the "radio-active" baths, and played cards and golf with one another. Roger Peckinpaugh remembered it as "a very close-knit group. We all worked very well together."[19]

While at the resort, Harris and others cooked up a memorable prank to play on Al Schacht, who was working out with the rookies in Florida in a last attempt to get his pitching career back on track. When the regulars got to Tampa, Harris told Schacht: "Al, I met a couple of the most beautiful women I have ever seen at Hot Springs, and I told them all about you. They're going to arrive here in a few days and rent a cottage, and you and I are going to visit them. These gals are all pepped up on meeting you. They think you're wonderful." At the team dinner table a few days later, Harris whispered into Schacht's ear, "It's all set, Al." Schacht got a haircut and shave, had his best suit pressed, and on the manager's instructions bought a twelve-dollar bottle of Prohibition liquor and a dozen oranges. A taxi took them into the darkness of the countryside to a cottage several miles outside Tampa. Harris knocked on the door. A man opened it, and Harris asked, "Is Margie in?"

"In one brief moment, the peace of the night was shattered," Schacht described the episode years later. "Without warning, the man pulled a revolver out of his pocket, aimed it at Harris's heart and shouted, 'So you're the dirty bums who are trying to break up my home!' With that he fired two shots through the screen at Harris. Bucky screamed in pain, 'My God', he cried, 'I'm shot. He got me.' And he fell off the porch, a crumpled heap, lying still—very still. For a few seconds I was stunned by the course of events, dreary thoughts racing through my head. Poor Bucky . . . what a nice guy he was . . . not a bad second baseman . . . and he sacrificed his life so that I could have some fun . . . maybe they'll make me manager. Not a single second had I allotted to my own safety until I was awakened out of my grief by a voice that boomed, 'And now I'll get you, you rat!'"

Leaping from the porch, Schacht took off as fast as he could, running headlong down the road back to Tampa. Ducking into the bushes whenever a car passed by, he ran and walked until finally reaching the hotel, exhausted. As he staggered into the lobby, the entire team was standing there. "You look a little pale, Al," one of them said as they cracked up laughing. It turned out that they had hidden in the bushes outside the house, several with guns ready to shoot in the air while Schacht scrambled for his life. Walter Johnson had been one of those, but laughed so hard he couldn't squeeze the trigger. "What really hurts," Schacht said of the episode years later, "is that they couldn't keep it to themselves. Even now every once in a while someone will shout, 'Hey, Al, how's Tampa Margie?'"[20]

Four months of hiking and hunting in the mountains around Reno had put Johnson in prime condition.[21] "I am in fine shape, never felt better in my life and expect to have a better season than the last one," he wrote F.C. Lane on January 14.[22] The legs causing so much trouble in 1923 had been built up and strengthened, and it was Johnson who set the pace for the rest of the team in their daily treks in the foothills of the Ozarks around Hot Springs. "The Mountain Goat," they started calling him. "He had most of us staggering around until we became accustomed to the uphill going," Bucky Harris recalled. "We returned to Tampa in fine condition."[23] A report from Hot Springs noted that "When some of the party return [from the mountain hikes] tired and ready to call it a day, Walter rests by playing from 18 to 36 holes of golf."[24] Upon the arrival of the veterans at the Florida camp on March 9, Frank Young of the *Post* wrote: "Those who have watched the comings and goings of the Griffmen to and from Tampa for the past several years expressed their surprise when Johnson made his appearance. The American League's greatest moundsman is the picture of health and looks better right now than he has at this time for any number of years back."

But it wasn't only Johnson's legs that had been restored to him at the advanced age of 36. For the first time since the injury in 1920 his arm was completely free of the tightness and soreness that had accompanied throwing. The knot above his elbow, "a little round ball" as he described it, had gotten progressively smaller each year, and now it was gone. Johnson planned to return to being primarily a fastball pitcher, and not mix up his pitches so much. "My pitching wing seems to be in as fine trim as it has been in any of my seventeen years with the Nationals," he said. "So I'm going to keep on shooting them in in the old way as long as the arm shows it will stand the gaff."[25] An encouraged Harris declared after Johnson's first workout at the Florida camp on March 10: "I can't imagine Walter ever having been faster than he is right now."[26]

Johnson's first test of the exhibition season on the 22nd against the St. Louis Cardinals was a good omen, holding them scoreless for four innings on one hit and no walks. Rogers Hornsby, facing Johnson for the second and last time in his career (the "knot-hole" home-run game in 1917 was the other), hit into a double play and popped up with men in scoring position both times. (Hornsby would hit .424, the major-league record, in 1924.) Against the three-time National League champion Giants on the 26th, Johnson was the winning pitcher, allowing a powerful New York lineup one run in four innings. The Giants expressed amazement at Johnson's speed. "If he was any better fifteen years ago than he is now, I'm glad I was in kindergarten," declared shortstop Travis Jackson.[27] "Walter Johnson, war-scarred veteran of 17 campaigns and holder of several major league records, is displaying mid-season form and has given Griffith's club an air of confidence," it was reported after the game. "Griffith, although not predicting a pennant for his club, feels confident that the Senators are going to cause considerable trouble in the American League."[28]

Johnson gave up four runs and a walk over 21 innings in his five exhibition appearances, all of them victories over National League clubs. Harris insisted on fighting for everything, even in meaningless exhibition games, to cultivate a winning attitude from the start. Remembering his rookie season of 1920, when Johnson caught a debilitating cold on the barnstorming trip back from Florida, Harris sent the veteran pitcher directly to Washington in advance of the full squad. It was decided that Johnson would get only well-spaced starting assignments this year; for the first time in his career there would be no relief jobs.[29]

The 1924 season opened on April 15 with a perfect spring day in Washington as President Coolidge and a record crowd of 26,000 packed into the newly-renovated ballpark. Manager Harris was presented a huge floral horseshoe for good luck, after which Walter Johnson caught the ceremonial toss with his bare hand. Coolidge autographed the ball, the fourth president to do so for Johnson's collection, and Billy Evans put another one into play. If his fine exhibition season had left anyone doubting the Big Train's return to old-time form, his blanking of the Athletics, 4–0, in the opener should have convinced them. The *Post* said of the day and the game: "No season ever started more propitiously."

One of the A's hits was a single by center fielder Al Simmons in his major-league debut. (Ten days later Simmons hit the first of 307 career home runs, also off Johnson.) Another "rookie" making his debut with Philadelphia was 30-year-old outfielder Paul Strand, whose last appearance in the big leagues had been in 1915 at the end of a three-year pitching tryout with the Boston Braves. Strand had converted himself into an outfielder, and with Salt Lake City in 1922 led the Pacific Coast League with a .384 batting average. The next year he paced the PCL again with a .394 average, 43 home runs, 187 RBI's, and 180 runs. His 325 hits in 194 games is still the record for organized baseball.[30]

After that performance Strand was put up for sale for $75,000. Excited by the prospect of another hard-hitting outfielder to team with Rice and Goslin, Griffith sent Joe Engel to size him up, but the scout's report was negative. While Griffith was mulling it over, Connie Mack, who was rebuilding his team, paid the price. After a strong exhibition season Strand opened the year batting third for Philadelphia. Knowing his boss would be among those eyeing Strand with great interest on opening day, Engel sought out his old teammate and friend, Walter Johnson, before the game. "I want you to do me a favor, Walter," he said. "When Strand comes up there, give him the works, please, for me."[31] In four trips to the plate Strand never came close to a hit, and for good measure Johnson sent him down on strikes the last time. (After hitting .228 in 47 games, Strand was gone from the major leagues.)

The inaugural game didn't appear to be any kind of omen at first, as the Nationals dropped quickly into the second division. A month later they fell into seventh place, and the judgment of those deriding Harris's promotion as "Griffith's Folly" seemed vindicated.[32] But in early June the team fought its way back to the .500 mark, then caught fire two weeks later, taking the last nine games of their first extended road trip. Johnson kicked off a personal six-game winning streak on May 23 with one of his greatest games, a 4–0 shutdown of Chicago in which he allowed one hit and one walk, faced 28 batters and struck out 14 (equalling his career best). He tied a league record by fanning six White Sox in a row. His 2–0 win at Detroit on June 6th gave Washington an important series over the second-place Tigers, who might have found their fans' partiality toward the visiting pitcher disconcerting. "Local fans repeatedly applauded Walter Johnson for his work, particularly in the second and fifth, when he struck out two men in both innings," it was reported.[33] Detroit player-manager Ty Cobb, who had made steady progress with the team since taking over from Hughie Jennings in 1921, tried desperately to rattle his young Washington counterpart, calling him "Baby face" and "Snookums". "Boot it! Boot it!" Cobb hollered from the third-base box whenever a ground ball came Harris's way.[34]

The Nationals got solid performances from all the veterans in 1924, but two positions were proving serious liabilities, particularly on defense, early in the year. Young Ossie Bluege spent the first part of the season on the bench in favor of Doc Prothro and his .333 batting. But the pudgy, short-armed Prothro was hurting the team in the field with his limited mobility, and a costly error at Cleveland early in June sealed his fate. After the game a frustrated Harris spotted Bluege in the shower. "You're playing third base tomorrow and from here on in, come hell or high water," he told him.[35]

The search to improve on Leibold for the third outfield spot had already seen four players come and go with no luck. Then the club bought Wid Matthews from Minneapolis and for a while, at least, the problem was solved. He had been a regular in 1923 with the Athletics but was pushed out this year by Simmons and Strand. A small, intense player ("A little pepperbox," one writer called him), Matthews made his Washington debut on June 5 with a triple, single, sacrifice, and assist. He hit .359 over the next three weeks, at the end of which the Nationals had taken over first place in the American League.[36]

On June 15 another "new" face joined the team, and although it's hard to imagine any coach or clown, or clown/coach, turning a franchise around, that's what happened following Al Schacht's return to Washington. As

Schacht himself put it in the first of his two autobiographies, *Clowning Through Baseball:* "My natural modesty prevents me from making any claims as a luck charm, but from the day I joined the club, the entire picture changed." Since his last appearance in the major leagues in 1921, Schacht had struggled to make a comeback with a number of minor-league teams. Appearing to have recovered his effectiveness in spring training this year, he then sustained a serious knee injury goofing around in batting practice against Walter Johnson. After a final unsuccessful journey to the minors convinced Schacht his playing days were over, he called Griffith to remind him of the promise made in 1920 after he filled in for Johnson and beat the Yankees. The Washington owner was true to his word, and Schacht replaced Jack Chesbro as the team's third-base coach.[37]

On the surface a simple case of returning a favor, the Old Fox rarely made any deal that didn't work out substantially to his benefit, and this was no exception. The Washington baseball club once again featured two "official" clowns when no other team had even one. But just as with Germany Schaefer and Nick Altrock, Schacht's talents weren't restricted to the comedic realm. Manager Harris welcomed the addition to his coaching staff. "They were both sound baseball men," he said of his assistants.[38]

Al Schacht was a born funnyman with an expressive face highlighted by big eyes and a prominent nose. He learned pantomime by imitating his teachers in New York's public schools, then pulled gags to amuse teammates throughout a long minor-league career. After riding a horse to the mound dressed in a top hat and tails over a baseball uniform, the costume that became his trademark, Schacht was anointed the "Clown Prince of Baseball" by Buffalo sportswriter Jack Yellen.[39] On a barnstorming trip north from spring training in 1921, Schacht and Altrock started doing comedy routines together, and their collaboration continued into the regular season to the delight of Washington fans. With a persistent sore arm raising doubts about his pitching career, Schacht began paying more and more attention to his gags and stunts.

The big break came when Yankees owner Jacob Ruppert hired the duo to entertain at the 1921 World Series, where they were a hit with the fans and received rave reviews from the writers. Over the next 15 years they gained national fame performing an endless variety of skits and satires of sporting and other events of the day at every conceivable venue, including World Series and All-Star games, basketball and hockey games, and tennis matches.[40] In the winter of 1927, with Joe Engel as manager and occasional participant in the sketches, they went onto the vaudeville and theatre circuits. ("I played on the same bill as Bing Crosby and the Rhythm Boys," Schacht recalled. "They got $350 a week and I was making $1,450.")[41]

What laughing audiences couldn't have guessed was the deep animosity between the two that only intensified over the years. At first Altrock had been happy to have another "second banana" to play off of, as he had with Germany Schaefer and Eddie Sawyer. But it was Schacht, with more in mind than Altrock's simple style of mugging and slapstick, inventing the increasingly sophisticated routines and satires that inspired the biggest laughs and elevated the act to success beyond the baseball world. The billing was always "Altrock and Schacht," but as the latter attracted more and more attention and praise he became the object of intense jealousy by the former. Their parodies of championship boxing matches took on a distinctly realistic appearance at times, and in 1929 they stopped talking to each other altogether. "That was the only way I could continue working with him," Schacht explained.[42]

The famous pair finally split up in 1936 when Schacht retired from coaching. Going out on his own as a single act he found even greater success, continuing to perform at the World Series (he did 27 of them in his career) and All-Star games while adding another 130 or so major- and minor-league games to his annual itinerary. During the Second World War he traveled through Africa, Europe, Asia, and the South Pacific, logging more than 300,000 miles to play 790 shows and appear at 310 hospitals. In 1946 Schacht got married and opened a restaurant in New York that became a famous gathering spot for athletes and other celebrities, making him wealthy in the process. Occasional personal appearances continued until his last performance at a game in Hartford, Connecticut, in 1973 at the age of 81. Al Schacht claimed to have performed live for more people than any entertainer in history, and with 60 years in front of stadiums full of them, he might be absolutely right.[43]

In his autobiography, Babe Ruth (winner of his only batting title in 1924) said of the '24 Nationals: "Washington got hot quicker than almost any club I ever saw."[44] They hovered around .500 until a Johnson victory at Philadelphia on June 21 pushed them over to stay. Four wins in three days at New York suddenly catapulted them past the Yankees, Tigers, Red Sox, and White Sox into the league lead. Never before had the Nationals been on top this late in the season, and 3,000 fans greeted their arrival at Union Station on June 25 after three weeks on the road. The next day a crowd of 23,000, including President and Mrs. Coolidge and their two sons, were on hand to see Johnson shut out the A's, 5–0, for the team's 10th straight win. "As I stood back of the plate," wrote umpire Billy Evans, "I marveled at Johnson's pitching as he mowed down the Athletics with consummate ease. As he struck out that dangerous hitter, Sammy Hale, on three fast balls to end the game, the thought came to me that in a pinch his fast one is just as puzzling as 18 years ago."[45]

Johnson's revival was one of the reasons for Washington's unexpected showing in the American League race (*Baseball Magazine* had picked them to finish seventh), but as Norman Baxter of the *Post* observed, it was part of a larger dynamic at work on the club: "Undoubtedly the greatest factor in the success of the Nationals has been that the veterans on the team—and there are many of them—have worked like Trojans for the youngest leader in baseball. It might not have been surprising to have found the Washington team slightly out of line because of refusal of some of the players to take the 'boy manager' seriously. There has been none of this evidently. If there had been it would have been impossible for Washington to lead the league. The veterans seem rather to have become infected with the enthusiasm of the manager. Johnson, Mogridge, Peckinpaugh and Judge have given themselves valiantly to the task of putting Harris and the ball club across. They have literally played their heads off and as a result they are today in a position that no outsider and few members of the team thought it would be possible for them to reach. There have been no geniuses, merely a bunch of hard-working and hard-fighting players."[46]

Harris did much to foster this spirit by constantly seeking the advice of the older men, particularly Griffith. While rooming with Donie Bush in 1923, Harris noticed that Bush never consulted with the owner. "I didn't think that was right," Harris said later. "It was his ballclub, after all." In contrast, he met with Griffith each morning to go over personnel matters and discuss strategy. "Clark Griffith was the smartest baseball man I ever knew," Harris said after his long career in the game. But Harris was gifted with his own strengths, too. "I think Bucky Harris was the best of all the player-managers," Al Schacht said. "He was smart, aggressive; he made the right moves."[47] Throughout the June western trip Harris made it his mission to infuse confidence into his charges, taking players aside individually to show them how at every position and man for man Washington was as good as or better than any team in the league.[48]

By the end of June the Nationals had built a four-game lead over the Yankees, and the first stirrings of a pennant-for-Washington feeling around the country were in evidence, much of it based on a desire to see Walter Johnson get his chance in a World Series. "If a vote of the nation was taken, Washington would finish in front by a dozen games," wrote Grantland Rice. "It would be worth more than an ordinary outlay of sentiment to have Walter Johnson in one World Series before the ancient wing begins to droop and lose its snap."[49] Poli's Theatre in Washington made the Nationals their guests for the June 30 performance of Gilbert and Sullivan's *HMS Pinafore.* In addition, DeWolf Hopper treated them to his inimitable rendition of the famous baseball poem, *Casey at the Bat,* after which the orator gave the team a few personal words of encouragement. Hopper had played hooky from rehearsal the day before, going out to the ballpark instead.[50]

For the next six weeks a fierce three-way struggle saw Washington, New York, and Detroit, never more than a few games from each other, trading places at the top of the league. The Tigers enjoyed their last moment of glory on August 3 when they beat the Yankees in front of 43,000 fans in Detroit. The Nationals lost five in a row in the sapping heat of St. Louis to drop several games behind both rival clubs,[51] and if Washington was going to fold up and be satisfied with an admirable second- or third-place finish, this was the time. But Johnson's win at Chicago on August 7 broke the club's six-game losing streak and the Nationals took the series there to stay in the race.

Once again the third outfield position was of great concern. Wid Matthews, who had helped so much during the team's first big push in June, had become a liability now. Opposing defenses began closing off the short right field area into which most of Matthews's hits were pulled, and as his average dropped the pressure worked on his nerves until Harris was finally forced to bench him.[52] Nemo Leibold was only adequate, particularly in the field. Viewing the acquisition of a solid center fielder as key to winning the pennant, Griffith assigned Joe Engel the task of finding one. He went to Sacramento and liked what he saw of their star, Earl McNeely—but not the price tag of $75,000 they had put on him. Not wanting to take responsibility for such a gamble, Engel insisted Griffith look the prospect over for himself. But with time running out Griffith put his faith in the scout's recommendation and cut a deal sending $35,000 and three players, including Wid Matthews, to Sacramento.[53] After debuting on August 12 in a 4–0 Walter Johnson win over Cleveland, McNeely hit .394 in his first 10 games and proved himself to be precisely the fast, rangy center fielder Griffith had in mind. Moving in immediately as the team's leadoff hitter, he batted .330 in the 45 games left in the season.

Another significant mid-season acquisition was Warren "Curly" Ogden, picked up in late June on waivers from the Athletics. Ogden's 2–9 career record (0–3 so far in 1924) and 1923 earned run average of nearly six runs a game wouldn't seem to have been much of a recommendation, but whatever hunch led the Nationals to add him to their staff paid off handsomely. A reliever almost exclusively at Philadelphia, Ogden became a potent starting pitcher with eight straight wins down the stretch, three of them shutouts—all the while suffering from a sore arm so painful that he walked the floor of his hotel room after each game, holding his arm and convinced he would never pitch again. Somehow trainer Mike Martin always had Ogden ready in time for his next start.[54]

⚾ ⚾ ⚾ ⚾ ⚾

My principal regret this season is the knowledge that I am not what I used to be as a pitcher. If I could have the strength and the speed and the endurance that I knew 10 years back, this pennant would be in and I don't mean to be at all boastful in making that statement. I know what I used to do with a losing ball club and I know well enough what I could do now with such a club as we have behind me. If the old right arm was young, I would pitch every other day from now on till the pennant was ours, and I wouldn't lose many games either. And it isn't all a matter of stuff. A young pitcher recuperates so quickly. Why, when I was young I could pitch today and go out and pitch tomorrow and feel fresh and energetic. Now it's a task to pitch once in three days. I'd be better once in four, but I shall try to get in there every third day. Pitching ball when you're young is a pleasure. When you're old it's a task and the task grows harder with every passing year. If I could only be for one short month the pitcher I used to be! But that's idle speculation and it's the realities that count. I am still good enough, I must be good enough to help the boys win a pennant.[55]

WALTER JOHNSON, AUGUST 30, 1924

The Nationals reclaimed second place and left the Tigers behind for good, beating them four out of five times in an important mid-August series that included a sparkling 8–1 Johnson victory on the 17th. Giving up four hits and no walks, he retired the side in order in seven of nine innings and ended the game with a flourish by striking out Ty Cobb to the cheers of 20,000 fans at Griffith Stadium. After that game and for the last six weeks of the pennant race, Johnson's normal break of four days between starts was cut to three. Harris had his two specialists, Marberry and Russell (72 relief appearances between them in 1924), and often took Johnson out after seven innings if he appeared to be tiring or the game was well in hand. Although leading the league with 38 starts in 1924, Johnson finished only 20 of them, Marberry alone saving five of his victories. In *Playing The Game* Harris wrote that one night during the final pennant drive Johnson told him that "if he could help Washington lead the league, he didn't care what happened to his arm. He added that he didn't mind if he never pitched in a world series."

Setting their sights now on the Yankees, the Nationals went on a nine-game winning streak to pull even with them behind Johnson's rain-shortened no-hitter in St. Louis on August 25. The only baserunners in a seven-inning, 2–0 victory came on two walks, and George Sisler commented afterward that "Under the dark sky out there today Johnson's pitches came over looking about the size of peas and we felt satisfied to connect regardless of where the ball went. In my estimation, Johnson right now is as good as he ever was."[56] The Nationals went to New York for the last series of the year between the deadlocked teams, four games in the last four days of August that would set the stage for the last month of the pennant race.

The first game on the 28th couldn't have given the team a bigger boost. Down by 6–3 after two home runs by Babe Ruth and another by Bob Meusel, Washington scored eight times in the eighth inning to put the game away, 11–6. The sudden torrent of runs triggered another surprising outburst, this one by the fans at Yankee Stadium. "That eighth inning explosion caused one of the wildest demonstrations ever seen anywhere," it was reported. "The big crowd stood and roared and howled encouragement as the fighting Griffs drove one pitcher after another from the rubber. A shower of straw hats followed every resounding wallop. The Washington dugout was bedlam, exuding dancing athletes, old gloves, towels, caps and shoes, and accompanied, as on a grand organ, by the roaring of some 25,000 fans."[57]

It was the first manifestation of a peculiar sight that became commonplace during the next month: crowds on the road showing a clear preference for the Nationals over their own teams. "Really, I felt almost at home at the Yankee Stadium the way those fans rooted for us," Walter Johnson said.[58] New York columnist and sportswriter Damon Runyon offered an explanation: "It will be a great thing for baseball if Washington gets into the world series," he wrote. "This is treasonable from a New Yorker, but true. New York has become satiated, blase, with baseball championships. It no longer appreciates the thrill of a world series. The country at large cannot work up much interest when two New York clubs are fighting for the championship of the baseball world. It was novel, thrilling for a couple of years to see the teams of the greater city struggle for supremacy; then it became monotonous."[59]

The desire to see a non-New York team reach the World Series accounted only partially for the phenomenon. The other, perhaps greater, sentiment was focused on one man—Walter Johnson—and its depth and sincerity was unmistakable in the reaction to his 5–1 victory over the Yankees the next day. "Although the large crowd (30,000, including Hazel Johnson, who came up for the game) gave nearly every player in the game a hand," it was reported, "the applause which Johnson drew when he started warming up, and also when he first went to the box, was greater than all of the others combined. When the old master fanned Ruth to end the alien first, the crowd nearly went wild."[60]

While the Nationals were gradually building a lead off "Bullet Joe" Bush, Johnson held the powerful New Yorkers scoreless for seven innings, pitching out of a bases-loaded jam with none out in the fourth and two other situations with runners on the corners and one out. Twice he struck out the dangerous Meusel to end an inning with two men on base. In the eighth, Wally

Schang's liner back to the box clipped Johnson's pitching hand at the base of the thumb, a heart-stopping moment for the Nationals (and for the Yankees, apparently, as they also gathered in concern around Johnson on the mound) before it was apparent the injury wasn't serious. Not taking any chances, Harris pulled him anyway, and as Johnson walked from the field the crowd, it was reported, "rose to its feet and gave him what veteran baseball reporters describe as the greatest ovation a player ever received in this city."[61] Goose Goslin was on a rampage in the series. After hitting for the cycle the day before, he went three for four with another home run and scored three of his team's five runs.

That night Johnson, Harris, and several other Nationals were guests of Will Rogers at his famous Ziegfeld Follies show on Broadway. In addition to being a movie actor, stage celebrity, rodeo performer, political commentator, philosopher, and beloved national icon, Rogers was also the country's most widely syndicated newspaper columnist. He described for his readers Johnson's visit to the show: "I have a custom of introducing prominent people of our audience every night, to the rest of the audience, and I have had some pretty big men, but I want to tell you that when I heard Walter was away back in the house I knew he was so bashful that he would never stand up if I introduced him. So I sneaked down off the stage and went out there and put my rope around his neck and with the aid of the other players I literally dragged him up on the stage and introduced him. Well, he got the biggest applause, and the most genuine, that I ever heard in our place, and mind you he had just beaten New York that day and this applause was in their town."[62]

Will Rogers was born (and still ranched) near Claremont, Oklahoma, 40 miles across the border from Coffeyville. He and Walter Johnson were in many respects kindred spirits, even sharing a certain physical resemblance. Rogers's high-pitched, Southern-Plains twang, which was to become one of the nation's most instantly recognizable voices with the advent of radio and "talkies," was a dead ringer for Johnson's. Country boys whose talents had brought them tremendous national celebrity, both were feted by officials and politicians all the way up to U.S. presidents. But while achieving a degree of acclaim and adulation known only to a select few, these men somehow managed to remain grounded in the simple, solid virtues of their youth on the frontier. Rogers rose to his greatest prominence applying plain common sense to the political and economic events of the day, stripping them bare for the average person. He was also a big baseball fan: "It should be made compulsory in the schools," he wrote only partly in jest. For Will Rogers, the saga of Walter Johnson and the pennant race of 1924 was a natural, bringing together a number of his favorite themes. His column of September 28, entitled "Everybody's Pulling For Walter," was devoted to it:

Away out west some 37 or 38 years ago a baby was born, which was not considered unusual in those days. It was found to be a boy baby, which also was not considered over 50 per cent unusual. In fact the whole thing went along in such a usual way, that for years there was nothing unusual about it. He was just tagged to be one of the hundred and ten million of us who are here for no apparent reason. He grew up kinder long and tall and awkward, and his folks knew and felt right away that he would never be the Prince of Wales, because he was not built for dancing. He was very modest and retiring, and it was almost a certainty that he would not be a politician. He had to work to make a living, he didn't have any advantages. He didn't get much schooling. He was just a big strong healthy country boy. Now what could a boy like that do in the next few years to have the eyes, and interest, and good wishes of the entire one hundred and ten million people of our whole country focussed on him, and to have his every move watched and reported to every little paper in the farthest corners of the land?

He is still just a big country boy, yet as I am writing this there is more real genuine interest in him than there is in a presidential election. What is this fellow that he can do this? How is it that one single individual can have the sincere good wishes of the President of the United States, the Congress, the Senate, the Judges of our Supreme Court, even the sincere good wishes of the other two Presidential candidates? (I suppose this is the only time in political history that three candidates ever agreed heartily on one thing.) He is not sick, yet there are lots and lots of people in all parts of our country that never saw him or hope to see him, that are actually praying for fate to smile on this big old country boy. In every conflict, or game or fight, people are generally divided. But not in this case. They are all for this country boy. Now what has he done to arrive on such a pedestal? No man in civil life, no philanthropist ever did. So what has he done? Why, he has just played. Nothing else in the world but played. But he has played so fair and so good, and given his all to the game, that any man, woman, or child in the United States that don't love Walter Johnson and admire him as a man, is not a good American.

I don't suppose that ever in the history of any sporting event has sentiment played so big a part as it is playing in the case of this one man this year. Mathewson, the great pitcher, was the idol of millions of well wishers, but he was on a winning team. He was in the limelight all the time. But here is a man, Johnson, that has been with a team at the bottom of the list so long that the only way he could ever get any satisfaction out of a newspaper was to stand on his head. He never grumbled, he could have sulked, and demanded and been traded to any other team in the league, and been with a pennant winner almost every year and made lots of money. Lots of them have done it and they are playing today and all has been forgotten. But not with this old country boy. That is why he stands in public estimation today where he does. Had he deserted Washington he would have just been known as a wonderful pitcher, perhaps losing fewer games with a good team than any pitcher the game ever knew. But as it is, he is known as a wonderful man, and today the entire baseball world is not pulling for Johnson the Pitcher; they are pulling for Johnson the Man.

If you want to know how a man stands, go among the people who are in his same business. I have had some mighty good friends, ballplayers, and I have been around them for years, and they are all a mighty fine class of real upstanding Americans. Walter Johnson is more universally liked among other ballplayers than any man that ever played ball. Ten out of 10 ballplayers will tell you he is the best fellow ever lived, and 9 out of 10 will tell you he is the best pitcher ever lived. If he had played with McGraw's Giants all these years and had lost a single game in his 18 years they would have released him for incompetency. Rain would have been the only thing that would have kept an opposing team from being beaten by him.

A great deal of the sudden success of the Washington team is due to the able management of Bucky Harris, the young manager. He deserves the credit, but what makes the sentiment of everybody with Washington is Walter Johnson. Harris is young and a comer, he has lots of time to win pennants, and will win them. But the people know that Walter can't go on much longer. They know that it is only due to the wonderful care he has taken of himself that he has lasted far beyond his allotted time. They want to see him get in there and get what has been coming to him for years.

Just think of the unheard of condition of everybody pulling for a team to win just because they want to see one man get a small part of what they know is his due. Even in New York among the rabid Yankee rooters if they must be beaten they want Walter to beat them. If Washington goes into the World Series with the Giants, the Giant fans may pull for the Giants to win the Series, but they will pull for Walter to win his games. I know McGraw and have been friendly with him as long as I have known Walter, and I know how McGraw loves to win, but if he is beaten I will wager that he would rather be beaten by Walter Johnson than any man living. If Walter gets into the World Series and should be so unfortunate as to be bombarded and have to retire from the game, which happens to the best of them at times, why I bet you out of that audience of 50 or 60 thousand you will see more old hard-boiled baseball fans wipe away tears as Walter goes to the bench than you ever saw shed at most men's funerals.

So good luck, Walter; win or lose, you will have the satisfaction of knowing that you carry more good wishes than any man that ever entered any event in the history of our country, and we will love you just the same if you never see a World Series, because you are an example to the American boy, the same as Abraham Lincoln *should be* to the politicians.[63]

Not to be outdone by Rogers, the manager of the rival Keith's Theatre in New York invited the entire Washington ballclub to their production the next night, with similar results. "The 'Fireball King' was given what is believed to be the greatest ovation ever accorded anyone at B.F. Keith's theatre," it was reported. "Hats, programs and everything else that was not nailed down were thrown in the air. A fan spied the Old Master, the word was passed along and the cheering started. It broke out anew later in the evening when Julia Sanderson, this week's headliner, whirled onto the stage and after a dainty windup hurled a bouquet straight into the big pitcher's lap. He was plainly flustered by the tribute. His face turned the color of Lee Fohl's [Red] sox, but he was equal to the occasion, gracefully thanking Julia and praising her control. Compelled to arise a half-dozen times in acknowledgement of the applause, Barney blushed and bowed awkwardly."[64]

After taking three out of four in New York (giving them 9 wins in 11 games there) and opening up a game-and-a-half lead over the Yankees, the Nationals returned to a tumultuous welcome at Union Station. Waiting until midnight for the train bearing their heroes was a crowd of 8,000 "frenzied fans, of all ages, sizes, and colors, bent on a single purpose—to give three cheers to the leaders of the American League," according to the *Post.* "A deafening cheer went up when Walter Johnson appeared at the gate. No greater acclaim could have been given a president or potentate returning as the leader of a victorious army than that extended to Walter."

It was the president acclaiming them, in fact, when the team was invited to the White House on September 5 to be congratulated by Calvin Coolidge on their fight for the pennant. Still mourning the sudden death of his 16-year-old son from blood poisoning two months earlier, Coolidge told the team it would give him great pleasure to attend the World Series and root for them. After shaking hands with each player and making a brief speech of encouragement for the coming weeks, the President walked over to Walter Johnson and asked the pitcher to show him how he held the ball, whereupon a baseball was brought out and Johnson demonstrated his grip. Coolidge took the ball and practiced what he had been taught, then showed Johnson the technique he had used as a boy playing on the sandlots of Plymouth, Massachusetts.

With Clark Griffith aboard and "in personal command," the Nationals took their two-game lead to Philadelphia for the start of a three-week road trip that would end the season. Johnson worked the first game on September 8, winning 8–4 for his 20th victory of the season and 10th straight. Washington took three of four from the fast-improving Athletics and moved west to Detroit, where Ty Cobb had almost personally kept his team in contention after losing first baseman Lu Blue for the season with a leg injury. At the age of 37 Cobb played in every Tigers game, going to the plate a career-high 625 times. Johnson outdueled rookie left-hander Earl Whitehill in the first game on September 13, but despite their fans' support for the visiting team even in the heat of a pennant race, the fighting Tigers took the last two games of the series.

Hours after the win at Detroit, Johnson learned of his near-unanimous selection as the American League's most valuable player for 1924. "The Big Train, always modest, could hardly speak for a moment," it was reported. "When he finally did get his bearings and the news was passed from player to player, he was almost carried off his feet in the rush which swooped to congratulate him. Time and again he repeated, 'I never dreamed of such a thing.'"[65] Taking 55 votes out of a possible 64 by the baseball writers, Johnson finished well ahead of the runner-up, another 36-year-old veteran, Eddie Collins of the last-place White Sox. Congratulatory telegrams poured in, including one from Collins himself. "It is indeed a consolation to me to be beaten by one as deserving as yourself," he wired. A message from Joe Engel lamented: "Let up. How am I going to make a living getting pitchers."[66]

After Washington dropped the last two games to Detroit while New York was sweeping Chicago, personal honors meant little. The Nationals and Yankees were now deadlocked at 82–59, with the Tigers still within striking distance at three games back. It was a somber trip across Lake Erie to Cleveland, where the Nationals had lost seven of eight games in their first two visits. Harris came up with a way to take advantage of the psychology of the moment, which clearly preferred Washington over the Yankees and Tigers, not just among fans but with many of the opposing ballplayers also. He instructed his players not to antagonize them unnecessarily; there was to be no riding from the bench. "Let's not make any enemies if we can help it," Harris told them. "Let's beat 'em, but treat 'em nice."[67]

Johnson's thrilling 3–2 win over the Indians on the 17th was the middle game of a three-game sweep that gave the club a much-needed shot in the arm. At Cleveland as elsewhere, the fans left no doubt where their sentiments lay. "Walter was tendered one of the greatest ovations of his life when he went to the mound," it was reported. The crowd "cheered and cheered throughout the fray and let the echo rebound with a farewell greeting when he fanned [Riggs] Stephenson for the final out in the ninth frame."[68] Moving into a late-summer steambath in St. Louis, nine runs in the first inning of the opener gave Washington a 15–9 win on the 19th. The next day, with the Nationals still in a virtual dead heat with New York, Johnson started with only two days' rest after the complete game win at Cleveland. Driven out after one inning of a wild 10-inning 15–14 loss, Johnson was the first of five Washington pitchers pounded in a game in which both teams lashed out 18 hits. Goslin put Washington ahead in the top of the tenth with his second homer of the day, but Fred Marberry lost it in the bottom half by throwing wild past second base with the bases loaded instead of taking the easy play at home. A lucky rain the next day stopped the game in the seventh inning with Washington ahead, and once again they held a two-game lead over the Yankees, who were taking their second straight loss at Detroit.

The St. Louis fans had gone so far in favoring the Nationals as to stand up en masse for the visitors' half of the seventh-inning stretch, a gesture that would be repeated by the Chicago crowds as the team moved into the Windy City for three games. But Harris heard that the White Sox players, alone among the western clubs, had no sympathy toward the Nationals in the pennant race. Nemo Leibold was told to go and mingle among his former teammates to see if this was true, and he reported back that it was indeed. "That's it," Harris told his men, "These guys would rather see the Yankees beat us for the pennant. There's nothing to be gained by being nice to the Sox, as long as they feel that way about it. Let's insult 'em first, and then beat their brains out."[69] In the first game on September 22, with a day's rest after his abortive start in St. Louis, Johnson went the distance and allowed only one earned run in an easy 8–3 win, his 13th consecutive victory and 23rd of the year. He hadn't lost a game since July 11. Washington took the next two games to sweep the series.

But if the red-hot Nationals, playing 20 games over .500 for the last month of the season, thought that winning consistently would guarantee them a pennant, they were mistaken. The World Champion Yankees, after all, had owned the flag for the last three years, taking it by a full 16 games in 1923. Unlike Washington, they were no strangers to the unrelenting pressure of a grueling pennant drive. As Washington swept Chicago, New York did the same to Cleveland to keep the margin between the contenders at two games. This magnificent Yankees club wasn't going down without a battle. Four-game sets for the Nationals at Boston and the Yankees at Philadelphia, the last of the season for both, would settle the issue.

The Nationals' opener on September 26 was a heartbreaking 2–1 loss to the Red Sox that had all the portents of a coming disaster. The Washington lead was suddenly pared down to a single game as New York beat the Athletics handily. Johnson's 13-game winning streak and a 31-game hitting streak by Sam Rice were both busted. Worse still, Johnson was hit on the elbow by a pitch and forced out of the game after the seventh inning when it stiffened up. Boston fans outdid all the other cities in their rousing support of the Nationals, but that provided little consolation. In the hotel that evening it looked like a team about to break. There was none of the usual kidding around, and the doubts were visible in their faces. Earl McNeely, who had played a terrible game that day, admitted candidly: "You know, it was the first time I realized just what our pennant chances really are. Before the game today I began thinking about the World Series and how wonderful it would be. And the whole thing scared me." Walter Johnson said later, "Everybody, from Clark Griffith on down, was in a pretty nervous state of mind, to say the least."[70] Two of them were so keyed up that instead of sleeping they spent each night walking up and down the street or just sitting in front of the Boston hotel.[71]

The situation didn't look any brighter the next day when George Mogridge gave up four runs in the first inning. But Harris rushed in Marberry to stop the Red Sox barrage, and he, Russell, and Zachary gave up only one more run the rest of the way. Having rallied from behind so many times in 1924, the Nationals did it once again, 7–5. The vociferous support of 20,000 Bostonians certainly helped. At one point they booed their own pitcher, Howard Ehmke, for striking out Peckinpaugh in a clutch situation. Soon the great news came in from Philadelphia that the Athletics had beaten the Yankees, 4–3. Washington's two-game lead was restored with two games to play, so the worst that could happen was a tie. But the next day was Sunday, and with blue laws still forbidding baseball on the Sabbath in Boston and Philadelphia, for the Nationals it meant an extra day of worry.

On Monday, September 29, assured of at least a tie for the pennant, the Nationals played confident, flawless baseball and beat Boston 4–2 to become champions of the American League. The improbable hero of the game was 28-year-old rookie outfielder Wade Lefler, a mysterious last-minute recruit from the Eastern League whose major-league career to that point consisted of a lone unsuccessful at-bat for the Boston Braves in their season-opener back in April. Batting for Marberry with the bases loaded in the deciding game on the 29th, Lefler doubled to bring in the three runs that decided the game. He had also driven in the only run in the 2–1 loss on Saturday. Curiously, the one appearance with the Braves and his five games (just one in the field) during these crucial, waning moments of the 1924 season would represent the sum total of Wade Lefler's big-league career. After boosting the Nationals with five hits, three of them doubles, in eight trips to the plate—including three-for-five in his pennant-winning role of pinch-hitter—Lefler would slip quietly and permanently back into obscurity.

Walter Johnson was in the bullpen, warming up just in case, when Harris's brilliant play on a hard-hit ball closed out the victory and clinched the pennant. "Then, when it was all over and his mates had raced joyously toward the clubhouse, Walter sauntered slowly across the field," it was reported. "As the great Walter neared the stand, 15,000 folks rose up and gave him a cheer that came right out of the heart of a nation. A few ran out to shake his hand; others patted him on the back; but Walter didn't hurry; neither did he look up in response to the noisy ovation. He kept his head down because there were tears in his eyes."[72] In the Washington clubhouse pandemonium reigned and tears rolled down many cheeks, including Griffith's. Harris, too, was crying as Johnson grabbed one leg and Altrock the other, boosting him up onto a sea of shoulders to be carried around the room in recognition of his part in leading the team to this point.[73]

In Philadelphia the Yankees were rained out of their game with the Athletics. Babe Ruth, a veteran of six World Series in his ten years in the league, was one of the first to get the news of the Nationals' victory at Boston. In the gathering twilight of a day already rendered dark and gloomy by an overcast sky, the irrepressible Ruth went around the lobby of the hotel waking up teammates dozing peacefully on the overstuffed chairs and couches. "You're not sleeping," he told them, "you're dead."[74]

CHAPTER 13

The Weight of Years

We recognize that there is something more in life than the grinding routine of daily toil, that we can develop a better manhood and womanhood, a more attractive youth, and a wiser maturity, by rounding out our existence with a wholesome interest in sport. To those who devote themselves to this enterprise in a professional way and, by throwing their whole being into it raise it to the level of an art, the country owes a debt of gratitude. They furnish us with amusement, with an outside interest, often times in the open air, that quickens the step, refreshes the mind, rejuvenates and restores us. We pitch with the pitchers, we go to bat with the batters, and make home runs with the hard hitters. The training, the energy, the intelligence which these men lavish upon their profession ought to be an inspiration for a like effort in every walk of life. They are a great band, these armored knights of the bat and ball. They are held up to a high standard of honor on the field, which they have seldom betrayed. While baseball remains our national game, our national tastes will be on a higher level and our national ideals on a finer foundation. By bringing the baseball pennant to Washington, you have made the National Capital more truly the center of worthy and honorable national aspirations.[1]

PRESIDENT CALVIN COOLIDGE, OCTOBER 1, 1924

The first question put to Bucky Harris after the Nationals locked up the pennant was whether Walter Johnson would pitch the first game of the World Series. "Will he pitch?" Harris shot back. "Well, there's one thing you've got right. Like to know who's going to pitch if he doesn't. Yes, sir, he surely has earned the honor of pitching the first game."[2]

Training rules were suspended for the last night in Boston. "The sky's the limit, boys," Harris told them. "Go to it, but remember that hard, serious work starts again tomorrow."[3] The final game the next day apparently was hard on the suffering players as they lost, 13–1. The most effective Washington pitcher was 48-year-old Nick Altrock, who gave up one run in the last two innings and scored the lone Nationals tally after his triple. Griffith, Harris, Rice, and Johnson passed up the celebrations and the game, heading back to Washington the night of the clincher.[4] When the train stopped at New Haven, Connecticut, Christy Walsh, who was Babe Ruth's agent and business manager, came aboard for a quick conference with Johnson in the Pullman washroom. A deal for the syndication of Johnson's account of the World Series, to be fashioned by one of Walsh's stable of ghostwriters, was consummated with a $1,000 advance. A total of $7,000 was eventually received from the venture.[5]

The nation's capital, meanwhile, was abuzz with word of the capture of the pennant, and reveling in celebration. Thousands downtown had stood through the afternoon in a cold, pouring rain to follow the game on large electric scoreboards put up during the pennant race. When the flash of victory came over the wires at 4:42 P.M., a wild outburst of cheering and shouting erupted. Umbrellas flew into the air, and traffic cops neglected their traffic. It had been a long time coming but now, as one writer put it, "No Washingtonian forevermore need hang his head in shame because his team is a chronic tailender. Bucky Harris and his gang of fighting Griffs have settled that for all time."[6] At the White House, the baseball fan in residence there—Grace Coolidge—brought the news to her husband, the president. A telegram was dispatched to manager Harris in Boston: "Heartiest congratulations to you and your team for your great work in bringing Washington its first pennant. We of Washington are proud of you and behind you. On to the world's championship!"[7] Of the torrent of messages pouring in to Walter Johnson, the most succinct was a cablegram from Ring Lardner in Biarritz, France. "Thataboy," it read.[8]

The city showed its appreciation to the team on October 1 with a parade along Pennsylvania Avenue for which a huge throng, estimated at 100,000, turned out to pack the historic route from the Capitol to the White House. A procession of mounted police, the U.S. Cavalry Band, the Washington Riding and Hunt Club in their scarlet hunting coats, and "ten of the city's most beautiful young girls, dressed in white and mounted on white horses," was followed by limousines carrying the ballplayers, many of whom seemed embarrassed by the attention. "Pennsylvania Avenue has been the scene of many a spectacle," the *Washington Post* noted. "Presidents, kings and potentates have trod its path. But the return of the Nationals was different. The joy of the cheering crowds was boundless." One reporter was struck by the enthusiasm of the female fans, and surprised by the particular object of it:

"There he comes! Isn't he grand? Isn't he just too sweet?" These were the endearing terms applied to the idol of Washington's feminine baseball fans. These sweet nothings were not broadcast to the unmarried young Beau Brummels of the Washington baseball team, but to a staid married man with a family—Walter Johnson! When the car bearing the greatest pitcher in the game rolled by, women fans along the route went wild. Flowers were hurled at him, kisses were thrown by fair hands and melting gazes from awe-struck eyes were leveled upon him. Not to Bucky Harris, young manager of the team, and known to be unmarried and very eligible; nor to "Muddy" Ruel, the handsome young catcher, who is the Beau Brummel of the team, nor to any of the unmarried ones did most of the feminine adulation go, but to the man who is known to be married, the regular old-fashioned father of four, Walter Johnson. Of course, the other members of the team got their fair share of the fair fans' applause. The fair fans even knew their names and called out greetings to them. But it was Walter who walked away with their hearts.[9]

The crowd followed the parade to its destination, the Ellipse behind the White House. After his speech saluting the "armored knights of the bat and ball," President Coolidge presented Bucky Harris with a loving cup as Johnson stood between the two. Harris received a gold key to the city, and that evening the team was thrown a banquet by 200 of its civic, business and professional leaders, a "dry" dinner in which even pocket flasks were banned. "The World Series will not be lost here tonight," it was declared. His eyes brimming with tears, Clark Griffith told the assemblage:

This is the happiest moment of my baseball career. My blood is tingling and to say I'm proud is putting it awfully mild. This team is the gamest ballclub I ever saw. It has met every crisis. About six times this season we were beaten and out of the race unless we came through, and we did. This team will bring home the world's flag. No team in the world can beat us. When I came in the old days and sunk my meager capital in the town, I was called a fool. But I have always had Walter Johnson to lean on.[10]

A two-minute demonstration for Harris was followed by the manager's introduction of the team. Johnson was called "the ace in the hole, or rather, aces back-to-back," and as he rose the crowd rose with him to cheer and clap as he stood smiling. To their demands for a speech, he just bowed his thanks.

At this moment of unbounded joy in Washington, a story was breaking in New York that cast a cloud over the coming World Series and even threatened its cancellation. Commissioner Landis had held hearings the previous day on an apparent bribe attempt to influence the National League pennant race by several members of the eventual champion New York Giants. Going into the final weekend of a campaign even more tense and exciting than the American

League's, the Giants had seen their once-commanding lead dwindle to just 1½ games ahead of Brooklyn. With the fireballer Dazzy Vance enjoying one of the best years any pitcher ever had, Brooklyn had won 24 of 28 games, including 15 in a row and four doubleheader sweeps in as many days, and picked up 12 games on New York in a span of 26 days. A three-game set with the seventh-place Phillies would end the Giants' season, while Brooklyn had two contests left with the last-place Boston Braves. Before their first game with Philadelphia on September 27, it was alleged, Giants utility outfielder Jimmy O'Connell offered $500 to Phillies shortstop Heinie Sand to avoid "bearing down hard." But Sand rebuffed O'Connell and reported the incident to his manager, Art Fletcher, and the matter was taken to Landis. O'Connell named Giants coach Cozy Dolan as the instigator and claimed that other Giants, including Frankie Frisch, Ross Youngs, and George Kelly, were privy to the bribe plan.[11] Ironically, the Giants clinched the pennant on the 27th anyway.

Ban Johnson exploded in vituperation against his archenemy John McGraw, demanding that the World Series be called off. Others wanted Brooklyn to represent the National League instead of New York. But Landis and National League President John Heydler, the other members of the Baseball Advisory Council, overruled Johnson and decreed that the Series go forward. The scandal, which ultimately resulted in the expulsion of O'Connell and Dolan from baseball, was overshadowed by the enormous public interest in the drama of Washington and Walter Johnson in their first World Series, and then by the excitement of the games themselves. The only lingering effects once play began were a solidification of popular sentiment favoring the Nationals and the boycott of the games in a pique by Ban Johnson.[12]

For the next two days, with thousands of fans queued up outside the ballpark clamoring for tickets, the Nationals practiced inside. Harris had declared the field off-limits to all but the team itself, with much of the secret activity focussing on bunting, squeeze plays, and other drills intended to counter a Giants defense said to be superior to any in the American League.[13] On October 2 Bucky Harris and Walter Johnson sat in front of a microphone, both for the first time, at Washington radio station WRC to thank the team's supporters and pledge victory in the World Series, their comments broadcast nationwide over the NBC network.

Johnson slept late in the mornings and played golf each day before heading for the ballpark. Reported Hazel Johnson: "Walter is placidity itself—eats well, sleeps well, and apparently he and excitement are utter strangers. But then he is always that way." She claimed to do enough worrying for both of them: "Under the anxiety that has been my part in the Johnson partnership, in following the team's grueling chase for the pennant I have already lost 15 pounds and two hairs have turned white."[14] The night before the start of the Series, Walter and Hazel, along with Mr. and Mrs. Roger Peckinpaugh and Muddy Ruel and his father and sister, had dinner together at the Wardman Park Hotel. As they were leaving, they ran into the Giants coming back from their workout. "It may have been imagination on my part," Hazel wrote, "but to me they appeared somewhat dejected. Certainly there was no manifest glow of confidence in their faces."[15]

But except for uncertainties created by the unfolding scandal, the dimensions of which were unknown at that point (and might be still), it's hard to imagine the Giants feeling anything but supremely confident. This was a John McGraw team, after all, his 10th pennant-winner in 23 seasons in New York and possibly the best of them all. Giants outfielder Billy Southworth, later a highly successful manager himself, recalled that "There was a glamour to being a Giant in McGraw's days unmatched anywhere in baseball."[16] Not only had this team taken four straight pennants, it had proved its mettle this year by holding steady, despite several key injuries, in the face of powerful onslaughts by the Dodgers and Pirates in the last month of the race. Christy Mathewson, covering the Series for the *New York World,* called it "A great ballclub, one which is intelligent and brilliant, led by a genius of the game . . . a team that is at its best in a crisis."

Unlike the championship Giants of Mathewson's heyday, however, the hallmark of this one was hitting, not pitching, the team average of .300 tops in the major leagues. They scored more runs than any other club, and only the Yankees hit more home runs.

Right fielder Ross Youngs was the third-best hitter in the league at .356, his eighth straight season over .300. Tragically, it was also Youngs's last great year, his life and brilliant career cut short at the age of 30 two years later by kidney disease.

First baseman Long George Kelly was a prodigious run-producer, hitting .324 and leading the major leagues in RBIs with 136, his fourth year in a row with more than 100. On June 14 he hit three home runs and drove in all eight of the Giants' runs; later in the season he homered in six straight games. In a game in 1923 he hit home runs in three consecutive innings. John McGraw said that "Kelly made more important hits for me than any player I ever had."[17] The 6-foot-4-inch slugger was an excellent first baseman, surprisingly agile and quick for his size, and often saw duty at second base and in the outfield under McGraw's various platooning schemes.

Switch-hitting second baseman Frankie Frisch, "the Fordham Flash," was one of the game's all-time greats at the position. The Giants' captain, Frisch batted .328 and tied Rogers Hornsby for the league lead in runs with 121.

Left fielder Emil "Irish" Meusel, like brother Bob of the Yankees one of the great "money hitters" in the game, drove in 102 runs in 1924 following totals of 132 and 125 in the previous two seasons.

Twenty-year-old Travis Jackson made sensational plays at shortstop and hit .302.

Veteran receiver Hank Gowdy, hero of the Boston Braves' 1914 World Series sweep and of the World War that followed it, hit .325 backing up starter Frank Snyder. Gowdy would catch every game during the Series.

Slick-fielding third baseman Heinie Groh, known for the unique design of his "bottle bat," had twisted a knee late in the season and was not expected to be ready for post-season play. Replacing him was 18-year-old Freddie Lindstrom, fresh out of high school, who had impressed McGraw with his clutch play in the closing days of the campaign.

Another rookie, Hack Wilson, only 5-foot-6 but tremendously strong, had taken over in center field, already showing the power that would make him one of the most feared hitters in baseball. Wilson's 56 home runs as a Chicago Cub in 1930 is still the National League record, his 190 RBIs that year the most ever in the major leagues.

Big Bill Terry, also in his first year, led the league in pinch-hitting appearances and toward the end of the season played first base against right-handed pitchers. A .341 lifetime hitter, Terry would be the last National Leaguer to top .400 in a season.

The team's pitching was ordinary at best, but with that crew behind them, ordinary was usually good enough.

Youngs, Kelly, Frisch, Wilson, Terry, Jackson, and Lindstrom would be inducted into baseball's Hall of Fame, while many other outstanding players, most of them proven veterans, filled out the Giants' roster. Their leader, John McGraw, merits consideration as the greatest manager of all time, his 10 pennants matched only by Casey Stengel's Yankees dynasty of the 1950s.

Muddy Ruel recalled the Giants "looking at us with tolerance and amused confidence . . . they had McGraw scowling from the bench—an awesome club, but not to us. We Senators were tough, too."[18] Indeed, except for home runs (Washington's 22 were last in the American league by far and only one more than George Kelly's total for the Giants), Nationals firepower stood up well even in comparison to the impressive New York lineup.

The main weapon was Goose Goslin, emerging in 1924 as one of the premier players in the game. Batting .344 with 12 homers and a league-leading 129 RBIs, his 17 triples were second in the circuit, his 299 total bases fourth. "If Walter Johnson was number one in the hearts of Washington fans, Goslin was certainly number two," Shirley Povich described the 23-year-old slugger. "They oohed and ah'd at the power in his throwing arm and chortled when the Goose threw runners out from deep left and right. But it was at bat that they loved Goslin and the plate-crowding stance he took before fastening a murderous glare on the pitcher. Even when he struck out, their disappointment was tempered by the gusto of his swing and the massive pirouette that was much like Ruth's. He was still using the same exaggerated closed stance, getting his tremendous power from a swing fuller than any other in the league. Actually, his back was nearly turned to the pitcher and he stood poised for the pitch while looking over his shoulder."[19]

Sam Rice had lined out 216 hits in 646 at-bats, league-leading totals both, for a .334 average. He scored 106 runs and his 24 stolen bases was third in the league.

Joe Judge hit .324 with 79 RBIs.

Earl McNeely and Doc Prothro had partial seasons of .330 and .333.

Harris, Peckinpaugh, Bluege, Ruel, and Leibold all hit between .250 and .300. Though lacking the glittering slugging pedigrees of the Giants, the Washington batting order was respectable nonetheless. In the field, both clubs were outstanding: quick, smart, great gloves everywhere you looked.

If the Giants held an edge at the plate, their pitching staff clearly suffered in comparison to that of the Nationals. To begin with, New York had no Walter Johnson. His 18th season was one of his very best, 23 wins against 7 losses and leading the league in wins and winning percentage (.767), earned run average (2.72), strikeouts (158) and strikeouts per game, shutouts (6), starts (38), and fewest hits per game. Johnson put in a yeoman 278 innings, won 13 in a row in the stretch drive, batted .283, and was flawless in the field.

Despite Johnson's accomplishments, more than one observer called attention to the Giants' preference for fastball pitchers, pointing to their success against Dazzy Vance as an example. Fred Lieb, baseball writer for the *New York Post* and chief scorer at the World Series, didn't think Johnson "would show the same effectiveness against New York that he has shown in the American League."[20]

The Giants didn't have a Fred Marberry, either. In his rookie season the big Texan had led both leagues in games pitched with 50 and set a new standard for saves with 15. Fellow reliever Allan Russell was second in the majors with eight saves and set his own record of 37 appearances without a start, a mark Marberry was to shatter with 55 the next year.

Beyond Johnson and Marberry, the two pitching staffs were remarkably similar, both stocked with seasoned, dependable veterans capable of winning consistently with good support. Between New York's Art Nehf (14–4), Virgil Barnes (16–10), Jack Bentley (16–5), and Hugh McQuillan (14–8); and

Washington's Tom Zachary (15–9), George Mogridge (16–11), and Curly Ogden (9–5), there was little to choose. Bentley, in addition to his fine pitching for the Giants, was a terrific hitter who had set a major-league record for pitchers in 1923 with his .427 average.

Jack Bentley was a curious case. A native of nearby Maryland, at the age of 18 he had been signed as a pitcher by Washington and spent four years with the club. When his arm went dead in 1916 he was released to the Baltimore Orioles of Jack Dunn, who transformed Bentley into a hard-hitting outfielder. Then in 1920 his arm came around. He was 16–3 with a league-leading 2.11 earned run average that year while also hitting .371 with 231 hits, 20 home runs, and 161 RBIs. In 1921 he went 12–1 on the mound and his .412 average, 246 hits, 24 home runs, and 47 doubles all paced the league. But just as with Lefty Grove and others, Dunn placed such a high price on Bentley ($100,000 plus two players) that no big-league team would touch him regardless of those fantastic accomplishments. Dunn made his money anyway, with the Orioles perennial league champions drawing tremendous crowds. To break up the dynasty, the other International League owners insisted in 1922 that Dunn honor major-league drafts of his players, so Bentley was sold to the Giants for $65,000 and three players. His dual effectiveness continued at New York, and for two of the next three years he was the best pinch-hitter in baseball.[21]

Both teams had been through the relentless grind of a long, tense pennant chase, but the Washington squad, lacking the depth of talent the Giants could call upon, was particularly battered and exhausted. Bucky Harris had been playing for two months with a broken bone in his foot; Ossie Bluege had his gimpy leg worked on and strapped by Mike Martin before each game; after playing in every one of Washington's 155 games, Roger Peckinpaugh's legs felt much older than his 33 years; Goslin and Rice appeared in 154 games each and Muddy Ruel had caught an amazing 147 of them, a new league record for catchers. The diminutive Ruel, who weighed only 150 pounds in top condition, was particularly run down after a year leading the league in putouts, assists, doubleplays, and chances per game. "By the end of that '24 season we were all worn down," Bluege remembered. "We all looked like scarecrows. We knew we'd been in a fight."[22]

The pitchers, too, were exhausted after being worked hard and often in the final weeks when the imperative was to capture the flag at all costs.[23] Here again the Giants' superior depth in starters had brought them through their pennant drive in better shape, with four regulars finishing the season in fine style. But with only three days to rest before the start of the World Series, followed by a game every day until the championship was decided, both staffs would be severely tested.

At first glance the contrast between John McGraw, heading into the twilight of his career, and Bucky Harris, the "boy manager," couldn't have seemed greater. But in the style of baseball they preferred, and the methods and strategies applied, they were of the same mold, emphasizing the old-time "inside baseball." Both sought to create runs with place-hitting, aggressive baserunning, bunting, and the hit-and-run, while blunting the opposition attack with pitching and defense. But the youthful Harris wasn't entirely on his own in battling the genius of McGraw, for always close at hand with the sage counsel of his years (and his intimate knowledge of McGraw) was another master of the game, the Old Fox himself, Clark Griffith.

However the individual talents on the two ballclubs compared, of incalculable advantage to the Giants in the coming struggle was their experience playing in the pressure-cooker atmosphere of the World Series. The heart of the team—Kelly, Youngs, Frisch, Meusel, and Nehf—had been together through the last three fall classics, 18 games in all, twice defeating the Ruthian Yankees to become World Champions. The Nationals, in stark contrast, had only two players, Roger Peckinpaugh and Nemo Leibold, with experience in post-season play, and their past performances were hardly encouraging. As the Yankees' shortstop against the Giants in 1921, Peckinpaugh had averaged .179 and became the "goat" of the Series when his error in the first inning of the final game allowed the only run, Nehf outdueling young Waite Hoyt, 1–0. Leibold was two for five in the 1917 White Sox victory over the Giants, but as a regular two years later hit a paltry .056.

The desire to see the upstart Nationals succeed against the powerhouse Giants, a feeling reinforced by the bad odor of the Dolan-O'Connell scandal, gave Washington an overwhelming edge in popular favor around the country. Even at their home field in New York the Giants would find a large part of the crowd rooting openly and unashamedly for Washington. To McGraw and his players, however, it made little difference. "I knew as well as anybody else that 90 percent of the people wanted to see Washington, and especially Walter Johnson, win," he said. "The mere fact of the whole country being against us made the players fight harder."[24] Fred Lindstrom recalled: "There was a lot of sentimental rooting for Walter. All of that was very nice, but neither I nor my teammates shared any of those feelings."[25] When the professional "layers" (bookmakers) sorted through the various factors on both sides, they called it a toss-up. Five to six, pick your team, were the odds reported, with a small advantage to Washington, 11 to 10, in the first game "as a result of Harris's promise to pitch Walter Johnson in the opener."[26]

During the first 12 years of his major league career, I believe Johnson could have won a world series singlehanded. A team looking at Johnson's great speed for the first time during that period of greatness would have found him almost unhittable. He is still a marvel after 18 years in the majors, most of the time with an also-ran club that forced him to continually extend himself to win.[27]

BILLY EVANS

Saturday, October 4, was a typical Indian Summer day in the nation's capital: not too hot, not too cold, a diaphanous haze dimming the early-fall sunlight. Perfect "Johnson weather," a local sportswriter called it.[28] By now the entire country was wired—literally—in anticipation of the World Series. Western Union alone had run 75,000 miles of cable to 125 scoreboards in cities around the country, while the wire services were hooked up to another 200 or so.[29] On the Pennsylvania Avenue side of its building, the *Washington Post* had erected a green magnetic diamond around which a baseball moved in replication of the action at the ballpark. Each day, thousands of those not fortunate enough to have tickets to the games gathered to watch while police diverted traffic around them.[30] Commercial radio, in its infancy in 1924, received a boost from the fledgling NBC network's live broadcast of Graham McNamee's play-by-play over affiliated stations in Washington, New York, and six other cities. "Crystal sets" were the hottest-selling item at department stores, and hundreds of them were set up in government and business offices throughout Washington.[31]

A large and distinguished contingent of print press, augmented by a sizeable number of ghostwriters and their "fronts," was on hand to report the spectacle. The Christy Walsh Syndicate alone featured the bylines of Babe Ruth, Ty Cobb, Walter Johnson, George Sisler, John McGraw, Nick Altrock, and Fred Lieb, who was probably the only one of this group to touch a typewriter during the Series. Bozeman Bulger of the *New York Evening World* served as Johnson's "ghost." Washington papers signed up many of the local ballplayers, and even a column by Hazel Johnson, which she wrote herself, could be found in the *Post* each day.

At first it looked as though a long-standing enmity between Ruth and Cobb might break out into open warfare at the World Series. Cobb had been quoted as saying that he "got quite a kick out of" sweeping the Yankees in the closing days of the pennant race, to which Ruth responded: "I see where [Cobb] gets a lot of happiness out of beating the Yankees those three games that cost us the pennant. I also see where he is coming up from Georgia to do some World Series writing. Maybe he's going to say some more things to make the Yankees feel bad. And maybe, as he did so much toward Washington winning the pennant, he's coming up to claim a share of the gate receipts from Clark Griffith."[32] But Christy Walsh conspired to get them into the same taxi to the opening game of the Series, and they declared a truce, spending most of the week side-by-side in the press box swapping cigars and stories. Their feuding days behind them for good, the greatest players in the game eventually became good friends.[33]

At the ballpark, meanwhile, Mike Martin finished slapping his liniment onto the long arm on which so many hopes were riding. As Johnson moved away from the table, Martin's eyes followed. He looked toward the ceiling as if in prayer, clenched his fists, and muttered "God, I hope he wins after all these years."[34] When Billy Evans came into the clubhouse to get a few baseballs signed for friends, he noticed Johnson's hand shaking as he scrawled his autograph.[35] Johnson was making no effort to conceal his anxiety about the task at hand. "I am doggone fidgety about my job this afternoon," he admitted to Babe Ruth that morning, "especially when you figure every last soul in the ball park expects me to win, including the President of the United States."[36] In a last comforting gesture before they went out to do battle, Bucky Harris came over and put his hand on Johnson's shoulder. "The boys are going to fight extra hard to see you win," Harris told him.[37]

Soon they moved through the tunnel between the clubhouse and the Washington dugout. Out on the field, the U.S. Army Band was playing behind home plate as a sea of reporters and photographers milled about. The stands were filling up early. "Let's toss a few," Johnson said to Sam Rice, but the cameramen closed in so tightly around them it became impossible. He went back to the bench, where a virtual parade of well-wishers came by. Many of Johnson's old compatriots were there, Clyde Milan, Cliff Blankenship, and Gabby Street among them. Babe Ruth offered a few helpful tips on Giants hitters gathered from his three years of World Series play against them.

Suddenly, Joe Judge ran up. "They're looking all over for you," he yelled, pointing to home plate and a beautiful new car with a huge floral horseshoe on the bumper. The seven-passenger Lincoln "touring car," at $8,000 the most expensive made in the United States, was presented to Johnson while the capacity crowd cheered wildly. Attached to the dashboard was a silver plaque inscribed, "To Walter Johnson, baseball's greatest pitcher, from his many friends." The car was the result of a hastily formed testimonial committee that raised the funds for it in less than a week, including President Coolidge's $10 check and $200 from Will Rogers accompanied by a note: "I understand that after 150 years of diligent search, Washington has at last found an honest man. In no city was such a man ever a bigger novelty. This should be the biggest lesson to official Washington since Lincoln told them they couldn't fool all the people all the time."[38] Johnson obliged the army of photographers by posing with the car. "One comfort about this ceremony, it was at homeplate," he later wrote. "I was getting closer to the pitcher's box, and the closer I got, the better I felt."[39]

There were more delays, though, and Johnson's restlessness was obvious as he wandered about the field, stopping to warm up briefly on several occasions.[40] At one point photographers got him together with Giants starting pitcher Art Nehf. "I felt sorry for him when we shook hands," Nehf recalled, "because his hand trembled so. I knew what he was thinking. He was thinking he mustn't let down the fans all over the country who were rooting, even praying for him."[41]

Eventually President and Mrs. Coolidge came down the aisle and took their seats in a flag-draped section next to the Washington dugout. It was only the second time a chief executive had so honored a World Series contest, Woodrow Wilson having attended the second game of the 1915 Series in Philadelphia. Sharing the White House box were Secretary of State Hughes, Secretary of War Weeks, and Speaker and Mrs. Gillette. Johnson's mother Minnie, who was about to see her first major-league game, had a prime seat adjacent to the presidential box and next to daughter-in-law Hazel Johnson.

"The stands were just packed with notables," Hazel told her readers. "You couldn't have thrown a ball without hitting an ambassador or senator or a cabinet officer or famous writer or an actor or prize fighter or some other distinguished individual."[42] The band played *The Sidewalks of New York* while the Giants were introduced, followed by the Nationals, who came out to the strains of *Dixie.* The teams lined up in front of the presidential box for the playing of *The Star-Spangled Banner,* after which Babe Ruth and Ty Cobb were brought over and introduced to the President. Bucky Harris handed him a new baseball.[43] The ceremonial toss was caught by umpire Tommy Connolly with one hand, and the crowd shouted in unison, "Play ball!"[44]

After 18 seasons in the major leagues, Walter Johnson finally took the mound in a World Series (the record wait until Joe Niekro made it in his 21st season in 1987). He was plainly nervous, an initial stage fright shared by the entire team.[45] Ironically, the first Giants batter was 18-year-old Freddie Lindstrom, exactly half Johnson's age with a big-league career of 79 at-bats behind him. He took two balls, one outside and one inside, then a called strike before lofting an easy fly to Earl McNeely in center. Frankie Frisch tried to lay down a bunt but popped it to Bluege, and Ross Youngs was called out on strikes. The veteran left-hander Nehf, whose best pitch was a sweeping curve, also set the Nationals down in order and the first inning was over without event.

Johnson worked carefully to George Kelly leading off the second, keeping the ball on the inside of the plate where the Giants slugger was weakest. But with the count three and two, Johnson grooved a fastball and Kelly lined it deep to left-center. Going back after the ball, Goslin was stopped one stride short by the three-foot fence guarding the temporary bleachers. He took a desperate, headlong dive into the crowd, but the ball sailed inches over his outstretched glove and landed five rows into the stands. A routine fly under ordinary conditions, in this game it was a home run that gave the Giants a 1–0 lead. In the third inning Frankie Frisch doubled with two outs but strayed too far off the bag, Ruel nailing him after a headlong dive. Youngs was again caught looking to open the fourth inning and again howled in protest at Connolly's call. Kelly also struck out, but Bill Terry swung late on a high fastball and drove a fly into the bleachers in left-center in the same vicinity as Kelly's shot in the second, Goslin staying in the park this time. Johnson fooled Wilson for the second time to strike out the side, but New York's lead was 2–0. In the bottom of the fourth Joe Judge became the first National to solve Nehf's offerings when he lined a single to right with two out.

Travis Jackson was Johnson's eighth strikeout victim, and his fifth straight, to open the fifth. Youngs struck out for the third time in a row in the sixth, and in the bottom half the Nationals got on the board. Leading off, McNeely dumped a double at Wilson's feet near the left field foul line, moved to third on an infield out, and scored on another with the Giants playing back. "Was there any clamor?" wrote Grantland Rice. "Was Babel quiet? Our ears are still throbbing." There was more noise to come when Johnson came up in the seventh with runners on first and second and two outs. The crowd rose to give their hero a long ovation and he almost obliged, smashing a liner over second base that Frisch intercepted with a leaping grab.

Ross Youngs finally got untracked in the eighth, doubling down the line in left with one out. A groundout moved him to third, and Terry was walked intentionally. The Giants attempted a double-steal, but instead of going after the slow-footed Terry at second, as McGraw might have expected, Ruel turned and fired instead on Youngs, who had ventured a step too far down the line at third. He scrambled to get back to the bag, but Bluege was waiting with the ball. The Nationals had a chance to tie the game in their half when Rice walked and stole second with two out, but Goslin was called out on strikes. Another sterling defensive play stopped the Giants from adding to their 2–1 lead in the ninth. Wilson opened with a single and was sacrificed to second. Hank Gowdy struck out, but Nehf cracked a hit into center and Wilson stormed around third. Rice scooped the ball up cleanly on one hop and fired it in the next motion, Ruel taking the throw five feet up the line and slamming it into Wilson's neck as he flew by, a play that electrified the crowd.

Down to their last chance in the bottom of the ninth, the Nationals struck quickly after Judge watched a third strike. Bluege shot a screamer into the hole at short that Jackson could only knock down, and Peckinpaugh brought him around with a double off the wall in left-center, tying the game. That occasioned a release of emotion built up through eight innings of the thrilling contest. "Did we mention the fact that there had been a racket in the sixth?" wrote Grantland Rice. "We take it back. Here came the cyclonic thunder of the day. Here came the crashing artillery of 38,000 human voices in one of the wildest vocal frenzies anyone ever heard. Hats went into the air; cushions sailed out upon the field; fans from the center field bleachers rushed out upon the grass to embrace one another." The demonstration lasted several minutes, after which hundreds of cushions and hats had to be cleared from the field. When play resumed Peckinpaugh moved to third on Ruel's grounder and Johnson came up with a chance to win the game for himself and turn it into an epic. The best he could do was a fly to center.

In the press box, Billy Evans abandoned all pretense of impartiality, yelling "Come on, you Big Train!" whenever Johnson was in a spot.[46] Even the normally stolid President was energized by the excitement swirling around him. Smoking cigars and clearly enjoying himself, Coolidge jumped up time and again to vigorously applaud the sensational plays. Frequently he leaned over to consult his wife, Grace, who was keeping the scorecard.

The thrills continued into extra innings. After Lindstrom struck out to begin the 10th, Frisch singled into left. Youngs popped up, but the Fordham Flash stole second to move into scoring position with the redoubtable Kelly coming up. Johnson rose to the occasion and sent Kelly packing on strikes to close off the threat. With one out in the Nationals' half, back-to-back singles by Harris and Rice put men on first and second. Nehf wasn't about to cave in any more than Johnson, however, and the crafty little lefty got Goslin to pop up and Judge to fly out to deep right. Before going out, both men sent line drives over first base only to watch them curve foul by a few feet. Each side was retired in order in the 11th.

Johnson had two strikes on Gowdy, the first batter in the Giants 12th, but then hit him squarely in the back. The first two pitches to Nehf were also strikes before he sent a dropping liner into center. For a moment McNeely froze with indecision before charging in to try for a shoestring catch. He caught the ball in his glove, but the impact of his knee hitting the turf jarred it loose. Gowdy had stopped midway between first and second, and McNeely saw that he might have a play. But he fumbled the ball trying to pick it up, then threw wild to the right of the bag, the ball rolling almost to the Giants dugout while Gowdy raced for third and Nehf pulled into second. It was the first error for either team. Jack Bentley pinch-hit for Lindstrom, and Johnson, pitching carefully to the dangerous left-handed hitter, walked him to load the bases with no outs. Billy Southworth came in to run for Bentley.

Frisch grounded sharply to Harris, who threw home to force Gowdy. Ross Youngs popped a Texas Leaguer into center field, and once again McNeely was slow starting for the ball. It dropped at his feet for a single as Nehf came in to score. The Giants tallied once more when the speedy Southworth tagged up on Kelly's long fly to Goslin in left. Joe Judge made a great diving stop of Terry's hot grounder but couldn't get to his feet in time to beat Terry to the bag, loading the bases for the fourth time in the inning. The crisis ended with Wilson's flyout to left, but the Giants were up, 4–2.

The game wasn't over just yet. Mule Shirley, a little-used rookie first baseman, batted for Johnson to lead off for the Nationals and reached second when Jackson lost his short pop fly in the sun, the ball dribbling through the shortstop's glove. McNeely flied out, but Harris brought Shirley home with a single to center. Sam Rice followed with an identical drive, Harris charging around to third. But when center fielder Southworth fumbled the ball momentarily, Rice unwisely took off for second and was thrown out by a full stride. Goslin hit a slow roller to Kelly, now playing second base, and he made a brilliant one-handed pickup and throw to first as Goslin streaked across the bag. Harris had already crossed the plate with the tying run, but umpire Bill Klem called Goslin out and the game was over. Goslin and Harris, joined by Altrock from his coaching box and Judge from the on-deck circle, surrounded Klem in protest, the squabble continuing even as the umpire left the field for the dressing rooms. President Coolidge passed right by Judge and Klem on his way through the underground exit, completely unnoticed by the arguing pair.[47] At one point a furious Goslin called the legendary umpire "Catfish," a nickname the players knew he despised. A man of unwavering dignity, Klem never forgave Goslin for the slight, not even years later when the slugger tried to apologize.[48]

Three hours of tense, stirring battle had left the Nationals and Walter Johnson with a bitter 4–3 defeat. It had been a wonderful contest, with spirited, heads-up play throughout. Eleven Giants and ten Nationals had been stranded on the bases. (American League RBI champion Goslin left men in scoring position three times.) Johnson's 12 strikeouts, six of them called, tied the World Series record as Youngs and Wilson succumbed three times and Kelly and Lindstrom twice. If not for the temporary bleachers, a sparkling first-game shutout would have been Johnson's reward, and satisfied the enormous expectations placed on him. But not all of the Giants' attack was cheap by any means, as they got to Johnson for 14 hits and six walks and forced him to extend himself to the fullest with almost every one of his 165 pitches.

To many observers, Johnson was no less a heroic figure for the loss. "From the last ditch of his baseball career, in his shining buckler of the strongest affection ever given by any community to a character in sport, the great Walter Johnson fought today and lost," observed Damon Runyon.[49] Grantland Rice wrote: "Today, 38,000 people paid him the homage due to greatness. Among those were the President and his wife, admirals, generals, cabinet members and other officials who help direct the affairs of the nation. They gave him the acclaim that few in this swift, tumultuous existence can ever hope to know. So what does it matter, after all, that Walter Johnson, the synonym for greatness in action and for greatness in integrity, lost his first world's series start? What is victory or defeat in any single encounter to be compared to a whirlwind of affectionate applause that a Caesar would have envied?"[50]

Those outpourings of love and respect, ironically, caused Johnson the most anguish, more so even than the defeat. "It wasn't losing the game that hurt," he confided that evening to his Nevada hunting partner Brewster Adams, "but think of my friends." When the subject of McNeely's error came up, the pitcher quickly threw it aside: "No one should blame the boy," he said. "He was just over-anxious, that's all."[51]

Sunday morning, I visited the disabled soldiers at the Walter Reed Hospital in Washington. My wife and mother wanted to personally bring our many world series flowers to the boys. And I must say that one look at their disfigured features and wasted bodies was enough to make any ballplayer forget all about such a trivial thing as losing a world series battle. Despite the sad surroundings, the situation was amusing. I was sorry for the boys and they were sorry for me. They hesitated talking about my lost game as one might avoid mentioning some poor lad's missing arm or leg. One fine fellow, with much difficulty, insisted on coming the length of the hospital corridor. An attendant pushed him in a chair. He couldn't shake hands because he had none. As we left this lad at the elevator he said, "Barney, we all know how you feel. A guy's a hero today and a dud tomorrow. Cheer up!"[52]

WALTER JOHNSON

The second game on Sunday, October 5, was even more exciting than the opener, if that was possible. Though lacking the special feature of the first appearances of Johnson and Washington in World Series action, plenty of drama was present from the outset in the knowledge that if the Nationals lost their cause was almost certainly hopeless. For eight innings the Giants managed only one run and four hits off nerveless Tom Zachary's "little nickel curve" and "little nickel knuckleball," as Freddie Lindstrom characterized them, his change of speeds and uncanny placement keeping them off-balance.[53] His teammates got to Jack Bentley quickly for two runs in the opening frame and added another along the way to take a 3–1 lead into the ninth inning, where the real fireworks took place. Zachary walked Frisch and he came all the way around to score on Kelly's long single to right, Rice's throw arriving a second too late. With two down, Kelly scored the tying run on a hit by Wilson, who moved to second on the play at the plate. Harris summoned Marberry, and the big Texan blew Jackson away on three pitches. Judge drew a walk to start the bottom half and Bluege bunted him to second. Peckinpaugh sent a scorcher down the line at third just out of reach of Lindstrom, Judge trotting in easily with the winning run.

The victory evened the Series at a game apiece, and spirits and confidence were high that evening on the train to New York.[54] Peckinpaugh's clutch double would prove costly, however. Accelerating around first base to reach second should there be a play at the plate, his right leg gave way, and the next day the shortstop's thigh was black and blue. Nonetheless, Mike Martin's ministrations and rolls of tape had him back at shortstop for game three.[55]

The Polo Grounds, home of the Series for the next three days, was the most oddly configured of the major-league ballparks, with the bleachers a mere 257 feet down the line in right field, 279 in left. From there the fences angled deeply away until meeting in dead center field—which no batter had ever reached on the fly— an incredible 484 feet from home.[56] Although much of the New York crowd was pulling for them, the Nationals fell apart in the strange environs, a breakdown far worse than the 6–4 score indicated. The offense was given nine walks and as many hits by the shaky New York pitching, but left 13 men on the bases. The defense awarded the Giants three unearned runs, and three of four Washington pitchers, including the surprise starter, Marberry, were ineffective, giving up 12 hits between them.

Almost as bad as the defeat was the loss of Peckinpaugh, for the rest of the Series it seemed, when his leg broke down while running out a ground ball in the second inning. He was replaced at shortstop by Bluege, who had played a total of six games at the position in his three years in the major leagues. But that was three games more than the new third baseman, Ralph "Boxcar"

Miller, had played all year, and those were at second base, not third. Miller was a journeyman who hadn't seen action in the big leagues since 1921 before being picked up late in the season. His nervousness showed in the sixth inning when he "let a softly hit grounder pass completely through his quaking legs," as the misplay was reported. Tommy Taylor, a 29-year-old rookie also added to the roster during the year, was the team's best utility infielder but had sprained his wrist during the pennant drive.[57]

George Mogridge started the fourth game in place of Johnson, who was given an extra day's rest after his marathon performance in the opener. The 35-year-old Mogridge had wilted toward the end of the year under the severe stress and overwork of the pennant grind, and Harris had planned to start Curly Ogden in the Series instead.[58] But Ogden's arm had given its all to the pennant cause, so Mogridge got the assignment of keeping Washington from slipping into the abyss, and the dependable veteran didn't let them down. Cool and collected throughout, he showed no fear of the precarious situation or the Giants, and neither did his teammates, jumping out to leads of 3–0, 5–1, and 7–2 on the way to a 7–4 win. Mogridge allowed only three hits in 7⅓ innings before Marberry came in to avenge his pounding of the day before by striking out Bentley and Kelly in the bottom of the ninth. With two out and two on the dangerous Kelly came up representing the tying run, but Marberry shut the door with three pitches. Goose Goslin, 3 for 15 in the first three games, emerged from his dormancy with a vengeance, going four for four with a home run and four RBIs while scoring two more. Grantland Rice estimated that four-fifths of the "buoyant and boisterous" New York crowd of 50,000 rooted for a Washington victory.[59] "One would have thought we were playing in our home town instead of on alien fields," Hazel Johnson wrote.[60]

With the Series tied at two games apiece, it was up to Walter Johnson in the pivotal fifth contest on October 8, the last in New York. After working out on the 6th the Nationals' ace had felt strong, with no ill effects from his 12-inning outing.[61] He was more concerned about his infield than his arm. The Nationals' lusty hitting the day before had rendered insignificant a rare error by Ossie Bluege, playing out of position at shortstop, and a second misplay in as many games by Miller at third. Johnson went to Roger Peckinpaugh and asked him to play in the fifth game, but the veteran shortstop had to decline the request—his mobility was almost non-existent. Johnson told him he didn't care, that it would be worth it to have him on the field and Bluege back at third.[62]

The Nationals' rearranged infield was unchanged, then, as the fifth game got underway. The sun was out, but an overnight rain had left a chill in the air, making it the coolest day of the Series. As Johnson moved with his loose, shambling gait (like he was still behind a plow, it was often said) to the mound, a burst of cheering echoed around the oval stadium, "a vocal tribute from Manhattan Island to the old speed king," one writer called it.[63] But there was to be no tribute from the Giants this day. Freddie Lindstrom set the tone in both halves of the initial frame, first with a leaping acrobatic snag of McNeely's vicious liner, robbing him of a double, then with a ringing single to center on Johnson's first offering.

There was no scoring until the New York third inning, after Johnson had blown a chance to help his own cause in the top. Smashing a liner against the left field wall only inches below the stands, he was surprised by Hack Wilson's quick recovery of the rebound. Storming around first base with his head down, Johnson suddenly realized that Wilson's throw would beat him by a mile. Putting the brakes on and turning back toward first was a futile gesture as Frisch's relay to Terry got him cold. McNeely and Harris followed with hits of their own but were stranded, and three hits in the inning had gone to waste. In the Giants half, Miller let Jackson's grounder go under his glove (scored a hit as Bluege fielded the ball behind him). Gowdy struck out but pitcher Jack Bentley singled to right, moving Jackson to third. Lindstrom chopped a "swinging bunt" roller to third, Miller coming in too slowly for a chance at either Jackson crossing the plate or the speedy Lindstrom at first. With runners on first and second, Frisch grounded to Bluege, who tossed to Miller for the force at third, but the hapless Miller instead tried to tag Bentley as he came down from second, and missed. The bases were loaded with one out and Ross Youngs at the plate. Youngs lined to right and Rice came up quickly to make the catch. Bentley tagged at third, but was cut down by Rice's throw to Johnson and the relay to Ruel. A serious crisis had been averted, but it left the Giants with a 1–0 lead.

The Nationals got the run back the next inning as Judge singled, went to second on a sacrifice, and came in on Miller's hit off the right-field wall. Miller's judgment was once again lacking, though, as he was cut down easily on a powerful throw by Youngs after trying to stretch the hit into a double. Kelly struck out to lead off the bottom of the fourth before Bill Terry cracked an incredible line drive all the way to the center-field wall, a blast John McGraw called "the longest line hit I ever saw made at the Polo Grounds. The ball hit the fence on a line at the furthest point from the plate in deep-center. The world series or any other game never saw a line drive like that, both for distance and speed."[64] Terry pulled into third before the ball was returned to the infield. Wilson followed with a hot grass-hugger back to the mound that Johnson snared with his glove while falling to the ground. Scrambling to his feet, Johnson wheeled on Terry, who had wandered down the line between third and home, and herded him back to the bag before tossing to Miller for the tag.

The Giants struck again quickly in the fifth. Gowdy opened with a single and Bentley lofted a "fluke" homer that landed a foot fair and a foot inside the upper deck railing down the abbreviated right field line, a routine pop fly in any other ballpark. There was more trouble with one out when Frisch doubled and Johnson hit Youngs with a pitch, but Bluege and Harris turned a beautiful double play on Kelly's grounder. In the seventh, sharp Washington defensive play helped Johnson out of difficulty again, as it had all day. Singles by Lindstrom and Youngs put runners on the corners with two out, and McGraw again put on the double steal. This time Ruel threw to second to nab the slower Youngs, who stopped and headed back to first. Harris tossed to Judge, who ran Youngs back toward second a few feet before giving the ball back to Harris. At that point Lindstrom made a dash for home, but Harris saw him and fired the ball to Ruel, who applied the tag on a close play to end the inning.

There was nothing flukey about Goslin's terrific liner into the right-field stands in the top of the eighth inning, which tied Babe Ruth's record of three home runs in a World Series. (Goslin's infield hit in the second was his sixth safety in a row, still the Series record.) The blow brought the Nationals to within a run at 3–2, but in the Giants half the bottom fell out. Kelly singled, Terry walked, and Johnson fumbled Wilson's bunt to load the bases with no outs. Kelly scored on Jackson's fly to left. Gowdy grounded to Miller, who forced Wilson at second as Terry moved to third. Pitcher Hugh McQuillan, who had relieved Bentley after Goslin's homer, dropped a Texas Leaguer into short left, scoring Terry, and Lindstrom's single—his fourth hit of the day and the Giants' 13th—tallied Gowdy. Bluege forced Lindstrom at second on Frisch's grounder to stop the carnage, but the damage was done. New York's 6–2 advantage held up through the Washington ninth, and the Giants led the Series, three games to two. The Nationals had to win the last two games.

As the Giants barrage persisted, and the game slipped further out of reach for Washington with each run passing over the plate, the crowd, which had cheered for Johnson at every opportunity throughout the afternoon, became more and more quiet. "As the dying shadows of a chill October day crept down from Coogan's Bluff, Walter Johnson stood on the mound of the Polo Grounds taking his punishment without a murmur," wrote Robert Small of the Associated Press. "There was a spirit of the dying gladiator in the air. The stands were silent; the spectators were stunned."

The crowd wasn't entirely mute, however. One man alone among the thousands insisted on bellowing the predictable: "Take him out! Take him out!" and he had the misfortune to be sitting in the same section as Billy Evans. Appalled fans around the man were already turning on him in outrage as Evans came charging over, yelling "Let him alone, let me have him. He's mine," and only the intervention of several spectators prevented a fight between the two. "I can stand for anything they call me when I'm out there," Evans later explained: "but it seemed a shame to razz a man like Walter, who was in there giving everything he had. It hurt to have someone shout that old line."[65]

On the train back to Washington that night, Bucky Harris correctly predicted that he would come in for some criticism over not removing Johnson during the Giants' assault. "They'll blame me for not using good judgment in not taking Walter from the game when he began to weaken," he confided to Brewster Adams. "Oh, I know it wasn't good baseball, but I wouldn't have pulled the big fellow from the box and made him walk those miles across the grounds to the clubhouse [through a gate in center field] to win all the games in the series."[66]

The drama of Johnson's second heartbreaking defeat in this moment of ultimate importance to his team was not lost on those whose job it was to describe the events for the rest of the world. "What took place yesterday at the Polo Grounds was a tragedy, one of the real tragedies of baseball," Fred Lieb told them. "Walter Johnson's great moment came, and it will leave a lifetime of tragic recollections."[67] Damon Runyon wrote: "A bright vision hung and held for just a moment over the Polo Grounds this afternoon—the vision of a tall, fresh-cheeked, fair-haired, brawny youth pitching with power, with blinding, dazzling speed. It was just a mirage of other years. Now it has vanished. The youth was gone. By some tragic quirk of the imagination there stood in his place an old fellow with stooping shoulders, as if they felt the great weight of years, whose arms lifted wearily and fell wearily, who glanced at the raging crowd around him with tired eyes. That was Johnson, once called the great; that seemingly old, old man! And that bright vision that passed so quickly—that also was Johnson, the Johnson that used to be. Almost mercifully the evening shadows closed over the stooped shoulders in the ninth inning, as he slowly trudged toward the distant clubhouse, keeping close to the walls above which sat the raging crowd."[68]

Not even the stirring spectacle of a stadium full of foreign fans standing in heartfelt applause as he passed by could console Johnson now, with his magnificent career ending at its most bitter moment. "As he shuffled from the pitcher's box, head down and arms hanging loosely at his sides, once more a loser, there were unmistakable tears in the veteran's eyes," Muddy Ruel recalled several years later:

When I went into the clubhouse after the contest had ended I found him sitting in front of his locker with his head in his hands. The big-hearted fellow who was always the first to console and sympathize with a teammate after a bit of poor playing was unable to reconcile himself for his own losses. Nothing that any other player might say could rouse him from his depression. My heart went out to Walter at that moment as it never had before for any player. It was the saddest spectacle I have ever witnessed in my years as a major league player. "Muddy," he said sadly as I placed an arm across his broad shoulders, "I would have cut off my right arm to win that ball game today. But I failed. And I've failed twice." He was broken-hearted because he felt that he had failed in the trust which had been placed in him by so many thousands, perhaps millions, of baseball followers. They and his teammates had depended upon him to bring victory to the Nationals' standard, and he had fallen down. "Never mind, old man," I said, trying to console him, "you'll beat 'em yet! This series isn't over yet, not by a long shot."[69]

Ruel knew, as everyone knew, that there wouldn't be another chance. But when Johnson, carrying young Bobby in his arms and tears still glistening in his eyes, boarded the train for the silent, funereal ride home, the one man in all the world who could lift his spirits at this moment came up and spoke the only words that could do it. Putting his hand on Johnson's pitching arm, Clark Griffith looked him straight in the eyes. "Don't think about it anymore, Walter," he told him, almost sternly. "You're a great pitcher. We all know it. Now tonight when we get home, don't stand around the box office buying seats for friends or shaking hands with people who feel sorry for you. Go home and get to bed early. We may need you."[70]

CHAPTER 14

Destiny, Waiting in the Wings

You know, I have heard people say that that 7th game in 1924 is perhaps the greatest ballgame ever played, in terms of importance and excitement and drama. That might be so. It sure had everything.[1]

FRED LINDSTROM

It was the greatest World Series game ever played, I'm sure. I'm inclined to think, indeed, that it was the most exciting game ever played under any circumstances.[2]

CHRISTY MATHEWSON

As their train pulled into Union Station at midnight, the Nationals weren't expecting much of a reception, certainly not the kind that had greeted the triumphal return from Boston with the pennant. To their surprise some 5,000 fans showed up, and not to blame or commiserate. From the cheering and raucous outbursts, a stranger might have thought the club ahead in the Series instead of behind. The players were acclaimed as heroes as they disembarked, and even the fallen warrior, Walter Johnson, heard nothing but support and affection. "Barney, my boy, we are with you!" was typical of the shouts coming from all over the vast concourse.[3] "The cheering made one's blood tingle," Johnson would recall, crediting the demonstration with a change in the team's demeanor. "That display of loyalty at midnight, totally unexpected after we had failed to win, acted like a powerful stimulant," he wrote. "The spirit of our ballclub changed overnight."[4]

The sixth game on October 9 began on a sad and dramatic note: a moment of silence for the sudden death that morning of Jake Daubert, the great Brooklyn and Cincinnati first baseman. Happier news for the Nationals was the return to the lineup of Roger Peckinpaugh, whose leg had been bandaged and strapped so tightly by Mike Martin that he could barely feel his foot touching the ground.[5] Ossie Bluege went back to his preferred spot, and it didn't take long to see the difference. Opening the game with a bunt to third, which would have been trouble for the slow-footed Ralph Miller, Freddie Lindstrom was thrown out easily by Bluege. Frisch doubled down the right field line, and Youngs hit a grounder to pitcher Tom Zachary, who turned on Frisch to trap him in a run-down while Youngs hustled to second. Kelly singled to center, bringing Youngs around to score, and New York had their first run—their only run, as it turned out.

From that point Zachary was masterful, allowing one other runner to reach second the rest of the game. Keeping ahead of the hitters all day, he walked none. All the offensive support he needed came in the fifth inning, which Peckinpaugh opened with a single to left. He limped to second on Ruel's sacrifice and then to third on Zachary's grounder to Kelly. Artie Nehf, pitching a brilliant game himself thus far, threw four straight balls to walk McNeely, who promptly stole second. Bucky Harris drilled a three-and-two pitch into right field for a single to score both runners, and that's the way the game ended: Washington 2, New York 1. Sam Rice, who wasn't having much of a Series at the plate, made three great catches, two of them run-savers. But aside from the Giant-killer Zachary, the Nationals' hero this day was Roger Peckinpaugh. His mobility limited by the leg wrappings, and in constant pain, he managed two of Washington's four hits and a walk in three trips to the plate. Five chances in the field were executed perfectly.

Peckinpaugh's last assist in the ninth inning was a spectacular game-saving play that ended his participation in the World Series. Kelly singled with one out, and Southworth came in to run for him. Irish Meusel drove a hard grounder through the mound on a path for center field, when out of nowhere came Peckinpaugh, streaking far over from his shortstop position. With a last, desperate leap into the air Peckinpaugh speared the bounding ball and somehow flipped it back to Harris at second, forcing Southworth. When his damaged leg hit the ground Peckinpaugh collapsed in a heap, rolling over and over in the dirt, writhing in agony. He was carried from the field by two teammates, his face twisted in pain and the now-useless leg hanging loosely beneath him. Tommy Taylor, a bandage on the wrist of his throwing hand, came in to play third as Bluege once again moved over to short. But with the winning run at the plate in the powerful figure of Hack Wilson, Zachary made sure it didn't matter who was playing where as he struck Wilson out on three pitches to end the game and even the Series.

Long after the end of the sixth game Bucky Harris sat in the locker room outlining his pitching plans for the next day, which included a brilliant piece of tricksmanship. Pledging his listeners, *Washington Herald* city editor Bryan Morse and prominent businessman and baseball fan George P. Marshall, to silence, Harris described his gambit. The most dangerous hitter on the New York ballclub, in his opinion, was neither Kelly, nor Youngs, nor any of the other established stars, but the rookie, Bill Terry, even though McGraw only used him against right-handed pitchers.[6] In three starts so far in the Series, Terry had six hits and three walks in 14 trips to the plate. Harris planned to start the lefty George Mogridge in the seventh game, which would keep Terry on the bench, but if Mogridge ran into trouble there would be righthanders coming in for the Nationals, and McGraw would immediately send Terry into the game.

Harris's idea was to start the all-but-disabled Curly Ogden instead, and have him pitch to the first batter. Then Mogridge would take over. Terry would be at first base against the right-handed Ogden. When Mogridge came in Terry might be lifted or McGraw might choose to leave him in. Either way was okay with Harris. The plan called for Marberry to follow Mogridge if that became necessary. "And if they get to Marberry," Harris told his eager listeners, "I'll put in Walter."[7] That evening Harris went to Clark Griffith's house to go over the idea, and found the boss approving. "That strategy sounded logical enough to me, even if it was a bit radical at first glance," Griffith recalled later.[8] The Nationals owner then telephoned Johnson, who had seemed particularly down in the dumps when he stopped by the Washington offices that afternoon to pick up tickets for the last game. Griffith told him to be ready to pitch, that he was in the plans for late-inning relief.[9] When Hazel heard the news, at first she was ecstatic. Then, when the ramifications sank in, she threw herself on the couch and cried, "Walter, you mustn't!"[10]

The 1924 World Series was the first since the Red Sox-Giants classic of 1912 to come down to a last deciding contest. Just as they had won the coin toss deciding where the Series would begin, Washington won again on a crucial second flip to determine the site of the finale. Judge Landis used a silver dollar given him by Clark Griffith, who had borrowed it from a long-time Nationals rooter for whom the coin had been a "good-luck piece." Harris called the flip correctly, and Griffith pocketed the dollar, which he carried with him for the rest of his life.[11] The morning of the last game a different sort of good-luck charm found its way to the Johnson home. A package arrived containing a horseshoe with numerous red, white, and blue ribbons tied to it, and accompanied by a note: "We, the undersigned players of the Honor Farm Ball Club of the Illinois State Penitentiary, send you this lucky emblem and trust that it will live up to its tradition." Not at all superstitious, Hazel nonetheless carried the horseshoe with her to the ballpark.[12]

The nation's capital was a strange place that day, October 10, 1924, with its entire population concerned with little else but baseball. "The situation was truly remarkable," it was described. "Government has been at a standstill; local business has been thrown out of joint; professional men have deserted their offices. Doctors waved away their patients and postponed important operations. Dentists paid no heed to the pleas of persons howling with an aching tooth; lawyers excused themselves from all clients, and in the shops purchasers could get nowhere with the sales persons who were demanding to know the latest word from the thousands of radio sets scattered all over the city."[13] A siege had been maintained all night (an estimated 5,000 persons stood in line at 4 o'clock in the morning) in front of ticket windows that wouldn't open until morning. Enterprising youngsters from the surrounding neighborhoods, many of whom had never held more than a dime, quickly grabbed up places they later sold for five or ten dollars.[14]

Every game of the 1924 World Series had been blessed with good weather, but this last day was the most beautiful of all, occasional cotton-puff clouds drifting lazily across a gorgeous blue sky, warm sunshine tempered by a cooling breeze. The federal establishment was out in full force for the denouement, as was the cream of Washington society, the feminine contingent of which used the occasion to show off the latest fall styles, the newly-fashionable Spanish influençe seen everywhere. Before the start of the game both teams, the umpires, and Judge Landis lined up in front of the presidential box for a picture. Flanked by managers Harris and McGraw, President Coolidge expressed to the gathering his appreciation for the game of baseball before sending them off with the edict, "May the better team win."[15]

Curly Ogden was supposed to pitch to the Giants' leadoff batter only, according to Harris's plan, then give way to Mogridge, who had been warming up out of sight under the stands. But when Ogden struck out Lindstrom on three pitches to start the game, and began walking to the bench as instructed, Harris waved him back to the mound. Maybe Ogden's arm had one last game left in it. But unable to take advantage of the reprieve, Ogden walked the next batter, Frisch, and the strategy went into effect. Mogridge came in to strike out Youngs and get Kelly on a grounder to Tommy Taylor at third, who was making his first World Series start in the 29th (and last) game of a brief major-league career. The Nationals went in order meekly in their half against Virgil Barnes, the Giants' own hurler from Kansas.

For five innings Mogridge held the Giants in his sway, just as he had in game four, giving up three hits and no walks. Barnes's screwball was even more of a mystery, though, as he rang up six strikeouts over that span, retiring the first 10 Nationals in order without a ball reaching the outfield. Only one runner had reached base against him, Bucky Harris in the fourth inning. Unfortunately for Barnes, Harris got to touch all the bases after driving a 3–2 pitch into the temporary bleachers in left. It was Harris's second home run of the Series, doubling his total for the regular season. (He would hit only nine homers in a 12-year career.)

In going after the ball Hack Wilson had tried to duplicate Goslin's balletic leap into the stands in the first game, but instead of clearing the barricade Wilson's ample girth made full contact with the top of it. The impact sounded "like a barrel of crockery being pushed down the cellar stairs," described Grantland Rice, as Wilson toppled head-first into the seats and the Washington crowd cheered wildly for Harris. Bleacher fans helpfully lifted Wilson to his feet and set him back onto the field where he tottered around for a few seconds before signaling that he was okay, a dramatic demonstration of which came moments later when Sam Rice sent a fast-sinking liner to left. Racing in at full speed Wilson made a headlong dive, picking the ball off just inches from the turf and then sliding another six feet on his belly before coming to a stop. It was the best of a handful of sparkling defensive plays that kept the crowd buzzing in the early going despite a lack of offensive fireworks.

In the top of the sixth Mogridge suddenly lost his control, and so did the infield. The willowy left-hander walked Youngs to start the inning before Kelly singled over second, Youngs advancing to third on the hit-and-run. McGraw had seen enough of Terry's futility against Mogridge (a weak grounder and a strikeout) by then, and sent Irish Meusel up to bat for him. That was Harris's signal to wave in Marberry, as Mogridge walked off to a standing ovation led by President Coolidge. Moments later a second ovation echoed through the stadium when Walter Johnson emerged from the Washington dugout, headed for the bullpen in right field. Waving to the crowd in acknowledgment, the first real grin in two days spread over his face.[16]

Meusel lined to Rice in deep right field, Youngs tagging easily with the tying run. Wilson followed with a single to center as Kelly raced to third. In this time of crisis the most dependable components of the Washington defense came unglued. Travis Jackson hit a sharp grounder to Joe Judge, who fumbled the ball momentarily in his desire to hurry a throw home. Realizing the play at the plate was lost to him with Kelly already streaking across, Judge stood frozen with indecision, holding the ball as Wilson went to second and Jackson made it safely to first. Then Gowdy hit a hard "grasscutter" straight to Bluege, who had been making sensational plays all game, and the inning should have been over on a routine double play. Instead, the ball went right through him, not even touching his glove as it rolled underneath. ("My worst error ever," Bluege would recall, "I looked up at second base just before the ball got to me.")[17] Wilson strolled home and Jackson pulled into third. Barnes lofted a fly to right field, Jackson holding on Rice's beautiful throw home, before a disgusted Marberry closed out the inning himself by striking out Lindstrom on three pitches. The Giants' 3–1 lead looked even larger when the Nationals went meekly again in the bottom of the sixth. Of 19 batters facing Barnes so far, Harris had been the only one to reach base.

The Washington defense, at least, recovered in the seventh inning, which opened with Ruel stretching far into the stands for Frisch's high foul near the screen. After Youngs walked, Tommy Taylor made a great play on Kelly's slow roller to short, racing in front of Bluege to cut the ball off and nip Kelly at first. Meusel bounced back to Marberry, who ran over to the line to make an unassisted tag. A glimmer of hope appeared in the bottom half when Harris led off with an infield hit into the hole at short. That woke the crowd up and started a round of cheering, which stopped suddenly when Rice hit the first pitch to Kelly, who was playing first base now, right at the bag. He stepped on it and threw to second for a tag on Harris to complete the double play. Goslin followed with a single to right, but Judge, swinging on the first pitch, flew out to center.

Wilson struck out on three pitches to start the Giants' eighth. Bluege made another error on Jackson's grounder, but with no damage this time as Gowdy flied to left and Marberry again shut the door on his own by striking out Barnes. The bottom half began inauspiciously with Bluege's foul pop to Gowdy. But Nemo Leibold batted for Taylor, who had struck out twice, and sent a shot down the third-base line past Lindstrom and into the corner. Leibold pulled up at second with a double. That brought up Muddy Ruel, who was hitless so far in the Series. Ruel punched a hard grounder toward the hole in right that Kelly could only knock down as Leibold went to third. Bennie Tate, a 23-year-old rookie backup catcher with a total of 43 at-bats in the major leagues, came up to hit for Marberry. As he did, Walter Johnson popped out of the dugout heading for the bullpen again, this time in a hurry. At that the crowd, brought to life by Leibold's hit and electrified by Ruel's, stood up with a roar, which intensified as Tate, after falling behind in the count, 1–2, took three outside pitches in a row from the rattled Barnes. The bases were loaded, and Mule Shirley came in to run for Tate. The din increased as McNeely took the first pitch for a ball, but was silenced a moment later when he hit a short fly to Meusel, who was in left field now with Wilson moving over to center.

As Harris walked up to the plate, Gowdy went over to the Giants bench to consult with McGraw. When play resumed Harris worked the count to two and two, then took two quick steps forward in the batter's box (perhaps to get at Barnes's screwball before it broke) and knocked a bouncing ball toward third. Lindstrom came in for the easy play, but just as he was about to grab the ball it hit something on the turf and took a 10-foot leap over the head of the surprised youngster, bounding on into left field. With two outs, Leibold and Ruel were running on Harris's swing and scored easily.

The game was tied, and now the crowd really went crazy. Many had come prepared for a celebration, and suddenly a cacophony of bells, whistles, and other noisemakers rang out from all over the park. Spectators jumped onto the field to show off their happiness, only to be quickly rounded up by police. Nowhere was the enthusiasm greater than in the presidential box, in the person of Grace Coolidge. "During the eighth inning, the ninth, and until the game ended, she scarcely sat down," it was reported. "Nor did she just cheer. She jumped up and down on both feet, waved her arms, yelled, called out, and did all the other things that the fair fans were doing."[18] Carried away by his wife's fervor, perhaps, "Silent Cal" dropped his cigar when the Nationals tied the game, and was reported to have "actually shouted on several occasions." But in contrast to the first lady's hearty applause and lusty yelling, "For the most part he just clapped his hands in his precise mechanical manner."[19]

With Shirley on second, Harris on first, and Sam Rice coming up, Artie Nehf was called in to replace Barnes. Nehf had gone seven innings the day before, but at least he was no stranger to this kind of pressure: it was his fourth straight appearance in the final game of a World Series, and he had won two of them. Once again Nehf proved worthy of the task, getting Rice on a grounder to Kelly to snuff out the Washington threat.

When all the game is young,
And pitching arms are keen;
When morning songs are sung,
Along the sporting green—
Then hey for any game, lad
Around the world of play;
Young blood will find its fame,
And stars will have their day.

But when the game is old,
And pitching arms are worn,
In search of fame and gold,
The aging nerves are torn,
And in the deadly swerve,
Where hearts must be unstrung,
God grant you find one curve, lad
You threw when you were young.[20]

GRANTLAND RICE

The drama of those last four innings is seared into my soul. I saw men crying unashamed, and men and women praying aloud. Call it an emotional debauch or just a paid performance, as you will. It was more than a ballgame to me. It was life and death.[21]

HAZEL JOHNSON

The packed stadium, in a continuous boil since Harris's hit tying the game, was quieted little by the end of the Nationals' rally. For now, as the teams changed sides for the ninth inning, the fans turned to the sight of Walter Johnson walking in to the mound. A tremendous shout went up all at once, followed by the chant, "Walter! Walter! Walter!" resounding through the rafters. "The park was in a fearful uproar," Clark Griffith remembered. "Utter strangers were hugging each other in the stands because Walter was getting one more chance in the series. It was his ball game now."[22] Uppermost in the minds of some, though, were the consequences of another failure. "Poor old Walter, it's a shame to send him in," sighed Christy Mathewson in the press box, knowing all too well the sting of defeat in a World Series.[23] Al Schacht said: "I wouldn't have given ten cents for Johnson's chances when he came in. He was tired."[24]

Even Hazel had doubts, despite her husband's assurances that morning that he was "primed for another battle." She told her readers the next day:

"I credited that to willingness of spirit rather than to strength of flesh. I could not believe he was ready."[25] Fearing that the strain of watching him pitch would prove too great, Hazel at first wanted to leave the stands and sit in the car before being convinced by her companion, California Congresswoman Mae Nolan, to stay. Hazel did insist, though, that they leave their grandstand boxes for the anonymity of the bleachers, in case her nerves snapped. She continued to clutch tightly the horseshoe that had been in her hands since the start of the game.[26]

Nobody in the ballpark was more keenly aware of the challenge at hand than the great pitcher himself. "I remember thinking, 'I'll need the breaks,'" he said years later, "and if I didn't actually pray, I sort of was thinking along those lines." A cloud of cigar and cigarette smoke had settled over the field, and Johnson took solace even in the little bit of cover it provided from the 30,000 pairs of eyes boring in on him.[27] As he reached the mound, Bucky Harris was there to meet him. "It was as though Harris introduced with some pride his Old Reliable," one observer thought.[28] Indeed, Johnson's previous losses and lack of rest notwithstanding, it might have just at that moment occurred to the young manager that for this ultimate situation he had at his disposal not merely the best pitcher on the team, or even the best in the league—he had The Greatest Pitcher in the History of Baseball to call upon. Harris patted Johnson on the back, telling him, "You're the best we've got, Walter. We've got to win or lose with you."[29]

The pitcher gritted his teeth and took the ball. "I never saw such a grim face as Johnson's when Harris gave him the ball," Clark Griffith recalled. "He grabbed the ball so hard the white showed through his knuckles." In the eighth inning, with the Nationals' cause looking increasingly hopeless, Griffith had moved from his box in the stands to a row of steps next to the dugout, positioning himself to escort President Coolidge out of the park through the ballplayers' tunnel. The moment he got there, the rally began that would tie the game. So the Old Fox, superstitious like so many baseball men, didn't budge for the rest of the inning, afraid even to sit down. He was still standing at the same spot when Johnson came in, and would remain there for the rest of the game.[30]

"Walter took his five warmups deliberately," it was reported, "but as the ball slapped into Ruel's big mitt with the crack of a rifle shot, the throngs were startled to the realization that the big fellow's fastball had somehow been restored to him."[31] Bucky Harris, watching Johnson intently, realized it, too. "When he warmed up, I knew he had all his stuff," Harris wrote in *Playing the Game.* Nonetheless, the Nationals skipper sent left-hander Tom Zachary, who had pitched a complete game the day before, and right-hander Paul Zahniser, who had seen no action in the Series, out to the bullpen. Having pinch-hit for Tommy Taylor, Harris had to bring in Ralph Miller to play third.

The final act of the World Series drama opened the way the production had kicked off a week earlier: Walter Johnson facing Freddie Lindstrom and the top of the Giants batting order. With the boy's four-for-four performance at the Polo Grounds etched clearly in his mind, Johnson pitched carefully before Lindstrom lifted a high infield pop-up halfway to third base. The nervous Miller staggered a few awkward steps underneath it, but made the catch. Then, with a 1–1 count on Frankie Frisch, disaster struck. Frisch leaned into a waist-high fastball and sent a terrific drive screaming into the deepest corner in right center field, between McNeely and Rice. Both of them raced after the ball, McNeely reaching it first after a carom off the bleachers, as Frisch dashed full-speed around the bases. McNeely summoned up a tremendous, desperate throw that reached the infield in time to stop the streaking Frisch at third. If not for the temporary stands, and McNeely's brilliant retrieval, the Fordham Flash would have completed the circuit. "The ball never seemed to stop rolling and I was crazy for fear Frisch would come clear home," Muddy Ruel recalled.[32]

The crowd slumped back in its seats at this stunning development, an ominous quiet settling over the ballpark. "Uh oh, this is curtains," Ossie Bluege said to himself at his shortstop position.[33] Ross Youngs walked to the plate, "swinging his clubs all the way from the dugout and veritably exuding vengeance at the mighty Johnson," it was reported.[34] Muddy Ruel said of Youngs: "He'd crouch at the plate and poise himself like lightning about to strike, his eyes boring in on a pitcher, tense as a violin string. I'll never forget that big white bat of his hanging over my head as I crouched behind the plate."[35] After a long conference on the mound, Harris decided to walk Youngs, a tough call with the major-league RBI champion George Kelly, who had homered off Johnson in the first game, next up. But Youngs batted from the left side and was three-for-six against Johnson since fanning in their first three confrontations in the opener. The right-handed Kelly was only two for nine facing Johnson, while also striking out three times against him. At the same time, he was the only Giant to have hit safely in every game, and if McGraw had been able to choose a batter to bring up at this critical time it would likely have been Long George Kelly.

Kelly moved into the batter's box "brimful of determination," Ty Cobb told his readers. "No batter likes to have the player preceding him purposely passed in a pinch," Cobb explained. "It is a deep thrust to his pride."[36] With the dangerous Frisch dancing up and down the line at third, Johnson wound up and fired a fastball for the heart of the plate. Kelly took a hard, sweeping cut at the ball, and missed. Wasting no time between pitches, Johnson soon swung his arm back and sent another to the same spot, and again the crouching Kelly uncoiled himself fully, swinging "like a gate," one writer described it, but again the ball crashed into Ruel's mitt untouched. At second base, Bucky Harris realized Johnson's strategy: "I could tell he was counting on his blinding speed to fool Kelly on three pitched balls. As Walter made ready to deliver his third pitch I said a little prayer. I knew he was demanding everything of his mighty right arm."[37] Kelly, the famed fastball hitter, must have known too, along with everyone else in the eerily silent ballpark, what was coming. But, as Grantland Rice wrote, "The tall Giant suddenly found himself facing the Johnson of a decade ago—blinding, baffling speed that struck him out and closed down on the rally with the snap of death."[38] "I can see that ball yet streaking in through Kelly's swing for strike three," Muddy Ruel recalled 20 years later.[39] It was reported that Kelly went down "angrily, and viciously."[40]

But Kelly was only the second out; the crisis wasn't over yet. Irish Meusel was the batter (but for Harris's strategy it would have been Terry), and the Nationals knew that with Frisch at third and Youngs, who had excellent speed himself, on first, McGraw would try to make something happen. As Meusel came up, "The field was cluttered with Senatorial conferences," it was reported.[41] The first pitch was fouled off, and Harris rushed in for another short discussion with Ruel. Meusel took a ball and Youngs took off for second. But Ruel made no throw, the Nationals conceding the base rather than make a play with the speedster Frisch on third. After taking another ball inside, Meusel swung on the next pitch and hit a sharp bounder down the line, an audible gasp going up from the crowd when they saw it heading for Ralph Miller. He fielded the ball cleanly, but followed with a wretched throw to first. Joe Judge, the smallest first baseman in the big leagues at 5 feet 8 inches, saved the game with a masterful stretch to take the throw as Frisch dashed across the plate in vain.

In the bottom of the ninth the Nationals mounted a one-out rally when Judge singled and Jackson muffed Kelly's double play throw on Bluege's tap to first. Judge went to third, and the crowd went wild. Nehf gave way to Hugh McQuillan, but the hapless Miller hit a grounder to Jackson, who made up for his error by starting a lightning-fast double play to close out the threat.

The game moved into extra innings, which Wilson opened by drawing a walk as Johnson shied away from his power zone. There was no such fear of Jackson and he fanned on four pitches, dropping his bat in disapproval of umpire Bill Dinneen's third-strike call. (Dinneen had been the pitching hero and last-game winner of the first World Series in 1903, coincidentally). Then it was Washington's turn for an inning-ending double play. After a pretty stop of Gowdy's grounder back to the box, Johnson wheeled and fired the ball to Bluege, who made the force at second and relayed to first. The Nationals went in order in the bottom half, the only excitement coming from Johnson's appearance at the plate with one out. A standing ovation for him turned into a roar when he drove a long fly to left-center, and for an electrifying moment the blast appeared to have a chance to reach the bleachers before Wilson hauled it in a dozen feet short of the fence.

Real trouble brewed again in the Giants 11th as the crippled veteran Heinie Groh made his first appearance of the Series, limping to the plate to bat for McQuillan. Assuming his odd stance with the bat lifted high over his head, Groh took a ball and a strike before lining a single into right field and limping to first base, where he was replaced by Billy Southworth. Lindstrom executed a perfect sacrifice bunt down the first-base line, Southworth moving to second. Once again facing the heart of the New York order with a runner in scoring position, Johnson was visibly nervous, reaching down to rub his hand in the dirt after every pitch. But with the count two and two on Frisch (who had 10 hits in the Series so far), Johnson crossed him up with a beautiful curve that started for the heart of the plate before sailing far outside. Frisch, one of the hardest batters in baseball history to strike out, flailed wildly at a ball that suddenly swerved out of his reach. That brought up Ross Youngs, precipitating another conference where it was again decided to pass him and pitch to Kelly instead. Youngs's fourth straight base on balls brought sporadic boos from those who never could abide the "cowardly" strategy of an intentional walk.

As Youngs trotted down to first base, Bucky Harris came in to the mound to pat Johnson on the back several times, continuing to shout encouragement while the tall, powerful figure of George Kelly stepped in to the batter's box. Kelly twisted into his exaggerated crouch, bent almost double over the plate, and took the first pitch for a strike. He swung on the next one and finally made contact, if only to foul it back, then refused to bite on a high fastball. On the next pitch Johnson put everything he had behind a hard, fast-breaking curve, which had worked on Frisch, and it worked on Kelly, too, as he unwound to make a full sweep of his big bat through the strike zone but met only air for strike three. As Johnson walked off the mound the crowd jumped to its feet and exploded. A "real inferno of noise," Muddy Ruel called it.[42]

They were still standing as Washington took its turn in the bottom of the 11th. Jack Bentley, who had pitched almost as much as Johnson in the fifth game, took over on the mound for the Giants. He got two quick outs before Goslin dropped a Texas Leaguer into right field between Youngs, Wilson, and Frisch, Goslin hustling to second. McGraw instructed Bentley to walk Judge in favor of the weaker-hitting Bluege, an unusual bit of strategy that had the lefty Bentley passing the left-handed hitter to face a right-handed one. With Bluege a dead pull-hitter, McGraw also brought Youngs's more powerful arm and faster legs over to left field, switching Meusel to right. Bluege hit a hard-hopping grounder to Jackson, who handled it skillfully and tossed to Frisch at second, forcing Judge to end the inning.

Meusel opened the 12th with a single to right, the third inning in a row New York's leadoff hitter had reached base. A fearful calm again settled over the exhausted crowd, whose emotions had been pulled back and forth all game. But Wilson went down on yet another deflating strikeout at the critical moment, and Jackson and Gowdy were easy outs. "I'd settled down to believe, by then, that maybe this was my day," Johnson said later.[43]

The Giants, too, were beginning to feel that it might be Johnson's day. The bottom half started quietly enough, with Ralph Miller going out on a routine grounder to Frisch. That brought up Muddy Ruel, the hitting bust of the Series for Washington, who seemed destined to continue in that role when he popped the first pitch high and foul behind the plate, and not 10 feet from it. The crowd issued a collective groan as the 15-year veteran catcher Hank Gowdy, who had handled 42 chances without a mishap so far in the Series, started back to make the easy play, pulling off and discarding his mask along the way. But as he got to where the ball should have been coming down, the wind started bringing it back toward the plate, and Gowdy drifted back with it. Putting his glove out to catch the ball and taking one last step to get into position, his left foot came down squarely on the inside of the upturned catcher's mask—and lodged in it. Gowdy tried to shake the mask off his foot, but it wouldn't budge. He stumbled and fell to one knee as the ball bounced off his glove and onto the ground. Clark Griffith would later claim: "That mask up and *bit* Gowdy. He was going to catch that pop foul and it grabbed him away from it."[44]

As seems to happen so often to batters given that kind of reprieve, Ruel took advantage of the second chance to drive a ball down the line in left, past Lindstrom and into the corner for a double, his first solid hit of the Series. Walter Johnson came to bat with another opportunity to put a monumental finish to the Series, but drilled the first pitch sharply on the ground slightly to Jackson's right at shortstop. Ruel pretended to take off for third, distracting Jackson, and he fumbled the ball. Ruel hurried back to second and Johnson was safe at first. The pitcher's sweater was rushed out to him while the crowd went into its umpteenth furor of the day.

Earl McNeely walked toward the plate. From the third-base coaching box Al Schacht waited to hear the familiar voice of the master strategist, John McGraw, barking out instructions from the dugout as he always did, moving his players around like so many pawns on a chessboard. McNeely was a pull-hitter ("Couldn't hit one to right if his life depended on it," Schacht recalled), and with a man on second McGraw would certainly switch right fielder Youngs and left fielder Meusel to get Youngs's superior arm into left, as he had done the previous inning. But this time the Giants dugout behind Schacht was silent.[45]

McNeely swung at the first pitch and fouled it back over the stands. Bentley sent him a fastball and McNeely swung at this one, too, knocking a hard, bouncing ball directly at Lindstrom, a few feet to the left of third base. Ruel, seeing that it was a perfect double play ball, decided to run as hard as he could and try to attract a tag. He could see Lindstrom holding his hands at his chest, waiting for the ball . . . then suddenly leap up into the air. Astonishingly, beyond all odds, it had happened again: the ball had hit a pebble—or something, perhaps the same something as in the eighth inning—and bounded completely over Lindstrom's head into left field. Ruel swerved back into the baseline, heading straight for third.[46] With Ruel the slowest runner on the team, Schacht had already considered the risks of sending him in on a sharp hit. If there was any chance at all, he would wave him around. Now Ruel was chugging toward Schacht, who circled his arm around and around like a windmill gone berserk, the signal to keep going.[47] Ruel made sure to stomp on the bag hard, then put his head down and charged for home as fast as he could go—but not nearly fast enough to suit Griffith ("It seemed like an eternity")[48] or Harris in the on-deck circle, convinced that the harder Ruel tried to run, the slower he moved.[49]

It didn't matter, though, because there was no throw to the plate, and never would be. Not expecting a routine ground ball to make it past Lindstrom, Meusel hadn't charged in on it, a costly lapse.[50] And when he did reach the ball, Meusel just picked it up casually, stuck it in his glove, and started running in toward the infield with Ruel still only halfway between third and home. It would forever be a mystery to the Nationals, as it was to John McGraw (who chewed out Meusel on the train back to New York), why there wasn't at least a desperation throw.[51]

There was no time to puzzle over such questions at the moment, for as Ruel crossed the plate to win the game and the World Series, the stadium exploded, the roiling, rocking stands pouring forth an instantaneous flood tide of humanity. Washington players rushed out from the dugout and Schacht and Altrock came in leaping and yelling from the coaching boxes toward the plate. For a moment the gray-clad Giants stood stunned and motionless, staring in disbelief as Ruel sealed their doom. After rounding first, McNeely turned to watch the events he had set in motion. Walter Johnson, in his gray,

"W"-monogrammed sweater, reached second base and stayed there, standing on the bag and looking straight toward home with a broad smile breaking over his face and tears welling up in his eyes.

In the next few instants they were all engulfed by a tidal wave of celebrating fans, sweeping up everyone in its surge toward the Nationals' bench. When the players recovered from their shock long enough to realize what was happening, they ran for the only exit: the Washington dugout, the same place the crowd was headed. Ruel, who wisely kept running, got there in time, and Harris and the others near the plate were close enough to be literally picked up by the leading edge of the human wave and forced through the opening to safety. But the last National to leave the field, the hero McNeely, had been seized by the mob, which in its affections tore his shirt apart and pulled the buttons off before police beat back enough of the seething mass in front of the dugout to allow his passage through. As for the luckless Giants, they were "being tossed around in the crowd like bits of driftwood in a running stream," Damon Runyon noted. All the while, hats, coats, cushions, newspapers, and other debris rained down from the grandstands upon the mad scene. In the press box "Hardened newspaper men sniffed their tears away," it was reported,[52] and Billy Evans was seen wiping his eyes with a handkerchief.[53]

Walter Johnson struggled in from second, his journey slowed by countless handshakes, hugs, kisses, and other delirious felicitations. Even under these wild circumstances, it was observed, "Walter, the Great Walter, in his supreme moment, was the same gracious Walter of old."[54] "I was so happy, it didn't seem real," he recalled years later. "They told me that President Coolidge kept watching me all the way into the clubhouse, and I remember somebody yelling, 'I'll bet Cal'd like to change places with you right now, Walter.' "[55]

As the presidential party stood watching the howling maelstrom swirl about below them, some in the mob began climbing on top of the dugout to lead the crowd in cheers. Fearing that the presidential box would be overrun in the frenzy, the Secret Service managed with great difficulty to clear a path for the chief executive into the dugout, where he disappeared through the exit. "The fates were kind in one respect," one account of the melee noted, "for the immense crowd did not care to bother with a mere President."[56] As they passed through the tunnel the Coolidges ran into the objects of the mob's passion, Walter Johnson and several other Nationals, as they were heading into the dressing rooms. The president and first lady shook hands with the pitcher and said how proud they were, while the president's secretary, Bascom Slemp, deliriously pounded Johnson on the back.[57]

The Nationals' clubhouse was a bedlam of shouting, hugging, exhilarated players. They shook Johnson's hand one by one "as though it were the handle on the town pump back in Coffeyville," it was reported, as Johnson repeated, "Gee, I was lucky, wasn't I?"[58] Clark Griffith burst through the door, tears running down his cheeks, and went about the room slapping his players on the back. Embracing Harris, the owner told him, "I'm certainly proud of you, Bucky boy." For his part, Harris was in a daze, forgetting to put on his clothes after showering. He paced back and forth, patting shoulders and squeezing hands, becoming so agitated at one point that Mike Martin started to worry about a nervous collapse. Martin urged him to quiet down, but the manager just laughed and said, "Get away from here, Mike, there's nothing the matter with me. I've just got to blow off steam," after which he stood in front of a mirror carefully combing his hair into a perfect part, still blissfully unaware, apparently, that he didn't have a stitch on.

A fully dressed Walter Johnson came over to shake Harris's hand one last time. "Bucky, I want to thank you for letting me go in today," Johnson told him, his eyes welling up with tears, before slipping out the door and into the crowd surrounding the players' cars. When the manager was asked, "Did Walter insist on going in this afternoon?" Harris turned on the reporter. "Why do you ask me that?" he said sharply. "Walter was my best bet. That's why I put him in. Anyone who thought Walter was through was a fool. I knew he was all right."[59]

Immediately after the game, and before the Washington locker room was closed to all but Nationals players and personnel, several of their vanquished foes stopped by to offer congratulations. John McGraw came in first to shake hands with Harris and Johnson.[60] Good-natured Hank Gowdy was the first Giants player to show up, crossing the room to shake hands with Johnson and tell him, "Walter, now that we have lost, I am truly happy it was you that pitched us out. I shall never regret losing to you." Ross Youngs and Frankie Frisch showed up after the door had been shut and a policeman posted to guard it, but when it opened briefly for someone to leave, Frisch spotted Johnson and called him over. "Your work was great, Walter," he said. "You and your team well deserve the victory. I hope we'll meet in the series again next year."[61] In his column about the Series, Frisch wrote: "So long as we had to be beaten, I am glad, and so is our whole ball club, that the victory is credited to Walter Johnson, a glorious triumph for one of the greatest pitchers that ever lived and one of the finest, cleanest men ever identified with baseball."[62]

Many years later, Fred Lindstrom would recall Jack Bentley's comment about the amazing events they had just witnessed: "Walter Johnson," said Bentley, "is such a lovable character that the good lord didn't want to see him get beat again."[63]

Destiny, waiting for the final curtain, stepped from the wings today and handed the King his crown. In the most dramatic moment of baseball's sixty years of history, the wall-eyed Goddess known as Fate, after waiting 18 years, led Walter Johnson to the pot of shining gold that waits at the end of the rainbow. It was something beyond all belief, beyond all imagining. Its crashing echoes are still singing out across the stands, across the city, on into the gathering twilight of early autumn shadows. There never was a ball game like this before, never a game with as many thrills and heart throbs strung together in the making of a drama that came near to tearing away the soul to leave it limp and sagging, drawn and twisted out of shape.

GRANTLAND RICE, NEW YORK HERALD TRIBUNE
OCTOBER 11, 1924

I was never swept by the Easter story until I saw the seventh game of the World's Series. I have seen Osiris die in the darkness and come back from his cavern into the sunlight to conquer. Mithra, Adonis, Krishna, Atlas, Hercules—all these I take to be symbols of the human spirit, and so without incongruity I may add Walter Johnson to the list. To see him throw the ball past the clubs of Giants was to be consoled with the thought of the might of man and the manner in which he may overcome all the forces of frailty if only he can get his soul and shoulders into living. And the legend was the more glamorous because of the fact that Johnson is primarily a fastball pitcher. In Olympus there is no change of pace. Johnson earned his place among the mighty myths because his weapon was not guile but power.

Accordingly it was tragic to see Johnson falter and fail. The reasons for that failure were familiar to us all. The grasp of man is never quite up to his reach. The body lags behind the will. There is no tick of time in the inner places where our wishes dwell. Then he took a rest of one day and returned with all his prowess. He returned for a little while as the Walter Johnson of ten years ago. The stone had been rolled away. I do not know a rational explanation, and so I think it is fair for me to call this happening, which I saw, a miracle. But though it was a miracle, it is also a universal principle in the emotional life of mankind. The road from the top down to despair is long, but the return may be no more than a night's journey. Every one of us is born again. We die in failure, and out of nothing, out of this very bleakness, we make for ourselves a new morning, a new hope, and a new strength.

Billy Sunday is welcome to whatever consolation of immortality he can find in hymn tunes and sermons, but when I want to reassure myself that the soul of man is too staunch to die, I will remember that Walter Johnson struck out George Kelly with one out and a runner on third base.

HEYWOOD BROUN, NEW YORK WORLD, OCTOBER 11, 1924

CHAPTER 15

Zenith

We have never seen anything in sport which quite equaled that moment. We have never seen anything in sport which sent such a buoyant thrill into so many million human hearts. Those last four innings of the world series comprise beyond all question the most dramatic stretch that sport has ever known. For over 30 minutes, millions of people looking on and listening in found their emotions torn into shreds and their nerves twisted out of shape. And five hours after the game was over the carnival was still raging with increasing intensity. In the space of two hours, Walter Johnson had come from a lone, dejected and broken figure in the shadows of the clubhouse to a personal triumph that no other athlete had ever drawn in all the history of sport.[1]

GRANTLAND RICE

After the last game of the 1924 world series I was alone with [Judge] Landis for a few moments on a little balcony outside his room in the Raleigh Hotel in Washington. Below us on Pennsylvania Avenue snake-danced a joy-maddened crowd. Washington's beloved Senators had just won the deciding 7th game, and saint Walter Johnson had been the winning pitcher in a 12-inning cliffhanger. Congressmen, department heads, merchants, barbers, bootblacks, janitors, secretaries—all joined in the frivolity. They blew trumpets and beat drums—some beat wash basins with large spoons. Anything that could make noise was being used in this joyous paean of victory. Landis put his hand on my shoulder and looked directly in my eyes as he said, "Freddy, what we are looking at now—could this be the highest point of what we affectionately call our national sport? Greece had its sports and its Olympics; they must have reached a zenith and then waned. The same for sports of ancient Rome; there must have been a year at which they were at their peak. I repeat, Freddy, are we looking at the zenith of baseball?"[2]

FRED LIEB

Police cleared a way through the teeming crowd so the new Lincoln carrying Walter Johnson, his elated wife, and misty-eyed mother could inch out of the stadium parking lot. A human sea parted before it, then a human river followed alongside for several blocks until Johnson could step on the gas and leave them trailing behind.[3] The mad mob at the ballpark raged on until dusk before spreading out onto a town exploding with sights and sounds even crazier than those at the scene of the triumph. The once staid and proper nation's capital was a Mardi Gras of confetti and noise.

"The firing of small cannon, the crack of pistols, the bang of firecrackers, the honk of automobiles and the overworked lungs of half-crazed baseball fans were blended into a deafening roar," the Associated Press reported. "Drums and sirens were coupled with racket makers and all of Washington was out to promote the noise. Traffic cops were lost in the melee as thousands of automobiles became twisted in a honking jam in the downtown streets. Thronging the streets in groups that ranged from three and four to long 'lock-step' processions, people seemingly in countless numbers paraded and cheered. Every person was equipped with some kind of noisemaker."

Revelers poured in from the nearby suburbs. A particularly memorable sight that evening was the fire department from nearby Cherrydale, Virginia. "That old boy who fiddled while Rome burned had nothing on the intention, at least, of the Cherrydale Fire Department," it was reported. "Apparatus and firefighters both came to Washington last night to join in the high carnival that marked the city's celebration. With women folk and firemen piled all over the three fire pieces they paraded the streets, taking on followers as they progressed. That is, until they could take on no more. The feelings of the firefighters were epitomized in the words displayed on a banner: 'Let Cherrydale Burn!' "[4]

As the melee on the streets gathered momentum, Walter and Hazel escaped to a favorite little restaurant on Vermont Avenue. Their hideout wasn't a secret for long, however, and before dinner was over some 200 telegrams had been delivered to the table.[5] From the campaign train of the Democratic presidential candidate, John W. Davis, came a typical wire: "I am glad to have the opportunity, for which I have waited a long time, to congratulate you on being a member of a world championship team and on your contribution to its victory."[6] The flood tide of messages from every part of the country and around the world was just beginning, some offering simple congratulations, others relating heartfelt stories from people of all walks of life describing the joy and inspiration Johnson's victory had given them. Eventually three large trunksful would go west with the family, and answering them at a rate of 75 per day would still leave some for the new year.[7]

Most of the world champion Nationals joined in the celebration. Harris, Griffith, and Landis were the honored guests at a Chamber of Commerce gala at the Willard Hotel, and a group of players danced the night away at the Wardman Park, only hours ago home of the vanquished New Yorkers.[8] The Giants were on their way to hook up with the Chicago White Sox in Montreal before embarking on an exhibition tour of Europe. (It would be the last major-league trip to the continent until 1992, when the St. Louis Cardinals played a Japanese all-star team in Barcelona, Spain). John McGraw, filing his final report for the Walsh Syndicate from the ship as it got under way, had "no regrets":

> The windup of that series has done more than any one thing since I was a boy to increase the affection that Americans have for our national sport. The whole game has been uplifted. My idea of the way that series should have ended was for Walter Johnson to come to bat in that last inning and drive the ball into the bleachers. Can you imagine anything more perfect—a more fitting climax to the greatest drama our game has ever known? As long as we had to lose it, I would be overjoyed right now if that grand player, Johnson, had hit the ball in the stands. In sailing away from home I still feel the thrills and can still see the remarkable scenes at Griffith Stadium. My new thrill is that baseball has grown in the affections of the public a thousand percent by virtue of Washington's victory.[9]

Hours after his triumph, Johnson was also traveling, heading to Rochester, New York, for another ballgame. Although a number of lucrative exhibition-game offers had come in toward the end of the season, Johnson instead decided to go along on Al Schacht's tour of the Northeast, for which the proceeds were to be split evenly among all the participants.[10] Then during the World Series, Rochester native George Mogridge heard from a friend, the captain of the police force there, about a crippled elderly man and his wife who were going to lose their home. A benefit game had been planned for October 11, and Mogridge was asked if he and some of his teammates would take part. Schacht and the others decided the tour would make its first stop in Rochester.[11]

Word must have been passed along as the train progressed northward, for at each stop a crowd was waiting on the platform to cheer Johnson and the other Nationals: Schacht, Mogridge, Joe Judge, and Nick Altrock. At Utica, New York, several hundred people charged onto the train to get to an exhausted Johnson, who sat patiently in his pajamas accepting their congratulations and signing autographs.[12] The train didn't reach Rochester until 9 in the morning, but several hours later the Washington contingent was at the ballpark to join the rest of the "American League All-Stars": Joe Bush, Charlie

Jamieson, Howard Ehmke, Steve O'Neill, and a husky 21-year-old Columbia University dropout who had played a few games for the Yankees at the tail end of the season—Lou Gehrig. Johnson pitched the first two innings, allowing a hit and no runs, as the All-Stars demolished a team of locals, 12–0, before a capacity crowd of 5,000. The benefit was a success, raising enough money to retire the couple's mortgage and set them up with a sizable nest egg. In keeping the commitment, Johnson had reportedly passed up $3,000 for a game in Brooklyn.[13]

After pitching five more innings over the next two days with the tour in Pennsylvania (giving him four appearances in as many days, five in six days), Johnson returned to Washington on the 13th. When Schacht apologized for talking him into the trip, the big pitcher told him, "Al, I wouldn't have missed this for the world."[14] Hazel, driving the Lincoln with Minnie Johnson, Bobby, Carolyn, and Brewster Adams aboard, had already left town early that morning. Johnson was in the capital just long enough to pick up his World Series check ($5,959.64) and confer with Clark Griffith about his plans to retire from the major leagues and buy a minor-league club.

Reluctantly, and only after pleading with his star to continue with Washington a while longer, the Nationals' boss agreed to let Johnson go—but only to acquire a controlling interest in a Pacific Coast League franchise. Any contract was to be submitted to Griffith first, it was stipulated, so the Old Fox could make sure his star was getting a fair deal.[15] The unconditional release necessary for Johnson to continue in organized baseball with another team was estimated to be a $100,000 concession. "If Clark Griffith grants the request for release contemplated by Walter," one writer claimed, "it will constitute the most costly bit of courtesy on record."[16]

Johnson left Washington convinced that his big-league career was over. "It was the psychological moment for me to say goodbye," he wrote a few months later. "My wish had been granted. I had pitched in a world series and I felt that I could now write a fitting close to my 18 years of major league service. That was the time to step aside and to prepare for the future."[17]

Missing connections with Hazel in St. Louis, Johnson slipped quietly into Coffeyville on October 17, foiling a reception committee planning to make a big deal out of his arrival. But three days later 15,000 people lined the streets for a "Walter Johnson Day" parade with floats and marching bands, followed by the last game he would pitch in Coffeyville, a bottom-of-the-ninth 4–3 victory by the local Sinclair Refiners over neighboring Caney. Johnson went the distance, giving up four hits and striking out 13. On occasion he cut loose with all of his stuff, causing the catcher to holler, "That looks like the Walter of old!" And who would know better than this particular receiver? It was none other than Gabby Street, coming over from Joplin where he managed their Western Association team. The 42-year-old Street caught the entire game, the two old friends having a grand time of it.[18]

From Kansas the family moved on to Reno. As Hazel and the children settled in for the winter, Johnson joined E.E. Roberts and 600 Nevadans on a special train bound for San Francisco to promote the upcoming Transcontinental Highway Exposition. A parade through the city kicked off a campaign to publicize the completion of the nation's first coast-to-coast highway, scheduled to take place in Reno in 1926.

Johnson continued on to Los Angeles for the first of three exhibitions on the West Coast. A crowd of 20,000 packed Washington Park (old Chutes Park) on October 26 to see him pitch for a team of local minor-leaguers and semipros against Vernon, one of the Pacific Coast League clubs up for sale. The Teapot Dome oil lease trial in Los Angeles had been postponed for the day to allow the defendant, E.L. Doheny, to participate in a charity function at the ballpark, and the oil baron's recent notoriety didn't stop the crowd from cheering as he came onto the field. After Johnson walked out to greet him they reminisced about Frank Johnson's job on Doheny's Santa Fe lease and the pitcher's own work there after school and during vacations. Johnson then lobbed a pitch to Doheny and autographed the ball, which auctioned for $500—Doheny making the winning bid himself. They both signed a ball that went for $100, and Johnson signed 50 more to be sold for charity. In return he was presented with a ball autographed by 50 movie stars.[19] In the game Johnson gave up one hit in the first six innings. After the first two batters in the seventh hit safely he turned it on again, and a pop-up and two strikeouts ended the inning. He was taken out, it was explained "so the Coast League sluggers might have a chance."[20]

Returning to San Francisco, Johnson was joined by George Weiss. Also checking in there was Joe Engel, dispatched by Griffith to keep tabs on the pitcher's activities. Although denied by the Nationals owner, reports circulated that Engel was carrying two contracts, for one and two years, should Johnson's dealings on the Coast turn sour—as they already had.[21] Discussions in the spring between Weiss and Cal Ewing, owner of the Oakland Oaks, had centered on a figure of $265,000,[22] but after Johnson's World Series victory and the media attention generated by it, the asking price had suddenly jumped to $450,000, a ridiculous sum for a franchise that had been the laughingstock of the league for a dozen years.[23] The major-league St. Louis Cardinals had recently been bought for $375,000.[24]

The first meeting with Ewing on October 28 wasn't encouraging, and neither was an exhibition the next day at the Oakland ballpark. After a luncheon in his honor at the Oakland Chamber of Commerce, Johnson took the mound for [Pirates coach Joe] "Devine's Major-League All-Stars" against "[Walter] Mails' Coast League All-Stars" and was once again masterful, giving up two hits in five innings of a 2–0 victory for the big-leaguers. The game had been intended as a demonstration of the city's enthusiasm for baseball, but when only 2,000 fans braved a chilly drizzle the local press declared it a big flop instead.

Hazel came over from Reno to join her husband for another trip south and a grand homecoming to the area where his ballplaying career had started 20 years earlier. After stopping at Santa Monica to visit his grandparents, John and Lucinda Perry, they arrived in Anaheim on the 30th. That evening Johnson served as the grand marshal of the first annual Anaheim Halloween Festival, a parade and "street dance" of seventy decorated floats with marching bands on both ends. From the lead car he waved at thousands of people lining the avenue, many of whom had known him as a bashful youngster.

Behind Johnson were cars filled with teammates from the old days at Olinda and Fullerton, and at a dinner afterwards at the Anaheim Elks Club they had a chance to get reacquainted. "The hero of the World Series was visibly moved by meeting so many of his old pals," it was reported, "and many a game was played over as they gathered around the banquet board."[25] Joe Burke, now the District Attorney of Los Angeles, was there, as were wealthy citrus farmer Guy Meats, Clare Head, Bob Isbell, and almost all of the others. Missing were Billy Elwell, who had made his home in Weiser, Idaho, and Jack Burnett, who had disappeared.

The parade and banquet were just a prelude to the main event, which the *Los Angeles Times* called "the greatest de luxe sandlot game Southern California has ever seen."[26] Several weeks earlier Fay Lewis, second baseman on the old Oil Wells team and now a prominent attorney and Exalted Ruler of the Anaheim Elks Lodge (of which the Meusel brothers were members), had contacted Johnson and Christy Walsh, the manager of Babe Ruth's tour of the Pacific Coast.[27] They agreed to participate in a charity game at the Brea Bowl, a semipro ballpark within shouting distance of the "flat" at Olinda. The contest was squeezed in on October 31, the day before Judge Landis's deadline for the end of exhibition play.[28]

On a sparkling Halloween day, stores in the area closed early and a holiday atmosphere prevailed over much of Orange County. Cars streamed in from miles around and a crowd estimated by the *Times* at 15,000 packed the stands and the surrounding hillsides that formed a natural amphitheater around the ballpark. Ruth's barnstorming team had been split up among the "Walter Johnsons," which included Donie Bush, Bob Meusel, Ken Williams and Jimmy Austin of the Browns, and the "Babe Ruths," with Ernie Johnson of the Yankees, Harvey McClellan of the White Sox, and old-timers Rube Ellis and 44-year-old Wahoo Sam Crawford. Local boys filled out the rosters, and Gavvy Cravath umpired.

Unfortunately for the many Johnson admirers on hand, including his grandparents and other relatives, his pitching was not one of the more notable features of a memorable day. With only a day's rest since the Oakland exhibition, and handicapped by a semipro catcher, Johnson was rocked for eight runs on eight hits, including four home runs. Two of those were by the Sultan of Swat himself, the second a mammoth blast judged to have traveled 550 feet. Johnson had never in his life given up more than two home runs in a game, and there is evidence that he was laying pitches into Ruth's power zone to thrill the crowd.[29] Nor would it be surprising if old pal Sam Crawford, who went 3 for 5 with a homer, likewise got a complimentary toss or two "down the pipe." But Johnson gave the fans a good look at his own specialty nonetheless, ringing up six strikeouts in five innings and sending the Bambino back on three pitches in their last confrontation.

Ironically, the pitching star of the game wasn't Johnson, but Babe Ruth. Making his first mound appearance in more than three years, the onetime premier lefthander of the American League took a shutout into the ninth inning before grooving a "gopher ball" to teammate and friend Meusel. He gave up six hits in a 12–1 victory, the 15th and final win of his team's undefeated tour of the Coast. One incident from the game, told by a witness 45 years later, could have come straight out of *The Babe Ruth Story*. "Babe Ruth hit a foul ball that bounced off a car and hit a boy in the head," he remembered. "He started bawlin' and Ruth walked over to him, handed him a silver dollar and said, 'Don't cry, kid—here.'"[30]

The next day Johnson looked up old friends still living in Olinda, his first visit there in 15 years.[31] He took a tour of Hollywood, where great sports fan Douglas Fairbanks showed Johnson and Babe Ruth around the set of his latest production, *The Thief of Bagdad*. Johnson had his picture taken with legendary director Erich von Stroheim and the casts of several films in progress. With movie-star looks of his own, the photogenic Johnson could easily pass for the leading man in these shots.[32] There was a brief scare when Hazel suffered an attack of appendicitis, her second that year. Checking into a Los Angeles hospital for observation, she was released after two days and the vacation continued another week before they returned to Reno.[33]

George Weiss, meanwhile, had been trying to complete the Oakland deal, but price was still the sticking point. On November 5 the owner of the San Francisco Seals, George Putnam, suggested publicly that the seven other clubs in the PCL put up whatever additional funds Johnson needed to buy the Oakland franchise. "The money that we give Johnson will be the best investment we ever made," Putnam declared, explaining that it would be more than repaid by increased attendance whenever he pitched.[34] With little apparent progress in the negotiations, Johnson took off on a hunting expedition into the western Nevada mountains with fellow pitchers Curly Ogden and Paul Zahniser, to whom he had extolled the wonders of the area during the season.[35] Also along was the shadow, Joe Engel. They returned several days later to a telegram calling Johnson back to Oakland.

On November 18 it was major news around the country that Walter Johnson had bought the Oakland Oaks. But the announcement, coming from Oaks owner Cal Ewing, was premature, based only on a $5,000 goodwill deposit by Weiss. No transfer papers had been signed— and none would be. As fast as an agreement seemed to have been struck, just as quickly the whole thing evaporated. Three days later Johnson was on his way back to Reno and Weiss was packing for a return to New Haven. The pitcher was quoted as feeling "forced into the Oakland deal before [I] was ready."[36] Frank Young of the *Washington Post* wrote, "It is quite likely that the Big Train discovered that the $385,000 price ticket—later reduced to $350,000—was about $200,000 too high."[37]

While Johnson and his companions took off again for bear-hunting in the Sierras, the collapse of the deal sparked rumors that he would buy, manage, or pitch for ballclubs in various parts of the country, including St. Paul, Spokane, Vancouver, Salt Lake City, and others. A few serious inquiries had been made, while other reports involved little more than idle speculation or wishful thinking by the press in those localities. But Clark Griffith took the situation seriously enough to emphasize publicly that Johnson would be released only to assume ownership of a team on the West Coast. "Neither Griffith nor other major-league club owners would tolerate the purchase by Johnson of a franchise nearer the big-league territory than the strip of country along the Pacific," it was reported.[38] At the same time, Griffith felt sanguine enough about the turn of events to pull Engel off the assignment. With the likelihood of a Johnson PCL deal greatly diminished, the Nationals owner announced that contract negotiations would take place only between the pitcher and himself.[39]

In late December Weiss wired Johnson that he had secured enough additional backing to enable them to offer Ewing the total in cash—another earlier stumbling block, it seems. Three days into the new year Johnson went to Oakland, but got no closer to the Oaks owner than a cursory phone call in which Ewing declared that plans had been completed for the coming season and the team was no longer for sale.[40] Discouraged, but not giving up just yet, Weiss made the cross-country trip once more to join Johnson in an attempt to buy the Vernon club, the original object of their interest the previous spring. A meeting on January 8 with Vernon owner Ed Maier at his home on Catalina Island went smoothly enough, with terms amenable to both sides quickly agreed upon.

There was a problem making the Vernon franchise unattractive at any price, however. A long-standing feud between Maier and the owner of the Los Angeles Angels, William Wrigley, Jr., was coming to a boil with the imminent completion of Wrigley's new ballpark in Los Angeles. Not only was Vernon to be denied use of the facility, but Wrigley announced his intention to bring the Salt Lake City club to Long Beach and have them play at the new park when the Angels were on the road—all part of his announced intention to drive Maier and his Vernon club out of Los Angeles. Wrigley told Johnson personally that regardless of who owned Vernon it would never be allowed to play at Wrigley Field.[41]

A disgusted Johnson left Los Angeles for Reno on January 29, never to return to the West Coast. What should have been a winter basking in the glow of a championship had instead been taken up chasing a chimera. As one Los Angeles newspaper editorialized: "It took 18 years for Johnson to attain his goal and taste the enduring sweets of success, but it only took the diseased Coast League political organ a few weeks to fill his cup with wormwood."[42] Tom Laird, sports editor of the *San Francisco Daily News,* declared that "Those responsible for the predicament in which Johnson has found himself should be proud. The assuming of a thumbs-down attitude against Johnson is the biggest mistake of their careers. Johnson would have added the color and prestige to the Coast League that it lacks, and always will lack, until men of his caliber are part and parcel of it. The Coast League needed Barney, but Barney does not need the Coast League!"[43]

Indeed, although Johnson left California frustrated by the futility of his efforts, at least now there would be no concern about jeopardizing the considerable estate he had built up. In addition to bank accounts and personal property, his holdings consisted of three farms in Kansas, three houses in Washington, real estate in Florida, oil stocks in California, a share in Weiss's New Haven club, and a recent investment with E.E. Roberts in six gold-mining claims in Nevada.[44]

Another $10,000 was realized from Christy Walsh's syndication of Johnson's autobiography, "My Pitching Years," a sixty-installment series running in newspapers around the country during the first two months of 1925.[45] That venture, too, ran into a bit of controversy when Johnson had to file suit in

New York Supreme Court to stop a competing syndicate from using a series of interviews he had done with journalist Lillian Barker over the past summer to advertise their own 12-part Johnson "autobiography."[46]

After his dreams of minor-league ownership had shipwrecked on the shoals of the Coast League, Johnson put them away for good. On his arrival in Hot Springs on February 23, he declared: "You can say that I'm through with the idea of being a minor league club owner. They gave me an awful runaround out on the coast."[47] It wasn't long before he was reflecting back on the episode philosophically. "I won't deny that the winter was something of a disappointment," he said a couple of months later, "And yet, perhaps it was better so. A ball club is a risky venture. I might not have made good."[48]

Who Enjoys the Greater Popularity, Walter Johnson or Babe Ruth?

In the United States there can be no doubt that Johnson is as widely and popularly known as Ruth. In the world as a whole the Home Run King may take precedence because of the salary that he has commanded. In point of popularity there is no doubt more genuine affection felt for the dean of the world's champions pitching staff than for Ruth. This was demonstrated by the heartfelt and universal wish of the baseball public last fall that Johnson might play a hero's part in the world series. Ruth probably enjoys the advantage in the matter of publicity. Not only the New York club but baseball as a whole has long been pushing Ruth to the front as the game's great figure. A hundred agencies have been working to create publicity for Ruth, while Johnson has, to a certain extent, written his own history in a more modest and unobtrusive way.

CLIPPING, JOHNSON SCRAPBOOK XIV

The announcement on February 9 that Walter Johnson had abandoned all hope of acquiring a PCL team and would return to the Nationals in 1925 kept the phones at Washington newspaper offices ringing throughout the night.[49] In Tampa, Al Schacht delivered the news to Clark Griffith and Bucky Harris as they came in from a golf match, after which they were observed "acting like a pair of school boys who had just received the top honors in their class."[50] Harris, the "Boy Wonder," as he was called now, said: "While for Barney's sake I'm sorry that he was not able to go through with his deal, as far as I'm concerned, I'm as happy as a kid at Christmas with a new toy. Walter's a great pitcher and we need him if we're to hang on to our American League and World titles."[51]

After three weeks of dickering with Griffith, first by phone from Reno and Hot Springs, then face-to-face in Tampa, Johnson signed a two-year contract for $20,000 per year. Having already surrendered much leverage by announcing an intention "to pitch for Washington as long as I am able," Johnson came down from reported original demands for a three-year deal at "quite a fancy figure per annum," perhaps as much as $30,000 a year.[52] He had received several theatrical offers, including an 18-week tour of vaudeville at $2,000 per week to do sketches and make a talk along with films of the World Series, but it's unlikely that Griffith or even Johnson himself took the prospect of a stage or screen career seriously.[53]

The settling of the salary matter wasn't the end of squabbling between the Nationals owner and his star. Johnson, arriving at the Florida training camp in typically good condition, planned to bring his arm around at the usual deliberate pace. But Griffith, not about to let the greatest baseball attraction on the planet lie fallow, put Johnson's name on a posted list of players going on the first exhibition tour around the state. After unsuccessfully trying to find Harris, Johnson went to Griffith's room. "Am I supposed to be trying to get in shape for the season, or what?" his complaint was reported. "You know I'm not ready to do any pitching and I'll come along faster if allowed to stay here and get my regular workouts, and I think you ought to let me stay." He stayed—this time.[54]

On March 14 Judge Landis presented the Nationals with tokens of their World Series victory, gold watch fobs with a diamond set in the middle of an embossed Capitol building. The mayor of Tampa gave Johnson and Harris mahogany bats made from the wood of a building said to have been constructed by Christopher Columbus and his men. At the ceremonies were Yankees owner Jacob Ruppert and Boston Braves owner Emil Fuchs, who was accompanied by Braves president Christy Mathewson in one of his last public appearances.[55]

Later in the month the Nationals left Florida for the trip home, a barnstorming tour of a dozen games against the New York Giants. Johnson tried to opt out of that trip, too, to remain in Tampa and continue with his training regimen. He told Frank Young of the *Post:*

> When I was younger I didn't mind it, for I could get by under almost any conditions, but it's different now. Traveling on trains, taxiing to hotels and later to ballparks, then sitting around on the bench waiting to work two or three innings and dragging back to the hotel again or hustling to make a train connection is not going to help an old fellow like me. I still need my regular workouts, including hikes, to round me into the best of physical condition, but, of course, I have to follow orders. If I get off on the wrong foot Griffith can't say that I didn't warn him.[56]

Having been subjected everywhere the team went to howls of disappointment over the absence of his star, however, Griffith put his foot down. "The Washington club is the South's contribution to big league baseball," he declared. "Everybody wants to see Johnson, even if he merely bats out flies for the outfielders before the games. He should have reported here a week earlier. If he had, he would now be ready and this ten-day trip wouldn't bother him in the least. As it is, I don't look for him to suffer any. If I did, I'd leave him here." For all their griping to the press, though, there was never any rancor evident between the two men. "No hard feelings were shown in the argument between the boss and the star pitcher," noted Kirk Miller of the *Times.* "They sat quietly in the hotel lobby and discussed the affair without anger on either side. Johnson refused to be convinced, but he accepted the order."[57]

Johnson's pitching career resumed on March 28 against the team he thought was the last he would ever face, the New York Giants. Trying to make a point to Griffith, perhaps, he began with two walks and hits by Frisch, Youngs, and Jackson for three quick runs. But from that point he was invincible, striking out Terry and Wilson to end the trouble and breezing through two more innings. In Johnson's last appearance against the Giants on April 11, a crowd of 15,000 at the Polo Grounds saw a close approximation of his performance in the last game of the World Series. Coming in with the bases loaded and two out in the fifth inning, he walked in a run before putting an end to the crisis, then shut them down the rest of the way on two inconsequential hits. The Nationals took the game, 9–4, and won again the next day to even the series at six games apiece after losing five of the first six.

Staying in New York for the season opener against the Yankees on April 14, the big news there—and everywhere else in baseball—was the "bellyache heard around the world," Babe Ruth's intestinal abscess, which had knocked him out a week earlier in North Carolina. Ruth underwent abdominal surgery on the 17th, and Johnson went to St. Vincent's Hospital to see the slugger later that day. Christy Walsh chronicled the visit in a syndicated article, "Barney Calls on Babe, is Barred":

> [Johnson] slipped past reporters on the outside and nurses on the inside. In fact, he got as far as room no. 19, where he was finally caught by the Bambino's nurse as he peeked through a crack in the door. "The big fellow was resting easy at one o'clock," said the Washington star. "He wasn't yet over the effects of the operation so he didn't recognize me when I stuck my head around the door. Naturally I expected he would have a nice, pretty little nurse and you can imagine my surprise when a big husky pair of hands came from behind and ordered me away from his patient. The

last time I saw Babe was in October in a little town near Los Angeles. He pitched an exhibition game against me and swatted me for two home runs. The big fellow looked a lot different today but I'm sure happy he is getting well. Our series against the Yankees lacked the old thrill without Babe." Asked what the nurses said when they discovered his identity, the World Series hero replied, "None of 'em knew me from Adam."[58]

By coincidence, Ruth's last article for the Walsh Syndicate before being sidelined was a comparison of Walter Johnson and Dazzy Vance. The Yankees had just finished a twelve-game barnstorming tour with Brooklyn when Ruth took ill, and his report was titled "Pitchers are Babe's last thoughts ere attack."

"Honestly, I don't think there is any comparison between the two," the slugger wrote. "Johnson was so much better when he was running on top form, that to compare him to any other speed ball pitcher would be like comparing Ty Cobb with a rookie. Of course, I'm talking about the Johnson of a few years ago. Even now he seems every bit as good as Vance and in many ways much better. What makes Vance a fine pitcher is his wildness. That might sound funny, but a fastball pitcher has to be a little wild to be good. I mean just wild enough so that batters won't know what's going to break loose next. If Vance, who is slower than Johnson, wasn't a little wild he would be a sucker for left-handers and an easy mark for right-handers. The difference between Johnson and Vance is this: Johnson was poison to any ball club. Vance is not hard for any team that likes fastball pitchers, such as the Yankees and Giants. I think that right now, with Johnson slowing up a lot, he is every bit as good a pitcher as Vance. In fact, I think he's better."[59]

After dropping the opener the Nationals took the last three games against the Yankees, an important start against the 1924 rivals even if they were minus Ruth. Clark Griffith wasn't depending on psychology to give his team a shot at another pennant, however. The World Series had exposed gaping weaknesses beyond the Washington starting lineup and front-line pitching, and in the off-season the Old Fox set about shoring things up. In a single week in December Griffith fixed the pitching staff when he picked up Stan Coveleski from Cleveland and Walter "Dutch" Ruether from Brooklyn, giving up little in return.

Coveleski (nee Stanislaus Kowalewski), a 35-year-old right-handed spitballer, had won more than 20 games for four years in a row (1918–21) at Cleveland. To his 24 victories in their pennant season of 1920 he added three more in the World Series to lead the Indians to the championship. Coveleski's spitball was said to be second only to Ed Walsh's in effectiveness, but he didn't rely on the pitch exclusively, mixing in a fastball, curve, slow ball and screwball.[60]

Ruether, 31, was a left-handed sidearm curveballer who had won 19 games for Cincinnati in 1919 (and another in the World Series) and 21 for Brooklyn in 1922. Griffith seemed to be carrying his fondness for older pitchers to an extreme, though, with the purchase of 40-year-old Vean Gregg from Seattle, where he had won 25 games in 1924. True, Gregg had won 20 or more in three straight years at Cleveland, but that was back in the Stone Ages of 1911–13. He hadn't thrown a ball in the major leagues since 1918.

Early in the season Griffith made two significant moves to bolster the Washington bench. In late April he traded Zahniser to the Red Sox for Joe "Moon" Harris, a 34-year-old veteran first baseman-outfielder who had been in the major leagues off and on since 1914. His sporadic career had included a two-year suspension for playing in an outlaw league. But in five seasons in the big leagues, the last three as a regular at Boston, Harris had never hit less than .300. Then early in June the Nationals traded George Mogridge and Pinky Hargrave to the Browns for 15-year veteran catcher Hank Severeid. After an undistinguished first 10 years in the majors, Severeid had suddenly blossomed, batting over .300 in the past five seasons as the starting receiver at St. Louis. Another old-timer, 37-year-old Bobby Veach, who had taken Davy Jones's spot alongside Cobb and Crawford in the first fabulous Detroit outfield, then made up the third wheel with Cobb and Harry Heilmann, was picked up on waivers in mid-August for the last 18 games of his distinguished career.

Walter Johnson's 1925 debut came in Philadelphia on April 18 before a record crowd of 35,000, who were thrilled by 6-foot-6-inch William Jennings Bryan "Slim" Harriss's 3–0 defeat of Washington's World Series star. After seven straight seasons (1915–21) at the bottom of the American League following Connie Mack's dismantling of the team, the Athletics had moved up a spot in the standings each year since. The addition this year of the highly-touted rookie battery of Lefty Grove and Mickey Cochrane to an already-improving team made them a possible contender for the flag.

Johnson's next start, the Washington curtain-raiser on April 22, was doubly exciting for Nationals fans. Getting a chance to show their appreciation for the events of the past October, finally, they continued cheering as their heroes blew away the Yankees, 10–1. After taking President Coolidge's ceremonial toss to begin the game, Johnson held the New Yorkers to an unearned run. (It was the last of his seven Opening Day starts for a U.S. chief executive, of which he won six.) Filling in for Babe Ruth in right field was the big college boy, Lou Gehrig, who was hoping to stick with the club this year. As an established star several years later, Gehrig wrote about his first appearance facing Walter Johnson.

"The first real discussion of Johnson I heard was on the train going to Washington in 1925. Johnson was due to pitch against us and the boys were talking about his fast ball. Some of the younger fellows were talking about his speed. Finally Babe spoke up. 'Say, you fellows never saw any swift at all. You should have seen that guy five years ago. You just see his arm swing and then the ump yells, "Strike three." ' I was literally scared to death when I stepped to the plate. The first pitch of Walter's was a fast ball inside, and I guess I jumped back 3 feet. Muddy Ruel was catching. 'Stand up there, kid,' Muddy said. 'He won't kill you. Only break a bone or two.' Walter struck me out that first time—and I was the easiest strikeout he ever got."[61]

The smiling, gifted slugger also singled in their only confrontation of 1925, and over the next two years had little difficulty solving Johnson's deliveries. Lou Gehrig was 10 for 20, with four home runs and a double, in their three years together in the league.

1925 was a memorable year at the plate for Johnson himself. Never having achieved a .300 average in any previous season, he inexplicably hit .433 that year, still the record for pitchers. His two pinch-hits were both spectacular game-winners, and the first one, against New York on April 24, brought about a change in league regulations.

Herb Pennock and Tom Zachary had been locked in a duel all day, the Yankees ace taking a 1–0 lead into the bottom of the ninth. With one out, the Nationals loaded the bases and Harris, having used up his right-handed pinch-hitters in the rally, wanted Johnson to bat. But the pitcher, sure that he wouldn't be called on to work, had already retired to the clubhouse and undressed for a shower. For 10 minutes the game waited while Johnson put his uniform back on, Yankees skipper Miller Huggins screaming bloody murder to the umpires all the while. Still buckling his belt, Johnson rushed out of the dugout, grabbed a bat along the way, and stepped up to the plate. He drilled Pennock's first pitch for a line single to bring in two runners and win the game. In June, Ban Johnson issued an edict that only players on the bench or warming up on the sidelines could be used as substitutes.[62]

At Cleveland on May 19 Johnson pinch-hit for Curly Ogden with two out, a man on, and the Nationals down 3–2, again in the ninth. This time he drove a mammoth blast over League Park's 45-foot right-field wall to win the game. According to Louis Dougher of the *Washington Times*, pitcher-turned-outfielder Smoky Joe Wood was the only other right-handed hitter to clear the wall in 15 years.[63] Two days later Johnson had three hits in four trips in a 6–2 win at Detroit, his sixth victory in a row after the opener. Although 13 for 26 with eight RBIs at that point, he wasn't even the best-hitting pitcher on the team. Dutch Ruether, in addition to his great work on the mound, was 12 for 22 with seven RBIs. The team as a whole was on a hitting rampage in 1925. After Johnson's seventh win in a row, 10–9 over the A's on May 27, they had scored 60 runs in support of the streak, five times giving him nine or more runs to work with.

The resurgent Athletics grabbed the league lead early in May, and by the end of the month had moved several games ahead of Washington. But just as in 1924, the fighting Griffs refused to let the team in front get out of range. For the next three months the two clubs traded places at the top while drawing away from the rest of the pack. In a historic game on June 1 in New York, the Nationals began a shift into higher gear to keep pace with the streaking A's.

Despite New York's shocking seventh-place standing, a crowd of 18,000 came out to Yankee Stadium on a Monday to see Babe Ruth in his first game of the year. Released from the hospital only five days earlier, he was described as "pale, almost delicate-looking," the same report noting that "His illness had done something he had been unable to do in training—it reduced him in weight almost to thinness."[64] Ruth left the game in the sixth inning after going 0 for 2 with a walk against Johnson in a 5–3 Washington win. Even a weakened Babe Ruth was nonetheless dangerous, driving a vicious liner into the right field seats inches foul before taking a base on balls.

Ruth's resurrection wasn't the most distinctive feature of the game, however. That was a seemingly routine pinch-hitting appearance in the ninth inning by Lou Gehrig against Fred Marberry, who had relieved Johnson in the eighth. It was the first of a record 2,130 consecutive games for Gehrig over the next 15 seasons. In a curious circle of events, the mark he would break—1,307, by Yankees shortstop Everett Scott—had ended the day before when Scott was replaced by Pee Wee Wanninger, for whom Gehrig was batting now to start *his* streak. The next day Wally Pipp, the Yankees' regular first baseman for the past 10 years, complained of a headache from an earlier beaning, and Gehrig replaced him. It would take a fatal illness to shake "The Iron Horse" off the position 14 years later.[65] Everett Scott was waived by New York on June 17 and claimed by Washington to spell Roger Peckinpaugh.

Fifteen thousand fans witnessed the raising of the World's Championship flag over Griffith Stadium on June 11. Judge Landis, National League President Heydler, Griffith, Harris, and Ty Cobb performed the ceremony, after which Cobb wrecked Johnson and the Nationals, 7–4. The Georgia Peach went 3 for 4 with two doubles, the first driving in two runs in the first inning. Ten days later Johnson was battered by Cleveland, 7–5, this time done in by Tris Speaker, who was 2 for 4 with four RBIs. Even as they watched talented youngsters like Gehrig, Grove, Simmons, Cochrane, and others coming into the league, old warriors Johnson, Cobb, and Speaker were all enjoying the last great season of their marvelous careers in 1925. Speaker would finish second in batting at .389, Cobb fourth at .378. With his 3–0 shutout of the Browns on June 16, Johnson became the first pitcher in the league to win 10 games.

Two days later he was presented with the Most Valuable Player Award for 1924. Players from the Nationals and St. Louis Browns formed an aisle of honor through which a smiling Johnson walked to accept the ornate scroll from President Coolidge, who had interrupted preparations for his summer vacation to do the honors. Even Ban Johnson, whose feud with Landis had kept him from the World Series and the championship flag-raisings, came to Washington for the ceremony. He made a brief speech stressing the example Johnson's life and career had set.

The first big showdown of the season between the Nationals and Athletics came in late June, a five-game home-and-away set starting on the 26th in Philadelphia. More than 30,000 fans saw Johnson outpitch Lefty Grove, 5–3, in the first of their three career head-to-head duels, Johnson victories all. The A's were shut down completely after the third inning, and Goose Goslin settled the matter with a three-run homer in the seventh.

Robert Moses "Lefty" Grove is considered by many experts the greatest lefthanded pitcher ever. Tall (6 feet 3 inches), with a blazing fastball and an intense hatred of losing, Grove's sparkling career record would be even more imposing if Jack Dunn hadn't kept him at Baltimore for five years, during which he won 108 games. Sold to Connie Mack for $100,600 (the $600 added to top the previous record of $100,000 paid for Babe Ruth) on October 11, 1924—the day after Johnson's victory in the World Series—Grove was 25 years old by the time of his debut with the Athletics and still managed to win 300 games in the major leagues. He led the American League in strikeouts his first seven seasons. As a boy growing up in western Maryland, Grove traveled to the capital just to see Walter Johnson play.

"I used to go from home to watch that bugger pitch," he told writer Donald Honig. "We'd take a train from Lonaconing down to Washington—three- or four-hour trip in those days—on Sunday to see him pitch. We idolized that guy. Just sat there and watched him pitch. Down around the knees—whoosh! One after the other. He had something all right. I pitched against a lot of guys and saw a lot of guys throw, and I haven't seen one yet come close to as fast as he was."[66]

For the last game of the series on the 30th, a crowd of 25,000 packed into Griffith Stadium to be treated to Johnson's best game of the year, a 7–0 gem in which he allowed the A's two scratch hits, no walks, while striking out seven. Retiring the first 16 hitters, he faced 29 in all and stopped Bill Lamar's

29-game hitting streak. He had now shut out the powerful Athletics (a .307 team average) for 15 straight innings. The victory was Washington's fourth in the five games, vaulting them into first place and knocking Philadelphia out of the lead for the first time since May 7.

On the first leg of a month-long road trip Johnson came down sick in Boston with flu-like symptoms and enlarged tonsils. Feeling well enough to travel after a couple of weeks, he joined the team in St. Louis in mid-July, but on the 17th in Detroit only 10 minutes of warming up left him exhausted. Looking pale and drawn and having lost weight, Johnson spent the rest of the trip recovering. Coming home seemed to restore the pitcher's health, and by the time of his 18th anniversary game on August 2 he was well enough to throw a two-hitter at the Tigers in a 5–1 win. The occasion prompted Ty Cobb to wax sentimental before the game, reminding Johnson that Ed Siever, the Tigers' pitcher in that first game in 1907, had since passed away. "We've seen a lot of them come and go, Barney, and we're still here," Cobb remarked.[67]

After trailing Philadelphia for almost a month, the Nationals pulled on top to stay on August 20, Zachary and Marberry combining for a 12-inning 1–0 win at Cleveland while the Browns were beating the Athletics. Johnson ran his second winning streak to five games at Detroit on the 22nd, a 20–5 explosion in which the Nationals got nine extra-base hits, including Johnson's tremendous clout over the left-field wall. Philadelphia moved into Washington for another five-game home-and-away series of "death grapples between the champion Griffmen and their powerful rivals," in one reporter's colorful phrasing. Of the 25,000 turning out for the first of them on September 1, he noted, "Flappers, flapper wives, flapperettes, and all other species of femininity appeared to be in the majority, the variety of color of their late summer frocks blending with the red, white and blue shirted physiques of the opposite sex."[68]

As to the game itself, Johnson defeated Slim Harriss and Jack Quinn, 7–3, shoving the Athletics 4½ games back. Once again Johnson helped his own cause, going 3 for 4 with two doubles. Roger Peckinpaugh, who was having an inspired season, was the other hero with three RBI's. The Nationals administered the coup de grace to the collapsing Athletics with a doubleheader sweep in Philadelphia on September 7. Johnson held the A's scoreless into the ninth inning (and went 3 for 4 again) in a thrilling 2–1 victory in the morning game against Lefty Grove. Philadelphia's defeat in the afternoon half of the twin bill was their twelfth in a row, putting them a full nine games behind and sealing their fate. The two games brought out a combined total of 66,000 fans—a record 36,000 for the afternoon contest alone—and they weren't pleased with the results.

"This may be the city of brotherly love but, according to the conduct of its inhabitants attending yesterday's ball games, that moniker means nothing where the professional diamond sport is concerned," it was reported. "Rabid Athletic rooters booed, jeered, and cursed every one of the champs on the field in both games. Their display of poor sportsmanship began with the start of the Nats batting practice in the morning and continued until the players left the field after the second engagement. Bucky Harris was the particular target for the blasphemous jibes and booing of the crowd. One Washington player escaped the universal displeasure of the Philadelphia rooters. Walter Johnson was cheered when his name was announced and at each of his appearances at the plate."[69]

Johnson picked up his 20th victory on September 11 before a huge Ladies Day crowd in Washington. On the 17th he wrenched his leg while sliding, but it seemed well enough to take the mound three days later. In that game he pulled up lame again while scoring in the seventh inning, and with the Nationals well in front in the race, Harris sat Johnson out for the rest of the year. On September 23 Peckinpaugh was voted the American League's Most Valuable Player for 1925, his clutch hitting and brilliant fielding throughout the year making him, in Joe Holman's words, "the richly rightful successor to Walter Johnson as MVP."[70] On September 24 it became official: Washington had won their second straight American League pennant. They would be returning to the World Series.

CHAPTER 16

The Great Sea Disaster

The Johnson who tied Pittsburgh batters into true lover's knots was not the nervous, high strung Johnson of a year ago who faced the Giants in his first world series test. He was the Johnson of 19 brilliant major league campaigns. Shuffling out into the middle of the diamond without the quiver of a pulse, with the broad shoulders slouching in the old way, the Coffeyville Cyclone turned on his famous smoke ball without a moment's delay and from that point on Pittsburgh's slugging hitters rested in the hollow of his broad and clammy hand. They never had a chance. That fast ball kept singing through the golden air with all the speed it ever carried when old Barney was a raw and untried youth, just off the Western plains. It came with a zip and a snap, with a baffling jump, and with this fast ball the famous veteran dished up a series of curves that broke everywhere except around the polished woodwork of Pittsburgh bats.

No one could have believed this venerable wing had been flapping in front of Major League bats for nearly 19 years. He was more like a great young pitcher just coming into his prime. For in every move there was all the smoothness and beauty of flawless rhythm, with all the ease and grace of the master working on a masterpiece. There was no sign of effort, no show of exertion as the long right arm of the veteran came sweeping through with a final snap of the wrist that left more smoke than a burning oil well. Sitting directly behind the plate, Johnson's curve ball and his hop proved to be a study in changing trajectories. The ball broke one way or another with terrific suddenness, fairly cracking as it reached the plate. In the face of this rifle it is not to be wondered that such keen-eyed troupers as Carey, Cuyler, Barnhart, Wright and others were helpless to the final pitch.

Apparently the marching years have passed Johnson by. They have missed him in their relentless march down the ancient highway of time. They may have beckoned to him and they may have called, but he neither saw nor heard. He was just a brawny, Western, sandy-haired youth that afternoon who had taken experience from the years and had given them none of his youth in return.[1]

GRANTLAND RICE, OCTOBER 8, 1925

There was no underdog sympathy for the Nationals going into the World Series of 1925.[2] Any notion that Washington's triumphs the year before over the world champion Yankees and the powerful Giants were flukes had been demolished along with the rest of the American League. Their 96–55 record, an improvement of 11 games over .500 from 1924, left Washington 8½ games ahead of the Athletics and a full 14 in front of the third-place Browns. This was an outfit commanding respect, solid in every department. The team's .303 batting average was third-highest in the major leagues, its earned run average and fielding percentage second-best. Rice hit .350, Goslin .334 with 18 homers (including three in one game) and a league-leading 20 triples, Joe Harris .323, Judge .314, Ruel .310; Coveleski was 20–5 with a league-leading 2.84 ERA, Johnson 20–7 with fewest hits per game, most strikeouts per game, second in strikeouts, third in ERA; Ruether was 18–7 and Marberry led the major leagues in saves and games pitched.

The National League champion Pittsburgh Pirates were no less impressive. Fighting back after the Giants had taken a commanding early lead in the race, the "Buccaneers" moved in front on July 1 and widened the gap over the rest of the season. Like Washington, they finished 8½ games in front. "The most violent clique of batters in the country," Westbrook Pegler called the Pirates,[3] who paced the major leagues in batting and slugging average, runs, doubles, triples, and stolen bases. Second baseman Eddie Moore was the only man in the starting lineup under .300 for the year, and he hit .298. From July 1924 to June 1925 they went 150 games without being shut out, the league record until 1993. The Pittsburgh lineup boasted three genuine superstars: Kiki Cuyler, Max Carey, and Pie Traynor.

Right fielder Kiki Cuyler was the Pirates' hitting leader, his .357 average coming on the heels of a .354 rookie season in 1924. He led the National League with 144 runs and 26 triples, and his 366 total bases is still the team mark. In September Cuyler strung together a record 10 straight hits. A fast and graceful runner in the field and on the basepaths, he would lead the National League in stolen bases four times. Rounding out the portrait of a complete ballplayer, Cuyler possessed a powerful, deadly-accurate arm.

Although he had managed a career-best .343 in 1925, 16-year veteran center fielder Max "Scoops" Carey couldn't hit like Cuyler, but in the other departments there was no comparison: as good as Cuyler was, Carey was even better. A protege of Honus Wagner during their eight years together with the Pirates,[4] Carey's 738 career stolen bases eventually passed his mentor's 722 (seventh and eighth on the all-time list). This was the last of his 10 years leading the league in thefts. In 1922 Carey stole 51 times in 53 attempts, an astonishing (and record) 96.2%. He holds National League career marks for outfield assists and double plays, and led the league in putouts nine times. On June 22, 1925, Carey claimed a unique mark by getting two hits in the same inning twice in one game.

There may never have been a better left-side infield combination than the Pirates' defensive wall of Pie Traynor at third and wide-ranging, rifle-armed shortstop Glenn Wright. Traynor led his league in putouts for seven straight years and was a great hitter besides, with a .320 career average and seven 100-RBI seasons. Wright led the 1925 team with 18 home runs and 121 RBIs, one of four Pirates with more than 100.

Pirates pitching was similar to that of the Giants of 1924: unspectacular, with no big stars, but more than adequate for the support they received. If you had to pick an ace it would be Ray Kremer, an 18-game winner as a 31-year-old rookie in 1924, 17–8 in 1925. Five on the staff won 15 or more games in 1925, but the best-known of the Pittsburgh pitchers was 43-year-old Charles "Babe" Adams, with a mere six victories. Almost at the end of a solid 19-year career, Adams was the only pitcher left whose career in the major leagues, which began in 1906, predated Walter Johnson's. (Cobb was the only other player.) The last link to the Pirates' last World Series in 1909, Adams had been the hero of their triumph over Detroit that year, winning all three of his starts and shutting out the powerful Tigers in the seventh game to take the Series. In their many years together in the big leagues, curiously, Adams and Johnson never met until the night before the opening of the 1925 Series, when Adams visited the Nationals' hotel for that purpose.[5]

The Bucs were led by another Hall-of-Fame manager, Bill McKechnie. Like John McGraw, McKechnie was a great practitioner of platooning.[6] This was the first of four pennants his teams would win in a 25-year managerial career.

The 1925 World Series opened in the "Iron City." As their train moved north, the Nationals' continued popularity was evident in the congregation of large groups of well-wishers at each stop along the way.[7] The Pirates' victory in the National League race was just as popular with fans in that section of the country, their offices overwhelmed with ticket requests from western Pennsylvania, Ohio, and West Virginia. Thousands of applications had to be denied after the 41,723 seats at the ballpark were quickly snatched up.[8]

Summer was gone in Pittsburgh by the opening of the World Series on October 7. In its place was a beautiful fall day, brilliant sunshine tempering a slight chill that warned of an early winter in the mountainous region, with an occasional bracing breeze to emphasize the point. Forbes Field was resplendent in red, white, and blue ceremonial drapery, a fitting stage for the baseball royalty on hand. The Sultan of Swat, Babe Ruth, was there, looking trim and dapper in his pinstriped three-piece suit, smoking a big cigar while hanging out in the Washington dugout before the game to shake hands and wish everybody luck. The Flying Dutchman, Honus Wagner, and the Georgia Peach, Ty Cobb, peerless adversaries of the 1909 fall classic, arrived just before the game and walked out to the plate together in acknowledgment of the thunderous applause greeting their appearance. They sat next to John McGraw in the press box, where the three spent the afternoon revisiting old times. Pennsylvania Governor Pinchot threw out the first ball to get the Series underway.

Walter Johnson might have pitched better games than the opening contest of the 1925 World Series, but from the comments of those who were there it's hard to believe that he ever had more on the ball. From his seat directly behind the plate Billy Evans had an excellent view of Johnson's deliveries. "He had just as much speed as he had over 18 years ago," Evans told Grantland Rice, "but he had a curve ball yesterday that he never had then."[9] The murderous Pirates lineup could muster only five hits and a walk in Washington's 4–1 victory. Ten times they went down on strikes, Cuyler, Wright, and Clyde Barnhart each victimized twice.

With the infield bathed in bright sunlight during the first six innings, Johnson threw numerous curves to the confused batters as they waited for the famous fastball. Later, as the shadows came creeping in over the pitcher's mound and stretched toward the batter's box until finally engulfing it, he turned on the heat, throwing only six curves in the last three innings, by Evans's count.[10] "I have watched Walter Johnson pitch a lot of ball games," Babe Ruth marvelled, "but I don't believe I ever saw him when he was better than he was yesterday. His fast one was breaking a good six inches, he had a sweeping curve that he mixed in to get the batters off balance, and he was just wild enough to be effective."[11]

Those watching the 37-year-old Johnson's performance from the field concurred. "In all the years I have seen Walter pitch, I have never seen him with more stuff," wrote Roger Peckinpaugh. "They tell me that the Pirates had a scout looking Walter Johnson over last week and he reported that 'the smoke ball king' had slipped so far that, taking his recent injury into consideration, the National Leaguers need not fear him at all. I guess that lad will be looking for another job tomorrow."[12] Muddy Ruel had a tough time of it all afternoon, jumping around behind the plate trying to grab Johnson's slants as they darted about. He dropped an estimated 20 pitches. "Walter was so good today that he made me look rotten," Ruel said after the game. "I don't believe I've ever had more trouble in holding the deliveries of a pitcher."[13] The Washington catcher had better luck with Pittsburgh's speed demons, cutting Carey down when he tried to steal in the opening frame and picking Cuyler off first base in the fourth.

The only run—and the only excitement for the subdued crowd—came in the bottom of the fifth inning. Pie Traynor, not known for his power, lifted a towering home run into the right-field bleachers, a blast described variously as "prodigious," "booming," and "terrific." But the solo blast brought the Pirates only to within two runs of the lead. Seeking to inject more offense into the Washington lineup, manager Harris played Moon Harris in place of Earl McNeely, and the move paid off almost instantly when he belted a home run in the second inning for the first score of the game. Sam Rice brought in two more runs in the top of the fifth with a bases-loaded single.

Johnson fairly breezed through the game. "Most of the Pirates looked puny when they tried to connect," Fred Lieb observed.[14] Westbrook Pegler noted that "Johnson did it so easily, with so little grunting and wrenching, with such casual grace, that the baffled young athletes of the resident squad are still wondering how, and are willing to believe the Swede was doing parlor magic. Having clubbed the pitchers of their own league all season the Pirates had some cause to think they would whale their way through the world series."[15]

Max Carey declared that he and the other Pittsburgh hitters were swinging wildly most of the time. "We just couldn't see Walter's fast ball," he said. "But it wasn't his speed alone that bothered us, for he used a wicked hook. I don't ever recall seeing a pitcher who combined such dazzling speed with such a sharp-breaking curve."[16] Oddly enough, Carey was hit twice by pitches, the crowd gasping audibly when his right arm took a Johnson fastball full-force in the opening frame. "For a moment it looked as if Carey's arm had been torn away at the shoulder," reported Grantland Rice. Carey grabbed the arm and danced up and down at the plate. He stayed in the game only to get plunked a glancing blow to the other arm in the ninth. After the game, a puzzled Carey asked teammate and former American Leaguer Stuffy McInnis, "I thought in the American League you could stand in the batter's box all season without that big guy ever hitting anyone. I'm up there four times and he hits me twice. Don't you think he likes me?"[17]

With little to cheer about on their own side, the multitude at Forbes Field showed their appreciation for the display of pitching prowess as Johnson came to bat in the eighth inning. "The crowd of 41,000 men and women, most of them Pittsburgh enthusiasts, rose and swept the field with a furious gust of applause for the magnificent old fellow," wrote Damon Runyon. "It was a sudden and unexpected and wholehearted tribute of admiration from a hostile fandom to a mighty enemy. Standing at the plate waiting his turn at bat, Johnson blushed beneath the tan of the baseball summer and lifted the long-beaked cap that covers more pitching brains than we shall see again in many a day. In all the 19 years of his big league career I doubt that Johnson has ever received a demonstration of greater admiration, not even in Washington."[18]

In the joyful Nationals dressing room after the game, amidst the handshaking and back-slapping, Mike Martin reminded everyone of his prediction that the veteran pitcher, in prime condition after a long rest, was ready for the game of his life. For his part, Johnson declared it the high point of his career. "I don't recall anything else in my professional career that made me feel happier than this victory," he said. "I failed to get anywhere in the last year's world series, for I don't feel that I cut such a great figure in the final 1924 contest as the fans have insisted I did. But in this opening game I believe I had more 'stuff' than I ever had before, even back in 1912 and 1913, when I was supposed to be at my best. I had long dreamed of winning the first game in a world series, and now that the dream has come true I'm so tickled I can scarcely find words to express my joy."[19]

The next day fans everywhere awoke to the shocking news of Christy Mathewson's death at Saranac Lake, New York, only hours after Johnson's glorious win. Especially saddened were the baseball men gathered in Pittsburgh for the World Series, most of whom had known and admired the great pitcher and gentleman for years. John McGraw was particularly hard hit by word of the passing of his friend and greatest player, leaving his reporting job immediately after the second game to be with the widow and serve as a pallbearer at the funeral. Before the game McGraw and other baseball dignitaries marched along with both teams, wearing black mourning bands on their uniform sleeves, to the flagpole in center field. The band played *Nearer, My God, to Thee* and *The Star Spangled Banner* before the flag was lowered to half-mast.[20]

Breaking through the pall was the game itself, more like what Pittsburgh fans had in mind after sitting through Johnson's dominating performance. The Pirates came out on top of a thrilling contest, 3–2. Coveleski started for Washington and acquitted himself well in spite of a sore back that had to be taped before the game. His opponent, Vic Aldridge, was equally effective, and going into the bottom of the eighth the game was tied at 1–1. The action to that point had been limited to home runs by Joe Judge and Glenn Wright—and Aldridge's beaning of Ossie Bluege in the sixth inning.

Dizzy from the impact, Bluege was taken out of the game and rushed to the hospital, where he was kept under observation for two days. The worried Nationals were relieved to hear that there was no fracture. According to Shirley Povich, the doctor told Clark Griffith, "In fact, we believe that Mr. Bluege's skull is the thickest we've ever x-rayed, for which he is fortunate."[21] Replacing Bluege was 21-year-old rookie Charles "Buddy" Myer, whose major-league career up to then consisted of four games at shortstop and eight trips to the plate.

Pittsburgh iced the game in the bottom of the eighth on Cuyler's booming home run into the right-field bleachers after Moore had reached base on Peckinpaugh's fumble. Washington blew a bases-loaded, no-out opportunity in the top of the ninth, although Bobby Veach drove in a run with a pinch-hit sacrifice fly before Aldridge shut the door. The Pirates pitcher had been tough in the clutch all day, stranding eight runners and escaping unscathed from an earlier bases-loaded, no-out jam in the fifth.

The scene shifted to Washington, where a driving rain forced postponement of the first game in the capital. It stopped that night, but left an early taste of winter, chilling gusts that sent shivers up the spines of frozen fans. Another shudder or two was triggered, no doubt, by the thought of a man like Christy Mathewson being lowered into his final resting place at Bucknell University. The sporting press seized upon the dramatic contrast between the two pitching heroes, one lying in a coffin, the other bathed in the brilliant sunlight of his greatest glory. Writer Jack Conway did the tale justice in a column entitled "Two American Idols":

They buried Christy Mathewson in a little Pennsylvania town Saturday, while 38,000 shivering fans in Griffith Stadium here stood with bowed heads and paid homage to the man who two decades ago was the idol of American youth—an idol without feet of clay. As the last note of the funeral dirge sounded, the huge crowd resumed its seat and, as if by common impulse, the eyes of every fan in the huge stadium turned toward the Washington bench where Walter "Barney" Johnson sat huddled in a huge sweater. Johnson is today what Matty was 15 or 20 years ago. He is the only ballplayer, not excepting Babe Ruth, who has threatened the throne upon which "Big Six" sat. To American youth Johnson and Matty will always be the symbols of honesty, sincerity, fearlessness, and modesty.

The destinies of these two crossed strangely on the road of time Wednesday, when one passed away in an Adirondack village and the other climbed to the Olympus of achievement in baseball. There will be much argument in the years to be as to whether "Matty" or Johnson was the greater, or, better to say, the greatest pitcher in baseball history. These two stand above all others. The part Matty played in 17 years campaigning as a Giant, in 4 world series, was written in great length in many newspapers. The sorrow hung like a pall over the carnival in Pittsburgh. So it is in Washington.

But in this city there will never be anyone to compare to Johnson. The big, pleasant-faced, slightly awkward Swede farmer from Idaho means more to the youth of Washington than has any President, or any ballplayer. Children stand in the streets in awe as his car passes and murmur under their breath: "There goes Walter Johnson." Older youngsters stand outside the ballpark gates for hours just to get a look at the big hurler as his car rolls through the gates into the park. And as he drives through the alley leading into the huge park they touch his car with loving fingers and look with shining eyes at the man who has meant more to baseball than any man since Matty. There will never be another Matty. And there will never be another "Barney."[22]

They had known each other only slightly, but Johnson's admiration for Mathewson led to his participation in an exhibition game to raise funds for a memorial to the great pitcher on July 7, 1926, at the Polo Grounds. Learning of plans for the game, Johnson sent a telegram to National League president John Heydler. "Although I am pitching here [D.C.] Monday," it read, "I would deem it a great privilege to pitch at least one inning in honor of Christy Mathewson at the memorial game on Wednesday."[23]

President Coolidge returned from a trip to Massachusetts in time to attend the third Series game, and for his trouble saw one of the great catches in World Series history. With the Nationals leading, 4–3, Fred Marberry relieved screwball pitcher Alec Ferguson in the top of the eighth and struck out the first two batters. But the next hitter, Pirates catcher Earl Smith, drove a ball deep into right center field. Sam Rice raced after it until running out of room at the temporary bleachers, where he leaped high into the air and was carried by his momentum into the stands. As he came down so did the ball, both of them disappearing into the mass of humanity. A few seconds later Rice popped up out of the crowd holding the ball. Umpire Cy Rigler's hand shot up, indicating an out.

Suspicious of Rice's delay in surfacing, McKechnie came charging out of the dugout, asking Rigler how he knew Rice had actually made the catch. But Rigler wasn't about to go back on a call, and McKechnie's protest to Judge Landis was denied.[24] After the game Landis called for the Washington outfielder and asked bluntly, "Sam, did you catch that ball?"

"Judge," Rice replied, "the umpire called Smitty out."

"That's exactly what I wanted you to say!" Landis declared, "and that's the way I want you to answer anybody else asking you that question."[25]

It became the standard reply for the rest of Rice's life, but was hardly enough to stanch the controversy. In 1965 Rice wrote a letter describing the details of the catch, sealed it in an envelope, and gave it to Baseball Hall of Fame president Paul Kerr to be opened upon Rice's death. When he passed away in 1974, the seal was broken. "At no time did I lose possession of the ball," the note read.[26]

There was never any doubt, either, in the minds of many who witnessed the game-saving play. "Old baseball men, players and writers searched their memories for a catch that could rival Rice's, but found none," the *Washington*

Star reported. "Clark Griffith, who played baseball when the game was in short trousers, declared he had never seen any catch approach it. 'It was a catch you are lucky to witness in a lifetime,' he observed. Nick Altrock was rendered speechless. All he could do in the clubhouse after the game was to murmur, 'How did he do it?'" But the furor over the play caused the first major-league rule change in five years. "A fair batted ball that goes over the fence or into a stand shall entitle the batsman to a home run," it stated.

Somehow Clark Griffith managed to jam 38,701 people into his little ballpark for Walter Johnson's second appearance on October 11. And despite the chilly weather, they had a grand time of it as their heroes had the game put away by the third inning. Goose Goslin drove an opposite-field home run into the left-field bleachers with two on, and Moon Harris pulled a solo shot into the same area. The back-to-back blasts gave Johnson three more runs than he needed in the 4–0 victory. The Pirates never mounted a threat, only one of them reaching third base all day. Of their six hits only two went out of the infield, Bucky Harris handling a record 13 chances at second base.

Johnson's performance was all the more remarkable considering that he reinjured his leg trying to stretch a hit into a double in the third inning. After one look at the "charley horse," Mike Martin told him to quit, but Johnson had him wrap it so he could stay in the game. For the next six innings Johnson pitched from the stretch to minimize the strain, and as Shirley Povich put it, "proved himself the best pitcher on one leg as well as two."[27] At 37 years, 11 months, he is still the oldest pitcher to throw a complete-game shutout in a World Series. "Yesterday's exhibition of pitching more than ever marks Johnson as one of the wonders of baseball," wrote John McGraw. "He was 20 percent better than against the Giants last year. Before him the Pirates were powerless. In fact, they looked a beaten club in practice. Washington had much more pep in practice, and they showed even more spirit on their dash to the field when the game began. This older club has shown more liveliness than the younger and faster one."[28]

McGraw wasn't alone in commenting on Pittsburgh's seeming lack of fight, and their players resented the insinuation. "We defeated the Giants in the most masterful fashion and never displayed the white feather," Stuffy McInnis declared. "We are unable to hit. Why? Because Walter Johnson was too much for us. And the way that Walter was 'smoking them' in was too much for anyone. I've been in World Series before with the Athletics and the Red Sox. No one will say that either of those clubs were yellow. Well, the Pirates of today are just as courageous as those A's and Red Sox. Do you think that any club could beat Walter these two days that he hurled against us? Not on your life. I've seen Johnson humble the Athletics and Red Sox just as he beat us."[29] The victory gave Washington a 3–1 lead in games, and the outcome seemed all but certain. No team had ever come back from such a deficit to win a World Series, and should the Pirates manage to take the next two games to pull even, the imposing figure of Walter Johnson loomed large over a final contest.

Stan Coveleski returned to the mound in game five despite his ailing back. The Pirates had been hard on left-handers all year, so Tom Zachary—the real pitching hero of the 1924 World Series—saw action only briefly in one game this year, and Dutch Ruether, the best southpaw in the league in 1925, didn't pitch in the Series at all. The strategy to go with right-handed pitching to the exclusion of the Nationals' fine lefties was one that Bucky Harris would no doubt rethink many times over the winter. The fifth game was deadlocked, 2–2, at the end of six innings, but the Pirates unloaded on Coveleski in the seventh for two runs and added two more off Zachary to coast to a 6–3 win. Vic Aldridge held the Washington attack in check once again for his second win. Ossie Bluege returned to the lineup, handling six chances flawlessly and hitting a double, but Fred Marberry was lost for the balance of the Series. After pitching to two batters in the ninth inning, the Nationals' stopper suffered a recurrence of the sore arm that had sidelined him for the last five weeks of the regular season.

The teams returned to Forbes Field to finish the Series. Alec Ferguson faced off against Ray Kremer again, both of them on only two days' rest, but this time the Pirates came out a run ahead, 3–2. Roger Peckinpaugh tied a Series record (Honus Wagner's, ironically) with his sixth error, fumbling a doubleplay ball in the third inning to let in two runs and nullify Goslin's third homer of the Series. Bucky Harris, the batting hero of the 1924 series, was the bust of this one (2 for 23). Harris had been badly spiked several weeks before the end of the season, and could barely grip the bat. He later admitted, "I shouldn't have played in that series at all."[30] He sent Veach up to bat for him with the tying run on third in the eighth.

The Pirates had pulled even at three games apiece now, and in his daily column Johnson thought the Nationals perhaps guilty of complacency. "I think that maybe our team was a little overconfident after winning three of the first four games, and let down," he wrote. "The team on the outside always fights harder than its rival. It is easier to work up a real fighting spirit in the challenger than it is to do the same thing to a title holder."[31] There was no evidence of a flagging spirit on the part of the pitcher himself, though. On the eve of the seventh game Harris sought Johnson out in the lobby of the hotel and asked if he could pitch the next day. His leg was sore and he would have only two days' rest, but Johnson replied, "I'll be ready." Harris turned to a group of newspapermen waiting for the pitching assignment for the last game. "Tell them," he said, "that the Senators will come back with the greatest pitcher baseball has ever known. We're stringing along with Barney."[32]

Then Washington got what seemed like a big break: it rained heavily on the 14th, and the game was postponed. Babe Ruth, analyzing the Series now from the warm comfort of his New York apartment, cited the soggy field (to slow down the Pirates' speedy runners) and the forecast for more gloomy weather (making Johnson's fastball harder to see) as advantages for the Nationals. "But dark or not," he wrote, "that extra day's rest ought to make the difference. And as for me—I'll be sitting there at the radio pulling for Barney, pulling for him to make it three straight wins. Who wouldn't? He's the greatest character in baseball today. We fellows in the American League do more than respect him—we love him."[33]

[It was] the wettest, weirdest and wildest game that 50 years of baseball has ever seen. Water, mud, fog, mist, sawdust, fumbles, muffs, wild throws, wild pitches, one near fistfight, impossible rallies—these were mixed up to make the best and the worst game of baseball ever played in this country. Players wallowing ankle-deep in mud, pitchers slipping as they delivered the ball to the plate, athletes skidding and sloshing, falling full length, dropping soaked baseballs—there you have part of the picture that was unveiled on Forbes Field this dripping afternoon. It was a great day for water polo. Johnny Weissmuller would have been in his element. The web-footed amphibians would have had a field day. But it was the last possible afternoon that you would pick for a game of baseball on which hung the championship of the country. And still the game was packed with more thrills to the square inch than any other game possibly could be. This is a broad statement, but it was a broad game—a game painted on a great canvas.

JAMES R. HARRISON, NEW YORK TIMES
OCTOBER 16, 1925

October 15, 1925, dawned in Pittsburgh in a shroud of fog and cold rain and ended the same way. In between, a ballgame, more or less, was played—the deciding game of the World Series. Rain had fallen off and on, sometimes very hard, for a day and a night. By the morning of the 15th Forbes Field was already heavily soaked. Puddles were evident in the outfield, along the baselines, even on the pitcher's mound. But as the afternoon approached, the rain let up to a fine drizzle and a capacity crowd came out to see their "Battlin' Bucs" pull off a miracle. With the Series running two days late already, and the weather forecast calling for more of the same, Judge Landis was determined to play the game. The Commissioner assembled both teams and explained the situation. "A lot of people have gone to a lot of trouble to come to this game," he told them. "I am not going to disappoint them. We are going to finish this game if it is humanly possible. I want you to give them a good game."[34]

With only two days' rest, the man who had brought the Pirates this far with his two complete-game victories, Vic Aldridge, was McKechnie's choice to start the finale. But this time he didn't make it out of the first inning, and when that was over so too, it seemed, was the game and the Series. Rice opened with a single and went to second on a wild pitch. Bucky Harris flied out and Goslin walked. Slipping and sliding on the slick rubber and muddy mound, and having difficulty gripping the wet ball, Aldridge found control impossible. Rice and Goslin advanced on another wild pitch, and Moon Harris walked, loading the bases. Judge also walked to force in the first run, and Aldridge was gone, replaced by Pirates relief ace "Jughandle Johnny" Morrison. Bluege greeted him with a single, scoring Goslin. Peckinpaugh grounded to short, Wright tossing to Moore at second for an apparent force. But Peckinpaugh's bat had tipped the catcher's mitt, it was ruled, and all runners were safe, including Moon Harris crossing the plate. Moore then fumbled Ruel's grounder, allowing Judge to score. With four runs in, the bases still loaded and one out, Johnson had a golden opportunity to blow the game wide open, but struck out instead. (Despite his fantastic season at the plate, Johnson was a batting flop in the Series, going 1 for 11.) Rice flied out to end the inning.

Things looked bleaker still for Pirates fans when Johnson struck out Cuyler and Barnhart to end the bottom of the inning after Carey had doubled. Bucky Harris's doubleplay cut off a rally in the second inning following singles by Wright and McInnis. But in the third inning Pittsburgh suddenly gave their partisans reason to hope, exploding for four hits and three runs to pull back into the game. Johnson was having the same problems as the Pittsburgh pitchers, slithering around on the wet, muddy mound, calling repeatedly for towels in a hopeless attempt keep the ball dry. His heavily taped leg was holding up well, though, and his arm felt fine. The Pirates were known for their murderous hitting binges, sometimes lasting an entire series. They had been quiescent in the first six games, getting 10 hits only once, but the quiet time was over. "I was putting on all my stuff, they were just hitting it, that's all," Johnson would say after the game.[35] Despite the awakening of Buccaneers' bats, Washington managed to keep the lead for most of the game. In the fourth inning Rice and Goslin singled before Moon Harris, the surprise hitting star of the Series for the Nationals, brought them around with a slashing double to make it 6–3. The Pirates got a run back in the fifth on back-to-back two-baggers by their great duo of Carey and Cuyler.

The drizzle turned to a steady rain after the third inning, and by the fifth it was pouring. A low-lying cloud cover made the day dark and gloomy. From the grandstand the outfielders were barely discernible in the mist, little more than ghostly, disembodied uniforms floating over the ground. Cigarettes being lit in the bleachers flickered like so many fireflies on a Fourth of July evening. The field was a soggy, muddy mess; it "resembled nothing so much as chicken a la King" to Ring Lardner.[36] Groundskeepers brought out occasional wheelbarrows of sawdust for the infield and pitcher's mound in a feeble attempt to soak up the water. Johnson went over several times to fill up his cap with sawdust to take back to the mound, and by the end of the game looked like he was covered with oatmeal.[37]

As the sixth inning ended, a waterlogged Landis, enduring the downpour from his box seat, turned to Clark Griffith sitting next to him. "You're the world champions," the commissioner told him. "I'm calling this game."[38] Incredibly, Griffith talked him out of it. "No, you can't do it," he replied. "Once you've started in the rain you've got to finish it."[39]

So "this baseball burlesque," as Joe Holman called it, continued. Dame Fortune, having bestowed a surfeit of good luck on Washington in 1924, cast a stone eye and turned her back on them now. ("Well, the good lord took it back the next year," Goose Goslin told Lawrence Ritter many years later. "Oh, that was ridiculous.")[40] Ray Kremer, having pitched two complete games in the past five days, with only a day's rest since the last one, took over for Pittsburgh in the top of the fifth. For three innings he kept the Nationals in check while the Pirates scored two more in the seventh to even the score at 6–6. Peckinpaugh, slipping badly in the slick outfield grass, dropped Moore's pop fly to start the inning. Carey shanked a Texas Leaguer down the line in left that Bluege, Goslin, and Peckinpaugh all went for, only to see it land a foot outside the foul line. They were turning away when umpire Brick Owens called the ball fair.[41] But Washington's protests fell on deaf ears. Carey, who was playing with two broken ribs from game six, pulled into second with his third double and fourth hit of the day while Moore crossed the plate. With two outs Pie Traynor slammed a ball to the wall in right center field, bringing Carey in with the tying run. Traynor tried to go all the way but was tagged out sliding through the deep mud at the plate.

In the top of the eighth Peckinpaugh tried to atone for his error, lifting a high fly into the temporary bleachers in left for a home run to put Washington back into the lead, 7–6. It didn't last long. The bottom of the inning started well enough when Wright fouled out to Judge and Rice pulled in McInnis's fly. Johnson had two strikes on Earl Smith when he doubled. Carson Bigbee, batting for Kremer, hit an ordinary fly ball to right field that would have been an out any other day. This day it sailed through the gloom unseen and over Rice's head for another double, tying the game once again. Moore walked—Johnson's first free pass, surprisingly. Carey hit a routine grounder to short, and Peckinpaugh, instead of going to first for the easy out, played for the force at second. But Bucky Harris, positioned toward first for the left-hand-hitting Carey, had no chance to reach the base in time. In addition, Peckinpaugh's throw was high and only a great leaping grab by Harris kept it from going over his head into right field. It was Peckinpaugh's eighth error of the Series, and the most costly.

Instead of an end to the inning, the bases were loaded with the Bucs' most dangerous hitter, Kiki Cuyler, coming to the plate. Cuyler worked the count to 2–2, slamming out several vicious line fouls. Then Johnson poured in a fastball that split the heart of the plate, waist-high, according to witnesses. To the Washington battery there was no doubt Cuyler had been struck out; Johnson walked off the mound and Ruel took off his mask, starting for the dugout.[42] But there was no strike call. Then, with the count full Cuyler jumped on a pitch shoulder-high and outside, drilling it to the opposite field over first base. The ball bounded on into the right field bullpen area, disappearing in the fog and shadows while all three runners came around to score, followed by Cuyler himself on Moon Harris's errant throw to the infield. After much confusion and discussion the umpires ruled that the ball had rolled under the tarpaulin in front of the right-field grandstand for a ground-rule double. Two runs were allowed, but Cuyler and Carey were sent back to second and third. Now it was the Pirates' turn to protest, McKechnie's screams of "It was a homer! It was a homer!" cutting through the patter of falling rain to be heard throughout the ballpark.[43]

Johnson got Clyde Barnhart on a pop-up to Bucky Harris to end the inning, but the damage was done. Waiting by the mound for Peckinpaugh to pass by on his way to the dugout, Johnson threw an arm around his devastated teammate's shoulders as they walked off the field.[44]

Coming in to protect the Pirates' 9–7 lead was Red Oldham, a journeyman curveballer who had been out of the major leagues for three years before being picked up by Pittsburgh late in the season. Oldham, curiously, had been singled out by Bucky Harris in his book *Playing the Game,* written earlier that year, as one of those pitchers with the "Indian sign" on Washington—beating the Nationals eight times in 1922 while pitching ineffectively against every other team in the league. But Oldham didn't need much voodoo at this point. Dusk was falling fast, taking away what little light had been forcing its way through the clouds. In the semidarkness Rice struck out, Bucky Harris popped up to Moore at second, and Goslin looked at a called third strike. The World Series was over.

The mood in the Washington dressing room matched the wretched climate outside. Walter Johnson dressed silently, an occasional teammate or reporter coming up to pat him on the back. Johnson's face was drawn and haggard, looking every one of his 37 years and more. A heartbroken Roger Peckinpaugh, the "goat" of the Series, wept openly. Responsible in large part for three of his team's losses, the American League's Most Valuable Player was, in Associated Press reporter Robert Small's phrase, "the most invaluable player ever in a World Series." Of nine Washington errors in the seven games, Peckinpaugh had committed an astonishing eight of them, the record still.

Most of the exhausted players said nothing as they prepared for the trip back home. "I feel pretty bad about it all," was all Bucky Harris had to say about the outcome, except for "1926 is another year." Just as after the fifth game of the 1924 Series, but worse this time, he was second-guessed for leaving Johnson in the game. As Harris boarded the train a Pittsburgh reporter asked, "What do you think of Johnson now?" The unapologetic manager fired back: "I think he's the greatest baseball pitcher of all time."[45] When the team arrived at Union Station a telegram was waiting there from Ban Johnson, who had avoided the Series in his continuing tiff with Landis. "You put up a game fight," the wire began. "This I admire. Lost the Series for sentimental purposes. This should never occur in a world series."[46]

Taking the remarks as an indictment of sticking with Walter Johnson, Harris quickly dispatched his reply. "I have no apologies or alibis," he wrote. "I went down with my best."[47] To reporters at the station Harris elaborated: "Sentiment played absolutely no part in my decision to pitch Johnson. He pitched wonderful ball. President Johnson's remarks, if his telegram has been correctly quoted, are gratuitous and would have been better left unsaid."[48] Within a few days Harris had succeeded in incurring the ire of the commissioner, also. Unhappy about negative comments in the press by Washington players regarding the umpiring in the Series, Landis summoned them, and the manager, to a meeting, where he was intent on having them apologize to the umpires for the remarks. The players made it to the meeting, but all the commissioner got from Harris was a wire saying he was too busy to attend.[49]

In light of the nine runs, 15 hits, and 26 total bases Johnson allowed in the game (the worst pounding ever given a pitcher in World Series history), Harris's comments might appear to be self-serving. But there were others who viewed the situation in a similar light. Oswin King of the *Dallas News* wrote:

Why manager Harris left Walter Johnson in the box in the final game, when he was being hit to all corners of the lot, was a puzzle to baseball fans all over the country. I believe Harris left Johnson in there because he had no one else who could pitch better than Big Barney. It was not Johnson's pitching, but Pirates hitting that turned the tide in the game. Johnson had all the stuff he ever had. I sat directly behind the catcher in the press box and saw every ball he pitched. He was not wild. The Pirates were simply on a hitting spree and they would have knocked any other pitcher out of the box. The darkness was in Johnson's favor. He depends on his speed and a low sweeping curve. His curve was breaking perfectly and his fast ball was coming in with such speed that it could not be seen from the press box, located about 50 feet behind the plate. If they could hit the mighty Walter Johnson under these circumstances, would it not have been futile to send in someone else? I believe that is the way Bucky Harris figured it and that was the reason Johnson was left in.[50]

Muddy Ruel, the man in the best position to know, agreed. "I have had many arguments about that game with persons who feel that Walter Johnson should have been removed," Ruel wrote two years later. "Bucky Harris has been charged with unnecessary sentimentality in allowing Walter to remain. I contend that Bucky was right in his judgement. We had confidence in Barney and I feel that if any Nationals' pitcher could have come through with a victory, Johnson was the man. He pitched a truly remarkable game in spite of the wet and slippery condition of the ball and the unstable footing, and but for some unusual and disheartening breaks he certainly would have won. Barney deserved better than the fate which was dealt to him on that occasion. He was a heroic figure, as he stood out there in the center of the diamond, his clothes covered with mud, shaking off the rain as best he could while he endeavored to control the course of a muddy, slippery ball. Pittsburgh players who took part in that game, I am sure, will readily testify with me to the splendid, though unsuccessful, battle which Walter Johnson waged on that day and to the speed of his fastball throughout the contest."[51]

Perhaps with the consolation of 1924, the grandest victory possible, in the back of his mind, the pitcher himself took the defeat philosophically. "Johnson turned from his preparations for the journey home long enough to remark: 'It was as fair for one as for the other,'" it was reported. "He was sorry, of course, but his head was held high and he looked forward to further conquests on the diamond. 'I gave them all I had but it wasn't enough', he said. 'My arm and my injured leg, wrapped in bandages, felt all right, all the way. They beat us and I guess that's all there is to it.'"[52] At Union Station Johnson's statement to the assembled Washington press was even more succinct. "I have no alibis to offer," he told them. "All I have to say is that the better team won."[53]

In a grave of mud was buried Walter Johnson's ambition to join that select panel of pitchers who have won three victories in one world series. With mud shackling his ankles and water running down his neck, the grand old man of baseball succumbed to weariness, a sore leg, wretched support and the most miserable weather conditions that ever confronted a pitcher. Probably the old veteran would have liked to have gone home and gone to bed, but he stuck it out with a great heart and a wise head against a team of youngsters who were just beginning to unleash the strongest batting attack in the game.

JAMES R. HARRISON, NEW YORK TIMES
OCTOBER 16, 1925

CHAPTER 17

The Old Master

Batters were still wary of Johnson's speed despite the fact he was nearing 40, and the customers always gasped in fear of tragedy on those rare occasions when the Big Train did hit a batter. One day early in 1926, with the White Sox in Washington, Eddie Collins took one of Johnson's fast balls in the leg. Collins went down instantly, and briefly it was feared that he had a fractured leg. Johnson raced to the plate where Collins was groveling in anguish, and stood there with grief on his face while first aid was given the injured player. Eventually, Collins got up, still hugging his leg in pain. When he decided to stay in the game, Johnson patted him gratefully on the back. Collins limped to first, and the fans applauded the gameness of the White Sox star who was apparently torn with pain. Johnson, relieved that he hadn't broken the leg, went back to his pitching. And from the trusting Johnson, Collins, the fraud, stole second on the first pitch![1]

SHIRLEY POVICH

After resting up for several days, Johnson was off to Florida for the winter. Hazel, the children, and Hazel's mother, Nora Roberts, took the train, while her husband drove the Lincoln accompanied by Al Schacht, Joe Engel, and Joe Judge. The family stayed at a house provided by the Chamber of Commerce of Daytona Beach, where Johnson planned to sell real estate for a large developer. For several years the great Florida land boom of the 1920s had been gaining momentum. Many ballplayers had been swept up in the frenzy, buying up lots in a dizzying array of future projects most of which never got off the drawing board. The four Washington players had done their share of that, but now they were to be on the selling end. Their timing couldn't have been worse. Over the summer the boom had collapsed, and by the time they got there no one was buying. In fact, everyone was selling, as Schacht hilariously detailed in a *Baseball Magazine* article, "Getting Rich from Florida Real Estate."[2] Johnson spent most of the winter playing golf, hunting, and fishing.

When the family returned at the end of spring training, it was to a new house in a new neighborhood: Alta Vista, Maryland, next to the Washington suburb of Bethesda. Purchased in July of 1925, the 8½ acre estate was originally to be for summer use only, an escape from the heat and humidity of the city. But after staying there briefly before the excursion to Florida, the Johnsons decided to make it their year-round residence. The Irving Street address was put up for sale, and for the next 10 years the spacious 11-room, white clapboard Victorian dwelling at Alta Vista was home.

Set back from the road by a large front yard and circular driveway, the property included a four-acre fruit orchard, a grape arbor, flower gardens, and a smaller house for domestic help. There were chicken coops with the latest in electric poultry-raising equipment, with which Johnson resumed his old hobby of raising purebred birds. It wasn't long before the place had taken on the appearance of a small farm, with a cow, a horse, and of course numerous dogs. A kennel was built where Johnson and Joe Engel raised prize-winning hounds together, and a side yard was fashioned into a baseball diamond.

The birth of Barbara Joan in July 1926 completed the family. Hazel's days were taken up largely with looking after the needs of her husband and five children, and supervising the affairs of the new, larger place. She loved to get out and drive around taking care of the family's business.[3] Most evenings were devoted to her "secretarial" duties, answering mail that by 1926 had reached staggering proportions—some 300 letters a day during the season. Hazel disposed of the standard questions herself, typing up short notes for Johnson's signature, but it wasn't unusual for the pitcher himself to spend an hour responding to a boy's question of "how to pitch" or the like. Countless autographed baseballs were sent out. The postage alone ran into hundreds of dollars a year, and stationery was bought in wholesale lots.[4]

Hazel's pet project was maintaining the scrapbooks into which she meticulously pasted articles, photos, letters, and other documents from Johnson's career. Clippings from local newspapers were supplemented by items from publications around the country sent by friends and strangers alike. Endless hours went into compiling these large books, which in the end numbered almost 30, a monumental record of Walter Johnson's years in the game. Hazel also took time to write poetry and an occasional magazine article.

In front of 25,000 frozen fans on a wintry April 13, 1926, in Washington, Walter Johnson's 20th season in the major leagues began with the pitching performance he considered his greatest: a 15-inning, 1–0 victory over the

Philadelphia Athletics and their ace, knuckleballer Eddie Rommel, who also went the distance. In a brilliant and thrilling display of pitching, defense and strategy, Johnson gave up six hits and three walks, struck out nine (five looking), and didn't allow a man to reach second base. "Barney's fast ball seemed to fairly hum as it shot across the plate," said Muddy Ruel.[5]

Johnson was presented a trophy beforehand for having been voted the most popular player in the league by American schoolboys in the NEA news service's "Great National Baseball Player contest." (Babe Ruth was second in the American League; Rogers Hornsby was the National League choice.) He then prepared for the last of eight career Opening Day ceremonial tosses caught by him personally, with Vice President Charles Dawes doing the honors this year in place of President Coolidge, who was mourning the death of his father. When Dawes's wild throw went flying past the waiting pitcher and bounced to third base, Johnson went over and picked up the opening ball instead, taking it to the mound to start the last of his 13 home openers. (He was 10–3, with six shutouts, in those games.) After the game it was widely reported that during it Johnson had reached his 111th shutout, 3,333rd strikeout, and 5,555th inning, but it was true only of the innings, according to later calculations.

The season's propitious beginning held up until mid-May, at which point Johnson's record was 6–1 and the Nationals were in second place, close behind the Yankees. But a month later the Nationals' ace had suffered the second-longest losing streak of his career, seven in a row, while the team had dropped into the second division. The revitalized Yankees had already salted away the pennant. A clue to the Nationals' troubles surfaced in July when Goose Goslin, despite a terrific year at the plate, was suspended indefinitely for "indifferent play." In New York on August 30 (following a 12–6 victory, ironically) Walter Johnson vented his frustration with the lackadaisical attitude of some on the team, according to this report:

> Walter Johnson, usually a calm individual, flared up after yesterday's victory over the Yankees and, once in the clubhouse, the veteran did not spare his bitterness over the poor support given him at certain times during the contest. Johnson told how he didn't think his supporters were taking the game seriously enough. He named names and told facts as he saw them. There is more than a little buzzing among the athletes as a result, Johnson's reputation lending weight to his words. While never mixed up in quarrels with umpires nor players, Johnson fights for every last advantage in a ball game. He always goes down with his colors flying. He doesn't like to see his teammates resting because of a long lead, but insists on their going through at top speed. This mental condition, customary in pennant winners, has proved a drawback to the champions all season. They have slumped mentally because of their slow start, and manager Harris seldom has been able to shake them out of it.[6]

Johnson's unusual action seemed to have had some effect, and his next start, a 5–1 win on "Walter Johnson Day" at Fenway Park on September 4, was the team's eighth victory in a row. With 15 wins and a month left in the season, Johnson hoped to close on a winning streak that would give him 20 for the year. Instead his final three decisions were losses, the last two 2–1 heartbreakers, leaving him at 15–16. Eight of the defeats were by one run, five by two runs. His 22 complete games ranked third in the league, his 262 innings and 125 strikeouts fourth. Although Johnson's earned run average climbed more than half a run from its 1925 level to 3.63, it was still better than the league average.

"Failure to reach the .500 mark would make it seem that Johnson slipped badly last season," wrote Billy Evans. "As a matter of fact, it was the Washington club more than Johnson that hit the toboggan. While Johnson isn't the Walter of 20 years ago, he is still a mighty pert pitcher, so good that his addition would considerably strengthen the pitching staff of any club in the majors."[7]

A sharp rally over the last six weeks of the season salvaged a respectable 81–69 season for Washington, good for fourth place, a deceptively short eight games behind the champion Yankees, who coasted through the last half of the campaign. Aside from the team's morale problems, the aging mound staff had to shoulder much of the blame. While the Nationals led the league in hitting, only Marberry avoided a marked decline among the pitchers. A disastrous trade sending Tom Zachary to the Browns for Joe Bush and Jack Tobin didn't help, as Zachary won 14 games for St. Louis while Bush went 1–8 and Tobin hit .212 for Washington. They were both gone by July, and Griffith would bring Zachary back with another trade in 1927.

On October 1, Johnson was among a small party of guests at Bucky Harris's wedding to Washington socialite Elizabeth Sutherland. Clark Griffith was the only other representative of the team present, much of the room in the small chapel having been reserved for President and Mrs. Coolidge, several of his cabinet members, and their entourages. Johnson stood at the rear looking over the heads of the assemblage, and was himself the focus of considerable attention, according to the *Washington Post's* account of the affair. "Many of the women guests queried, 'Which one is Johnson?'" it reported. "When Walter was pointed out, several women commented at once, 'Isn't he wonderfully good-looking?' In answer, one woman guest remarked, 'Washington could have won the pennant on his looks.'"[8]

In character, Charles Lindbergh seems to be another Walter Johnson, and his influence for clean morals and pure living will, we can confidently believe, be felt for generations. As the life of our own Walter Johnson has been an inspiration to uncounted millions of American boys, so too shall the life of Lindbergh. Physical stamina and gameness are splendid attributes, and the world pays its tribute to them, as in the case of Lindbergh, but lasting fame goes to the men who not only possess these, but modesty and moral strength also. In many respects, Lindbergh and Johnson are of a similar type, each possessed of high ideals and strong, manly hearts. Each has striven to accomplish things in a fair manner. Each has loathed the doings of things not in keeping with wholesome ideals and are setting examples that may safely be emulated by aspiring young Americans.[9]

EDITORIAL, AUGUST 2, 1927

A few days into the new year of 1927 Walter Johnson delivered to Clark Griffith what would turn out to be his last contract to pitch for Washington, a one-year deal at the same $20,000 salary. Johnson had been intimating that this might be his final season, but there was no public announcement to that effect.[10] A youth movement was underway on the pitching staff, with Johnson and the other veteran hurlers little more than stopgaps while a new rotation was being put together. "We are rebuilding our pitching staff, as everybody knows," Harris said. "Our plans call for Johnson and Covey to work only when they feel at their best. Walter is going to pick his own spots."[11]

Stopping at Daytona Beach for a few days of fishing and an inspection of orange groves he owned near there, Johnson arrived at the Tampa training camp on February 25. His first full workout the next day was a revelation to the large group of rookie hurlers assembled there. Denman Thompson of the *Washington Star* described the scene:

> He lobbed the ball not more than half a dozen times and then started breezing it over in his characteristically effortless fashion, but with such speed that the resounding whacks made by impact of the sphere with coach Jack Onslow's glove could be heard all over the park as the recruits, who have been carefully nursing their juvenile wings for two weeks hung around and marveled. "He's a wonder," was the tribute paid by trainer Mike Martin when Johnson disappeared into the clubhouse. "He has the greatest arm of any pitcher the game ever produced. For him, throwing a ball involves no more labor than snapping your fingers does for you, and so far as his wing is concerned, he will be able to pitch when he is 60."

Another admirer of the pitcher's talents that day was evangelist and former big-league ballplayer Billy Sunday, who had walked over from his hotel after learning of Johnson's arrival at nearby Plant Field. The world-famous preacher borrowed a catcher's mitt and took a few pitches from the veteran, drawing the interest of everyone on the field and especially the photographers present. When Johnson finished his workout with a few laps around the track, the 66-year-old Sunday insisted on jogging alongside. They ran a quarter-mile shoulder to shoulder before Sunday veered off through the gate and toward his hotel, still trotting. "The old boy fooled me," Johnson declared. "I thought he'd go about fifty yards or so."[12]

The first two weeks of the spring camp showed Johnson to be in top form, looking forward to the 1927 campaign with optimism. "My arm feels good," he said. "I'm in fine shape, feel okay, and don't see why I shouldn't have a successful season."[13] Neither did anyone else who had seen him throw. Billy Evans said so to Griffith and Harris as they stood together watching Johnson throw batting practice on March 9. "I had just mentioned that Walter seemed in great shape and very fast for so early in the season," the umpire wrote. "Both Harris and Griffith agreed with me, expressing the belief that the 'Old Master' was in for a big year."[14]

But suddenly Johnson was on the ground, toppled by a line drive off the bat of Joe Judge. There had been time only to flinch away before the ball crashed into the outside of his left ankle. Not realizing the seriousness of the situation, Nick Altrock and Al Schacht ran over and goofed around as Johnson rolled on his back in pain, holding his leg. They started a chorus of *London Bridge is Falling Down* before Schacht, imitating a fight referee, counted ten as though the fallen pitcher was a knocked-out boxer. Between winces Johnson laughed at the stunts along with the rest of the players gathered around, but none of them could have guessed that Schacht was in reality, as Shirley Povich put it, "tolling the fatal decimal [ten-count] over the greatest pitching career in major-league history."[15]

Johnson was helped back to the clubhouse, where Mike Martin gently removed his stockings to reveal an ugly black-and-blue lump the width of the baseball that had caused it. An ice pack was applied and soon the swelling disappeared. Martin's prognosis was that the pitcher would be working out again in three days unless the fibula (the smaller bone) had been broken, which would make the situation quite different. That night and the following day, in spite of intense pain, Johnson clung to the more hopeful scenario, limping about and even going to the ballpark to work out. But the leg wouldn't support the slightest attempt at running, and a concerned Martin ordered an x-ray, which confirmed his worst fear. The fibula had sustained a complete 45-degree fracture 3½ inches above the ankle. The leg was set in a cast up to the knee and Johnson retired to his hotel room, while the team went off on a two-day road trip. A rookie was left behind to attend to his needs, and Mike Martin stayed behind also, abandoning the team to "hover over his patient like a hen with 19 chickens," it was reported.[16]

"Words cannot tell you how sorry I am over your injury," Judge wired from the road. That it happened to be the Nationals' first baseman, one of Johnson's best friends on the team, whose hit put him down was doubly ironic. Judge had sent a drive off Johnson's other ankle a few days earlier, with little effect that time, and in 1917 Judge's own ankle had been broken sliding home in a Johnson victory at Detroit.

The accident cast a gloom over the Washington camp. For Bucky Harris, hoping for as many as 20 wins from his ace, it represented a grave blow to the team's pennant chances.[17] Taking the mishap more to heart than anyone, even the pitcher himself, was Clark Griffith, perhaps the only one to foresee its ultimate portent. In his public pronouncements, though, the club owner was philosophical. "Of course, if Barney can't take his turn until the season is gone a month, somebody else will have to take his place, that's all," Griffith declared. "It's a heavy loss to have Johnson out of it for the early breakaway from the tape, but some other pitcher will step into the breach and deliver. That's always the way. He's going to stop someday anyway, and somebody will have to replace him. That goes for all of us, too. He's no exception."[18]

Accompanied by business manager Eddie Eynon, Johnson made a premature exit from the Tampa camp on March 13, pushed onto the train in a wheelchair for the sad trip home to begin a six-week convalescence. Griffith called off his daily golf match for a doleful farewell at the station.

After almost a month of nothing more strenuous than reading, playing cards, and listening to the radio, Johnson traded the cast for a smaller and lighter one that enabled him to hobble around outdoors for a while each day. He could visit the kennels with his two dozen dogs and tour the hennery, home now to such noble fowl as Rhode Island Red, White Leghorn, and Buff Rock chickens, along with Bourbon Red turkeys. His first public appearance came on April 8 at a testimonial luncheon for the team at the Raleigh Hotel in Washington, where Johnson was visibly overcome by a 10-minute standing ovation from the 400 attendees following an introduction in which it was proclaimed: "There is no man living in North America who has the love of more people than Walter Johnson."[19]

Four days later, on crutches and wearing a business suit instead of a uniform, he was at Griffith Stadium to see Stan Coveleski beat the Red Sox in the opening game. Receiving the ceremonial toss from President Coolidge in Johnson's place was another 21-year veteran of the American League, the "Grey Eagle," Tris Speaker. The two old warriors were now teammates, Griffith having signed Speaker when Cleveland dumped him following charges that he, Ty Cobb, and others tried to fix a game in 1919. Cobb, the only major-leaguer with more seniority than Johnson and Speaker, also switched teams in the wake of the scandal, leaving Detroit after 22 seasons to finish his career with Connie Mack at Philadelphia.

With his leg healing on schedule, Johnson began light workouts at the stadium toward the end of April, wearing a metal brace from the bottom of his shoe to the top of his calf. He pitched his first batting practice on May 2 and surprised everybody, including himself, with his speed after the two-month layoff. When the team left for its first western swing Johnson went along, but only to work out. He had hoped to pitch against the league-leading Yankees at the end of the trip, but Harris scheduled his first start for May 30 against the Red Sox, doormats of the circuit. For the sake of the pitcher's morale, and the team's, the manager wanted Johnson's belated debut to be successful. Tuning up with five innings of an exhibition against the International League Baltimore Orioles on May 24, Johnson gave up two runs on five hits and struck out three. There didn't seem to be any lingering handicap from the injury.

Before a Memorial Day crowd of 20,000 at Griffith Stadium, Johnson made a belated start to his final season. Like so many of his previous curtain-raisers it was a beauty, a 3–0 whitewash of the Red Sox in which he gave up three hits, walked none, and faced only 29 batters, the last of 11 career complete games in which fewer than 30 of the opposition made it to the plate. Although the box score gave the impression of a return of the old Johnson, the real clue to this performance was the single strikeout registered. The famous fastball was seldom in evidence, curves and perfect control proving the keys to victory instead. By the end he was clearly exhausted but there was nothing in his movements to suggest a recently broken leg. Boston had put that to the test from the start, but got only outs and a broad smile from the pitcher as he darted off the mound quickly to field their bunts before the strategy was abandoned.

More speed was apparent in his second start four days later, a 5–3 loss to St. Louis in which he struck out six, but it was absent again in a 7–1 loss to Cleveland on June 9. "Deprived of his famed speed ball by Father Time or one of his descendants," wrote Shirley Povich in the *Post,* "Johnson again resorted to curves, which were slammed back at him." A concerned Harris kept the struggling veteran on the bench through consecutive series with Chicago and Detroit, and when Johnson came back on the 21st the fastball was again missing in action during an 8–2 pounding by the Athletics.

The first indication of significant firepower left in the long right arm came on a spectacular July 4th in New York. An estimated 75,000 fans, the largest crowd ever to see a baseball game to that point, jammed into Yankee Stadium for a holiday doubleheader. A 10-game winning streak had moved the Nationals into second place, although the magnificent 1927 Yankees—perhaps the greatest baseball team ever—maintained a double-digit lead, a gap they would steadily widen over the rest of the season.

After Washington starter Hollis "Sloppy" Thurston had been knocked around for eight runs in the first four innings of the opener, Johnson was sent in for mop-up duty. For three innings the veteran gave the multitude a glimpse of his past, holding the New York sluggers scoreless and striking out Babe Ruth and Lou Gehrig in succession in one inning, Tony Lazzeri and Pat Collins in the next. But in the eighth inning the roof fell in, a three-run homer by Gehrig the big blow of a four-run barrage before Johnson struck out Bob Meusel and Lazzeri to stop the carnage. The 12–1 defeat looked almost respectable by the end of the second contest, a 21–1 catastrophe.

Another encouraging appearance followed on July 9 in a 3–2 win at Cleveland, a five-hitter with eight strikeouts, four in a row at one point. His next start was a second straight complete-game victory over White Sox ace Ted Lyons on the 17th. Suddenly Johnson was the ace of the staff again, with three wins in a row and the only complete games by a Washington pitcher in three weeks. In Washington on July 28 he beat the White Sox again, allowing one earned run in a 12–2 rout. "The White Sox were not fond of Johnson's pitching," Shirley Povich reported. "Johnson has left some of his burning speed along his 20-year trail of service, but he actually had 'em backing away from the plate yesterday." That game brought his record for the year to five wins and four losses. It was also the last of 417 victories in the major leagues.

Not long after the end of the 1926 season, preparations had begun for a celebration of the 20th anniversary of Walter Johnson's debut with Washington, to take place on August 2, 1927. A testimonial committee was organized with Secretary of Commerce Herbert Hoover serving as honorary chairman, and Clark Griffith arranged with Ban Johnson to schedule a home game with Detroit on that date. Johnson told Griffith that the league would also like to formally honor the pitcher in some way.

"In making the announcement that District fans could put a circle around the August 2 date on next year's calendar," reported Frank Young of the *Post,* "president Griffith also took the occasion to amend a statement he made some time ago to the effect that he would trade any player on his team provided he was offered what he considered the better of the deal. 'Walter Johnson is the lone exception,' he said. 'I wouldn't trade him for ten times his value as a player. He started his brilliant career here and here he will end it.

This is one time where I will rate sentiment higher than money or material anyone has to offer.'"[20]

As the day approached, a drumbeat of press attention helped ensure the affair's success locally, but the event also drew considerable interest elsewhere. "August the second, which is Tuesday, don't forget the national anniversary celebration of Walter Johnson at Washington, D.C.," Will Rogers noted in his syndicated column. "He is the other Swede that Lindbergh copied in showing the world how to be great and still be modest. Do something to help round out a great sportsman's career. Remember next Tuesday the only man in America that stayed a hero for 20 years."[21] On August 2 and 3 newspapers around the country ran editorials extolling Johnson's life and career, most of them making particular mention of his salutary example for the nation's youth.

Griffith Stadium was decked out like a World Series game on the anniversary day, with huge American flags draping down from the upper grandstands. The Army Signal Corps had installed an amplification system so the ceremonies at home plate could be heard by the 20,000 fans and admirers showing up to honor the great pitcher.

A letter from President Coolidge, from his vacation in the Black Hills of South Dakota, was read to the crowd. "It is a pleasure to me as one of Walter Johnson's host of friends to join in the tribute to be paid to him on the occasion of his twentieth anniversary," Coolidge wrote. "Others may speak with greater authority of his wonderful record, but I am sure that I speak for all when I say that his has been a fine and wholesome influence for clean living and clean sport and that he will remain one of the outstanding figures in our great national pastime of baseball."[22]

Secretary of State Frank Kellogg served as master of ceremonies. His brief speech touched off a lengthy ovation, after which he presented the honoree with gifts.[23] The Nationals and Tigers donated their receipts from the game, a check for $14,746. A testimonial fund brought another $1,500 and a large silver service. A second silver set came from his teammates, and Joe Engel trotted out with four pedigreed fox hounds from a famous kennel in Alabama. Johnson was awarded the American League Distinguished Service Medal, a gold medallion with an embossed figure of him pitching, circled by 20 diamonds, one for each year in the league. It was said to have cost the league $2,000.

Johnson seemed to be enjoying the affair, smiling at the playful antics of the irrepressible Altrock and Schacht as they joked and clowned about while the gifts were brought out. The good-natured joshing of a jovial crowd also helped keep things light. "You'd better keep an eye on it, Walter," someone bellowed as the gold medal was passed around among the assembled ballplayers. At another point Secretary Kellogg held up a package and announced with the discretion of his years in the foreign service, "Here is a beautiful bottle of perfume from France, for Walter from a lady whose name it is not necessary to recall." Johnson smiled bashfully, and a fan cried out, "Look out, Walter, your girlfriend is in the stands."

The pitcher's composure began to crumble, though, when four veterans from Walter Reed Hospital came up on crutches with a bronze serving tray they had made. They were followed by a crippled District of Columbia employee, pushed up in his wheelchair to present a tiny bird-dog puppy on behalf of his fellow city workers. Now Johnson was fighting back tears. When the gifts had all been tendered, the crowd demanded a speech but he was barely up to it. Walking slowly to the microphone and pausing, overcome with emotion, when he got there, Johnson simply told them: "There's lots I'd like to say, but I can't. It's been a wonderful day and I want you all to know that I appreciate it."[24]

As part of the publicity for the gala, the team had advertised a special treat for those also present at Johnson's first game on August 2, 1907: they would be greeted personally by the pitcher himself. The result, predictable enough in hindsight, was that every one of the 500 "I was there at Walter's first game" badges had been taken an hour and a half before the game, after which another 5,000 spectators claimed the distinction also. The greeting had to be called off, although the names and addresses of the self-styled "first-gamers" were taken and Johnson sent them all hand-signed form letters with his apology for not being able to fulfill the ludicrous promise.

Another idea, to have the umpire behind the plate for the first game, Billy Evans, do the honors at this one also, almost didn't come off either. At a game in Washington four days earlier Evans had suffered a knee injury and was on crutches the day of the anniversary. Broken-hearted at the prospect of missing the game ("He actually had tears in his eyes at the possibility that he would be unable to officiate," reported fellow arbiter Bill McGowan), Evans called the first half-inning before being replaced.[25] Evans and Tommy Connolly were the only umpires left in the American League from the time of Johnson's debut, and Evans's partner in the 1907 game, Jack Sheridan, had long since passed away.

Tris Speaker was another veteran who wasn't going to let an injury, a sprained wrist in his case, keep him from participating in the historic game. His doctor doubted the wrist would be strong enough for Speaker to play until later in the week, but the outfielder had other plans. "If it is possible, I certainly will be in that game," he told Frank Young of the *Post,* "and if my injury has not healed enough to let me go the route, I am going to ask Harris to let me play one inning anyway, just so I can say that I was in it."[26]

One last tribute came after the Nationals took the field for the start of the game. The players stood with their hats off and heads bowed as a barbershop quartet led the assemblage in the singing of *Auld Lang Syne.* "This old Scotch song seemed to touch the Old Master's heartstrings," the *Post* reported. "His mates, sensing this, rushed about him and tried to 'josh' him back into his normal mood. He appeared quite overcome momentarily, but a few jokes and pats on the back soon brought back the old-time Johnson smile."

The game itself was something of an anticlimax. For the first four innings Johnson put everything he had on the ball, sending the first twelve Tigers went down in order, four on strikeouts. "On the day that the fans wanted to please Walter Johnson, Johnson tried to please the crowd," noted Shirley Povich.[27] But in the fifth inning Detroit exploded for four runs on five straight hits. Then Johnson settled down and the Tigers managed just one hit in the next three frames as Washington took a 5–4 lead into the ninth inning. When he walked the first batter in the top of the ninth and threw two balls to the next, Harris pulled him, anniversary or no. Both runners scored and the Nationals eventually lost the game, 7–6, the official scorer pinning the loss on reliever Garland Braxton. Under today's rules Johnson would have taken the defeat, but in a sense it was justice 20 years after the fact for his first loss in 1907, a defeat he wouldn't have been charged with under modern scoring procedures.

The Johnson anniversary game was the lead story in the *Washington Star,* relegating President Coolidge's pithy but dramatic declaration, "I do not choose to run" (for another term), to a secondary position. At his news conference the famously succinct president spent more time speaking of Walter Johnson than of himself. "I think he stands out as a fine character," the president said. "I do not suppose all the youth of America would care to be big league ballplayers, but I know they all would profit if the character of Walter Johnson was emulated by them."[28]

Johnson saw action in only a handful games during the last two months of the season. With the Yankees holding a huge lead over the rest of the league, Bucky Harris wanted to test the young prospects making up the bulk of the staff. A 7–3 loss at Detroit on August 22 was Johnson's last complete game, last defeat, and last decision, giving him a 5–6 record on the year.

In a curious twist of fate, Walter Johnson's last appearances in the major leagues happened to coincide with two of the most famous sporting events in American history. His final pitching performance, and his last game in Washington, came on September 22 when he gave up six runs to St. Louis before being lifted with one out in the fourth. Browns outfielder (and former

Above: Ghostwriting impresario Christy Walsh (at right) and his stable of bylines for the 1924 World Series: Fred Lieb (probably the only one to do any writing), Nick Altrock, Ty Cobb, Babe Ruth, John McGraw, Walter Johnson, and George Sisler. By arranging for Cobb and Ruth to share a cab to the opening game, Walsh ended years of animosity between the two superstars.

Above and right: October 1, 1924.
A crowd of 100,000 turned out to see their American League champions parade down the "Avenue of the Presidents" to the Washington Monument grounds, where President Coolidge, flanked by Walter Johnson and Bucky Harris, saluted the "armored knights of the bat and ball."

Left: October 4, 1924. After an 18-year wait, Johnson gets his chance in a World Series. Giants starter Art Nehf, playing in his fourth straight fall classic, said later: "I felt sorry for him when we shook hands because his hand trembled so. He was thinking he mustn't let down the fans all over the country who were rooting, even praying, for him."

Below: A gift from the fans of Washington before the first game: an $8,000 Lincoln touring car adorned with a horseshoe of flowers. "One comfort about this ceremony," Johnson recalled, "it was at home plate. I was getting closer to the pitcher's box, and the closer I got, the better I felt."

Above: Muddy Ruel heads home to make Washington the World Champions. Earl McNeely rounds first as the stadium begins to explode in celebration. Johnson's profile can barely be seen at right as he looked on from second base at the realization of his dream.

Opposite Top: In Hollywood with Douglas Fairbanks and Babe Ruth, November, 1924.

The Washington Post.

WASHINGTON: SATURDAY, OCTOBER 11, 1924—TWENTY-TWO PAGES — TWO CENTS.

JOHNSON IS HERO AS NATIONALS WIN DECISIVE GAME OF WORLD SERIES, 4-3; CITY IN CARNIVAL, CELEBRATES VICTORY

POST-SCRIPTS

WHIRLWIND OF JOY SWEEPS CAPITAL IN BIG DEMONSTRATION

Milling Crowds Combine Armistice and Mardi Gras Outburst.

PRESIDENT VOICES JOY AT RESULT OF SERIES

WORKERS IN BUILDINGS RAIN CONFETTI STORM

GRIFFMEN TRIUMPH IN 12-INNING BATTLE AS CITY GOES WILD

Walter Johnson Pitches to Victory in Last Four Innings.

HE AND HARRIS BEAT M'GRAW STRATEGY

BUCKY GETS HOME RUN AND LATER TIES SCORE

President, Rejoicing With Nats, Felicitates Both Ball Teams

JOHNSON'S BLAZING TRIUMPH A FITTING CLIMAX, HARRIS SAYS

Successful Boy Manager Praises Mates for Fighting Spirit.

Nats Split $148,991.63, Each Player Receiving $5,370 as Series Share

Nats' Victory Keeps Young From Altar

Harris Used All but 2 Nat Players in Series

Above*:* On the set of the movie "The Top of the World" with director George Melford, actress Anna Q. Nilsson, Hazel Johnson, and actor James Kirkwood. Johnson received movie offers himself after the World Series.

Above: President Coolidge presenting the 1924 American League Most Valuable Player Award at Griffith Stadium on June 13, 1925. League president Ban Johnson and Clark Griffith look on.

Above: Johnson was used as a pinch-hitter 110 times in his career, and his .433 batting average in 1925 is still the record for pitchers.

Top Left and Right: Carolyn Ann Johnson on Al Schacht's oversized glove, 1924, and Barbara Joan two years later.

Above: At the house on Irving Street in Washington, 1924: Walter, Jr., Carolyn, Hazel, Bobby, and Eddie.

Above: With evangelist Billy Sunday at spring training in Tampa, Florida, 1927, Johnson's final season as a player.

Right: With heavyweight boxer Ben Pound.

Below: With umpire Billy Evans on Johnson's 20th-Anniversary Day, August 2, 1927. Evans had been behind the plate for Johnson's first game and many of the pitcher's notable appearances since. Despite suffering a leg injury several days earlier, he umpired the first inning of the anniversary game on crutches.

Above: Secretary of State Frank Kellogg presents the American League Distinguished Service Medal. "Others may speak with greater authority of his wonderful record," President Coolidge wrote from his vacation in South Dakota, "but I am sure that I speak for all when I say that his has been a fine and wholesome influence for clean living and clean sport." In announcing his plans for 1928 that same day, the president was briefer: "I do not choose to run," he said.

Top: With Lou Gehrig, 1927. (The Sporting News Charles Conlon collection)

Above: With Grover Cleveland Alexander and Gabby Street, 1930.

Top: At Cleveland with second baseman Boze Berger, 1935.

Above: Signing to manage Washington, October 15, 1928. (Mark Stang)

Top: In 1938 as manager of the Dr. Pepper semipro team with son Eddie Johnson, a baseball and basketball star at the University of Maryland who went on to play in the Yankees organization.

Above Left: Receiving news of victory in his first venture into politics, winning the Republican nomination for Commissioner of Montgomery County, Maryland.

Above: The contented farmer in Germantown, Maryland. "I'm happy out here," Johnson said in 1936 following his retirement from baseball. "I guess I'll always be a country boy."

Left: President Truman consoles Minnie Johnson at the dedication of the Walter Johnson Memorial at Griffith Stadium on June 22, 1947. The President, who had grown up just a few miles from Johnson on the other side of the Kansas-Missouri border, called him "one of my great athletic heroes." The Memorial now stands at the Walter Johnson High School in Bethesda, Maryland. (National Baseball Library)

Nationals teammate) Frank "Blackie" O'Rourke made the last hit off a Johnson delivery and also became his final strikeout victim. That same day, before a mammoth crowd of 150,000 at Soldier's Field in Chicago, heavyweight champion Gene Tunney withstood ex-champion Jack Dempsey's rabbit punches and a seventh-round knockdown, waiting out the famous "long count" to recover and retain the crown.

On September 30, 1927, Johnson played in his last game. In the ninth inning of a 4–2 loss to the Yankees in New York, he pinch-hit for Tom Zachary, who had given up Babe Ruth's record 60th home run an inning earlier. Completing the day's ironies—and his major-league career—Johnson flied out to Ruth.

For the next two weeks Johnson pondered his future in baseball, undecided about whether to call it quits or go another year. The broken ankle had drastically altered the course of his season, no doubt, but even after it had healed there were disturbing signs of slippage in the great veteran's abilities. On many occasions he was fine for the first few innings only to see his effectiveness suddenly vanish. The leg problems dogging him for the past few seasons continued to be a nuisance. "My arm is as good as ever, but there are other troubles," Johnson admitted. "The leg I broke bothers me a lot, and not where it was broken. You see, when the legs are bad and you lose the old 'zip' on the ball, you find pitching a lot harder and you find that you are not effective. I figure another season at any rate will be enough. Perhaps when I settle down for the winter I may not pitch in 1928. It's worth plenty of thought."[29]

Johnson's appearance with George Weiss at the last two games of the World Series in New York prompted rumors that they were once again looking to buy a minor-league team, Providence of the Eastern League the reported target this time.[30] After the third game of the Yankees' sweep of the Pirates on October 7, he needed the help of police to free him from the large crowd of fans descending on his box. "Walter Johnson watched the game from close to the Yankees dugout, and following the victory was mobbed by admirers," it was reported. "He signed scorecards and baseballs until tired and had to have police protection to get out of the park."[31]

On October 14, Johnson walked into Clark Griffith's office and asked for an unconditional release. The fact that he didn't seem to weigh heavily in the team's pitching scheme ultimately decided the issue. Despite a great deal of speculation in the press as to the veteran's plans, there had been no communication from Griffith, and Johnson took it as a sign that perhaps he was no longer wanted. "I didn't want Griff to feel that he was paying me for something I had done in the past," he explained. "We didn't do very well this year, and they wanted to build up the club with plenty of young fellows. Griff didn't send me a contract and I just decided it was time for me to get out."[32]

The surprised owner tried to talk Johnson out of it, it was reported, but in the end agreed to the request, telling him, "I won't stand in your way. If you really want your release, you are entitled to it. You can do as you wish." The impression that Griffith didn't want Johnson to return was "all wet," according to this account, which quoted the Nationals' boss as having said a few days earlier: "[Johnson] is one player I wouldn't sell for a million dollars, and I'll never voluntarily take his name off the payroll." Asked why Johnson hadn't been tendered a contract, Griffith replied, "Why, I haven't sent any player a contract. I never send them out until the middle of the winter."[33] In a letter to Johnson the next day, Griffith wrote: "I deeply regret that our day of parting associations has arrived, and I am granting your request solely with the belief that it is being of service to you."[34] He told a reporter, "I hate the thought that Walter will not be with us next season."[35]

Walter Johnson announced his retirement on October 15, 1927. Later that day—almost as if to emphasize the voluntary nature of the action—he made a marvelous exhibition-game appearance pitching for the Warrenton, Virginia "All-Stars" (local ballplayers, along with Johnson, Sam Rice, and Joe Judge) against the Philadelphia Phillies in a benefit for the Boy Scouts. In four innings he didn't allow a hit and struck out six, getting four-time National League home-run champion Cy Williams twice. "If there is anything wrong with Johnson it was not noticeable," the *Post* reported. "He had the National League entry in the palm of his hand during his stay on the mound."

Walter Johnson wasn't the only monumental baseball figure stepping down at this time. He wasn't even the only notable Johnson in baseball to do so, coincidentally. Just two days later, on October 17, American League founder Ban Johnson stepped down after 27 years presiding over the circuit. His once-majestic power over league affairs had been eroding for some time, the endless battles with Judge Landis and National League president John Heydler making him a liability to the game, in the opinion of many team owners.[36] The final straw for the one-time "Czar of Baseball" was his public castigation of the commissioner for bringing the Cobb-Speaker affair into the open after Johnson had arranged for their accuser, former Red Sox pitcher Dutch Leonard, to receive $20,000 in return for his silence.[37]

A month later, Billy Evans retired after 22 years as an American League umpire. He was hired by Alva Bradley, head of a syndicate buying the Cleveland Indians, to become baseball's first general manager. Roger Peckinpaugh quit after 17 years as a player to become the Tribe's manager. Zack Wheat ended his 19-year career, and Eddie Collins moved to the front office at Philadelphia.

Tris Speaker received his unconditional release from Washington to move to the Athletics, where he and Ty Cobb would play their final seasons together in 1928. After 12 years with the St. Louis Browns, George Sisler was sold to the Nationals, and Rogers Hornsby was traded by the New York Giants.

Johnson cleared waivers without interference from the other clubs, and on November 5 Clark Griffith signed the release making him a free agent for the first time in 20 years. Johnson held virtually every American League and 20th-century career pitching mark, and the assorted records for seasons and games stretched out for pages. His totals of 110 shutouts and 3,508 strikeouts were considered unassailable. (Cy Young's old record of 2,803 strikeouts had been surpassed by 25%.) In the flood of editorials following his retirement, however, the statistical record was given only passing mention. Most of the tributes focused on the man.

"Johnson unquestionably leaves the national game with more friends than any other athlete of the sports world," wrote Frank Young of the *Washington Post.* "With all the glory that was his, he never lost his modest and unassuming manner and is the idol of fans and players alike. His private life has been the same open book as that on the diamond, and his record, both as a citizen and a player, will stand as more of a monument to baseball than the one to be erected at the Griffith Stadium."[38]

CHAPTER 18

A Tough Time

A few minutes later batting practice began, and who was pitching but Walter Johnson, "The Big Train," retired as a player and managing the [1929] team. He signaled me to step into the batter's box, and I walked in with a bad case of the jitters. Johnson was then 42 years old, but he still had something that I had never seen before: a fastball with a hop. Whoever heard of that in the Quarter League? I kept missing his pitches altogether or popping them foul. The other guys were crowding around the batting cage and growling. "Okay," they'd say after each pitch, "That's it. That's it! Get him out of there!" I was dying. By the time Mr. Johnson waved me away, I'd taken about 20 cuts and hadn't hit a fair ball.[1]

HANK GREENBERG

Before a [1932] spring training game against Cincinnati, he took the mound to throw some batting practice. The Cincinnati players closed in around the batting cage to get as near as possible to a Walter Johnson pitch, even a middle-aged Johnson. Among them was Babe Herman, a .393 hitter just two years before with Brooklyn. Heinie Manush, an old friend of Herman's, was about to step in and take his licks. He saw the little-boy-at-the-circus expression on Herman's face and invited Babe into the cage. Herman eagerly accepted.

"Johnson threw 4 or 5 balls that I just couldn't get around on," Herman said. "When I got out of the cage I asked Manush for cripe's sake why Johnson was retired. Heinie laughed. "You've seen all he's got," he said. "A half-dozen pitches and then it's gone. In another few days he'll crank it up again. But it's something to see, isn't it?"[2]

DONALD HONIG

When I went up to Cleveland in 1935, Walter Johnson was the manager. Oh, Walter was a great fellow. He was all baseball. Any time you got in a general conversation with him, it would revert to baseball. And he had a great arm. As old as he was, his legs weren't holding up too good. But the arm was, sure. I can remember we were in spring training down in New Orleans, and we had a catcher with us, Charlie "Greek" George. He was a college boy, and he used to ride Johnson, tell him, "I could wear you out hitting you with a tie pin." Walter got tired of the Greek needling him. This particular day, Walter said—I heard this myself—"Greek, get your bat and get up there." Walter threw five or six warm-up pitches on the sidelines, then he went out to the mound. Walter threw exactly 13 pitches, and the Greek hasn't fouled one yet, because the Greek had a blind spot right above his letters. Swing and a miss, swing and a miss. Knocked the air out of the ballpark.[3]

ROY HUGHES

It didn't take long after the announcement of Walter Johnson's retirement from the Nationals before offers started coming in. That evening he received a call from E.B. "Ned" McLean, owner of the *Washington Post.* McLean's friend and fellow newspaper magnate, Paul Block, was buying the Newark Bears of the International League, and he had McLean ask Johnson not to make any firm arrangements without talking to him first.[4] During the next few days rumors floated about of a "substantial offer" to pitch for the Boston Braves, a "determined effort" by Jack Dunn to get Johnson to manage the Baltimore team, and feelers from other major- and minor-league clubs.[5] At a meeting with Block at McLean's estate on October 26, Johnson agreed to manage the Bears. In a scheduled radio talk that evening on behalf of the Washington Boys Club, he announced his departure from the city that was so much a part of his life for so long:

Well, folks, after over 20 years on the Washington team, I am about to leave you. I have nothing but good will for the officials of the Washington ball club. I consider Stanley Harris as good a manager as I ever saw, and I hope that you folks will get back of him and help him to win another pennant next year. There never was a finer bunch of men on one ball club, and I am sorry that I have to leave them. My greatest regret is that my new work will take me away from Washington. I know I shall never forget the fine way in which I have been treated, and one of these days I am coming back home to stay.[6]

A two-year deal was inked the next day for what was said to be the highest salary ever paid a player-manager in the minor leagues, although no figures were given out. The contract said nothing about pitching, but it was understood that in addition to his managerial duties Johnson would be taking a regular turn on the mound.

Some questioned whether he had the right disposition to be a successful manager—too friendly and easygoing, many baseball men thought—but the Newark position was universally regarded as an appropriate place for the baseball hero to land. The city of half a million (about the same as Washington) had supported the team well over the years; a new stadium, superior to some in the big leagues, had just been built; and Paul Block was a wealthy, enthusiastic young owner whose stated principles could have come from Johnson himself. "The Newark team may not do any better, and perhaps not as well, as last year [third place]," Block declared, "but if I have my way it will play ball in an honorable, clean, sportsmanlike manner, and I hope to give Newark many reasons for being proud of its team." All advertising signs were removed from the ballpark because Block thought it looked better without them.[7]

For the selection of Walter Johnson to run his ballclub Block received congratulatory telegrams from Mayors Thomas Raymond of Newark and Jimmy Walker of New York, and a letter from President Coolidge. "Newark is to be felicitated on obtaining Walter Johnson to manage its baseball team," the president wrote. "This selection is assurance that clean character and true sportsmanship are as highly valued as are experience and ability."[8]

Johnson himself was elated. "I realize the ups and downs of a manager's life," he said, "but I am looking forward with a lot of pleasure to this new job of mine. Every ballplayer dreams of the time when he can try out certain ideas and theories, and I feel that I am now going to have my chance."[9] He outlined a dozen of those ideas for the press:

1) Every player must hustle every minute. No athlete who loafs will be kept in the lineup.

2) Every player will be treated individually. Those who need coaxing will be coaxed. Those who need driving will be invited to follow orders.

3) No player will be scolded for mechanical errors. They are part of the game.

4) No player will cheat. That is, pitchers will not be allowed to roughen the ball or use any substance to make the ball do tricks.

5) No rowdyism or useless arguing with fans or umpires will be tolerated. Suspended athletes are a dead loss to the club.

6) Every player will be allowed, generally speaking, to use his own judgement until he proves he can't think for himself. This will apply to pitchers, baserunners, and others.

7) No player's natural batting or pitching style will be changed.

8) No attempt will be made by Johnson to signal for the various balls to be pitched, to give orders for every play.

9) Every player will be expected to practice to correct any weakness he shows.

10) Every player must obey orders and practice self-control.

11) Every player will be told to forget alibis and talk and think of victory. Believe in yourself.

12) Fight for every game as if the pennant depended on it. But don't fight or argue with players of your own club, no matter what the provocation.[10]

Kirk Miller of the *Washington Times,* dean of the capital's sporting press, took issue with those disparaging Johnson's chances out of hand. "Some of the smartest baseball folks we know are shaking their heads dubiously over the prospect of success for Barney as a pilot, minor league or otherwise," he wrote. "They said the same thing about Bucky Harris a few years back, if we are not mistaken. But to get back to Johnson, we would like to ask why he shouldn't make a real good manager. He has over 20 years of the best kind of experience behind him. Naturally a reticent, self-effacing soul, Johnson has never paraded his baseball knowledge. But it is impossible to figure any man of Walter's natural intelligence and splendid background in baseball not having the stuff in him of which managers are made. 'Walter's too easy-going,' many have said. True, Walter has seemed easy-going, but he's had no reason to be otherwise. But that doesn't prove he can't 'bear down' on those of whom he has a right to expect support. When one man's success is in the hands of those working for him, he is usually a different fellow than when he, himself, was in the ranks. There is a strange psychology behind the fact that so many are putting a limit on how far Walter can go in baseball. He should, in our opinion, be able to master things pretty well in Newark and perhaps step up to the major leagues as manager, maybe to Washington—who knows?"[11]

There wouldn't be much of a chance to settle the issue one way or the other in 1928. In February Johnson came down with a bad case of the flu, and although not fully recovered by the end of the month made the two-hour drive from Daytona Beach, where the family spent the winter, to St. Augustine to open the Bears' training camp. Fighting an intermittent fever, for the next two weeks Johnson made sporadic visits to the camp, even working out once and throwing a few pitches. A trip to Augusta, Georgia, for an exhibition game with the New York Giants was the knockout blow. After a week in bed with no improvement, Johnson—pale, weak, and 20 pounds underweight—wired

Dr. Harry Kaufman, the Nationals' team physician in Tampa. Kaufman came immediately but couldn't determine the cause of Johnson's infirmity. He advised checking into the Riverside Hospital in Jacksonville, where an examination found both kidneys badly infected. As his condition deteriorated, Hazel took up a bedside vigil.

On March 26 came the shocking news from Kansas of the death of Johnson's sister Blanche, just 28 years old, of complications from appendicitis and intestinal flu. Minnie Johnson, who had been visiting the family in Florida, hurried back to Coffeyville to be with her four other children and Blanche's husband, John Burke, and their two little boys. Too ill himself to attend the funeral, and getting no better in Jacksonville, Johnson asked to go back to Washington. Dr. Kaufman agreed with the idea and on March 29, along with Eddie Eynon and Mr. and Mrs. Clark Griffith, he took Johnson to the train station where they boarded an express for the 20-hour trip to the capital. Hazel returned to Daytona Beach to prepare the rest of the family to follow.

Johnson's diminished figure and gaunt visage were a startling sight to those meeting him at Union Station. "Walter reached out a hand of greeting to several friends but did not smile," it was reported. "The words he spoke were muttered and indistinct. His eyes surveyed the drab train sheds with a dismal rain dripping down the sides and he shuddered. His face was drawn and peaked. His massive frame seemed shrunken."[12] But once in Washington's Emergency Hospital, where Dr. Kaufman was chief of staff, Johnson's improvement was dramatic. Just being home was a tonic, it seemed. "He appeared to be glad to be back in the attentions of Clark Griffith and Eddie Eynon, officials of the Washington club whose interest in Walter now is personal, not official," wrote Kirk Miller. "Johnson couldn't have received greater attention were he being counted on to pitch the opening game for Washington this year."[13] After a good night's sleep his temperature was nearly normal.

Hundreds of inquiries flooded the hospital and newspaper offices, and letters and telegrams poured in. Judge Landis wired from Chicago: "Don't worry about the ball club. Worry never built up a team nor won a ball game nor got a man out of a hospital. I can assure you that among those of us who are on our feet in health are an entirely sufficient number of worriers and you may safely leave to them that part of the season's job. What all of us want, including millions of men and women and boys and girls, is that you just get well."[14] North Pole explorer Commander Richard E. Byrd sent an autographed copy of his book *Skyward,* while dozens of flower baskets overwhelmed Johnson's room and had to be spread around the hospital.

Johnson listened by radio as Washington started their season on April 10, 1928, the first time the opener was officially scheduled a day ahead of the rest of the league in order to highlight the appearance of the president. Under the leadership of Newark coach George McBride, Johnson's Bears started their season at home on the 18th with a 6–0 victory. Hazel Johnson and 12-year-old Walter, Jr. were there representing the recovering manager, and before returning to the capital she rented a house in nearby Maplewood. Eight days later, after five weeks in the hospital and still showing the ravages of the disease, Johnson was declared well enough to leave. The family went straight to Newark, where they were greeted at the station by 300 fans. Wearing a suit, heavy coat, and hat instead of a baseball uniform, Johnson sat in the dugout for the first time on April 28th, watching the Bears lose to Buffalo, the 1927 league champions. After another loss the next day, the team left on an 18-day road trip, their manager staying behind to continue his recovery.

His weight and health almost back to normal, Johnson took charge of the club in Rochester on May 14. Two days later that city held a "Walter Johnson Day" to repay his act of kindness there after the 1924 World Series. "Walter Johnson Day" in Newark, delayed several months by the illness, took place on June 23, a motorcade through the downtown ending at the ballpark with gifts and tributes. Nick Altrock and Al Schacht (who pitched for Newark's last pennant-winner in 1913) came from Washington to entertain the large crowd, highlighting their show with a slow-motion burlesque of the Dempsey-Tunney fight with Tom Heeney, Tunney's next opponent, playing the referee.

Newark's starting pitcher against Buffalo was Walter Johnson, in a token gesture quickly abandoned after Bison outfielder Maurice Archdeacon walked on a 3–1 count. It was Johnson's only mound appearance of the year—and the only official minor-league pitching performance of his career, although he did put himself into six other games as a pinch-hitter, getting a single. A groundout on September 16 became Walter Johnson's last official act as a player in organized baseball. Doctors cautioned against trying to work himself into condition to pitch, recommending a continued steady strengthening instead.

There was more than enough to deal with as manager anyway. Hovering around .500 all season, the Bears jockeyed between second and seventh place in the eight-team circuit's bunched-up pennant race. Paul Block had tried to buy himself a championship, picking up former major-league stars at tremendous salaries for the minor leagues. Jack Fournier, Jack Bentley, Hugh McQuillan, Bill Lamar, and Rube Lutzke, all at the end of their big-league careers in 1927, were signed, along with other recent major-leaguers Al Mamaux, Cliff Lee, and ex-Nationals Allan Russell and Roy Carlyle.

In addition to a wealth of proven talent, though, came some bad attitudes and resentment at having fallen to the minor-league level. Two weeks after taking over, Johnson let ex-teammates Russell and Carlyle go. He wanted to do the same with the two biggest headaches on the team, "Good Time Bill" Lamar and "Handsome Hugh" McQuillan, both of whom were out of shape, lackadaisical, and showed no regard for training rules. Block had invested a lot of money in the pair, however, and it wasn't until mid-August that Johnson, after suspending the pair twice, finally placed them on waivers. Injuries and illness also hurt the team badly, 15 or 20 victories having been expected from Johnson himself. Mamaux, a 25-game winner for the Bears in 1927, was out for nine weeks when an infection developed from being hit by a batted ball and contributed only 15 victories

Newark finished seventh with an 81–84 record, 10½ games behind champion Rochester. Some 300,000 fans, tops in the International League, came out in support of the team and to see Walter Johnson, but the season was a major disappointment for Block nonetheless. Johnson wasn't happy either, blaming himself for not getting rid of the "bad actors" before they could affect team morale.[15] As late as August Block was still trying to buy ex-major-league talent to salvage the season, while Johnson urged him to jettison that strategy and develop younger, more enthusiastic ballplayers out of the lower minors instead.[16] With a clean bill of health from the doctors, though, Johnson was planning to take a regular turn on the mound himself in 1929.[17]

The one man everybody is pulling for to make the grade this year is the one man everybody says won't make it. This man is Walter Johnson, now a managerial novice in the big leagues. The indictment against Johnson is that there is too much Pollyanna in his blood and not enough Simon Legree. Being human himself, he has always tried to be human with his fellow men. Apparently you can't do this and succeed in baseball. I don't know whether this is actually so or merely a theory bequeathed to the moderns by the frontiersmen of the sport.[18]

JOE WILLIAMS, NEW YORK TELEGRAM

Clark Griffith made the short trip from Washington to Baltimore on July 22 for the purpose of scouting Newark infielder Wes Kingdon—or so he told reporters. Pictures were taken as the Washington owner shook hands with his former star, Walter Johnson, now in a foreign uniform; a nostalgic scene, the photographers probably thought. Griffith was interested in a reunion with Johnson, that much was true, but not to dwell on the past. It was the future he was thinking about, one that would include Walter Johnson at the helm of the Nationals if the Old Fox had his way. Over dinner that night Griffith made the offer, but a surprised Johnson told his old boss he was satisfied with the job at Newark, and his contract had another year to run besides. The subject came up casually between the two men on several other occasions over the summer,[19] but took on a new urgency for Griffith after he fired Bucky Harris on October 1—and appeared in a different light to Johnson.

Washington got off to a terrible start in 1928, 20 games behind the Yankees and out of the race before the end of May. A late-season rally pulled the team into the first division, but with their first losing record in five years. In addition, Harris was miserable at the plate, hitting only .204 and virtually turning his second-base job over to rookie Jackie Hayes by the end of the year. At the age of 31 he was washed up as an active player. Rumors circulated that fame, wealth (Griffith had rewarded him after 1925 with a 3-year deal at $30,000 annually), and marriage into a prominent family had gotten Harris caught up in the Washington social scene to the detriment of his duties as team leader. His stunning decline as a player was more the result of prematurely aged legs, though, and the Washington owner never lost his affection for Harris personally or his admiration for his talents as a manager. There would be two more stints as leader of the Nationals in Harris's 29-year, Hall-of-Fame managerial career.

None of that mattered as the 1928 season ended, however. The back-to-back pennants of 1924–25 had whetted the city's appetite for victory, and the heralded 'Boy Wonder' of such a short time ago was out of favor with the fans, some of whom took to booing him on a regular basis. Griffith had to do something. First he arranged with Detroit owner Frank Navin for Harris to take over the Tigers. Then, in a roundabout manner to avoid accusations of tampering, a serious violation of baseball law, Griffith went about securing Johnson's release from Newark. Ned McLean was once again the agent, asking Paul Block for the personal favor of Johnson's release to come back to Washington. Block wired McLean: "As it was you who actually got him for my Newark baseball club, I dislike to refuse your request, much as I would like to keep him at the head of our team."[20] Johnson returned from an assignment covering the World Series (the Yankees' second straight sweep) to find Block reluctantly agreeable to a release. "It had been my hope that you would be with Newark for many years," the owner lamented.[21] Tris Speaker, whose major-league career had just ended at Philadelphia, would take Johnson's place at Newark.

On October 15, after negotiating with Griffith by phone and then taking the night train to Washington, Johnson signed a three-year contract to manage the Nationals at a reported salary of $25,000 per year. A contingent from the club of Eynon, Engel, Martin, Schacht, and Judge were in Griffith's office to witness the event, along with a small group of local sportswriters. Johnson smiled broadly while shaking hands and accepting congratulations. "It's great to be back home," he told them.[22] For his part Griffith positively beamed throughout the proceedings, breaking out some prohibited "stimulating beverages" and even indulging a bit himself, a rare loosening of his usual office decorum.[23] The owner's unabashed glee at the turn of events was easily understood, and reuniting with a good friend and associate of long standing played but a part in it. The appointment of Johnson had eased the Old Fox out of a jam. "Clark Griffith has at one stroke placated the fans who resented the dismissal of Stanley Harris and earned the enthusiastic approbation of all sports followers in the capital," it was noted.[24]

In private, Griffith expressed reservations about whether Johnson had the personality to be a successful manager,[25] but in public he cited Johnson's Newark experience in answer to the "too easy-going" question. "Any doubts I had in this respect are gone now," Griffith told Frank Young of the *Post.* "When he suspended both Hugh McQuillan and Bill Lamar late in the season for breaking training rules, I knew that he realized his responsibilities and would not dodge them. Naturally, I believe that Johnson will prove a fine manager here or I would not have signed him."[26]

The return of the Big Train was a big story that day, but happened to be overshadowed—quite literally—by the arrival of another, newer, form of transportation. Thousands of residents were awestruck by the sight of the huge dirigible *Graf Zeppelin,* "the queen of the German air," sailing over the city in completion of the first trans-Atlantic passenger flight.

Spring training, 1929, brought Johnson back together with many old friends and former teammates. Clyde Milan was a holdover from Harris's coaching staff along with Altrock and Schacht, and became Johnson's roommate again. Sharing a table in the dining room and conferring constantly about baseball and other matters, they fell in with each other just as they had as rookies in 1907.[27] Hazel Johnson and Margaret Milan also took up where they left off, and when the season started could be found sitting together at every home game.[28] Johnson's own appointment as coach, former catcher Patsy Gharrity, had been playing outlaw ball since his retirement in 1923 and had to be reinstated into organized baseball by Judge Landis. Old Joe Cantillon visited the Tampa training camp, and when the team went to Augusta, Georgia, to play the Giants, newly retired Ty Cobb came to the ballpark. Asked by a reporter if he thought Johnson would be a capable manager, Cobb replied, "Sure, Walter's got it in him to make good. Who wouldn't work for a guy like that?"[29]

The team Johnson took over was not highly regarded, however. The annual

Associated Press preseason sportswriters poll picked them to finish fifth, with just one of the 66 scribes predicting a Washington pennant and 32 judging them good enough only for sixth or lower. The 1929 Nationals were an ungainly combination of aging veterans from the championship years—Rice, Goslin, Judge, Bluege, Ruel, and Marberry were still the core of the team—and promising youngsters. Less than two years after his initiation into the major leagues in the 1925 World Series, Buddy Myer had been traded to Boston, where he blossomed into a star. Johnson wanted him back, and Griffith—never too proud to rectify a bad trade—sent five players (an estimated $100,000 worth of talent) to reclaim him from the Red Sox. In midseason Myer was switched from third base to second, where he would shine for Washington for a dozen years. Another Johnson favorite was 22-year-old shortstop Joe Cronin. Dropped by Pittsburgh after a two-year tryout (he had watched the 1925 World Series from the Pirates bench), the slick-fielding Cronin was picked up by Joe Engel for a mere $7,500 but had yet to prove he could hit big-league pitching. He lost his job altogether for a time in 1929, in fact, moved out by Bluege while Myer was tried out at third. Once that experiment was over, Cronin went back in to stay.

With two exceptions, the staff was an unimposing collection of unproven youngsters and proven mediocrities. Thirty-six-year-old Sad Sam Jones, who would win 229 games over the course of a 22-year career, had paced Washington pitchers with 17 victories in 1928 after being claimed on waivers. Fred Marberry would be the big man in 1929, starting 26 games in addition to his league-leading relief duties, giving the team 250 innings and 19 wins in the dual roles.

Following a deceptively successful exhibition season in which the Nationals compiled the best record in baseball, 21 wins in 27 outings, Johnson's major-league managerial career began with the home opener on April 17, 1929. In a scene that would be repeated each year of Herbert Hoover's disastrous term in office, Johnson walked to the presidential box with Clark Griffith, shook hands with President Hoover, and handed him a baseball for the opening toss. A 13–4 lambasting by the Athletics set the tone for the season.

The first few weeks were plagued by rain and bitter cold; it was snowing when the team pulled into Cleveland on May 3. Johnson came down with a bad cold that triggered a recurrence of his kidney problems. When his fever climbed to 102 degrees, Griffith personally rushed him back to Washington, staying up all night in Johnson's stateroom applying ice packs to his sweating brow. In a repeat of the scene at Union Station a year earlier, Johnson was wheeled from the train and taken to Emergency Hospital. Before going to his room he dropped in on another patient, 12-year-old Robey Whitfield, whose leg had been amputated several weeks earlier after an auto accident. Whitfield had been the star pitcher on his school team, and after reading about the mishap Johnson sent him a note of consolation. Now he put a commiserating hand on the pale youngster's shoulder.

"Good morning, Robey," he said. "I certainly was sorry to read about your misfortune, but you see, you have company. I guess we'll be floor mates for a little while."

"Yes, sir," the boy answered in a barely-audible voice. "I'm sorry you're sick, too, but I'm sure glad to meet you. Gee, I wish I could pitch like you!"

"Well, never mind, son," Johnson told him before being taken away. "If we can't do the thing we want most, there is always something else."[30]

With early treatment Johnson was in the hospital less than a week this time, rejoining the team after a 12-day absence. When Robey Whitfield was released, Johnson invited him to the stadium where they watched a game side-by-side in the Washington dugout.

By the end of May the season's prospects had already vanished for the Nationals, who were run over—physically and psychologically—by the rampaging Philadelphia Athletics, winners in 13 of 14 confrontations between the two teams in the first six weeks. On August 1 Washington was tied for seventh place, 20 games below .500. Most observers attributed the team's breakdown more to the decline of several key players (Goslin was 100 points below his league-leading average of a year earlier) than a failure of Johnson's leadership. The manager himself made no attempt to dodge responsibility.

"While we may have been overrated as a result of our spring exhibition record, it's a cinch that we ought to be better off than we are right now," he admitted. "The only thing that I can find to blame for this state of affairs is my own mismanagement. By switching a pitcher here or pulling a player there I could have saved a lot of those tough games, but at that I guess we've all got to learn our lessons in any profession. I'm not through as a manager. I may have had my bumps this year, but I've learned something. I've passed up lots of chances to better our standing, but those who are writing me out of the picture would do well to remember that 1930 is another year."[31]

Griffith took decisive action to squelch rumors that Johnson would be replaced. On July 17 he held a clubhouse meeting, his first since stepping down as manager in 1920, to tell the players that Johnson would not only be there at least through the end of his three-year contract but was being given the authority to fix salaries for everyone but the rookies. Griffith also discounted reports of a planned housecleaning of the veterans. "If you play well, hustle all the time, and work earnestly for Walter, the Washington club wants you," he declared. In a press conference after the meeting, the owner expressed confidence in his manager.

"Johnson knows baseball; knows the men in it; knows how well they are fulfilling their contracts, and he knows how to deal with them," Griffith stated. "I am confident he will handle the task well. Johnson is no manager to be trifled with. How foolish are these stories about Walter's softness. To hear them you'd think he had no courage at all. Why, Johnson has the heart of a lion. And he has this heart, this courage, in his position as manager now. No one should be fooled into believing Johnson is too soft to handle his job just because he is naturally amiable. Walter can be hard as iron and cold as stone when it is necessary and his ballplayers know that."[32]

In late July, with the team about to go on the road for most of the next month, Johnson instituted morning drills at the stadium. Convinced that their abilities were not being reflected in the games, he stressed heads-up tactics and had them practicing plays again and again. "I've always objected to morning drills in mid-summer," he said, "but something has to be done about this ball club. There's no excuse for some of the games we've kicked away. Alibis can go just so far. What I want is results and I'm ready to go to the limit to get them."[33]

It worked. The Nationals went 14–6 on the road trip and in the last two months of the season posted the best record in the American League, closing with a 35–23 run. "Only a few weeks ago the Griffs were a dull, conservative combination with no future, a dismal present, and a hopeless past," wrote Bob Thayer of the *Washington Herald* in mid-August. "Today they are real fighters who promise to make a spirited bid against tough odds for a first division finish. Why this sudden transformation? Many answers could be given, but none seems more logical than the obvious one—the boys are finally playing the ball of which they are capable." The 71–81 Nationals edged Bucky Harris's Tigers, after trailing them by 14 games at one point, for fifth place. They finished out of the first division for the first time in seven years.

That fall Clark Griffith joined the trend toward major-league ownership of minor-league "farm teams," buying the Chattanooga Lookouts of the Southern Association. Relinquishing management of Altrock and Schacht's off-season stage act, Joe Engel became part-owner and president of the club. A state-of-the-art facility, Engel Stadium, was built, the stage on which "The P.T. Barnum of the Bushes," as Fred Lieb dubbed Joe Engel, presided for the next 35 years. Never depending on his teams alone to draw crowds into the ballpark, Engel the impresario conducted a virtual three-ring circus for the fans. "Make 'em laugh" was his motto: "Even a good ball club needs a little meringue on top," he declared.[34]

There were beauty pageants, circus parades, rabbit chases, an elephant hunt, and countless other crazy stunts Engel cooked up to swell the gate. A league-record 26,000 fans showed up when he gave away a $15,000 house with a car in the garage in the middle of the Depression. One year he traded one of his players for a turkey, explaining that the turkey had a better year. Among students of baseball history Engel's most famous episode came on April 2, 1931, when he signed a 17-year-old girl, Virne "Jackie" Mitchell, to pitch for the Lookouts in an exhibition game against the Yankees. Mitchell struck out Babe Ruth and Lou Gehrig in an apparent Engel set-up.

The Nationals' rally in the last third of the 1929 season had impressed few baseball men. The steady slide from third place to fifth in the past three years, along with an absence of substantial changes in the roster for 1930, gave many the impression of a washed-up franchise that would be saved from the bottom of the league only by the awful Red Sox and their six-year lease on the cellar. The Associated Press poll picked Washington for seventh place, not one of the 65 voters predicting a finish higher than fourth. "If [Johnson] can get [Washington] out of the second division, it will be proof of managerial genius," wrote Bill Slocum.[35] "I think we're going to get a flock of laughs out of the boys who are picking us for seventh place," Johnson responded. "We're not that kind of club."[36] Griffith also exuded confidence as the season approached. The veterans were showing new life and the youngsters beginning to fulfill their promise, all at the same time. The club went 17–2 in exhibition games, taking the last 11 in a row.

Success carried into the regular season in 1930, with victories in 10 of the first 12 games, including six out of seven against the Athletics. Late in May the Nationals held a four-game lead over Philadelphia before slumping. By mid-June the team had fallen several games back when they were suddenly reinvigorated by a momentous trade, probably the best in franchise history. Goose Goslin still hadn't regained his batting eye, hitting only .268, and was sent to St. Louis for outfielder Heinie Manush and pitcher Alvin "General" Crowder. Manush had twice hit .378, winning the batting title in 1926 and losing by a point to Goslin two years later. He was third in the league in 1929 at .355 and having another fine year in 1930. Crowder's career had begun with the Nationals in 1926–27 before being sent to St. Louis in the trade by which Tom Zachary was reclaimed. The leading pitcher in the American League in 1928 at 21–5, Crowder fell to 17–15 the next year and was 3–7 at the time of the trade for Goslin.

The St. Louis press and fans screamed bloody murder. Most regarded a straight Manush-for-Goslin trade as a steal for Washington, considering that the Nationals slugger appeared to be washed up. Throwing in Crowder, one of the best pitchers in the league, made it a crime. According to one account it was Browns owner Phil Ball's personal pique with the departing players that had prompted him to suggest the crazy deal to Griffith.[37]

Two trades with the White Sox the same week brought the Nationals a superb pinch-hitter in Dave "Sheriff" Harris and a talented first baseman in the exotic personage of Art "The Great" Shires. A big, handsome Texan with wavy golden hair and an irrepressible ego, Shires was also a wonderful athlete (a professional boxer in the off-season until Judge Landis forbade it), and although an offbeat personality would keep him from realizing his potential, Shires proved a worthy backup to Joe Judge in 1930. He was of great value just sitting on the bench, the competition of his .369 hitting spurring Judge on to his best season in years.

A record regular-season crowd of 35,000 at Griffith Stadium saw the Nationals sweep a July 4 doubleheader from the Yankees, giving them 13 wins in 14 games. The high point of the season came three days later when a victory at Boston pulled Washington ahead of the Athletics by a half-game with a record of 49–25. The lead held up for several days before Washington stopped winning and Philadelphia didn't, the powerful A's regularly crushing their opponents by lopsided margins. The Nationals' fate was sealed on a 7–12 road trip ending July 28 in St. Louis, after which they had fallen 6½ games back. The pitching rotation, the backbone of the team until then with six starters consistently going the distance, suffered a catastrophic collapse. And with Marberry a full-time starter this year and Garland Braxton gone in the trade for Shires, there were no relief specialists to fall back on. With the sole exception of Sam Jones, the entire staff became starters and relievers, and before long any semblance of a regular rotation evaporated.

Several times on the western swing the Washington manager seriously considered going in himself for late-inning relief. In top shape after pitching batting practice all year, Johnson felt physically capable, according to *The Sporting News,* and only Griffith's jaundiced view of the move kept him from doing it. "However, unless he gets the desired results from his present staff members," it was reported, "the Big Train may be expected to be seen in action on the mound in the near future."[38]

As the team returned to Washington for an important two-game set with the Athletics, Johnson had more on his mind than pitching, or managing, or anything related to baseball. Hazel was seriously ill. With the Nationals on the road for most of July, she had decided to drive the children to Kansas to visit their grandmother. The trip was difficult, and shortly after arriving home she had collapsed from exhaustion.

It had been a trying winter and spring. Just before Christmas, 12-year-old Eddie came down with a bad throat infection that kicked off problems with his congenitally weak kidneys. He was sick off and on for months, missing school for the rest of the year. In January came the sad news of Joe Cantillon's death at his home in Hickman, Kentucky. Then Clyde Milan accepted a job managing Birmingham of the Southern Association. "Every once in a while Walter gets to grieving over Clyde's departure," Hazel wrote Margaret Milan. "He will miss him terribly."[39]

Then on March 13, 14-year-old Walter, Jr. was roller-skating a block from the house when a drunk driver slammed into him. Both legs were broken, one with a compound fracture that cut a vein and caused heavy bleeding and impaired circulation. Amputation was a possibility for a while, and the break had to be reset three times before it healed. He was in the hospital for two months and spent several more recuperating at home. With her husband away at the Nationals' new camp at Biloxi, Mississippi, Hazel had a lot to deal with by herself. "It has been hard on me," she wrote Mrs. Milan. "[But] outside of a few gray hairs and the loss of a few pounds, I am still intact."[40]

By July young Walter was getting along better, using a cane and walking with only a slight limp. A perfect recovery was predicted. As the team's three-week road trip approached, Hazel was thinking about taking one herself, she told Margaret Milan. "I may go somewhere and do something while he's gone this trip," she wrote. "Mrs. Johnson wants us to come out to Kansas for a visit and I may drive out. Really need a rest, tho, instead of a trip! Still, a change is good once in a while. Home always looks so good when you get back."[41] They had just bought a new Ford, and Hazel had enjoyed a recent jaunt to Philadelphia, so she made the decision to go. Several of the children developed upset stomachs on the way to Coffeyville. "I remember it was a rough trip. We were all ill," recalled Carolyn Johnson Thomas.[42] There was also the heat.

July, 1930, was the hottest month on record in U.S. history. Soaring temperatures gripped much of the country for the entire summer, accompanied by a drought that in some areas would persist for years.[43] This was the beginning of the "dust bowl" devastation of the early 1930s, a natural phenomenon contributing its share of misery to the financial failures of the Great Depression. At Fort Smith, Arkansas, 50 miles from Coffeyville, temperatures of 100 degrees or higher were recorded on 17 days during the month.[44] On her way back to Washington, Hazel met the team at St. Louis on July 20. That day at Sportsman's Park it was 104 degrees in the locker rooms, a sizzling 114 at third base.[45] Her husband and Clark Griffith both urged Hazel to put the car on the train and travel with the team on its final swing north and then home, but she chose to keep going.[46]

Reaching home on July 29, Hazel took to bed immediately, exhausted. Instead of getting stronger overnight she grew weaker, and the next morning was taken to Georgetown Hospital. Specialists were called in but all they could do at that point was express the hope that rest would restore her. There was no disease or organic breakdown, and no particular treatment available for her deteriorating condition—she had simply driven herself past the point of complete exhaustion. The next day, July 31, Johnson was called at the stadium and told that his wife had taken a turn for the worse. Rushing to her bedside, he stayed there until 4:30 in the morning, when Hazel passed away. "Aware that the end was near," the *Washington Post* reported, "Mrs. Johnson's last thoughts were of her five children and the home to which she devoted her life. The 'Big Train' promised her that he would keep the children with him and, shortly after, she died, her hand in the clasp of the man to whose success she materially contributed."[47]

The most important person in Johnson's life, his inseparable companion, was gone. "He idolized her, and her every thought and consideration was for Walter," wrote Vincent Flaherty. "It was a story-book marriage. There was never a happier one."[48] Johnson never fully recovered from the loss. From that point on there would always be a hint of sadness to him. "It was a tragedy that was to leave its mark on him for the rest of his life," Shirley Povich observed.[49] For three days he refused to leave Hazel's side, sitting by the coffin weeping and accepting the condolences of friends. In truth he was inconsolable. Johnson wouldn't eat or sleep, and concern mounted about the state of his own health, which he brushed aside, saying "She would have done as much for me."[50] Not religious in a formal, churchgoing sense, he repeated, "I can't understand how God could do this to me."[51]

Indeed, a relentless series of personal tragedies had crashed down upon Walter Johnson during the past decade. Until the age of 33 his had been a charmed life in that respect as in so many others. The only close relative to have passed away was his grandmother, Phoebe Higbee Johnson, at the age of 84 in 1913. But in a span of nine years beginning with the deaths of Frank Johnson and the baby Elinor in 1921, he lost his father, daughter, grandfather (John L. Perry in 1925), mother-in-law (Nora Roberts in 1926), sister, and finally, in the cruelest blow of all, his beloved wife. The contrast between Johnson's nature, so consistently gentle and kind, and the pain visited on him by these heartbreaks, is striking. But as suddenly as they had begun, the family tragedies stopped. Thirteen years would pass before the next one, the death of grandmother Lucinda Perry in 1943 at the age of 93.

Johnson had lost not only his friend, lover, and partner in life. Gone was the mother of his five children. Coming to take care of them at first was Hazel's friend Addie Hugenin, a Capitol Hill secretary who had worked for E.E. Roberts. Of great help also were Mr. and Mrs. Thomas Flaherty, close friends of the family who had no children of their own. Tom Flaherty, a postal union official, was godfather to the children, and he and his wife were known as "Uncle Tom" and "Aunt Therese." After Hazel's death they doted on the children. Five rambunctious youngsters proved to be too much for Addie Hugenin, however, and that fall Johnson turned to his mother for help. Minnie Johnson put her house in Coffeyville for rent and came East with her son-in-law, John Burke, and his children, Jack and Jim. Minnie stayed on to help her son raise the children, and never returned to Kansas to live. At the age of 63 she took on the task of bringing up her third family, having first assumed much of that role as the oldest of 10 children on a frontier farm, then with her own. Over the course of a long and productive life Minnie Johnson played a substantial role in the raising of 22 children.

The men of the Washington baseball team, all of them fond and admiring of Hazel Johnson, were deeply shaken by the tragedy. Al Schacht's reaction was typical: "This is the most terrible thing that could have happened," he told a reporter. "We all love Walter and we realize what this means to him. She was a wonderful woman— her heart was as big and full of thoughtfulness for others as a human heart can be. Nothing that I can remember has affected me this way."[52] Team captain Joe Judge served as acting manager as the ballclub went to New York and took two games from the third-place Yankees, who had closed to within a game of Washington. A third contest there was cancelled so the team could serve as honorary pallbearers at Hazel's funeral on August 4.

Clark Griffith left up to his grieving manager the timing of his return, while at the same time expressing the feeling that the sooner Johnson got back into action the better it would be for him.[53] That advice was taken, and four days after the funeral Johnson was once again in uniform. The team broke out of its month-long slump, winning 21 of 30 in August to leave the Yankees in the dust and keep the red-hot A's from running away with the race. Washington closed to within 5½ games on September 4 before cooling off to a .500 pace for the rest of the season while Philadelphia continued to burn its way through the schedule. The Nationals finished eight games behind the Athletics and ahead of New York by the same margin. They had won the head-to-head competition with the A's, 12 games to 10, and their 94–60 record was two games better than the 1924 championship year. None of that was much consolation without a pennant, however. Johnson's old pal Gabby Street had better luck with his St. Louis Cardinals, capturing the first of two straight National League flags after a startling late-season rally.

"It was a tough time to be in that league," recalled Roger Peckinpaugh, who managed Cleveland to fourth-place finishes behind Philadelphia, New York, and Washington every year from 1930 through 1933. "We were up against two great ball clubs. On the one hand you had Connie Mack's Athletics, with Foxx, Simmons, Grove, Cochrane. And on the other hand there were the Yankees, with Ruth, Gehrig, Lazzeri, Dickey, Combs and those fellows. It was discouraging. You knew you were doomed the day the season opened, with those two monsters in the league."[54]

For Walter Johnson and his Nationals there was no better example of that frustration than in 1931. Two months into the season, after a road trip on which they had captured 15 of 16 games (including 12 in a row), and with an overall record of 37–17, Washington still trailed the 39–13 Athletics. On July 23, at 57–32, they had fallen seven games behind Philadelphia's 107-win pace. Worse still was the last-minute loss of the runner-up spot, after holding onto it for four months, to the surging Yankees. Second place barely eluded the Nationals again in 1932 when a tremendous September rally, in which they won 24 of their last 28, fell a game short of the A's. That year it was the Yankees who won 107 games.

Johnson was tendered a one-year contract for 1932 to replace the expired three-year deal, a clear signal that it was to be a make-or-break year for the Nationals manager. Therefore no one, least of all Johnson himself, was surprised when Griffith called him into the office and, in effect, asked permission to fire him. It was a painful task for the club owner after their long and close association.

"We need a change, Walter," he told him, according to one account of the conversation. "How are you fixed? If you don't need the job, let me get a new manager."

"It's all right with me, Griff," Johnson replied. "In fact, I think it's a good idea."[55]

The only bright spot for Johnson came with the appointment of his successor, 26-year-old Joe Cronin. Personally fond of the good-natured, hardworking shortstop, Johnson had proudly overseen Cronin's sudden explosion into a star of the first order in 1930, when he hit .346 and was named the American League's Most Valuable Player. "He's a fine boy and a good hustler," Johnson said. "I'd like to see him go ahead and have a big year. I'll be pulling for him."[56] The feeling was mutual, and Cronin was always quick to point to his development under Johnson. Griffith had seen in him the potential to spark the team in the manner of the original "Boy Wonder," Bucky Harris, and that's exactly what happened. In desperate financial straits with the deepening of the Depression (attendance had dropped from 614,000 to 371,000 between 1930 and 1932), the Old Fox also saw an opportunity to save himself the cost of Johnson's big salary.

At a testimonial banquet before 700 Washingtonians at the Shoreham Hotel on November 30, 1932, Walter Johnson bade farewell to the Nationals more than a quarter-century after joining the team. With a stone-faced Clark Griffith sitting a few feet away, Johnson professed to be slightly baffled by the attention. "This is the first celebration ever given me in honor of losing my job," he declared with a grin. "I've been feted for victories and crowned for defeats, but never before eulogized for being fired."[57]

The assessments of Johnson's performance as leader of the Nationals vary widely. His excellent record—the best of any manager in the 84-year history of the capital's major-league teams—has often been discounted on the grounds that the talent under him was better than his direction of it. At first glance the capture of the pennant in 1933 under Cronin seems to support that argument. And some members of those teams, including such personal Johnson friends as Ossie Bluege and Al Schacht, would flatly declare him a failure. It was his handling of pitchers, ironically, that brought the most criticism.[58] Not long after his retirement from the game Johnson addressed that point:

> Where I have been criticized the most is in my handling of pitchers. Since I was a pitcher myself for more than 20 years, I might suppose that was one department of the game that I knew something about. I don't say that I've always handled our pitchers correctly, but I never knew a manager who did. Pitching will always remain baseball's biggest problem, and a manager gropes in the dark when he puts a pitcher on the slab or yanks him off. Only the event can tell whether or not the choice was a correct one.[59]

At the time of Johnson's firing, the senior members of Washington's sporting press—Kirk Miller of the *Times,* Frank Young of the *Post,* and Joe Holman of the *Herald*—all put up a strong defense of his tenure, attributing many of the team's failings to factors no manager could have overcome. Shirley Povich has written that Johnson's pleasant personality was a victim of the pressures of the job at times, but said of his performance: "He had no apologies [to make] for his record as a manager. He was a very decent manager."[60] The coloration of sentimentality might seep into the judgment of local writers, but there were more distant observers who held the same view. Fred Lieb summed up Johnson's administration of the Washington ballclub this way:

> Some of the moves on the baseball chessboard are difficult to fathom. I judge Johnson's release was dictated by economic reasons, as was the sale of Simmons, Haas and Dykes by the Athletics. Johnson drew a salary of $20,000 last year. Maybe the move is necessary. I judge the Senators paid no cash dividends last season, even though they had a pretty snappy team. Every now and then I heard someone in baseball say, "Walter Johnson is a great fellow, but no manager." I don't know what a man

needs to be termed a manager. In 1930 the team finished 2nd. In 1931 the Yanks nosed out Washington for 2nd place in the last series of the season. This year the Athletics beat the Senators for 2nd by about the same slim margin. Washington finished with a higher percentage than the Cubs, the National League champions. The Senators held the Yanks to an even break in 22 games, by far the best showing made against them this year. What more could one have expected of the Senators? Certainly it did not figure to beat such clubbing crews as the Yankees and Athletics. Even so, it was the fastest-moving team in the American League last September. In fact, I was told that the players were working their heads off in an effort to save the managerial head of Walter Johnson. To have beaten the Yankee club it would have been necessary for the Senators to play .700 ball, and only two clubs in American League history have finished with .700 percentages, the Yankees of 1927 and the Athletics of 1931. What sluggers had Walter Johnson to match those of the Athletics and Yankees, who drove out 173 and 160 home runs, respectively? Everything considered, I believe it was quite a feather in Johnson's cap that he finished only a game behind the strong Philadelphia club. I am sorry to see Walter drop out of the big time. Johnson is a big leaguer, if there ever was one.[61]

To be booed by the Cleveland fans is to be booed by the best in the business. There may be no truth to the report that Cleveland game-goers eat their young, but they don't stop very short of being carnivorous where Cleveland managers are concerned. But a Cleveland manager has not only the wolfish fans to contend with. He must battle an unpredictable front office and a hypercritical Cleveland press. Nowhere around the baseball circuit is a manager hamstrung by a city's correspondents in the manner that it happens in Cleveland. Here, the baseball writers treat the game as something akin to life and death. In their columns, they pontificate. With eagle eyes, they watch a manager's every move. When the Indians are licked, the game has not ended as far as the baseball correspondents are concerned. It is replayed on the sports pages and Cleveland managers are often made to look very stupid indeed by the second-guess. Editorials follow in the wake of Cleveland defeats and it was a matter of this type that once occasioned aroused fans to picket the ballpark with a threat of patronizing no more games unless a manager were fired. The greatest travail of a Cleveland manager spawns, however, from the business office, where they do such very strange things. The suspicion is that the Cleveland ownership doesn't quite know what the baseball business is all about.[62]

SHIRLEY POVICH, 1939

After firing Roger Peckinpaugh earlier in the day, Cleveland general manager Billy Evans flew to Washington on June 7, 1933. Two days later it was announced that Walter Johnson would take over as manager of the Indians. Satisfaction was expressed throughout the baseball world, and especially by Clark Griffith, Joe Cronin, and the other members of the Washington ballclub, that Johnson had landed on his feet and back in the big leagues. And with seven children and several adults to care for, no one seemed happier than Johnson himself. "I know the club has some good talent and I believe it can be whipped into a winner," he declared.[63] But aware of it or not, Johnson was heading into a buzzsaw.

Over a period of some 15 years, from the late 1920s into the 1940s, the history of the Cleveland franchise is a study in the consequences of failure to live up to expectations. Although finishing in the first division consistently, and usually winning more than 80 games, only rarely was there a serious challenge for the pennant. The hopes of Indian fans were being dashed constantly. Periodically the mood got ugly and not even such hometown heroes as Tris Speaker, Roger Peckinpaugh, and Steve O'Neill were spared retribution. His popularity as a pitching idol ancient history now, an outsider like Walter Johnson didn't stand a chance. In 1937, Shirley Povich outlined the scenario in a piece entitled "Cleveland Fans Still Same Old Bunch."

> The folks out here haven't changed much. They're still whooping that the Indians will win the pennant. It's a seasonal shout with Cleveland fans. They read all winter that the Indians are an improved ball club and they yelp all spring that the Indians are the class of the league. Come summer, they don't want a pennant—that's impossible—they want the manager's scalp. That's been the routine for the past dozen years. Cleveland clubs, on paper, did indeed seem to measure up nicely. They had hitting, they had an acceptable defense, and apparently they had the best pitching staff in the league. The only thing they lacked was the ability to win sufficient ball games. That particular deficiency was ascribed variously to bum management, dissension on the ball club, and tough luck. The athletes were never blamed.[64]

Contributing to an often-poisonous atmosphere surrounding those teams were the efforts of local baseball writers to run the club with their typewriters, backing favorite players and second-guessing management without regard for its effect on team harmony. The proprietary attitude of the Cleveland press was made clear to Johnson not long after his arrival.

"Come down to the office and we'll get together on the situation," a reporter suggested.

"What situation?" Johnson asked.

"Well," the writer replied, "two heads are better than one. We'll talk over the running of the team."[65] The invitation was rejected out of hand, ending Johnson's honeymoon with the newspapers before it began.

Cleveland ballplayers had grievances of their own, foremost among them an austerity program imposed by the owners and carried out by Evans. As the Depression took its toll, costs were pared. After posting more than 20 wins in each of the past four seasons, the ace of the Indians staff, Wes Ferrell, was asked to take a $6,000 *cut* in salary. Ferrell refused, electing to play without a contract in 1933, while others signed—and some played—less than enthusiastically. The hitters on the club were unhappy with the move that year into new Municipal Stadium, a cavernous ballpark with seating for 80,000 and field dimensions to match: the center field fence was 470 feet from the plate. The team's batting average and power production dropped from near the top of the league in 1932 to close to the bottom the next year. In 1934 the Indians returned to the smaller League Park, with a corresponding rebound in hitting.

The Indians finished 1933 under Johnson the way they had begun under Peckinpaugh, playing .500 ball. For the fifth straight year the team's destiny was fourth place. With the Athletics depleted by the sale of Al Simmons, Jimmy Dykes, and Mule Haas to the White Sox (the start of a wholesale liquidation of Connie Mack's marvelous team), and the Yankees showing their age, the Nationals swept easily to the American League pennant. Reporting on the World Series as a newspaper correspondent, Johnson visited with the new "Boy Wonder," Joe Cronin, in the Washington dugout before the first game at the Polo Grounds. Two days later more than 300 writers covering the Series, including such other baseball luminaries as Babe Ruth, Honus Wagner, and John McGraw (only a few months before his death), were received by the new President, Franklin D. Roosevelt, at the White House. Ruth and Johnson were personally presented to the president.

In part to relieve his homesickness, perhaps, in 1934 Johnson brought Sam Rice and catcher Moe Berg to the Indians from Washington, and Pat Gharrity came in as a coach. The Associated Press poll predicted a fifth-place finish for Cleveland, with 65 of the 87 voters judging them no better than a second-division team, and not one believing they could win the pennant. The Indians got off to a good start, nonetheless, closely trailing the Yankees and Tigers through the first two months of the season and even taking the lead briefly in late May.

Joe Cronin made Johnson an American-League coach for the second All-Star game on July 10, his only game at the position in 28 years in the big leagues. From the first-base coaching box at the Polo Grounds he witnessed one of the great events in the history of the annual classic: Carl Hubbell's consecutive strikeouts of Ruth, Gehrig, Foxx, Simmons, and Cronin. The

American League overcame that humiliation to win, 9–7, with Cleveland players the stars for their side: outfielder Earl Averill drove in three runs, while pitcher Mel Harder shut out the National League on one hit over the last five innings for the victory. Afterwards, Cronin credited Johnson for his contribution to the win by keeping Harder out of the Cleveland rotation for several days before the game (at Cronin's request). "Walter, I owe you a great deal of thanks," he told him.[66]

The first serious trouble in Cleveland came just after the All-Star break when a game was lost to New York on a ninth-inning rally in which the Yankees made only one hit but were given six walks. With the Indians in a slump for the better part of a month, the writers jumped on the loss as an example of Johnson's weakness in handling the pitching staff. The criticism was muted when the team took off on a winning streak to pull within seven games of the lead, principal owner Alva Bradley taking the opportunity to praise the manager and announce his new contract for 1935. "We are satisfied with the progress he has made with the club and in the development of young players," Bradley declared.[67] Additional support came from *Baseball Magazine,* which laid into the "irresponsible fraternity" of the Cleveland sporting press:

> Alva Bradley, President of the Cleveland club, did well to disregard the senseless criticism of Walter Johnson, and to sign that deservedly popular character to an extended contract for next season also. The storm that assailed Johnson came from the chronic kickers who infest every ball park, and was foolishly fanned by the Cleveland sport writers. Just what they expect of Johnson is problematical. Under his management Cleveland has become a powerful club, strong in pitching, strong in attack. Though probably not of championship calibre, the club has earned and deserves local support rather than local criticism. Owner Bradley, while admitting that Walter had made some mistakes, pointedly asked, who was free from mistakes? He allowed it to be known that the Cleveland club was not being run by local sport writers. This irresponsible fraternity, entirely lacking in business experience, are quite out of their province when they attempt to coerce the owner in the selection of a manager.[68]

Rallying to Johnson's defense in a more personal way was another towering figure nearly at the end of his time in the game: Babe Ruth. In the Cleveland Hotel nursing an injured ankle, Ruth summoned to his room the two Johnson daughters, Carolyn, 11, and eight-year-old Barbara, who were staying at the hotel with their father. Too young to be aware of the controversy, and with little idea what he was talking about, they listened as Ruth cautioned them to ignore the criticism of Johnson in the newspapers. "I don't know whether you girls have seen any bad comments about your Dad," he told them, "but if you have, don't pay a bit of attention to them, because he's just a fine, fine person."[69]

The Indians won 85 games in 1934, finishing third behind the Tigers and Yankees to break the fourth-place hex at last. Joe Cronin's Nationals plummeted to seventh.

During his time at Cleveland Walter Johnson didn't confine his activities entirely to the dugout, but had some interesting experiences on the pitching mound also. Like many minor-league clubs trying to survive the Depression, the Indians farm team at Toledo installed a lighting system. In an exhibition game there on August 9, 1933, Johnson pitched for the Indians—his first appearance in a night game. With a crowd of 6,800 on hand he retired nine of ten Toledo batters during a three-inning stint, a walk the only blemish on his record.

In a spring training contest at Lafayette, Louisiana, on March 25, 1934, Johnson was the winning pitcher for an Indians split squad against the Kansas City Blues. The other Cleveland team was in New Orleans playing the minor-league Pelicans, and taking the mound for them was the greatest female athlete of the time, Babe Didrikson. She went two scoreless innings, hit two line drives (one fair and one foul), and "looked as if she had been playing baseball in fast company all her life," according to the *Cleveland Plain Dealer*. "Barney and Babe" was the heading over box scores of the exhibitions.

On June 5, 1934, the Indians manager made himself the starting pitcher in a game against Michigan State University at East Lansing. Not in the least awestruck by Johnson's storied past, apparently, the collegians roughed him up for three hits in the first inning, topping it off with a grand-slam home run to take a four-run lead. But over the next eight innings only one other MSU runner reached base as Johnson went the distance in a 14–4 Indians victory. Pitching his first complete game in seven years (and his last ever), Johnson also got three hits and drove in five runs himself.

The most bizarre exhibition appearance came at the end of the season on September 30, 1934, in a two-inning old-timers game between halves of a Cleveland-Chicago doubleheader at League Park. Sixty-seven-year-old Cy Young pitched for the "Antiques" of Nap Lajoie, Terry Turner, Elmer Flick, Steve O'Neill, Bill Bradley, and Lee Fohl. Johnson's "Has-Beens" included Roger Peckinpaugh, Bill Wambsganss, Earl Moore, and Glenn Liebhardt. Relieving Moore in the second inning, Johnson got one out before his attempted pick-off of Lajoie at second base turned the game into a near-riot, as the *Plain Dealer* reported:

> The game between two teams of old-time big league ballplayers at League Park yesterday ended in a brawl. The Has-Beens were leading 3 to 1 in the last of the second

inning. In a baffling movement, one of the Has-Beens' outfielders (they had 5) sneaked in from center field in an attempt to pick Larry Lajoie off second base. Safety Director Martin Lavelle, umpiring behind the plate, called Lajoie safe. Roger Peckinpaugh, shortstopping for the Has-Beens, started for Lavelle. The rest of the team came with him. They milled about the safety director, who went down in the crush. Immediately a dozen policemen swarmed on the field and headed for the players. They shoved back the irate Has-Beens and, making a flying wedge, escorted Lavelle from the field. As one fan remarked, "That Peckinpaugh always was a scrappy son-of-a-gun."

The beginning of the end at Cleveland came even before the start of the 1935 season, when the Associated Press poll forecast a pennant for the Indians. Based on the 1934 performances of veterans Earl Averill (.313, 31 home runs), Mel Harder (20–12), and Willis Hudlin (15–10), and youngsters Joe Vosmik (.341), Bill Knickerbocker (.317), Odell Hale (.302), Monte Pearson (18–13), and especially first baseman Hal Trosky, with one of the greatest rookie seasons ever (.341, 35 home runs, 142 RBIs), Johnson himself declared that he had the makings of the strongest club in the league.[70] Six weeks into the season they had done little to change that opinion, trailing closely behind the White Sox and Yankees for the lead.

Then Johnson created a firestorm of protest in the Cleveland press with the release of long-time Indians Willie Kamm and Glenn Myatt on May 23. "They were no longer useful to me as players, and I felt they were an antagonizing influence upon the ball club," Johnson explained.[71] A slump over the next several weeks weakened his position, and some writers portrayed the situation as a manager's jealousy over the popularity of veteran players among fans and players. A predicted uprising against Johnson failed to materialize, though, when the team returned from a losing road trip. "Anti-Johnson Bomb Turns Out to be a Dud," *The Sporting News* reported of the first game back in Cleveland on June 8, where cheers for the embattled manager overwhelmed scattered boos.

"I'm 100% for Walter and I think the whole team is for him," Earl Averill declared. "The boys have found that Walter is on the level and has plenty of guts." Pitcher Oral Hildebrand, who had been disciplined several times by Johnson, said: "I've had trouble with Walter, but I'm for him. I think he's OK and I think the fans should be for him. I mean it. I was telling one of the other boys that in case of a showdown, I'd be for Walter, and he was surprised. He thought I was still sore, but I'm not."[72] The departure of Kamm and Myatt produced little sympathy anywhere but in the newspapers, and a winning streak that carried the club to within two games of the lead on July 1 dampened the controversy over their release.

From there the club took a dramatic nosedive, however, losing 15 of 19 to drop into the second division and bring renewed claims of Johnson's incompetence and calls for his head. It didn't help that Averill was lost for six weeks when a firecracker exploded in his hand, the latest in a series of mishaps plaguing the team. In Washington on July 22 old friends showed their support with a "Walter Johnson Day" at Griffith Stadium, presenting a scroll signed by thousands of them. "Today he is under fire as manager of the Cleveland club," wrote Shirley Povich of the *Post,* "the target of fourth-wit Cleveland fans and newspaper writers who for two years have been heaping abuse on Johnson because he has failed to win a pennant with a fourth-place ball club. In Washington folks still think of Walter Johnson as Walter Johnson."[73]

On August 5, 1935, Alva Bradley announced Johnson's "voluntary resignation" as manager of the Indians. The action was a foregone conclusion since a two-hour meeting between them on the 2nd, after which Johnson asked waiting reporters, "What are you fellows going to write about after I go back to the farm?"[74] According to some reports, he had been fired at the meeting but urged Bradley to postpone the announcement until the Indians returned from a three-day trip to Detroit. The slumping Indians weren't likely to do well against the powerful Tigers, and Johnson thought it important that his successor, coach Steve O'Neill, get off on the right track.[75] Bradley agreed, and Cleveland was indeed swept by Detroit. Herman Goldstein of the *Cleveland News* described Walter Johnson's "last mile" as manager of the Indians:

> It was an unhappy trip for everybody. Bruce Campbell, during the night, had been stricken with spinal meningitis and left in a Detroit hospital. We all liked Bruce and we were all afraid for him. Johnson knew, as did the baseball writers, that he was through as manager. In the Cleveland Hotel that evening, Billy Evans was waiting to meet Walter to make it official. We knew that, too. On the ride back, Johnson sat in a card game with some of the ballplayers. He had his coat off, his shirt unbuttoned, his necktie draped loosely around his shoulders. When the train pulled into the terminal, everybody hurried off but Johnson. I stayed on the train, thinking I would walk up with the manager. But he was in no hurry. He stood and stretched, fiddled with his necktie, stood around. I could understand his thinking. Once he left the train he was walking toward the guillotine. I finally left the train, feeling very sorry for Walter Johnson. A great ballplayer, he was far from a great team manager, but a nice guy, a very nice guy.[76]

CHAPTER 19

Mountain View

I'm happy out here. I was raised on a farm and never have gotten the dirt out of my shoes. I guess I'll always be a country boy.[1]

WALTER JOHNSON, 1936

Knowing that anything short of a pennant in 1935 would make his future at Cleveland precarious at best, Walter Johnson prepared for life after baseball. In January he bought a 553-acre farm near the small town of Germantown, Maryland, an hour and a half from Washington by automobile, and in April the Alta Vista property was put up for sale and the family moved onto the farm. In August it became a welcome refuge from the traumatic events at Cleveland. "What a relief to get back to the country, to get away from it all," Johnson told a visiting reporter upon his return. The day after his firing Johnson was already able to speak philosophically about it. "That's baseball," he said. "If the job were mine again, I'd go about it the same way."[2]

"Mountain View Farm," so named for the prominent sight of nearby Sugarloaf Mountain, had in recent years been home mostly to a herd of sheep. It was a beautiful place, with a main house and several tenant bungalows on a hill surrounded by large oak trees, overlooking the rest of the property. A 150-acre forest of oak, maple, and pine stood out amid the cultivated land, and a variety of fruit trees were spread around. Wild mallard ducks made their home in the spring-fed creek. Johnson built up a sizable dairy operation that shipped 100 or so gallons of milk into Washington each day. His interest in birds was apparent in the chickens, turkeys, pheasants, peacocks, geese, and ducks wandering about, and of course there were dogs everywhere.

Walter Johnson's existence after baseball was hardly the sob story some writers later tried to make of it: a forlorn, lonely figure forgotten by the game and relegated to laboring in the isolation of the countryside. In truth, except for some resentment over his treatment at Cleveland, which he quickly put behind him, and the absence of Hazel, which he never got over, Johnson's life at Germantown had everything he wanted. Was he sorry to be out of baseball? His son, Eddie Johnson, who took to the farm life immediately and is still at it 60 years later, doesn't think so.

"Baseball was a living for him," he said, "and I think if he had it to do over again he probably would have preferred to be a hunter or a farmer, that's where he really liked to be. I always did have that feeling, because he liked to hunt and be outside so much. He was the type of fellow that just couldn't wait to get into some old clothes, and get a dog. He liked to travel with his own people, hunters and people like that. Now maybe I'm not entirely accurate in saying that he would have been happier, maybe that's just my own feelings. But fame, and people bugging him and everything . . . why he certainly never gloried in that."[3]

There was plenty of work on the farm, to be sure, but also lots of help. A professional dairyman, responsible for the milking operation, lived there; brother-in-law John Burke, a warm, good-humored Irishman, was the gardener; Minnie Johnson took charge of the household, which included a full-time maid and cook; the four boys (Walter, Jr. was in Washington, married and working for the FBI by personal appointment of J. Edgar Hoover) and two girls shared the daily chores. Additional labor was hired as the seasons required. Johnson was no country squire sitting on the porch surveying his domain, but that wasn't his style anyway. Most of the time he did the work he wanted when he wanted to do it. "He was content to be the Maryland farmer," wrote Shirley Povich, "to hunt with his dogs and watch them win field trials. On any day he could be seen in his hip boots, corduroys and windbreaker, puttering around with his brood of rare australorp chickens, feeding the wild mallard ducks and bourbon turkeys, milking his cows, or racking the underbrush with his two pet bird dogs, Ben and Quail."[4]

Three or four times a week, at night mostly, Johnson indulged in his favorite pastime: roaming the countryside with his purebred English hounds (there were three dozen of them at one point) hunting fox and raccoons. These expeditions were more of a chase than a hunt, actually, the animals rarely caught and let go when they were; the pursuit was the thing. Sometimes the dogs would be set loose while Johnson stayed at the house or drove to a nearby hilltop to listen for the sounds of a trail being picked up. He could tell from the barking exactly what was happening, which hounds were in the lead, even, from their distinctive pitch. "There's Old Betsy, and there's Lightning . . . there's Screamer," he'd say.[5]

Sportswriters showed up on occasion when his name was in the news, or to get his opinion about some development in baseball, or sometimes, in the case of Joe Holman, or Vincent Flaherty, or Shirley Povich, just to visit an old friend. "Never expected to see you on a farm," Johnson greeted Joe Williams of the *New York World-Telegram* when he dropped by one day. "You can't get any stories around here, but if you're interested in a nice sow. . . . "[6] Clark Griffith, Bucky Harris, Ossie Bluege, Joe Judge, and others from the old days came out to chat or play cards. Johnson and Sam Rice, who had a large chicken farm not far away, were especially close during this time, visiting each other often. It was always a happy occasion when Rice's car was spotted making its way up the long driveway to the house at Germantown, the children remember.[7]

After 30 years in the game, though, baseball was never far from Johnson's mind. "Often I think about the old days while jobbing around on the farm," he said not long after his retirement. "I'd like to pitch again to Cobb and Jackson and all the rest. I'm still wondering how I could have stopped them."[8] And as one of the great figures in its history, Walter Johnson was never far off baseball's horizon. Clark Griffith, on the occasion of his 66th birthday in November 1935, named his all-time team and surprised no one with the choice of Johnson for his pitcher, calling him "the greatest ballplayer of them all." "If he had had a team behind him in his prime, I don't think he ever would have lost a game," Griffith declared. "He was so far ahead of any other pitcher that I don't think we oughta pick a second fellow." He finally chose Christy Mathewson for the second team.[9]

In February 1936, results of the first Baseball Hall of Fame election were announced. With 226 members of the Baseball Writers Association naming up to ten players each, five greats received the 75% of the vote necessary for enshrinement. Ty Cobb was on 222 ballots, missing from only four. Babe Ruth and Honus Wagner received 215 votes each, Mathewson 205, and Walter Johnson 189, or 84%. Pitchers Cy Young, with 111 votes, and Grover Cleveland Alexander, with 55, missed out.

Later in the month Johnson was back in the national headlines with his attempt to support George Washington's childhood legend of throwing a silver dollar across the Rappahannock River. The director of the George Washington Bicentennial Commission, Congressman Sol Bloom, declared the feat physically impossible, but after inspecting the site at Fredericksburg, Virginia, Johnson agreed to defend the (probably apocryphal) story as part of the first president's 204th birthday celebration. In throwing metal washers and half-dollar pieces across the Potomac River, though, he found them difficult to control, tending to curve or sail straight up or down after 50 or 60 feet. Two days before the event Johnson reported from Germantown: "I am still practicing with a dollar against my barn door. Arm getting stronger, barn door weaker."[10]

The story attracted national attention, and 8,000 curious spectators crowded the shores of the Rappahannock on February 22 along with reporters and newsreel cameras. The event was carried live over the CBS radio network. A preliminary toss with a lead washer fell five feet short, followed by a second practice throw with a coin that cleared the river easily. The third and official toss with a silver dollar minted in 1796 was the best yet, sailing over the opposite shore by 25 feet after traveling an estimated 317 feet in all.

A few days later Walter Johnson was off to spring training in Florida—only this time it was Walter, Jr., who had been signed by the Philadelphia Athletics. A Maryland man acquainted with Connie Mack had recommended Walter and another boy after seeing them pitch for a local semipro team, and Mack agreed to take them south. "He's got the makings, all right," Johnson said of his 20-year-old namesake, who was an inch taller at 6 feet 3 inches and almost as broad at 190 pounds. "The boy has a good strong arm and a good physique. Walter's green and has plenty of time to come along. I'm hoping Connie will farm him out to some small league where the other kids will be green, too."[11] The touching scene at Union Station, as the father sent his son off on the familiar journey, was described by Vincent Flaherty:

> "So long, son, take care of yourself and don't forget, I'll be thinking of you." If there's an ounce of sentimentality in your soul, you'd have batted the mist from your eyes when old Walter Johnson bid goodbye to his son. It was beautiful, delicately so. For the first time in 29 unmatched years, the old Walter Johnson wasn't going south. And it was a strain, he seemed eager to go. He was fidgety, nervous, stomping around the train-shed platform like an old fire-horse. It seemed like he was fighting a battle within himself to keep from boarding the train. Grasping his son's hand firmly, he gave his boy advice that he never had when he broke into baseball. "Above all, son," the immortal Walter said, "don't give up. Don't get discouraged, no matter what happens down there. Don't overwork yourself. Take care of your arm and don't be too anxious to make good. There's plenty of time for you."[12]

The advice was disregarded, however, and after pitching two scoreless innings of an A's intersquad game on March 4 young Walter had a sore arm that would plague him the rest of the summer. He spent six weeks with Des Moines of the Western League, pitching ineffectively in five games before being released. Brief stints the next year with Norfolk of the Piedmont League and Tarboro of the Coastal Plain League and in 1939 with Augusta of the South Atlantic League made up the balance of his career.

A more likely professional prospect was younger brother Eddie Johnson, star of the baseball and basketball teams and president of the Student Government Association at the University of Maryland. "A sure-fire major-league shortstop," American League umpire Bill McGowan predicted.[13] Eddie was a three-year starter for a fast college team that included Clark Griffith's nephew Sherry Robertson, who would play 10 years with Washington; Hugh Keller, brother of Yankees slugger Charlie "King Kong" Keller and Nationals catcher Hal Keller; and Fritz Maisel, Jr., whose father had been an American League contemporary of Walter Johnson.

A slick fielder with a near .400 average during his career at Maryland, Eddie was recruited by the Red Sox, Pirates, and Yankees before signing with New York, whose farm system director, George Weiss, had an inside track. After graduating in 1939 he went to Easton of the Eastern Shore League, hitting .274 in 63 games and making the league's All-Star team before breaking his collarbone toward the end of the season. In 1940 Eddie moved up to Norfolk, which had just lost its double play combination of Gerry Priddy and Phil Rizzuto, but tore a muscle in his leg during the first exhibition game. After trying to play through the injury for two weeks he went back to Germantown to recover—and never returned to baseball. The Yankees wanted him back, but instead he took over the farm, raced thoroughbred horses with Walter, Jr., and got married and started a family. "It's probably just as well," Eddie says with the modesty of his famous dad, "I wouldn't have done much. I probably would have kicked around the minors for awhile."[14]

He also claims that of the three boys it was the youngest, Bob, who was blessed with the most natural ability. "Bobby was probably the best athlete of us all, and would have been a great ballplayer if he had kept it up," Eddie recalled. "He could hit, he could run, he could throw, he could really do everything. But he never got away, he got married and had a couple of kids and went to work, and he played sandlot ball around. But he had tremendous potential. Boy, he could do it all . . . big, 200 pounds and all. But—I don't know if it was his temperament or what—he just didn't want to go away and try."[15]

The father's association with baseball continued despite the demands of the farm. Providing color commentary for the Mutual radio network's broadcast of the opening games in 1936 and 1937, he picked up good reviews for his work. "Johnson has a remarkable radio voice, by the way," wrote Bob Considine of the *Washington Herald*. "His handling of the opening game here won him fame all over the section. His voice has the haunting twang Will Rogers had, and his everlasting simplicity of style sits well with any brand of listener."[16] At the 1937 All-Star game at Griffith Stadium, Johnson saw Earl

Averill's line drive break Dizzy Dean's toe, the beginning of the end of Dean's brief but dazzling mound career. Later that summer there came his first opportunity to see the fireballing 18-year-old Cleveland Indians phenom being widely heralded as the "next Walter Johnson"—Bob Feller.

Hired by a Chicago radio station as a guest announcer on White Sox games for several weeks, Johnson saw Feller pitch against them on August 22. When the Nationals came through Chicago a few days later, Shirley Povich asked him about it. "I don't know if he is as fast as I was," Johnson told him, "but he's the fastest thing I've seen in 20 years. That boy can pour that ball in there."[17] Eventually Povich pinned him down on the matter. "I popped the question," he related, "'Tell me, Walter, does Feller throw that ball as fast as you did?' He dropped his head and thoughtfully ran a hand through his hair. Now the Johnson modesty was colliding full tilt with the honesty of the man. For a moment, it seemed an unfair question. His honesty finally prevailed. The Big Train shook his head. 'No,' he said. It hurt to do it, but Walter had to tell the truth."[18]

An Iowa farmboy signed by the Indians at the age of 16 in July 1935—while Walter Johnson was the Cleveland manager, coincidentally—Feller would forever pitch in Johnson's shadow, in a sense. The relative speed of their fastballs quickly became a subject of debate, and with Johnson so recently retired there were plenty of observers qualified to compare them. Steve O'Neill was one. He batted against Johnson for 16 seasons, managed Feller for two years, and claimed the distinction of being the last person in the major leagues to catch Johnson (Indians batting practice) and the first to catch Feller (a 1936 exhibition game against the Cardinals in which Feller struck out eight of the first nine hitters). "No man in baseball history could throw a ball faster than Walter Johnson—including Bobby Feller," O'Neill declared.[19] After watching Feller pitch the first night game in Cleveland, Nap Lajoie said, "He's almost as fast as Walter Johnson."[20]

If he hadn't lost four prime years to World War II, Feller's numbers would certainly rank him with the handful of true pitching immortals, but to his credit he never argued with the prevailing opinion that as hard as he could throw, Johnson had thrown even harder. "In my opinion Walter Johnson has to be the fastest pitcher of all time," Feller told writer Donald Honig, "for the simple reason that he didn't have a curveball and he struck out so many hitters. I would say he had to be a harder thrower than I was. People who saw us both in our prime generally say that."[21] "I've always considered Walter Johnson the greatest pitcher of all time," Feller wrote in his autobiography. "He won 416 games for the Washington Senators with perennially bad teams. If he had been able to change teams, he might have won another hundred games."[22]

Johnson received a big hand when introduced at the World Series in New York that fall, and his 50th birthday on November 6, 1937, was the occasion for a gala party attended by more than 400 guests at the Mayflower Hotel in Washington. Hosted by radio personalities Arthur Godfrey, Clem McCarthy, and Arch McDonald, the affair was carried live by the NBC network. During the proceedings a letter arrived from the White House and was read to the crowd:

> Dear Walter, It is a pleasure to join with other fans in honor of one who has done so much to advance the national sport. As one of those fans who has followed your career with admiration and interest, and as one farmer to another, I send you heartiest greetings. Very sincerely yours, Franklin D. Roosevelt.[23]

An association with the Dr. Pepper Company began in 1937, Johnson becoming a spokesman and "promotional director" for the Washington area bottler for 1,000 shares of stock and a $5,000 salary. He also got a sporty fire-engine-red Oldsmobile with the Dr. Pepper logo emblazoned on both sides to drive around on his promotional rounds. In 1938 he managed the company's baseball team, which played the fastest semipro clubs in the Washington area and included several stars from the 1937 National Football League champion Washington Redskins: Cliff Battles, Riley Smith, and Charlie Malone.

As shortstop for the Dr. Pepper team, Eddie Johnson got to hit against his famous father. "Dad would pitch batting practice," he remembered. "I was fresh from the University of Maryland and I had seen a lot of big, strong pitchers, maybe wild but they could throw the ball because they were 20 years old and they knew how to throw. So the first time I came up for batting practice against Dad, I was swinging way late, and I just couldn't understand it because his motion was so slow and easy, sidearm. But the ball got there long before you knew it was going to. I thought I was a pretty good college ballplayer, and I'm swinging way late on these things and he wasn't even trying to throw hard—all he was doing was just putting it across the plate. That was my first realization of just how fast he really must have been."[24]

In the fall of 1938 Johnson was elected to the five-man Board of Commissioners of Montgomery County, Maryland, the only victorious Republican in the face of a Democratic sweep. Agreeing to run for the post on the condition that he wouldn't have to campaign or make speeches, his report of expenditures listed 50 cents for "printed cards."[25] Most of the Board's business was taken care of at weekly meetings, and the position paid $1,800 a year. That money and the salary from Dr. Pepper provided a welcome income during bleak Depression years when most farms could do little more than break even.

Baseball celebrated its Centennial in 1939, for those still believing the Abner Doubleday myth, and among the notable events of a memorable year for the game was the return of Walter Johnson to the major-league arena. On February 2 he was elected president of the National Association of Professional Baseball Players, an organization founded in 1924 to aid needy ex-ballplayers. Then came the surprising news that Johnson would do the radio announcing for the Nationals in 1939, a development brought about by historic circumstances in the annals of baseball broadcasting.

This was still the era when ballclubs were leery of putting their games on the radio, fearing damage to live attendance. For five years, from 1934 through 1938, the three New York teams had kept an agreement among themselves not to broadcast at all. But in 1939 Larry McPhail, who had seen the promotional value of the medium in Cincinnati before becoming general manager at Brooklyn, decided to break the ban, bringing the popular Reds announcer, Red Barber, with him to do Dodgers games. The other New York teams vowed to retaliate with bigger broadcasting signals and better personalities at the mike. The Yankees recruited Arch McDonald, the wildly successful voice of the Washington Nationals, paying him $27,800—"More than Joe DiMaggio," it was reported—to come to New York.[26]

Writer and publicist Joe Holman suggested to Clark Griffith that local hero Walter Johnson would make an appealing presence to replace McDonald on the Washington broadcasts,[27] and when advertising rights were sold to the breakfast cereal Wheaties, Johnson was part of the package.[28] That fouled up the plans of the station, CBS affiliate WJSV, to give the job to a young network assistant from New York named Mel Allen.[29]

On March 22, 1939, Johnson arrived at the Florida spring training camp of the Nationals, just like the old days, only this time it was to familiarize himself with the team in preparation for his radio work. Much of it was already quite familiar: coaches Clyde Milan and Nick Altrock, manager Bucky Harris, owner Griffith, trainer Mike Martin, second baseman Buddy Myer, center fielder Sammy West, and the last of his old teammates still playing for Washington, Ossie Bluege, beginning his 18th and final season. Sportswriters had been touting two rookie fastball pitchers, Walt Masterson and a young Cuban named Roberto Ortiz, even invoking comparisons with Walter Johnson, who joked that he was there to "get a look at all these pitchers down here who can throw faster than I did."[30]

Walking onto Tinker Field in Orlando the next day wearing a new Washington uniform, he watched for a while as the team worked out, then started warming up himself. "Johnson just about disrupted the regular workout," reported Vincent Flaherty, "for the Big Train was the only working ballplayer on the field. The rest had turned spectators."[31] "He tossed a dozen or so half-hard pitches while the rookies and veterans stood open-mouthed and then he cut one loose," it was reported. "It almost took the glove off a proud little recruit catcher named Grimes. Again, in that lazy, incredibly smooth sidearm motion he whizzed the ball over. Walter threw as much and as hard as any Nat pitcher who has been in spring training for 7 weeks. When it was over he mused, 'My arm's all right. If the old legs were only still good. But my arm's as good as it ever was.' Johnson was the object of rookie Roberto Ortiz's undiluted idolatry. The big Cuban fastballer, mouth wide open, stood fascinated as he watched the amazing performance. 'He's a no-peetch now?' asked Ortiz, unable to believe there is no place on a pitching staff for the Big Train. 'Ooh,' added Roberto, 'he's a fast. Ball go whoosh.' "[32]

Johnson had a wonderful time in Florida, hitting fungoes and pitching batting practice, besieged by admirers and autograph seekers wherever the team traveled. Just before leaving camp in early April he saw the top teams in the Negro National League that year, Washington's Homestead Grays and the Newark Eagles, play at Tinker Field. "Curious Washington [Nationals] players flocked to the game," Shirley Povich described the occasion in his column, "and went away with a deep respect for colored baseball. Walter Johnson sat in a box at the game, profoundly impressed with the talents of the colored players. 'There,' he said, 'is a catcher that any big league club would like to buy for $200,000. I've heard of him before. His name is [Josh] Gibson. He can do everything. He hits that ball a mile. And he catches so easy he might as well be in a rocking chair. Throws like a rifle. Bill Dickey isn't as good a catcher. Too bad this Gibson is a colored fellow.' "[33]

After broadcasting a Washington game on May 9, Johnson took his first airplane flight, traveling to New York to play in a charity softball game for a crowd of 14,000 at Madison Square Garden. With New York Senator Wagner, Mayor LaGuardia, and Father Flanagan of Boys Town umpiring, Johnson pitched for Robert Ripley's "Believe it or Nots" against Lowell Thomas's "Nine Old Men," with Babe Ruth, Gene Tunney, Bugs Baer, Edward Bowes, Colonel Stoopnagle, Heywood Broun, Arch McDonald, and Graham McNamee.

On June 12 Johnson took the train to Cooperstown, New York, for the opening of the Baseball Hall of Fame and Museum, one of a dozen living legends gathered to dedicate the Hall and the plaques immortalizing their deeds for future generations. Sportswriter (and later director of the Hall of Fame) Ken Smith described the ceremony:

Through the Hall of Fame portal, one by one as they were presented, walked the mightiest stars of the Twentieth Century—heroes whose deeds on the diamond were still fresh in the memory of the audience. "Walter Johnson." What writer or painter could possibly envision a better picture of an athletic idol for old and young to admire than this bronzed, curly-haired, stalwart American citizen? His simple spoken response reflected a deep and matchless humility which only the truly great know: "I am glad I was able to do enough to merit an honor of this magnitude." The pathos was complete as Walter Johnson wrapped his great arms around the shoulders of "Old Pete" [Alexander].

Johnson and Ty Cobb shared a dining car for the long ride back from Cooperstown, treating a small crowd of listeners to tales of the old days.[34]

More than 200 former big-leaguers assembled in Boston on July 11 to form the Association of Retired Major League Players. Johnson was elected to the board of governors and called upon to speak. The next day more than 60 old-timers squared off in a geriatric version of the All-Star game played in New York the day before. The National League, behind the pitching of Alexander and Kid Nichols, won 8–4 over an American League aggregation that included Tris Speaker, Eddie Collins, Frank Baker, Harry Hooper, Duffy Lewis, and Joe Wood. 72-year-old Cy Young pitched the first inning and Johnson the second, allowing a run on three hits, one of them by George Kelly.[35]

Joe Holman's original idea had been for Johnson to be the relaxed half of a radio team, sort of a baseball Will Rogers. "I knew Johnson to be a no-hurry man," Holman wrote later, "one who performed best when taking his time. Color commentary, I sensed, would give him ample opportunity to make best use of his homespun delivery."[36] Instead, probably for financial reasons, Johnson ended up alone at the mike, with little time for anything but the play-by-play and public address announcing, which was also part of the job. In July he got help after taking flak from political opponents for missing the Board of Commissioners meetings. Another broadcaster came on board so Johnson could attend to his county duties, and on the other days they rotated air time—still not what Holman had envisioned.[37]

Johnson got decent reviews for his performance, nonetheless, and everything worked out all right as it was. "I enjoyed broadcasting the ballgames here last year," he wrote to a friend, "and I am sure I didn't keep anyone away from the game."[38] But Arch McDonald's folksy expressions and down-home Arkansas drawl, which had worked so wonderfully at Chattanooga and Washington, flopped miserably in the Big Apple. McDonald gratefully returned to those who appreciated him, putting an end to Walter Johnson's career at the microphone.

There's a guy who really could throw that onion.[39]

BABE RUTH, 1942

In 1940, Johnson's political allies talked him into running for Congress. His primary campaign in Maryland's 6th District was hardly more vigorous than his run for the commissioner's post, with few appearances and little in the way of an agenda, but again he won handily. "I am not going to make any promises," he declared in one of his few speeches, "but I don't have anybody to take care of. That's the only way I want to run."[40] His strategy was simple: "I just tell them that I'll try to do my best and hope they'll believe me."[41]

Aside from a few speeches, the only pitching Johnson did in the campaign came after a Memorial Day ceremony at the Tomb of the Unknown Soldier in Thurmont, Maryland. He went one inning of an exhibition game against a "colored" CCC camp team from Gettysburg, giving up one hit and striking out two before stepping down to umpire the rest of the game. Johnson appeared at the Republican National Convention in Philadelphia on June 27, blushing and bowing to the applause of 16,000 attendees after an introduction by GOP chairman Joseph Martin. Presented with a cap and baseball by the rookie politician from Maryland, Martin demonstrated his grip and throwing technique. "That's the funniest thing I ever saw," said one observer. "Joe Martin showing the greatest fastball pitcher in the history of baseball how to throw a fastball."[42]

The high point of the campaign came on September 16, 1940, in Coffeyville, Kansas, of all places. The Republican presidential candidate, Wendell Willkie, had taught high school there before entering the law, and chose it as the location for his campaign kickoff rally. Johnson returned to Coffeyville for the first time in years to introduce Willkie, both of them revisiting scenes of their earlier lives there and renewing acquaintances with old friends. "I am proud of my old home town and never more proud to be present today to introduce the next president of the United States," Johnson told the gathering of 20,000. "Thank you very much, Walter," Willkie prefaced his address on the evils of totalitarianism and the dangers of a third Roosevelt term. "You were my boyhood hero when I lived in Coffeyville and you are my hero now. I hope you will be throwing them out in Congress."[43]

Johnson's own campaign got an assist from a fellow old-time ballplayer when the editor of the *Bethesda Journal* received this letter late in October:

It has come to my attention that Walter Johnson is a candidate for Congress from Maryland. I have not heard Walter's views on national affairs and I don't know what local questions are before him, but I do feel so strongly as to his qualities of character that I am writing you in his behalf. I have known Walter for 32 years and have had every opportunity to size him up. I have never known Walter to take short cuts or do a cheap thing. We opposed each other in baseball. I know that if honor had not always been first with him he could have improved his record vastly by letting one fly at the batter's head occasionally in order to loosen him up. He never once deviated from right. He is the kind of man who can be banked upon to keep his word to his supporters. No consideration of expediency will cause him to change his convictions. Walter will not make flowery speeches or promises he does not intend to keep. I venture to say that during the campaign he will not enjoy putting on the political front.

We need men like Walter in our representative bodies—men who will vote constructively and who are too independent to be swayed unduly by any one man. He is conscientious enough to examine things for himself and I am sure will preserve an open mind willing to listen to advice and weigh its wisdom. I hope that those who read this letter will not consider it presumptuous coming from me, a non-resident. I think so highly of the man's integrity that I can't resist recommending him to the voters of his district. This you can count on: If Walter is elected he will always be the same man he has been and now is. That quality should help to make him a good Congressman. Ty Cobb, Menlo Park, Calif.

But it was Johnson's opponent, William Byron, who captured the endorsements that counted in the game of politics. On election eve Johnson's home newspaper, the *Montgomery County Sentinel,* editorialized: "In complete fairness it is proper to suggest that Mr. Byron is entitled to return to Congress. His opponent, Walter Johnson, is beloved and respected throughout the United States as a baseball hero, but hero worship should not be the basis on which national legislators are selected."[44] Byron instructed his campaign manager to abstain from any personal attacks.[45]

Johnson's alliance with the Republican platform of isolationism and opposition to Roosevelt's big-government "dictatorship" swayed the heavily Democratic electorate against him, giving the victory to the able and popular young incumbent. He polled 52,000 votes to Byron's 60,000 in the midst of a nationwide Democratic sweep in which Roosevelt demolished Willkie by four million votes. "It has been a fine campaign and I wish the best success to Representative Byron," Johnson said in his brief concession speech.[46] There was a tragic footnote to the election on February 27, 1941, when Byron was killed in a plane crash near Atlanta while on congressional business. His wife, Katherine, won a special election three months later to become the first woman representative from Maryland, and she was eventually succeeded by both her son and daughter-in-law, the seat remaining in the Byron family for more than half a century. Johnson won easy re-election to his commissioner's seat in 1942 to remain the lone Republican on the board.

On May 28, 1941, Johnson threw a pitch from the mound at Griffith Stadium to break a radio beam that inaugurated a new era at the old ballpark: night baseball. The toss actually sailed three inches wide of the plate and missed the beam, but electrical engineers threw a switch as the ball smacked into catcher Jake Early's mitt, flooding the field with light from the $120,000 system. None of the 25,000 present knew the difference.[47]

Walter Johnson's next few mound appearances came in support of a larger cause—the United States effort in World War II. Baseball staged many special exhibitions to sell war bonds during the course of the conflict, and the attraction at Yankee Stadium on August 23, 1942, was two great figures of the game's past, Walter Johnson and Babe Ruth, facing each other between games of a New York-Washington doubleheader.

Not having swung a bat in four years, Ruth went to the ballpark on the 21st for a 100-pitch batting practice. Johnson hadn't held a ball since turning on the lights at Griffith Stadium more than a year earlier, but decided against any preparation.[48] "My daughter [Carolyn, living in New York] warned me that Ruth had done some hitting in the stadium on Friday and suggested that I do a little training too," he said. "I told her that after half an hour of throwing I would be no good pitching to the Babe."[49] And Johnson wasn't planning to exert himself in the exhibition anyway, he told a reporter at Toots Shor's restaurant the night before: "The fans want to see the Babe hit a homer. He's drawing the crowd. If I can get the ball up there, I'm going to throw one he can hit over the fence."[50] But Ruth wasn't the only object of interest, as writer Tom Meany's account of Johnson's arrival at Yankee Stadium made clear:

> The high esteem in which Walter was held in his own profession was evidenced when he walked into the Yankee dressing room. One of the players approached him with a baseball to be autographed. That's about as high as a ballplayer can get in the way of compliments. Lefty Gomez turned Joe DiMaggio's attention to Johnson's long arms.
>
> "No wonder he was so great," said Lefty. "He's got arms like a gorilla. He could probably lace his shoes without bending over."
>
> "Looks like he's in shape right now," observed Joe. "Speaking as a hitter, from what I've heard of the guy I'm just as pleased he's not working regularly now—even with Washington."
>
> Johnson, with a shy smile, nodded to the Yankees around the locker room and walked into manager McCarthy's office with George Weiss, head of the Yankee farm system, and Paul Krichell, the ivory hunter.[51]

When Ruth arrived, the two legends greeted each other warmly and chatted briefly about golf and farming.[52] After dressing, Ruth came over and sat down next to Johnson, who had been chatting with humorist Bugs Baer. Their conversation was reported by sportswriter Frank Graham:

"Lay it in there so I can hit it," [Ruth] said. "I'm getting old and I can't reach for a ball like I used to."

"I'll lay it in there," Walter said.

"I'll try not to hit it back at you," Ruth said.

"You know," Walter said, "I was thinking about that coming up here today. I always had to think about it when I was pitching to you."

The Babe laughed. "I promise," the Babe said. "And you promise me one thing, too. Don't hit me in the head. I can't move as fast up there as I could when I was a young fellow. But I never had to worry when you were pitching." Walter picked up his glove out of the locker. "Come on, Babe. It's about time we got out there. I'll lay 'em in there and you hit 'em good. That's what they want to see."[53]

Announcer Mel Allen proclaimed, "Doing the pitching today, Walter Johnson," and the huge crowd of almost 70,000 responded with a tremendous ovation as Johnson ambled out to the mound. The players in both dugouts moved to the top of the steps to get a better view of a man most of them knew only as one of the game's immortals, now throwing from the mound just a few feet away, flesh and blood. Yankees shortstop Phil Rizzuto was surprised by Johnson's motion. "My gosh, he's pitching sidearm," he exclaimed, "a fastballer pitching sidearm."[54] New York manager Joe McCarthy said, "Look at him, he still looks like a pitcher, doesn't he?"[55] But as usual it was Yankees pitching great Lefty Gomez, coming to the end of a career in which he had once been the hardest thrower in the league himself, with the best line. "At 55," Gomez sighed, "he's faster than me."[56]

After Johnson had tossed a dozen warmup pitches to his catcher, Washington coach and former Yankee Benny Bengough, Mel Allen made the announcement everyone was waiting for: "The next batter, Babe Ruth."[57] The words had only a moment to reverberate around the massive ballpark before being drowned out by a roar that one writer said "struck with the impact of a physical force."[58] Out of the Yankees dugout came the big slugger in a moment he described in his autobiography as "one of the great thrills of my life in the game."[59] On only one other occasion since the end of his American League career had he returned to "The House That Ruth Built"—Lou Gehrig's farewell in 1939.[60]

In a further touch of nostalgia, Billy Evans moved into place behind Bengough to umpire the exhibition. After a ball, a strike, another ball, and a fly to right, Ruth connected for an arching drive a few rows into the lower stands in right. "No cheer ever to greet any of the 714 homers Ruth had hit in championship games or any of the 15 he exploded in the world series matched the mighty roar as the Babe swung," reported the *New York Times.*[61] Ruth managed only a single in the next 14 pitches, although he did smash two substantial fly outs. Johnson cranked up a real fastball once, just for old time's sake, and grinned as Billy Evans's arm shot up for a called strike.[62] Mostly the pitches came in right over the plate, medium speed, but the Babe was out of shape and looked bad more than once trying to connect. He knew it was time to go, and his cue came on the 20th pitch. Getting a hold of the ball with everything he had left, Ruth drove a mammoth blast high into the third tier in right field.

"I knew I couldn't top that," he said later. Ignoring Evans's protestations that the ball had landed foul, Ruth trotted around the bases and across the plate, where Johnson met him. Putting their arms around each other, the two legends walked off the field together. "They were still yelling for us as we disappeared into the Yankee dugout and started down to the dressing room," Ruth recalled. "We walked along, gabbing and signing autographs, but there was a kind of sadness in both of us. Walter had been the greatest pitcher in the league; I had been the greatest slugger. But he was no longer part of the game, and the same was true of me."[63]

A year later on August 26, 1943, Johnson and Ruth reprised their act at the Polo Grounds but this time an all-time all-star team, many wearing the uniform of their greatest fame, assembled to play the field behind Johnson: George Sisler at first, Eddie Collins at second, Honus Wagner at short, Frankie Frisch at third, and Tris Speaker, Duffy Lewis, and Red Murray in the outfield. The inventor of shinguards, 63-year-old Roger Bresnahan, was the catcher. Connie Mack "managed" the squad, and Bill Klem was the umpire. Looking even rustier than the year before, Ruth finally connected on the 18th pitch to thrill the fans with a long drive into the upper stands. The old-timers' exhibition was part of an all-day extravaganza that included a game between a combined Yankees-Dodger-Giants all-star team and a top service team managed by Major Hank Gowdy.

The ballplayers weren't the only stars of this spectacular affair, which also brought out some of the cream of Hollywood and Broadway. James Cagney, Carole Landis, Ralph Bellamy, Ethel Merman, Cab Calloway, Joe E. Lewis, and Milton Berle were among those entertaining. Irving Berlin sang his stirring *God Bless America.* The most touching moment came when boxing champion and war hero Barney Ross limped to the microphone to thank the participants "on behalf of those who are here, those who are gone, and those who are going."[64]

The war-bond drive took Johnson on his last visit to Kansas, flying to Wichita for the annual Knights-Shriners baseball game on June 25, 1944. Pitching an inning for both sides with "some snap on the ball," according to the *Wichita Eagle,* he gave up a run on one hit and struck out two. Dave Woods came from Humboldt to see his childhood pal and left with a ball inscribed "Best wishes always to my first catcher."[65]

At yet another war-bond appearance, Johnson took the mound at Griffith Stadium for the last time on July 7, facing alumni of Washington's 1933 pennant-winning team before a game with the Browns. Baseball's megaphone pioneer, E. Lawrence "One-armed" Phillips, delivered the old cry of "Jawnnnn . . . son and Ru . . . ellll!" and White Sox coach Muddy Ruel and umpire Bill McGowan took their positions behind the plate. "More than a trace of his famed fastball" was in evidence as Johnson got Washington manager Ossie Bluege and St. Louis manager Luke Sewell on pop-ups. Joe Kuhel, who was still holding down first base for the 1944 Nationals, grounded out softly to end the inning. The exhibition continued for a bit when 67-year-old Nick Altrock came up to the plate with knees trembling, swung twice and missed, then traded his bat for another one eight inches wide. After fouling one off with the massive club, Altrock turned, tipped his hat to Johnson, and retired—the last batter to face a Walter Johnson pitch.[66]

On August 4 Johnson made his final appearance in uniform, traveling with Clark Griffith to Philadelphia for the celebration of Connie Mack's 50th anniversary as a manager. With 30,000 in attendance at Shibe Park, Mack's hand-picked team of all-time greats was called out onto the field to tremendous ovations: Sisler, Collins, Baker, Wagner, Dickey, Grove, Johnson, Speaker, Ruth, and Simmons; only Cobb and Cochrane were absent. The comedy team of Abbott (wearing an A's uniform) and Costello (in Yankees garb) were on hand to perform their baseball specialty, *Who's on first?*

Griffith prevailed on Johnson to come in from Germantown to help dedicate the 1945 season opener to President Roosevelt, who had died several days earlier on April 12. Appropriate to the mood of the country, rain fell on the scheduled date of the 16th, but on April 20 Johnson marched to the flagpole in center field with Griffith, American League President Will Harridge, and Secretary of War Patterson to raise the flag and lower it back to half-mast. A few minutes later he stood with Griffith, Ossie Bluege, and Yankees skipper Joe McCarthy, watching with 25,000 fans as Speaker of the House Sam Rayburn threw out the first ball. Just a few feet away was a young Congressman and protege of Rayburn's, Lyndon Johnson. Before the ceremonies, Walter Johnson had caused a stir in the Washington dugout. The *Washington Star* reported:

A tall, broad-shouldered, pigeon-toed and slightly stooped fellow wearing a blue suit and gray hat climbed up the stairs to the dugout, peered inquisitively at the players, then lumbered in and sat down beside Clyde Milan. "Hi ya, Walter," said Milan casually, hardly taking his eyes off the field. "Who's that?" asked Lt. Bert Shepard, the army flyer who may do some pitching for the Nats this season. "That's Walter Johnson," Ossie Bluege replied. Shepard looked admiringly at the old speedball king, sitting crosslegged in the center of the dugout, alternately puffing on a cigar stub and exchanging remarks with Milan. At the opposite end of the bench a knot of rookies gaped at the great man with the unashamed curiosity of tourists. For a minute you wondered which would be the first to step up and ask for an autograph. The Cubans chattered excitedly in Spanish and the others simply stared in mute awe.

The first indication that something was wrong came toward the end of March 1946, when Johnson started feeling a strange numbness in his left arm. At dinner a couple of weeks later he had to ask for help cutting a steak after dropping his knife several times. Eddie Johnson took his father to Dr. Larkin, the Washington team physician, who admitted him into Georgetown University Hospital the next day, April 9. The first public report from Dr. Larkin noted only a "little rise in blood pressure. He has been working hard and is exhausted. His condition at the present time, however, is good." Johnson would be in the hospital for a week, he predicted.[67]

But the initial diagnosis of the doctors there was that Johnson had suffered a cerebral hemorrhage, and had only days to live. At this terrible news, family members were summoned from around the country and a vigil began at the hospital. Several days later Clark Griffith was at the bedside talking about the old days when Johnson suddenly asked, "You remember what I did 20 years ago tomorrow, don't you?" "I sure do," Griffith told him. "That was the day you beat Eddie Rommel in 15 innings." Johnson smiled at the memory of the game he considered his greatest.[68]

His condition deteriorated rapidly, however, and soon there was a complete paralysis of the left side of his body and loss of speech. More sophisticated x-rays revealed the true source of the problems: a large, malignant, inoperable brain tumor. Radiation treatments were begun, but all they could do was keep the tumor in check. A recovery was out of the question. Johnson improved temporarily after each series of treatments, alert and in reasonably good spirits for a time, even taking an occasional ride in a wheelchair. But as soon as the tumor started growing again he would fall back, sometimes awake but unable to speak, other times slipping into a deep coma. The pattern repeated itself for months.

During the first extended coma Carolyn Johnson Thomas, who had just delivered Johnson's seventh grandchild on April 20, was standing by the bed holding her father's hand. He had been out for some time, the doctors told her, and wouldn't know she was there. She was startled, therefore, when he asked, "How's that fine baby boy?" and wanted to know what she had named him.[69] It would no longer be assumed that Johnson was completely unaware, even when he appeared to be unconscious. The family kept a more or less constant attendance, sometimes violating hospital rules to sneak three-year-old "Bunky" (Eddie Johnson, Jr.), his granddaddy's constant pal on the farm, in to see him.[70] Old teammates and other friends came by to visit. "It breaks your heart to see him lying there," Ossie Bluege told a reporter, "knowing that there isn't a thing in this world you can do for him except to sit with him as long as the nurses will allow."[71]

Clark Griffith came every day, and even during Johnson's periods of coma or speechlessness sat by the bed, holding his hand while carrying on a one-way conversation, often reminiscing about the times they had shared together. Sometimes he felt a squeeze of the hand when Johnson was touched by something he said. On one occasion Griffith became concerned when tears flowed from Johnson's eyes, and alerted the doctor, Thomas Keliher. "Don't worry," Dr. Keliher assured, "you're good for him."[72] Each day Griffith brought a single rose to the hospital. "I took the earth from the pitcher's box in which Walter Johnson worked so long," Griffith told the doctor, "and made a special rose garden of it. I felt that anything enriched by Walter's sweat was semi-sacred. These roses are from that bed."[73]

On September 21, 1946, a testimonial evening for Walter Johnson was held at Griffith Stadium. The 24,000 who showed up pushed the season's attendance over a million for the only time in Washington history, and a check for $5,000 from the Nationals and Red Sox was presented to Eddie Johnson. Griffith was overcome with emotion during his presentation speech and had to ask Arch McDonald to take over. The broadcaster remembered Johnson as a "a gentleman and a gentle man." Another $5,000 came from an anonymous donor, possibly George Weiss. Worried about mounting hospital bills, Eddie had asked his father about taking out a bank loan and was told to contact Weiss, who had never repaid Johnson's investment many years earlier in the New Haven ballclub. During the latter part of Johnson's illness, Clark Griffith started picking up the bills from the hospital, until eventually they were sent directly to him. Joe Engel called Eddie from Chattanooga with an offer of money or anything else he could do to help.[74]

During periods of lucidity Johnson continued to follow baseball. His doting, adoring nurse, Daisy Barnwell Jones, made sure he was well taken care of in that respect as in all others, folding the daily papers back to the sports page for his careful scrutiny.[75] He listened intently to the 1946 World Series, a seven-game classic rivaling the thrills of 1924.[76]

On the occasion of Johnson's 59th birthday on November 6, and again on Thanksgiving Day, the 26th, small parties were held in his room with members of the family and a few close friends, and both occasions brightened his spirits considerably. Then on December 6 he took a dramatic turn for the worse, lapsing into a coma from which he would only briefly emerge in the following days. Nurse Jones arrived for duty at 7 P.M. on Tuesday, December 10, and was greeted by the usual squeeze when she took Johnson's big hand into her own. But an hour later she could see that he was fading fast and notified Dr. Keliher, who called the family. At 11:40 in the evening, with his children gathered around him, Walter Johnson died in his sleep.

"Mr. Johnson died like he lived—with quiet dignity," wrote Daisy Barnwell Jones. "Heaven and earth stood in awesome silence at his passing. The ever-present streetcar forever tearing around the corner like a freight train was behind schedule—strangely missing. Not one car passed by, not one voice was heard, save the noisy press down the hall. The night supervisor, a saintly Sister in long black garb, making her usual rounds, looked in upon the death scene, heard the voices of the press, picked up the phone on the desk just outside Mr. Johnson's room and whispered, 'We hear you.' With that, all was silent, in the halls, on the street, in his room, everywhere. As gently as a feather wafted out the window, and just as silently, his soul took its flight."[77]

Epilogue

To millions of Americans—particularly to keen followers of baseball—Walter Johnson, who died last night at Georgetown University Hospital, was best known as the greatest pitcher the game ever produced. But he was more than that. Despite a degree of adulation earned by few in any walk of life, he was an utterly unspoiled individual, a simple, direct soul whose depth of character was best exemplified as husband and father and whose monument is a career that for modesty and moderation stands as a model for the youth of the nation. According to Clark Griffith, it is conjectural whether Johnson ever fully realized his monumental stature in baseball, but if he did it was not reflected in his attitude on or off the playing field.[1]

DENMAN THOMPSON, WASHINGTON STAR
DECEMBER 11, 1946

The day after Walter Johnson's death was one of immeasurable sadness in Clark Griffith's office, as in so many other places in Washington and around the country. Bob Addie of the *Washington Times-Herald* described the scene:

> Griffith peered through the pale gold of the afternoon sunlight yesterday out beyond the quiet stands and for the hundredth time, he said, "It was better that way. He suffered too much." The energy seemed to be drained out of Griffith. He looked like the outline of a tree in mid-winter, and the twin peaks of snowy eyebrows that have snapped and waggled so furiously in all the old gentleman's bouts down through the years now seemed to hang lank and limp. Those keen old eyes always throwing off sparks like a smithy's forge looked glazed and tired. Occasionally they would puddle up when Griff kept recalling those precious moments with his friend who was gone. "I went to see him just before the end," Griff said. "He still kept holding on, still fighting like he had done all this time, and you felt that he might even beat it yet. He was unconscious but still fighting. Even though we've been expecting it all this time," Griff said wistfully, "it's hard to believe Walter is gone. He was so strong, so uncomplaining. We'll never see his like again."[2]

President Harry Truman, who had grown up just across the Kansas-Missouri border from Johnson at about the same time, was "greatly grieved to hear of the death of one of his great athletic heroes," press secretary Charles Ross announced, adding that Mr. Truman had admired him as both ballplayer and man.[3]

The historical coincidences running throughout Johnson's life continued to the end with the death, also of cancer, of famed sportswriter, columnist, and *Guys and Dolls* creator Damon Runyon in New York the same day. Runyon had also been born in Kansas, three years before Johnson, and the contrasting paths taken by the two as the result of an interest in sports was the subject of much commentary: Runyon the personification of urbanity and Johnson, happiest without a building in sight. "Life is a river and change is sure, but the passing of men like Damon Runyon and Walter Johnson tinges the fact with melancholy," lamented one editorialist. "Philosophy of whatever brand cannot dissemble the truth that it isn't the same United States it was on Monday."[4]

On December 13, 1946, a thousand seats in the nave of the Washington Cathedral were filled with people from all walks of life. Dignitaries of the highest level sat next to ballpark vendors, all of them brought there by the same impulse: to pay their last respects to Walter Johnson. The Dean of the Cathedral, The Reverend John Suter, gave thanks "for all the goodness and the courage which have passed from the life of this, Thy servant, into the life of others, leaving the world richer for his presence . . . for a life's task faithfully and honorably discharged, for gracious affection and kindly generosity, for sadness without surrender, and weakness endured without defeat."[5] Graying comrades who had supported Johnson in the heat of countless battles on long-ago ballfields—Joe Judge, Sam Rice, Ossie Bluege, Muddy Ruel, Roger Peckinpaugh, Tom Zachary, Mike Martin, and Nick Altrock—strained their muscles now to carry him to his final resting place. Clark Griffith, Clyde Milan, Bucky Harris, and the others walked alongside him for the last time.

Surrounded by family and friends, amid the rolling green hills of Maryland he loved to wander with his dogs, Walter Perry Johnson was laid to rest. A small granite marker in the Rockville Union Cemetery gave not the slightest hint that here was anything but the most ordinary of men who had led the most ordinary of lives. Next to it was another marker, identical in all but the inscription: "Hazel Lee Johnson." During his final illness, when it became clear there would be no recovery, Johnson had told the hospital chaplain, The Reverend Edward Duff: "Father, I guess I'm gonna be seeing Hazel . . . it's been a long time."[6]

APPENDIX I

Was He the Greatest?

The Senators beat the Yankees out that season [1933] and faced the Giants in a World Series Damon [Runyon] covered from the press box for his column. But Ring [Lardner] didn't have to pay off any of his losing bets; he died in his East Hampton home on September 25, 1933. A few weeks before that Damon had visited Ring for the last time in a New York hospital. The two great ironists were noted for their long silences. Ring was propped up on his back in bed, reading a magazine, and didn't hear his guest come in. Damon removed his hat, dropped his cigarette to the floor and ground it out, and cleared his throat. Ring's eyes rolled up from the magazine and performed their act of recognition.

"Hello, Damon," he said quietly. The magazine fell on the covers in front of him.

"Hello, Ring," Damon said. He sat down on the edge of the sick man's bed.

Silence fell over the room. Half an hour went by; a nurse took Ring's temperature and pulse and left again; still nothing was said. Ring lay back and glared at the ceiling. Damon sat on the edge of the bed, frowning and staring down at his new shoes, which were too tight and hurt his feet. (Ring's last published piece, an O.O. McIntyre parody that would appear in the New Yorker *a few weeks after his death, would have a line about "Damon Runyon's tight shoes.") Finally Ring made a small, impatient noise and said, "Damon, who was the greatest pitcher in the world?"*

"Matty," Damon said. Ring, Damon knew, was a Walter Johnson man—he'd always favored the "Big Train," even over Matty. Hearing Damon's reply to his question, Ring rolled his eyes again, away from Damon this time, and turned over on his side.

"Goodbye, Damon," he said.

"Goodbye," Damon said.[1]

TOM CLARK, THE WORLD OF DAMON RUNYON

The short answer to the question, "Was Walter Johnson the greatest pitcher who ever lived?" is "Yes." The long answer is also yes—it just takes longer. The following is a brief history of how others, employing various methods of evaluation, have answered the broader question: "Who was the greatest pitcher in baseball history?"

A good place to begin is with Johnson's American League contemporaries, because if they didn't consider him the greatest, the argument ends there. Babe Ruth[2] and Ty Cobb[3] did, for starters. Joe Jackson[4], Napoleon Lajoie[5], Eddie Collins[6], Tris Speaker[7], Sam Crawford[8], and Joe Wood[9] had the same view, as did many others. National Leaguers of Johnson's era, many of whom saw Johnson only rarely if at all, usually picked Christy Mathewson or Grover Cleveland Alexander. And many old-timers swore by such 19th-century giants as Cy Young and Amos Rusie. Some were willing to concede superiority to a "modern," however, including Charley Farrell, a big-league catcher from 1888 to 1905 before becoming a scout.

"For 30 years I have seen pitchers," he said in 1913. "I caught [Jouett] Meekin and Rusie when they were believed to be the greatest of all. I believed in that day that the man would never live who could put more speed on a ball than Rusie, but I am frank to admit that I was mistaken. Walter Johnson is the greatest pitcher I have ever laid my eyes on. The game has never seen his equal. While there have been many other great pitchers, I am positive that Johnson is the greatest of them all."[10]

Among the great writers covering the game during Johnson's time, it's not hard to find those who agreed with Farrell's assessment, including Grantland Rice[11], Fred Lieb[12], Ring Lardner[13], and—contrary to the story leading off this section—Damon Runyon[14].

But individual opinions, even of those who actually observed Johnson and the other pitchers of his era and eras before and since, are just that—opinions, inconclusive in themselves. An impressive list might be compiled of judgments similar to those above, but instead of favoring Johnson they would single out Mathewson or Alexander or Young, or perhaps Grove, Feller, Hubbell, Paige, Spahn, Koufax, Gibson, Seaver, Carlton, Ryan, Clemens, or others. Only a totality of choices can impose any kind of consensus on the question, and for this we must turn to the various polls and surveys conducted over the years:

1936—**The first Hall of Fame election.** This was the first significant vote on the matter, despite its restriction to careers ending after 1900. Two hundred twenty-six members of the Baseball Writers Association of America named ten players each, and two pitchers—Christy Mathewson with 205 votes and Walter Johnson with 189—received the 75% of the vote needed for enshrinement. Cy Young, with 111 votes, and Pete Alexander, with 55, fell short. Although some have seen in Mathewson's greater total a resolution of the question of the greatest pitcher to that point in the game's history, others have noted the disproportionate New York membership in the BBWAA as well as a general sympathy for the tragic circumstances of Big Six's early demise.

1950—***Big-Time Baseball.*** For a book by this name, 164 sportswriters and 76 prominent figures in sports, government, and the arts—from Fred Astaire, Ernest Hemingway, Groucho Marx, and Ronald Reagan to Bill Veeck, Max Carey, and Ralph Kiner—were given one vote for each position. Walter Johnson was the pitcher on 117 of the 240 ballots, while Mathewson was on 72, Alexander 16, and Lefty Grove 11.[15]

1951—The All-America Board of Baseball. Writer, promoter, and sports agent Christy Walsh's All-America Board had been naming annual all-star teams since 1924. To name an all-time team he mailed nominating ballots in 1950 to more than 500 sportswriters, who were to put up six candidates for each position. As in the first Hall of Fame ballot they were restricted to 20th-Century players. Walsh's 12-member All-America Board, consisting of such writers as Joe Williams, John Carmichael, and H.G. Salsinger, and chaired by Connie Mack, then voted on the finalists. Late in 1951 the team was announced, and the next year Walsh's book, *Baseball's Greatest Lineup,* was published based on the results. Nominated were 82 different pitchers, with Walter Johnson getting the most recommendations. Of the six pitchers chosen by the board, Johnson was the only unanimous selection. Mathewson, Young, Alexander, Hubbell, and Grove were the others.[16]

1969—Baseball Centennial team. A committee of Baseball Writers Association members, working from a list of Hall of Famers and nominations from fans, chose an all-time team. Walter Johnson was the right-handed pitcher, followed by Mathewson and Young. Lefty Grove was the left-hander, followed by Koufax and Hubbell.[17]

1987—***Players' Choice.*** For this book a questionnaire was mailed to 5,000 present and retired major-league players and coaches, from which 645 responses were received. In a survey necessarily skewed to players of more recent vintage (only 7% of the respondents were active during the era of 1910–1929), Walter Johnson was the surprising choice for right-handed pitcher, with 17.6% of the votes. Bob Feller was close behind with 16.9%, followed by Bob Gibson with 13.2, Tom Seaver, and Dizzy Dean. Koufax was chosen best left-hander by a wide margin over Grove and Spahn.[18]

In 1994, *Inside Sports* magazine chose Johnson the top pitcher in its selection of the 20 greatest players of all time. He was ranked 6th overall, behind only Ruth, Cobb, Mays, Aaron, and Williams.[19] Also in 1994, *Baseball*

Digest rated Johnson the greatest right-hander (and Koufax the lefty).[20] *Sports Illustrated's* 1992 "Dream Team," on the other hand, had Mathewson the best right-handed pitcher (with Spahn the lefty).[21] Johnson got the nod as top pitcher and was ranked 9th among all players in Maury Allen's 1981 *Baseball's 100.*[22] He was declared the best by Okrent and Lewine in their *The Ultimate Baseball Book* of two years earlier.[23]

Of the various statistical analyses, Ted Oliver's 1944 "pitchers' rating manual," *Kings of the Mound,* which emphasizes wins-above-team, rates Johnson the greatest, followed by Alexander, Young, Mathewson, and Grove.[24] *The Bill James Historical Abstract,* published in 1985, names Johnson the best right-hander (career and peak), followed by Young, Seaver, Mathewson, and Alexander. Grove is the best left-hander, according to James, and also his pick for top pitcher of all time.[25] John Thorn and John Holway's 1987 *The Pitcher* also chooses Grove.[26] *Total Baseball,* first published in 1989 by Thorn and Pete Palmer, rates Johnson the top pitcher and 7th among all players behind Ruth, Cobb, Aaron, Williams, Mays, and Lajoie.[27] Ralph Horton, in his 1993 treatise, *Baseball's Best Pitchers,* also rates Johnson number one,[28] as does John McCarthy in 1994's *Baseball's All-Time Dream Team,* which rebuts the Grove partisans by arguing that any comparison of their magnificent records must take into account the fact that in his big-league career Johnson pitched half again as much as Grove.[29]

Bill James decried the years Grove spent languishing in Baltimore while Jack Dunn held him back from the major leagues, but Grove was no great shakes pitching for a strong second-place club in 1925 when he finally did get a chance, and anyway the "what if" game is silly in this context, and endless. What if Alexander had never touched alcohol? What if Feller hadn't gone to war? What if Satchel Paige had been white? What if Earl Averill hadn't broken Dizzy Dean's toe? What if Rube Waddell had been serious?, etc., etc. Well, what if during his prime years Walter Johnson had pitched for a team with Al Simmons, Jimmie Foxx, Mickey Cochrane and the other great players Grove had behind him? With that crew piling up runs for him, Johnson could have loafed through the majority of his games and saved himself for the close ones. Five hundred wins would have been a certainty, 550 not out of the question. What if Grove had been with the Nationals of Johnson's prime years instead of with one of the great teams in the game's history? Would he have won 250 games? What if Johnson had possessed Grove's fiery temperament? Addressing that question in 1915, Grantland Rice wrote:

> A bunch of ball players the other night were discussing the case of Walter Johnson as a pitcher. It was agreed that Johnson would be almost unhittable, beyond

all range, if he ever adopted the tactics used by most successful slabmen—that is, the policy of shooting a stray shot at the batsman's onion once in a while. This system has kept many pitchers up in the winning ranks, as it has a decided tendency to drive the athlete back from the plate and work upon his nerves.[30]

Taking a unique approach to the "who was greatest?" proposition in 1991 were University of Dayton economists who calculated modern salaries for 250 former major-league stars based on their best 13 years in the case of pitchers and 11 years for hitters. Lou Gehrig topped the list at $7.83 million, with Walter Johnson second at $7.51 million. Babe Ruth came in a surprising third at $7.49 million. At the time of the study, Roger Clemens had the highest current salary of $5.4 million.[31] The turn of the century will undoubtedly be the occasion for a number of 20th-Century "all-time great" teams, and it will be interesting to see who comes out on top.

APPENDIX II

The Best Games

In a career with 417 major-league victories; 110 shutouts, of which 38 were 1–0 cliffhangers; 28 games of two hits or less, and 45 with ten or more strikeouts; seven Opening Day shutouts, and six appearances in two of the greatest World Series ever played; in a career of such sweep, a list of fifty of Walter Johnson's greatest games would still leave out many brilliant performances. Here are fifteen of the best.

1. April 14, 1926—Washington 1, Philadelphia Athletics 0, in 15 innings. This is the game Johnson believed to be his masterpiece, and who's to argue with the master himself? Well into his 39th year and starting his 20th season in the major leagues, the Big Train thrilled a capacity Opening Day crowd in Washington by blanking their 1925 pennant rivals until the home team could score in the bottom of the 15th. The powerful A's managed just six hits, nine of them going down on strikes (five times called), and not one saw second base all day. Knuckleballer Eddie Rommel also went the distance in this classic pitching duel.

2. October 10, 1924—Washington 4, New York Giants 3, in 12 innings. The most dramatic and exciting mound appearance of his—or anyone else's—career. After losing both starts in the World Series he waited 18 years for, and with one day's rest after a 13-hit pounding by the Giants in game five, Johnson is summoned for the ninth inning of a 3–3 tie in the deciding contest. With most of official Washington, including President and Mrs. Coolidge, among the 35,000 electrified spectators, Johnson held McGraw's greatest lineup in check for four innings until the Nationals finally pushed over a run in the bottom of the 12th for the only championship in their history. New York got to him for three hits and three walks, putting men on base in every frame, but Johnson also struck them out five times, always at the crucial moment. Major-league RBI leader Long George Kelly went down swinging with runners on second and third and one out in the ninth inning. In the eleventh Johnson struck out Frankie Frisch with a man on second and one out, then fanned Kelly again with two on to end the inning.

3. **July 1, 1920**—Washington 1, Boston 0. Johnson's only nine-inning no-hitter missed being a perfect game by an error. It was a one-runner game, much rarer than a no-hitter. He struck out ten Red Sox and got six of them to foul out, four to the catcher. In the ninth inning Johnson struck out two left-handed pinch-hitters before Joe Judge's miraculous stop to save the no-hitter. Ironically, Johnson started the game not feeling up to snuff and immediately following it came down with the only serious sore arm of his career. But in between he "never pitched a greater game, to my knowledge," said Bucky Harris.[1]

4. **May 11, 1919**—Washington 0, New York Yankees 0, in 12 innings. In this duel to a draw with spitballer Jack Quinn, Johnson gave up two hits, one walk, and faced a near-minimum 37 batters (two runners were thrown out). Between a single in the first inning and a walk in the tenth, he retired 28 batters in a row. The first legal Sunday game in New York, it was Yankees owner Jacob Ruppert's misunderstanding of the new statute, rather than darkness, that stopped it. New York right fielder George Halas was hitless in five trips to the plate, and after going 0-for-4 the next day abandoned his brief major-league baseball career (22 at-bats). Soon Halas would turn his attention to founding the National Football League.

5. **April 14, 1910**—Washington 3, Philadelphia 0. In the first of his 14 Opening Day games, Johnson held a great Athletics team (American League champions that year and four of the next five) to one hit—on a misplay caused by interference from the roped-in outfield crowd. Among the record throng were President Taft and Vice President Sherman, unwinding at the ballpark after a morning meeting with suffragists who hissed and booed the chief executive for his opposition to the women's vote. In a hastily-arranged ceremony that was to become one of America's most hallowed traditions, Taft tossed a ball to the pitcher—Walter Johnson—to start the game. But instead of taking the ball to the mound he put it aside and the next day sent it to the White House, where the president inscribed: "To Walter Johnson, with the hope that he may continue to be as formidable as in yesterday's game. William H. Taft."

6. **September 25, 1910**—Washington 3, St. Louis 0. At the other end of Johnson's first great season, an even better performance than the opener: one hit, no walks, 11 strikeouts. The first of two one-runner games in his career, this one also fell shy of a perfect game by the slimmest of margins—a scratch bounder that shortstop George McBride missed "by an inch or two," the *Washington Post* reported.

7. **May 15, 1918**—Washington 1, Chicago 0, in 18 innings. The longest shutout victory ever (equalled by Carl Hubbell in 1933). Johnson blanked the 1917 World Champions for the equivalent of two full games. Lefty Williams, one of the eight Black

Sox barred for life in the 1919 scandal, also went the distance in this peculiar marathon in which nine players were used by each side and not a single error was committed.

8. SEPTEMBER 7, 1908—Washington 4, New York 0. This sparkling Labor Day two-hitter over Jack Chesbro, in which Johnson walked none and struck out five, qualifies for the list because it was his third shutout in four days.

9. AUGUST 28, 1913—Boston 1, Washington 0, in 11 innings. Mentioned for years afterwards as Johnson's greatest game. In the first 10 innings the only baserunner for the World Champion Red Sox was Steve Yerkes with a single in the second. Then 26 straight batters went down before Yerkes singled again with one out in the 11th, reaching third when the ball went through center fielder Clyde Milan's legs. A fielder's choice and another hit ended the game, in which Johnson walked none and struck out ten, threw 17 strikes before a ball was called, threw 69 strikes out of 96 pitches, struck out Hall-of-Famer Harry Hooper three times (twice on three pitches), and struck out five in a row. The loss ended Johnson's 14-game winning streak and killed a chance to better his own (and Joe Wood's) record of 16 set a year earlier. Of Milan's disastrous error, Johnson said only: "Well, you know Zeb doesn't do that very often."

10. MAY 23, 1924—Washington 4, Chicago 0. The pennant race hadn't begun in earnest yet, but it must have gladdened his mates to see the return of Johnson's full powers in his 18th season after three years of steady recovery from an arm injury. One hit, one walk, a career-high 14 strikeouts (six in a row), 28 batters faced.

11. OCTOBER 11, 1925—Washington 4, Pittsburgh 0. For the second time in the World Series, Johnson shut down a vaunted Pirates attack, the major-league leaders in batting and slugging average, runs, RBIs, doubles, triples, and stolen bases. Of their six hits only two made it out of the infield. The achievement of a prized World Series shutout (the oldest pitcher ever to do that, at 37 years, 11 months) came before a Griffith Stadium crowd of 36,000 and gave the Nationals a seemingly insurmountable 3–1 edge in games. After pulling a leg muscle in the third inning while running the bases, Johnson pitched even better than before—proving himself, in the words of Shirley Povich, "the best pitcher on one leg as well as two."[2]

12. MAY 30, 1927—Washington 3, Boston 0. The first outing of Johnson's 21st campaign after breaking a leg in spring training. His fastball didn't make the trip to Boston for this Memorial Day, but you'd never know it from the result: three hits, no walks, 29 batters faced. It was the last of Johnson's incredible total of 110 complete-game shutouts, a record as safe as any in the game.

13. **August 2, 1907**—Detroit 3, Washington 2. Exactly one week after arriving in Washington from an Idaho town league, teenager Johnson forced the powerhouse Tigers of Cobb and Crawford to bunt for their only run in the first seven innings. Pulled for a pinch-hitter in the ninth inning after giving up two runs on six hits, Johnson's major-league debut left Detroit's ace Wild Bill Donovan predicting: "If nothing happens to that fellow, he will be a greater pitcher in two years than Mathewson ever dared to be."[3]

14. **June 9, 1907**—Weiser 11, Emmett 0. The only perfect game Johnson ever pitched at any level, this second no-hitter in a row might have been the final straw that made Washington manager Joe Cantillon decide to go after him. Eighteen Emmett "Prune-pickers" went down on strikes.

15. **April 15, 1905**—Fullerton Union (California) High School 0, Santa Ana High School 0, in 15 innings. The 17-year-old Johnson had already shown promise in a handful of games for the Olinda Oil Wells semipros, but this was the first real indication of what was to come. Twenty-seven of the Southern California high school champion Santa Ana Saints went down on strikes before his sweeping sidearm deliveries, Johnson's highest total ever. More than 50 years later, Santa Ana's captain and cleanup hitter, Garland Ross, still vividly recalled the schoolboy Walter Johnson: "For the most part, we just went up to the plate, took our three swings, and walked back to the bench," he said. "I remember we all kept saying to the next batter, 'he ain't got a thing but a fast ball' and that was true. But what a fast ball! It came up to the plate like a pea shot out of a cannon."[4]

APPENDIX III

Numbers

SCHEDULE A

WALTER JOHNSON

Career Pitching Summary, Washington A.L. 1907–1927

																						RELIEF						
Year	**W**	**L**	**T**	**PCT**	**ShO**	**G**	**GS**	**CG**	**IP**	**R**	**ER**	**ERA**	**AB**	**H**	**OBA**	**HR**	**SO**	**BB**	**HBP**	**WP**	**BK**	**G**	**GF**	**IP**	**ERA**	**W**	**L**	**SV**
1907	5	9	0	.357	2	14	12	11	110+	35	23	1.88	408	100	.245	1	70	20	2	4	0	2	2	5+	3.38	0	2	0
1908	14	14	1	.500	6	36	30	23	256+	75	47	1.65	921	194	.211	0	160	53	11	13	1	6	6	17	4.24	0	1	1
1909	13	25	0	.342	4	40	36	27	296+	112	73	2.22	1120	247	.221	1	164	84	15	12	0	4	3	12+	3.55	1	2	1
1910	25	17	1	.595	8	**45**	**42**	**38**	**370**	92	56	1.36	1278	**262**	.205	1	**313**	76	13	**21**	0	3	3	8+	2.08	1	1	1
1911	25	13	0	.658	**6**	40	37	**36**	322+	119	68	1.90	1228	292	.238	8	207	70	8	**17**	0	3	3	6	0.00	1	1	1
1912	33	12	2	.733	7	50	37	34	369	89	57	**1.39**	1321	259	**.196**	2	**303**	76	16	11	0	13	13	51	0.35	6	2	2
1913	**36**	7	1	**.837**	**11**	48	36	**29**	**346**	56	44	**1.14**	**1239**	232	**.187**	**9**	**243**	38	9	3	0	12	11	35	0.26	7	0	2
1914	**28**	18	1	.609	**9**	**51**	**40**	**33**	**371+**	88	71	1.72	**1321**	**287**	.217	3	**225**	74	11	**14**	1	11	9	27+	4.55	4	3	1
1915	**27**	13	1	.675	**7**	47	**39**	**35**	**336+**	83	58	1.55	**1205**	258	.214	1	**203**	56	19	7	0	8	8	8+	1.04	2	0	4
1916	**25**	20	2	.556	3	48	38	**36**	**369+**	105	78	1.90	**1319**	**290**	.220	0	**228**	82	9	9	0	10	10	29+	1.82	4	3	1
1917	23	16	1	.590	8	47	34	30	326	105	80	2.21	1173	248	.211	3	**188**	68	12	8	0	13	12	39+	1.82	5	1	3
1918	**23**	13	0	.639	**8**	39	29	29	326	71	46	**1.27**	1149	241	.210	2	**162**	70	8	8	0	10	10	29+	0.92	3	4	3
1919	20	14	1	.588	**7**	39	29	27	290+	73	48	**1.49**	1073	235	**.219**	0	**147**	51	7	4	1	10	10	21+	2.53	2	4	2
1920	8	10	0	.444	4	21	15	12	143+	68	50	3.13	549	135	.246	5	78	27	5	5	1	6	6	22	4.50	1	2	3
1921	17	14	1	.548	1	35	32	25	264	122	103	3.51	1007	265	.263	7	**143**	92	2	7	0	3	2	6	4.50	1	1	1
1922	15	16	0	.484	4	41	31	23	280	115	93	2.99	1060	283	.267	8	105	99	7	3	0	10	9	25	3.24	1	1	4
1923	17	12	0	.586	3	42	34	18	261	112	101	3.48	977	263	.269	9	**130**	73	**20**	2	0	8	8	12	3.00	1	2	4
1924	**23**	7	0	**.767**	**6**	38	38	20	277+	97	84	**2.72**	1041	233	**.224**	10	**158**	77	10	4	0	0	0	0	—	0	0	0
1925	20	7	0	.741	3	30	29	16	229	95	78	3.07	867	217	**.250**	7	108	78	7	1	0	1	1	2	0.00	1	0	0
1926	15	16	0	.484	2	33	33	22	260+	120	105	3.63	986	259	.263	13	125	73	5	2	0	0	0	0	—	0	0	0
1927	5	6	0	.455	1	18	15	7	107+	70	61	5.10	407	113	.278	7	48	26	7	1	0	3	2	7	5.14	0	0	0
21yrs	417	279	12	.599	110	802	666	531	5914+	1902	1424	2.17	21649	4913	.227	97	3508	1363	203	156	4	136	128	366	2.19	41	30	34
World Series																												
1924	1	2		.333	0	3	2	2	24	10	6	2.25	89	30	.337	3	20	11	1	1	0	1	1	4	0.00	1	0	0
1925	2	1		.667	1	3	3	3	26	10	6	2.08	99	26	.263	1	15	4	2	0	0	0	0	0	—	0	0	0
2 yrs	3	3		.500	1	6	5	5	50	20	12	2.16	188	56	.298	4	35	15	3	1	0	1	1	4	0.00	1	0	0

Sources: Frank J. Williams, *The Baseball Encyclopedia, Total Baseball*

Bold = Led League

WALTER JOHNSON
Major League Managerial Record, 1929–1935

Year	Club	Pos	Won	Lost	Pct
1929	Washington	5	71	81	.467
1930	Washington	2	94	60	.610
1931	Washington	3	92	62	.597
1932	Washington	3	93	61	.604
1933	Cleveland	4	49	51	.490
1934	Cleveland	3	85	69	.552
1935	Cleveland	3	46	48	.489
7 Years			530	432	.551

WALTER JOHNSON
Career Batting and Fielding Summary, Washington A.L. 1907–1927

																		PINCH-HIT		FIELDING					
Year	G	AB	H	BA	SA	1B	2B	3B	HR	BB	HP	TB	R	RBI	SH	SB	SO	AB	H	POS	PO	A	E	DP	PCT
1907	14	36	4	.111	.167	3	0	1	0	1	–	6	3	1	4	0	–	0	0	P	5	20	3	1	.893
1908	36	79	13	.165	.253	8	3	2	0	6	–	20	7	5	5	0	–	0	0	P	4	56	4	3	.938
1909	40	101	13	.129	.188	9	3	0	1	1	–	19	6	6	3	0	–	0	0	P	15	73	7	1	.927
1910	45	137	24	.175	.277	15	6	1	2	4	0	38	14	12	1	2	–	0	0	P	23	90	6	3	.950
1911	42	128	30	.234	.344	21	5	3	1	0	0	44	18	15	6	1	–	2	1	P	14	95	4	8	.965
1912	55	144	38	.264	.403	26	6	4	2	7	0	58	16	20	6	2	–	5	0	P	15	93	4	4	.964
1913	54	134	35	.261	.433	22	5	6	2	5	0	58	12	14	1	2	14	5	2	P-OF(1)	21	82	0	7	1.000
1914	55	136	30	.217	.326	22	4	1	3	10	0	45	23	16	5	2	27	3	0	P-OF(1)	30	102	5	8	.964
1915	64	147	34	.231	.374	21	7	4	2	8	0	55	14	17	5	0	34	12	2	P-OF(4)	23	95	6	7	.952
1916	58	142	32	.232	.324	26	2	4	1	11	0	46	13	7	4	0	28	9	2	P	17	72	6	2	.937
1917	57	130	33	.254	.362	20	12	1	0	9	0	47	15	15	2	1	30	9	1	P	16	82	0	2	1.000
1918	65	150	40	.267	.367	31	4	4	1	9	0	55	10	18	4	2	18	20	5	P-OF(4)	17	70	2	5	.978
1919	56	125	24	.192	.272	19	1	3	1	12	0	34	13	8	4	1	17	14	3	P-OF(3)	16	69	1	6	.988
1920	33	64	17	.266	.422	12	1	3	1	3	0	27	7	8	2	0	12	11	2	P-OF(2)	5	28	1	0	.971
1921	38	111	30	.270	.333	23	7	0	0	6	0	37	10	10	2	0	14	2	0	P	4	51	1	2	.982
1922	43	108	22	.204	.259	18	3	0	1	2	0	28	8	15	2	0	12	2	0	P	11	66	0	2	1.000
1923	42	93	18	.194	.290	12	3	3	0	4	0	27	11	13	6	0	15	0	0	P	13	51	2	7	.970
1924	39	113	32	.283	.389	22	9	0	1	3	1	44	18	14	2	0	11	1	0	P	9	53	0	2	1.000
1925	36	97	42	.433	.577	33	6	1	2	3	1	56	12	20	6	0	6	6	2	P	5	37	0	2	1.000
1926	35	103	20	.194	.272	14	5	0	1	3	0	28	6	12	3	0	11	2	0	P	11	38	1	1	.982
1927	26	46	16	.348	.522	12	2	0	2	3	0	24	6	10	1	0	4	7	1	P	5	25	0	3	1.000
21 Yrs	933	2324	547	.235	.342	388	94	41	24	110	2	795	242	256	74	13	253	110	21	P-OF	279	1348	53	76	.968
World Series																									
1924	3	9	1	.111	.111	1	0	0	0	0	0	1	0	0	0	0	0	0	0	P	1	4	1	2	.833
1925	3	11	1	.091	.091	1	0	0	0	0	0	1	0	0	0	0	3	0	0	P	0	4	0	0	1.000
2 Yrs	6	20	2	.100	.100	2	0	0	0	0	0	2	0	0	0	0	3	0	0	P	1	8	1	2	.900

Sources: *TotalBaseball, BaseballEncyclopedia*

SCHEDULE B

MAJOR LEAGUE RECORDS

21*	Seasons one club, pitcher (1907–27)
21	Seasons one club, consecutive, pitcher (1907–27)
9	Seasons 300+ innings, consecutive
9*	Games won vs one club, season (Chicago, 1912)
110	Shutouts won
38	Shutouts won 1–0
23	Shutouts won vs one club (Philadelphia)
7	Shutouts won opening game
2*	Seasons 10+ shutouts
4*	Seasons leading major leagues, shutouts
2*	Seasons leading major leagues, shutouts, consecutive
7*	Seasons leading league, shutouts
3*	Seasons leading league, shutouts, consecutive
18*	Innings shutout game (May 18, 1918)
8	Seasons leading major leagues, strikeouts
12	Seasons leading league, strikeouts
8	Seasons leading league, strikeouts, consecutive
18*	Seasons 100+ strikeouts, league
4*	Strikeouts, inning (April 15, 1911)
15	Strikeouts, game, relief
0	Home runs allowed, fewest, season, most innings (371, 1916)
65	Shutouts lost
26	Shutouts lost 1–0
5*	Shutouts lost vs one club, season (Chicago, 1909)
5	Shutouts lost, month (July, 1909)
203	Hit batsmen
4*	Wild pitches, inning (September 21, 1914)
41	Triples, pitcher
.433	Batting average, season, pitcher (1925)

Note: Walter Johnson holds the 20th-century major-league records for innings pitched (5,914), batsmen faced (23,433), at bats (21,649), complete games (531), wins (417), and shutouts (110).

* = tied

AMERICAN LEAGUE RECORDS

5,914	Innings
9	Seasons 300+ innings
18	Seasons 200+ innings
5*	Seasons leading league, innings
4	Seasons leading league, innings, consecutive
23,433	Batsmen faced
5	Seasons leading league, batsmen faced
4*	Seasons leading league, batsmen faced, consecutive
21,649	At bats
4*	Seasons leading league, at bats and consecutive
666	Games started
531	Complete games
6	Seasons leading league, complete games
4	Seasons leading league, complete games, consecutive
1.14	Earned run average, lowest, season, 300+ innings
417	Games won
66	Games won vs one club (Detroit)
16*	Games won, season, consecutive
6*	Seasons leading league, games won
4	Seasons leading league, games won, consecutive
2*	Seasons 30+ games won and consecutive
12	Seasons 20+ games won
10	Seasons 20+ games won, consecutive
55⅔	Innings scoreless, consecutive
28	Batsmen retired, consecutive, extra-inning game (May 11, 1919)
3,508	Strikeouts
7*	Seasons 200+ strikeouts, consecutive
279	Games lost
4,913	Hits allowed
10	Shutouts lost, season (1909)
2,324	At bats, pitcher
542	Hits, pitcher
242	Runs, pitcher
269	Putouts, pitcher
1,606	Chances, pitcher
1,337	Assists, pitcher
1.000	Fielding percentage, season, most chances, pitcher (103, 1913)
3	Seasons leading league, fielding percentage, pitcher
0	Errors, fewest, season, most chances, pitcher (103, 1913)

WORLD SERIES RECORDS

3* Games started, Series (1925)
3* Complete games, Series (1925)
2* Games lost, Series (1924)
30 Hits allowed, Series (1924)
11* Walks allowed, Series (1924)
2* Double plays, Series (1924)
9* Runs allowed, game (October 15, 1925)
15 Hits allowed, game (October 15, 1925)
8 Doubles allowed, game (October 15, 1925)
9 Extra-base hits allowed, game (October 15, 1925)
25 Total bases allowed, game (October 15, 1925)
Oldest pitcher, shutout game (37 years, 11 months, October 11, 1925)
Source: *The Book of Baseball Records,* Elias Sports Bureau, 1994 edition
* = tied

SCHEDULE C

ANALYSIS OF CAREER GAMES

	WON-LOST		VS ALL CLUBS				
				Combined	Home	Road	Shutouts
Total	417	279	Detroit	66 - 42	35 - 20	31 - 22	12
Starter	376	249	Chicago	63 - 39	37 - 16	26 - 23	14
Relief	41	30	NewYork	61 - 38	29 - 15	32 - 23	21
Complete	339	187	Philadelphia	59 - 39	36 - 16	23 - 23	23
Home	233	117	Cleveland	59 - 41	30 - 18	29 - 23	12
Road	184	162	St. Louis	56 - 37	33 - 16	23 - 21	13
Extra-inning	50	38	Boston	53 - 43	33 - 16	20 - 27	15
One-run	145	131		417 -279	233 -117	184 -162	110
Two-run	68	50					
1-0	38	26					
2-1	38	26					

Winning streaks of 16, 14, 13, 10, and 10 games in a season, 25 streaks of 5 or more.

16 straight wins over Chicago (1912–14), 15 over St. Louis (1910–12), 12 over Detroit (1912–14) and New York (1912–14).

28 games of two hits or less, 24 of them 9+-inning complete games: 2 no-hitters (one of seven innings), 8 one-hitters (one of six innings), 18 two-hitters (one of eight innings, one of five innings); also 25 three-hitters and 62 four-hitters for a total of 115 games of four hits or less.

45 games of 10 or more strikeouts: 35 won, 8 lost, 2 tied.

Source: Frank J. Williams

Notes

CHAPTER 1

1. Walter Johnson, "My Pitching Years," syndicated newspaper series, *Washington Times*, January-February 1925.
2. Donald Smith, "Minnie Johnson Nears 100," *Washington Star*, March 5, 1967.
3. F.C. Lane, "75,000 Pitches Without a Sore Arm!" *Baseball Magazine*, August 1934.
4. Johnson, "A Quarter Million Strong," *American Legion Magazine*, n.d., Johnson family archives; Johnson, "My Twenty Years On the Mound," as told to Lillian Barker, syndicated newspaper series, *Washington Post*, November-December 1924.
5. Roger Treat, *Walter Johnson, King of the Pitchers* (New York: Julian Messner, 1948).
6. Johnson, "My Pitching Years."
7. Treat, *Walter Johnson, King of the Pitchers.*
8. Johnson, "My Twenty Years on the Mound"; Lane, "75,000 Pitches Without a Sore Arm!"
9. Vincent X. Flaherty, "Life Story of Walter Johnson," *The Sporting News Baseball Register*, 1947.
10. Johnson, "A Page From My Book of Experience," *The Blue Diamond Magazine*, July 1924.
11. Treat, *Walter Johnson, King of the Pitchers.*
12. Flaherty, "Life Story of Walter Johnson"; Johnson, "My Pitching Years." *Baseball Magazine* editor F.C. Lane, after staying with the Johnsons for a week in 1915, wrote: "Johnson's father and mother are quiet, wholesome people of the type that informs the backbone of the nation. There is nothing in the least affected in their open hospitality." F.C. Lane, "At Coffeyville with Walter Johnson," *Baseball Magazine*, April 1915.
13. Clipping, n.d., scrapbook VIII(1924). Johnson explained his childhood behavior this way: "I guess I don't deserve any special credit for not running wild when I was a kid, because that kind of thing never seemed to appeal to me. I didn't get any kick out of the idea, as they say nowadays. Then as I got older I was working too hard." Frank Heaton, clipping, n.d., scrapbook VIII(1924).
14. Johnson, "My Pitching Years."
15. Johnson, "Some of My Early Experience," n.d., manuscript, Johnson family archives.

16. Johnson, "My Pitching Years."
17. *Boston Globe*, September 9, 1912.
Walter Johnson seems to have been the only one in his family so blessed, although his uncle, Ray Perry (who was actually two years younger) did play for the Olinda Oil Wells several years after Johnson. Of his father, he said: "[Frank Johnson] was not a ballplayer, [but] I have seen him throw and his swing was with that naturalness which surely indicates pitching ability. It may be that my pitching is a direct inheritance. If it was, it was apparently limited to me, for my three brothers, though rabid baseball fans, have never shown any inclination toward playing the game themselves either in the amateur or professional ranks." Johnson, "My Twenty Years on the Mound."
18. *Humboldt Union*, April 13, 1901. April 6, 1901: "Severe Drought." July 27, 1901: "No rain yet to do much good. The damage in Allen county from the drought is very large."
19. Lane, "75,000 Pitches Without a Sore Arm!"
20. Johnson, "Some of My Early Experience."
21. *Humboldt Union*, December 19, 1946.
22. *Humboldt Union*, March 9, 1901; *Kansas City Star Magazine*, August 25, 1974.
23. *Chanute Tribune*, December 12, 1946. Dave Woods: "Johnson was a good pitcher then, but we never dreamed that he would be the most famous hurler in the world."
24. Johnson, "My Pitching Years": "It wasn't a very good indication of my future ideas on discipline, but as my brother, Leslie, remarked in later years, it was the only time I ever 'laid down' in the pitcher's box." See also *Humboldt Union*, December 19, 1946.
25. Johnson, "My Life So Far," *Baseball Magazine*, August 1912.
26. *Humboldt Union*, November 16, 1901.
27. Johnson, "My Twenty Years on the Mound": "We had had a bad year in Kansas. There is nothing like a drought that makes a farmer think of moving to another part of the world to try his luck"; *Humboldt Union*, March 8, 1902: "Escape inclement weather by joining the homeseekers excursion to California, via Santa Fe route. Rate $25 from Humboldt."
28. *Humboldt Union*, April 26, 1902; Johnson, "My Pitching Years."
29. Lawrence Ritter, *The Glory of Their Times* (New York: Morrow, 1966).
30. *Historical Guide to Carbon Canyon Regional Park* (Santa Ana, California: Environmental Management Agency, 1975).
31. Johnson, "What I Think About Hunting," *Baseball Magazine*, June 1913.
32. Nora Brown McMillan, "Memories of Early Olinda," *Historical Guide to Carbon Canyon Park.*
33. *Anaheim Bulletin*, September 6, 1957.

34. McMillan, "Memories of Early Olinda."
35. Mildred Yorba MacArthur, *Orange County Historical Volume III* (Whittier, California: The Historical Volume and Reference Works, 1963); Johnson, "My Pitching Years"; Earl Gustkey, "When the Big Train Ran On a Rural Track," *Los Angeles Times*, June 2, 1970.
36. Steve Grimley, "Johnson Remembered As Baseball's Hardest Thrower," *Orange County Register*, February 12, 1978; MacArthur, "Long Arm From Olinda," *Westways*, October 1978.
37. Joseph C. Burke, "How Walter Johnson Got His Start In Baseball," *Cincinnati Enquirer*, September 20, 1913; Johnson, "My Pitching Years."
38. Johnson, "A Quarter Million Strong."
39. Johnson, clipping, n.d., scrapbook XVIII(1927).
40. Burke, "How Walter Johnson Got His Start in Baseball"; Johnson, "My Pitching Years."
41. Johnson, "My Pitching Years"; Johnson, "Some of My Early Experience"; Gustkey, "When The Big Train Ran on a Rural Track": Hollis Knowlton (Johnson's high school teammate): "I can remember he played catcher with no mask and played about 10 feet behind the plate. I got on first and tried to steal once. He threw me out by 30 feet."
42. Johnson, "My Pitching Years"; Johnson, "Some of My Early Experience"; *Washington Herald*, July 27, 1907.
43. Grantland Rice, *Washington Star*, December 11, 1946.
44. Johnson, "The Meanest Thing In Baseball," *Baseball Magazine*, September 1917.
45. Johnson, "My Pitching Years."
46. Burke, "How Walter Johnson Got His Start in Baseball"; Johnson, "My Pitching Years."
47. Burke, "How Walter Johnson Got His Start in Baseball"; Bob Guild, "Anaheim Shares Claim to 'Big Train' With Olinda," *Anaheim Bulletin,* March 11, 1939;
48. Burke, "How Walter Johnson Got His Start in Baseball."
49. "The Lucky Thirteen," *Fullerton Union High School yearbook*, June 14, 1905; McMillan, "Memories of Early Olinda"; Gustkey, "When the Big Train Ran on a Rural Track"; Johnson, "My Pitching Years."
50. MacArthur, *Orange County Historical Volume III.*
51. *Cleveland Plain Dealer*, August 17, 1919; Johnson, "My Life So Far"; Johnson, "My Pitching Years."

    According to teammate Hollis Knowlton, it took the intervention of Fullerton Union's principal for Johnson to pitch for the school: "Downey was beating us 6–0 one day and I said to our captain, Bob McFadden—we had no coaches in those days—'Why not let Walter pitch some?' Well, he said to me, 'I'm the captain here.' Later, I talked to our school principal, Prof. W.R. Carpenter. He said that after school one day he'd come down by the school barn and let Walter pitch some to him. Walter threw a half-dozen balls at him at normal speed and then he threw a hard one and it knocked Prof. Carpenter's glove off. He said to Bob McFadden, who was standing there, 'Better let this boy pitch, Bob.'" Gustkey, "When The Big Train Ran On a Rural Track."

52. "Walter Johnson, One of Nation's Top Ballplayers, From Fullerton," clipping, n.d., Fullerton Library files; MacArthur, *Orange County Historical Volume III.* According to Bob McFadden, the game almost didn't take place because of Collins:

> We didn't have a catcher who could catch Walter's fastball. So we found a grammar school boy, Collins, who could catch it—most of the time. Well, Santa Ana got wind of the fact before the game that we had a grammar school boy on our team and at first threatened not to play us. But we talked them into it and we played the game.— Gustkey, "When the Big Train Ran on a Rural Track."

53. Burke, "How Walter Johnson Got His Start in Baseball."
54. *Anaheim Gazette*, April 6 and 13, May 18, June 1, 1905.
55. Johnson, "Some of My Early Experience."
56. *Anaheim Gazette*, July 20, August 3, 1905.
57. MacArthur, *Orange County Historical Volume III.*
58. Flaherty, "Life Story of Walter Johnson"; *Dearborn Independent*, October 6, 1923; Joe Scherrer, "Today is Special For Big Train's Brother," *Corpus Christi Times*, April 13, 1953; Eddie West, "Walter Johnson Went Up 50 Years Ago Today," *Santa Ana Register,* August 11, 1957.
It's not clear exactly when or for how long Johnson attended the business school. Eddie West, whose father played with Johnson for the Santa Ana team several years later, wrote that Johnson attended the business school while pitching for Guy Meats's Olive team in the fall of 1906. When Johnson went to Weiser, Idaho, in March, 1907, it was reported that he "returns from the west, where he has been attending school." *Idaho Daily Statesman*, April 9, 1907.
59. MacArthur, *Orange County Historical Volume III.*
60. *Anaheim Gazette*, October 19, 1905.
61. $25 per game—Burke, "How Walter Johnson Got His Start in Baseball"; "$1.50 a day"—MacArthur, *Orange County Historical Volume III.*
62. Burke, "How Walter Johnson Got His Start in Baseball"; Johnson, "My Pitching Years"; Abe Kemp, clipping, n.d., scrapbook X(1924).
63. Complete statistics for Walter Johnson's California semipro games, including a game-by-game listing and more detailed account of his experiences there, can be found in "The California Comet?: Walter Johnson in the Golden State" by Henry W. Thomas and Charles W. Carey in *Grandstand Baseball Annual 1995*,

available from P.O. Box 4203, Downey, CA 90241–1203. The following is a yearly summary:

( )= number of games for which that statistic is available

Year	G	GP	W	L	T	IP	R	H	BB	K	AB	H	PO	A	E
1904	1	1				3				6					
1905	31	23	12	9	1	206(22)	79(22)	124(18)	27 (16)	182(18)	89	9 (23)	47	36	3 (23)
1906	17	14	12	2		124	36	44	8	113	31	7 (8)	8	0	0 (8)
1907	19	17	9	5	3	151	26	68	16	196	55	16 (18)	7	31	3(19)
1908	13	12	4	6	2	115	34	48(11)	16 (11)	133(11)	46	9	5	26	1(12)
1909	17	15	12	3		134	41	91	26	122	55	14	2	31	3
1910	8	8	8	0		72	5	21	2 (6)	97	15	6	6	12	1
Total	106	90	57	25	6	805(89)	221(88)	396(83)	95 (80)	849(83)	291	61 (87)	75	136	11(85)

64. Johnson, "My Pitching Years"; *Fullerton Tribune*, April 19, 1906; *Boston Globe*, September 27, 1912.
65. Johnson, "My Pitching Years."

CHAPTER 2

1. Johnson, "My Pitching Years."
2. Ibid.
3. *Portland Oregonian*, April 20, 1906.
4. There has been some question about whether this game—Johnson's only appearance in the minor leagues prior to his ascension to the major leagues—was official, but the evidence seems clear that it was not. The contest was not on the league schedule, according to local papers and the May 5, 1906, issue of *The Sporting News*. *Sporting Life* reported the Tacoma-Grays Harbor games of April 28 and 29 and May 1, but the April 30 contest is conspicuously absent. It was not included in the standings compiled by the *Tacoma Ledger*, and on April 29 the paper reported: "Monday afternoon the Tacoma and Grays Harbor teams will play an exhibition game for the benefit of the Red Cross ... The game will not count in the championship series. President Lucas stated last night that while exhibition games are contrary to the rules of the league, the object of the relief work is so worthy that it was decided to waive all objections and help the good cause."
5. *Portland Oregonian*, April 30, 1906.
6. Johnson, "Some Experiences of a Speed King," *St. Nicholas Magazine*, October 1914.
7. *Portland Oregonian*, May 4–6, 1906. May 5: "League Will Hold"; May 6: "Its Future Assured."
8. Johnson, "My Pitching Years."
9. Johnson, "My Twenty Years on the Mound."
10. Johnson, "My Pitching Years." Johnson is unequivocal here about how he happened to go to Weiser. But he gave Lillian Barker a different account and there is support for this other version in a letter from Weiser manager J.B. Coakley to the *Weiser Signal* in 1924. Here are those accounts:

Johnson: "[Jack] Barnett[sic] felt worse than I did. He helped me scout around for a berth somewhere in the Northwest. He heard that Weiser, Idaho was a live ball town and was in the market for a pitcher. So he telegraphed to that city stating that he knew a man, and if they wanted him they could get him by sending transportation and an advance of $50. It didn't take long for them to answer."—Johnson, "My Twenty Years on the Mound."

Coakley: "Here is the true story of Johnson's coming to Weiser: I was manager of the Weiser team in May, 1906. Reading an article in the *Portland Oregonian* that on account of the earthquake in California, ballplayers of that section were arriving in Portland, Seattle and Tacoma looking for positions and thinking this is a good chance to get a battery to compete with Caldwell and Boise, who had strong teams, I wrote to the *Oregonian* asking them to put me in communication with some of the players. I received a telegram asking what I would pay for a battery. I answered giving my terms and received another telegram stating terms accepted and battery on the road. This can be verified by files of the telegraph company."—*Weiser Signal*, n.d., scrapbook X(1924).

11. Betty Derig, *Weiser, The Way It Was* (Weiser, Idaho: Rambler Press, 1987).
12. Will Wedge, "Weiser Was Wild Ball Burg," *New York Sun*, May 9, 1924; Johnson, "My Pitching Years."
13. Herold Ruel, "Catching a Speed King," newspaper series, n.d., scrapbook XVIII (1927).
14. Johnson, "My Pitching Years."
15. *Weiser World*, April 13, 1906: "Mr. James Coakley, manager of the Weiser team, said [at the league's organizational meeting in Caldwell] that the league will be composed of amateur players from their respective localities and that no professionals will be employed." But soon Coakley would be casting about for professionals cut loose from their teams by the earthquake. He resigned as Weiser manager on May 13.
16. Clipping, Reno, Nevada, newspaper, n.d., scrapbook XV(1925).
17. Johnson, "My Pitching Years."
18. *Weiser Signal*, June 13, 1906.
19. Johnson, "My Pitching Years."
20. *Weiser Signal*, June 13, 1906.
21. Johnson, "My Pitching Years."
22. *Weiser Signal*, July 7, 1906; *Emmett Index*, July 5, 1906.
    Senator Borah is perhaps best remembered for having declared, after Germany's invasion of Poland in September 1939: "If only I could have talked with Hitler, all this might have been avoided." Charles Krauthammer, "Peace in Our Time," *Washington Post*, June 24, 1994.
23. *Weiser Signal*, July 9, 1906.
24. *Weiser Signal*, July 11, 1906.
    A complete statistical listing of Johnson's Idaho games as well as a more detailed account of his experiences there can be found in "The Weiser Wonder: Walter

Johnson in Idaho" by Henry W. Thomas in *Grandstand Baseball Annual 1995*, available from P.O. Box 4203, Downey, CA 90241–1203.

25. MacArthur, *Orange County Historical Volume III.*
26. Walter H. Nagle, *Five Straight Errors On Ladies Day* (Caldwell, Idaho: Caxton Printers, 1965).
27. Johnson, "My Pitching Years"; "Some Experiences of a Speed King"; "Some of My Early Experience."
28. There is some evidence that a tryout with the Giants had been prearranged. In its account of a 1–0 Pasadena victory over Anaheim on March 3, 1907, the *Pasadena Daily News* called Johnson "the lanky twirler who is to be given a tryout by 'Mugsy' McGraw."
29. Johnson, "My Pitching Years"; "My Twenty Years on the Mound."
30. Shirley Povich, *The Washington Senators, An Informal History* (New York: G.P. Putnam's Sons, 1954). There is little doubt that this much-used "quote" is apocryphal, but it's too good not to include.
31. John F. Carmichael, *My Greatest Day in Baseball*, (New York: A.S. Barnes and Company, 1945).
32. Wedge, "Weiser Was Wild Ball Burg."
33. Johnson, "What I Think About Hunting," *Baseball Magazine,* June 1913; Jim Poore, "Former Batboy Still Remembers Big Train Johnson," *Idaho Daily Statesman*, August 11, 1981.
34. Johnson, "Some of My Early Experience."
35. *Idaho Daily Statesman*, April 9, 1907.
36. Johnson, "My Life So Far."
37. The scoreless innings streak almost didn't get off the ground. On May 12 at Mountain Home he gave up three runs in the first inning, but a fierce wind and dust storm made play impossible and the game was cancelled after the top of the second.
38. Johnson, "Some Experiences of a Speed King."
39. H.F. Manchester, "When Walt Johnson Pitched As Dark Horse For 'Hicks'," *Boston Herald,* May 9, 1926; Johnson, "Some of My Early Experience."
40. Manchester, Ibid; *Weiser Signal*, June 5, 1907; *Idaho Daily Statesman*, June 4, 1907; *Nampa Leader*, June 4, 1907.
41. *Weiser Signal*, June 5, 1907.
42. *Idaho Daily Statesman*, June 10, 1907. Ironically, in 1913 Walter Johnson did break Jack Coombs's record of 53 (or 52—sources differ) consecutive scoreless innings, set in 1910.

    Tacoma manager Mike Lynch must have blanched reading this account in his local paper:

    Idaho Boy-Pitcher Astonishes Fans—Record of 57 Straight Scoreless Innings: His name is Walter Johnson. He is 19 years of age and is tall and strong as an ox. He has arms that for length would put Fitzsimmons to blush. The clubs he has pitched against are not amateurs. The clubs in the Idaho league are exceptionally strong. With proper care of himself Johnson should make his mark in the baseball world.—*Tacoma Daily Ledger*, June 12, 1907.

43. *Weiser Signal*, June 8 and 13, 1907.
44. Johnson, "Some Experiences of a Speed King."

A coincidental event that helped Johnson's reputation make its way out of the Northwest was the spectacular Haywood-Pettibone-Moyer murder trial beginning May 8, 1907, in Boise and lasting through the summer. Officers of the Western Confederation of Miners were accused of slaying businessmen and government officials in several states, including former Idaho Governor Frank Steunenberg in Caldwell in 1905. In one of the most celebrated murder trials in American history, U.S. Senator William Borah served as special prosecutor with legendary attorney Clarence Darrow leading the defense. Reporters from all over the country poured into Boise. This is the account of Robert T. Small, who covered the trial for a Washington newspaper:

It was the privilege of this writer to meet and watch Walter Johnson work in his bush league days. He stood in the center of a diamond laid out in lava dust and fringed with sagebrush. About 50 newspapermen constituted themselves into big league scouts when they first came into contact with Walter Johnson. The Moyer-Haywood-Pettibone trials at Boise, Idaho, had taken them from the effete east into the heart of the west. The trials lasted for months. There were no court sessions on Sunday—but there was baseball. No one of those Eastern writers will ever let fade the memory of the first Sunday that Walter visited the Idaho metropolis [May 26] and the unknown took the mound. The writer, feeling a Columbus complex, and being a resident of Washington at the time, promptly wired to the late Tom C. Noyes, who was president of the Nationals, telling him there was a 'cyclone' worth giving the once-over. Sad was the lot of the discoverer when Noyes, under whom he had labored seven years as a reporter [Noyes also owned the *Washington Star*], wired back his thanks and the information that Walter had already been observed and was about to sign on the dotted line.—Clipping, source unknown, n.d., scrapbook IX(1924; *Washington Post*, July 27, 1907.

These are a few of the more credible and interesting claims of other "near-signings" of Walter Johnson:

DETROIT TIGERS —"Do you know that Johnson was tipped off to me several months ago?", remarked [Hughie] Jennings to a group of friends yesterday. "Yes, sir; they came to me and told me of his wonderful record, but I did not pay any attention to it. Whenever they talk about a fellow going through 85 innings without allowing a run and striking out 166 men in 12 games, we consider it a joke. But since I have seen him I guess that dope was right and I regret that I did not take the chance."—*Washington Post*, August 7, 1907.

If the late Frank J. Navin had had any confidence in William Yawkey's knowledge of baseball, Walter Johnson would have joined Detroit instead of Washington. Yawkey, who owned the Detroit club at that time, walked into Navin's office one morning and handed him a letter from a friend of his, advising Yawkey to buy the "best pitcher in the country." Navin scoffed.

"Where is this phenom pitching?", asked Navin.

"It says here in the letter that he's pitching independent ball out in Weiser, Idaho", Yawkey told him.

"This friend of yours, what does he do?"

"He's a cigar salesman. He travels all around the west."

"So you want me to go to the expense of sending a scout out there on the word of a cigar salesman?", said Navin as he pigeon-holed the letter. Navin never ignored a tip after that but, unfortunately, there were no more Johnsons setting the prairie leagues on fire. —H.G. Salsinger, "Tigers Spurned Johnson For Free," *Baseball Digest*, August 1946.

New York Highlanders—Clark Griffith: "Every time I hear praise for Johnson it makes me sore, because if it had not been for Billy Hogg's [New York Highlanders '05–08] forgetfulness he would now be wearing a New York uniform. Three weeks before he joined the Washington team, Hogg received a letter from a friend at Weiser, Idaho, telling him to have me come out and get Johnson. Hogg put the letter in his locker and never gave it a thought until the day after Johnson pitched his first game. Then he saw the account of the game in the paper and showed me the letter." —*Washington Post*, September 9, 1907.

Cleveland Naps—"Walter Johnson, the Idaho phenom that Cleveland was a trifle late in trying to sign, pitched a splendid game for Washington." —Henry P. Edwards, *Cleveland Plain Dealer*, August 21, 1907.

Henry P. Edwards: "Along in midseason, 1907, I received a letter from a friend, a former manager of an amateur team in Cleveland, who had gone west and settled in Weiser, Idaho. J.A. Siffert was his name. In that letter Siffert wrote: 'We have a pitcher here in Weiser I think could make good in the American League. I would like to see [Cleveland owner] Charley Somers get him. He has not allowed a run for 85 innings and in his last game he struck out 22 men.' I called up Somers at once and read the letter to him. 'Wire Siffert to send this pitcher on at once and we will make it all right with him. Tell him to sign up for Cleveland without delay', was Somers' reply. Before the message left Cleveland, however, a news item came over the wires that Cliff Blankenship, scouting for the Washington club, had signed a young pitcher by the name of Walter Johnson in Weiser, Idaho. If Siffert had but wired, instead of sending his tip by mail, the speed king might have been wearing a Cleveland uniform these many years." —Clipping, n.d., scrapbook IV(1920).

Pittsburgh Pirates—George Moreland: "I was tipped off by an umpire named McGuire that a fellow named Walter P. Johnson had pitched some great ball around Idaho and the coast towns. I relayed my information to my very good friend, Fred Clarke, manager of the Pirates. The Pirates that season were training at Hot Springs, Ark.. Clarke said he wasn't interested in Johnson, pointing out that his team was all set and that they would break camp in two days. I told him I had it on good authority that young Johnson was surefire big league timber. Clarke and the Pirates could have taken a look at Johnson for $18, which would have covered the train fare from Weiser to Hot Springs and return. But the Pirates did not make the investment. As it turned out, there would have been no return ticket to Weiser necessary if Johnson had reported to the Pirates. The Pittsburgh club would have acquired the greatest pitcher of them all for exactly $9."—George Moreland, *Balldom* (Youngstown, Ohio: Balldom Publishing, 1914).

Fred Lieb: "There are many tales going around as to how Walter Johnson got his first big league start. It is true that the Pittsburgh club lost Johnson's services because it wouldn't pay Walter's train fare from Weiser, Idaho to Pittsburgh. In the summer of 1907, the manager of the Weiser club for whom Johnson was pitching wrote Fred Clarke, then manager of the Pirates, that he had the greatest pitching prospect in the world and suggested that Clarke look him over immediately. Most big league clubs get many such letters in the course of a season, and the fare wasn't worth the gamble. In the meantime a traveling friend of Joe Cantillon wired him telling of this young phenom at Weiser. He was so insistent that Cantillon sent Cliff Blankenship out to Idaho to look him over." Elias, "Important Games and Famous Players Series, #17,"—February 11, 1920, scrapbook III.

45. *Tacoma Ledger*, June 22, 1907.
In one of his first appearances with St. Louis, a doubleheader with the Giants on July 9, Burnett doubled twice off Christy Mathewson, then doubled and tripled against "Iron Man" McGinnity.
46. Johnson, "My Pitching Years"; Johnson, "How Walter Johnson Became a Big Leaguer," clipping, source unknown, September 27, 1924, scrapbook IX.
47. West, "Walter Johnson Went Up 50 Years Ago Today"; Gustkey, "When The Big Train Ran on a Rural Track."
48. *Washington Post*, March 25, 1917.
49. Johnson, "How Walter Johnson Became a Big Leaguer"; *Idaho Daily Statesman*, June 29, 1907.
50. Johnson, "My Pitching Years."
51. Cliff Blankenship, "How Walter Johnson Became a Big Leaguer": "When the fans at Weiser found that I had signed him they were ready to lynch me. I finally consented to allow him to pitch an important game and then got away as quickly as possible."

Corroborating sources for Blankenship's time in Weiser are: *Weiser Signal*, June 29, 1907 and July 11, 1911; *Washington Star*, June 30, 1907; *Idaho Daily*

Statesman, June 30, 1907; *Coffeyville Journal*, October 23, 1912; Denman Thompson, *Washington Star*, February 2, 1930; Louis Dougher (*Washington Times* sports editor) manuscript, n.d., Johnson family archives; Johnson, "Some of My Early Experience"; Carmichael, *My Greatest Day in Baseball.*

52. Johnson, "My Pitching Years."
53. *Weiser American*, July 4, 1907, quoting the *Butte Miner*, June 30, 1907; *Caldwell Tribune*, July 6, 1907.
54. *Idaho Daily Statesman*, June 30, July 1, 1907; *Caldwell Tribune*, July 6, 1907; *Washington Star*, February 2, 1930; Johnson, "My Pitching Years."
55. *Weiser Signal*, July 10 and 24, 1907; *Idaho Daily Statesman*, July 16 and 22, 1907. Johnson's 1907 Weiser statistics: 14 W, 2 L; .056 ERA, 146 IP, 10 R, 45 H, 12 BB, 214 K; .340 BA, 59 AB, 20 H; 48 C, 4 E.
56. *Idaho Daily Statesman*, July 24, 1907; Johnson, "My Twenty Years on the Mound."

    The game against Vale on July 21 wasn't reported until the October 17, 1907, issue of the *Weiser American*.
57. Gustkey, "When The Big Train Ran on a Rural Track."
58. Carmichael, *My Greatest Day in Baseball;* Dougher manuscript.

CHAPTER 3

1. Joe Cantillon: "There was nothing of the 'rube' about him, as the term is generally applied to young ballplayers from the bush. He realized he didn't know very much about pitching and was always a good listener, also a keen observer, trying to do as he was instructed while he watched those who had more experience and knowledge of the game." (Cantillon, unpublished manuscript, n.d., Johnson family archives).
2. Shirley Povich, interview with the author, May 1992.

    Chicago sportswriter Charles Dryden coined the expression, according to Ring Lardner biographer Jonathan Yardley. Yardley, *Ring* (New York: Random House, 1977).
3. *Sporting Life*, April 1, 1905.
4. *Washington Post*, October 22, 1906: "Cantillon's reputation as a brainy baseball man is well known."
5. *Washington Star*, February, 1, 1930.
6. *Washington Star*, May 23, 1907.
7. *Washington Star*, February 2, 1930; *Washington Post*, January 26, 1938.
8. *Washington Star*, February 2, 1930.
9. *Washington Star*, June 23, 1907. Cantillon, too, had heard from baseball pals of his in the West that several American and National League clubs were interested in Milan.

10. Denman Thompson, *Washington Star*, n.d., scrapbook XXV(1929); *Washington Post*, March 5, 1953.
11. *Washington Post*, August 30, 1907.
12. Fred W. Lange, *History of Baseball in California and Pacific Coast Leagues, 1847–1938* (San Francisco: 1938).
13. *Washington Post*, August 30, 1907; Johnson, "My Pitching Years"; clipping, n.d., scrapbook X(1924).

    There is another person who might have played a significant role in Washington's "discovery" of Johnson. According to Ben Minor, the club's attorney in 1907 (and later president), Charles E. McCoy, an employee of the Interstate Commerce Commission, was traveling in Idaho on business and saw Johnson pitch. McCoy and Minor worked in the same building in Washington, and he came in and told Minor about the young phenom, Minor dismissing it as the typical tall tale from the bush leagues. Several weeks later McCoy called on Minor again, telling Minor this time that if he wasn't interested in Johnson, he would tell his friend John Taylor, owner of the Boston Red Sox, about him. Minor instructed Cantillon to check Johnson out, and Blankenship was sent to Idaho.

    This story, the source of which seems to be Minor himself, was written about several times in the mid-teens while he was president of the team. Clark Griffith, who worked for Minor as Washington manager during those years, told the story in 1927 on the occasion of Johnson's 20th anniversary with the club. McCoy, still living in Washington in 1937, apparently confirmed it to Shirley Povich at that time. Cantillon, though, makes no mention of McCoy, or Minor, or any prompting other than Shea's in his numerous (including contemporaneous, which the McCoy story is not) accounts of how he got Johnson for the Nationals. But perhaps Minor caused Cantillon to finally act on Shea's pleadings, or the process might already have been underway when Minor broached the matter. In any case, the frequency and consistency with which the story was repeated over the years requires mention of it here. The sources are:

    1) J. Ed Grillo, *Washington Star*, March 21, 1915.
    2) Clipping, n.d., 1916, Baseball Hall of Fame files.
    3) Clipping, August 2, 1927, scrapbook XIX.
    4) Shirley Povich, *Washington Post*, November 5, 1937.

14. *Washington Post*, June 10, 1907.

    A surprising number of inaccuracies found their way into the initial reporting, local and national, of Johnson's "signing" with Washington. The name was misspelled "Johnston" on occasion, and as late as January, 1908, *The Sporting News* was still calling him "Oscar", a curious mistake repeated several times in the first few weeks. Their first report, on July 4, has him being "of independent fame around Salt Lake City." The *Washington Herald* was convinced for a long time that Johnson was from Montana. Most egregious of all was the *Washington Star*'s initial article, on June 30, purportedly quoting Blankenship's "letter" (there hadn't been enough time for a letter from Idaho) to Nationals president Tom Noyes, apocryphal almost in its entirety:

> I have signed a pitcher by the name of Oscar Johnson. He was recommended to me by a friend in Kansas City. I came here immediately and watched Johnson work in a couple of games, and then to satisfy myself went in and caught behind him.

While Johnson was still in Idaho, a full two weeks prior to his arrival in Washington, the *Star* reported his appearance in Chicago and went so far as to fabricate a quote from the manager: "Cantillon got over the shock toward midnight and says he may pitch young Johnson today." The degree of error in these stories is astonishing and difficult to understand, particularly in the case of the *Star*, whose owner, Tom Noyes, also owned the ballclub and should have been privy to the real story.

15. *Washington Post*, July 1, 1907.
16. Billy Evans: "His coming was the talk of the town. All his records preceded him and perhaps no player ever came into the big league with such glowing press notices. His wonderful feats were treated rather lightly, however, as most of the fans figured that most any old pitcher could do the same as Johnson against rube teams." "Evans Dissertates on Walter Johnson," *Washington Star*, November 16, 1908.
17. Evans, syndicated column, n.d., scrapbook XIX(1924).
18. Evans, "Evans Dissertates on Walter Johnson."
19. *Washington Post*, July 27, 1907.
20. *Washington Herald*, July 27, 1907.
21. J. Ed Grillo, manuscript, c. 1915, Johnson family archives; *Washington Post*, July 28, 1907.
22. *Washington Star*, July 28, 1907; *Sporting Life*, August 24, 1907. "Johnson resembles Waddell in the box. Joe Cantillon is praying that the resemblance will not go any further."
23. *Washington Star*, August 1, 1907.
24. *Washington Times*, August 2, 1907.
25. Johnson, "My Pitching Years."
26. Johnson: "I made up my mind that morning that the ball was the same size as ever, and the bats no larger than those I had been accustomed to. I also reached the conclusion that the big league players were human beings, just like the young men out at Weiser." Johnson, "Some Experiences of a Speed King."
27. Evans, "Evans Dissertates on Walter Johnson."
28. James C. Delahanty, clipping, n.d., scrapbook V(1923).

29. Johnson, "My Pitching Years."
30. "It was interesting to watch Johnson pitching to the players of both teams yesterday in practice. He was apparently lobbing the ball over without any curve, but very few of the batters could connect safely with the ball." *Washington Star*, August 2, 1907.
31. Clipping, n.d., scrapbook X(1924).
32. Johnson, "My Pitching Years."
33. Bryan Morse, *Washington Herald*, August 2, 1932.
34. *Washington Star*, August 2, 1907.
35. Ritter, *The Glory of Their Times.*
36. Ty Cobb with Al Stump, *My Life in Baseball—The True Record*, (Garden City, New York: Doubleday and Company, 1961): "On August 2, 1907, I encountered the most threatening sight I ever saw on a ballfield."
37. *Washington Star*, August 3, 1907.
38. Clipping, August 2, 1927, scrapbook XIX.
39. *Washington Post*, August 2, 1907; *Washington Times*, August 2, 1907: "Prize package."
40. *Washington Herald*, August 3, 1907: "Standing-room only"; *Washington Star*, August 2, 1907: "They turned out in such large numbers as to overflow the stands, and went behind the ropes in right field"; Morris Bealle, *The Washington Senators* (Washington, D.C.: Columbia Publishing Company, 1947).
41. *Washington Post*, August 3, 1907.
42. Cobb, *My Life in Baseball.*
43. *Washington Star*, August 3, 1907.
44. Davy Jones letter to Lee Allen (Hall of Fame historian), April 13, 1963.
45. Cobb, *My Life in Baseball.*
46. *Washington Herald*, August 3, 1907:

    "He-e-ah-a-a-ya
    We-e-ah-a-a-ya
    Ye-e-ah-a-a-ya
    Hah-wah-yah
    Wah-yah-hah
    Yah-hah-wah."

    Gibberish such as this enlivened the doubleheader at the ballpark yesterday afternoon. As Hughey [sic] Jennings drew upon his unidentified vocabulary to give utterance to his 'He-e-ahs' and "We-e-ahs," he danced about in the coaching box, going through outlandish, monkeylike contortions, and all the while pulling for dear life for the success of his Tigers. He pulled literally and figuratively—pulled grass up by the roots and then pulled it to pieces; pulled his arms back and forth and fairly pulled his muscles out of place. He was a sight to see, was Jennings. An escaped patient from St. Elizabeth's could not have given a weirder performance.

47. *Washington Times, Washington Herald, Washington Post*, August 3, 1907. In an interesting coincidence, the front pages headlined a $29 million fine levied against John D. Rockefeller and his Standard Oil Co. by Federal Judge Kenesaw Mountain Landis, the "heaviest fine ever imposed by any court for any offense."
48. *Washington Post*, August 3, 1907. Charley O'Leary, Tigers shortstop: "Say, after that fellow pitched me a couple, I wished he had missed the train. He sent one so fast, I couldn't see it, and I thought it was going to take my block off, so I ducked and this foolish Sheridan, the umpire, called it a strike."

    J. Ed Grillo: "It is questionable whether a 19-year-old lad ever broke into baseball who made a better showing as a pitcher than Johnson did yesterday. The writer saw Cy Young when he first broke into fast company and he was 40 times rawer than is Johnson. Even the great Mathewson did not have what Johnson had at his command when he broke into the game. Furthermore, he is a mere boy. What will he be when he grows up?"
49. Cobb, *My Life in Baseball*; clipping, n.d., scrapbook XIX(1927). Cobb: "We all said then that we had met the coming master of American League pitchers."
50. *Washington Post*, August 3, 1907.
51. Johnson, "My Pitching Years."
52. *Washington Star*, August 8, 1907. "The latter pair of bingles(ninth inning) was simply the result of Johnson slowing up under manager Cantillon's directions to take it easy."
53. *Washington Times*, August 8, 1907. "Elmer Flick was the most peevish man on the grounds. He simply couldn't locate the ball, and didn't realize he had struck out until umpire Sheridan shooed him away from the plate. In the eighth inning, after he had struck out, Flick went to the coaching box at first and moaned his disgust to umpire Evans, while he took a fiendish delight in seeing Terry Turner slam the air three times. After Turner failed to connect with the second strike, Flick remarked to Evans, 'I wonder how far he missed that one by?' 'No further than you missed your third one,' was Evans's comforting rejoinder. 'He couldn't have,' confessed Elmer."
54. *Washington Post*, August 9, 1907. The immediate and unflinching comparisons to Young and Mathewson, generally regarded the top pitchers in the history of the game to that point, are particularly striking. Ed Grillo, *Post* baseball writer and ex-president of the Toledo American Association club, echoed Joss's comparison the next day in a letter to Cincinnati Reds owner August Herrmann: "Cantillon has picked up a pitcher that I would like to have seen you get. Johnson is his name. He hails from Idaho, is only nineteen years old and looks to be the greatest find of recent years. He will be another Cy Young." Letter file, Baseball Hall of Fame.
55. *Washington Post*, August 8, 1907. "If he had won the world's championship he

could not have been given a much greater ovation than he was yesterday"; *Washington Star, Cleveland Press*, August 8, 1907.

56. *Weiser Signal*, August 21, 1907.
57. Ibid; *Fullerton Tribune*, August 28, 1907; *Washington Post*, February 17, 1909; Johnson, "My Pitching Years"; Blankenship, "How Walter Johnson Became a Big Leaguer," September 27, 1924, scrapbook IX. Blankenship claimed a role in the signing: "When it came to signing a contract he showed good judgment, holding out for higher money, and it was only through my efforts that he finally did sign."

    Ty Cobb reportedly earned $1,200 for his first full season in 1906. *Washington Star*, September 12, 1907; St. Louis Browns shortstop Bobby Wallace was the highest-paid player in either league at $6,500. *Washington Post*, August 16, 1907.
58. Johnson, "Some Experiences of a Speed King."
59. *Washington Star*, September 25, 1912.
60. F.C. Lane, "Milan the Marvel," *Baseball Magazine*, May 1914; *Washington Herald*, April 8, 1911; Denman Thompson, *Washington Star*, n.d., scrapbook XXV(1929).
61. *Washington Star*, December 11, 1946.

    Shirley Povich on Johnson's attitude about these things: "There never was any feeling among his teammates that he was a prude. They put him down for what he was—a country boy. Milan and the neighborhood kids were his chief pals." Povich, "Walter Johnson, The Big Train", *Sport Magazine*, January 1950.
62. Treat, *Walter Johnson, King of the Pitchers*.
63. Denman Thompson, *Washington Star*, n.d., scrapbook XXV(1929).

    Their 16 seasons together has since been exceeded by Sam Rice/Joe Judge with Washington 18 years, Lou Whitaker/Alan Trammell with Detroit 18 years, Roberto Clemente/Bill Mazeroski with Pittsburgh 17 years, and equalled by Carl Hubbell/Mel Ott with the New York Giants. *Baseball Research Journal*, Society for American Baseball Research, 1978.
64. Robert L. Tiemann, "Walter Johnson's Shutouts," n.d., n.p., Society for American Baseball Research.
65. Johnson, "My Twenty Years on the Mound."
66. John McCallum, *The Tiger Wore Spikes* (New York: Praeger Publishers, 1975). Cobb: "I later learned that after we beat him the first time, Walter went back and practiced fielding bunts for hours." Johnson told about it years later: "I figured I would have won [the first game] if I'd known how to field bunts. I practiced fielding until I was pretty fair at it." *Washington Star*, August 4, 1937.
67. *Washington Herald*, August 3, 1907; Johnson, "What Records Mean to a Manager," *Baseball Magazine*, March 1935; Frank Young, *Washington Post*, n.d., scrapbook XXV(1929).

In his two seasons with Johnson on the Nationals, ironically, Cliff Blankenship never caught him in a game. Why the Nationals were carrying four catchers (Blankenship, Heydon, Kahoe, and Warner) on their roster at the same time is a mystery.

68. *Washington Post*, September 29, 1907.
69. *Washington Post*, August 29, 1907. Kahoe was said to have "handled the deliveries of as many star pitchers as any catcher in the country, and should be a good judge of a twirler."
70. Johnson, "My Pitching Years."
71. Steven H. Heath, "An Analysis of the Walter Johnson Shutouts," *Baseball Quarterly Reviews*, Vol. 4, 1989. To put the 1–0 shutout record—38—in perspective, Grover Cleveland Alexander is next with 17.
72. Even as the *Post* was hailing Johnson, that same day there was evidence that baseball was not yet the respectable profession that he, Billy Evans, and others would help make it. In St. Louis, Evans's skull was fractured by a soda bottle thrown by a fan objecting to a call. It was reported that "the bottle burst in a thousand pieces against Evans's skull, and he fell bleeding and unconscious across the plate." The assailant, a rooter for visiting Detroit, was chased down by a mob of St. Louis fans and about to be lynched with the flagpole rope before the huge crowd was beaten away by 50 cops wielding nightsticks. *Washington Star*, September 16, 1907.
73. Johnson, "My Twenty Years on the Mound."
74. *The Sporting News*, October 31, 1907.

CHAPTER 4

1. *Anaheim Gazette*, October 17, 1907.
2. *Santa Ana Register*, November 7, 1907: "$5 a game"; Jay Berman, "The Early Days of Sports in Orange County," *Orange Coast Magazine*, July 1990.
3. West, "Walter Johnson Went Up 50 Years Ago Today."
4. Johnson batted .132 (19 for 144) in California games, 1905–07 (through the San Diego series), for which batting statistics are available, and .111 (4 for 36), at Washington in 1907. His only hitting success to this point had come at Weiser, .317 (26 for 82 in games where batting statistics are available, including the one game at Tacoma).
5. Unknown Washington newspaper, January 1908, HOF clipping file.

In the letter, Johnson also denied rumors, which cropped up briefly in the Washington press, of his playing in the "outlaw" California League: "I never thought of playing outlaw ball here," he wrote. "There's good money in it, but I intend to stick to Washington as long as I can." The semipro circuits in which Johnson and other professionals played in the off-season were not seen as any kind of threat or competition to those leagues operating under the aegis of the National Agreement, and were therefore not deemed to be "outlaw."

6. MacArthur, *Orange County Historical Volume III.*
7. Clipping, *Iola* [Kansas] *Register*, n.d., 1908, scrapbook III.
8. *Los Angeles Times*, March 1 and 5, 1908.
9. *Washington Post*, March 12, 1908.
10. *Washington Star*, March 17, 1908.
11. *Washington Star*, April 7, 1908.
12. Clipping, *Iola Register*, scrapbook III.
13. *Washington Post*, June 8, 1908.
14. Johnson, "My Pitching Years."
15. Alan Gould, "Gabby Street, Ace of the Cards," Associated Press series, n.d., scrapbook XXV(1929).
16. Johnson, "Some Experiences of a Speed King."
17. Johnson, "My Pitching Years."
18. *Washington Star*, August 21, 1908.

    Overlooked in the coverage of Street's catch was the record indicating that it had been done before. According to the *Washington Post* of August 26, 1894, Pop Schriver, a catcher with Cap Anson's Chicago Colts, had the day before caught a ball tossed by Clark Griffith from a window at the top of the monument. However, Griffith later told Shirley Povich that the attempt had failed, the first ball falling wide of the waiting catcher and the second popping out of Schriver's mitt, dribbling to the ground. They were then run off the monument grounds by police, ending the venture. Povich, *The Washington Senators.*
19. Seymour Siwoff, *The Book of Baseball Records*, (New York: Siwoff, 1994).
20. Johnson, "My Pitching Years," *Washington Post*, December 14, 1924.

    Ed Grillo of the *Washington Post* ascribed a degree of premeditation to Johnson also in his performance in New York. "Johnson is pitching these games at his own request," he wrote on Sunday, September 6. "It seems that some few days before the Nationals left for New York, some of the players and their friends were talking about pitching feats, during which Johnson's name was mentioned. During the course of the discussion someone remarked that he did not believe any pitcher could work three days in succession and pitch winning ball. Some of the players thought that Johnson could turn the trick, while others doubted it. Finally, Johnson was consulted and after having the subject explained to him, remarked in that characteristic, quiet way of his that he would like to try it." *Washington Post*, September 7, 1908.
21. Fred Lieb, "Johnson's 16-Victory String Snapped in Relief Role by Questionable Ruling," *The Sporting News*, February 15, 1945.
22. Johnson, "My Twenty Years on the Mound."

23. Johnson, "My Pitching Years."
24. *Washington Post*, February 1, 1930.
Bob Considine tells the following story: "Monday night [Johnson] went to [Washington] with the team. In the fifth inning of Tuesday's game, the stumblebum pitcher Cantillon had in the box began to get his brains splattered. Cantillon ordered Johnson to go in as relief. 'But I put my foot down that time,' Walter told me years later, in his shy way. 'I told Cantillon I didn't intend to throw another ball at least until Wednesday.' " *Washington Post*, December 15, 1946.
Rarely mentioned is a virtually identical performance the previous year by Philadelphia A's pitcher Jimmy Dygert, who pitched shutouts on October 1, 3 and 4 (second game of a doubleheader), 1907. Perhaps because the games were not consecutive, but more likely because it was the only notable accomplishment in his career, Dygert's feat is all but forgotten while Johnson's became legendary.
25. Johnson, "The Greatest Players I Ever Saw," *Baseball Magazine*, October 1929.
26. J. Ed Grillo, *Washington Post*, September 12, 1908.
27. Denman Thompson, *Washington Star*, February 26, 1927.
28. Johnson, letter to F.C. Lane, March 12, 1919, HOF files.
29. F.C. Lane, "The Greatest Pitcher On the Diamond Today," *Baseball Magazine*, January 1916.
30. Ibid.
31. "Only Weakened Legs Keep Walter From Being Top Hurler," March 24, 1929, clipping, source unknown, misc. scrapbook.
32. Johnson, "The Greatest Players I Ever Saw"; "My Pitching Years."
33. *Washington Post*, October 20, 1908.
Of the $100 fine, Johnson later wrote: "I took the matter up with Cantillon and he advised me to write to [Ban] Johnson, giving the exact circumstances [of his participation in the Logan Square series], and said he thought the fine would be cancelled. I heard nothing more until Spring and supposed it was dropped. But when I returned to the club I was surprised to receive a fine for $50. The original sum had been cut in half, but I was obligated to pay the $50. I didn't like it very well, but nothing more was said about it." Johnson, "Why I Signed With The Federal League," *Baseball Magazine*, April 1915.
34. *Chicago Tribune*, October 18, 1908.
35. *Washington Post*, October 23, 1908.
36. *Washington Post*, October 16, 1908.
37. *Atlanta Journal*, October 7, 1908.
38. *Washington Star*, November 11, 1908.
39. *Chicago Record-Herald*, October 21, 1908, quoting from *Collier's*.
40. *Los Angeles Herald*, October 19, 1908.
41. *Los Angeles Herald*, November 8, 1908. A crowd of 5,000, half "colored" and half

white, watched the Angels beat "the heretofore invincible [they had won 34 of 35 games] Giants, the pride of darktown." *Los Angeles Herald*, November 9, 1908.

42. Alan Gould, "Gabby Street, Ace of the Cards."

Cantillon (who was serving a suspension) invited Johnson to join him in watching a game in street clothes from the grandstand. "Manager Joe Cantillon and his famous pitcher," the *Post* reported, "occupied a box near the Washington bench this afternoon. Joe and Walter were dressed in dapper suits of light material. They were the cynosure of all eyes, and chatted pleasantly all through the game. Some admirers in the grandstand sent Walter a big bouquet of American Beauties. The big Idaho boy blushed, and so did Joe. It was said they came from a lady admirer." *Washington Post*, July 2, 1909.

43. *Washington Post*, September 1, 1909.
44. *Fullerton Tribune*, September 22, 1909.
45. J. Ed Grillo, *Washington Post*, September 22, 1909.
46. *Washington Post*, October 18, 1908.
47. Robert Tieman and Mark Rucker, *Nineteenth Century Stars*, Society for American Baseball Research, 1989: "When Ban Johnson was moving the American League to major league status in 1901, McAleer was probably his most successful recruiter [other than Griffith], luring many National Leaguers into the Johnson fold."
48. Joe Quinlan, *Sports Collectors Digest*, March 30, 1990.
49. Cantillon managed the Millers from 1910–1923; scouted for the White Sox 1924–25; managed Little Rock (A.A.) 1926–27; A.A. supervisor of umpires, 1928. Bill James, in his *Historical Baseball Abstract*, called the Cantillon brothers' Minneapolis Millers, made up almost entirely of former major leaguers, "the outstanding minor league team of this time. About 1909 they started concentrating on getting the best major league players available. The question of how they built their team is no different, really, than the question of how any major league team of the time built their strength. They made good trades and put out the money when they had to." Former Nationals pitcher "Long Tom" Hughes was 31–10 for the Millers in 1910. Many other ex-Washington players found a home there, including Dave Altizer, Otis Clymer, Nick Altrock, and Gavvy Cravath. Cantillon had Cravath for a couple of years before selling him to the National League, where he won six home run titles. Other former big-league stars employed by the Cantillons included the great Pirates pitcher Sam Leever, Claude Rossman, and Jimmy Williams. Early in 1910 they bought Rube Waddell from the Browns and he gave them two productive years, winning 20 games in 1911, his last year in baseball. *Washington Star*, August 20, 1912, February 2, 1930; Bill James, *The Bill James Historical Abstract* (New York: Villard Books, 1985).
50. *Washington Post*, September 12, 1908.
51. Johnson, "My Pitching Years."

52. Poore, "Former Batboy Still Remembers Big Train Johnson."
53. *New Orleans Picayune*, December 20, 1909.
54. Flaherty, "Life Story of Walter Johnson."
55. *Los Angeles Herald*, February 14, 1910: "Development work is being rushed day and night in all of the oil fields in the Olinda district. The wells owned by the Santa Fe Company produced 1,100,000 barrels of oil during the past year, a heavy increase over the previous year."

CHAPTER 5

1. J. Ed Grillo, manuscript, n.d., Johnson family archives.
2. *Washington Post*, October 1, 1909.
3. *Washington Post*, November 7, 1909.
4. Cobb, *My Life in Baseball.*
5. *Washington Herald*, April 8, 1911.
6. *Washington Herald*, March 16, 1910.
7. *Washington Post*, March 29 and 31, 1910; *Washington Herald*, April 8, 1911.
8. *Washington Herald*, April 10, 1910.
9. Bob Addie, *The Sporting News*, April 6, 1974.
10. Johnson, "My Pitching Years."
11. *Washington Post*, April 16, 1910.
12. Ed Grillo, *Washington Post*, April 16, 1910; William Howard Taft, letter to Walter Johnson, April 15, 1910, Johnson family archives.
13. *Washington Post*, May 12, 1910.
14. Ibid. This terrible editorial advice, offered with even worse timing, might have cost Brewer his job. He was gone from the *Post* about 22 years sooner than Johnson from the Nationals.
15. *Washington Star*, September 3, 1911.
16. Bob Feller tied the record in 1938 and Nolan Ryan broke it with 41 in 1974.
17. Bealle, *The Washington Senators.*
18. *St. Louis Globe-Democrat*, October 23, 1910.
19. David Pietrusza, *Major Leagues* (Jefferson, North Carolina: McFarland & Company, 1991).
20. *Washington Post*, October 28, 1910.
21. *Coffeyville at 100*, centennial booklet, n.d., Coffeyville Historical Society.
22. *The Gunfighters.* (New York: Time-Life Books, 1974).
23. Lane, "At Coffeyville With Walter Johnson"; *Coffeyville Journal*, October 23, 1912.
24. Johnson, "This is the Life," manuscript, c. 1918, Johnson family archives.
25. *The Best Short Stories of Ring Lardner* (New York: Charles Scribner's Sons, 1957).

26. *Washington Post*, March 30 and 31, 1911.
27. *Washington Post*, March 15, April 7, 1911.
28. Shannon and Kalnesky, *The Ballparks* (New York: Hawthorn Books, 1975).
29. Johnson's other known three-pitch innings occurred on May 26, 1913, August 29, 1915, and June 1, 1917.
30. Hugh Fullerton, "The Greatest Game of Baseball," *Liberty Magazine*, April 20, 1929.
31. *Washington Post*, July 2, 1911, quoting Sid Mercer of the *N.Y. Globe*.
32. *Anaheim Gazette*, November 2, 1911, quoting *Sporting Life*.
33. Shirley Povich, *Washington Post*, April 7, 1939.
34. *New York Age*, October 19, 1911.

CHAPTER 6

1. Clipping, n.d., scrapbook IX(1924).
2. Povich, "Clark Griffith—50 Years in Baseball," *Washington Post*, parts 1–10, January 16–25, 1938.
3. Povich, *The Washington Senators*.
4. Povich, "Clark Griffith—50 Years in Baseball", part 18, February 2, 1938.
5. Johnson, "My Pitching Years."
6. Flaherty, "Life Story of Walter Perry Johnson."
7. Bob Considine, *Washington Herald*, clipping, n.d., 1935, Johnson family archives.
8. Joe Holman, *Wonderful Walter Johnson,* n.d. unpublished manuscript, Johnson family archives; Considine.
9. Clipping, n.d., scrapbook XXVII(1930).
10. Eddie Collins, "Twenty-One Years of Baseball," *North American Newspaper Alliance*, 1926, scrapbook XVII.
11. Povich, "Clark Griffith—50 years in Baseball," part 20, February 4, 1938.
12. Robert McConnell, "The Non-Home Run Hitters", *Baseball Research Journal*, 1983. Foster also holds the record for consecutive at-bats without a home run, 3,278, from opening day, April 20, 1916, through the end of his career in 1923.
13. Povich, *The Washington Senators*; Bob Considine, clipping, *Washington Herald*, 1935, misc. scrapbook; Clark Griffith: "Eddie Foster was the best hit-and-run man I or any other man ever owned."

    Povich also credits Griffith with inventing the "squeeze play" in 1904 while he was managing the Highlanders. Povich, "Clark Griffith—50 Years in Baseball," *Washington Post*, January 28, 1938.

    It was being hit by a Walter Johnson pitch that indirectly led to Foster's acquisition by Washington. He had started the 1910 season at shortstop for the New York Highlanders, and on their first trip to Washington on April 22, 1910, Johnson hit him in the ribs with a fastball, sending him to the hospital. Foster never regained his form that year (.133 BA) and was dispatched to Rochester, where Griffith grabbed him. *Washington Post*, March 12, 1917. Johnson also hit Birdie Cree in the head in the same game, knocking him unconscious for five minutes. *Washington Post*, April 23, 1910.

14. Guy Waterman, "The Upstart Senators of 1912–1915," *The National Pastime*, 1993.
15. Povich, *The Washington Senators*; Fred Lieb, "The P.T. Barnum of the Bushes: Jester Joe Engel, Chattanooga Club Chief," *The Sporting News Baseball Register*, 1953.
16. *Washington Post*, March 11, 1912; *Washington Herald*, March 18, 1915; Frank T. Sullivan, clipping, August 16, 1925, scrapbook XIV.
17. Povich, "Clark Griffith—50 Years in Baseball," part 18, February 2, 1938; Johnson, "My Pitching Years."
18. Johnson, "My Pitching Years."
19. McGraw, "My Thirty Years In Baseball," *North American Newspaper Alliance*, n.d., scrapbook IV(1922).
20. Johnson, "My Pitching Years."
21. William B. Mead and Paul Dickson, *Baseball, The President's Game* (Washington, D.C.: Farragut Publishing Company, 1993).
22. Martin letter to the author, December 11, 1978. Martin went 0 for 3, with a walk, in his first game against Johnson after the injury.
23. Paul Zingg, *Harry Hooper* (Chicago: University of Illinois Press, 1993). Lord broke his finger on July 10, 1910.
24. *Washington Post*, April 23, 1910.
25. Donald Honig, *Baseball When The Grass Was Real* (New York: Coward, McCann & Geoghegan, 1975).
26. Ritter, *The Glory Of Their Times*. Sam Crawford: "Walter was a wonderful person, too, you know. He was always afraid he might hit somebody with that fast ball. A wonderful man, in every way. Warm, and friendly, and wouldn't hurt a soul. Easily the greatest pitcher I ever saw."

    George McBride: "It's true that he didn't like to hit anybody. He didn't like them to hang over the bag [plate] like Cobb did." Ritter, "George McBride: 'I Took Honus Wagner's Job'," *The National Pastime*, 1985.
27. Grantland Rice, "The Sportlight," *Washington Post*, March 9, 1915.
28. Jack Martin: "[Johnson] came into the clubhouse to check on me. A real fine guy and I'm glad I had the pleasure to know him. His ball that hit me was an accident and not intentional." Letter to the author, December 11, 1978.
29. *Society for American Baseball Research Bulletin*, February 1994.
30. Povich, "Clark Griffith—50 Years in Baseball", part 19, *The Washington Post*, February 3, 1938.

31. Joe Wood interview with Lawrence Ritter, from *The Glory Of Their Times* documentary film, 1970, Cappy Productions, Inc.
32. *The Washington Star*, June 7, 1912.
33. F.C. Lane, "Thirteen Seasons Of Marvelous Pitching," *Baseball Magazine*, April 1920.
34. A.B. M'Ginley, clipping, n.d., scrapbook XVIII(1927).
35. *Washington Star*, June 11, 1912.
36. Johnson, "My Pitching Years": "It was that spirit in 1912 that made us hustle almost to a pennant."
37. *Washington Star*, July 22, 1912. Under the headline "Griffith Secures Altrock To Assist Schaefer In Coaching Sketch," it was noted that "The acquisition of Altrock gives Griffith the greatest pair of baseball comedians in captivity."
38. Bealle, *The Washington Senators*.
    Among Schaefer's repertoire of stunts and gags were an imitation of Hughie Jennings's physical and vocal contortions and umpires' gesticulations, impromptu speeches to the spectators, and walking the baseline as if it were a tightrope. *Cleveland News*, June 13, 1912.
39. Stanley Milliken, *Washington Post*, March 15, 1914.
    "Both Altrock and Schaefer were shrewd baseball men," Fred Lieb confirmed. Fred Lieb, "Comedians and Pranksters of Baseball," *The Sporting News* booklet, 1958.
40. Billy Evans: "Until the coming of the lively ball most of the glamor of the diamond centered around the pitcher. He was the big hero."Clipping, n.d., scrapbook V(1924.
41. *Washington Star*, July 30, 1912.
42. Eugene C. Murdock, *Ban Johnson, Czar of Baseball* (Westport, Connecticut: Greenwood Press, 1982).
43. Billy Evans, "Umpires American League Team," *Collier's,* October 19, 1912.
44. *The Sporting News*, September 12, 1912.
    Johnson: "Griff knew how to work up the fans through the newspapers." "My Pitching Years."
45. Ritter, *The Glory of Their Times.*
46. Ibid.
47. *Washington Post*, September 7, 1912; Emil Rothe, "The War of 1912, The Wood-Johnson Duel," *Baseball Research Journal*, 1974
48. Ed Grillo, *Washington Star*, December 4, 1914.
49. Shirley Povich, quoting Eddie Ainsmith, *Washington Post*, February 29, 1932.
    Johnson: "Stopping in our clubhouse after the game umpire Evans explained, 'One more like that last one, Walter, and I could be a dead umpire.' " "My Pitching Years."
50. Collins, "Twenty-One Years of Baseball," *North American Newspaper Alliance*, n.d., 1926, scrapbook XVII.
    Eddie Plank went all 19 innings for Philadelphia in this game.
51. John Daley, a shortstop with the Browns for 17 games in 1912 (his entire major

league career) claimed authorship of this expression in an interview with *The Sporting News* commemorating his 100th birthday in 1987: "On July 20, 1912, [Daley] took a third strike from Hall of Famer Walter Johnson, who had been brought in as a reliever in the top of the ninth. On a full count, Daley said, 'the next pitch I never saw. I just heard it smacking into the catcher's mitt. Strike three. When the Browns' George Stovall asked me about it, I said, 'You can't hit what you can't see.' The writers used to sit down at the field level in the front row. The next day, one of them wrote about the kid who couldn't hit what he couldn't see. A couple of years ago, some fellow claimed he was the originator of the phrase. I told him I'm the one who did it, and he could look it up.' " *The Sporting News*, June 22, 1987. Unfortunately, confirmation of Daley's story couldn't be found in any of the Washington or St. Louis papers. Daley, however, also mentioned it some years earlier in a taped interview with Baltimore sports broadcaster Ted Patterson. Daley did strike out against Johnson on the day in question, and his other details also check out.

Around the end of the 1912 season there was a flurry of similar quotes. In the September 26, 1912, *Anaheim Gazette*, in a long interview (undoubtedly picked up from another source, but unattributed) with Hal Chase about Walter Johnson, Chase says, "It's an old saying in baseball, 'When you can't see 'em you can't hit 'em.' " The *Boston Globe* of September 27, containing an interview with Johnson, ends with, "How can you hit 'em when you can't see 'em—answer me that!" The *Coffeyville Journal*, October 28: "We believe it was Mr. Larry Lajoie who expressed himself about our Walter's work in the following well- chosen words: 'You can't hit what you can't see.' " In time, the quote would be attributed to Ty Cobb, Lu Blue, Ping Bodie, and others.

52. Evans, "Umpires American League Team."
53. Ed Grillo, *Washington Star*, September 3, 1911: "It is questionable whether there is a better centerfielder in the league than Milan. It is by no means a certainty that either Speaker or Cobb is his superior in this respect;" Grillo, *Washington Star*, March 21, 1915: "Milan is today considered one of the star outfielders of the American League, classing right up with Speaker and Cobb."
54. Shirley Povich, *Washington Post*, March 5, 1953: " 'Jimmy McAleer showed me how to play the outfield,' said Milan. 'He'd been a great outfielder himself.' " Johnson: "Milan, while not a colorful player like Cobb or Speaker, was, I think, one of the great outfielders of all time. Jimmy McAleer worked hard with Milan, and within two years had developed him into a great player." Clipping, Detroit newspaper, n.d., scrapbook V(1923).
55. Lane, "Milan the Marvel."
56. F.C. Lane, "One Hundred and Twenty-Two Feet Per Second," *Baseball Magazine*, September 1912.

57. Clipping, n.d., misc. scrapbook, Johnson family archives.
58. Lane, "One Hundred and Twenty-Two Feet Per Second."
59. *Washington Post*, March 21, 1915.
60. *Washington Herald*, October 18, 1912.
61. *Washington Post*, April 6, 1913.
62. *Washington Post*, March 21, 1915.
63 *Washington Post*, October 19, 1912.
64. *Washington Post*, March 21, 1915.
65. *Coffeyville Journal*, October 23, 1912.
66. *Chanute* (Kansas) *Tribune*, December 12, 1946.
67. *Ottawa* (Kansas) *Herald*, November 21, 1966.
68. Billy Evans, "Baseball on the Inside," clipping, n.d., scrapbook III (1919–20).

CHAPTER 7

1. Treat, *Walter Johnson, King of the Pitchers*.
2. *Washington Star*, March 11, 1913.
3. Denman Thompson, *Washington Star*, December 11, 1946.
4. Even before he was with Washington, Griffith had an eye on these possibilities, somehow arranging an audience for his New York Highlanders with Teddy Roosevelt, who was by all accounts not a fan of the game, at the White House on May 5, 1908.
5. Clipping, unknown Detroit paper, "Personal and Confidential" column, n.d., scrapbook V(1923).
6. *Washington Star*, May 18, 1913.
7. Thomas Kirby, *Washington Post*, May 9, 1913.
8. The current method of computing scoreless-inning streaks disregards outs in the inning in which the streak is broken. Under that method of calculation, Johnson's streak would be 55–2/3 innings. There was one out when it was broken, making 56 innings of three outs each—the figure used for many years.
9. Red Smith, "The Big Train and His Buddies," *New York Herald Tribune*, December 14, 1946.
10. *Washington Post*, July 26, 1913.
11. *Anaheim Gazette*, August 7, 1913.
12. Paul R. Paddock, "Walter Johnson Sends Greetings," *Weiser Semi-Weekly Signal*, September 29, 1924. "Walter is a married man now with three boys and a girl, but he wanted to know about the girl he used to go with in Weiser."

    That relationship might have been a factor in the following events: his return to Weiser in 1907; his rejection of several offers from professional teams, including Washington; the delay in his departure from Weiser after the end of the 1907 season there; all of the above.

13. *Washington Times-Herald*, April 26, 1913.
14. Hazel Johnson personal scrapbook, Johnson family archives.
15. Clipping, source unknown, n.d. (June 1911), Hazel Johnson scrapbook.
16. Clipping, source unknown, n.d. (March 1913), Hazel Johnson scrapbook.
17. Clipping, source unknown, n.d., Hazel Johnson personal scrapbook; Flaherty, "Life Story of Walter Perry Johnson."
18. *Washington Daily News*, June 17, 1925.
19. Postcard, Johnson family archives—The "J" was added, no doubt, to avoid seeming to presume that he was the only Walter from whom she might be receiving a card.
20. Shirley Povich, *Washington Post*, February 4, 1938.
21. *Washington Star*, August 1, 1913.
22. *The Sporting News*, June 19, 1913.
23. *Washington Star*, September 1, 1913.
24. Johnson, "Some Experiences of a Speed King," *St. Nicholas*, October 1914.
25. *Washington Star*, August 29, 1913.
26. Denman Thompson, *Washington Star*, December 11, 1946.
27. *Washington Post*, September 25, 1913; *Washington Star*, September 25 and 27, October 1 and 3, 1913.
28. *Washington Times*, October 12 and 13, 1913.
    Betting by players and managers on games in which they were not directly involved was common until after the Black Sox scandal and the appointment of Judge Landis as commissioner in the early '20s.
29. *New York Age*, October 9, 1913.
    Although several books and articles refer to a supposed Williams-Johnson pitching duel, won by Williams, 1–0, the author could find no evidence of it. If they had pitched against each other, the game certainly would have attracted the same kind of attention as those Johnson pitched against Frank Wickware, Gunboat Thompson, and Dick McClelland. Stories of a Williams-Johnson matchup are probably the result of confusing the Johnson-Wickware game and the Williams-Alexander game, which took place the same day, October 5, 1913.
30. Johnson's known appearances against black teams:

Date	Location	Team	Vs	Score	IP	R	ER	H	BB	K
06/19/07	Weiser,Id	Weiser	Rastus Rufus	12-7	PROBABLY PLAYED, DIDN'T PITCH					
10/18/08	Los Angeles	Olive	LA Giants	5-6	11	6	–	9	1	20
01/30/10	Santa Ana,Ca	S.A.	Occidentals	3-0	9	0	0	2	0	15
10/15/11	New York,NY	ML A/S	Lincoln Giants	5-3	9	3	–	6	0	14
10/05/13	Schenectady	All-Am	Mohawk Giants	0-1	5	1	1	2	0	11
10/11/14	New York, NY	NYFD	Lincoln Stars	0-2	9	2	–	5	2	8
06/01/40	Thurmont,Md	?	Gettysburg CCC	?	1	0	0	1	0	2
Totals				W2-L3	44	12	–	25	3	70

Sportswriter Sam Lacy, who saw Walter Johnson and Joe Williams pitch, told the author that he thought they were about equal in speed. There are these anecdotal comparisons from two men who played against both of them:

"Robert Berman, a semipro catcher around New York, often played against Joe Williams and in 1918 joined the Washington Senators briefly as a teammate of Johnson. Which was faster? 'There was no comparison,' Berman said. 'I think Johnson was faster than Williams.' But, Berman maintained, Williams was faster than either Paige or Cannonball Dick Redding. 'It gripes me when the papers claim that Satchel Paige was the fastest black pitcher that ever lived,' he said. 'Smokey Joe Williams, to my mind, was the fastest.' "—John Holway, *Blackball Stars* (Westport, Connecticut: Meckler Publishing, 1988).

Chet Hoff—"We played the Cuban Stars, the Lincoln Giants, and all them teams from New York [during Hoff's 10 years in semipro ball beginning in 1918]. They were as good as major leaguers. Smokey Joe Williams played against us. He would have been a good pitcher in the majors. He could throw almost as hard as Walter Johnson. Walter Johnson was fast. This guy was fast, too! But I think Walter Johnson was the fastest in them days. When I was playing baseball, I thought Johnson was the best pitcher."—James Riley and Renwick Speer, "1991 Marks Chet Hoff's 100th Birthday," *Baseball Research Journal*, 1991.

Johnson was the favorite major-leaguer of some African-American fans, according to the memoirs of the Delany sisters of New York. "Sadie and I loved Walter Johnson, a pitcher for the Washington team," they wrote. "If he was pitching in New York, we were there!"—Sarah and A. Elizabeth Delany with Amy Hill Hearth, *Having Our Say, the Delany Sisters' First 100 Years* (New York: Kodansha America, 1993).

31. *The Sporting News*, October 13, 1913: "Johnson could not see himself going to Cuba to make $500 for a month's work when he might pick up three times that amount pitching exhibition contests around New York in half the time."
32. *Collier's*, October 12, 1912.

CHAPTER 8

1. Clipping, source unknown, n.d., scrapbook VIII(1924).
2. *Washington Post*, December 11, 1946.

The earliest version of this story found by the author appeared in a Newark newspaper in 1929, told by catcher Ray Haley (Bos-Phi. A.L., 1915–17). The game was said to be against the Athletics and in Washington.(Clipping, source unknown, n.d., scrapbook XXII(1929)).

A 1947 magazine article contained a version dubbed "official" by Clark Griffith, it claimed: The game was in Detroit with Ainsmith catching, Jack Sheridan the umpire, and Sam Crawford the victim. Gene Coughlin, "Walter

Johnson—Salesman For the Golden Rule," *American Weekly*, June 8, 1947.

3. Official National Commission figures, HOF files.
4. Charles C. Alexander, *Ty Cobb* (New York: Oxford University Press, 1984).
5. Johnson, "What I Pitch to Babe Ruth and Why," *Baseball Magazine*, September 1920; Johnson, "My Life So Far": "I would rather face any batter in the game than Baker. He hits me harder than any other player. Sam Crawford used to be my 'hoodoo,' but now it's Baker."; Letter to F.C. Lane, March 12, 1919, HOF files: "I believe Frank Baker has won more games from me than any other man with a bat."
6. *Washington Post*, May 24, 1914: "It is reported in Washington circles that Joe Boehling made the remark that 'all you have to do to get Baker is to send a beaner at his head and then give him three strikes.' "
7. Povich, "Walter Johnson."
8. *Washington Post*, May 24, 1914.
9. Povich, "Walter Johnson."

   Baker told John Steadman, longtime sportswriter for the *Baltimore Sun*, that it was the catcher, Eddie Ainsmith, who called for the knockdown pitch. Asked by Steadman what he did when Johnson threw at him, Baker replied: "It was either duck or no dinner." John Steadman letter to the author, January 2, 1995.
10. Johnson, "The Meanest Thing In Baseball."
11. Margaret Milan, letter to Carolyn Johnson Thomas, May 8, 1961, Johnson family archives.
12. Johnson family archives.
13. Flaherty, "Life Story of Walter Perry Johnson."
14. *Washington Times*, June 24, 1914.
15. *Cleveland Plain Dealer*, June 13, 1914.
16. *Washington Daily News*, June 17, 1925.
17. Clipping, source unknown, n.d.(presumably June 25, 1914), Hazel Johnson personal scrapbook.
18. Clipping, source unknown, October 1914, HOF files.
19. *Baseball Magazine*, April 1915.
20. Clipping, source unknown, n.d., 1915, HOF files.
21. Johnson, "My Pitching Years."

   The story that Joe Engel was responsible for Jack Dunn's discovery of Babe Ruth, the source of which apparently was Engel himself, has been repeated so many times that it might as well be told again here. This is from *Babe, The Legend Comes To Life*, by Robert Creamer:

   > Engel was a colorful man and a fascinating raconteur. One of the stories he loved to tell concerned the time he went back to Emmittsburg one Sunday to pitch for the alumni in a commencement day game. (He had the day off because Sunday baseball was not allowed in Washington then). There was a preliminary game between the Mount St.

Mary's freshmen and an "orphanage" team—St. Mary's of Baltimore. The St. Mary's pitcher caught Engel's eye, partly because of his fastball and partly because of his haircut. Ruth—he was the pitcher, of course—no longer wore his hair cropped short but instead was wearing it in the most mature hair style that he, Engel, had ever seen on a school kid. Clipped on the side, it "roached" or waved over the forehead, in the mode highly favored by bartenders and other cool cats of the day.

Beyond the haircut, Engel was singularly impressed by the young lefthander's sidearm speed. 'He really could wheel that ball in there,' he said, 'and remember, I was used to seeing Walter Johnson throw. This kid was a great natural pitcher. He had everything. He must have struck out 18 or 20 men in that game.' Later that afternoon, as Engel was pitching for the alumni, he spotted Ruth again, still in baseball uniform but now sitting with the school band banging away at a big bass drum. That night, on his way back to join the Senators, Engel ran into Dunn. Dunn was 40, twice Engel's age, but he knew and liked the flip young pitcher. In his book on Ruth, Tom Meany recreated the dialogue between the two.

" Where you been working, Slick?" asked Dunn.

"Aw, just pitching against some college kids."

"That's where you belong. See anybody that looked any good?"

"Yeah. There was some orphan asylum from Baltimore playing in the first game and they had a young lefthand kid pitching for them who's got real stuff.' Engel paused. 'He can beat hell out of a bass drum."

"You don't happen to remember his name, do you?" asked Dunn, reaching inside his coat for a pencil and an old envelope.

"I think they called him Ruth," said Engel.

Whether or not this was Dunn's first report on Ruth is impossible to determine.—Robert Creamer, *Babe, The Legend Comes to Life* (New York: Simon and Schuster, 1974).

22. Johnson, "Why I Signed With the Federal League."
23. *Washington Post*, May 24, 1914.
24. *Washington Post*, May 25, 1914.
25. *Washington Star*, June 4, 1914.
26. Harold Seymour, *Baseball, The Golden Age* (New York: Oxford University Press, 1971).
27. *Washington Star*, July 16, 1914.
28. Johnson, "Why I Signed With the Federal League."
29. Ibid.
30. *Washington Star*, October 10, 1914.
31. Clipping, source unknown, n.d. (July 1914), Hazel Johnson scrapbook.
32. *Washington Post*, July 28, 1914.

33. *Washington Star*, October 29, 1914.
34. *Arkansas Gazette*, October 31, 1914.
35. Seymour, *Baseball, The Golden Age.*
36. Johnson, "Why I Signed With the Federal League."
37. "The Famous Minor Letter From the President of the Washington Club to Walter Johnson," *Baseball Magazine*, April 1915.
38. Johnson, "Why I Signed With the Federal League."
39. Povich, *The Washington Senators.*
40. Clipping, source unknown, December 3, 1914, HOF files.
41. Johnson, "Why I Signed With the Federal League."
42. Clipping, source unknown, December 26, 1914, HOF files.
43. *Detroit Free Press*, December 5, 1914.
44. Associated Press, December 4, 1914.
45. Seymour, *Baseball, The Golden Age.*
46. *Washington Star*, December 11, 1946.
47. Robert Boyd, source unknown, October 12, 1925, scrapbook XV.
48. Johnson, "Why I signed With the Federal League."
49. Clipping, source unknown, n.d., HOF files.
50. *Washington Star*, December 11, 1946.
51. Povich, *The Washington Senators.*
52. Clipping, source unknown, December 26, 1914, HOF files.
53. *Washington Times*, January 2, 1915.

CHAPTER 9

1. Arthur Daley, "The Fireball Throwers," *New York Times*, March 20, 1953. Braves manager George Stallings: "When [Johnson] struck Evers out, Johnny came back to me and remarked, 'That was the fastest ball that ever passed me at the plate. I didn't see it until it was on top of me, and although I wanted to swing, it was too late.' " *Washington Post*, April 11, 1915.
2. Clipping, source unknown, March 6, 1915, HOF files.
3. *Washington Post*, March 9, 1915.
4. Ibid.

The erroneous notion that Grantland Rice originated "The Big Train" somehow got into the baseball literature and was repeated so often that eventually Johnson came to believe it himself. Taylor Spink, *The Sporting News*, September 3, 1942. In a Newark radio interview in 1928, however, in response to the question, "Why do they call you 'The Big Train'?" Johnson replied: "That's something I can't answer. I suppose some sporting writer pinned that on me. But I really do not know why I am called that." Norman St. Denis, clipping, unknown Newark newspaper, n.d., scrapbook XXII(1928). In a lengthy profile of Johnson in 1926, Rice used the nickname "Old Barney" eight times and "The Coffeyville Express" twice—but never "The Big Train." At one point he writes, "also sometimes known as Old Barney and the Coffeyville Express," almost as if he was purposely trying to avoid the much more famous moniker, which he certainly wouldn't do if he was its creator. Grantland Rice, "The Coffeyville Express," *Collier's*, June 5, 1926.

5. *Washington Post*, March 26, 1915.
6. *Washington Post*, May 26, 1916.
7. Carmichael, *My Greatest Day In Baseball*. From more than 2,000 games in his great career, Sisler picked his pitching win over Johnson as his "Greatest Day in Baseball": "Every American kid has a baseball idol. Mine was Walter Johnson, the 'Big Train.' Come to think about it, Walter is still my idea of the real baseball player. I was so crazy about the man that I'd read every line and kept every picture of him I could get my hands on." Of beating Johnson, Sisler wrote: "For a minute I thought maybe I'd go over and shake his hand and tell him that I was sorry I beat him, but I guess that was just the silly idea of a young kid who had just come face to face with his idol and beaten him."
8. Alan Trammell and Lou Whitaker, in their 18th season together with Detroit in 1994, tied the record.
9. Steve Wulf, "The Secrets of Sam," *Sports Illustrated*, July 9, 1993.
10. Al Kermisch, "Sam Rice's Batting Record Purified," *Baseball Research Journal*, 1981.
11. Povich, *The Washington Senators*.
12. Povich, "The Washington Senators," *Sport Magazine*, December 1951.
13. Bob Considine, *Washington Herald*, November 1935, misc. scrapbook.
14. Dan Schlossberg, *The Baseball Book of Why* (Middle Village, N.Y: Jonathan David, Inc., 1984).
15. *Washington Star*, February 25, 1940.
16. Povich, *The Washington Senators*.
17. *Washington Post*, August 15, 1915.
18. Donald Honig, *The Man In The Dugout* (Chicago: Follet Publishing Co., 1977).
19. J.G. Taylor Spink, *The Sporting News*, December 25, 1946.
20. Johnson, "The Greatest Players I Ever Saw."
21. Spink, *The Sporting News*, December 25, 1946.
22. J.G. Taylor Spink, "End of Line For Big Train," *The Sporting News*, December 18, 1946.
23. Johnson, "The Greatest Players I Ever Saw."
24. Ritter, *The Glory of Their Times*.
25. Cobb, *My Life in Baseball*.

26. Ward Mason, "Oscar Vitt," *Baseball Magazine*, August 1916.
27. Povich, "Walter Johnson, The Big Train."
28. Cobb, *My Life in Baseball.*
Cobb told the same story to Shirley Povich 20 years earlier. "If it hadn't been for his kind nature, he'd have owned me," Cobb said. *Washington Post*, May 9, 1940.
29. *Washington Post*, May 9, 1940.
30. Steven H. Heath, "Ty Cobb vs. Walter Johnson," *Baseball Quarterly Reviews*, Fall 1992. Cobb faced Johnson 368 times in 103 games. He had 119 hits in 322 official at-bats, including 1 home run, 7 triples, and 19 doubles. Johnson hit Cobb with a pitch only once—in 1910, *before* Cobb started crowding the plate on him.
31. Cobb, *My Life In Baseball.*
Cobb told Arthur Daley, "Walter was the finest and most decent man I ever met." *New York Times*, June 9, 1968; "The only man Ty Cobb openly admired during his stormy career was pitcher Walter Johnson." Jack Shea, "The Georgia Peach," *Sport Magazine*, November 1948.
32. Johnson, "My Pitching Years"; Ken Smith, *Baseball's Hall of Fame* (New York: A.S. Barnes & Co., 1947); Cobb, *My Life In Baseball.*
33. Al Stump, *Cobb* (Chapel Hill, North Carolina: Algonquin Books, 1994); Alexander, *Ty Cobb.*
34. Vincent X. Flaherty, *Washington Times-Herald*, April 7, 1939. Although many of the details vary between Flaherty's version of the story, as told to him by Johnson, and that presented by Charles Alexander in *Ty Cobb*, taken from contemporary reports, this must surely be the same incident.
35. Johnson, "My Pitching Years."
36. Ritter, "George McBride: 'I Took Honus Wagner's Job.'"
37. *Washington Post*, March 8, 1917; Ibid.
38. Margaret Milan letter to Carolyn Johnson Thomas, May 8, 1961.
39. Clipping, source unknown, scrapbook XXVI(1929).
40. Povich, "Walter Johnson, The Big Train."
41. Lane, "The Greatest Pitcher On the Diamond Today."
42. Gregory Kallen, "Major League Baseball During the Great War," *Rounding Third, Major League Baseball in Washington*, Preservation Press, 1979. The patriotic Gowdy, a coach with the Cincinnati Reds in 1942, also made himself one of baseball's first enlistees in the Second World War.
43. J.V. Fitzgerald, *Washington Post*, June 24, 1917.
44. *Boston Globe*, September 28, 1917.
45. Rogers Hornsby, *My War With Baseball* (New York: Coward-McCann, 1962).
46. Johnson, "This is the Life,", unpublished manuscript, n.d. (c. 1918), Johnson family archives.

CHAPTER 10

1. Kallen, "Major League Baseball During the Great War."
2. Kermisch, "Sam Rice's Batting Record Purified."
3. Creamer, *Babe*.
   Ruth hit a second home run off Johnson on June 30 to beat him in the tenth inning. Those two homers by Ruth on May 7 and June 30, 1918, were the only home runs given up by Johnson from September 1917 to May 1920. Raymond Gonzales, "Home Runs Off the Big Train," *Baseball Research Journal*, 1979.
4. Carl Hubbell also pitched an 18-inning shutout win on July 2, 1933; Ed Summers of Detroit pitched an 18-inning shutout tie game on July 16, 1909.
5. *Washington Post*, July 12, 1918.
6. Creamer, *Babe*; Kallen, "Major League Baseball During the Great War."
7. J.V. Fitzgerald, *Washington Post*, August 5, 1918. Griffith is called "the dominant factor in the affairs of the American League at present."
8. Povich, "Clark Griffith—50 Years in Baseball," *Washington Post*, February 6, 1938.
9. Povich, *The Washington Senators*.
10. Kallen, "Major League Baseball During the Great War."
11. Stanley Grosshandler, *Baseball & The Great War* (New York: Dutton, 1990).
12. Johnson, "My Honest Opinion Of My Own Pitching," *Baseball Magazine*, May 1919.
13. Clipping, source unknown, n.d., scrapbook III(1919).
14. George Halas, the legendary National Football League pioneer and owner/coach of the Chicago Bears football team, had five of his 22 major league at-bats in this game, going 0-for-5 with two strikeouts. In an exhibition game against the New York Giants on April 20, another football (and Olympic) great, Jim Thorpe, went 2-for-5 in one of his last major-league appearances, a game in which Johnson pitched the first 6 innings.
15. Louis Dougher, *Washington Times*, July 25, 1919.
16. Frank Young, *Washington Post*, June 2, 1929. "[Engel's] main trouble [pitching] was an inability to locate the plate, and one of the best stories told of him while a player comes from Minneapolis in this connection. In one game he walked 16 players, and that night someone asked manager Cantillon for a pass to the next day's game. 'See Joe Engel,' was the reply, 'he issues most of the passes on this club.' … He was a notoriously bad hitter, and Griffith used to say that Engel used himself as a test in judging a pitcher's ability, that 'If [Engel] can get even a foul off him, he's no good.' "
17. Holman, *Wonderful Walter Johnson*.
18. Frank Young, *Washington Post*, June 2, 1929.
19. Lieb, "The P.T. Barnum of the Bushes."

20. Young, *Washington Post*, June 2, 1929.
21. Lieb, "The P.T. Barnum of the Bushes."
22. Ibid; Johnson, "My Pitching Years"; Povich, *The Washington Senators.*
23. Harris interview with Larry Amman.
24. Stanley Harris, *Playing The Game* (New York: Grosset & Dunlap, 1925).
25. Harris's 479 putouts at second base in 1922 was the major-league record for more than 50 years, and is still the American League record, as is his five years leading the league in doubleplays. He led the league in putouts four years.
26. Clipping, source unknown, n.d., scrapbook XXV (1929).
27. Alex Haas, "Batters Hit By Pitchers," *Baseball Historical Review*, 1981.
28. Bob Considine, *Washington Herald*, n.d., 1935, misc. scrapbook.
29. Harris, *Playing The Game.*
30. Larry Amman, unpublished manuscript, Johnson family archives; Ossie Bluege interview with Amman; *Literary Digest*, April 18, 1925.
31. Seymour, *Baseball, The Golden Age.*
32. Povich, "Clark Griffith—50 Years in Baseball," *Washington Post*, February 7, 1938.
33. *Washington Times-Herald*, July 12, 1942.
34. Povich, *The Washington Senators.*
35. Bealle, *The Washington Senators.*
36. Povich, "Clark Griffith—50 Years in Baseball."
37. Ritter, *Glory of Their Times.*
38. Schacht interview with Larry Amman. Griffith's exaggerated reputation for tightfistedness was cemented into legend for all time in 1934 by the sale of pennant-winning manager and all-star shortstop Joe Cronin, who also happened to be married to Griffith's niece and ward Mildred Robertson, to the Red Sox for \$250,000 (\$225,000 and Boston shortstop Lyn Lary). "No ballplayer in the world is worth \$250,000," the owner explained. Povich, "Clark Griffith—50 Years in Baseball," *Washington Post*, February 16, 1938.
39. *Washington Post*, June 10, 1942.
40. Ogden Nash, "Line-up For Yesterday: An ABC of Baseball Immortals," from Charles Einstein(ed.), *The Fireside Book of Baseball* (New York: Simon & Schuster, 1956).
41. *Boston Globe*, May 7, 1924; *Washington Post*, March 24, 1939.
42. Johnson, "When I Was a Shine Ball Pitcher," *Baseball Magazine*, January 1921.
43. Lyall Smith, *Detroit Free Press*, reprinted in *Baseball Digest*, Jan-Feb 1957.
44. Whitney Martin, *Washington Post*, December 12, 1946.
45. John Thorn and Peter Palmer, *The Hidden Game of Baseball* (Garden City, New York: Doubleday & Co., 1985).
46. Johnson, "The Greatest Batters I Have Ever Faced," *Baseball Magazine*, June 1925.
47. Dan Daniel, *The Sporting News*, December 25, 1946.

48. Harris, *Playing The Game.*
49. Al Schacht, *My Own Particular Screwball* (Garden City, N.Y.: Doubleday & Co., 1955).
50. Telegram, Johnson family archives.
51. Clipping, source unknown, n.d., scrapbook III (1919–20).

Among those at Johnson's no-hitter was Thomas P. "Tip" O'Neill, Speaker of the House in the 1980s. In his memoirs O'Neill described the impression it made on him:

> I was seven and a half. The Washington Senators were a terrible team, but the legendary Walter Johnson was on the mound, and from our seats in the centerfield bleachers we saw Johnson pitch the only no-hitter of his career, as the Senators defeated the Red Sox, 1–0. At one point I watched in amazement as Johnson retired 6 Boston batters on 6 consecutive pitches. I've always wondered whether that was some kind of record, but this turns out to be one of the few statistics in baseball that nobody keeps track of. I also counted the number of pitches thrown by each pitcher. I had read that baseball managers did this, and that when a pitcher reached a certain quota—maybe 115 pitches—it was time to bring somebody in from the bullpen. I've always loved working with numbers, and throughout my career in politics I was known as a guy who knew how to count. Who knows? Maybe it all began with counting Walter Johnson's pitches at Fenway Park. — Thomas P. O'Neill, *Man of the House* (New York: Random House, 1987).

52. J.V. Fitzgerald, *Washington Post*, July 6, 1920.
53. Schacht, *My Own Particular Screwball.*
54. Creamer, *Babe.*
55. Cullen Cain, source unknown, June 1921, scrapbook IV.
56. Clipping, source unknown, n.d. (early August 1920), scrapbook III(1919–20).
57. Schacht, *My Own Particular Screwball.*
58. *Washington Post*, December 12, 1946.
59. Bill McGowan, source unknown, n.d., scrapbook IX(1924).
60. Schacht, *My Own Particular Screwball.*
61. Clipping, source unknown, n.d., scrapbook III(1919–20).
62. Johnson letter to F.C. Lane, May 10, 1923, HOF files.

The exact nature of Johnson's arm injury is unknown, and the wide variety of descriptions of symptoms and effects doesn't make it any easier to determine. Johnson himself always called it a "cold which settled in my arm." But he also several times described a hard, round knot "in the shape of a little round ball" that formed just above the elbow, apparently on the inside of his arm. Another time he said, "The doctors have advised complete rest. They think a muscle or ligament between the elbow and shoulder is liable to be torn loose if the arm is exerted too much." One article has Dr. Knight's diagnosis as "an inflammation due to a cold settling in the shoulder," while another quotes Griffith as saying Johnson "merely tore the lining off a bone."

63. Joe Holman, *Washington Times*, June 16, 1930.

CHAPTER 11

1. *San Francisco Examiner*, February 6, 1920.
2. *Washington Herald*, April 10, 1909.
3. Charles Gandil, "This is My Story of the Black Sox Scandal," *Sports Illustrated*, September 17, 1956.
4. Eliot Asinof, *Eight Men Out* (New York: Holt, Rinehart and Winston, 1963). Clark Griffith may have been referring to Sullivan in this story, told in a spring training "fanning bee" in 1930: "Why, the bare announcement that Johnson was going into the box one day caused a man to faint. This is the gospel truth. It was in Boston, and betting there in those days was rampant. A big shot, on the occasion of a Washington visit, had wagered $2,500 to $1,000 on the Red Sox. [Hugh] Bedient was in the box for Boston. I don't remember which of our pitchers was working. In the 5th inning the score was 3 to 0 in favor of the Red Sox and the gambler, whose bet was well known to the Washington team, was having a great time guying our boys. Germany Schaefer fired back at him, 'We'll win this game yet; it's as good as in.' These sounded like idle words, however, until the 7th when, with 2 runs over in a Washington rally and 2 men on, Schaefer hit the fence for a double and the Senators were ahead. When the side was retired, with several Washington pitchers warming up in the bullpen, I motioned to the bench and Johnson, pointing to himself, asked, 'me?' I nodded, and Walter started with that lanky stride toward the pitcher's box. That Boston gambler took one look at the approaching player, turned pale and then fainted—cold. They carried him off, and Washington won the game." *Washington Star*, February 22, 1930.
5. Johnson, "Some of My Early Experiences."
6. *Humboldt Union*, May 24, 1921. In a letter to "a friend" (possibly Dave Woods) back in Humboldt, Johnson wrote: "We are getting cleaner and finer boys in the game every day, and I hope before long the so-called 'roughneck' will be a thing of the past."
7. Johnson, "The Greatest Batters I Have Ever Faced"; Johnson, "The Greatest Players I Ever Saw": "I shall never believe that he [Jackson] was a bad fellow at heart. He was easily and terribly misled by his associates."
8. Editorial, "Walter Johnson: Sportsman," *New York Evening World*, n.d., scrapbook VIII(1924).

   Walter Johnson's reputation for honesty and forthrightness was so well known that it's unlikely that he was ever directly approached by the gambling sorts that hovered around the game before and after the Black Sox scandal. That didn't give him immunity from their attempts to influence events, however, as this episode from 1924 illustrates:

On opening day, when Walter Johnson trailed into Griffith Stadium he was approached by a niftily dressed young fellow who asked Johnson if he desired to cross up the gamblers.

"Why, what do you mean?" asked Johnson.

"Well, all the wise bettors in town are wagering that the first ball you pitch this afternoon will be a strike. Why not cross them up by throwing a wide one?" was the suggestion made.

Johnson only smiled and walked away. Remember that the first ball pitched was a strike. Recently while pitching against Ruth at the local park Johnson was accused by the "cheap gamblers" of laying one through the groove so Babe could homer. The "wise boys" had bet that Ruth would not hit one against him. On arriving at the park yesterday Johnson received an unsigned letter in which the writer attempted to place Johnson in the same type of player who would throw a game. Of course he had no comeback. He did not desire any and was not particularly interested in the anonymous letter. Those are but a few of the ways that bettors try to fix things and get back at a player when the gambler happens to lose.—*Washington Herald*, April 28, 1924.

9. Seymour, *Baseball, The Golden Age.*
10. *Coffeyville Journal*, February 1922, scrapbook IX; Clipping, source unknown, October 1921, scrapbook IV. Johnson: "The ball this year [1921] was really made livelier than ever before . . . . A deader ball will be used from this season on."

    In a May 15, 1920, letter to Neil "Foxy Grandpa" Uhl—apparently still involved in the game at the age of 70—Johnson made some curious comments about the balls: "I sent you five baseballs today, they are not very good but all we had. They saved a lot of the old ones and sent them back to the factory the other day. The balls have been no good and they are trying to have them made better or else sell them cheaper. They are hard to get, though, as they are." (HOF files).
11. Clipping, source unknown, August 3, 1927, scrapbook XIX.
12. Seymour, *Baseball, The Golden Age.*
13. Clipping, source unknown, n.d., scrapbook IX(1924); Clipping, source unknown, n.d., scrapbook III(1919–21): "Johnson does not discolor the ball in the slightest degree, not even to the extent of spitting on his glove or rubbing in a little dirt. He really prefers to work with a sphere absolutely unsullied and has been known to call for a new ball when that he was using had become accidentally scuffed to the degree that other hurlers connive to get it in."
14. Clipping, source unknown, August 3, 1927, scrapbook XIX.
15. Ibid.
16. Yardley, *Ring.*

17. Clippings, sources unknown, n.d., scrapbook III(1919–21).
Josh Clarke, former major leaguer and brother of the Pirates great outfielder/manager Fred Clarke, was made the first manager of the Coffeyville team. Both Clarkes lived at nearby Winfield, Kansas.
18. *Washington Herald*, March 15, 1921.
19. Clipping, source unknown, March 27, 1921, scrapbook III.
20. Clipping, source unknown, May 8, 1921, scrapbook III.
21. *N.Y. Daily News*, August 24, 1942.
22. Povich, *Washington Post*, March 13, 1989.
23. Schacht, *My Own Particular Screwball*; Johnson, "My Pitching Years."
24. Clipping, source unknown, May 16, 1921, scrapbook III.
25. Johnson, "The Reflections Of An Old Timer," *Baseball Magazine*, February 1922.
26. Salsinger, *Detroit News*, June 10, 1921.
27. *Detroit News*, June 11, 1921.
28. Clipping, source unknown, n.d., scrapbook IV(1921).
29. Clipping, source unknown, n.d., scrapbook XXV(1929).
30. Johnson letter to F.C. Lane, January 15, 1922, HOF files.
31. *Washington Star*, January 20, 1922: "The hurler also stated [in a letter to Griffith accompanying his contract] that he was disposing of his holdings in Coffeyville and would in the very near future take up residence with his father-in-law in Nevada. It seems that the loss of his little daughter Elinor and his father has cast a damper over the once sunny disposition of the great pitcher and he is more than anxious to get away from the scene of all his sorrows."
32. Johnson letter to Hazel Johnson, n.d., Johnson family archives.
33. Johnson family archives.
34. Johnson, "The Reflections Of An Old Timer."
35. Cullen Cain, source unknown, March 18, 1922, scrapbook IV.
36. Clipping, source unknown, April 13, 1922, scrapbook IV.
37. Clipping, source unknown, n.d., scrapbook IV(1922–23). Johnson's statement is ironic in light of his own problems as a manager.
Milan was reunited with his "discoverer," Joe Cantillon, at Minneapolis, where he averaged .296 in 101 games in 1923. The next year he hit .316 as player-manager of George Weiss's New Haven club, and in 1925 batted .324 while managing Memphis to a Southern Association pennant. Of Milan's minor-league managing career, Frank Young of the *Washington Post* said in 1929: "He has had marked success. He has consistently turned out first-flight teams in the bushes by making real players out of the crudest kind of ivory." Clipping, n.d., scrapbook XXV (1929).
38. David W. Toll, "E.E. Roberts and the Politics of Personal Liberty," *Nevada* magazine, n.d., Johnson family archives.

39. Associated Press, September 29, 1929.
40. Toll, "E.E. Roberts and the Politics of Personal Liberty": "The only way to put the bootleggers out of business," Roberts said in a speech from the pulpit of a Reno church, "is to place a barrel of good corn whiskey on every downtown street corner, with dippers attached, and signs inviting passersby to help themselves to all they want, free of charge. That is the way to eliminate the problem of whiskey and graft."
41. *New York Times*, March 21, 1931.
42. Toll, "E.E. Roberts and the Politics of Personal Liberty", quoting from an interview with John Cahlan for the oral history program at the University of Nevada.
43. Ibid, quoting from an interview with John Sanford.
44. Ibid.
45. Johnson letter to F.C. Lane, December 10, 1922, HOF files.
46. *Washington Herald*, March 15, 1923.
47. Johnson, letter to F.C. Lane, May 10, 1923, HOF files: "I am not foolish enough to think that I can pitch like I used to but believe I can hold my own for a year or two yet ... will admit that I have used my arm pretty hard but I don't believe there ever was an arm like mine and don't be surprised if you see me pitching four or five years from now."
48. Johnson, "My Pitching Years."
49. Denman Thompson, *Washington Star*, n.d., scrapbook V(1924).
50. Bealle, *The Washington Senators*.
51. Povich, "Clark Griffith—50 Years in Baseball," *The Washington Post*, February 8, 1938.
52. Shirley Povich, "The Old Fox," *Regardies,* June/July 1983.
53. Johnson, "What I Pitch to Babe Ruth and Why": "Peck has done our club more injury than Ruth ever did."
54. Peckinpaugh interview with Larry Amman.
55. Povich, "The Old Fox."
56. J.P. Glass, *Cleveland Plain Dealer*, n.d., scrapbook XXIII(1928).
57. Harris interview with Larry Amman. Bluege had the edge, in Harris's opinion, because of a better arm.
58. Bob Considine, *Washington Herald*, 1935, misc scrapbook.
    Bluege retired from the Minnesota Twins in 1971, ending a 50-year association with the Griffith baseball franchise as player, coach, manager, farm-system director, controller, and executive secretary.
59. Povich, "Bluege Last Link To Heyday of Senators," *Washington Post*, October 16, 1985.
60. Povich, "The Old Fox."
61. Bluege interview with Larry Amman.
62. Povich, "The Old Fox."

63. Schlossberg, *The Baseball Book of Why*.
64. Harris, Bluege interviews with Larry Amman; Holman, *Wonderful Walter Johnson*.
65. Frank Graham, *New York Sun*, n.d., scrapbook XXVI(1929).
66. Ruel, "Catching a Speed King," n.d., scrapbook XVIII(1927).
   In 1924, Ruel's father said: "It was 15 years ago when I took my boy to see Walter Johnson pitch. 'Muddy' had on knee pants. Even then he was a rabid baseball fan. The game was half over when he turned to me and said: 'Wouldn't it be great to catch Walter Johnson.' " Clipping, source unknown, n.d., scrapbook IX(1924)).
67. Harris interview with Larry Amman.
68. Marberry's status as the first great relief specialist should be beyond dispute. His 59 relief appearances in 1926 wasn't topped until 1942, his 22 saves that year not until 1949; his 55 games without a start in 1925 wasn't bettered until 1942; Marberry was the first pitcher with 100 career saves, and the next one wouldn't do it until 11 years after his retirement; he led the American League in saves five times; he holds the records for most years leading both leagues in games pitched(6) and games finished(5). Bill James: "Firpo Marberry was a landmark. Marberry was the first truly outstanding pitcher to be used primarily in relief over a period of several seasons.... Whether or not his career had the longevity that is expected of a Hall of Famer, this I don't know—but for an 11-year period, 1924 through 1934, Marberry was as valuable to his team as any pitcher in baseball except Lefty Grove." Bill James, *The Bill James Historical Abstract* (New York: Villard Books, 1985).
69. Schacht interview with Larry Amman.
70. Bluege interview with Larry Amman.
71. Povich, *The Washington Senators*.
72. Bluege interview with Larry Amman. Bluege called Leibold *"a fine gentleman."*
73. *Washington Senators 1957 media guide*.
74. Clipping, n.d., scrapbook VI(1924).

CHAPTER 12

1. William Fowler, manuscript, presumed unpublished, n.d., Johnson family archives. The same story was related by an unknown writer in the *Detroit Athletic Club News*, July 1921.
2. *The Sporting News*, March 17, 1924.
3. Clipping, source unknown, n.d., scrapbook X(1924).
4. Denman Thompson, *Washington Star*, n.d., scrapbook V(1923–24).
   Weiss was still recovering from injuries suffered in a December train wreck in which New Haven manager and former Tigers pitching great Wild Bill Donovan was

killed. Milan replaced Donovan at New Haven, which became something of a farm club of the Nationals. *Washington Herald*, March 6, 1924.

5. Clipping, source unknown, n.d., scrapbook V.
6. Frank Young, *Washington Post*, n.d., scrapbook V.
7. John Dugan, *Washington Herald*, n.d., scrapbook V.
8. Povich, *The Washington Senators*; Harris interview with Larry Amman.
9. Povich, "Clark Griffith—50 years in Baseball," *Washington Post*, February 10, 1938.
10. Povich, *The Washington Senators.*
11. Holman, *Wonderful Walter Johnson*; Larry Amman, "The Clown Prince of Baseball," *Baseball Research Journal*, 1982. Al Schacht: "His [Harris's] example meant a lot. He was a tough one at second. If a runner came in high on a double play, he wouldn't hesitate to put the ball right between the guy's eyes. Babe Ruth tried to up-end Bucky once. Bucky sidestepped him, gave him the hip, and knocked Ruth onto the outfield grass."
12. Walter Johnson: "When Bucky Harris, almost a kid, was named to run the club, I was the most surprised player in the bunch." Johnson, "My Pitching Years."
13. Povich, *The Washington Senators.*
14. Clipping, source unknown, March 2, 1924, scrapbook V.
15. Povich, *The Washington Senators.*
16. Holman, *Wonderful Walter Johnson*; Larry Amman, unpublished manuscript. "Harris did not hesitate to assert his authority when it was necessary. He fined rookie pitcher Byron Speece $50 for public drunkenness. He benched Jim Prothro for not running out a ground ball."
17. Harris interview with Larry Amman.
18. Holman, *Wonderful Walter Johnson.*
19. Peckinpaugh interview with Larry Amman. Ossie Bluege (on the 1924 team): "I liked them all. They were all fine fellows." Bluege interview with Larry Amman.
20. Al Schacht, *Clowning Through Baseball* (New York: A.S. Barnes & Co., 1941.); "Schacht Shows Mid-Season Form In Dodging Bullets," clipping, source unknown (probably a Tampa newspaper), n.d., scrapbook IV.
21. Johnson, "My Pitching Years." The great shape these activities left him in "kept me from being forced out of baseball," Johnson wrote.
22. Johnson letter to F.C. Lane, January 14, 1924, HOF files.
23. Harris, *Playing The Game.*
24. Clipping, source unknown, n.d., scrapbook V.
25. *Washington Post*, March 7, 1924.
26. *Washington Star*, March 10, 1924.
27. *Washington Herald*, June 28, 1924.
28. Clipping, source unknown, March 27, 1924, scrapbook VI.

29. Harris, *Playing The Game.*
30. Bob Davids, *Minor League Baseball Stars*, Society for American Baseball Research, 1978.
31. Povich, *The Washington Senators.*
32. Ibid.
33. Clipping, source unknown, n.d., scrapbook VI.
34. Povich, *The Washington Senators.*
35. Honig, *The Man In The Dugout*; Bluege interview with Larry Amman.
36. Beale, *The Washington Senators.*
Bucky Harris: "We obtained [Matthews] when we were in desperate straits for an outfielder who could hit. He supplied the needed punch. More than that, he furnished an inspiring example of courage and fighting spirit. He helped infuse new life in the club." Harris, *Playing The Game.*
37. Schacht, *Clowning Through Baseball*; *My Own Particular Screwball.*
38. Harris interview with Larry Amman.
39. Amman, "The Clown Prince of Baseball."
40. Their routines included infield practice with Schacht at third and Altrock, pretending to be drunk, at first, Schacht throwing a rubber baseball that bounced off Altrock's head; a slow-motion pitching and batting sequence; a golf outing with Schacht the caddy and Altrock the duffer using a bat to "golf" a baseball all over the park, then getting down on all fours and using the bat like a billiard cue to knock it into the "cup"; Schacht taking over as conductor of the band, leading the musicians in frenzied versions of their songs while Altrock pretended to play the tuba and other instruments. Their grand finale was an elaborate burlesque of dancer Ruth St. Denis's "Death Dance," which she performed with a live snake—a string of frankfurters in their routine. 50,000 fans at the first game of the 1922 World Series at the Polo Grounds witnessed their greatest act, a recreation of the bullfighting scene from Rudolph Valentino's famous movie *Blood and Sand.* The "bull" was a goat which Schacht got to chase him by stuffing cabbage leaves into his clothes, while Altrock, in drag, played the swooning senorita. Schacht, *My Own Particular Screwball*; *Washington Post*, October 8, 1921.
41. Rich Marazzi, "Al Schacht, The Clown Prince of Baseball", *Baseball History*, Winter 1986.
42. Lieb, "Comedians and Pranksters of Baseball"; Schacht, *My Own Particular Screwball*: "I knew for sure Nick and I would never hit it off when I first saw what he was like with too much to drink. He spied me in the hotel and insisted I go out drinking with him. I refused. He shouted I was nothing but a 'Jew Kike bastard!' I knew he was under the weather, but I didn't like it. I never did."
43. Charles Einstein, *The Fireside Book of Baseball*, 3rd edition; Marazzi, "Al Schacht, The Clown Prince of Baseball."

More recent baseball fans have been exposed to Schacht's genius, most of them without knowing the source, unfortunately, in the performances of baseball comedian Max Patkin. Having appropriated much of Schacht's material and even his title of "The Clown Prince of Baseball," Patkin, who bears a striking physical resemblance to Schacht, has been doing his act throughout the minor league circuits for years. Part of his routine can be seen in the movie *Bull Durham*.

44. Babe Ruth with Bob Considine, *The Babe Ruth Story* (New York: E.P. Dutton & Co., 1948).
45. Clipping, source unknown, n.d., scrapbook VI.
46. Baxter, *Washington Post*, n.d., scrapbook VI.
47. Amman, "The Clown Prince of Baseball."
48. Harris, *Playing The Game*.
49. Clipping, source unknown, n.d., scrapbook VI.
50. Clipping, source unknown, n.d., scrapbook VI.
51. Ossie Bluege on St. Louis in July and August: "Remember, both St. Louis teams used that field. It was as hard as concrete, and felt like running on hot coals. The ground crew would water it down after practice. There was so much steam rising it hit you in the face. I saw a number of guys faint standing on the infield. At night the air in the hotel rooms was sweltering. You couldn't get a fan. You'd douse yourself with water and hope you'd get some sleep. The next day you'd go to the ballpark feeling like a wrung-out dishrag." Interview with Larry Amman.
52. Joe Holman, *Wonderful Walter Johnson*.
53. Frank Young, *Washington Post*, June 2, 1929.
54. Povich, *The Washington Senators*.
55. F.C. Lane, "If I Were Only Young Once More," *Baseball Magazine*, November 1924.
56. Clipping, source unknown, n.d., scrapbook VI.
57. Clipping, source unknown, n.d., scrapbook VI.
58. Clipping, source unknown, n.d., scrapbook IX.
59. Damon Runyon, source unknown, n.d., scrapbook VII.
60. Clipping, source unknown, n.d., scrapbook IV.
61. Ibid.
62. Will Rogers, "Everybody Is Pulling For Walter," *New York Times*, September 28, 1924.
63. Ibid.
64. Clipping, source unknown, n.d., scrapbook IV.
65. Clipping, source unknown, n.d., scrapbook VII.
66. Telegrams in Johnson family archives.
67. Povich, *The Washington Senators*.
68. Clipping, source unknown, n.d., scrapbook VII.

69. Povich, *The Washington Senators.*
70. Johnson, "My Pitching Years."
71. Muddy Ruel, "Catching a Speed King," 1927, scrapbook XVIII: "Even in those hectic days, Walter Johnson was the same level-headed fellow, with a friendly smile and handclasp for those who sought him out. The night we arrived in Boston for that crucial series, a reporter intercepted him in the hotel lobby and Barney willingly and graciously sat down with him for an interview. He did this in spite of the fact that we had just concluded a long, tedious train journey from the west and Walter expected to be called on duty the next day. 'The same old Walter,' said the reporter as he went down the steps. 'Long live the King!.' "
72. Clipping, source unknown, n.d.[probably Sepember 30, 1924], scrapbook VIII.
73. John Dugan, *Washington Herald*, September 30, 1924.
74. John Kieran, *New York Herald*, September 30, 1924.

CHAPTER 13

1. *Washington Post*, October 2, 1924.
2. Clipping, source unknown, n.d., scrapbook VIII(1924).
3. Frank Young, *Washington Post*, September 30, 1924.
4. Johnson, "My Pitching Years."
5. Christy Walsh, *Adios to Ghosts* (New York: 1937).
6. Clipping, source unknown, n.d., scrapbook VIII(1924).
7. Clipping, source unknown, n.d., scrapbook IX(1924).
8. Lardner telegram, October 1, 1924, Johnson family archives.
9. Margaret Ruth Triggs, source unknown, n.d, scrapbook IX(1924).
10. *Washington Post*, October 2, 1924; clippings, source unknown, n.d., scrapbook IX(1924).
11. Lowell Blaisdell, "Mystery and Tragedy: The O'Connell-Dolan Scandal," *Baseball Research Journal*, Society for American Baseball Research, 1982.
12. Clipping, source unknown, n.d., scrapbook X(1924); Harold Johnson, *Who's Who in Major League Baseball* (Chicago, Buxton Publishing Co., 1933); *Baseball Magazine*, December 1924.
13. Clipping, source unknown, n.d., scrapbook IX(1924).
14. *Washington Post*, n.d., scrapbook IX(1924).
15. *Washington Post*, October 4, 1924.

   To get away from the siege of phone calls and visitors at their home on Irving Street, the Johnsons moved into a suite at the Arlington Hotel in downtown Washington. Even so, as he later recalled for Shirley Povich, Johnson was up late the night before the first game of the Series trying to get tickets for his friends. *Washington Post*, October 7, 1937. In "My Pitching Years" he wrote: "There was so much excitement and confusion that Mrs. Johnson insisted we slip out of the city so I could get a little quiet and a good night's sleep. We got as far as the sidewalks but there was such a stampede of baseball fans that we turned around and went back. It was better staying in Washington than making one's way through such a jam. I figured if I shook hands with everybody, I'd lose my pitching arm, and if I didn't I'd lose some friends."

16. Carmichael, *My Greatest Day in Baseball.*
17. John McGraw, *My Thirty Years In Baseball* (New York: Boni & Liveright, 1923).
18. Carmichael, *My Greatest Day in Baseball.*
19. Povich, *The Washington Senators.*
20. Clipping, source unknown, n.d., scrapbook IX(1924).
21. Bob Lemke, "Jack Bentley Was the First 'Next Babe Ruth'," *Sports Collectors Digest*, February 4, 1994.
22. Bluege interview with Larry Amman. On Ruel: "He was awfully worn down."
23. Clipping, source unknown, October 1, 1924, scrapbook IX. Johnson: "We have just finished a terrific grind lasting more than a month. Our pitchers are tired."
24. Clipping, source unknown, n.d., scrapbook VIII(1924).
25. Donald Honig, *The October Heroes* (New York: Simon & Schuster, 1979).
26. Henry L. Farrell, United Press, n.d., scrapbook IX(1924).
27. Billy Evans, source unknown, n.d., scrapbook VI(1924).
28. Heinie Miller, *Washington Herald*, n.d. (probably October 5, 1924), scrapbook IX.
29. Clipping, source unknown, n.d., scrapbook VIII(1924).
30. Shirley Povich, "The Old Fox."

    5,000 fans gathered in a chilling rain in front of an electrical diamond at the *Winnipeg* (Canada) *Free Press*. "Sympathies were almost entirely with the Washington Senators," it was reported. Caption to picture, source unknown, n.d., scrapbook VIII.
31. "When Washington Won the World Series," *The Transmitter* (C & P Telephone Co. magazine), November 1924.

    This was the network's second year of broadcasting the World Series. McNamee became the first nationally-famous baseball announcer, his voice associated with the postseason classic for many years.
32. Clipping, source unknown, n.d., scrapbook X(1924).
33. Walsh, *Adios to Ghosts*; Alexander, *Ty Cobb*; Johnson, "My Pitching Years."
34. Heinie Miller, *Washington Herald*, n.d., scrapbook IX(1924); Frank T. Sullivan, source unknown, August 16, 1925, scrapbook XIV.
35. Billy Evans, source unknown, n.d. (1930), misc. scrapbook.
36. Clipping, source unknown, n.d., scrapbook IX(1924).

    Ruth went to Johnson's hotel for the interview after being refused admittance to Griffith Stadium. "If the editors that hired me to write up this world series knew what I went through today, they'd give me a raise right off the bat," Ruth wrote.

"I went out to the ballpark this morning to do some interviewing. They wouldn't let me in the press gate so I tried the public entrance. I found that barred, and a big burly cop wouldn't even let me in the players gate—'Ballplayers only,' he says. And for the first time in my life I couldn't get into a ballpark."

37. Johnson, "My Pitching Years."
38. Rogers letter to E.B. McLean, owner of the *Washington Post*, September 29, 1924; *Washington Post*, n.d., scrapbook IX(1924).
39. Johnson, "My Pitching Years."
40. Grantland Rice, source unknown, n.d., scrapbook IX(1924).
41. Clipping, source unknown, n.d., scrapbook IX(1924).
42. Hazel Johnson, *Washington Post*, October 2, 1924.
43. Clipping, source unknown, n.d., scrapbook IX(1924).
44. Johnson, "My Pitching Years."
45. Ruel, "Catching a Speed King"; John B. Keller, *Washington Star*, n.d., scrapbook VIII(1924).
46. Robert Small, Associated Press, n.d., scrapbook VIII(1924).
47. Amman manuscript.
48. Holman, *Wonderful Walter Johnson*.
49. Clipping, source unknown, n.d., scrapbook VIII(1924).
50. Clipping, source unknown, n.d., scrapbook IX(1924).
51. Clipping, source unknown, n.d., scrapbook X(1924).
52. Johnson, "My Pitching Years."
53. Honig, *The October Heroes*.
54. John B. Keller, *Washington Star*, October 6, 1924.
55. Ralph Peckinpaugh (son of Roger) interview with Larry Amman.
56. Amman manuscript.
57. Damon Runyon, source unknown, n.d., scrapbook IX(1924).
58. Harris, *Playing The Game*; Louis Dougher, *Washington Times*, n.d., scrapbook IX(1924).
59. Grantland Rice, *New York Herald Tribune*, October 8, 1924.
60. Hazel Johnson, *Washington Post*, October 8, 1924.
61. Johnson, syndicated column, October 7, 1924, scrapbook IX.
62. Ralph Peckinpaugh interview with Larry Amman.
63. Associated Press, October 9, 1924, scrapbook X.
64. Clipping, source unknown, n.d., scrapbook IX(1924).
65. Herbert Corey, source unknown, n.d., scrapbook IX(1924); clipping, source unknown, n.d., scrapbook VIII (1924).
66. Clipping, source unknown, n.d., scrapbook VIII(1924).
67. Clipping, source unknown, n.d., scrapbook IX(1924). Lieb did point out that "If Johnson's defeats mean the loss of this series for the Nationals, it will not be the

first time that a great star has fallen down in this post-season competition. Hans Wagner hit only .200 in the 1903 series; Cobb hit feebly in 1907 and 1909, and Babe Ruth batted .116 two years ago."

68. Clipping, source unknown, n.d., scrapbook X(1924).
69. Ruel, "Catching a Speed King."
70. Carmichael, *My Greatest Day in Baseball.*

CHAPTER 14

1. Honig, *The October Heroes.*
2. *New York World*, n.d., scrapbook IX(1924).
3. Hazel Johnson, *Washington Post*, October 10, 1924; Clipping, source unknown, n.d., scrapbook IX(1924).
4. Johnson, "My Pitching Years."
5. J.P. Glass, source unknown, n.d., scrapbook XXVIII(1930). Johnson: "[Peckinpaugh] could hardly move."
6. Harris, *Playing the Game.*
7. Morse, *Washington Herald*, n.d., scrapbook IX(1924); Harris, *Playing the Game*: "True, the Giants had beaten him twice, but it didn't seem in the cards that they could turn the trick again—if he was right."
8. Carmichael, *My Greatest Day in Baseball.*

   Harris had used the same ploy successfully in the waning days of the pennant race. On September 24 in Chicago he faced another platooning manager in Johnny Evers, who alternated lefthanded hitters Maurice Archdeacon and Harry Hooper with righthanders Johnny Mostil and Roy Elsh. Fearing the former pair more than the latter, Harris wanted to start a lefty against them, but knew they would come in immediately if the Nationals' righthanded bullpen duo of Marberry and Russell had to be called on for relief. He started Ogden, and true to form, Evers's lefthanded hitters were in the lineup. After one batter Harris brought in Zachary, and it wasn't long before Archdeacon and Hooper were replaced. Zachary finished the game, as it happened, but if Harris had needed to go to the bullpen, the lefthanded hitters would have been gone.(Amman manuscript).
9. Clipping, source unknown, n.d., scrapbook VIII(1924).
10. Clipping, source unknown, n.d., scrapbook VIII(1924). The source for this vignette was Brewster Adams, who was in the Johnson apartment when it happened.
11. Morris Siegel, *Washington Post*, August 30, 1951.
12. Hazel Johnson, "Walter Johnson's Fan Mail," *Liberty Magazine*, June 19, 1926; Johnson, "My Pitching Years": "She clutched it so tightly during those exciting moments that when the game was over the iron shoe had dug into her palms and left a perfect imprint."

13. Clipping, source unknown, n.d., scrapbook IX(1924).
14. Harold K. Phillips, source unknown, n.d., scrapbook IX(1924).
15. Clipping, source unknown, n.d., scrapbook VIII(1924).
16. Billy Evans recounted a conversation that morning with the still-disconsolate Johnson:

The day of the last game in Washington I again strolled into the dressing room shortly before game time, with some more balls to be autographed. No one was in sight. Then over at the far end of the room I saw Johnson. He was sitting on a trunk, his knees drawn up to his chin. He was gazing into space. He didn't see me.

"Hello, Walter."

"Hello, Billy, how are you?"

"Great. How do you feel?" He shook his head sadly. "Not so good, Billy."

"Listen, Walter, you're not thinking for a minute that those two defeats will wipe out the 18 years of wonderful pitching you have been through, do you?"

"Billy, that's nice of you to say such things, but I want to tell you that those games counted far more with me than the sum total of the hundreds I have pitched in my career."

"Walter," I said, "I've come back with more balls for you to sign." A sad smile crossed his face.

"Gee, Billy, I didn't think there'd be anybody wanting me to sign a ball now."

"Don't you believe it. You'll always be the same old Walter Johnson to the fans, and don't let anybody, yourself included, tell you different. Now sign the balls."

And he did. And his hand as he traced his signature was as firm and steady as of old.—Clipping, source unknown, n.d., 1930, misc. scrapbook; clipping, source unknown, n.d., scrapbook XIX(1927).

17. Bluege interview with Larry Amman.
18. Margaret Ruth Triggs, *Washington Post*, October 11, 1924.
19. Clipping, source unknown, n.d., scrapbook IX(1924).
20. Clipping, source unknown, n.d., scrapbook IX(1924).
21. Hazel Johnson, "Walter Johnson's Fan Mail."
22. Carmichael, *My Greatest Day in Baseball.*
23. Heywood Broun, source unknown, n.d., scrapbook IX(1924).
    Mathewson: "I must admit that I never thought Walter would be able to do it. I thought to myself that it was a crime to put Walter in there, that he hadn't a chance because he had been beaten twice, the second time much worse than the first, and because he hadn't had proper rest for such a trying situation as this." *New York World*, n.d., scrapbook IX(1924).
24. Schacht interview with Larry Amman.
25. Hazel Johnson, *Washington Post,* October 11, 1924.

26. Johnson, "My Pitching Years": "She was afraid of her nerves, afraid she would disgrace the family in case I lost again."
27. Carmichael, *My Greatest Day in Baseball.*
The heavy smoke on the field that day was still vivid in Al Schacht's mind more than 50 years later: "The fans were awfully nervous in the last few innings. They were smoking one cigarette right after another. And so there was a cloud of smoke that had settled over the field. It just hung there." Schacht interview with Larry Amman.
28. Clipping, source unknown, n.d., scrapbook IX(1924).
29. Carmichael, *My Greatest Day in Baseball.*
30. Clipping, source unknown, n.d., scrapbook X(1924).

Muddy Ruel: "Some thought it was mere sentiment which caused Bucky Harris to send Walter Johnson into the battle on that Friday afternoon. Only 2 days before, the speed king had dismally failed in his efforts to stop the slugging McGrawmen. Pitchers as a rule require more than one day's rest between games. There was no idea of sentiment, however, in the mind of our 27 year-old pilot, as he selected Johnson for box duty, and it was furthest from our thoughts as we dug our spikes into the dirt and prepared to fight for the deciding contest.

"We had confidence in Barney's ability because we knew that his heart would be in every pitch that he sent speeding up to the plate. There was another reason for our confidence, unknown to the spectators, a seemingly unbelievable fact, but nevertheless a true one. Walter Johnson, warming up a day or two after pitching a full game, has apparently more speed for a few innings than on the previous occasion. His fast ball is considerably faster and it comes up to the plate as light as a feather, almost impossible to see, let alone to bat against. Barney had been warming up, and we had all noted his speed and the lightness of his fast ball. The Giants who faced Walter during the last 4 innings of that game can also bear testimony to these facts."—Ruel, "Catching a Speed King," 1927, scrapbook XVIII.

31. Carmichael, *My Greatest Day in Baseball.*
32. Bill Madden, "Bluege Hails the Big Train," *The Sporting News*, May 23, 1983.
33. Kirk Miller, *Washington Times*, n.d., scrapbook XXII(1928).
34. Carmichael, *My Greatest Day in Baseball.*
35. Clipping, source unknown, n.d.(probably October 11, 1924), scrapbook VIII(1924). Cobb: "I don't recall that I ever witnessed a battle between pitcher and hitter that thrilled me as did that contest between Johnson and Kelly."
36. Harris, *Playing the Game.*
37. Grantland Rice, *New York Herald Tribune*, October 11, 1924.
38. Carmichael, *My Greatest Day in Baseball.*
39. Holman, *Wonderful Walter Johnson.*
40. Clipping, source unknown, n.d., scrapbook VIII(1924).

41. Carmichael, *My Greatest Day in Baseball.*
42. Ibid.
43. Ritter, *The Glory of Their Times.*

Ossie Bluege: "I can still see Gowdy on Muddy's foul ball. He was kicking the mask, kicking it, looking down at it. Then the ball fell right through him." Bluege interview with Larry Amman.

Fred Lindstrom: "By that time, I suppose, even a callow, 18-year-old boy like myself, who knew nothing about fate, should have begun to see the light. Washington was supposed to win this game and that's all there was to it." Honig, *October Heroes.*

44. Schacht interview with Larry Amman.
45. Carmichael, *My Greatest Day in Baseball.*
46. Schacht, *My Own Particular Screwball.*
47. Carmichael, *My Greatest Day in Baseball.*
48. Spink, "End of Line for Big Train."
49. Fred Lindstrom: "You know, I don't think [Ruel] could have scored if Irish Meusel had anticipated my not taking the ball. If Meusel had been running in the moment the ball was hit I don't think Ruel, a slow runner, would have even tried to score." Honig, *October Heroes.*
50. Spink, "End of Line for Big Train"; Holman, *Wonderful Walter Johnson*; Harris interview with Larry Amman: "To this day I don't know why Meusel didn't throw home. I believe he might have caught Ruel at the plate."

    Ossie Bluege: "One thing I still don't understand is why Meusel didn't make a throw home. He might have had a chance. But he just picked up the ball and ran off the field. I don't know why." Bluege interview with Larry Amman.
51. Thomas L. Cummiskey, source unknown, n.d., scrapbook IX(1924.)
52. Joe Williams, *New York World Telegram*, April 29, 1931.

    Billy Evans: "I think that a kind of Providence, watching over all things great and small, created that opportunity for Walter Johnson. Created it for him and then stood by him through it all to carry him to the triumph he so justly deserved." Source unknown, n.d.(1930), misc. scrapbook.
53. Clipping, source unknown, n.d., scrapbook IX(1924).
54. Carmichael, *My Greatest Day in Baseball.*
55. Clipping, source unknown, n.d., scrapbook IX(1924).
56. Clipping, source unknown, n.d., scrapbook IX(1924); *New York Times*, n.d. (probably October 11, 1924), scrapbook IX(1924).

    President Coolidge issued this formal statement on the Series: "Naturally, in Washington, we were pleased to see Walter Johnson finish the game pitching for our home team and make a hit in the last inning that helped win the series. It has to be kept in mind that, though he was not successful in the two games which he pitched, that it was his skill that has won the pennant and put Washington into the world's series. Everyone was pleased to see him come back at the close of the last game. The three contests which I have witnessed maintained throughout a high degree of skill and a high class of sportsmanship that will bring to every observer an increased respect for and confidence in our national game. It would be difficult to conceive a finer example of true sport." Clipping, source unknown, n.d., scrapbook IX(1924).

57. Schacht, *Clowning Through Baseball.*
58. *Washington Star,* October 11, 1924. " 'I'm the happiest man in the world—the happiest man in the world,' the Big Train laughed to a Star reporter in the dressing room. 'Tell everybody I'm tickled to death and anything else along the same line you can think of. I'll stand back of anything you say, as I can't express my feelings in words at all right now. I can never thank Bucky enough for having confidence in me again after my two failures, and I'm happy I didn't disappoint him and my friends.' "
59. Spink, "End of the Line for Big Train."
60. John B. Keller, *Washington Star*, October 11, 1924.
61. Clipping, source unknown, n.d., scrapbook IX(1924).
62. Honig, *October Heroes*. Lindstrom: "McGraw didn't have much to say about it. He had seen enough baseball in his life to know when something had been taken out of his hands."

CHAPTER 15

1. Rice, "The Greatest Thrill of 1924," *Collier's,* January 10, 1925.
   Ty Cobb: "I have had a day to cool off since the world series ended and to think it all over, but the more I turn the things that happened over in my mind the harder it is to cool off. All the thrills of the series come to life again and absolutely freeze me in amazement. One way and another there never was a series like it. I doubt if there ever will be a series like it. Fiction couldn't possibly improve on the plot or the fight the Giants and Senators put up. It was simply uncanny. I have been around baseball a long, long time, but I never saw anything like it. As a fan I got a terrific kick out of it all. As a baseball man it just about paralyzed me with thrills." Clipping, source unknown, n.d., scrapbook VIII(1924).
2. Fred Lieb, *Baseball As I Have Known It* (New York: Coward, McCann & Geoghegan, 1977).
   Visiting the Supreme Court the next day, Landis said: "Friday's struggle was a perfect game not only from the viewpoint of the spectators in the stands, but also from an artistic point of view. I never had seen anything like it before and probably never will again. I regard it as the greatest game ever played." Clipping, source unknown, n.d., scrapbook IX (1924).

3. Francis P. Daily, source unknown, n.d., scrapbook IX(1924).
4. Clipping, source unknown, n.d., scrapbook IX(1924).
5. Carmichael, *My Greatest Day in Baseball.*
6. Associated Press, n.d., scrapbook IX(1924).
7 Carmichael, *My Greatest Day in Baseball.*
8. Clipping, source unknown, n.d., scrapbook IX(1924).
9. Clipping, source unknown, n.d., scrapbook VIII(1924).
10. *Washington Post*, September 25, 1924.
11. Clipping, source unknown, n.d., scrapbook XXII(1928).
12. Schacht, *My Own Particular Screwball.*
13. *Rochester Democrat and Chronicle*, October 12, 1924.
14. Schacht, *My Own Particular Screwball.*
15. Clipping, source unknown, n.d., scrapbook X(1924); *Washington Post*, n.d., scrapbook X(1924). Griffith: "I told [Johnson] that if his deal went through and it looked all right to me, I would not stand in his way, in view of his past service to the club and of the further fact that he is nearing the end of his baseball career."
16. George Chadwick, source unknown, n.d., scrapbook X(1924).
17. Johnson, "The Greatest Batters I Have Ever Faced," *Baseball Magazine*, June 1925.
18. *Coffeyville Journal*, October 21, 1924.
19. Clipping, source unknown, n.d., scrapbook X(1924).
20. *Washington Post*, October 27, 1924.
21. *Washington Times*, November 22, 1924; clipping, source unknown, n.d., scrapbook X(1924).
22. Dan Parker, source unknown, n.d., scrapbook X(1924).
23. *Anaheim Plain Dealer*, October 28, 1924.
24. Clipping, source unknown, n.d., scrapbook X(1924), quoting Sid Keener of the *St. Louis Times.*
25. *Anaheim Bulletin*, October 31, 1924.
26. *Los Angeles Times*, November 1, 1924.
27. *Anaheim Gazette*, October 9, 1924.
28. Clipping, source unknown, n.d., scrapbook X(1924).
29. Eddie West, "Golden Day: Ruth, Johnson at Brea," *Orange County Register*, October 30, 1974. "Those who played, and still live around these parts, say that Johnson never threw a curve and the home run pitch he made to the Babe was 'Complimentary'—right down the pipe.

"Forrest B. 'Bus' Callan of Anaheim, was prevailed upon to catch Johnson on this occasion. In later years Bus recalled the game:

'I used to be a pretty good catcher, but I was pretty rusty by then. Honestly, when he threw in some of those fireballs, I couldn't see them. We had a short conference at a spot between home plate and the pitcher's mound and I said, "Walter, I just can't see the ball." He replied, "Just put your mitt where you want me to throw and I'll throw into it," and he did! Since I couldn't see the fast balls coming, I couldn't jerk my mitt back as one does to ease the shock in catching them. I got a beautifully sprained wrist.'

"When Babe Ruth came up to bat for the first time, Walter and Bus had another conference. Johnson whispered, 'Bus, the crowd wants to see Babe make some home runs and we don't want to disappoint them. The first two times I'll throw him easy ones that he can't miss. The last time I'll fan him.' And so the enthusiastic spectators saw the Babe smack two home runs. He came up to bat the third time with his usual confidence. Johnson bore down and on the third ball thrown umpire 'Beans' Reardon called him out. Babe's short temper got the better of him. He slammed down his bat and left the diamond." —Leo J. Friis, *Kleinigkeiten*, Orange County Pioneer Series #4, 1975.

30. Earl Gustkey, "The Day Ruth and Johnson Came To Orange County," *Los Angeles Times*, August 4, 1970.
    Another of the five local boys playing for the "Walter Johnsons" was centerfielder Vic Ruedy, later Anaheim's superintendent of parks under whose jurisdiction Anaheim Stadium, home of the major-league California Angels, was opened in 1966.
31. *Fullerton News*, November 6, 1924.
32. Photographs in Johnson family archives.
33. *Anaheim Plain Dealer*, November 7, 1924.
34. Clipping, source unknown, n.d., scrapbook X(1924). San Francisco, Los Angeles, and Seattle were said to be the only PCL franchises turning a profit. Several were in bad shape financially, and the league overall was not prospering, according to this account.
35. Johnson and Zahniser bagged a deer apiece. Two years later Zahniser recalled one of the kills: "We went hunting one day, and finally killed a big buck deer. I tried to help tote that deer back to the car, which was stationed a half mile or so away. But I finally had to give it up. 'Never mind,' said Walter, 'I can manage it,' and he did. He slung that big deer over his shoulder and set out across the country at so fast a pace that I had trouble keeping up with him. And it was no pose on Walter's part, either. He actually thought nothing of the thing." Clipping, source unknown, n.d., scrapbook XVII(1926).
36. Clipping, source unknown, n.d., scrapbook X(1924).
37. Frank Young, *Washington Post*, January 25, 1925. Johnson: "I was sorry to see our deal slip down at Oakland. It made me look like a bum."
38. Clipping, source unknown, n.d., scrapbook X(1924).
39. Denman Thompson, *Washington Star*, November 25, 1924.
40. Clipping, source unknown, n.d., scrapbook X(1924).

41. *Washington Post*, January 8, 1925; *San Francisco Chronicle*, January 31, 1925.
42. Clipping, source unknown (Los Angeles newspaper), n.d., scrapbook X(1924). The PCL had been under a cloud since 1919, when the pennant was fixed by Vernon players bribing Salt Lake City players during a crucial late-season series.
43. Tom Laird, *San Francisco Daily News*, n.d., scrapbook X(1924).
On June 17, 1925, J.H. Stevens, president of the Merchants National Bank of Sacramento, wrote Johnson with a proposal that he and local resident Harry Hooper take over the Sacramento PCL club, with the bank to finance the purchase. Citing his two-year contract with Washington and other commitments, Johnson declined. Zingg, *Harry Hooper* (Chicago: University of Illinois Press, 1993).
44. Johnson, "My Pitching Years."
45. Walsh, *Adios to Ghosts*.
46. *New York Times*, January 23, 1925. The suit against the Thompson Feature Service, asking for $50,000 in damages, was dismissed on the grounds that eight of the twelve parts had already run. According to a disclaimer run by the *Washington Post* (which carried the series) on November 23, 1924, Barker had represented to Johnson only that she would write a series of short articles on his life based on the interviews. Instead they came out as "My Twenty Years on the Mound, by Walter Johnson."

Barker also used the president of the United States to promote her project, writing Coolidge about Johnson and then placing his reply conspicuously at the lead of the first article, making it appear to be an endorsement. "My Dear Miss Barker," it read, "I don't know that I can do much better than to adopt the terms of your own letter to me in expressing my feeling about the athletic career of Walter Johnson. Through a strikingly long and notable experience he has been, as you suggest, not only the admirable athlete, but always a gentleman and a good citizen. This combination of parts has won for him a place in the affection of the American sport-loving community well-nigh unique among the great figures of our national athletics. The fine loyalty, the unswerving purpose always to do his best, even when the great reward was not seemingly in sight, have made him a figure deserving of all admiration. Most sincerely yours, Calvin Coolidge." *Washington Post*, November 16, 1924.
47. Dan Parker, source unknown, n.d., scrapbook X(1924–25).
48. Johnson, "The Greatest Batters I Have Ever Faced."
49. *Washington Herald*, February 10, 1925.
50. Universal Service, February 9, 1925.
51. Frank Young, *Washington Post*, February 10, 1925.
52. Frank Young, *Washington Post*, February 17, 1925.
"I do not blame Griff for getting his men as cheaply as he can. That's good

business," Johnson said during the negotiations. Dan Parker, source unknown, n.d., scrapbook X(1924–25). Aided by the second million-dollar gate in World Series history, the Nationals turned a profit of $149,511.47 in 1924. Povich, "Clark Griffith—50 Years in Baseball," *Washington Post*, February 13, 1938.

53. Clipping, source unknown, n.d., scrapbook X(1924–25). The offer came from Washington theatrical producer Tom Moore, said to be "of the opinion that Johnson possesses many of the qualities necessary to the making of a capable screen star."
54. Clipping, source unknown, n.d., scrapbook X(1924–25).
55. Ray Robinson, *Matty—An American Hero* (New York: Oxford Press, 1993).
56. Frank Young, *Washington Post*, March 26, 1925.
57. Kirk Miller, *Washington Times*, n.d., scrapbook X(1924–25).
58. Christy Walsh Syndicate, April 17, 1925.
59. Christy Walsh Syndicate, April 11, 1925.
60. Clipping, source unknown, n.d., scrapbook XIV(1925). "The rugged Pole is undoubtedly the best exponent of the moist delivery that has worked in either league since Ed Walsh passed out."

    Bucky Harris: "Coveleski's ball 'exploded' more than any other spitballer's." Harris interview with Larry Amman.
61. Lou Gehrig, "Gehrig Struck Out On First Appearance Against Old Master," chapter 15 of a series, source unknown, n.d., scrapbook XVIII(1927). Gehrig: "A lot of people used to say baseball as a profession was a waste of time. All I can say to that is that any game which will produce a man like Walter Johnson after 20 years of competition is worthwhile."
62. Clipping, source unknown, n.d., scrapbook XIV(1925).
63. According to another article, "The number of home runs made over this wall by righthand hitters can be counted on the fingers of one hand." Clipping, source unknown, n.d., scrapbook XIV(1925).
64. Clipping, source unknown, n.d., scrapbook XIV(1925).
65. Eric Nadel and Craig R. Wright, *The Man Who Stole First Base* (Dallas: Taylor Publishing, 1989).

    As the Nationals' announcer in 1939, coincidentally, Walter Johnson was in the studio doing a simulated broadcast of the last game of Gehrig's streak—and his career—against Washington in Yankee Stadium on April 30, 1939.
66. Donald Honig, *Baseball When the Grass Was Real* (New York: Coward, McMann & Geoghegan, 1975).
67. Frank T. Sullivan, source unknown, n.d., scrapbook XIV(1925).
68. Francis P. Daily, source unknown, n.d, scrapbook XIV(1925).
69. Clipping, source unknown, n.d., scrapbook XIV(1925).
70. Holman, *Wonderful Walter Johnson*.

CHAPTER 16

1. Clipping, source unknown, scrapbook XV(1925).
2. Holman, *Wonderful Walter Johnson*; Fred Lieb, *The Pittsburgh Pirates* (New York: Putnam's Sons, 1948): "The pre-series predictions installed the Senators as a heavy favorite following their strong season finish"; Steve Bailey, *Walter Perry Johnson: A Biography* (Master's thesis, Arizona State University, May 1990): "Most of the critics and baseball men picked the Senators. Oddly enough, the professional gamblers strung along with Pittsburgh. The odds out of New York were 6 to 5, Pirates."
3. Westbrook Pegler, source unknown, n.d., scrapbook XV(1925).
4. Johnson, *Who's Who in Major League Baseball.*
5. Amman manuscript.
6. James, *The Bill James Historical Abstract.*
7. Povich, *The Washington Senators.*
8. Lieb, *The Pittsburgh Pirates.*
9. Grantland Rice, source unknown, October 8, 1925, scrapbook XV(1925).
10. Billy Evans, source unknown, n.d., scrapbook XV(1925); Associated Press, October 8, 1925.
11. Babe Ruth, source unknown, October 8, 1925, scrapbook XV(1925).
12. Roger Peckinpaugh, source unknown, n.d., scrapbook XV(1925).
13. John Keller, *Washington Star*, October 8, 1925.
14. Lieb, *The Pittsburgh Pirates.*
15. Westbrook Pegler, source unknown, n.d., scrapbook XV(1925).
16. Denman Thompson, *Washington Star*, October 8, 1925.
17. Lieb, *The Pittsburgh Pirates.*
18. Damon Runyon, International News Service, October 7, 1925.
19. Keller, *Washington Star*, October 8, 1925.
20. Lieb, *The Pittsburgh Pirates*; Robinson, *Matty—An American Hero.*
21. Povich, *The Washington Senators.*
22. Jack Conway, source unknown, n.d., scrapbook XV(1925).
23. Clipping, source unknown, n.d., scrapbook XVII(1926).

    In the memorial game Johnson went two innings for the Nationals against the Giants, giving up no runs while striking out four, despite having pitched a complete game two days earlier.
24. Lieb, *The Pittsburgh Pirates.*
25. Holman, *Wonderful Walter Johnson.*
26. Wulf, "The Secrets of Sam."
27. Povich, *The Washington Senators.*
28. McGraw, source unknown, n.d., scrapbook XV(1925).

    Fred Lieb: "That doughty American League hater, John McGraw—still feeling the sting of his defeat the year before—also did his best to keep up the fighting spirit of the Pirates. 'Keep after them; never give up', he advised." Lieb, *The Pittsburgh Pirates*.

29. Clipping, source unknown, October 12, 1925, scrapbook XV(1925).
30. Harris interview with Larry Amman.
31. Johnson, source unknown, n.d., scrapbook XV(1925).
32. Ford Frick, source unknown, October 14, 1925, scrapbook XV(1925).
33. Ruth, source unknown, n.d. (probably October 15, 1925), scrapbook XV(1925).
34. Robert L. Burnes, "Walter Johnson's Toughest Defeat," *Baseball Digest*, February 1963.
35. Johnson, source unknown, n.d., scrapbook XIV(1925).
36. Ring Lardner, *Washington Post*, October 16, 1925.

Bluege: "We were standing in puddles. You'd look up for a pop-up and get hit with that driving rain right in the eyes." Bluege interview with Larry Amman.

37. Burnes, "Walter Johnson's Toughest Defeat."
38. Bluege, Harris interviews with Larry Amman.
39. Paul Green, *Forgotten Fields* (Waupaca, Wisconsin: Parker Publications, 1984).
40. Ritter, *The Glory of Their Times*.
41. Povich, "Clark Griffith—50 Years in Baseball," *Washington Post*, February 8, 1938.

Bluege: "That ball that Carey hit was at least a foot foul. I saw it hit. Owens was the umpire at third. He never would give us a break."—Bluege interview with Larry Amman.

Ruel: "Max Carey sent a drive down the left field line which appeared to be foul to many of us, but was declared fair and went for a two-base hit."—Ruel, "Catching the Speed King."

42. Holman, *Wonderful Walter Johnson*; Ruel, "Catching the Speed King": "Confidently I started to remove my mask, believing that the Pirate had been struck out, but the umpire ruled differently."

Bluege: "Walter had two strikes on Cuyler and split the middle of the plate and McCormick called it a ball. Moon McCormick, a National League umpire—and they were always partial to the National League, of course, don't forget that."—Green, *Forgotten Fields*.

"Just as George Washington never told a lie, so it has been said that Walter Johnson never offered an alibi. He came as close to it as he ever will the other day in discussing the last world series. There were some who protested at the time that a third strike should have been called [on Cuyler], but Johnson never uttered a complaint. Even now he refuses to make excuses, but he let drop a remark full of meaning. 'I had Cuyler struck out,' he said. And that's the closest Walter has ever come to offering an alibi."—*New York Times*, March 15, 1926.

43. Lieb, *The Pittsburgh Pirates.*
Goose Goslin told Lawrence Ritter that Cuyler's hit, too, was foul, although Goslin was playing left field and Cuyler's ball was down the right field line. He might have been confusing it with Carey's hit the previous inning. "Kiki Cuyler hit a ball down the right field line that they called fair, and that won the game for Pittsburgh," he said. "It wasn't fair at all. It was foul by two feet. I know it was foul because the ball hit in the mud and *stuck* there. The umpires couldn't see it. It was too dark and foggy." Ritter, *The Glory of Their Times.*
44. Leonard Koppett, "Walter Johnson, Greatest Pitcher of Them All," *Baseball Digest*, February 1965, quoting Ford Frick.
45. Frank Sullivan, source unknown, n.d., scrapbook XV(1925).
46. Clipping, source unknown, n.d., scrapbook XV(1925).
47. *Washington Post*, November 10, 1977.
48. Associated Press, October 16, 1925.

Harris told Larry Amman: "I thought about it [taking Johnson out] a couple of times, but many of the hits off him were fluky. He was the best I had." In response to the question, "Suppose Marberry had not had that sore arm. Would you have brought him in?" Harris replied: "Yes. Definitely." Harris interview with Larry Amman.

49. Povich, *The Washington Senators.*
50. Oswin King, *Dallas News*, November 8, 1925.
51. Ruel, "Catching the Speed King."
52. Clipping, source unknown, n.d., scrapbook XV(1925).
53. *Washington Post*, n.d., scrapbook XV(1925).
Judging from the statistical results of the Series, the teams were as well matched as the overall result would indicate. The similarity in some of the numbers is striking. The Nationals hit .262 and scored 26 runs, the Pirates hit .265 and scored 25. Each team had 16 extra-base hits, 17 walks, and 32 strikeouts.

In an article entitled, "Peck Defeats Johnson in Great Sea Disaster," H.I. Phillips wrote: "All the [Pirates'] victory proved, besides the fact that baseball can be played at night and at sea … ." Phillips, Associated Newspapers, October 16, 1925.

CHAPTER 17

1. Povich, *The Washington Senators.*
2. F.C. Lane, "Getting Rich From Florida Real Estate," *Baseball Magazine*, July 1926.
3. Virginia Chatham Moore, "Mrs. Walter Johnson, As I Know Her," c. 1926, manuscript in Johnson family archives.
4. Hazel Johnson, "Walter Johnson's Fan Mail."
5. Ruel, "Catching a Speed King."
6. Clipping, source unknown, n.d., scrapbook XVII(1926).

7. Clipping, source unknown, n.d., scrapbook XVII(1926).
8. *Washington Post*, October 2, 1926.
9. Clipping, source unknown, August 2, 1927, scrapbook XVIII(1927).
10. NEA news service, n.d., scrapbook XVII(1927).
11. Clipping, source unknown, n.d., scrapbook XVIII(1927).
12. Bob Thayer, *Washington Herald*, February 26, 1927.
13. Denman Thompson, *Washington Star*, February 26, 1927.
14. Billy Evans, source unknown, n.d., scrapbook XVIII(1927).
15. Povich, "Walter Johnson, The Big Train."
16. Clipping, source unknown, n.d., scrapbook XVIII(1927).
17. Billy Evans, source unknown, n.d., scrapbook XVIII(1927).
18. Bob Thayer, *Washington Herald*, n.d., scrapbook XVIII(1927).
19. Clipping, source unknown, April 9, 1927, scrapbook XVIII(1927).
20. *Washington Post*, October 26, 1926.
21. Will Rogers, *New York Times*, July 29, 1927.
22. Coolidge letter to Johnson testimonial committee, July 26, 1927, Johnson family archives.
23. Clipping, source unknown, n.d., scrapbook XIX(1927). Kellogg: "Your sterling qualities, both as a ballplayer and as a citizen, have made your name known throughout the country and have gained for you admirers in all sections. Your name stands for what is best in sports and your personal life is held as an example for the youth of the country."
24. Clipping, source unknown, n.d., scrapbook XIX(1927).
25. Frank Young, *Washington Post*, n.d., scrapbook XIX(1927).
26. Ibid.
27. Shirley Povich, *Washington Post*, August 3, 1927.
28. *New York Times*, August 3, 1927.
29. Clipping, source unknown, n.d., scrapbook XVIII(1927).
   In an interview with F.C. Lane in 1934, Johnson reiterated that it was his legs, not his arm, that forced him to step down from the mound. "It wasn't my arm that went bad," Johnson told him. "In fact, the old arm is pretty good even now. It wasn't the arm, it was the legs. Pitchers, like all other players, grow old in their legs. I might have staggered along and pitched a few more games here and there, but I would have been no credit to myself and no great benefit to my ball club. I knew when it was time to quit, and fortunately I didn't have any battle with father time. That's always a losing battle and a ballplayer knows it." Lane, "75,000 Pitches Without a Sore Arm!"
30. Clipping, source unknown, October 15, 1927, scrapbook XVIII(1927).
31. *Washington Herald*, October 8, 1927.
32. Frank Getty, United Press, n.d., scrapbook XVIII(1927). In this interview, con-

ducted on October 16 at the house in Alta Vista, Johnson made little effort to hide his disappointment with his treatment by the Nationals, although it's less clear what he had been expecting or hoping for. After candidly admitting "my days of usefulness to the Washington club as an active player were about over," he went on to lament: "I had rather hoped to wind up my baseball career right here in Washington, but—well, I guess it just wasn't to be." Bucky Harris had another year to go on his contract to manage the club, and it doesn't seem likely Johnson would have been interested in a coaching job. Perhaps he really did want to go out with one more year, hoping Griffith or Harris would come to him with an offer of spot starts or a relief role or some combination of those. But Washington already had the two best relievers in the league in Fred Marberry and Garland Braxton, and a full complement of young starting pitchers. The idea that Johnson wanted to keep pitching is buttressed by his statement that if he was claimed by another team on waivers, he would consider going with that club. "If I received the right offer from someone who really wanted me—why, I might keep on," he said. Whether Griffith would have let Walter Johnson go for the waiver price is another matter altogether.

Johnson's managerial aspirations were also stated plainly for the first time: "Walter was asked if he would consider accepting the management of one of a number of major league clubs now casting about for pilots for 1928. 'Why, yes,' he replied without hesitation. 'Like every ballplayer, I'd be glad to have charge of a major league club and at least see if I could make a success of it.'" Although saddened by the thought of leaving the Washington ballclub, and possibly the city also, Johnson managed to keep things in perspective. Toward the end of the interview he admitted, "I'm one of the lucky ones. Sometimes life is pretty hard on a ballplayer."

33. Gene Kessler, source unknown, n.d., scrapbook XVIII(1927).
34. Griffith letter to Johnson, October 15, 1927, Johnson family archives.
35. Clipping, source unknown, n.d., scrapbook XVIII(1927).
36. Johnson, *Who's Who in Major League Baseball.*
37. *Washington Post*, October 18, 1927.
38. Frank Young, *Washington Post*, October 16, 1927.
There was talk of a Johnson monument at the stadium as early as his retirement in 1927. It materialized twenty years later following his death.

CHAPTER 18

1. Greenberg, *The Story of My Life* (New York: Times Books, 1989).
2. Donald Honig, *Baseball America* (New York: MacMillan, 1985).
3. Bill Hugo and Bob Littlejohn, "The Roy Hughes Story Bag," *Baseball Research Journal*, 1991.

4. Frank Getty, United Press, n.d., scrapbook XVIII(1927).
5. Clipping, source unknown, n.d., scrapbook XVIII(1927).
6. Clipping, source unknown, n.d., scrapbook XVIII(1927).
7. Clipping, source unknown, n.d., scrapbook XXII(1928).
8. Coolidge letter to Paul Block, November 1, 1927, copy in Johnson family archives.
9. J. Earle Moser, source unknown, n.d., scrapbook XVIII(1927).
10. Rodger Pippen, *Baltimore News*, October 28, 1927.
11. Kirk Miller, *Washington Times*, n.d., scrapbook XVIII(1927).
12. Alfred Reck, United Press, March 30, 1928.
13. Kirk Miller, *Washington Times*, March 31, 1928.
14. Landis telegram to Johnson, March 31, 1928, Johnson family archives.
15. Gus Bock, *Newark Evening News*, n.d., scrapbook XXIII(1928).
16. Frank Fagan, *Newark Star-Eagle*, n.d., scrapbook XXIII(1928).
17. Gus Bock, *Newark Evening News*, n.d., scrapbook XXIII(1928).
18. Joe Williams, *New York Telegram*, n.d., scrapbook XXV(1929).
19. Frank B. Ford, source unknown, n.d., scrapbook XXV(1929).
20. Frank Fagan, *Newark Star-Eagle*, n.d., scrapbook XXV(1929).
21. Frank B. Ford, source unknown, n.d., scrapbook XXV(1929).
22. John B. Keller, *Washington Star*, October 15, 1928.
23. Holman, *Wonderful Walter Johnson*.
24. John B. Keller, *Washington Star*, n.d., scrapbook XXV(1929).
25. Schacht, *My Own Particular Screwball*. According to Schacht, Griffith told him:

> I feel I owe him this chance after all he did for me as a pitcher. I know he'll be a poor manager to start, because I really don't think he's the type. But I'll give him a three-year contract, and maybe he'll pick up enough experience to make a good leader.

26. Frank Young, *Washington Post*, n.d., scrapbook XXV(1929).
27. Denman Thompson, *Washington Star*, n.d., scrapbook XXV(1929).
28. Margaret Milan letter to Carolyn Johnson Thomas, May 8, 1961, Johnson family archives.
29. *Washington Times*, April 10, 1929.
30. *Washington Star*, May 7, 1929.
31. Bob Thayer, *Washington Herald*, n.d., scrapbook XXVI(1929).
32. John B. Keller, *Washington Star*, July 17, 1929.
33. Thayer, *Washington Herald*, n.d., scrapbook XXVI(1929).
34. Lieb, "The P.T. Barnum of the Bushes."
35. Clipping, source unknown, n.d., scrapbook XXVII(1930).
36. Bob Thayer, *Washington Herald*, n.d., scrapbook XXVII(1930).
37. Bill Stern, *Bill Stern's Favorite Baseball Stories* (New York: Doubleday & Co., 1951).

38. *The Sporting News*, July 31, 1930.
39. Hazel Johnson letter to Margaret Milan, n.d.(1930), Johnson family archives.
40. Ibid.
41. Ibid.
42. Carolyn Johnson Thomas interview with the author.
43. *Washington Post*, August 2, 1930.
44. *Washington Star*, August 1, 1930.
45. *Washington Post*, July 21, 1930.
46. Holman, *Wonderful Walter Johnson*.
47. *Washington Post*, August 2, 1930.
48. Vincent Flaherty, "The Greatest of Them All," *Los Angeles Examiner*, June 1946.
49. Povich, "The Washington Senators."
50. *Washington Star*, August 4, 1930.
    Johnson's exhaustion might have been the genesis of Ty Cobb's claim that "Walter Johnson tried to kill himself when his wife died." The author found no evidence to support the assertion, made during the last days of Cobb's own life. Al Stump, "Ty Cobb's Wild Ten-Month Fight to Live," *True*, December 1961.
51. Flaherty, "The Greatest of Them All."
52. *Washington Times*, August 1, 1930.
53. *Washington Star*, August 4, 1930.
54. Honig, *The Man in the Dugout*.
55. Povich, "The Washington Senators."
56. Associated Press, October 27, 1932.
57. Tom Doerer, *Washington Star*, December 1, 1932.
58. Bluege and Schacht interviews with Larry Amman; Honig, *The Man in the Dugout*; Schacht, *My Own Particular Screwball*.
59. F.C. Lane, "Storm Center of the Cleveland Club," *Baseball Magazine*, September 1935.
60. Povich interview with the author, May 1992.
    In the author's interview with Monte Weaver, a 22-game winner as a rookie for the Nationals in 1932, Weaver seemed surprised that anyone would ask whether Johnson was a good manager. "I couldn't see anything wrong with his management the year I was with him," he answered. "He was the nicest manager I had, I think. He was awfully good to his players." Monte Weaver interview with the author, May 13, 1992.
61. Lieb, "Cutting the Plate" column, source unknown, n.d., scrapbook XXIX (1930–46).
62. Povich, *Washington Post*, May 9, 1939.
63. *Washington Star*, June 9, 1933.
64. Povich, *Washington Post*, May 5, 1937.

65. *Washington Star*, August 1935, misc. scrapbook.
66. *Washington Post*, July 11, 1934.
67. Associated Press, July 20, 1934.
68. *Baseball Magazine*, September 1934.

Kirk Miller of the *Washington Times* was even more caustic in his condemnation of the Cleveland sportswriters. "That riding they gave Walter Johnson back in Cleveland was no sporadic attack," he wrote. "It was an organized second-guessing campaign led, as I understand it, by one gentleman of my profession who had ambitions to emulate the precedent set by the late William C. Veeck [Sr.] who, in his capacity as a reporter, once told the Chicago Cub management he could run a club better than the man who was getting paid for it—and was forthwith given the job. At the moment of this verbal and typographical onslaught against one of the noblest men the game has produced, Johnson's club was not holding some despised position in the league. There were 4 and sometimes 5 other managers in the circuit who would have gladly traded team positions in the standings with Walter's Indians when he was getting hazed. And that was what Walter couldn't understand and, to tell you the truth, a lot of his friends in Washington couldn't comprehend it either. If the Clevelanders had flopped to the bottom of the league, and shown no fight whatever, Walter is of the opinion the worst they could have said about him wouldn't have been too bad. But there he was, in midseason, knocking at the door, not too far away from the thick of things, and they do their best to throw him an anchor." Kirk Miller, *Washington Times*, n.d., scrapbook XXIX(1930–46)).

69. Carolyn Johnson Thomas interview with the author.
70. Lane, "The Storm Center of the Cleveland Club."
71. Ibid.
72. *The Sporting News*, June 5, 1935.
73. *The Washington Post*, July 22, 1935.
74. International News Service, August 6, 1935.
75. Bill Corum, "Why Sir Walter is Great—Story of Johnson's Dismissal Comes to Light," *Des Moines Register*, October 17, 1936; Flaherty, "Life Story of Walter Perry Johnson."
76. Herman Goldstein, *The Sporting News*, December 25, 1946.

CHAPTER 19

1. Dillon Graham, Associated Press, February 29, 1936.
2. Associated Press, August 6, 1935.
3. Eddie Johnson interview with the author.
4. Povich, "Walter Johnson, The Big Train."
5. Eddie Johnson, Carolyn Johnson Thomas interviews with the author.

6. Joe Williams, *New York World-Telegram*, December 16, 1936.
7. Barbara Johnson Pogue interview with the author.
8. *Washington Star*, n.d. (August 1935), scrapbook XXIX (1930–46).
9. Bob Considine, *Washington Herald*, November 20, 1935. In addition to Johnson, Griffith's all-time team included catcher Buck Ewing; Sisler, Lajoie, Wagner, and Baker in the infield; and Cobb, Ruth, and Speaker in the outfield. The manager was Clark Griffith.
10. Associated Press, February 20, 1936.
11. Vincent X. Flaherty, *Washington Herald*, n.d.(February 1936), scrapbook XXIX (1930–46).
12. Ibid.
13. Bill McGowan, *Washington Times-Herald*, March 31, 1939.
14. Eddie Johnson interview with the author.
15. Ibid.
16. Bob Considine, *Washington Herald*, n.d.(1937), misc. scrapbook.
17. Shirley Povich, *Washington Post*, August 28, 1937.
18. Povich, "Walter Johnson, The Big Train."
19. Daley, "The Fireball Throwers." "I still think that Johnson was as fast then [at Cleveland] as he ever was," O'Neill said. "But his legs were gone. There was nothing wrong with his arm, though. When he'd throw in those bullets in batting practice, even our best hitters couldn't touch him—fellows like Averill and Vosmik and all the rest."
20. J.M. Murphy, "Napoleon Lajoie, Modern Baseball's First Superstar," *The National Pastime*, Spring 1988.
21. Honig, *Baseball When the Grass Was Real.*
22. Bob Feller with Bill Gilbert, *Now Pitching, Bob Feller* (New York: Birch Lane Press, 1990).
23. Franklin D. Roosevelt letter to Johnson, November 6, 1937, Johnson family archives.
24. Eddie Johnson interview with the author.
25. *Washington Star*, November 30, 1938.
26. *Washington Post*, March 17, 1939.
27. Holman, *Wonderful Walter Johnson.*
28. Povich, "Walter Johnson, The Big Train."
29. Curt Smith, *Voices of the Game* (South Bend, Indiana: Diamond Communications, 1987).
30. *Washington Times-Herald*, March 23, 1939.
31. *Washington Times-Herald*, March 24, 1939.
32. *Washington Star*, March 24, 1939.
33. *Washington Post*, April 7, 1939.

34. Ken Smith, *Baseball's Hall of Fame.*
35. *Boston Globe,* July 13, 1939.
36. Holman, *Wonderful Walter Johnson.*
37. *Washington Star,* July 19, 1939.
38. Johnson letter to Eleanor Fleitman, January 3, 1940, copy in Johnson family archives.
    Johnson's broadcast of a Washington-Cleveland game on September 21, 1939, survives as part of WJSV's "radio time-capsule" recording of that day's programming.
39. Joe Cummiskey, "The Babe and Walter—Dressing Room Vignettes," *Baseball Digest,* November 1942.
40. *Washington Star,* March 1, 1940.
41. *Washington Star,* May 8, 1940.
42. *Washington Post,* June 28, 1940.
43. *Washington Star,* September 17, 1940; *New York Times,* September 18, 1940.
44. *Montgomery County Sentinel,* November 7, 1940.
45. Shirley Povich, *Washington Post,* June 9, 1940.
46. *Montgomery County Sentinel,* November 10, 1940.
47. Shirley Povich, *Washington Post,* May 29, 1941.
48. *New York Sun,* August 24, 1942.
49. *New York World Telegram,* August 24, 1942.
50. Stan Frank, *New York Post,* August 24, 1942.
51. Tom Meany, "The Babe and Walter—Dressing Room Vignettes," *Baseball Digest,* November 1942.
52. Joe Cummiskey, "The Babe and Walter—Dressing Room Vignettes."
53. *New York Telegraph,* December 12, 1946.
54. Shirley Povich, *Washington Post,* August 24, 1942.
55. Stan Frank, *New York Post,* August 25, 1942.
56. Taylor Spink, *The Sporting News,* September 3, 1942.
57. *New York Herald Tribune,* August 24, 1942.
58. Stan Frank, *New York Post,* August 24, 1942.
59. Ruth with Considine, *The Babe Ruth Story.*
60. *New York Times,* August 21, 1942.
61. James Dawson, *New York Times,* August 24, 1942.
62. Povich, *Washington Post,* August 24, 1942.
63. Ruth with Considine, *The Babe Ruth Story.*
64. *New York Times,* August 27, 1943.
65. *Humboldt Union,* July 1944.
66. *Washington Post, Washington Star,* July 8, 1944.
67. *Washington Star,* April 10, 1946.

68. Denman Thompson, *Washington Star*, December 11, 1946.
69. Carolyn Johnson Thomas interview with the author. The boy's name was Henry W. Thomas III.
70. Eddie Johnson interview with the author.
71. Frank Graham, "The Big Train," *Baseball Magazine*, February 1947.
72. Francis Stann, *Washington Star*, December 11, 1946.
73. Dr. Thomas Keliher letter to Carolyn Johnson Thomas, November 5, 1982, Johnson family archives. "Your father had the finest natural good manners of any person I have ever taken care of," Keliher wrote. "He was particularly kind and courteous to his nurses."
74. Eddie Johnson interview with the author.
75. James Austin, *Washington Post*, August 15, 1946.
76. *Washington Star*, December 11, 1946.
77. Daisy Barnwell Jones, *My First Eighty Years* (Baltimore: Gateway Press, 1985).

EPILOGUE

1. Shirley Povich has often told the following story to illustrate the kind of admiration Johnson inspired:

   "The reverence in which the Big Train was held was typified one day by Edward T. Folliard, Pulitzer Prize-winner of the *Washington Post* and historian of virtually all important national and international events of the past 20 years. Speaking before a brilliant assemblage in the National Press Club, Folliard was introduced as a famous war correspondent, an on-the-spot reporter at White House conferences when history was made, and an authority on national affairs. When asked what was his greatest thrill, he said unhesitatingly: 'That was the day when I covered Walter Johnson's attempt to throw a silver dollar across the Rappahannock River, as George Washington had done. As a small boy in Washington, I was a Johnson fan. That day, when Johnson threw the dollar across the Rappahannock, I got my greatest thrill. You see, I was the fellow who held Walter Johnson's coat.' " Povich, "Walter Johnson, The Big Train."

2. Bob Addie, *Washington Times-Herald*, December 12, 1946.
3. *Washington Star*, December 11, 1946.

   President Truman dedicated the Walter Johnson Memorial at Griffith Stadium on June 21, 1947. "I am honored and privileged to be called upon to unveil this plaque to a man who in my opinion is the greatest ballplayer who ever lived," he said. "He was a great ballplayer, a great American, and a great citizen of the United States." *Washington Star*, June 22, 1947. The memorial was moved to the Walter Johnson High School in Bethesda, Maryland, in 1962.
4. "Runyon and Johnson," clipping, source unknown, Kansas State Historical Society.

Another sad and ironic coincidence wasn't noticed at all, because its implications weren't known at the time. On November 26, two weeks before Johnson's death, Babe Ruth checked into a hospital in New York. He made it out after several months, but this was the beginning of the end for him also.

5. Povich, "Walter Johnson, The Big Train."
6. Flaherty, "Life Story of Walter Perry Johnson."

APPENDIX I

1. Tom Clark, *The World of Damon Runyon* (New York: Harper & Row, 1978).
2. Ruth with Considine, *The Babe Ruth Story*.
3. Cobb with Stump, *My Life in Baseball, The True Record*; Shea, "The Georgia Peach."
4. Lane, "The Greatest Pitcher on the Diamond Today."
5. "Twenty Years Ago in the *Star*," *Washington Star*, 1933, misc. clippings: "Larry Lajoie, who has played 18 consecutive years as a major leaguer, says Walter Johnson of the Nationals is the greatest pitcher he ever faced."
6. F.C. Lane, "Collins the Great," *Baseball Magazine*, March 1915. Collins: "[Johnson] is so great that he overshadows all the rest in my opinion by a wide margin"; Collins, "Twenty-one Years of Baseball," North American Newspaper Alliance, 1926, scrapbook XVII.
7. Clipping, source unknown, n.d., scrapbook XXVIII (1930). In a radio talk with Grantland Rice in 1930, Speaker names Johnson the greatest pitcher of all time, and Johnson, Ruth, and Cobb as the three greatest players in the history of the game.
8. Ritter, *Glory of Their Times*.
9. Honig, *October Heroes*.
10. *Washington Star*, August 29, 1913.
11. Grantland Rice, "The Coffeyville Express": "It is my belief that, given an even break in team strength, Johnson, year in and year out, was the hardest man to beat that ever sent a ball flashing over the plate."
12. Lieb, *Baseball As I Have Known It*.
13. Damon Runyon: "Mr. Ring Lardner, the old-time baseball reporter, was earnestly pecking away at the keys of a typewriter when I eased myself into his quarters in a downtown hotel(New York) the other day. He gave me a very sour look, and then continued pecking, by way of a hint to make it short. But I know how to deal with these old-time baseball reporters. 'The greatest pitcher that ever lived,' I remarked, 'was . . . '

    'Walter Johnson,' completed Mr. Ring Lardner, pushing his typewriter aside with an impatient gesture, and turning to confront me. 'That's the name—Walter Johnson. Oh, I know you were going to say Mathewson. You New York sportswriters make me tired putting Mathewson away as the greatest pitcher.'

'Why,' I said, 'I ...'

'Don't ever ask sportswriters about such things,' interrupted Mr. Ring Lardner, rudely. 'Ask baseball players. I traveled with the club that hit against Mathewson, and I also traveled with the club that hit against Johnson. Frank Chance's Cubs was the club that hit against Mathewson, and they didn't worry the least bit when they knew they were going to meet Matty. But when Fielder Jones's White Sox knew they would be up against Walter Johnson the next day, you heard of more stomach aches and lame legs and touches of the flu, and other indispositions than you would believe possible among one small group of athletes.'" Damon Runyon, *New York American*, May 18, 1933.

14. Runyon: "Allowing that figures don't lie, the greatest pitcher in the history of baseball must have been Walter Johnson. The figures that Jawn J. McGraw says don't lie would indicate that Walter Johnson performed more prodigies of pitching valor during his big league service than even the great Mathewson. I doubt if any pitcher ever lived who had more speed than Johnson in his youth." Damon Runyon, *New York American*, April 13, 1928.
15. Harold Hart and Ralph Tolleris, *Big-Time Baseball* (New York: Hart Publishing, 1950).
16. Christy Walsh, *Baseball's Greatest Lineup* (New York: Barnes & Co., 1952).
17. *The Sporting News*, August 2, 1969.
18. Eugene and Roger McCaffrey, *Players' Choice* (New York: Facts on File Publications, 1987).
19. Dave Nightingale, "Baseball's Greatest Players of All Time," *Inside Sports*, June 1994.
20. *Baseball Digest*, April 1994.
21. *Sports Illustrated*, October 1992.
22. Maury Allen, *Baseball's 100* (New York: A & W Publishers, 1981).
23. Daniel Okrent and Harris Lewine, *The Ultimate Baseball Book* (Boston: Houghton Mifflin Company, 1979).
24. Ted Oliver, *Kings of the Mound* (Los Angeles: Ted Oliver, 1944).
25. James, *The Bill James Historical Abstract.*
26. John Thorn and John Holway, *The Pitcher* (New York: Prentice Hall Press, 1987).
27. John Thorn and Pete Palmer, *Total Baseball* (New York: Warner Books, 1989).
28. Ralph Horton, *Baseball's Best Pitchers* (St. Louis: Horton Publishing Co., 1993).
29. John P. McCarthy, Jr., *Baseball's All-Time Dream Team* (Cincinnati: Betterway Books, 1994).
30. Grantland Rice, "Sportlight" column, *Washington Post*, March 9, 1915.

    Babe Ruth: "No one could ever throw a ball as hard as Walter. Yet everybody who ever hit against him took a toe hold on the plate. They knew that Walter wouldn't throw at them and that he wouldn't doctor up the ball so that it might 'take off' and skull them. Walter always believed in getting along without any sharpshooting. If he had gone in for any trickery, he would have left behind him a pitching record which nobody ever would have touched. What he did leave behind was greater—a remarkable pitching record and a wonderful name." Ruth with Considine, *The Babe Ruth Story*.

31. Michael Hiestand, "Old-Timers Would Profit Nowadays," *USA Today*, July 10, 1991.

APPENDIX II

1. Harris, *Playing the Game*.
2. Povich, "The Washington Senators."
3. *Washington Post*, August 3, 1907.
4. "Walter Johnson, One of Nation's Top Ball Players, From Fullerton", clipping, source unknown, n.d., Fullerton (California) Library Clipping file.

Bibliography

INTERVIEWS

Johnson, Edwin R.. June 1978 and November 1992.
Lacy, Sam. December 1994.
Pogue, Barbara Johnson. November 1987.
Povich, Shirley. May 1992.
Thomas, Carolyn Johnson. November 1987 and November 1992.
Weaver, Monte. May 1992.

ARCHIVAL SOURCES

Anaheim Library, Anaheim, California. Walter Johnson file.
Coffeyville, Kansas, Historical Society. Walter Johnson file.
Fullerton Library, Fullerton, California. Walter Johnson file.
Idaho State Historical Society, Boise, Idaho. Clippings.
Intermountain Cultural Center & Museum, Weiser, Idaho. Clippings.
Kansas State Historical Society, Topeka, Kansas. Walter Johnson file.
Martin Luther King Library, Washington, D.C.. Walter Johnson file.
Montgomery County, Maryland, Historical Society. Walter Johnson file.
National Baseball Library, Cooperstown, New York. Walter Johnson file.
Walter Johnson personal scrapbooks. Volumes I-XXIX (1919–1930) and miscellaneous clippings, Johnson family archives.
Washington Historical Society, Washington, D.C.. Clippings.

NEWSPAPERS

Anaheim Bulletin
Anaheim Gazette
Anaheim Plain Dealer
Atlanta Journal
Baltimore News
Baltimore Sun
Bethesda Journal
Boston Globe
Boston Herald
Caldwell Tribune
Chanute Tribune
Chicago Record-Herald
Chicago Tribune
Cleveland News
Cleveland Plain Dealer
Cleveland Press
Coffeyville Journal
Dallas News
Dearborn Independent
Des Moines Register
Detroit Free Press
Detroit News
Emmett Index
Fullerton News
Fullerton Tribune
Humboldt Union
Idaho Daily Statesman
Iola Register
Kansas City Star
Los Angeles Examiner
Los Angeles Herald
Los Angeles Times

Montgomery County Sentinel
Nampa Leader
New Orleans Picayune
New York Age
New York American
New York Daily News
New York Globe
New York Herald Tribune
New York Post
New York Sun
New York Telegram
New York Telegraph
New York Times
New York World
New York World-Telegram
Newark Evening News
Newark Star-Eagle
Orange County Register
Ottawa (Ks) Herald
Pasadena News
Portland Oregonian
Rochester Democrat and Chronicle
San Diego Union
San Francisco Chronicle
San Francisco Daily News
San Francisco Examiner
Santa Ana Evening Blade
Santa Ana Register
Schenectady Union-Star
Spokane Spokesman-Review
Sporting Life
Sporting News
St. Louis Globe-Democrat
St. Louis Times
Tacoma Daily Ledger
Tulsa World
Washington Daily News
Washington Herald
Washington Post
Washington Star
Washington Times
Washington Times-Herald
Weiser American
Weiser Signal
Weiser World
Whittier News
Wichita Eagle

BOOKS

Alexander, Charles C.. *Ty Cobb* (New York: Oxford University Press, 1984).

Allen, Maury. *Baseball's 100* (New York: A & W Publishers, 1981).

Asinof, Eliot. *Eight Men Out* (New York: Holt, Rinehart and Winston, 1963).

Bailey, Steve. *Walter Perry Johnson: A Biography* (Master's thesis, Arizona State University, May 1990).

Bealle, Morris. *The Washington Senators* (Washington, D.C.: Columbia Publishing Company, 1947).

Carmichael, John F.. *My Greatest Day in Baseball* (New York: A.S. Barnes and Company, 1945).

Clark, Tom. *The World of Damon Runyon* (New York: Harper & Row, 1978).

Cobb, Ty, with Al Stump. *My Life in Baseball—The True Record* (Garden City, New York: Doubleday and Company, 1961).

Creamer, Robert. *Babe, The Legend Comes to Life* (New York: Simon and Schuster, 1974).

Curran, William. *Big Sticks, The Batting Revolution of the Twenties* (New York: William Morrow & Co., 1990).

Davenport, John W.. *Baseball's Pennant Races: A Graphic View* (Madison, Wisconsin: First Impressions, 1981).

Davids, L. Robert. *Minor League Baseball Stars* (Washington, D.C.: Society for American Baseball Research, 1978).

Delany, Sarah and A. Elizabeth with Amy Hill Hearth. *Having Our Say, the Delany Sisters' First 100 Years* (New York: Kodansha America, 1993).

Derig, Betty. *Weiser, The Way It Was* (Weiser, Idaho: Rambler Press, 1987).

Einstein, Charles, editor. *The Fireside Book of Baseball* (New York: Simon & Schuster, 1956).

Feller, Bob with Bill Gilbert. *Now Pitching, Bob Feller* (New York: Birch Lane Press, 1990).

Friis, Leo J.. *Kleinigkeiten* (Orange County Pioneer Series #4, 1975).

Green, Paul. *Forgotten Fields* (Waupaca, Wisconsin: Parker Publications, 1984).

Greenberg, Hank. *The Story of My Life* (New York: Times Books, 1989).

Grosshandler, Stanley. *Baseball & The Great War* (New York: Dutton, 1990).

Harris, Stanley. *Playing The Game* (New York: Grosset & Dunlap, 1925).

Hart, Harold and Ralph Tolleris. *Big-Time Baseball* (New York: Hart Publishing, 1950).

Holway, John. *Blackball Stars* (Westport, Connecticut: Meckler Publishing, 1988).

Honig, Donald. *Baseball America* (New York: MacMillan, 1985).

______. *Baseball When the Grass was Real* (New York: Coward, McMann & Geoghegan, 1975).

______. *The Man In the Dugout* (Chicago: Follet Publishing Co., 1977).

______. *The October Heroes.* (New York: Simon & Schuster, 1979).

Hornsby, Rogers. *My War With Baseball* (New York: Coward-McCann, 1962).

Horton, Ralph. *Baseball's Best Pitchers* (St. Louis: Horton Publishing Co., 1993).

James, Bill. *The Bill James Historical Abstract* (New York: Villard books, 1985).

Johnson, Harold. *Who's Who in Major League Baseball* (Chicago: Buxton Publishing Co., 1933).

Jones, Daisy Barnwell. *My First Eighty Years* (Baltimore: Gateway Press, 1985).

Lange, Fred W.. *History of Baseball in California and Pacific Coast Leagues, 1847–1938* (San Francisco: 1938).

Lardner, Ring. *The Best Short Stories of Ring Lardner* (New York: Charles Scribner's Sons, 1957).

Lieb, Fred. *Baseball As I Have Known It* (New York: Coward, McCann & Geoghegan, Inc., 1977).

______. *Comedians and Pranksters of Baseball* (St. Louis: The Sporting News, 1958).

______. *The Pittsburgh Pirates* (New York: G.P. Putnam's Sons, 1948).

MacArthur, Mildred Yorba. *Orange County Historical Volume III* (Whittier, California: The Historical Volume and Reference Works, 1963).

McCaffrey, Eugene and Roger. *Players' Choice* (New York: Facts on File Publications, 1987).

McCallum, John. *The Tiger Wore Spikes* (New York: Praeger Publishers, 1975).

McCarthy, John P., Jr..*Baseball's All-Time Dream Team* (Cincinnati: Betterway Books, 1994).

McGraw, John. *My Thirty Years in Baseball* (New York: Boni & Liveright, 1923).

Mead, William B. and Paul Dickson. *Baseball, The President's Game* (Washington, D.C.: Farragut Publishing Company, 1993).

Moreland, George. *Balldom* (Youngstown, Ohio: Balldom Publishing, 1914).

Murdock, Eugene C.. *Ban Johnson, Czar of Baseball* (Westport, Connecticut: Greenwood Press, 1982).

Nadel, Eric and Craig R. Wright. *The Man Who Stole First Base* (Dallas: Taylor Publishing, 1989).

Nagle, Walter H.. *Five Straight Errors On Ladies Day* (Caldwell, Idaho: Caxton Printers, 1965).

Okrent, Dan and Harris Lewine. *The Ultimate Baseball Book* (Boston: Houghton Mifflin Company, 1979).

Oliver, Ted. *Kings of the Mound* (Los Angeles: Ted Oliver, 1944).

O'Neill, Thomas P.. *Man Of The House* (New York: Random House, 1987).

Pietrusza, David. *Major Leagues* (Jefferson, North Carolina: McFarland & Company, 1991).

Povich, Shirley. *The Washington Senators, An Informal History* (New York: G.P. Putnam's Sons, 1954).

Reichler, Joseph L., editor. *The Baseball Encyclopedia* (New York: MacMillan, 1985).

Ritter, Lawrence. *The Glory of Their Times* (New York: Morrow, 1966).

Robinson, Ray. *Matty—An American Hero* (New York: Oxford Press, 1993).

Ruth, Babe, as told to Bob Considine. *The Babe Ruth Story* (New York: E.P. Dutton & Co., 1948).

Schacht, Al. *Clowning Through Baseball* (New York: A.S. Barnes & Co., 1941).

______. *My Own Particular Screwball* (Garden City, N.Y.: Doubleday & Co., 1955).

Schlossberg, Dan. *The Baseball Book of Why* (Middle Village, N.Y.: Jonathan David, Inc., 1984).

Seymour, Harold. *Baseball, The Golden Age* (New York: Oxford University Press, 1971).

Shannon and Kalnesky. *The Ballparks* (New York: Hawthorn Books, 1975).

Siwoff, Seymour. *The Book of Baseball Records* (New York: Siwoff, 1994).

Smith, Curt. *Voices of the Game* (South Bend, Indiana: Diamond Communications, 1987).

Smith, Ken. *Baseball's Hall of Fame* (New York: A.S. Barnes & Co., 1947).

Stern, Bill. *Bill Stern's Favorite Baseball Stories* (New York: Doubleday & Co., 1951).

Stump, Al. *Cobb* (Chapel Hill, North Carolina: Algonquin Books, 1994).

Thorn, John and John Holway. *The Pitcher* (New York: Prentice Hall Press, 1987).

Thorn, John, and Pete Palmer. *The Hidden Game of Baseball* (Garden City, New York: Doubleday & Co., 1985).

______. *Total Baseball* (New York: Warner Books, 1989).

Tiemann, Robert L. and Mark Rucker. *Nineteenth Century Stars* (Society for American Baseball Research, 1989).

Treat, Roger. *Walter Johnson, King of the Pitchers* (New York: Julian Messner, 1948).

Walsh, Christy. *Adios To Ghosts* (New York: 1937).

______. *Baseball's Greatest Lineup* (New York: Barnes & Co., 1952).

Yardley, Jonathan. *Ring* (New York: Random House, 1977).

Zingg, Paul. *Harry Hooper* (Chicago: University of Illinois Press, 1993).

ARTICLES

"A Neighbor." "And What a Best It's Been These Sixteen Years," *Dearborn Independent*, October 6, 1923.

Amman, Larry. "The Clown Prince of Baseball," *Baseball Research Journal*, 1982.

Berman, Jay. "The Early Days of Sports in Orange County," *Orange Coast Magazine*, July 1990.

Blaisdell, Lowell. "Mystery and Tragedy: The O'Connell-Dolan Scandal," *Baseball Research Journal*, 1982.

Burke, Joseph C.. "How Walter Johnson Got His Start in Baseball," *Cincinnati Enquirer*, September 20, 1913.

Burnes, Robert L.. "Walter Johnson's Toughest Defeat," *Baseball Digest*, February 1963.

Coughlin, Gene. "Walter Johnson—Salesman for the Golden Rule," *American Weekly*, June 8, 1947.

Cummiskey, Joe. "The Babe and Walter—Dressing Room Vignettes," *Baseball Digest*, November 1942.

Daley, Arthur. "The Fireball Throwers," *New York Times*, March 20, 1953.

Evans, Billy. "Umpires' American League Team," *Collier's*, October 1912.

______. "Evans Dissertates On Walter Johnson," *Washington Star*, November 16, 1908.

Flaherty, Vincent X.. "Life Story of Walter Perry Johnson," *The Sporting News Baseball Register*, 1947.

Fullerton, Hugh. "The Greatest Game of Baseball," *Liberty Magazine*, April 20, 1929.

Gandil, Charles. "This Is My Story of the Black Sox Scandal," *Sports Illustrated*, September 17, 1956.

Gonzales, Raymond. "Home Runs Off the Big Train," *Baseball Research Journal*, 1979.

Graham, Frank. "The Big Train," *Baseball Magazine*, February 1947.

Grimley, Steve. "Johnson Remembered as Baseball's Hardest Thrower," *Orange County Register*, February 12, 1978.

Guild, Bob. "Anaheim Shares Claim To 'Big Train' With Olinda," *Anaheim Bulletin*, March 11, 1939.

Gustkey, Earl. "The Day Ruth and Johnson Came to Orange County," *Los Angeles Times*, August 4, 1970.

______. "When the Big Train Ran on a Rural Track," *Los Angeles Times*, June 2, 1970.

Haas, Alex. "Batters Hit By Pitchers," *Baseball Historical Review*, 1981.

Heath, Steven H.. "An Analysis of the Walter Johnson Shutouts," *Baseball Quarterly Reviews*," Vol. 4, 1989.

______. "Ty Cobb vs. Walter Johnson," *Baseball Quarterly Reviews*, Fall 1992.

Hiestand, Michael. "Old-Timers Would Profit Nowadays," *USA Today*, July 10, 1991.

Hugo, Bill and Bob Littlejohn. "The Roy Hughes Story Bag," *Baseball Research Journal*, 1991.

Johnson, Hazel. "Reflections of a Baseball Pitcher's Wife," *Liberty Magazine*, May 30, 1925.

______. "Walter Johnson's Fan Mail," *Liberty Magazine*, June 19, 1926.

Johnson, Walter. "A Page From My Book of Experience," *The Blue Diamond Magazine*, July 1924.

______. "A Quarter Million Strong," *American Legion Magazine*, n.d., Johnson family archives.

______. "My Honest Opinion Of My Own Pitching," *Baseball Magazine*, May 1919.

______. "My Life So Far," *Baseball Magazine*, August 1912.

______. "My Pitching Years," 60-part syndicated newspaper series, *Washington Times*, January-February 1925.

______. "My Twenty Years On The Mound" (as told to Lillian Barker), 12-part syndicated newspaper series, *Washington Post*, November-December 1924.

______. "Some Experiences of a Speed King," *St. Nicholas Magazine*, October 1914.

______. "The Greatest Batters I Have Ever Faced," *Baseball Magazine*, June 1925.

______. "The Greatest Players I Ever Saw," *Baseball Magazine*, October 1929.

______. "The Meanest Thing in Baseball," *Baseball Magazine*, September 1917.

______. "The Reflections Of An Old Timer," *Baseball Magazine*, February 1922.

______. "What I Pitch to Babe Ruth and Why," *Baseball Magazine*, September 1920.

______. "What I Think About Hunting," *Baseball Magazine*, June 1913.

______. "What Records Mean To A Manager," *Baseball Magazine*, March 1935.

______. "When I Was a Shine Ball Pitcher," *Baseball Magazine*, January 1921.

______. "Why I Signed With The Federal League," *Baseball Magazine*, April 1915.

Kallen, Gregory. "Major League Baseball During the Great War," *Rounding Third, Major League Baseball in Washington*, 1979.

Kermisch, Al. "Sam Rice's Batting Record Purified," *Baseball Research Journal*, 1981.

Koppett, Leonard. "Walter Johnson, Greatest Pitcher of Them All," *Baseball Digest*, February 1965.

Lane, F.C.. "75,000 Pitches Without A Sore Arm!", *Baseball Magazine*, August 1934.

______. "At Coffeyville With Walter Johnson," *Baseball Magazine*, April 1915.

______. "Collins the Great," *Baseball Magazine*, March 1915.

______. "Getting Rich From Florida Real Estate," *Baseball Magazine*, July 1926.

______. "If I Were Only Young Once More," *Baseball Magazine*, November 1924.

______. "Milan the Marvel," *Baseball Magazine*, May 1914.

______. "One Hundred and Twenty-Two Feet Per Second," *Baseball Magazine*, September 1912.

______. "The Greatest Pitcher On the Diamond Today," *Baseball Magazine*, September 1912.

______. "The Greatest Pitcher on the Diamond Today," *Baseball Magazine*, January 1916.

______. "The Storm Center of the Cleveland Club," *Baseball Magazine*, September 1935.

______. "Thirteen Seasons of Marvelous Pitching," *Baseball Magazine*, April 1920.

Lemke, Bob. "Jack Bentley Was the First 'Next Babe Ruth'," *Sports Collectors Digest*, February 4, 1994.

Lieb, Fred. "Johnson's 16-Victory String Snapped in Relief Role by Questionable Ruling," *The Sporting News*, February 15, 1945.

______. "The P.T. Barnum of the Bushes: Joe Engel, Chattanooga Club Chief," *The Sporting News Baseball Register*, 1953.

MacArthur, Mildred Yorba. "Long Arm From Olinda," *Westways,* October 1978.

Madden, Bill. "Bluege Hails the Big Train," *The Sporting News*, May 23, 1983.

Manchester, H.F.. "When Walt Johnson Pitched As Dark Horse For Hicks," *Boston Herald,* May 9, 1926.

Marazzi, Rich. "Al Schacht, The Clown Prince of Baseball," *Baseball History*, Winter 1986.

Mason, Ward. "Oscar Vitt," *Baseball Magazine*, August 1916.

McConnell, Robert. "The Non-Home Run Hitters," *Baseball Research Journal*, 1983.

McMillan, Nora Brown. "Memories of Early Olinda," *Historical Guide to Carbon Canyon Regional Park*, 1975.

Tom Meany. "The Babe and Walter—Dressing Room Vignettes," *Baseball Digest*, November 1942.

Moore, Virginia Chatham. "Mrs. Walter Johnson, As I Know Her," unpublished (?) manuscript, n.d. (c. 1926), Johnson family archives.

Murphy, J.M.. "Napoleon Lajoie, Modern Baseball's First Superstar," *The National Pastime*, 1988.

Nightingale, Dave. "Baseball's Greatest Players of All Time," *Inside Sports*, June 1994.

Poore, Jim. "Former Batboy Still Remembers Big Train Johnson," *Idaho Daily Statesman*, August 11, 1981.

Povich, Shirley. "Bluege Last Link To Heyday of Senators," *Washington Post*, October 16, 1985.

______. "Clark Griffith—50 Years in Baseball," 30-part series, *Washington Post*, January-February 1938.

______. "The Old Fox," *Regardies*, June/July 1983.

______. "The Washington Senators," *Sport Magazine*, December 1951.

______. "Walter Johnson, The Big Train," *Sport Magazine*, January 1950.

Rice, Grantland. "The Coffeyville Express," *Collier's,* June 5, 1926.

______. "The Greatest Thrill of 1924," *Collier's,* January 10, 1925.

Riley, James and Renwick Speer. "1991 Marks Chet Hoff's 100th Birthday," *Baseball Research Journal*, 1991.

Ritter, Lawrence. "George McBride: *'I Took Honus Wagner's Job'*," *The National Pastime*, 1985.

Rogers, Will. "Everybody Is Pulling For Walter," *New York Times*, September 28, 1924.

Rothe, Emil. "The War of 1912, The Wood-Johnson Duel," *Baseball Research Journal*, 1974.

Ruel, Herold. "Catching a Speed King," syndicated newspaper series, source unknown, n.d. (1927), Johnson scrapbooks.

Salsinger, H.G.. "Tigers Spurned Johnson For Free," *Baseball Digest*, August 1946.

Scherrer, Joe. "Today is Special For Big Train's Brother," *Corpus Christi Times*, April 13, 1953.

Shea, Jack. "The Georgia Peach," *Sport Magazine*, November 1948.

Smith, Donald. "Minnie Johnson Nears 100," *Washington Star*, March 5, 1967.

Smith, Red. "The Big Train and His Buddies," *New York Herald Tribune*, December 14, 1946.

Spink, J.G. Taylor. "End of Line For Big Train," *The Sporting News*, December 18, 1946.

Stump, Al. "Ty Cobb's Wild Ten-Month Fight to Live," *True*, December 1961.

Thomas, Henry W.. "The Weiser Wonder: Walter Johnson in Idaho," *Grandstand Baseball Annual*, 1995.

______. and Charles W. Carey. "The California Comet?: Walter Johnson in the Golden State," *Grandstand Baseball Annual*, 1995.

Toll, David E.. "E.E. Roberts and the Politics of Personal Liberty," *Nevada Magazine,* n.d., Johnson family archives.

Waterman, Guy. "The Upstart Senators of 1912–15," *The National Pastime*, 1993.

Wedge, Will. "Weiser Was Wild Ball Burg," *New York Sun*, May 9, 1924.

West, Eddie. "Golden Day: Ruth, Johnson at Brea," *Orange County Register*, October 30, 1974.

______. "Walter Johnson Went Up 50 Years Ago Today," *Santa Ana Register,* August 11, 1957.

"When Washington Won the World Series," *The Transmitter* (C&P Telephone Co. magazine), November 1924.

Wulf, Steve. "The Secrets of Sam," *Sports Illustrated*, July 9, 1993.

OTHER SOURCES

Amman, Larry. Transcripts of interviews with Bucky Harris, Ossie Bluege, Al Schacht, Ralph Peckinpaugh (son of Roger), Stan Coveleski; unpublished manuscript on the Washington Nationals of 1924–25.

Chapman, Stanley C., editor. *The Lucky Thirteen*, Fullerton Union High School yearbook, vol. I, No. I, June 14, 1905.

Coffeyville at 100, centennial booklet, n.d., Coffeyville Historical Society.

Coolidge, Calvin. Letter to General Anton Stephan, chairman, Walter Johnson Testimonial Committee, July 26, 1927, Johnson family archives.

______. Letter to Paul Block, November 1, 1927, Johnson family archives.

Griffith, Clark. Letter to Walter Johnson, October 15, 1927, Johnson family archives.

Holman, Joe. *Wonderful Walter Johnson*, unpublished manuscript, n.d., Johnson family archives.

Johnson, Hazel. Letters to Margaret Milan, January-July, 1930, Johnson family archives.

Johnson, Walter. Letter to Eleanor Fleitman, January 3, 1940, copy in Johnson family archives.

______. Letters to F.C. Lane and Neil Uhl, various dates, National Baseball Library.

______. Letters to Hazel Johnson, 1913–1930, Johnson family archives.

______. Audiotape, broadcast of Cleveland Indians at Washington Nationals, September 21, 1939, Johnson family archives.

Jones, Davy. Letters to Lee Allen, March 25 and April 13, 1963, National Baseball Library.

Keliher, Dr. Thomas. Letter to Carolyn Johnson Thomas, November 5, 1982, Johnson family archives.

Martin, Jack. Letter to the author, December 11, 1978.

Milan, Margaret. Letter to Carolyn Johnson Thomas, May 8, 1961, Johnson family archives.

Roosevelt, Franklin D.. Letter to Walter Johnson, November 6, 1937, Johnson family archives.

Steadman, John. Letter to the author, January 2, 1995.

Taft, William H.. Letter to Walter Johnson, April 15, 1910, Johnson family archives.

Tiemann, Robert L.. "Walter Johnson's Shutouts," n.d., Society for American Baseball Research.

Various authors. Manuscripts from Walter Johnson scrapbooks, publishing histories unknown, Johnson family archives.

Various correspondents and dates. Telegrams to Walter Johnson, Johnson family archives.

Washington Senators 1957 media guide. Franchise attendance figures, 1901–56.

Wood, Joe. Videotape, *The Glory of Their Times*, 1970, Cappy Productions, Inc..

Index